ORGANIZATIONAL BEHAVIOR

McGRAW-HILL SERIES IN MANAGEMENT
Consulting Editors
Fred Luthans and Keith Davis

Arnold and Feldman: Organizational Behavior

Bartol and Martin: Management

Boone and Bowen: Great Writings in Management and Organizational Behavior

Boone and Kurtz: Management

Cascio: Managing Human Resources: Productivity, Quality of Work Life, Profits

Certo and Peter: Selected Cases in Strategic Management

Certo and Peter: Strategic Management: Focus on Process

Certo and Peter: Strategic Management: Concepts and Applications

Daughtrey and Ricks: Contemporary Supervision: Managing People and Technology

Davidson and de la Torre: Managing the Global Corporation: Case Studies in Strategy and Management

Davis and Newstrom: Human Behavior at Work: Organizational Behavior

Dilworth: Production and Operations Management: Manufacturing and Non-Manufacturing

Dobler, Burt, and Lee: Purchasing and Materials Management: Text and Cases

Feldman and Arnold: Managing Individual and Group Behavior in Organizations

Frederick, Davis, and Post: Business and Society: Management, Public Policy, Ethics

Hodgetts: Effective Supervision: A Practical Approach

Hodgetts and Luthans: International Management

Hoffman and Moore: Business Ethics: Readings and Cases in Corporate Morality

Jauch and Glueck: Business Policy and Strategic Management

Jauch and Glueck: Strategic Management and Business Policy

Jauch and Townsend: Cases in Strategic Management and Business Policy

Katz and Kochan: An Introduction to Collective Bargaining and Industrial Relations

Koontz and Weihrich: Essentials of Management

Koontz and Weihrich: Management

Kopelman: Managing Productivity in Organizations: A Practical, People-Oriented Perspective

Kuriloff and Hemphill: Starting and Managing the Small Business

Levin, Rubin, Stinson, and Gardner: Quantitative Approaches to Management

Luthans: Organizational Behavior

Luthans and Thompson: Contemporary Readings in Organizational Behavior

Miles: Theories of Management: Implications for Organizational Behavior and Development

Miles and Snow: Organizational Strategy, Structure, and Process

Mills: Labor-Management Relations

Mitchell and Larson: People in Organizations: An Introduction to Organizational Behavior

Molander: Responsive Capitalism: Case Studies in Corporate Social Conduct

Monks: Operations Management: Theory and Problems

Newstrom and Davis: Organizational Behavior: Readings and Exercises

Pearce and Robinson: Corporate Strategies: Readings from *Business Week*

Porter and McKibbin: Management Education and Development: Drift or Thrust into the 21st Century?

Prasow and Peters: Arbitration and Collective Bargaining: Conflict Resolution in Labor Relations

Quick and Quick: Organizational Stress and Preventive Management

Rue and Holland: Strategic Management: Concepts and Experiences

Rugman, Lecraw, and Booth: International Business: Firm and Environment

Sayles: Leadership: Managing in Real Organizations

Schlesinger, Eccles, and Gabarro: Managing Behavior in Organizations: Text, Cases and Readings

Schroeder: Operations Management: Decision Making in the Operations Function

Steers and Porter: Motivation and Work Behavior

Steiner: Industry, Society, and Change: A Casebook

Steiner and Steiner: Business, Government, and Society: A Managerial Perspective, Text and Cases

Steinhoff and Burgess: Small Business Management Fundamentals

Sutermeister: People and Productivity

Walker: Human Resource Strategy

Weihrich: Management Excellence: Productivity through MBO

Werther and Davis: Human Resources and Personnel Management

Wofford, Gerloff, and Cummins: Organizational Communications: The Keystone to Managerial Effectiveness

Yoffie: International Trade and Competition

ORGANIZATIONAL BEHAVIOR

SIXTH EDITION

FRED LUTHANS
George Holmes Professor of Management
University of Nebraska

McGRAW-HILL, INC.
New York   St. Louis   San Francisco   Auckland   Bogotá   Caracas
Lisbon   London   Madrid   Mexico   Milan   Montreal   New Delhi
Paris   San Juan   Singapore   Sydney   Tokyo   Toronto

ORGANIZATIONAL BEHAVIOR

International Edition 1992.

Exclusive rights by McGraw-Hill Book Co-Singapore. This book cannot be re-exported from the country to which it is consigned by McGraw-Hill.

3   4   5   6   7   8   9   0   KHL SW   9   6   5   4   3

ISBN 0-07-039166-1

This book was set in Garamond Stemple by Better Graphics, Inc.
The editors were Alan Sachs, Dan Alpert, and Peggy Rehberger;
the designer was Charles A. Carson;
the production supervisor was Kathryn Porzio.

Library of Congress Cataloging-in-Publication Data

Luthans, Fred.
    Organizational behavior/Fred Luthans.—6th ed.
        p.   cm.—(McGraw-Hill series in management)
    Includes bibliographical references and indexes.
    ISBN 0-07-039166-1
    1.   Organizational behavior.   I. Title.   II. Series.
HD58.7.L88   1992
658.4—dc20   91-17026

When ordering this title, use ISBN No: 0-07-112687-2

Printed in Singapore.

FOR
KAY, KRISTIN, BRETT, KYLE, AND PAIGE

ABOUT THE AUTHOR

FRED LUTHANS is the George Holmes Distinguished Professor of Management at the University of Nebraska at Lincoln. He received his B.A., M.B.A., and Ph.D. from the University of Iowa and did some postdoctoral work at Columbia University. While serving in the armed forces, he taught at the U.S. Military Academy at West Point. A prolific writer, he has published a number of books and over one hundred articles in applied and academic journals. His book *Organizational Behavior Modification*, coauthored with Robert Kreitner, won the American Society of Personnel Administration award for the outstanding contribution to human resources management, and a more recent book titled *Real Managers* is the result of a four-year research study that observed managers in their natural settings. *International Management*, coauthored with Richard Hodgetts and also published by McGraw-Hill, is his latest book. His articles are widely reprinted and have brought him the American Society of Hospital Personnel Administration award. The consulting coeditor for the McGraw-Hill Management Series, Professor Luthans is also the editor for *Organizational Dynamics* and co-editor for *International Human Resources Management Review*. He has been very active in the Academy of Management over the years and was elected a Fellow in 1981. He is a former president of the Midwest Region. He was vice president, program chair of the National Academy meeting in Boston in 1984, and was president in 1986 for the celebration of the fiftieth anniversary of the Academy of Management and the Centennial of the academic field of management. Also active in the Decision Sciences Institute (DSI), he was elected a Fellow in 1987. Professor Luthans has a very extensive research program at the University of Nebraska and teaches courses in organizational behavior and management at both the graduate and undergraduate levels. He has been a visiting scholar at a number of universities in the United States and has lectured at universities and conducted workshops for managers in Australia, Mexico, and most countries in Europe and Asia. He has been on the Executive Committee of the annual Pan Pacific Conference since its beginning. This international experience and interest is reflected in his approach to the field of organizational behavior. He currently serves on the Board of Directors of the Foundation of Administrative Research. In addition, he is an active consultant to both private- and public-sector organizations and conducts workshops on behavioral management both in this country and abroad.

CONTENTS IN BRIEF

PREFACE   **xxvii**

PART 1   THE FOUNDATION FOR ORGANIZATIONAL BEHAVIOR   **1**
     1   An Introduction to Organizational Behavior   **3**
     2   The Background and Methodology   **18**

PART 2   THE BASIC BUILDING BLOCKS OF ORGANIZATIONAL
     BEHAVIOR: A MICRO PERSPECTIVE   **51**
     3   Perception   **53**
     4   Personality   **83**
     5   Micro Variables Applied: Job Attitudes, Satisfaction,
        and Commitment   **107**

PART 3   THE HEART OF ORGANIZATIONAL BEHAVIOR:
     MOTIVATION, LEARNING, AND LEADERSHIP   **143**
     6   Motivation Theory: Needs and Processes   **145**
     7   Motivation Applied: Job Design and Goal Setting   **180**
     8   Learning Theory: Reinforcement and Punishment   **206**
     9   Learning Applied: Organizational Behavior Modification   **235**
     10   Leadership Theory: Background and Processes   **267**
     11   Leadership Applied: Styles and Performance   **297**

PART 4   THE DYNAMICS OF ORGANIZATIONAL BEHAVIOR:
     GROUPS, INTERACTIVE BEHAVIOR, CONFLICT, STRESS,
     POWER, AND POLITICS   **343**
     12   Group Dynamics   **345**
     13   Interactive Behavior and Conflict   **369**
     14   Job Stress   **398**
     15   Power and Politics   **425**

PART 5   THE PROCESSES AND STRUCTURE OF ORGANIZATIONAL
     BEHAVIOR   **463**
     16   Communication   **465**
     17   Decision Making   **492**
     18   Organization Theory and Design   **516**

PART 6   THE ENVIRONMENTAL CONTEXT OF ORGANIZATIONAL
         BEHAVIOR: ORGANIZATION CULTURE, INTERNATIONAL
         ORGANIZATIONAL BEHAVIOR, AND CHANGE   **559**
         19   Organizational Culture   **561**
         20   International Organizational Behavior   **582**
         21   Organization Change, Development, and the Future **609**

         REFERENCES   **637**

         ACKNOWLEDGMENTS FOR EXPERIENTIAL EXERCISES   **641**

         INDEXES   **643**

CONTENTS

PREFACE | **xxvii**

PART 1 | THE FOUNDATION FOR ORGANIZATIONAL BEHAVIOR | **1**

1 | An Introduction to Organizational Behavior | **3**
Learning Objectives | **4**
The Challenges Facing Management | **4**
The Changing Environment Going into the New Millennium | **5**
A New Perspective for Management | **7**
What Is Organizational Behavior? | **7**
Approaches to Organizational Behavior | **9**
    Cognitive Framework | **10**
    Behavioristic Framework | **11**
    Social Learning Framework | **11**
    Organizational Behavior Framework | **13**
Summary | **14**
Questions for Discussion and Review | **14**
References | **15**
Real Case: It's a Worldwide Problem | **15**
Case: How Is This Stuff Going to Help Me? | **16**
Case: Conceptual Model: Dream or Reality? | **17**

2 | The Background and Methodology | **18**
Learning Objectives | **19**
The Early Practice of Management | **19**
    Pioneering American Managers | **19**
    Organizational Specialists | **21**
    Scientific Managers | **21**
    The Human Relations Movement and
      the Hawthorne Studies | **23**
Behavioral Science Foundation | **25**
    Anthropology | **25**
    Sociology | **27**
    Psychology | **28**
Research Methodology | **29**
    The Overall Scientific Perspective | **29**
    Starting with Theory | **30**
    The Use of Research Designs | **31**

Experimental Designs	**31**
The Validity of Studies	**31**
Case Design	**32**
Survey Design	**33**
Reliability and Validity of Measures	**34**
The Validity Concept	**35**
Content and Predictive Validity	**35**
Construct Validity	**36**
Summary	**37**
Questions for Discussion and Review	**37**
References	**38**
Real Case: Things Will Never Be the Same	**39**
Case: Too Nice to People	**40**
Case: Dilemma for Program Evaluation	**41**
Integrative Contemporary Case for Part 1	**42**
Dispelling the Myths That Are Holding Us Back	**42**
Experiential Exercises for Part 1	**48**
Exercise: Synthesis of Student and Instructor Needs	**48**
Exercise: Work-Related Organizational Behavior: Implications for the Course	**48**

PART 2	THE BASIC BUILDING BLOCKS OF ORGANIZATIONAL BEHAVIOR: A MICRO PERSPECTIVE	**51**
3	Perception	**53**
	Learning Objectives	**54**
	The Nature and Importance of Perception	**55**
	Sensation versus Perception	**55**
	The Senses	**55**
	Definition of Perception	**56**
	Subprocesses of Perception	**56**
	Perceptual Selectivity	**58**
	External Attention Factors	**58**
	Internal Set Factors	**61**
	Perceptual Organization	**68**
	Figure-Ground	**68**
	Perceptual Grouping	**69**
	Perceptual Constancy	**70**
	Perceptual Context	**70**
	Perceptual Defense	**71**
	Social Perception	**73**
	Characteristics of Perceiver and Perceived	**73**
	Attribution	**74**
	Stereotyping	**74**
	The Halo Effect	**75**
	Impression Management	**76**

The Process of Impression Management	**76**
Employee Impression Management Strategies	**77**
Summary	**78**
Questions for Discussion and Review	**78**
References	**79**
Real Case: Is Patriotism for Sale?	**80**
Case: Space Utilization	**80**
Case: Same Accident, Different Perceptions	**81**

4 Personality — **83**

Learning Objectives	**84**
The Meaning of Personality	**84**
The Self-Concept: Self-Esteem and Self-Efficacy	**85**
Person-Situation Interaction	**86**
The Development of Personality	**86**
Adult Life Stages	**87**
Immaturity to Maturity	**88**
Major Determinants of Personality	**90**
Biological Contributions	**90**
Cultural Contributions	**94**
Contributions from the Family	**95**
The Socialization Process	**97**
More Immediate Situational Considerations	**98**
Summary	**102**
Questions for Discussion and Review	**102**
References	**103**
Real Case: Looking for an Equal Chance	**104**
Case: Cheerleader versus Activist	**105**

5 Micro Variables Applied: Job Attitudes, Satisfaction, and Commitment — **107**

Learning Objectives	**108**
The Nature and Dimensions of Attitudes	**108**
Components of Attitudes	**108**
Antecedents of Work-Related Attitudes	**109**
Functions of Attitudes	**109**
Changing Attitudes	**111**
Job Satisfaction	**113**
What Is Meant by Job Satisfaction?	**114**
Measuring Job Satisfaction	**114**
Job Satisfaction of American Employees	**118**
Influences on Job Satisfaction	**121**
Outcomes of Job Satisfaction	**122**
Organizational Commitment	**124**
The Meaning of Organizational Commitment	**124**
The Outcomes of Organizational Commitment	**125**
Summary	**126**

Questions for Discussion and Review   **127**
References   **127**
Real Case: Surprisingly, Positive Attitudes   **129**
Case: Doing His Share   **130**
Case: Measuring Job Satisfaction in a Hospital   **131**

Integrative Contemporary Case for Part 2   **132**
The New Work Ethic: You Cannot Work Too Hard
or Too Long   **132**
Experiential Exercises for Part 2   **140**
Exercise: Self-Perception and Development
of the Self-Concept   **140**
Exercise: He Works, She Works   **140**

PART 3   THE HEART OF ORGANIZATIONAL BEHAVIOR:
MOTIVATION, LEARNING, AND LEADERSHIP   **143**

6   Motivation Theory: Needs and Processes   **145**
Learning Objectives   **146**
The Meaning of Motivation   **146**
Primary Motives   **147**
General Motives   **148**
The Curiosity, Manipulation, and Activity Motives   **148**
The Affection Motive   **148**
Secondary Motives   **149**
The Power Motive   **149**
The Achievement Motive   **150**
The Affiliation Motive   **152**
The Security Motive   **153**
The Status Motive   **154**
Work-Motivation Approaches   **154**
The Content Theories of Work Motivation   **156**
Maslow's Hierarchy of Needs   **156**
Herzberg's Two-Factor Theory of Motivation   **159**
Alderfer's ERG Theory   **161**
The Process Theories of Work Motivation   **162**
Vroom's Expectancy Theory of Motivation   **162**
The Porter-Lawler Model   **165**
Equity Theory of Work Motivation   **167**
Attribution Theory   **169**
Summary   **172**
Questions for Discussion and Review   **173**
References   **174**
Real Case: Keeping Them Motivated   **176**
Case: Star Salesperson   **177**

Case: What Do They Want? **177**
Case: Tom, Dick, and Harry **178**

7 Motivation Applied: Job Design and Goal Setting **180**
Learning Objectives **181**
Job Design **181**
  Background on Job Design **181**
  Job Enrichment **183**
  The Job Characteristics Approach to Task Design **184**
  Guidelines for Redesigning Jobs **187**
  A Social Information Processing Approach **189**
Quality of Work Life and Sociotechnical Design **190**
  The Volvo Project **190**
  Self-Managed Teams **191**
Goal Setting **193**
  Theoretical Background of Goal Setting **193**
  Research on the Impact of Goal Setting **195**
  The Application of Goal Setting to Organizational
    System Performance **197**
Summary **199**
Questions for Discussion and Review **200**
References **201**
Real Case: Made By Hand **203**
Case: The Rubber Chicken Award **204**
Case: Specific Goals for Human Service **205**

8 Learning Theory: Reinforcement and Punishment **206**
Learning Objectives **207**
Types and Theories of Learning **207**
  Connectionist, Behavioristic Theories of Learning **208**
  Cognitive Theories of Learning **210**
  Social Learning Theory **213**
Reinforcement: The Key to Learning **214**
  The Law of Effect **214**
  Definition of Reinforcement **215**
  Positive and Negative Reinforcers **216**
  Escape-Avoidance Learning: A Special Case
    of Negative Reinforcement **217**
  Ways to Identify Positive Reinforcers **218**
  Organizational Reward Systems **218**
Techniques of Administering Reinforcement **224**
  Fixed Ratio Schedules **224**
  Fixed Interval Schedules **224**
  Variable or Intermittent Schedules **225**
  Administration of Reinforcement in Human
    Resources Management **226**

The Effect of Punishment   **227**
    The Definition of Punishment   **227**
    Administering Punishment   **228**
Summary   **229**
Questions for Discussion and Review   **229**
References   **229**
Real Case: Thanks for the Favor   **231**
Case: Contrasting Styles   **232**
Case: Volunteers Can't Be Punished   **233**

9   Learning Applied: Organizational Behavior Modification   **235**
Learning Objectives   **236**
The Steps of Organizational Behavior Modification   **237**
    Step 1: Identification of Critical Behaviors   **237**
    Step 2: Measurement of the Behaviors   **239**
    Step 3: Functional Analysis of the Behavior   **240**
    Step 4: Development of an Intervention Strategy **243**
    Step 5: Evaluation to Ensure Performance Improvement **244**
Experience with the Application of Organizational Behavior
    Modification   **245**
    Manufacturing Applications of O.B. Mod.   **247**
    Nonmanufacturing Applications: Health and
        Service Industries   **253**
Behavioral Self-Management   **256**
    The Meaning and Background of Self-Management **256**
    Strategies for Behavioral Self-Management   **258**
    Applications of Self-Management   **259**
Organizational Behavior Modification in Perspective   **259**
Summary   **263**
Questions for Discussion and Review   **263**
References   **263**
Real Case: Forget the Raise, How about a Nice Bonus?   **265**
Case: Up the Piece Rate   **265**
Case: A Tardiness Problem   **266**

10 Leadership Theory: Background and Processes   **267**
Learning Objectives   **268**
What Is Leadership?   **268**
The Background and Classic Studies on Leadership   **270**
    The Iowa Leadership Studies   **270**
    The Ohio State Leadership Studies   **271**
    The Early Michigan Leadership Studies   **272**
Established Theories of Leadership   **272**
    Trait Theories of Leadership   **273**
    Group and Exchange Theories of Leadership   **275**

Contingency Theory of Leadership	**276**
Path-Goal Leadership Theory	**280**
Emerging Theoretical Frameworks for Leadership	**283**
Charismatic Leadership Theories	**283**
Transformational Leadership Theory	**285**
A Social Learning Approach	**286**
Substitutes for Leadership	**287**
Summary	**289**
Questions for Discussion and Review	**290**
References	**290**
Real Case: Presidential Leadership	**293**
Case: He Sure Looked Good	**294**
Case: The Missing Ingredient	**295**

11	Leadership Applied: Styles and Performance	**297**
	Learning Objectives	**298**
	Leadership Styles	**298**
	Style Implications of the Classic Studies and the Modern Theories	**299**
	Managerial Grid Styles	**302**
	Hersey and Blanchard's Life-Cycle, or Situational, Approach	**304**
	Likert's Four Systems of Management	**305**
	Vroom-Yetton Leadership Model	**309**
	Women and Leadership	**311**
	From Leadership Styles to Managerial Activities	**313**
	What Do Managers Do?	**314**
	What Do Successful Real Managers Do?	**317**
	What Do Effective Real Managers Do?	**318**
	Implications of the Real Managers Study	**318**
	Leadership Skills and Techniques for the Future	**319**
	Summary	**320**
	Questions for Discussion and Review	**321**
	References	**321**
	Real Case: Leading Them into the 21st Century	**323**
	Case: If It Is Good Enough for Us, It Is Good Enough for Them	**323**
	Case: The Puppet	**324**

Integrative Contemporary Case for Part 3	**325**
Farewell, Fast Track	**325**
Experiential Exercises for Part 3	**333**
Exercise: Motivation Questionnaire	**333**
Exercise: Job Design Survey	**335**
Exercise: Role Playing and O.B. Mod.	**337**
Exercise: Leadership Questionnaire	**339**

PART 4 THE DYNAMICS OF ORGANIZATIONAL BEHAVIOR: GROUPS, INTERACTIVE BEHAVIOR, CONFLICT, STRESS, POWER, AND POLITICS **343**

12 Group Dynamics **345**
   Learning Objectives **346**
   The Nature of Groups **346**
       The Dynamics of Group Formation **347**
       Types of Groups **349**
       Implications from Research on Group Dynamics **350**
   Committee Organization **353**
       The Nature and Functions of Committees **354**
       Positive Attributes of Committees **355**
       Negative Attributes of Committees **356**
       "Groupthink": A Major Problem with Committees and Groups **358**
   The Dynamics of Informal Groups **359**
       Norms and Roles in Informal Groups **359**
       Informal Managerial Roles **360**
       Informal Organization Structures **364**
   Summary **364**
   Questions for Discussion and Review **365**
   References **365**
   Real Case: The Mario Brothers Strike Again **366**
   Case: The Schoolboy Rookie **367**
   Case: The Blue-Ribbon Committee **368**

13 Interactive Behavior and Conflict **369**
   Learning Objectives **370**
   Intraindividual Conflict **370**
       Conflict Due to Frustration **370**
       Goal Conflict **374**
       Role Conflict and Ambiguity **376**
   Interpersonal Conflict **378**
       Transactional Analysis **378**
       The Johari Window **384**
       Strategies for Interpersonal Conflict Resolution **385**
   Intergroup Behavior and Conflict **387**
       Intergroup Behavior in Organizations **387**
       The Impact of, and Strategies for, Intergroup Conflict **389**
   Organizational Conflict **391**
       Structural Conflict **391**
       The Role of Conflict in Today's Organizations **392**
   Summary **393**
   Questions for Discussion and Review **394**

References   **394**
Real Case: Do Just the Opposite   **395**
Case: Drinking up the Paycheck   **396**
Case: Arresting the Neighbor's Kid   **396**

14 Job Stress   **398**
Learning Objectives   **399**
The Meaning of Stress   **399**
The Background of Stress   **400**
The Causes of Stress   **401**
    Extraorganizational Stressors   **401**
    Organizational Stressors   **403**
    Group Stressors   **405**
    Individual Stressors: The Role of Dispositions   **405**
The Effects of Job Stress   **410**
    Physical Problems Due to Stress   **411**
    Psychological Problems Due to Stress   **412**
    Behavioral Problems Due to Stress   **412**
Coping Strategies for Stress   **413**
    Individual Coping Strategies   **414**
    Organizational Coping Strategies   **416**
Summary   **418**
Questions for Discussion and Review   **418**
References   **419**
Real Case: Getting along without the Boss   **422**
Case: Sorry, No Seats Are Left, Have a Nice Flight   **423**
Case: A Gnawing Stomachache   **423**

15 Power and Politics   **425**
Learning Objectives   **426**
The Meaning of Power   **426**
    The Distinctions between Power, Authority,
       and Influence   **427**
    The Classifications of Power   **428**
    Contingency Approaches to Power   **432**
    A More Macro View of Power   **437**
Political Implications of Power   **438**
    A Political Perspective of Power in Organizations   **438**
    Specific Political Strategies for Power Acquisition   **440**
    A Final Word on Power and Politics   **443**
Summary   **443**
Questions for Discussion and Review   **444**
References   **444**
Real Case: Fighting Back   **446**
Case: Throwing away a Golden Opportunity   **447**

Integrative Contemporary Case for Part 4   **449**
　　　Superteams at Work   **449**
Experiential Exercises for Part 4   **458**
　　　Exercise: Groups and Conflict Resolution   **458**
　　　Exercise: Power and Politics   **460**

PART 5   THE PROCESSES AND STRUCTURE OF ORGANIZATIONAL
　　　　　BEHAVIOR   **463**

　　16   Communication   **465**
　　　　Learning Objectives   **466**
　　　　Historical Background of the Role of Communication   **467**
　　　　　Fayol's Contribution   **467**
　　　　　Barnard's Contribution   **468**
　　　　　Modern Perspective   **469**
　　　　The Definition of Communication   **470**
　　　　　Management Information Systems   **471**
　　　　　Telecommunication Technology   **472**
　　　　　Nonverbal Communication   **474**
　　　　　Organizational and Interpersonal Communication   **475**
　　　　Interpersonal Communication   **477**
　　　　　The Importance of Feedback   **477**
　　　　　Other Important Variables in Interpersonal
　　　　　　Communication   **479**
　　　　Superior-Subordinate Communication   **479**
　　　　　The Purposes and Methods of Downward
　　　　　　Communication   **479**
　　　　　Media Used for Downward Communication   **481**
　　　　　Ways to Improve Downward Communication   **481**
　　　　Subordinate-Initiated Communication   **482**
　　　　　Methods of Improving the Effectiveness of Upward
　　　　　　Communication　.   **483**
　　　　　Types of Information for Upward Communication   **484**
　　　　Interactive Communication in Organizations   **484**
　　　　　The Extent and Implications of Interactive
　　　　　　Communication   **485**
　　　　　The Purposes and Methods of Interactive
　　　　　　Communication   **485**
　　　　Summary   **487**
　　　　Questions for Discussion and Review   **487**
　　　　References   **487**
　　　　Real Case: 800 to the Rescue   **489**
　　　　Case: Doing My Own Thing   **490**
　　　　Case: Bad Brakes   **491**

17 Decision Making   **492**
     Learning Objectives   **493**
     The Nature of Decision Making   **493**
     Behavioral Decision Making   **495**
          Decision Rationality   **496**
          Models of Behavioral Decision-Making   **496**
     Behaviorally Oriented Decision-Making Techniques   **503**
          Traditional Participative Techniques   **504**
          Modern Participative Techniques   **504**
          Participation Techniques in Perspective   **506**
     Creativity and Group Decision-Making   **506**
          The Process of Creativity   **506**
          Group Decision Making   **508**
          The Delphi Technique   **509**
          The Nominal Group Technique   **510**
     Summary   **511**
     Questions for Discussion and Review   **511**
     References   **512**
     Real Case: Getting Additional Information   **514**
     Case: Harry Smart or Is He?   **515**

18 Organization Theory and Design   **516**
     Learning Objectives   **517**
     The Bureaucratic Model   **517**
          The Characteristics of Bureaucracy   **518**
          Bureaucratic Dysfunctions   **519**
          The Modern View of Bureaucracies   **520**
     Modifications of Bureaucratic Structuring   **522**
          Centralization and Decentralization   **522**
          Flat and Tall Structures   **524**
          Departmentation   **525**
          The Staff Concept of Organization   **529**
     The Roots of Modern Organization Theory   **530**
          The Organization as an Open System   **532**
          Information Processing View of Organizations   **533**
          Contingency and Ecological Organization Theories   **534**
     Modern Organization Designs   **535**
          Project Designs   **535**
          Matrix Designs   **538**
     Summary   **541**
     Questions for Discussion and Review   **542**
     References   **542**
     Real Case: People Are the Real Key   **544**
     Case: The Grass is Greener—or Is It?   **545**
     Case: The Outdated Structure   **545**

Integrative Contemporary Case for Part 5 — **547**
    Managing in Times of Uncertainty — **547**
Experiential Exercises for Part 5 — **554**
    Exercise: Organizations — **554**
    Exercise: Paper Plane Corporation — **555**

PART 6   THE ENVIRONMENTAL CONTEXT OF ORGANIZATIONAL BEHAVIOR: ORGANIZATION CULTURE, INTERNATIONAL ORGANIZATIONAL BEHAVIOR, AND CHANGE — **559**

19   Organizational Culture — **561**
Learning Objectives — **562**
The Nature of Organizational Culture — **562**
    Definition and Characteristics — **562**
    Uniformity of Culture — **563**
    Strong and Weak Cultures — **564**
    Types of Cultures — **568**
Creating and Maintaining a Culture — **568**
    How Organizational Cultures Start — **568**
    Maintaining Cultures through Steps of Socialization — **570**
    Changing Organizational Culture — **573**
Summary — **577**
Questions for Discussion and Review — **577**
References — **578**
Real Case: Look Out World, Here We Come — **579**
Case: Out with the Old, in with the New — **580**
Case: Keeping Things the Same — **581**

20   International Organizational Behavior — **582**
Learning Objectives — **583**
The Impact of Culture on International Organizational Behavior — **584**
    How Do Cultures Vary? — **584**
    Behavior across Cultures — **586**
    Dimensions of Cultural Difference — **588**
Communication in an International Environment — **593**
    Communication Breakdown across Cultures — **593**
    Improving Communication Effectiveness across Cultures — **595**
Motivation of Personnel across Cultures — **596**
    The Meaning of Work — **596**
    Motivational Differences across Cultures — **598**
Managerial Leadership across Cultures — **600**
    Personal Values — **600**

	Managers' Background	**600**
	Interpersonal Skills	**601**
	Decision Making	**602**
	Summary	**603**
	Questions for Discussion and Review	**604**
	References	**604**
	Real Case: Everybody's Everywhere	**606**
	Case: I Want Out	**607**
	Case: Getting the Facts	**607**
21	Organization Change, Development, and the Future	**609**
	Learning Objectives	**610**
	The Changing Environment	**610**
	Organization Development: The Modern Approach to the Management of Change	**614**
	The Historical Development of OD	**615**
	OD Techniques	**615**
	The Impact of a Possible Paradigm Shift on OD-Techniques	**619**
	OD in Perspective	**620**
	The Future of Organizational Behavior	**622**
	Summary	**624**
	Questions for Discussion and Review	**624**
	References	**624**
	Real Case: Meeting the Challenges of the Next Century	**626**
	Case: The High-Priced OD Consultant	**627**
	Integrative Contemporary Case for Part 6	**628**
	Stepping up to the Challenge of Change	**628**
	Experiential Exercise for Part 6	**634**
	Exercise: Organization Development at J. P. Hunt	**634**
	REFERENCES	**637**
	ACKNOWLEDGMENTS FOR EXPERIENTIAL EXERCISES	**641**
	INDEXES	
	Name Index	**643**
	Subject Index	**651**

PREFACE

We are now well into the 1990s and the widely known saying that "the only certainty is change" is truer than ever before. The dizzying rate of change and the accompanying uncertainty has had and will continue to have a tremendous impact on our organizations and the way they are managed. The challenge is clear: in order to be competitive, and even survive, organizations of all types can no longer afford to just do business as usual. How can things get turned around and back on track as we move toward the year 2000? Technologically, most organizations are doing great. On the human side, however, most organizations need to do better. There is no question that to move ahead there is a desperate need for human as well as technologically oriented managers.

To genuinely like people and to want to work with them has become a basic prerequisite for effective management. Yet, however important and necessary it is to enjoy people, it is not sufficient. Managers must also understand and be able to apply innovative techniques to better manage their human resources. This is where the study and application of organizational behavior becomes so important in the years ahead.

Like the previous editions, this latest version provides a strong conceptual framework for the study, understanding, and application of organizational behavior. The previous edition recognized that we are now in a global economy and this international perspective is continued and expanded upon in this edition. Besides having an entire chapter devoted to international organizational behavior, there are international examples in the text discussion, highlighted "International Application Examples" placed in chapters throughout, and some end-of-chapter real cases from the international arena. However, the real strength of the book over the years has been its research base and its comprehensive, readable coverage of the important topics of the field of organizational behavior. This latest edition should enhance this reputation because it has been thoroughly revised and updated to include new research findings and the latest topics. Just as the actual practice side of management can no longer afford to slowly evolve, neither can the academic side of the field. With the world turned upside down for most organizations today, drastically new thinking, approaches, and techniques are needed both in the practice or management and in the way we study and apply the field of organizational behavior.

Conceptual Framework. The book contains twenty-one chapters in six major parts. Part 1 provides the foundation for the study and application of organizational behavior. The introductory chapter points out some reasons for the emerging importance of organizational behavior, defines the field, and presents the various approaches including the cognitive, behavioristic, social learning, and organizational behavior conceptual frameworks. The second chapter provides a historical, behavioral science, and methodological foundation. After this foundation is laid, the subsequent parts of the book progress from a micro to a macro perspective and units of analysis.

The second part takes a very micro approach with chapters on perception and personality and a more applied chapter on job attitudes, satisfaction and commitment. This pattern of having relatively theoretical chapters followed by an applied chapter is continued in Part 3. Called "The Heart of OB", this part contains theory followed by applied chapters on motivation, learning, and leadership. Part 4 moves away from micro oriented concepts and applications and explores the dynamics of organizational behavior with chapters on groups, conflict, stress, and power and politics. Part 5 focuses on the processes and structure of organizational behavior. There are chapters on communication, decision making, and then very macro oriented organization theory and design. The last part provides the environmental context for organization behavior. There are chapters on organization culture, international organizational behavior, and change and development. These six parts and twenty-one chapters are fairly self-contained. Thus, a whole part, selected chapters, or even sections of chapters, could be dropped or studied in a different sequence without damaging the flow or content of the book.

New Topical Coverage. A number of new topics are added to this edition. These include topics such as the following:

impression management	personal control and learned
self-esteem	helplessness
self-efficacy	psychological hardiness
positive and negative affectivity	employee empowerment
prosocial and citizenship	telecommunication technology
behaviors	active listening
organizational commitment	behavioral decision making
attribution errors	judgmental heuristics and biases
SIPA (social information processing	creativity process
approach) model of job design	divergent thinking
self-managed teams	cognitive complexity
control theory	social decision schemes
pay for performance	status quo tendency
cognitive resource theory	organizational ecology theory
transformation leadership styles	population ecology
charismatic styles of leadership	learning organization
women and leadership	diverse workforce
managerial activities	paradigm shift

Pedagogical Features. As with the previous edition, there are several strong pedagogical features. First, each chapter opens with a contemporary (all but three are new for this edition) vignette drawn from the real world. These opening vignettes set a relevant applications perspective for the student and help to relate the more theoretical content of each chapter to real events, real people, and real organizations. Second, to further reflect and reinforce the applications orientation of the text, self-contained, set-off real-world application examples appear in each of the chapters. As mentioned earlier, some of these are "International Application Examples" to maintain the global perspective throughout the text. To keep these applications examples timely, most are new to this edition.

Besides the opening vignettes and the applications examples, the text also features experiential exercises and cases. The end of each major part contains exercises to get students involved in solving simulated problems or experiencing first-hand organizational behavior issues. Besides the usual end-of-chapter short discussion cases, there is also a "Real Case" at the end of each chapter. These cases are drawn from recent events (most are new to this edition) and are intended to enhance the relevancy and application of the theories and research results presented in the chapter. The same is done for each of the six major parts. A new, longer, integrative real case that is relevant to the preceding chapters is placed at the end of each part. These end-of-chapter and end-of-part real cases serve as both examples and a discussion vehicle. It is suggested that students read them, especially the longer end-of-part ones, even if they are not discussed in class. The intent is that they can serve as outside readings as well as discussion cases.

This edition also contains learning objectives that start off each chapter. These objectives should help students better focus and prepare for what follows in the chapter. Finally, the chapters have the usual end-of-chapter summaries and review and discussion questions.

Intended Audience. Despite the significant changes and additions, the purpose and the intended audience of the book remain the same. Like the earlier editions, this edition is aimed at those who wish to take a totally up-to-date, research-based approach to organizational behavior and human resources management. It does not assume the reader's prior knowledge of either management or the behavioral sciences. Thus, the book can be used effectively in the first or only course in four-year or two-year colleges. It is aimed primarily at the behavioral follow-up course to the more traditional introductory management course, or it can be used in the organizational behavior course in the M.B.A. program. I would like to acknowledge and thank my many colleagues in countries around the world who have used previous editions of the book and point out that the cultural and international perspective and coverage should make this new edition very relevant and attractive. Finally, the book should be helpful to practicing managers who want to understand and more effectively manage their most important asset—their human resources.

Acknowledgments. Every author owes a great deal to others, and I am no exception. First and foremost, I would like to acknowledge the help on this as well as many other writing projects that I have received from Professor Richard M. Hodgetts of Florida International University. He has been an especially valued colleague and friend over the years. Next, I would like to acknowledge the interaction I have had with my colleagues John Schaubroeck, Steve Sommer, and Doug May in the organizational behavior area at the University of Nebraska. In particular,

I would like to acknowledge the total support and standards of excellence provided by my departmental chairman, Sang M. Lee. Linda Rohn, Debbie Burns, and especially Cathy Jensen from the Management Department staff have been very helpful. Dean Gary Schwendiman has also been very supportive. In getting started in my academic career, I never want to forget the help, encouragement, and scholarly values I received from Professors Henry H. Albers and Max S. Wortman. Over the years, I have been very lucky to have been associated with excellent doctoral students. I would like to thank them all for teaching me as much as I have taught them. In particular, I would like to mention Professors Elaine Davis of Saint Cloud State University, Tim Davis of Cleveland State University, Marilyn Fox of Mankato State University, Avis L. Johnson of the University of Akron, Robert Kreitner of Arizona State University, Diane Lockwood of Seattle University, Mark Martinko of Florida State University, Harriette S. McCaul of North Dakota State University, Nancy C. Morey of Western Illinois University, James L. Nimnicht of Central Washington University, Stuart A. Rosenkrantz of the University of Central Florida-Daytona Beach, Carol Steinhaus of Indiana University–Purdue University at Fort Wayne, Linda Thomas of the University of Nebraska-Omaha, Kenneth Thompson of DePaul University, Robert Waldersee of the University of New South Wales, Australia, Dianne H. B. Welsh of Eastern Washington University, and Steve Williams of the National University of Singapore, as having had an especially important impact on my recent thinking about organizational behavior. I am also very grateful to those professors who used the previous editions of the book and gave me valuable feedback for making this revision. In particular, I would like to thank: Charles Kuehl, University of Missouri, St. Louis; Jeffrey K. Pinto, University of Maine; Robert J. Rush, Wheeling Jesuit College; Allen B. Shub, Northeastern Illinois University; Jack L. Simonetti, University of Toledo; Ronald J. Sivitz, Pace University; David Turnipseed, Georgia Southern University; and Robert H. Vaughn, Lakeland Community College, who read and gave their comments on the manuscript. I would also like to take this opportunity to publicly acknowledge the support and dedication I have received from my McGraw-Hill editors over the years. In particular, I feel very fortunate to have worked with Alan Sachs in recent years. I would also like to thank my editing supervisor Peggy Rehberger. Finally, as always, I am deeply appreciative and dedicate this book to my wife and children, who gave me the time and encouragement to complete this book.

FRED LUTHANS

ORGANIZATIONAL BEHAVIOR

PART **1**

THE FOUNDATION
FOR ORGANIZATIONAL
BEHAVIOR

1

An Introduction to Organizational Behavior

A pressing question for the years ahead is whether America can effectively compete in the world marketplace. This is true in all industries, but the most visible and perhaps the most critical is in manufacturing in general and automobiles in particular. The Japanese, of course, have made dramatic inroads in America's market share, and the Europeans are not far behind. General Motors has countered this competition with a new car line produced in a new plant that is intended to meet the competition and go beyond.

GM's Saturn plant in Spring Hill, Tennessee, is considered the grand experiment in American manufacturing and a working laboratory for human resource management. GM committed eight years and $3.5 billion to launch the Saturn. Its huge plant is the most self-reliant assembly plant built in the United States since Henry Ford's Rouge River complex in 1927. However, it is not technology which separates the Saturn plant from other manufacturing facilities. Rather, the Saturn plant represents a profound change in the way people are managed. The plant has 165 work teams that have been given more power than workers at any other GM plant, or even any Japanese plant. Saturn workers are empowered to do the following: interview and approve new hires for their teams; decide by consensus how to run their own area (when workers see a problem, they can pull on a blue handle and shut down the entire line); and have budget responsibilities (one team rejected a piece of equipment and went to another supplier for a replacement that was deemed to be safer). All employees are on salary and bonuses are based on quality.

Much is at stake on whether this radical experiment will work. As Lester Thurow, the dean of MIT's Sloan Management School, noted: "Saturn will have enormous psychological impact on American business. If Saturn is successful, it will prove that it's possible to junk the old bureaucracies, change the corporate culture, change the adversarial relationships between union and management, and put it all back together right. If they succeed, it will be a big positive for America. If not, it will be a huge downer."

Learning Objectives

- **Present** the major challenges facing today's management.
- **Analyze** the changing environment going into the new millennium.
- **Define** the organizational behavior approach, explaining how it differs from other approaches to managing people.
- **Relate** the various approaches to organizational behavior including the cognitive, behavioristic, and social learning frameworks.
- **Explain** a conceptual framework for the study of organizational behavior.

The opening vignette indicates that effective management is facing enormous challenges, but some new ways of managing people are being tried, which is what this book is all about. Organizational behavior is involved with the study and application of the human side of management. This introductory chapter simply gives the perspective and approach to the field. After a discussion of the challenges currently facing management, the new perspective of taking an organizational behavior approach is presented. Next, the definition and characteristics of organizational behavior, and how it differs from other behaviorally oriented approaches, are explained. The chapter concludes with the behavioral science perspectives and a conceptual framework for organizational behavior.

THE CHALLENGES FACING MANAGEMENT

Although the field of organizational behavior has been around for at least the past twenty-five years, as we move toward the year 2000, the new millennium, there are still significant human-oriented problems facing organizations. In the past decade, managers were preoccupied with restructuring their organizations to improve productivity and meet the competitive challenges in the international marketplace. Although the resulting "lean and mean" organizations offered some at least short-run benefits in terms of lowered costs and improved productivity, they won't be able to meet the challenges that lie ahead. Specifically, they:

1. *Won't be fast enough* to match the product development time of foreign competitors or to spot an opportunity in fractionating consumer markets.
2. *Won't be keen enough* to deliver the higher levels of service customers will increasingly demand or to achieve leaps in productivity beyond the easy gains everybody got from screwing down on costs.
3. *Won't be smart or sensitive enough* to manage a polyglot work force or to satisfy its best employees, baby-boomers facing a sort of collective mid-life crisis (Is that all there is to my work?).[1]

These challenges in the years ahead are just examples of the need for new thinking and new approaches to management. We have made too many mistakes, if not out and out blunders, in the past. Here are a sampling of things that have gone wrong in American business:

1. Xerox launched the first commercial fax machine over twenty-five years ago, but going into the 1990s they had 7 percent of the U.S. market while Japanese companies had two-thirds.
2. Raytheon in 1947 sold its first Radarange, a microwave oven marketed to restaurants. When the company introduced a household version twenty years later, sales boomed. Now four out of five American homes have microwaves. But three out of four microwaves sold here are made in the Far East.
3. American-owned companies built 80 percent of the autos sold in the United States in 1979. Over the following decade, U.S. carmakers shuttered thirteen North American car and truck assembly plants, while eleven new plants opened under Japanese management. The Big Three's share of domestic sales fell to 67 percent.[2]

What is wrong, and what can managers do about it? Well, first of all, there is no reason to panic or surrender to the Japanese, or the Germans, or anyone else. America is still the most productive nation in the world and all indicators point to a continuing strong economy in the future. By the same token, there is no question that the approaches that have been used in the past to manage organizations and people will not be sufficient for the future. Before examining and defining the proposed organizational behavior perspective and approach, let us review the major environmental changes facing managers as we move toward the new millennium.

THE CHANGING ENVIRONMENT GOING INTO THE NEW MILLENNIUM

The global, one-world economy has arrived. The so-called "Golden Triangle" of North America (United States, Canada, and Mexico), the Pacific Rim (Japan and the newly industrialized countries or NICs of South Korea, Taiwan, Hong Kong, and Singapore), and the European Community or EC (Western and now Central and Eastern European countries) will dominate this global economy in this decade.[3] However, the rest of the world and especially the export-driven countries of Southeast Asia such as Thailand, Malaysia, and Indonesia will also become major players in the global marketplace in the years ahead. This global competitiveness will perhaps be the biggest challenge facing the field of management going into the new millennium.

A second major challenge is that we have already entered the second generation of the Information Age. The first generation was characterized by automated data processing. This second generation has moved to automated decision making and telecommunications. Decision support and expert systems and E-mail, putting every member of the organization in direct communication with everyone else, even around the world, have become commonplace. Such an information explosion has tremendous implications for the field of management.

Still another major challenge that is of particular importance to the field of management is the "Quality Service Revolution" that is occurring around the world. Quality of products and services has become the competitive edge in the world marketplace. The International Application Example shows how Toyota has done it.

Toyota's Rapid Inch-Up

Just about every organization today understands the competitive edge that quality can provide. For many, however, the question becomes how to do it. For example, how should a quality emphasis be introduced and at what point should additional quality be added? Toyota provides an excellent answer to this question. Their answer: Build the best product you can and then continually make improvements. That's why even the new General Motor's Saturn plant cannot match Toyota's cost advantage. Toyota has learned two things that are bound to help it keep ahead of the competition. First, improved quality often results in lower costs. Rather than moving in opposite directions, quality and low cost usually move in the same direction. Those with the poorest quality tend to have the highest costs and vice versa. Second, by continually improving the quality of its product, Toyota puts the competition at an extreme disadvantage. One consultant has referred to this Toyota strategy as "rapid inch-up." Every year the products get better and better. And this is no easy feat, given that the firm introduces more new models every year than any other auto firm. Nevertheless, the company's market growth shows that customers worldwide agree that Toyotas are excellent cars. The firm currently holds almost 45 percent of the Japanese auto market and it sells more than 1 million cars and trucks in the United States each year. At present, Toyota is the third largest auto firm in the world and the fourth largest in the United States.

What is also impressive about Toyota's approach is its behavioral orientation. No one at the company is ever satisfied with the current product quality. As the chief of personnel puts it, "Our current success is the best reason to change things." What he means is that the firm's permanent dissatisfaction with its performance produces exemplary results. This is in direct contrast to many of its competitors who are quick to point out that the latest auto industry ratings show that their cars meet some of the highest quality standards in the world. While Toyota is continually mentioned in these ratings, it is only a sign to the management that previous goals have been met. But whether the cars currently coming down the line will also be the best is another matter. This undoubtedly helps explain why quality will continue to be a dominant thrust at Toyota and why the firm is likely to remain one of the world's best auto companies.

Whereas price, brand loyalty, attractive design, and technical innovation are still important to consumers in developed countries, the quality of products has surged ahead in relative importance. Also, the delivery of quality in the exploding service sector has become critical.[4]

Importantly, there is accumulating evidence that the delivery of quality products and service to customers has a direct impact on the success of organizations. For example, the Profit Impact of Market Strategy (PIMS) study, conducted by the U.S.-based Strategic Planning Institute utilizing comprehensive data from over 3,000 firms over a fifteen-year period, found that those judged to have the best quality products and service come out on top.[5] The key, of course, is to realize that the human resources of the firm, not advertising slogans nor statistical quality control, deliver quality goods and services.[6] The challenge for organizations across the world is to have their human resources deliver quality products and—especially—service to each other (internal customers) and to customers and clients.

A NEW PERSPECTIVE FOR MANAGEMENT

How is management going to meet the challenges outlined above? Management is generally considered to have three major dimensions—technical, conceptual, and human. The technical dimension consists of the manager's expertise in computers or accounting or engineering or marketing. There seems little question that today's managers are technically competent. They know the technical requirements of their jobs inside and out. This is a major reason why this country remains the most powerful in the world. American managers have the technical know-how to get the job done. But few today would question that at least in the past, most practicing managers either ignored the conceptual and human dimensions of their job or made some overly simplistic assumptions.

Although there were certainly exceptions, most managers thought, and many still do, that their employees were basically lazy, that they were interested only in money, and that if you could make them happy, they would be productive. When such assumptions were accepted, the human problems facing management were relatively clear-cut and easy to solve. All management had to do was devise monetary incentive plans, ensure security, and provide good working conditions; morale would then be high, and maximum productivity would result. It was as simple as one, two, three. Human relations experts, industrial psychologists, and industrial engineers supported this approach, and personnel managers implemented it.

Unfortunately, this approach has not worked out in practice. Although no real harm has been done, and some good actually resulted in the early stages of organizational development, it is now evident that such a simplistic approach falls far short of providing a meaningful solution to the complex challenges facing today's management. The assumptions have been questioned and for the most part have been invalidated by research and experience.

The major fault of the traditional approach is that the assumptions overlook far too many aspects of the problem. Human behavior at work is much more complicated and diverse than is suggested by the economic-security–working-conditions approach. The new organizational behavior approach assumes that employees are extremely complex and that there is a need for theoretical understanding backed by rigorous empirical research before applications can be made for managing people effectively. The transition has now been completed. The traditional human relations approach no longer has a dominant role in the behavioral approach to management. Few people would question that the organizational behavior approach, with its accompanying body of knowledge, dominates the behavioral approach to management now and will do so in the foreseeable future.

WHAT IS ORGANIZATIONAL BEHAVIOR

Now that organizational behavior has become the widely accepted approach, it is beginning to develop and mature as an academic discipline. As with any other relatively new academic endeavor, however, there have been some rough spots and sidetracks in its development. Besides the healthy academic controversies over theoretical approach or research findings, perhaps the biggest problem that organizational behavior has had to face is an identity crisis. Exactly what is meant by *organizational behavior*? Is it an attempt to replace all management with behavioral science concepts and techniques? How, if at all, does it differ from good old applied or industrial psychology? Fortunately, these questions have now largely been answered to the satisfaction of most management academicians, behavioral scientists, and management practitioners.

Figure 1.1 shows in very general terms the relationships and emphasis of organizational behavior (OB) and the related disciplines of organization theory (OT), organization development (OD), and personnel/human resources (P/HR). As shown, OB tends to be more theoretically oriented and at the micro level of analysis. Specifically, OB draws from many theoretical frameworks of the behavioral sciences that are focused at understanding and explaining individual and group behavior in organizations. As with other sciences, OB accumulates knowledge and tests theories by accepted scientific methods of research. In summary, *organizational behavior* can be defined as the understanding, prediction, and control of human behavior in organizations.

Although Figure 1.1 is not intended to portray mutually exclusive domains for the related fields, because the lines are becoming increasingly blurred and there is not universal agreement of what belongs to what among academics or practitioners, most people in the field would generally agree with what is shown. Organization theory tends to be more macro oriented than OB and is concerned primarily with organization structure and design. Yet, as in this text (Chapter 18), OT topics are included in the study and application of OB. Organization development, on the other hand, tends to be both more macro and more applied than OB. But also like

FIGURE 1.1
The relationship of organizational behavior to other closely related disciplines.

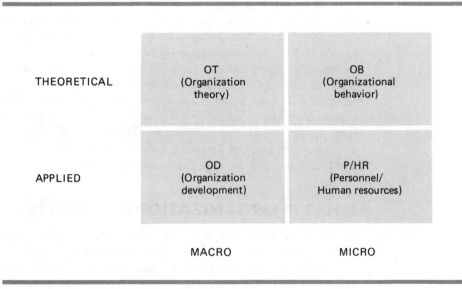

	MACRO	MICRO
THEORETICAL	OT (Organization theory)	OB (Organizational behavior)
APPLIED	OD (Organization development)	P/HR (Personnel/ Human resources)

OT, as in this text (Chapter 21), OD topics are included in the study and application of OB. Finally, as shown, P/HR tends to have a more applied focus than OB. The personnel/human resources function is a part of practicing organizations as much as the marketing, finance, or production/operations functions are.

Personnel or human resource managers (the more modern term is the latter) are hired and found with this title in practicing organizations; organizational behaviorists are not. Yet, somewhat confusingly, those managers who apply and draw from the field of organizational behavior (whether they be marketing managers, finance managers, hospital administrators, operations managers, store managers, academic administrators, office managers, *or* personnel/human resource managers) are called "human resource managers." They are called human resource managers and have a human resource management role (in addition to their other technical, functional, role), because they all manage people. Thus, all managers, regardless of their technical function, are human resource managers in this view because they deal with human behavior in organizations. These managers need to have an understanding and perspective of organizational behavior.

Organizational behavior represents the *behavioral* approach to management, not the whole of management. Other recognized approaches to management include the process, quantitative, systems, and contingency approaches. In other words, organizational behavior does not intend to portray the whole of management. The charge that old wine (applied or industrial psychology) has merely been poured into a new bottle (organizational behavior) has also proved to be groundless. Although it is certainly true that the behavioral sciences make a significant contribution to both the theoretical and the research foundations of organizational behavior, it is equally true that applied or industrial psychology should not be equated with organizational behavior. For example, organization structure and management processes (decision making and communication) play an integral, direct role in organizational behavior, as in this text (Part 5), but have at most an indirect role in applied or industrial psychology. The same is true of many important dynamics and applications of organizational behavior. Although there will probably never be total agreement on the exact meaning or domain of organizational behavior—which is not necessarily bad, because it makes the field more exciting—there is little doubt that organizational behavior has come into its own as a field of study, research, and application.

This book on organizational behavior attempts to provide the specific, necessary background and skills to make the managers of today and tomorrow as effective with the conceptual and human dimensions of management as they have been in the past with its technical dimensions.

APPROACHES TO ORGANIZATIONAL BEHAVIOR

Although organizational behavior is extremely complex and includes many inputs, the cognitive, behavioristic, and social learning frameworks can be used to develop an overall framework. After first examining these approaches, the last section of the chapter presents an organizational behavior framework that conceptually links and structures the rest of the book.

Cognitive Framework

The cognitive approach to human behavior has many sources of input. The chapters in the next part will provide some of this background. For now, however, it can be said simply that the cognitive approach gives people much more "credit" than the other approaches. The cognitive approach emphasizes the positive and free-will aspects of human behavior and utilizes concepts such as expectancy, demand, and incentive. *Cognition,* which is the basic unit of the cognitive framework, is the act of knowing an item of information. Under this framework, cognitions precede behavior and constitute input into the person's thinking, perception, problem solving, and processing information.

The classic work of Edward Tolman can be used to represent the cognitive approach. Although considered a behaviorist in the sense that he believed behavior to be the appropriate unit of analysis, Tolman felt that behavior is purposive, that it is directed toward a goal. In his laboratory experiments, he found that animals learned to expect that certain events would follow one another. For example, animals learned to behave as if they expected food when a certain cue appeared. Thus, Tolman believed that learning consists of the *expectancy* that a particular event will lead to a particular consequence. This cognitive concept of expectancy implies that the organism is thinking about, or is conscious or aware of, the goal. Thus, Tolman and others espousing the cognitive approach felt that behavior is best explained by these cognitions.

Contemporary psychologists carefully point out that a cognitive concept such as expectancy does not reflect a guess about what is going on in the mind; it is a term that describes behavior. In other words, the cognitive and behavioristic theories are not as opposite as they appear on the surface and sometimes are made out to be—for example, Tolman considered himself a behaviorist. Yet, despite some conceptual similarities, there has been a controversy throughout the years in the behavioral sciences on the relative contributions of the cognitive versus the behavioristic framework. As often happens in other academic fields, this debate has gone back and forth through the years.

Because of the recent advances from both theory development and research findings, there has been what some have termed a "cognitive explosion" in the field of psychology.[7] Applied to the field of organizational behavior, a cognitive approach has traditionally dominated through units of analysis such as perception (Chapter 3), personality (Chapter 4), attitudes and job satisfaction (Chapter 5), motivation (Chapter 6) and goal setting theory (Chapter 7). Very recently, there has been renewed interest in the role that cognitions can play in organizational behavior in terms of advancement in research on how managers make decisions and in the area of social cognition. The behavioral decision making area is concerned with the cognitions involved in judgement and choice[8] and will be given attention in Chapter 17. Social cognition involves the process of understanding or making sense of people's behavior[9] and is especially relevant to organizational behavior in terms of social perception (Chapter 3) and attribution theories of motivation (Chapter 6). In other words, both the traditional and newer approaches to cognitive theory and application play an important role in the framework of this text. However, before discussing the specific input that the cognitive approach can make to the study of organizational behavior, it is necessary to have a better understanding of the behavioristic approach.

Behavioristic Framework

Chapters 8 and 9 will discuss the behavioristic school of thought in psychology. Its roots can be traced to the work of Ivan Pavlov and John B. Watson. These pioneering behaviorists stressed the importance of dealing with observable behaviors instead of the elusive mind that had preoccupied the earlier psychologists. They used classical conditioning experiments to formulate the stimulus-response (S-R) explanation of human behavior. Both Pavlov and Watson felt that behavior could be best understood in terms of S-R. A stimulus elicits a response. They concentrated mainly on the impact of the stimulus and felt that learning occurred when the S-R connection was made.

Modern behaviorism marks its beginnings with the work of B. F. Skinner. Recently deceased, Skinner is widely recognized for his contributions to psychology. He felt that the early behaviorists helped explain respondent behaviors (those behaviors elicited by stimuli) but not the more complex operant behaviors (those behaviors which are not elicited by stimuli but which simply occur; operant behaviors are emitted by the organism). In other words, the S-R approach helped explain physical reflexes; for example, when stuck by a pin (S), the person will flinch (R), or when tapped below the kneecap (S), the person will extend the lower leg (R). On the other hand, Skinner found through his operant conditioning experiments that the consequences of a response could better explain most behaviors than eliciting stimuli could. He emphasized the importance of the response-stimulus (R-S) relationship. The organism has to operate on the environment in order to receive the desirable consequence. The preceding stimulus does not cause the behavior in operant conditioning; it serves as a cue to emit the behavior. For Skinner, behavior is a function of its consequences.

Both classical and operant conditioning are given more detailed attention in Chapter 8. For now, however, it is important to understand that the behavioristic approach is environmentally based. It implies that cognitive processes such as thinking, expectancies, and perception do not play a role in behavior. However, as in the case of the cognitive approach, which includes behavioristic concepts, some psychologists feel that there is room for cognitive variables in the behavioristic approach. In particular, a social learning approach has emerged in recent years that incorporates both cognitive and behavioristic concepts and principles.

Social Learning Framework

The cognitive approach has been accused of being mentalistic, and the behavioristic approach has been accused of being deterministic. Cognitive theorists argue that the S-R model, and to a lesser degree the R-S model, is much too mechanistic an explanation of human behavior. A strict S-R interpretation of behavior seems justifiably open to the criticism of being too mechanistic, but because of the scientific approach that has been meticulously employed by behaviorists, the operant model in particular has made a tremendous contribution to the study of human behavior. The same can be said of the cognitive approach. Much research has been done to verify its importance as an explanation of human behavior. Instead of polarization and unconstructive criticism between the two approaches, it now seems time to recognize that each can make an important contribution to the study of human behavior. The social learning approach tries to integrate the contributions of both approaches.

It must be emphasized that the social learning approach is a behavioral approach. It recognizes that behavior is the appropriate unit of analysis. However, unlike a strict or radical behavioristic approach, under the social learning approach it is felt that people are self-aware and engage in purposeful behavior. Under a social learning approach, people are thought to learn about their environment, alter and construct their environment to make reinforcers available, and note the importance of rules and symbolic processes in learning.[10]

Although a number of psychologists are associated with social learning, the work of Albert Bandura is probably the most representative of this approach.[11] He takes the position that behavior can best be explained in terms of a continuous reciprocal interaction between cognitive, behavioral, and environmental determinants. The person and the environmental situation do not function as independent units but, in conjunction with the behavior itself, reciprocally interact to determine behavior. Bandura explains that "it is largely through their actions that people produce the environmental conditions that affect their behavior in a reciprocal fashion. The experiences generated by behavior also partly determine what a person becomes and can do, which, in turn, affects subsequent behavior."[12] The triangular model shown in Figure 1.2 takes this work of Bandura and translates it into relevant units of analysis and variables in organizational behavior.

FIGURE 1.2
A social learning approach to organizational behavior.

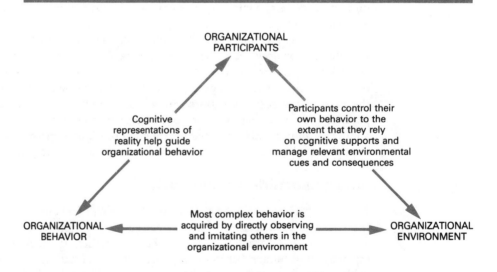

The specifics of social learning, such as vicarious or modeling processes, the role of cognitive mediating processes, and the importance of self-control procedures, will be discussed in Chapters 8 and 9. But for now, it can be said that social learning, with its very comprehensive, interactive nature, serves as an excellent conceptual framework and point of departure for the study of organizational behavior.[13]

Organizational Behavior Framework

Organizational behavior has the advantage of being a relatively young and growing field of study. It can legitimately borrow, in an eclectic manner, the best from the various established frameworks for human behavior. Traditionally, most writers on organizational behavior have taken a humanistic, cognitive approach. For example, Douglas McGregor, who wrote the classic *Human Side of Enterprise* in 1960, took a humanistic approach, and well-known theorists such as Victor Vroom and Lyman Porter depended mainly on cognitive concepts in their writings on organizational behavior. In the last few years, the behavioristic model has begun to be utilized in theorizing and research on organizational behavior. In many ways, what the field of organizational behavior has been going through in recent years is a replay of the behavioristic-versus-cognitive controversy that has existed and, in many respects, still exists in psychology. Now, in organizational behavior, as in the more established behavioral sciences, the time seems to have come to recognize the contributions of both approaches and to begin to synthesize and integrate both into a comprehensive framework for organizational behavior. The social learning approach provides a good foundation for such an eclectic organizational behavior framework.

The reason for presenting the cognitive and behavioristic frameworks was to better understand, not evaluate, the complex phenomena collectively called *human behavior.* Understanding human behavior in organizations is also a vital goal for a conceptual framework for organizational behavior. In addition, however, because organizational behavior is not a basic behavioral science such as psychology or sociology, two other especially desirable goals besides understanding are prediction and control. The field of organizational behavior serves as the basis for modern human resources managers. Prediction and control of human resources are critical to the goals of a new approach to management that will help solve the problems and meet the challenges identified in the introductory comments of the chapter. Thus, the goals of a conceptual framework for organizational behavior are to understand, predict, and control human behavior in organizations.

The cognitive approach seems essential to the understanding of organizational behavior. The behavioristic approach can also lead to understanding, but perhaps even more important is the contribution it can make to prediction and control. For example, on the basis of Edward Thorndike's classic law of effect, the behavioristic approach would say that organizational behavior followed by a positive or reinforcing consequence will be strengthened and will increase in subsequent frequency and that organizational behavior followed by an unpleasant or punishing consequence will be weakened and will decrease in subsequent frequency. Thus, organizational behavior can be predicted and controlled on the basis of managing the contingent environment.

If the three goals of understanding, prediction, and control are to be met by a conceptual framework for organizational behavior, both the cognitive and the behavioristic approaches become vitally important. Both the internal causal factors, which are cognitively oriented, and the external environmental factors, which are behavioristically oriented, become important. In other words, the social learning approach that incorporates both cognitive and behavioristic concepts is an appropriate conceptual framework for organizational behavior that will help understand, predict, and control.

Summary

The chapter started by pointing out the emerging importance of organizational behavior in light of the significant challenges facing managers now and as we move toward the new millennium. Next, organizational behavior was precisely defined as the understanding, prediction, and control of human behavior in organizations, representing human resource managers (broadly defined) and the behavioral approach to management.

Everyone is concerned with human behavior. Yet philosophers, theologians, behavioral scientists, managers, and the person on the street have still not completely reached a true understanding of human behavior in general or of organizational behavior in particular. All people think they are experts and are defensive about their views. The difference between the behavioral science approach and the other approaches is that behavioral scientists use the methods of science and take an understanding, rather than an evaluating, approach.

The most widely recognized frameworks from the behavioral sciences are the cognitive approach, the behavioristic approach, and the emerging and more integrative social learning approach. The cognitive model gives the human being more "credit" and assumes that behavior is purposive and goal-oriented. Cognitive processes such as expectancy and perception help explain behavior. The behavioristic approach deals with observable behavior and the environmental contingencies of the behavior. Classical behaviorism explained behavior in terms of S-R, whereas more modern behaviorism gives increased emphasis to contingent consequences, or R-S. The social learning approach emphasizes that the person, the environment, and the behavior itself are in constant interaction with one another and reciprocally determine one another. This social learning approach incorporates both cognitive and behavioristic elements and is used as the conceptual framework for organizational behavior used by this book.

Questions for Discussion and Review

1. What are some of the major challenges facing today's and tomorrow's organizations?
2. What are generally considered to be the three major dimensions of management? How do they compare and contrast with one another now, and what is needed in the future?

3. How does organizational behavior relate to, or differ from, organizational development? Organization theory? Personnel and human resources management?
4. In your own words, identify and summarize the various theoretical frameworks for understanding organizational behavior.
5. How does the social learning approach differ from the cognitive approach? How does the social learning approach differ from the behavioristic approach?
6. Explain the conceptual framework for organizational behavior that is used in this book. Does it meet the goals of understanding, prediction, and control?

References

1. Walter Kiechel III, "The Organization that Learns," *Fortune*, March 12, 1990, p. 133.
2. Thomas A. Stewart, "Lessons from U.S. Business Blunders," *Fortune*, April 23, 1990, p. 128.
3. John Naisbitt and Patricia Aburdene, *Megatrends 2000*, Morrow, New York, 1990, Chap. 1.
4. D. Keith Denton, "The Service Imperative," *Personnel Journal*, March 1990, pp. 66–74, and Michael J. Mandel, "There's a Silver Lining in the Service Sector," *Business Week*, March 4, 1990, pp. 60–61.
5. B. Uttal, "Companies that Serve You Best," *Fortune*, December 7, 1987, pp. 98–116.
6. Fred Luthans, "Quality Is an HR Function," *Personnel*, May 1990, p. 72.
7. Ronald E. Riggio, *Introduction to Industrial/Organizational Psychology*, Scott, Foresman/Little, Brown, Glenview, Ill., 1990, p. 16.
8. See R. J. Herrnstein, "Rational Choice Theory," *American Psychologist*, March 1990, pp. 356–367; Robin M. Hogarth, *Judgment and Choice*, 2d ed., Wiley, New York, 1987; and Max H. Bazerman, *Judgment in Managerial Decision Making*, 2d ed., Wiley, New York, 1990.
9. See Stephen Worchel, Joel Cooper, and George Goethals, *Understanding Social Psychology*, 4th ed., Dorsey Press, Chicago, 1988, Chap. 2, and Robert S. Wyer, Jr., and Thomas K. Srull, *Memory and Cognition*, Erlbaum, Hillsdale, N.J., 1989.
10. Spencer A. Rathus, *Psychology*, 4th ed., Holt, Rinehart and Winston, Fort Worth, Tex., 1990, p. 410.
11. Albert Bandura, "Social Learning Theory," in J. T. Spence, R. C. Carson, and J. W. Thibaut (eds.), *Behavioral Approaches to Therapy*, General Learning Press, Morristown, N.J., 1976; Albert Bandura, *Social Learning Theory*, Prentice-Hall, Englewood Cliffs, N.J., 1977; Albert Bandura, "The Self System in Reciprocal Determinism," *American Psychologist*, April 1978, pp. 344–358; and Albert Bandura, *Social Foundations of Thought and Action: A Social-Cognitive Theory*, Prentice-Hall, Englewood Cliffs, N.J., 1986.
12. Bandura, *Social Learning Theory*, p. 9.
13. See Tim R. V. Davis and Fred Luthans, "A Social Learning Approach to Organizational Behavior," *Academy of Management Review*, April 1980, pp. 281–290; Robert Kreitner and Fred Luthans, "A Social Learning Approach to Behavioral Management: Radical Behaviorists Mellowing Out," *Organizational Dynamics*, Autumn 1984, pp. 61–75; and Fred Luthans and Robert Kreitner, *Organizational Behavior Modification and Beyond*, Scott, Foresman, Glenview, Ill., 1985.

REAL CASE: IT'S A WORLDWIDE PROBLEM

During this decade, the effective application of organizational behavior theories and techniques is going to be a challenge not only for American firms but for international companies as well, because of the coming world labor shortage. More and more firms around the globe are going to be competing for the available work force, and only the best are going to be successful. The reason for this new development is quite simple: The population growth of the world has not kept pace with the human resource needs of the global economy. Consider some of the specific challenges that will face some nations.

In Japan, the elderly population is growing at nearly six times that of the United States. As a result, new human resource management ideas will have to be introduced—including rewarding employees more for their contribution to the company and less for their seniority with the firm. Equality of women in the workplace is also going to be forced on Japanese firms as they begin to realize that, in order to hire and retain women, it will be necessary to promote them into managerial positions. There will also be greater concern for helping Japanese employees deal with their family responsibilities. Over two-thirds of all Japanese senior citizens live with their children. Therefore, to meet its social responsibilities, the Japanese government is now building 9,000 new day-care centers for the elderly. There are going to be a great number of changes in Japan during this decade, and these are going to greatly affect what goes on in the workplace.

The same is true in Europe. Germany, for example, has the oldest work force in Europe and companies there are now scurrying to attract and retain young people. One way is by encouraging people to work past the typical retirement age of sixty. Another way is improving benefit packages and promotion opportunities. There is also a current move toward training people for service sector jobs, since this area will grow faster than manufacturing during the upcoming decades. Other countries in Europe are following similar approaches. In the process, business organizations are now developing improved methods of managing employees in the workplace, including more effective communication practices and motivation and leadership approaches.

The same work-force pattern is taking place in the United States. The only major difference is that the Americans may be better positioned for the worldwide labor shortage because they have long encouraged immigration and have been able to attract highly talented people from other parts of the world. Nevertheless, as the ethnic makeup of the work force changes and international competition intensifies, American firms are going to find themselves relying increasingly on more effective organizational behavior concepts and techniques to motivate and lead their people.

1. In what way is the worldwide labor shortage changing the environment of the global, one-world economy?
2. How is this shortage resulting in a new perspective for management? Is this perspective more technical or behavioral in focus?
3. How does this case help explain the close linkage between organizational behavior and personnel/human resources? Why is it important for a manager of the 1990s to be able to link these two areas?

**Case:
How Is This
Stuff Going
to Help Me?**

Jane Arnold wants to be a manager. She enjoyed her accounting, finance, and marketing courses. Each of these provided her with some clear-cut answers. Now the professor in her organizational behavior course is telling her that there are really very few clear-cut answers when it comes to managing people. He has discussed some of the history of behavioral management and says that behavioral science concepts play a big role in the course. Jane is very perplexed. She came to school to get answers on how to be an effective manager, but this course surely doesn't seem to be heading in that direction.

1. How would you relieve Jane's anxiety? How is a course in organizational behavior going to make her a better manager?
2. Why did the professor start off with a brief introduction to the behavioral science framework?
3. How does a course in organizational behavior differ from courses in fields such as accounting, finance, or marketing?

Case: Conceptual Model: Dream or Reality?

Hank James has been section head for the accounting group at Yake Company for fourteen years. His boss, Mary Stein, feels that Hank is about ready to be moved up to the corporate finance staff, but it is company policy to send people like Hank to the University Executive Development Program before such a promotion is made. Hank has enrolled in the program; one of the first parts deals with organizational behavior. Hank felt that after fourteen years of managing people, this would be a snap. However, during the lecture on organizational behavior the professor made some comments that really bothered Hank. The professor said:

> Most managers know their technical job but do a lousy job of managing their people. One of the problems is that just because supervisors have a lot of experience with people, they think they are experts. The fact is that behavioral scientists are just beginning to scratch the surface of understanding human behavior. In addition, to effectively manage people we also have to somehow be able to better predict and control organizational behavior. Some models are just beginning to be developed that we hope will help the manager better understand, predict, and control organizational behavior.

Hank is upset by the fact that his professor apparently discounts the value of experience in managing people, and he cannot see how a conceptual framework that some professor dreamed up can help him manage people better.

1. Do you think Hank is justified in his concerns after hearing the professor? What role can experience play in managing people?
2. What is the purpose of a conceptual framework such as the one presented in this chapter? How would you weigh the relative value of studying theories and research findings versus "school-of-hard-knocks" experience for the effective management of people?
3. Using the conceptual framework presented in the chapter, how would you explain to Hank that this could help him better manage people in his organization?

2

The Background and Methodology

■ The Illumination Studies at the Hawthorne Works of Western Electric: A Serendipitous Discovery

Several years ago, Western Electric phased out and shut down its Hawthorne Works outside of Chicago. However, back in 1924 the now famous illumination studies were conducted at the huge plant. The studies attempted to examine the relationship between light intensity on the shop floor of manual work sites and employee productivity. A test group and a control group were used. The test group in an early phase showed no increase or decrease in output in proportion to the increase or decrease of illumination. The control group with unchanged illumination increased output by the same amount overall as the test group. Subsequent phases brought the level of light down to moonlight intensity: the workers could barely see what they were doing, but productivity increased. The results were baffling to the researchers. Obviously, some variables in the experiment were not being held constant or under control. Something besides the level of illumination was causing the change in productivity. This something, of course, was the complex human variable.

It is fortunate that the illumination experiments did not end up in the wastebasket. Those responsible for the Hawthorne studies had enough foresight and spirit to accept the challenge of looking beneath the surface of the apparent failure of the experiments. In a way, the results of the illumination experiments were a serendipitous discovery, which, in research, is an accidental discovery. The classic example is the breakthrough for penicillin which occurred when Sir Alexander Fleming accidentally discovered green mold on the side of a test tube. That the green mold was not washed down the drain and that the results of the illumination experiments were not thrown into the trash basket can be credited to the researchers' not being blinded by the unusual or seemingly worthless results of their experimentation. The serendipitous results of the illumination experiments provided the impetus for the further study of human behavior at work and, most scholars would agree, mark the beginning of the field of organizational behavior.

- **Trace** the early background of American management through pioneers such as William C. Durant.
- **Present** the organizational specialists in the history of management through examples such as Henri Fayol and Alfred P. Sloan.
- **Discuss** the scientific management movement under Frederick W. Taylor.
- **Relate** the early human relations movement through the Hawthorne studies.
- **Identify** the behavioral sciences of anthropology, sociology, psychology, and social psychology.
- **Explain** research methodology through theory building and the experimental, case, and survey designs.
- **Define** reliability and the various types of validity.

Although the illumination studies at Hawthorne may be thought of as the single most important beginning of the field of organizational behavior, there are obviously other important historical and academic foundations. The purpose of this chapter is to trace through this foundation and background. The first section explores the early practice of management. Next, the emergence of the more directly relevant human relations movement is examined. The last half of the chapter is concerned with the parallel foundation for organizational behavior that comes from the behavioral sciences. After a very brief overview of anthropology, sociology, and psychology, the research methods and perspective coming from the behavioral sciences are given attention. In total, this management and behavioral science foundation serves as the point of departure for the more specialized—but more directly relevant—topics for organizational behavior in the rest of the book.

THE EARLY PRACTICE OF MANAGEMENT

Although there have been managers and management as long as there have been organized civilizations, the beginning of management as we know it today is really a product of this century.

Pioneering American Managers

William C. Durant, the founder of General Motors, is an outstanding example of the initial phase of the practice of management in the twentieth century. In 1908 he laid the building blocks for the company that was to become the largest manufacturing concern in the world. Durant had the necessary entrepreneurial skills to build the giant corporation's foundation. It was essentially a one-man operation in which Durant made all major decisions, and he preferred subordinates who were yes-men. All pertinent information and records were carried in his head. His day-to-day activities and decision making were based on hunch, experience, and intuition.

Other famous pioneering managers were Henry Ford, Cornelius Vanderbilt, Andrew Carnegie, and John D. Rockefeller. All these men were brilliant but sometimes ruthless. They possessed the qualities necessary for the initial stages of industrialization. However, when the industrial revolution began to mature and become stabilized, this approach was no longer appropriate. Although Durant's style was highly effective in the early days of General Motors, after a while "chinks began to appear in the armor."[1] By 1920, General Motors was in serious financial trouble. Within a few weeks' time Durant himself had lost nearly $100 million. There were many contributing causes to the General Motors crisis. For example, insufficient use of accounting and inventory control was a big problem.[2] However, two major difficulties stood out from the rest: Durant refused to utilize staff advice, and he failed to come up with an organizational plan that could hold together the tremendous corporate structure he had created.

Some of Durant's behaviorally oriented shortcomings are exemplified by his handling of two brilliant subordinates, Walter Chrysler and Alfred P. Sloan. Chrysler, who at the time headed the Buick Division of General Motors, remembered how he pleaded with Durant to

> . . . please, now say what your policies are for General Motors. I'll work on them; whatever they are. I'll work to make them effective. Leave the operations alone; the building, the buying, the selling, and the men—leave them alone, but say what your policies are.[3]

Chrysler also told of an almost unbelievable encounter he had with Durant:

> Once I had gone to New York in obedience to a call from him [Durant]; he wished to see me about some matter. For several days in succession I waited at his office, but he was so busy he could not take the time to talk with me. . . . During a lull I gained his attention for a minute. "Hadn't I better return to Flint and work? I can come back here later." "No, no. Stay right here." I waited four days before I went back to Flint; and to this day I do not know why Billy [Durant] had required my presence in New York.[4]

Because of this kind of shabby treatment, Chrysler eventually quit General Motors and founded what was to become one of that company's biggest competitors.

A similar blunder was Durant's treatment of Alfred P. Sloan. In May 1920, when General Motors was in the beginning of its decline, Sloan submitted to Durant an ingenious plan of organization. The plan reflected many insights into the company's problems and contained some logical solutions. Durant apparently ignored the plan completely. Sloan was so distraught over the outright rejection without discussion or consultation that he was about to resign from the company when the du Pont family assumed control of the corporation. In December 1920, Pierre S. du Pont resubmitted Sloan's organizational plan to the board of directors, and this time it was accepted. Sloan was made president of the company and was allowed to implement his plan. Using his new methods of management, he practically single-handedly rescued General Motors from the sure-death management methods used by Durant. The early pioneers, such as Durant, played a necessary initial role, but it was organizational specialists such as Sloan who then perpetuated and strengthened what they had founded.

Organizational Specialists

Two successful practicing managers, the French engineer and executive head Henri Fayol and General Motors' Alfred P. Sloan, best represent the "Great Organizers." Fayol's career embodied many different phases. He made his initial mark as a practicing mining engineer. Then, as a research geologist, he developed a unique theory on the formation of coal-bearing strata. This experience gave him a keen appreciation for the technical side of enterprise. However, the major portion of his career was spent practicing, and then writing about, the managerial functions and process.

In 1888, Fayol became managing director of Comambault, the well-known French combine. When he assumed the top position, no dividend had been paid for three years and bankruptcy was approaching. Fayol's ingenious managerial and organizational methods soon paid off. The decline was shortly reversed, and the combine was able to make a significant contribution to the French cause during World War I. Fayol retired in 1918, but through writing and speaking engagements he succeeded in popularizing his theories and techniques of management. He maintained that the successful practicing manager should be able to handle people and should have considerable energy and courage.

Alfred P. Sloan is the other outstanding historical example of a Great Organizer. His basic organizational plan was for General Motors to maintain centralized control over highly decentralized operations. Although the du Ponts undoubtedly influenced Sloan, he is widely recognized as having made a tremendous managerial contribution.[5] His plan is largely responsible for the success story of General Motors. Ernest Dale states: "Sloan's organization study—the report on which the G.M. reorganization was based—is a remarkable document. Almost entirely original, it would be a creditable, if not a superior, organization plan for any large corporation today. It is a landmark in the history of administrative thought."[6] In the first year after the du Ponts installed Sloan as president, the company almost doubled its manufacturing capacity. The reorganization went hand in hand with increased productivity and higher profits.

After he retired, Sloan wrote *My Years with General Motors*, an instant best-seller when it came out in 1964. Peter Drucker, the famous management writer and consultant, recently called Sloan's autobiography the best book on management ever written. One of the insights that Drucker particularly likes in Sloan's book concerns the manager's approach to his or her people:

> The job of a professional manager is not to like people. It is not to change people. It is to put their strengths to work.[7]

The Great Organizers were concerned primarily with overall managerial organization in order for their companies to survive and prosper. The scientific management movement around the turn of the century took a narrower, operations perspective. Yet the two approaches were certainly not contradictory. The managers in both cases applied the scientific method to their problems, and they thought that effective management at all levels was the key to organizational success. The two approaches differed chiefly in that the scientific managers worked from the bottom of the hierarchy upward, whereas the organizationalists worked from the apex downward. In other words, both had essentially the same goals, but they tried to reach them from different directions.

Frederick W. Taylor is the recognized father of scientific management. Although the validity of some of Taylor's accomplishments has been questioned,[8] comprehensive analysis of Taylor's work concludes: "With respect to the principle of scientific decision making techniques such as time study, standardization, goal setting, money as a motivator, scientific selection, and rest pauses, Taylor's views were fundamentally correct and have been generally accepted."[9] The accompanying Application Example, A First-Rate Company, indicates that the scientific management approach by Taylor is still alive and well in some modern applications.

Taylor dramatically contributed to increased productivity through his scientific management philosophy and principles. In Taylor's words, this approach can be summarized as (1) science, not rule of thumb; (2) harmony, not discord; (3) cooperation, not individualism; (4) maximum output, in place of restricted output; and (5)

Application Example
||||➡

A First-Rate Company

Frederick Taylor believed that by choosing a "first-rate" person and then training that individual carefully, he could obtain first-rate performance. In recent years, his idea of first-rate performance has taken a number of different forms. One way is expressed through top-quality performance. In fact, an international award is now given to the firm that has the highest quality. This Deming award, named after an American engineer who introduced quality control in Japan, is highly coveted. Thus far, the only American recipient has been Florida Power and Light (FPL). After eighteen months of scrutinizing the quality service delivered by FPL, the Deming committee concluded that FPL deserved the honor. How did it do it? Here are some examples of the things that FPL did to become a first-rate company:

- Power-line installation has been made faster and easier because of a simple template developed by a team of linemen. The device holds plastic pipe in place as cable is pulled through. Previously, pipes would often shift, causing costly delays.
- Meter readers' dog-bite injuries have declined since the adoption of a team's suggestion that hand-held computers be programmed to beep a warning when the reader punches in the address of a house known to have a dog on the premises.
- Suggestions from the company's various divisions have produced solutions to problems such as: how to reduce the number and duration of power outages; how to replace existing transmission-line components with stainless steel to reduce corrosion from salt spray; and how to prevent bird droppings from corroding power lines.

Quite obviously, many of the criteria that Taylor envisioned as leading to a first-rate company are being met by FPL.

the development of each person to his or her greatest efficiency and prosperity.[10] These concepts obviously recognize and even emphasize the importance of the human element at work.

The Human Relations Movement and the Hawthorne Studies

Although the early pioneers and organizational specialists and, as pointed out above, even the scientific managers recognized the behavioral side of management, the human relations movement focused directly on the importance of human beings at work. Although there were varied and complex reasons such as the Great Depression of the 1930s and the labor union movement, the Hawthorne studies marked the beginning.

Relay Room Studies. The illumination studies (as discussed in the opening vignette of the chapter) were the first phase, but they were followed by a study in the relay room which tried to test specific variables such as length of workday, rest breaks, and method of payment. The results were basically the same as those of the illumination studies: each test period yielded higher productivity than the previous one. Even when the women were subjected to the original conditions of the experiment, productivity increased. The conclusion was that the independent variables (rest pauses and so forth) were not by themselves causing the change in the dependent variable (output). As in the illumination experiments, something was still not being controlled.

Bank Wiring Room Studies. The final phase was the bank wiring room study. As in the preceding relay room experiments, the bank wirers were placed in a separate test room. The researchers were reluctant to segregate the bank wiring group because they recognized that this would alter the realistic factory environment they were attempting to simulate. However, for practical reasons, the research team decided to use a separate room. Unlike the relay room experiments, the bank wiring room study involved no experimental changes once the study had started. Instead, an observer and an interviewer gathered objective data for study. Of particular interest was the fact that the department's regular supervisors were used in the bank wiring room. Just as in the department out on the factory floor, their main function was to maintain order and control.

The results of the bank wiring room study were essentially opposite to those of the relay room experiments. In the bank wiring room there were not the continual increases in productivity that occurred in the relay room. Rather, output was actually restricted by the bank wirers. By scientific management analysis—for example, time and motion study—the industrial engineers had arrived at a standard of 7312 terminal connections per day. This represented 2½ equipments. The workers had a different brand of rationality. They decided that 2 equipments was a "proper" day's work. Thus, 2½ equipments represented the management norm for production, but 2 equipments was the informal group norm and the actual output. The researchers determined that the informal group norm of 2 equipments represented restriction of output rather than a lack of ability to produce at the company standard of 2½ equipments.

Of particular interest from a group dynamics standpoint were the social pressures used to gain compliance to the group norms. The incentive system dictated that the more an individual produced, the more money the individual would earn. Also, the best producers would be laid off last, and thus they could be more secure by producing more. Yet, in the face of this management rationale, almost all the workers restricted output. Social ostracism, ridicule, and name-calling were the major sanctions utilized by the group to enforce this restriction. In some instances, actual physical pressure in the form of a game called "binging" was applied. In the game, a worker would be hit as hard as possible, with the privilege of returning one "bing," or hit. Forcing rate-busters to play the game became an effective sanction. These group pressures had a tremendous impact on all the workers. Social ostracism was more effective in gaining compliance to the informal group norm than money and security were in attaining the scientifically derived management norm.

Implications of the Hawthorne Studies. Despite some obvious philosophical[11] and methodological limitations by today's standards of research (which will be covered at the end of this chapter), the Hawthorne studies did provide some interesting insights that contributed to a better understanding of human behavior in organizations. For instance, one interesting aspect of the Hawthorne studies is the contrasting results obtained in the relay room and the bank wiring room. In the relay room, production continually increased throughout the test period, and the relay assemblers were very positive. The opposite was true in the bank wiring room; blatant restriction of output was practiced by disgruntled workers. Why the difference in these two phases of the studies?

One clue to the answer to this question may be traced to the results of a questionnaire administered to the women in the relay room. The original intent of the questions was to determine the health and habits of the women. Their answers were generally inconclusive except that *all* the operators indicated they felt "better" in the test room. A follow-up questionnaire then asked about specific items in the test room situation. In discussions of the Hawthorne studies, the follow-up questionnaire results, in their entirety, usually are not mentioned. Most discussions cite the women's unanimous preference for working in the test room instead of the regular department. Often overlooked, however, are the women's explanations for their choice. In order of preference, the women gave the following reasons:

1. Small group
2. Type of supervision
3. Earnings
4. Novelty of the situation
5. Interest in the experiment
6. Attention received in the test room[12]

It is important to note that novelty, interest, and attention were relegated to the fourth, fifth, and sixth positions. These last three areas usually are associated with the famous Hawthorne effect. Many social scientists imply that the increases in the relay room productivity can be attributed solely to the fact that the participants in the study were given special attention and that they were enjoying a novel, interesting experience. This is labeled the *Hawthorne effect* and is, of course, a real problem with all human experimental subjects. But to say that all the results of the relay room experiments were due to such an effect on the subjects seems to ignore the important impact of the small group, the type of supervision, and earnings. All these variables (that is, experimental design, group dynamics, styles of leadership and supervision, and rewards), and much more, separate the old human relations movement and the modern approach to the field of organizational behavior.

BEHAVIORAL SCIENCE FOUNDATION

So far the chapter has traced the historical foundation for organizational behavior through the practice of management. This section provides the other key foundataion for organizational behavior, the behavioral sciences. A working knowledge of the behavioral sciences and their research methods is a necessary prerequisite for the study of organizational behavior. A behavioral science foundation is what separates the organizational behavior approach from the older, more simplistic human relations approach. The disciplines of anthropology, sociology, and psychology and their accompanying rigorous research methods make an important contribution to a better understanding of human behavior in modern organizations.

Anthropology

A basic behavioral science foundation starts with the discipline of anthropology. *Anthropology* is literally defined as the science of man. The term combines the Greek stem *anthropo* ("man") and the noun ending *logy* ("science"). Although there are many subfields within anthropology and different units of analysis, cultural anthropology with the culture unit of analysis is most relevant to organizational behavior. Chapter 19 is devoted specifically to organizational culture and the International Application Example on the next page demonstrates the importance of culture to international management, which will be covered in Chapter 20. However, to serve as a foundation for the study of organizational behavior it is important to understand how anthropologists define and use "culture."

Definition of Culture. There are numerous definitions of *culture*. After a survey of more than a hundred of them many years ago, it was concluded that the following was the most comprehensive definition: "Culture consists of patterns, explicit and implicit, of and for behavior acquired and transmitted by symbols, constituting the distinctive achievement of human groups, including their embodiments in artifacts."[13] A modern definition of "culture" would be "the acquired knowledge that people use to interpret experience and generate social behavior."[14] This latter view of culture emphasizes both *content* and *meaning* and is most applicable to organizational behavior.

> ## Do's and Don'ts in the Middle East
>
> At first, the OPEC oil cartel and—more recently—the war in the "Persian Gulf," or as #2 below notes more accurately the "Arabian Gulf," has brought considerable attention to the Middle East. The media coverage during the war gave many new insights, but how much do we really know about their culture and customs? Here are some sound guidelines of do's and don'ts when interacting with those in the Middle East:
>
> 1. Local Islamic religious custom demands that everything stop five times a day for prayers. While you are not expected to kneel or face Mecca, do not interrupt or display impatience while your host is praying.
> 2. Never refer to the "Persian Gulf." This body of water is known as the "Arabian Gulf."
> 3. While it is customary to shake hands with your host, do not be surprised if the individual welcomes you with a kiss on both cheeks. It is good manners to return the gesture at the same time.
> 4. The business week runs from Saturday to Thursday. Expect to work on Sunday.
> 5. If you are invited to the home of your host, do not be surprised if his wife is not on hand. She is probably in the kitchen preparing the meal and will not appear at the table. Do not inquire about her; this is considered impolite. Most entertainment is done with other men; wives are seldom seen.
> 6. Do not ask for an alcoholic drink. Arabs do not drink alcoholic beverages; it is a violation of their religion.
> 7. Unless your host provides you with a knife and fork, be prepared to eat with your fingers. Watch your host and let him take the lead. Also remember that eating is done with the right hand only.
> 8. During conversation, stay away from religion and politics. The growth and development of the country you are visiting is a good, safe topic.

Characteristics of a Culture. Although there is not complete agreement on the underlying theories, most modern anthropologists agree on certain characteristics of culture. In brief, there is general agreement that culture is:

1. *Learned.* It is not genetic or biological, but, of course, it does interact in complex ways with human biology.
2. *Shared.* People as members of groups or organizations share culture; it is not special to single individuals.
3. *Transgenerational.* It is cumulative in its development and is passed down from one generation to the next.
4. *Symbolic.* It is based on the human capacity to symbolize, to use one thing to represent another.
5. *Patterned.* It is organized and integrated; a change in one part will bring changes in another part.
6. *Adaptive.* It is based on the human capacity to adapt, as opposed to the more genetically determined adaptive process of most other animals.

Depending on the theoretical position of the anthropologist, other characteristics could be added, but for organizational behavior purposes the characteristics of learned, shared, symbolic, and patterned are especially relevant.

Significance of Culture. The important role that culture plays in human behavior may be one of the most underrated concepts in the behavioral sciences. Culture dictates what people learn and how they behave. One management theorist points out the nature and significance of culture by making an analogy with the sea: "We are immersed in a sea. It is warm, comfortable, supportive, and protecting. Most of us float below the surface; some bob about, catching glimpses of land from time to time; a few emerge from the water entirely. The sea is our culture."[15]

Because of the sudden popularity of culture applied to modern organizations, there is the danger of misusing the concept. Recently, some anthropologists are cautioning that the concept of culture is being over-applied and misapplied, particularly in the form of so-called "corporate culture." For example, one anthropologist recently noted that corporate culture has been used as an excuse for inefficiency and managerial stupidity. "When Ford had twenty-two levels of management and Toyota five, the difference was not in corporate culture but in sheer competence."[16]

It is important to recognize that when culture is applied to the field of organizational behavior, there are two distinct levels. One application of culture is as a set of general attributes of people (such as the things discussed in the previous section—learned, shared, and adaptive). In addition, culture can be used to identify the specific content of a *particular* group of people, such as blue-collar workers versus white-collar workers or high-tech employees versus customer service employees, and to treat organizations "as if" they were cultures, as Chapter 19 does.

Sociology

Although anthropology has made a big contribution to the understanding of organizational behavior, and in the future will undoubtedly make a bigger one, the behavioral science discipline of sociology is more widely recognized. *Sociology* is traditionally defined as the science of society. To the uninformed, its purposes and goals are often unclear. Many equate sociology with social work and the solving of social problems. Some even relate sociology to the political philosophy of socialism. In reality, sociology is at the same time narrower and broader than the areas with which it is often confused.

Contemporary sociology is characterized by rigorous methodology with an empirical emphasis and conceptual consciousness. The major thrust common to all areas of sociology is toward the goal of understanding interdependent social behavior. The primary units of analysis studied by modern sociologists, going from the largest to the smallest, are the society, the institution, the organization, the group, and norms and roles. Most relevant to the study of organizational behavior are the latter three—the organization, the group, and norms and roles. In fact, whole chapters and parts of other chapters of this book are devoted to these units of analysis. Chapters 12 and 13 (on groups) and Chapter 18, which deals with the macro perspective of organizational behavior, as well as many of the contemporary organizational development techniques covered in Chapter 21, are sociologically based.

Psychology

Whereas sociology plays a big part in the macro perspective, psychology is the most significant foundation for the micro approach to organizational behavior. As Chapter 1 indicated, the micro perspective dominates contemporary organizational behavior, so it follows that a grounding in psychology is necessary.

Modern *psychology* is almost universally defined as the science of human behavior, although psychology has many different schools of thought and units of analysis.[17] In particular, the cognitive and behaviorist approaches discussed in the last chapter have had the most impact of late on the orientation of modern psychologists. On the whole, however, contemporary psychologists take an eclectic theoretical approach and generally divide themselves into areas such as experimental, clinical, and social. The social area is particularly relevant to organizational behavior.

There are many slight variations in the definitions of *social psychology*. One comprehensive definition is that it is the study of individual behavior in relation to the social environment. The most important part of the social environment is other persons, individually and collectively. More simply, *social psychology* is defined as the study of individual behavior within a group. This definition points out the close ties that social psychology has to psychology (individual emphasis) and sociology (group emphasis).

The logical breakdown for analysis and study in social psychology is the individual, the group, and the interaction between the individual and the group. The last-named provides the key difference between the study of social psychology and the study of psychology and sociology. An example is the approach taken in the study of groups. Social psychology is more concerned with why an individual joins a group (affiliation) and wants to remain a member of the group (cohesion). The social psychologist focuses primarily on group structure and function only to the extent that they affect individual behavior. Besides the study of groups, topics of general interest to the social psychologist include:

1. *Attitudes,* their formation and change
2. *Communication research,* the effect that networks have on individual and group efficiency and satisfaction
3. *Problem solving,* the analysis of cooperation versus competition
4. *Social influences,* the impact of conformity and other social factors on individual behavior
5. *Leadership,* especially the identification and function of leaders and their effectiveness

More specialized theories (such as cognitive dissonance) and analysis (such as approach-avoidance conflict) are also a vital part of social psychology.

As these topics indicate, social psychology is very closely related to organizational behavior. This is evidenced by the overall orientation and table of contents of this book. Part 4, in particular, borrows heavily from the theories and research findings of social psychology. Moreover, a mutually beneficial relationship seems to exist between the disciplines of social psychology and organizational behavior. One of the major purposes of this book is to help develop and refine this relationship.

RESEARCH METHODOLOGY

All the behavioral sciences discussed so far depend upon a rigorous research methodology in order to better understand human behavior. This search for the truth of why humans behave the way they do is a very delicate and complex process. In fact, the problems are so great that many scholars, chiefly from the physical and engineering sciences, argue that there can be no precise science of behavior. They maintain that humans cannot be treated like chemical or physical elements; they cannot be effectively controlled or manipulated. For example, the critics state that, under easily controllable conditions, 2 parts hydrogen to 1 part oxygen will always result in water and that no analogous situation exists in human behavior. Human variables such as motives, learning, perception, values, and even "hangovers" on the part of both subject and investigator confound the controls that are attempted. For these reasons, behavioral scientists in general and organizational behavior researchers in particular are often on the defensive and must be very careful to comply with accepted methods of science.

The Overall Scientific Perspective

Behavioral scientists in general and organizational behavior researchers in particular strive to attain the following hallmarks of any science:

1. The overall purposes are understanding/explanation, prediction, and control.
2. The definitions are precise and operational.
3. The measures are reliable and valid.
4. The methods are systematic.
5. The results are cumulative.

Figure 2.1 summarizes the relationship between the practical behavioral problems facing today's human resources managers and unanswered questions, research methodology, and the existing body of knowledge. When a question arises or a problem evolves, the first place to turn for an answer is the existing body of knowledge. It is possible that the question can be immediately answered, or the problem solved, without going any further. Unfortunately, this usually is not true in the case of organizational behavior. One reason is that the amount of knowledge directly applicable to organizational behavior is relatively very small, primarily because of the newness of the field.

It must be remembered that behavioral science is relatively young and that organizational behavior is even younger—it is really a product of the 1970s. The Hawthorne studies go back over sixty years, but a behavioral science–based approach to the study and application of organizational behavior is very recent. The sobering fact is that many questions and problems in organizational behavior cannot be directly answered or solved by existing knowledge. Thus, a working knowledge of

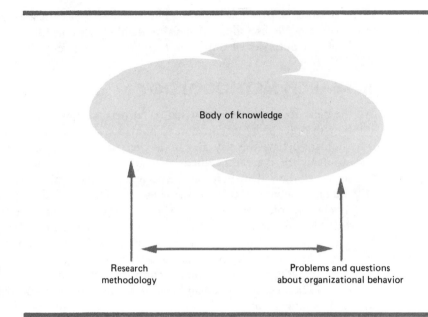

FIGURE 2.1
Simple relationships between problems, methodology, and knowledge.

research methodology becomes especially important to future managers, both as knowledgeable and critical consumers of the rapidly expanding literature reporting the results of organizational behavior research and as sophisticated practitioners who are capable of applying appropriate research methods to solve difficult problems in the workplace.

Starting with Theory

It has often been said (usually by theoreticians) that there is nothing so practical as a good theory. Yet students of organizational behavior are usually "turned off" by all the theories that pervade the field. The reason for all the theories, of course, is the newness of the field and the fact that there are not yet many definitive answers. The purpose of any theory, including all those found in organizational behavior, is to explain and predict the phenomena in question; theories allow the researcher to deduce logical propositions or hypotheses that can be tested by acceptable designs. Theories are ever-changing on the basis of the research results. Thus, theory and research go hand in hand.

John Miner, in the introductory comments in his book *Theories of Organizational Behavior*, gives several criteria for how to "know a good theory when we see one":

1. It should contribute to the goals of science by aiding understanding, permitting prediction, and facilitating influence.
2. There should be clear boundaries of application so that the theory is not used in situations for which it was never intended.
3. It should direct research efforts toward important, priority problems and issues.

4. It should produce generalizable results beyond single research efforts.
5. It should be readily subject to further testing by using clearly defined variables and operational terms.
6. Not only should it be confirmed by research directly derived from it, but it should also be consistent within itself and with other known facts.
7. It should be stated in the simplest possible terms.[18]

The Use of Research Designs

The research design is at the very heart of scientific methodology; it can be used to answer practical questions or to test theoretical propositions/hypotheses. The three designs most often used in organizational behavior research today are the experimental, the case, and the survey designs. All three have played important roles in the development of meaningful knowledge. The experimental design is borrowed largely from psychology, where it is used extensively, and the case and survey designs have traditionally played a bigger role in sociology. All three designs can be used effectively for researching organizational behavior.

Experimental Designs

A primary aim of any research design is to establish a cause-and-effect relationship. The experiment method offers the best possibility of accomplishing this goal. All other factors being equal, most researchers prefer this method of testing hypotheses. Simply defined, an experiment involves the manipulation of independent variables to measure their effect on, or the change in, dependent variables, while everything else is held constant or controlled. Usually, an experimental group and a control group are formed. The experimental group receives the input of the independent variables, and the control group does not. Any measured change in the dependent variable in the experimental group can be attributed to the independent variable, assuming that no change has occurred in any other variable and that no change has occurred in the control group. The controls employed are the key to the successful use of the experimental design. If all intervening variables are held constant or equal, the experimenter can conclude with a high degree of confidence that the independent variable caused the change in the dependent variable.

The Validity of Studies

The value of any research study is dependent on its validity, that is, whether the study really demonstrates what it is supposed to demonstrate. In particular, a study must have both *internal validity* and *external validity* in order to make a meaningful contribution to the body of knowledge. A study has internal validity if there are no plausible explanations of the reported results other than those reported. The threats to internal validity include but are not limited to:

1. *History.* Uncontrolled intervening events that occur between the time the pre-experiment measurement is taken and the time the postexperiment measurement is taken.
2. *Maturation.* Changes in the subject or subjects with the mere passing of time, irrespective of the experimental treatment.

3. *Testing.* The effect of previous testing on a subject's present performance.
4. *Instrumentation.* Changes in measures of subject performance due to changes in the instruments or observers over time.
5. *Regression.* Changes in performance due to subjects' going from extreme scores to more typical scores.
6. *Selection.* Changes due to the differences in the subjects rather than the treatment.
7. *Ambiguity about direction of causation.* Does A cause B, or does B cause A? This is a problem with correlational studies.
8. *Local history.* Changes due to the unique situation when the experimental group received the treatment.[19]

Laboratory studies usually control these threats to internal validity better than field studies do. But, as Daniel Ilgen has pointed out, this control afforded by the laboratory is purchased at the price of generalizability and relevance. "As a result, many behavioral scientists decry the use of any laboratory research and dismiss results obtained from such as irrelevant or, worse yet, misleading for the understanding of naturally occurring human behavior."[20]

But, in general, the threats can be minimized, even in field settings, by *pretests* (these allow the investigator to make sure that the experimental and control groups were performing at the same level before the experimental manipulations are made, and they give measurement over time); *control groups* (these permit comparison with experimental groups—they have everything the same except the experimental manipulation); and *random assignment* (this pretty well assures that the experimental and control groups will be the same, and it allows the correct use of inferential statistics to analyze the results). Thus, the threats to internal validity can be overcome with careful design of the experiment. This is not always true of external validity, which is concerned with the generalizability of the results obtained. In order for a study to have external validity, the results must be applicable to a wide range of people and situations. The field experiment tends to have better external validity than the laboratory experiment because at least the experiment takes place in a real setting.

In general, the best strategy is to use a number of different designs to answer the same question. The weaknesses of the various designs can offset one another. Normally, the research would start with a laboratory study to isolate and manipulate the variable or variables in question. This would be followed by an attempt to verify the findings in a field setting. This progression from the laboratory to the field may lead to the soundest conclusions. However, free observation in the real setting should probably even precede laboratory investigations of organizational behavior problems or questions.

Case Design

The case design makes a complete examination and analysis of one or a few behavioral entities (worker, supervisor, work group, department, organization) over an extended period. The purpose is to discover and analyze *every* aspect of the particular case under investigation. The case researcher typically uses field observation, existing records, and questionnaires and interviews to gather data. As applied to organizational behavior research, the case design should not be confused with the case-study approach used by social workers and psychotherapists or even with the "case" approach widely used in courses in business policy. The case method as used in organizational behavior research is much more rigorous and comprehensive.

The actual conduct of case research is most crucial to its success. Three areas are generally recognized as being crucial for successful case research:

1. *The attitude of the investigator.* In order for the case technique to be successful, the investigator must be alertly receptive and must be seeking rather than testing. The investigator should be continuously reformulating and redirecting as new information is uncovered.
2. *The intensity of the study.* An effective case analysis should obtain all information unique to the particular unit being studied and also those features which are common to other cases.
3. *The integrative ability of the investigator.* The case approach must rely on the talent of the researcher to successfully pull together many diverse findings into a unified interpretation. The final interpretation should not, however, merely reflect the investigator's predisposition.

If careful attention is given to key points such as those just outlined, the case technique can be a very effective research design. The depth of analysis attained through the technique is its major advantage. With the increasing importance of qualitative measures (techniques which try to fully describe and then interpret the meaning, not the frequency, of naturally occurring events in organizations)[21] in organizational behavior research, the case approach has taken on new respectability. This is especially true of the so-called single-case experimental designs, which can overcome the threats to internal validity, and also of the traditional control group experimental designs.[22] However, like the experimental design, single-case designs can have a problem with external validity.[23]

It is generally neither practical nor logical to generalize the results of one case analysis to other cases or to the whole. This limitation drastically reduces the external validity of the case method for building a meaningful body of knowledge. The case method does not normally provide enough evidence to prove cause and effect. On the other hand, this method does usually uncover some very meaningful insights, research questions, and hypotheses for further testing by an experimental design. In addition, its generalizability can be enhanced by replication. A case could also be made for single-case studies actually being more useful to management practitioners than large-survey studies. As one research methodologist points out, large-group comparisons may not generalize to individual cases, but it is these individual, single cases that practitioners must deal with on a day-to-day basis.[24]

Survey Design

The third major design available to researchers on human behavior is the survey. This easy-to-use technique depends upon the collection of empirical data via questionnaires and interviews. It is extremely useful in dealing with some questions and problems of organizational behavior. In particular, it is useful to get at information and attitudes from a large group of subjects. The only way to get at people's feelings is to ask them in a survey or an interview.

The survey can overcome the generalizability problems facing the experimental and case designs. Whereas the case is restricted to a single unit, or to very few units of analysis, the survey has very broad coverage. Another advantage is that the survey collects original data that are adaptable to statistical analysis. Its major drawback is the lack of depth of information obtainable from the two major data collection tools: the questionnaire and the interview. Because of this limitation, some scholars within—and many outside—the behavioral sciences have totally discredited the survey as a legitimate research design. Some of this criticism, especially that relating to some of the early surveying done in the behavioral sciences, is certainly justified. Even today, some surveys concentrate only on "dust-bowl" empiricism (gathering data for data's sake) and neglect the necessary planning and design aspects. In addition, overdependence on questionnaire-generated data may be highly misleading.

An indirect measurement technique, questionnaires reflect perceptions of behavior rather than the actual behavior in the real setting. "The prospects of discovering, for example, whether leaders really do structure subordinates' paths to goals (e.g., the path-goal approach) or whether such procedures can actually be effective is more likely to be answered through real-time, in-situation observational studies, than through questionnaire investigations which are many times removed from the actual behavior."[25] For example, there is evidence that the way subordinates describe their managers' behavior on standardized questionnaires is not necessarily the same as the way the managers are observed to behave in the actual day-to-day organizational setting.[26] Observational studies are beginning to reveal managerial behavior that is quite different from what has been typically portrayed by both non-research-based management textbooks and research-based studies that have depended solely on questionnaires or interviews describing managerial behavior.[27]

There is little doubt that the field of organizational behavior has depended too much on questionnaire instruments to obtain data for all three designs—experimental, case, and survey. A multiple-measures approach that gives a degree of convergence among the various data collection techniques is needed for the future.

The key is that organizational behavior researchers need to use all the measurement techniques. In particular, more attention should be given to observational techniques that allow measurement of the interactive nature of behaviors, persons, and situations. In their rush for respectability, organizational behavior researchers may be guilty of bypassing the most widely recognized first stage of any scientific development—observation of naturally occurring events. Obviously, it is much easier to ask than to observe, and this path of least resistance is the one that has too often been followed in accumulating knowledge about organizational behavior.

RELIABILITY AND VALIDITY OF MEASURES

Although multiple measures can help in the search for knowledge about organizational behavior, the crux of the problem of quality of research still gets down to the reliability and validity of the measures that are used. Although reliability is not as important as validity, in order for a measure to be valid, it must also be reliable. Measurement *reliability* refers to the *accuracy* of measurement and the *consistency* of results. Reliability is not nearly as difficult to achieve as validity. Normally, all that is required for a high degree of reliability is control over the measurement conditions. However, even though the measures are reliable, it does not automatically follow that they will be valid. The measures may be accurately and consistently measuring the wrong variables. The major challenge facing organizational behavior researchers comes not from reliability but from validity.

The Validity Concept

Validity has been mentioned throughout this discussion. It is *the* key concept for determining the value of any research. Exactly what is meant by this important concept? Very simply, *validity* is present when the measure is measuring what it is supposed to measure. Much of the confusion about validity results from the adjectives that are used with the term. For example, *face* validity, which most measures depend upon, is a pseudo type of validity and refers only to the surface appearance of the measure. In someone's subjective judgment, the measure is valid. This is a normative, as opposed to an empirical, judgment. It is now recognized that face validity is not sufficient and can be very misleading. Now attention is being focused on the different types of empirically derived validity. An examination of these different types of validity is vital to the understanding of research and to the understanding of organizational behavior in general.

Content and Predictive Validity

In content validity the criterion is the representativeness of the measure. Obviously, this is quite subjective and can slip into being mere face validity. Predictive validity, on the other hand, calculates an objective, statistical relationship between the measure's predictors and an outside criterion. Figure 2.2 shows how this approach to predictive validity can be used.

In the bivariate scatterplot, a strong positive correlation is shown between a questionnaire score and a performance criterion. Each dot represents an employee's score on the questionnaire and his or her resulting level of performance. If a manager wanted to use this questionnaire to predict who would be successful performers if they set the score as indicated, the "hits" would far outnumber the "misses." In other words, this questionnaire would have predictive validity in this case. The hits (in quadrant 1 those who would have been selected and would have turned out to be successful and in quadrant 4 those who would not have been selected and would have turned out to be unsuccessful) show the value of such predictive measures. On the other hand, the misses, even though in the minority, are sacrificed. Especially of concern would be those in quadrant 3—they would not have been selected but would have turned out to be successful. Can the organization or the society as a whole afford these misses? Obviously, the answer depends on the type of job (for example, in selecting astronauts, the selection score would be set so high that there would be no misses in quadrant 2 and a lot of misses in quadrant 3) and on the social consciousness/responsibility of the organization (for example, is the organization eliminating minorities and/or women in quadrant 3 who would have turned out to be successful?). Such a predictive validity assessment, however, is extremely valuable for many measures used in the research process.

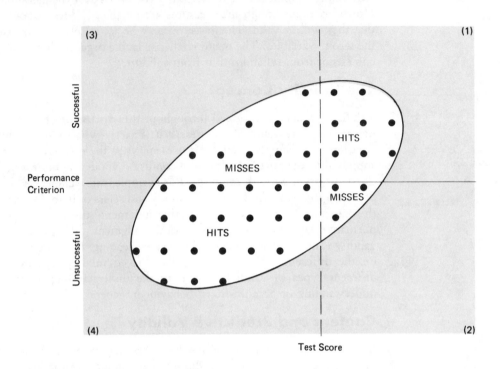

FIGURE 2.2
A predictive va-
lidity scatterplot.

Construct Validity

Both content and predictive (that is, criterion-related) validity have proved to be useful for determining the value of relatively simple measures used in the research process. But for measuring more complex concepts or constructs such as personality dimensions (aggressiveness or confidence), motivation (needs or expectancies), and leadership, construct validity becomes the most important issue.

In the final analysis, the other forms of validity become subsumed by construct validity; it is the crux of measurement and has significant implications for how research is done in the whole field of organizational behavior. Robert Guion, a recognized expert on validity, supports this view when he states: "All validity is at its base some form of construct validity. . . . The most salient of the traditionally identified aspects of validity—the only one that is salient—is construct validity. It *is* the basic meaning of validity."[28]

Unlike content or predictive validity, construct validity draws on a number of studies and sources in order to make an evaluation. Thus, it is both a logical and an empirical process.[29] The construct validation approach would involve what measurement experts call a *nomological network* (that is, a system of interrelated concepts, propositions, and laws), in which observable characteristics are related to other observables, observables are related to theoretical constructs, or one theoretical construct is related to another theoretical construct.[30]

Summary

This chapter first gave a historical foundation for organizational behavior from the practice of management. At the turn of the century, pioneering managers, exemplified by General Motors founder William C. Durant, dominated. Their often ruthless, one-person style then gave way to the approach used by organizational specialists (Fayol and Sloan) and scientific managers (Taylor). These latter managers recognized the human element, but the human relations approach in general and the Hawthorne studies in particular gave focal attention to the behavioral side of management.

The last half of the chapter provided a behavioral science foundation for organizational behavior. The academic discipline of anthropology, defined as the science of man, concentrates primarily on the role that culture plays in human behavior. Sociology is directly concerned with social behavior—in societies, institutions, organizations, and groups—and with roles and norms. Psychology, the science of human behavior, is vital to the micro analysis and understanding of organizational behavior. Social psychology is closest to overall behavioral science and organizational behavior.

The behavioral sciences depend upon rigorous research methodology to accumulate knowledge. This tradition has carried over to the field of organizational behavior. Experimental designs, case designs, and survey designs are used. Each of these has advantages and disadvantages, but the real issue surrounding quality research in organizational behavior is measurement reliablity and validity. Reliability has to do with accuracy and consistency, and validity is present when the measure is indeed measuring what it is supposed to measure. Validity is the more important concept and can be broken down into the categories of content, predictive, and construct validity. Each is important, but construct validity is the ultimate test of most of the measures used on important constructs such as personality, motivation, and leadership in the organizational behavior field.

Questions for Discussion and Review

1. How did pioneering managers such as William Durant differ from the organizational specialists such as Henri Fayol and Alfred P. Sloan in their practice of management?
2. In the Hawthorne studies, how do you explain the fact that in the relay room experiments there were continual increases in productivity, while in the bank wiring room study there was deliberate restriction of output?

3. Why do you feel the Hawthorne studies made such an important historical contribution to the study of organizational behavior?
4. Why is the study of culture important to organizational behavior?
5. What are the major units of analysis studied by modern sociologists? Which one do you think is most relevant to organizational behavior? Why?
6. How does social psychology relate to sociology? To psychology?
7. What are the strengths and weaknesses of the three major research designs?
8. What is validity? What is its relationship to reliability? What are the differences between content, predictive, and construct validity?

References

1. Ernest Dale, *The Great Organizers*, McGraw-Hill, New York, 1960, pp. 73–74.
2. Ibid., p. 74.
3. Walter P. Chrysler, with Boyden Sparkes, *Life of an American Workman*, Dodd, Mead, New York, 1950, p. 148. (Originally published in 1937.)
4. Ibid., pp. 156–157.
5. Dale, op. cit., p. 84.
6. Ibid., p. 86.
7. Peter Drucker, "The Best Book on Management Ever," *Fortune*, April 23, 1990, p. 152.
8. Charles D. Wrege and Amedeo G. Perroni, "Taylor's Pig-Tale: A Historical Analysis of Frederick W. Taylor's Pig Iron Experiments," *Academy of Management Journal*, March 1974, pp. 6–27.
9. Edwin A. Locke, "The Ideas of Frederick W. Taylor: An Evaluation," *Academy of Management Review*, January 1982, p. 14.
10. Frederick W. Taylor, *The Principles of Scientific Management*, Harper, New York, 1911, p. 140.
11. For example, see Lyle Yorks and David Whitsett, "Hawthorne, Topeka, and the Issue of Science versus Advocacy in Organizational Behavior," *Academy of Management Review*, January 1985, pp. 21–30.
12. C. E. Turner, "Test Room Studies in Employee Effectiveness," *American Journal of Public Health*, June 1933, p. 584.
13. Alfred L. Kroeber and Clyde Kluckhohn, "Culture: A Critical Review of Concepts and Definitions," *Papers of the Peabody Museum*, vol. 47, no. 1, Harvard University, Cambridge, Mass., 1952, p. 181.
14. J. P. Spradley, *The Ethnographic Interview*, Holt, New York, 1979, p. 5.
15. Ross A. Webber, *Culture and Management*, Irwin, Homewood, Ill., 1969, p. 10.
16. Lionel Tiger, "When 'Corporate' and 'Culture' Clash," *The Wall Street Journal*, April 9, 1990, p. A-10.
17. See Robert S. Feldman, *Understanding Psychology*, McGraw-Hill, New York, 1990, pp. 18–20, for a review of the historical development and major models.
18. John B. Miner, *Theories of Organizational Behavior*, Dryden Press, Hinsdale, Ill., 1980, pp. 7–9.
19. Thomas D. Cook and Donald T. Campbell, "The Design and Conduct of Quasi-Experiments and True Experiments in Field Settings," in M. D. Dunnette (ed.), *Handbook of Industrial and Organizational Psychology*, Rand McNally, Chicago, 1976, pp. 224–246; also see Terence R. Mitchell, "An Evaluation of the Validity of Correlational Research Conducted in Organizations," *Academy of Management Review*, April 1985, pp. 192–205.
20. Daniel R. Ilgen, "Laboratory Research: A Question of When, Not If," in Edwin A. Locke (ed.), *Generalizing from Laboratory to Field Settings*, Lexington Books, Lexington, Mass., 1986, p. 257.
21. John Van Maanen, James M. Dabbs, Jr., and Robert R. Faulkner, *Varieties of Qualitative Research*, Sage, Beverly Hills, Calif., 1982.
22. Michel Herson and David H. Barlow, *Single Case Experimental Design*, Pergamon, New York, 1976; Judi Komaki, "Alternative Evaluation Strategies in Work Settings: Reversals and Multiple Baseline Designs," *Journal of Organizational Behavior Management*, Summer 1977, pp. 53–77; Fred Luthans and Tim R. V. Davis, "An Idiographic Approach to Organizational Behavior

Research: The Use of Single Case Experimental Designs and Direct Measures," *Academy of Management Review*, July 1982, pp. 380–391; and Ronald L. Taylor and Gary L. Adams, "A Review of Single-Subject Methodologies in Applied Settings," *Journal of Applied Behavioral Science*, vol. 18, 1982, pp. 95–103.

23. Alan E. Kazdin, "Obstacles in Using Randomization Tests in Single-Case Experimentation," *Journal of Educational Statistics*, Fall 1980, pp. 253–260.

24. M. M. Kennedy, "Generalization from Single Case Studies," *Evaluation Quarterly*, November 1979, pp. 661–678.

25. Tim R. V. Davis and Fred Luthans, "Leadership Reexamined: A Behavioral Approach," *Academy of Management Review*, April 1979, p. 244.

26. Fred Luthans and Diane Lockwood, "Toward an Observation System for Measuring Leader Behavior in Natural Settings," in J. G. Hunt, D. Hosking, C. Schriesheim, and R. Stewart (eds.), *Leaders and Managers: International Perspectives of Managerial Behavior and Leadership*, Pergamon, New York, 1984, pp. 117–141.

27. Colin P. Hales, "What Do Managers Do?" *Journal of Management Studies*, January 1986, p. 22; Fred Luthans, Stuart A. Rosenkrantz, and Harry Hennessey, "What Do Successful Managers Really Do?" *Journal of Applied Behavioral Science*, vol. 21, no. 3, 1986, pp. 255–270; Stephen J. Carroll and Dennis A. Gillen, "Are the Classical Management Functions Useful in Describing Managerial Work?" *The Academy of Management Review*, January 1987, pp. 38–51; and Fred Luthans, Richard M. Hodgetts, and Stuart A. Rosenkrantz, *Real Managers*, Ballinger, Cambridge, Mass., 1988.

28. Robert M. Guion, "Content Validity: Three Years of Talk—What's the Action?" *Public Personnel Management*, November–December 1977, p. 410.

29. Wayne Cascio, *Applied Psychology in Personnel Management*, Reston Publishing, Reston, Va., 1978, p. 95.

30. Lee J. Cronbach and Paul E. Meehl, "Construct Validity in Psychological Tests," *Psychological Bulletin*, July 1955, pp. 281–302.

REAL CASE: THINGS WILL NEVER BE THE SAME

After 1917, when the Bolsheviks took over the government of Russia, private industry became outlawed. However, going into the 1990s under the government of Mikhail Gorbachev, things changed dramatically. The Soviet Union introduced a number of major changes that were designed to create economic reform over a 500-day period. If these changes became successful, the economy would supposedly move from being government-controlled to being responsive to the free market. In the change to a market economy, the methods used for managing human resources in Soviet organizations would also undergo dramatic change. Here are some of the proposed changes, as well as the time period during which they were scheduled to occur.

First 100 Days

- An inventory is to be put together of the state property that will be sold off.
- Collective farms and state lands will be broken up into individual plots and sold off to farm workers.
- A sell-off of state companies is scheduled to begin.
- Three-quarters of foreign aid to countries such as Cuba is to be affected; also, the secret police's budget is to be cut by 20 percent and defense spending trimmed by 10 percent.

Days 101–250

- Half of all the restaurants and shops in the Soviet Union are to be in private hands.

- The sale of the nation's largest industries is to begin.
- Prices are to be lifted on many, but not all, consumer goods.

Days 251–400

- Forty percent of all Soviet industry is to be in the hands of individual shareholders, worker groups, and foreigners.
- Two-thirds of the service sector from auto repair to barber shops is to be in private hands.
- Price controls are to remain only on selected critical items such as oil, gas, drugs, and a few other commodities.

Days 401–500

- A new banking system is to be completed and a foreign exchange market will shift into high gear.
- Seventy percent of industry and 90 percent of retail trade and construction is to be in private hands.
- Longtime restrictions on migration within the Soviet Union are to be loosened so that unemployed workers can travel to find new jobs.

1. Under the old Soviet system, how important were scientific management ideas? Why?
2. Would the Soviets have used human relations ideas prior to their economic reforms? Why or why not?
3. How likely is it that, under the new economic system, Soviet management will have to turn toward a more behavioral-science–based approach to managing people? Defend your answer.

**Case:
Too Nice to
People**

John has just graduated from the College of Business Administration at State University and has joined his family's small business, which employs twenty-five semiskilled workers. The first week on the job his dad called him in and said, "John, I've had a chance to observe you working with the men and women for the past two days and, although I hate to, I feel I must say something. You are just too nice to people. I know they taught you that human relations stuff at the university, but it just doesn't work here. I remember when the Hawthorne studies were first reported and everybody at the university got all excited about them, but believe me, there is more to managing people than just being nice to them."

1. How would you react to your father's comments if you were John?
2. Do you think John's father understood and interpreted the Hawthorne studies correctly?
3. What phases of management do you think John's father has gone through in this family business?

**Case:
Dilemma for
Program
Evaluation**

Jane Dewy has just been assigned to the training department of a large federal agency. She is assigned to program evaluation and works directly with the training and development program for first-line supervisors. She has been charged with constructing a method of measuring the effectiveness of some of the agency's training programs. The usual evaluation procedure is to administer a reaction questionnaire, which is given to the supervisors at the end of the training program. The trainees have consistently rated the program very highly. Jane is skeptical though. She thinks that anyone who receives a week off from work to go to a training program at a vacation resort might think the program was great. She wants to find another means of evaluating the program, a means that will truly measure its results and effectiveness. She has thought of sending a questionnaire to the subordinates whom the trainees supervised, but she feels uncomfortable about sending out such questionnaires. She knows how trite and meaningless they can be. She remembers how she and most of the other trainees in training programs that she participated in over the years treated surveys—as a joke and a waste of time. Yet she has to do something to evaluate the effectiveness of the training program. She reasons that sending out another questionnaire is better than nothing.

1. Is sending out another questionnaire Jane's only alternative?
2. How could she design an experiment to evaluate the program? What would be the independent variable? What would be the dependent variable or variables?
3. Besides program evaluation, what are some other direct applications of research methodology by practicing managers?

INTEGRATIVE CONTEMPORARY CASE FOR PART 1

Dispelling the
Myths that Are
Holding Us
Back*

Most horror films have sequels, and this one is no exception. In the 1980s, millions of Rust Belt workers watched helplessly as imports took their jobs and their futures, leaving them only unwanted skills and wrecked communities.

Now, it's everyone else's turn. From the drugstore clerk to the high-paid banker, America's competitive failures are hurting almost everybody. The damage is not as obvious as a shuttered factory, but it's real: smaller paychecks, fewer good jobs, and a hungrier and meaner future.

Americans want to believe their trade agonies are over. But BUSINESS WEEK's new analysis of how foreign trade affects all sectors of the economy shows that no one is safe. Competing in world markets requires hard truths rather than comforting myths. Here's how the global economy will affect Americans in the 1990s.

MYTH: *American workers have become productive members of the global economy.*

REALITY: *Some have, but the share of the work force in the exporting sector is small—and shrinking.*

Hospital Staffing Services Inc. (HSS) is one of the country's newest exporters—with a twist. Since July, the Fort Lauderdale (Fla.) personnel agency has been supplying trained American nurses to British hospitals. The hospitals are pleased, the nurses enthusiastic, and the company's president, Leonard J. Cass, is eyeing the rest of Europe and the Far East. "We see a world of opportunities internationally," says Cass.

Success stories such as this one are heartwarming but misleading. A company such as HSS may place a handful of nurses abroad, but it still depends on the U.S. market for almost all its business—and that's typical. Only a small number of U.S. industries ship a significant fraction of their output overseas. The exporting sector is still mostly composed of high-profile stalwarts such as aircraft, business services, chemicals, and computers. And for all the fuss about the U.S. becoming more export-oriented, hardly any additional industries have joined the exporting sector in the past 10 years.

Moreover, success overseas is not translating into job creation at home. In recent years, it's been harder to find a job in the exporting sector than in the rest of the economy. Boeing—the country's top exporter—has cut its work force by about 3,000 this year, even though orders for commercial aircraft may exceed last year's record. And even before the recent round of layoffs, employment in the computer industry had dropped by 5% since 1986. Indeed, the exporting sector now employs only one-eighth of the work force—and this share is eroding.

The reason? Although many exporters have been expanding output and sales, they're also boosting productivity by shedding jobs and substituting capital for labor. And successful industries have been spinning off production to smaller suppliers, either at home or abroad, to take advantage of lower wages.

These trends show no sign of abating. Using government employment forecasts, BUSINESS WEEK is projecting an increase of 9.6% in the size of the exporting sector over the next 10 years, far less than projected national employment growth of 14.6%. True, the exporting sector could expand faster if import-competing industries such as machine tools and autos regain market share in the U.S.—or if some domestic industries learn how to be big exporters. Barring these competitive gains, the proportion of Americans producing for world markets will just continue to shrink in the 1990s.

MYTH: *Foreign trade lifts everyone's standard of living.*

REALITY: *Only workers in the exporting sector are winners from the global economy.*

The accounting and consulting firm Arthur Andersen & Co. is a strong advocate for liberalizing international trade in services, and no wonder. Last year, revenues from overseas offices climbed by 35%, much faster than the 14% growth of U.S. revenues. And the almost 1,000 non-U.S. partners share costs, such as the expense of running Andersen's 145-acre in-house training facility, located near Chicago. "From the standpoint of the U.S. partners," says Lawrence A. Weinbach, Arthur Andersen's managing partner and chief executive, "[international expansion] was an outstanding thing to do."

But most people have reason to regard the global economy with dismay. Hurt by the direct and indirect effects of foreign competition, real earnings outside the exporting sector have dropped by 6% since 1980. And import competition is still keeping wage gains well below the rate of inflation in industries such as industrial machinery and machine tools, despite their recent revival.

By comparison, foreign trade has boosted the living standards of Americans smart or lucky enough to hold jobs in the exporting sector. There, average real wages have risen by 5.2% since 1980, according to BUSINESS WEEK calculations. Some did much better. Employees in industries such as computers, chemicals, and accounting services saw their living standard increase by 7% to 10% in the 1980s, beating the national averages by a mile. "What's driving wages is world market growth and competitiveness," says James K. Galbraith, a University of Texas economist. "Export success means rising wages."

The benefits from export success are showing up in surprising places—for example, college campuses. Education exports—mostly tuition and room and board paid by foreign students—now total about $5 billion a year. That's why the exporting sector includes part of higher education, even though the service never crosses the U.S. border. Indeed, foreign students have provided more than 20% of the increase in total college and graduate enrollment since 1985, and foreign graduate students now fill the nation's doctoral programs.

This worldwide demand for a U.S. education has helped pay for the 17% increase in real earnings received by college instructors since 1983.

The global market for U.S. movies and television programs is also boosting pay in the entertainment industry. Foreign revenues accounted for about 42% of the $12.5 billion raked in by the film industry last year, and workers are sharing in the gains. For example, under the Writers Guild contract, feature-film screenwriters get royalties on sales to overseas television and on foreign videocassette sales—a market that has more than doubled since 1985.

Companies that compete well abroad may even be able to protect their workers from the looming U.S. recession. At Boeing Co., domestic orders for commercial aircraft have plunged so far this year, but foreign orders are up by more than $3.6 billion. This success is helping Boeing afford the 1989 labor settlement that granted generous wage increases to its unionized employees. And the good times have spilled over to suppliers such as Seattle-based Airborne Express, which handles international air cargo—mainly spare parts and voluminous technical manuals—for Boeing. Thanks to Boeing's orders, Airborne has added five new trucks and doubled its international staff in Seattle since last year.

MYTH: *You can hide from the global economy.*

REALITY: *Global competition is pushing down wages, even in domestic industries.*

Foreign competition is a distant echo for most retail salesclerks. Unlike assembly-line workers, they probably won't be elbowed aside by imports. Even if a Japanese or German-owned store opened up across the street, it would still need U.S. workers.

But for these apparently insulated workers, America's trade troubles mean more competition for jobs. The import-competing sector lost 1.7 million jobs in the 1980s, while exporting industries, facing tough foreign competition, could not fill the gap. This means that most new entrants into the labor market are forced to shoehorn themselves into a job in a domestic industry, such as retailing or construction.

People who lack a college degree are being hit especially hard as the U.S. increasingly competes internationally on the basis of its skilled workers. According to calculations done for BUSINESS WEEK by the Center for Regional Economic Issues in Cleveland, 26% of workers in the export sector now have college degrees, vs. 16% in the import-competing sector. "When U.S. manufacturers get bashed for foreign competition, well-paid jobs for workers without college degrees disappear," says Lawrence F. Katz, a Harvard University economist.

A large pool of less-skilled labor has produced a steep decline in the wages of workers in the domestic sector. Real earnings there have dropped almost twice as much as earnings in the seemingly more vulnerable import-competing sector. Indeed, the biggest wage loser of the 1980s was retailing, a domestic industry, where real earnings for nonsupervisory workers fell by 13%.

For the same reason, some manufacturing industries that are insulated from foreign competition are also paying lower wages. For instance, in the printing industry, which faces almost no import competition, a proliferation of small print shops has added 205,000 production jobs to the industry since 1980, a fat 29% increase. But average real wages fell by 1.2% during that time.

Labor-force growth will slow in the 1990s, which may ease downward pressure on wages. But the long-term trend favoring skilled labor is likely to continue. "As more industries open up to the global market, it will be harder for unskilled American workers to compete," says Clifford Johnson, an economist at the Children's Defense Fund. "This doesn't bode well for dropouts or even for non-college-grads who don't get specialized training."

MYTH: *White-collar workers are safe from international competition.*

REALITY: *The global economy spares no one.*

Mark D. Wolf, a 36-year-old market researcher for a large New Jersey insurance company, is no stranger to the global economy. In previous jobs, he's helped bid for a West German cellular telephone license and was squeezed out by cutbacks at a British-owned advertising agency. Now, he's working in an industry in which imports are not yet a big presence. But that doesn't make him feel safe from foreign competitors. "They're coming," worries Wolf.

That's a new fear for white-collar workers, who once felt protected from the ravages of international competition. In the 1980s, managers and professionals prospered no matter which part of the economy they worked in. Import-competing industries such as mining and industrial machinery continued to boost their employment of college graduates, even as they were laying off production workers. The financial services boom provided jobs for more than 700,000 college graduates. And the U.S. ran big trade surpluses in business services such as accounting, law, and management consulting. Not surprisingly, managerial salaries since 1982 have risen by 8.7%, adjusted for inflation, while blue-collar salaries have fallen by 1.5%.

But now, high-flying white-collar workers are being hit by the same streamlining and productivity improvements that made other export industries competitive. There are fewer and fewer job opportunities at the big U.S.-based multinationals, which provide the highest-paying and most prestigious jobs. Since the early 1980s, multinationals have steadily reduced their U.S. employment, according to Commerce Dept. figures. Downsizing, spin-offs, and competitive pressures have taken their toll. Now, less than 20% of the work force is employed by a U.S.-based global company, down from 25% in 1982.

Of course, there are still some industries in which strong international growth is shielding white-collar workers from the recent wave of layoffs. For example, most drug companies are not paring back staff, responding in part to strong demand for their products in Europe and Japan. At Merck & Co., foreign sales account for about 46% of total revenue, which is partially insulating the company and its employees from U.S. economic woes.

But employees in banks, one of the main sources of white-collar growth in the 1980s, have no such protection. Few U.S. banks have the size and the muscle to compete actively in the global market for financial services. Since 1985, they've closed almost 100 foreign branches, reducing their overseas presence. This means that when the domestic economy slows, U.S. banks can't rely on foreign markets to pick up the slack.

And competitive problems in the computer industry are starting to hurt the engineers and other white-collar employees who make up much of its work force.' Data General Corp. has announced plans for laying off 17% of its employees, and Digital Equipment Corp. is intending to pare 6% of its workers. At the same time, imports of computers and related equipment are soaring. So far in 1990, imports of office machinery—mostly computers and parts—are up by 7.1% over last year, far outpacing office-machinery export growth of 3.4%.

And it could get worse. "We are witnessing a big decline in financial services and what might be the beginning of a steep decline in computers," says Stephen S. Cohen, director of the Berkeley Roundtable on the International Economy (BRIE). If this happens, college graduates will find good jobs getting scarcer in the 1990s, just as blue-collar workers did in the last decade.

MYTH: *Most Americans are going to prosper in the 1990s.*

REALITY: *Without changes, much of the decline in living standards is yet to come.*

Leaner and meaner, employing a smaller share of the work force, U.S. industry has staged a spectacular export boom over the past four years. The trade deficit, in real terms, has been sliced by more than 60% since 1986. Exports now make up almost 15% of the U.S. economy, up from 12% in 1980. And strong foreign demand for U.S. goods and services is keeping much of the Midwest and Northwest healthy amid the national slowdown.

But the overall volume of imports has continued to grow, and key industries such as machine tools, while showing near-record exports, have ceded almost half the domestic market to imports. Even if a recession narrows the trade deficit further by reducing demand for imports, a weak economy won't help U.S. manufacturers sell more goods at home.

And much of the price for declining competitiveness has yet to be paid. To be sure, average wages and salaries, in real terms, have only risen by a meager 3.7% since 1983. But even this dismal performance required massive borrowing from foreigners and the sales of real estate and companies such as MCA Inc. to finance the huge trade deficit—a dissipation of national wealth that can only make Americans poorer in the long run. Robert Z. Lawrence, an economist at the Brookings Institution, estimates that America's competitive troubles will eventually reduce living standards by about 3%, erasing most of the gains from the economic expansion of the 1980s.

Moreover, other countries are turning in far better performances. Manufacturing wages in Japan and Germany have risen by 18% and 14% in real terms since 1980. And with a large portion of their work force in the exporting sector, those countries are better prepared to benefit from trade in the future.

If Americans want this type of growth in living standards, they will need to compete better in the global economy. It's not enough just to let a few big exporters worry about world markets. These days, the lack of competitiveness in the U.S. is everybody's problem.

1. Which of the myths in the case did you find most surprising? Which do you disagree with? Have situations described changed since the case was written?
2. How will the realities of the global economy directly affect you?
3. How can the study of organizational behavior help U.S. organizations and their management better compete in the global economy?

EXPERIENTIAL EXERCISES FOR PART 1

EXERCISE: Synthesis of Student and Instructor Needs

Goals:
1. To "break the ice" in using experiential exercises
2. To initiate open communication between the students and the instructor regarding mutual learning goals and needs
3. To stimulate the students to clarify their learning goals and instructional needs and to commit themselves to these
4. To serve as the first exercise in the "experiential" approach to management education

Implementation:
1. The class is divided into groups of four to six students each.
2. Each group openly discusses what members would like from the course and drafts a set of learning objectives and instructional aims. The group also makes up a list of learning/course objectives which they feel the instructor wants to pursue. (About twenty minutes.)
3. After each group has "caucused," a group spokesperson is appointed to meet with the instructor in an open dialogue in front of the class about course objectives.
4. The instructor meets with each group representative at the front of the classroom to initate an open dialogue about the semester of learning. (About thirty minutes.) Several activities are carried out:
   a. Open discussion of the learning objectives of both the students and the instructor
   b. Recognition of the constraints faced by each party in accommodating these goals
   c. Identification of areas of goal agreement and disagreement, and feasible compromises
   d. Drafting a set of guidelines for cooperation between the parties, designed to better bring about mutual goal attainment

EXERCISE: Work-Related Organizational Behavior: Implications for the Course

Goals:
1. To identify course topic areas from the participant's own work experience
2. To introduce experiential learning

Implementation:
Task 1: Each class member does the following:

1. Describes an experience in a past work situation that illustrates something about organizational behavior. (Some students have had only part-time work experience or summer jobs, but even the humblest job is relevant here.)

2. Explains what it illustrates about organizational behavior. (Time: five minutes for individuals to think about and jot down notes covering these two points.)

Task 2: The class forms into triads and each triad does the following:

1. Member A tells his or her experience to member B. Member B listens carefully, paraphrases the story back to A, and tells what it illustrates about organizational behavior. Member B must do this to A's satisfaction that B has understood fully what A was trying to communicate. Member C is the observer and remains silent during the process.
2. Member B tells his or her story to C, and A is the observer.
3. Member C tells his or her story to A, and B is the observer. (Each member has about five minutes to tell his or her story and have it paraphrased back by the listener. The instructor will call out the time at the end of each five-minute interval for equal apportionment of "airtime" among participants. Total time: fifteen minutes.)

Task 3: Each triad selects one of its members to relate his or her incident to the class. The instructor briefly analyzes for the class how the related story fits in with some topic to be studied in the course, such as perception, motivation, communication, conflict, or leadership. The topic areas are listed in the table of contents of this book.

PART **2**

THE BASIC BUILDING BLOCKS OF ORGANIZATIONAL BEHAVIOR: A MICRO PERSPECTIVE

3 Perception

■ Perceptions in the Auto Wars

The automotive industry has been one of the most competitive in the world in recent years. The big question for auto manufacturers is: When people buy a car, what are the major influences affecting their purchase decision? Recent results show that purchasers have a wide variety of perceptions and sometimes these seem to be contradictory. For example, since a majority of Americans report that they own a U.S.-made car, American auto makers hold a large share of the national market. On the other hand, Americans also say that the most important thing they are looking for in a new car is reliability and this, in their minds, is the major area where U.S. car makers are lacking. Does this then mean that Japanese and German cars will gain market share over the next decade? Maybe not, because, contrary to common belief, Americans say that they are more likely to buy a U.S.-made car than a foreign car the next time they purchase a new car. Surprisingly, while 22 percent of people in a recent survey reported that they own or lease Japanese cars, only 12 percent of those surveyed said that they would buy Japanese the next time.

But if foreign cars have higher quality, why are most Americans saying they will not purchase them now or in the near future? One reason may be that American consumers perceive the quality of U.S.-made cars as increasing. Over 70 percent of those surveyed reported that U.S. auto quality is now almost as high as that of the Japanese. Additionally, many buyers look for things other than quality—comfortable interiors, styling, engineering, and good dealer relationships. American cars are perceived to be far superior to foreign autos on each of these four points. In fact, of those sampled only 17 percent felt that Japanese car dealers were better than American car dealers, while 71 percent felt just the opposite.

Despite these encouraging survey results, Detroit has to be careful not to perceive them as an indication that Americans are and will remain loyal. Ninety-six percent of those surveyed said that reliability was very important; 43 percent said that the Japanese produced cars with fewer defects. Unless Detroit can overcome this negative perception of the quality of their autos, consumers will surely buy foreign-made cars. What most of those surveyed seem to be saying is: We are going to buy an American car the next time out, but if the quality is not at least as good as that of a foreign make, we are then going to have to switch. Detroit has a few more years in which to change current perceptions. If it cannot, market share is likely to fall dramatically.

■■■■■■■ Learning Objectives

- **Define** the overall nature of perception, explaining how it differs from sensation.
- **Discuss** perceptual selectivity, including the external attention factors and internal set factors.
- **Explain** perceptual organization, including figure-ground, grouping, constancy, context, and defense principles.
- **Identify** the dimensions of social perception, including attribution, stereotyping, and halo.
- **Examine** the processes and strategies of impression management.

This chapter isolates one of the human cognitive processes—perception. As indicated earlier, cognitions are basically bits of information, and the cognitive processes involve the ways in which people process that information. In other words, the cognitive processes suggest that, like computers, humans are information processors. However, today's complex computers are very simple information-processing units when compared with *human information processing*.

People's individual differences and uniqueness are largely the result of the cognitive processes. Although there are a number of cognitive processes (imagination, perception, and even thinking), it is generally recognized that the perceptual process is a very important one that takes place between the situation and the behavior and is most relevant to the study of organizational behavior. For example, the observation that a department head and a subordinate may react quite differently to the same top management directive can be better understood and explained by the perceptual process. Also, recent research indicates that things such as age perceptions can affect promotion and performance. One such study found that a merger largely failed because one company's forty-year-old executives and the other company's sixty-five-year-old executives differed over which group was better able to make decisions.[1] It was a matter of differing age perceptions.

In this book, perception is presented as an important cognitive process in understanding organizational behavior. The environment (both antecedent and consequent), plus other psychological processes such as learning and motivation and the whole of personality, is also important. However, for the most part, although much of the material on perception is basic knowledge in the behavioral sciences, it has been largely overlooked or not translated for use by those in the organizational behavior field. All the topics covered in this chapter are concerned with understanding organizational behavior, and they have many direct applications to organization and management practice.

The first major section presents a theoretical discussion of the general nature and significance of the perceptual process. The relationship between sensation and perception is clarified, and some of the important perceptual subprocesses are discussed. The second section covers the various aspects of perceptual selectivity. Both external factors (intensity, size, contrast, repetition, motion, and novelty and familiarity) and internal ones (motivation, personality, and learning) are included. The third section is concerned with perceptual organization. The principles of figure-ground, grouping, constancy, and context are given primary emphasis. The next section focuses on social perception—the phenomena of attribution, stereotypes, and the halo effect. Finally, attention is given to impression management, which has direct implications for organizational behavior.

THE NATURE AND IMPORTANCE OF PERCEPTION

The key to understanding perception is to recognize that it is a unique *interpretation* of the situation, not an exact recording of it. In short, perception is a very complex cognitive process that yields a unique picture of the world that may be quite different from reality.

Recognition of the difference between the perceptual world and the real world is vital to the understanding of organizational behavior. A specific example would be the universal assumption made by managers that subordinates always want promotions, when, in fact, many subordinates really feel psychologically *forced* to accept a promotion. Managers seldom attempt to find out, and sometimes subordinates themselves do not know, whether the promotion should be offered. In other words, the perceptual world of the manager is quite different from the perceptual world of the subordinate, and both may be very different from reality. If this is the case, what can be done about it from a management standpoint? The best answer seems to be that a better understanding of the concepts involved should be developed. Direct applications and techniques should logically follow complete understanding. The rest of the chapter is devoted to providing a better understanding of the cognitive process of perception.

SENSATION VERSUS PERCEPTION

There is usually a great deal of misunderstanding about the relationship between sensation and perception. Behavioral scientists generally agree that people's "reality" (the world around them) depends on their senses. However, the raw sensory input is not enough. They must also process these sensory data and make sense out of them in order to understand the world around them. Thus, the starting point in the study of perception should clarify the relationship between perception and sensation.

The Senses

There is not full agreement as to the differences and similarities between sensation and perception. The physical senses are considered to be vision, hearing, touch, smell, and taste. There are many other so-called "sixth senses." However, none of these sixth senses is fully accepted. The five senses are constantly bombarded by numerous stimuli that are both outside and inside the body. Examples of outside stimuli include light waves, sound waves, mechanical energy of pressure, and chemical energy from objects that one can smell and taste. Inside stimuli include energy generated by muscles, food passing through the digestive system, and glands secreting behavior-influencing hormones. These examples indicate that sensation deals chiefly with very elementary behavior that is determined largely by physiological functioning. In this way, the human being uses the senses to experience color, brightness, shape, loudness, pitch, heat, odor, and taste.

Definition of Perception

Perception is much more complex and much broader than sensation. The perceptual process can be defined as a complicated interaction of selection, organization, and interpretation. Although perception depends largely upon the senses for raw data, the cognitive process may filter, modify, or completely change these data. A simple illustration may be seen by looking at one side of a stationary object, for example, a statue or a tree. By slowly turning the eyes to the other side of the object, the person probably *senses* that the object is moving. Yet the person *perceives* the object as stationary. The perceptual process overcomes the sensual process and the person "sees" the object as stationary. In other words, the perceptual process adds to, and subtracts from, the "real" sensory world. The following are some organizational examples which point out the difference between sensation and perception:

1. The purchasing agent buys a part that she thinks is best, not the part that the engineer says is the best.
2. A subordinate's answer to a question is based on what he heard the boss say, not on what the boss actually said.
3. The same worker may be viewed by one supervisor as a very good worker and by another supervisor as a very poor worker.
4. The same widget may be viewed by the inspector to be of high quality and by a customer to be of low quality.

Subprocesses of Perception

The existence of several subprocesses gives evidence of the complexity and the interactive nature of perception. Figure 3.1 shows how these subprocesses relate to one another. The first important subprocess is the *stimulus* or *situation* that is present. Perception begins when a person is confronted with a stimulus or a situation. This confrontation may be with the immediate sensual stimulation or with the total physical and sociocultural environment. An example is the employee who is confronted with his or her supervisor or with the total formal organizational environment. Either one or both may initiate the workings of the employee's perceptual process. In other words, this represents the stimulus situation interacting with the person.

In addition to the situation-person interaction there are the internal cognitive processes of *registration, interpretation,* and *feedback*. During the registration phenomenon, the physiological (sensory and neural) mechanisms are affected; the physiological ability to hear and see will affect perception. Interpretation is the most significant cognitive aspect of perception. The other psychological processes will affect the interpretation of a situation. For example, in an organization, employees'

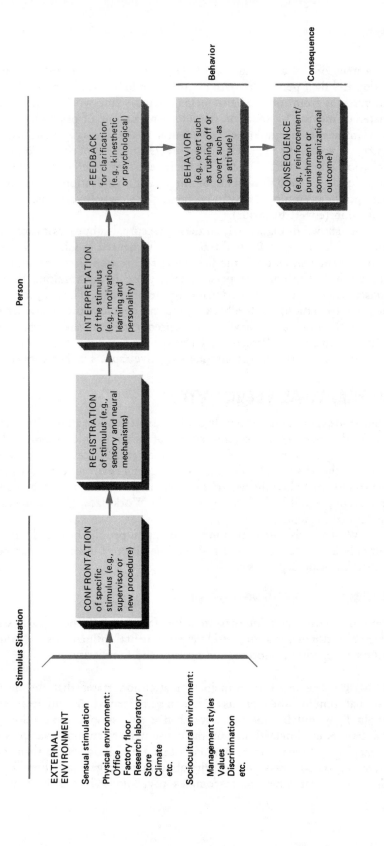

FIGURE 3.1
The subprocesses
of perception.

interpretations of a situation are largely dependent upon their learning and motivation and their personality. An example would be the kinesthetic feedback (sensory impressions from muscles) that helps assembly line workers perceive the speed of materials moving by them on the line. An example of psychological feedback that may influence an employee's perception is the supervisor's raised eyebrow or a change in voice inflection. The behavioral termination of perception is the reaction or behavior, either overt or covert, which is necessary if perception is to be considered a behavioral event and thus an important part of organizational behavior. As a result of perception, an employee may move rapidly or slowly (overt behavior) or make a self-evaluation (covert behavior).

As shown in Figure 3.1, all these perceptual subprocesses are compatible with the social learning conceptual framework presented in Chapter 1. The stimulus or environmental situation is the first part; registration, interpretation, and feedback occur within the complex person; then there is the resulting behavior; and the consequences of this behavior make up the final part. The subprocesses of registration, interpretation, and feedback are internal cognitive processes that are unobservable, but the situation, behavior, and consequences indicate that perception is indeed related to behavior. Perceptual selectivity and organization, which are discussed next, play a key role in the internal cognitive aspects of perception.

PERCEPTUAL SELECTIVITY

Numerous stimuli are constantly confronting everyone all the time. The noise of the air conditioner or furnace, the sound of other people talking and moving, and outside noises from cars, planes, or street repair work are a few of the stimuli affecting the senses—plus the impact of the total environmental situation. Sometimes the stimuli are below the person's conscious threshold. The accompanying Application Example, Subliminal Perception in the Workplace, gives some examples of this subliminal perception.

With all this stimulation impinging upon people, how and why do they select out only a very few stimuli at a given time? Part of the answer can be found in the principles of perceptual selectivity.

External Attention Factors

Various external and internal attention factors affect perceptual selectivity. The external factors consist of outside environmental influences such as intensity, size, contrast, repetition, motion, and novelty and familiarity.

Intensity. The intensity principle of attention states that the more intense the external stimulus, the more likely it is to be perceived. A loud noise, strong odor, or bright light will be noticed more than a soft sound, weak odor, or dim light. Advertisers use intensity to gain the consumer's attention. Examples include bright packaging and television commercials that are slightly louder than the regular program. Supervisors may yell at their subordinates to gain attention. This last example also shows that other, more complex psychological variables may overcome the

Application Example ⊪⟹

Subliminal Perception in the Workplace

Subliminal perception involves giving a message below the person's level of consciousness. This device has been banned in uses such as advertising to get people to buy a product without their awareness. For example, flashing on a movie theater screen, "Go get a cola, you are thirsty" so fast that the person is unaware of the message but stimulated to obey it is not permitted. Recently, however, some business organizations have begun to use this approach to cut employee and customer theft, reduce employee accidents and injuries, and even increase productivity. For example, Proactive Systems Inc., a company that specializes in this approach (although it is careful to point out that what it is doing is really not subliminal and does not violate any constitutional rights) has been successful in conveying messages such as "Stay honest, don't steal, obey the law" to discourage shoplifting in retail stores such as Jay Jacobs, a Seattle-based chain with 102 stores. To cut down accidents, Proactive Systems puts out messages, in places such as warehouses, that whisper, "Slouch is ouch, life straight is great." One large company is using the approach to increase productivity by repeatedly subjecting employees to the phrases, "I feel good about my job," "I like myself," and "My job is important." A spokesperson for the company states that since the system was installed, "turnover has dropped, productivity has gone up and morale seems to have improved."

simple external variable. By speaking loudly, the supervisor may actually be turning the subordinates off instead of gaining their attention. These types of complications enter into all aspects of the perceptual process. As with the other psychological concepts, a given perceptual principle cannot stand alone in explaining complex human behavior. The intensity principle is only one small factor in the perceptual process, which is only a part of the cognitive processes, which are only a part of what goes into human behavior. Yet, for convenience of presentation and for the development of basic understanding, these small parts can be effectively isolated for study and analysis.

Size. Closely related to intensity is the principle of size. It says that the larger the object, the more likely it will be perceived. The largest machine "sticks out" when personnel view a factory floor. The maintenance engineering staff may pay more attention to a big machine than to a smaller one, even though the smaller one costs as much and is as important to the operation. A 6-foot 4-inch, 250-pound supervisor may receive more attention from his subordinates than a 5-foot 10-inch, 160-pound supervisor. In advertising, a full-page spread is more attention-getting than a few lines in the classified section.

Contrast. The contrast principle states that external stimuli which stand out against the background or which are not what people are expecting will receive their attention. Figure 3.2 demonstrates this perceptual principle. The black circle on the right appears much larger than the one on the left because of the contrast with the background circles. Both black circles are exactly the same size. In a similar manner,

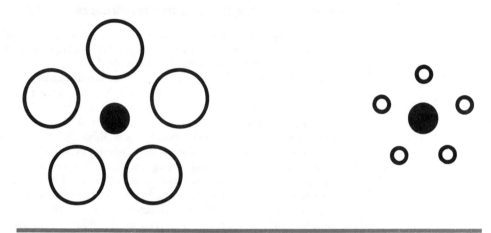

FIGURE 3.2
The contrast principle of perception: Which black circle is larger?

plant safety signs which have black lettering on a yellow background or white lettering on a red background are attention-getting; and when the 6-foot 4-inch, 250-pound supervisor mentioned above is placed next to a 5-foot 4-inch, 130-pound supervisor, the smaller one will probably receive as much notice as the bigger one. A worker with many years of experience hardly notices the deafening noise on the factory floor of a typical manufacturing operation. However, if one or more of the machines should come suddenly to a halt, the person would immediately notice the difference in noise level.

The contrast principle can be demonstrated by the experience of some companies with training disadvantaged, unskilled workers. In designing these training programs, some firms have found that they have more success when they conduct the initial sessions in the disadvantaged person's own environment. The familiar location relieves some of the tension and creates a more favorable learning atmosphere. However, at some point the disadvantaged person must make the transition to the organizational environment. A regular, quiet classroom in the organization does not seem to be enough. One company learned that when the entire training of the disadvantaged trainees was conducted in a clean, quiet factory classroom, their subsequent performance was very poor. Fortunately, the company did not jump to the conclusion that the workers were "no good" or untrainable. Instead, through rational behavior analysis, the company discovered that the poor performance was due to the extremely loud noises that occurred on the assembly line. The workers were not accustomed to the noise because their training had taken place under nice, clean, quiet conditions. When the workers were placed on the noisy factory floor, the contrasting din drew all their attention and adversely affected their performance. To solve this problem, the company conducted the training sessions right next to the noisy factory floor. By the end of the training sessions, the workers were used to the noise, and they performed very well when subsequently placed on the job.

Repetition. The repetition principle states that a repeated external stimulus is more attention-getting than a single one. Thus, a worker will generally "hear" better when directions for a dull task are given more than once. This principle partially explains why supervisors have to give directions over and over again for even the simplest of tasks. Workers' attention for a boring task may be waning and the only way they hear directions for the task is when the supervisors repeat themselves several times. Advertisers trying to create a unique image for a product which is undifferentiated from its competitors—such as aspirin, soap, and deodorant—rely heavily on re-petitious advertising.

Motion. The motion principle says that people will pay more attention to moving objects in their field of vision than they will to stationary objects. Workers will notice materials moving by them on a conveyor belt but they may fail to give proper attention to the maintenance needs of the stationary machine next to them. In addition, the assembly line workers may devote their attention to the line of slowly moving materials they are working on and fail to notice the relatively nice working conditions (pastel-colored walls, music, and air conditioning). Advertisers capitalize on this principle by creating signs which incorporate moving parts. Las Vegas at night is an example of advertisement in motion.

Novelty and Familiarity. The novelty and familiarity principle states that either a novel or a familiar external situation can serve as an attention getter. New objects or events in a familiar setting or familiar objects or events in a new setting will draw the attention of the perceiver. Job rotation is an example of this principle. Changing workers' jobs from time to time will tend to increase the attention they give to the task. Switching from a typewriter to a word processor may not motivate the clerical staff, but it will increase their attention until they become accustomed to the new job. The same is true for the previously mentioned disadvantaged people newly trained for their first job assignments. The work environment is a completely novel experience for them. If supervisors use familiar street jargon in communicating with the employees, they may receive more attention from them. However, once again, this approach could backfire unless properly handled. The same is true in a foreign context. The accompanying International Application Example shows some of the blunders U.S. advertising language has made in foreign countries.

Internal Set Factors

The concept of *set* is an important cognition in selectivity. It can be thought of as an internal form of attention getting and is based largely on the individual's complex psychological makeup. People will select out stimuli or situations from the environ-ment that appeal to, and are compatible with, their learning and motivation and with their personality. Although these aspects are given specific attention in Part 3 and the next chapter, a very brief discussion here will help in the understanding of percep-tion.

Sometimes It Doesn't Translate

While marketing people in the United States have produced some outstanding advertisements, it is not always possible to take these same ads and use them in other countries. Why not? Because the perceptions are not the same. Here are some classic examples.

1. "Schweppes Tonic Water" was initially translated to the Italian as "il water." However, the copywriters quickly corrected their mistake and changed the translation to "Schweppes Tonica." In Italian "il water" means water in the bathroom commode.
2. When Pepsi-Cola ran an ad slogan of "Come Alive with Pepsi," it did very well in the United States. However, the company had to change its slogan in some foreign countries because it did not translate correctly. In German the translation of "Come alive" is "Come out of the grave." In Asia the phrase is translated, "Bring your ancestors back from the grave."
3. When General Mills attempted to capture the British market with its breakfast cereal, it ran a picture of a freckled, red-haired, crew-cut grinning kid saying, "See kids, it's great!" The company failed to realize that the typical British family, not so child-centered as the U.S. family, would not be able to identify with the kid on the carton. Result: sales were dismally low.
4. General Motors initially had trouble selling its Chevrolet Nova in Puerto Rico. It failed to realize that while the name "Nova" in English means "star," in Spanish the word sounds like "no va," which means "it doesn't go."
5. Rolls-Royce attempted to market one of its models in Germany under the name "Silver Mist." It soon discovered that the word "mist" in German means "excrement."

Learning and Perception. Although interrelated with motivation and personality, learning may play the single biggest role in developing perceptual set. Read the sentence in the triangle below:

TURN
OFF THE
THE ENGINE

It may take several seconds to realize there is something wrong. Because of familiarity with the sentence from prior learning, the person is perceptually set to read "Turn off the engine." This illustration shows that learning affects set by creating an *expectancy* to perceive in a certain manner. As pointed out in Chapter 1, such expectancies are a vital element in the cognitive explanations of behavior. This view states simply that people see and hear what they expect to see and hear. This can be further demonstrated by pronouncing the following words very slowly:

M-A-C-T-A-V-I-S-H
M-A-C-D-O-N-A-L-D
M-A-C-B-E-T-H
M-A-C-H-I-N-E-R-Y

If the last word was pronounced "Mac-Hinery" instead of "machinery," the reader was caught in a verbal response set.

There are many other illustrations that are commonly used to demonstrate the impact of learning on the development of perceptual set. Figure 3.3 is found in many introductory psychology textbooks. What is perceived in this picture? If one sees an attractive, apparently wealthy young woman, the perceiver is in agreement with about 60 percent of the people who see the picture for the first time. On the other hand, if an ugly, poor old woman is seen, the viewer is in agreement with about 40 percent of first viewers. Obviously, two completely distinct women can be perceived in Figure 3.3. Which woman is seen supposedly depends on whether the person is set to perceive young, beautiful women or old, ugly women. How did you come out?

How Figure 3.3 is perceived can be radically influenced by a simple learned experience. When first shown a clear, unambiguous picture of a beautiful young woman (Figure 3.4) and then shown Figure 3.3, the person will almost always report seeing the young woman in Figure 3.3. If the clear picture of the old woman is seen

FIGURE 3.3
Ambiguous picture of a young woman and an old woman. (*Source:* Edwin G. Boring, "A New Ambiguous Figure," *American Journal of Psychology,* July 1930, p. 444. Also see Robert Leeper, "A Study of a Neglected Portion of the Field of Learning—The Development of Sensory Organization," *Journal of Genetic Psychology,* March 1935, p. 62. Originally drawn by cartoonist W. E. Hill and published in *Puck,* Nov. 6, 1915.)

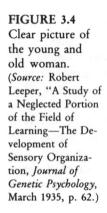

FIGURE 3.4
Clear picture of the young and old woman.
(*Source:* Robert Leeper, "A Study of a Neglected Portion of the Field of Learning—The Development of Sensory Organization, *Journal of Genetic Psychology,* March 1935, p. 62.)

Old woman

Young woman

first (Figure 3.4), the viewer will subsequently report seeing the old woman in Figure 3.3.

In addition to the young woman–old woman example, there is a wide variety of commonly used illusions that effectively demonstrate the impact of learned set on perception. An illusion may be thought of as a form of perception that badly distorts reality. Figures 3.5 and 3.6 show some of the most frequently used forms of perceptual illusion. The two three-pronged objects in Figure 3.5 are drawn contrary to common perceptions of such objects. In Figure 3.6*a*, the length of the nose (from the tip to the X) is exactly equal to the vertical length of the face. In Figure 3.6*b*, the height of the hat is exactly equal to the width of the brim. Both shapes in Figure 3.6*c* are exactly the same size, and in Figure 3.6*d* the lines *AX, CX, CB,* and *XD* are of equal length.

FIGURE 3.5
Common Illusions.

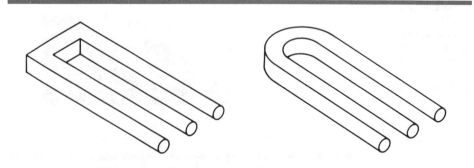

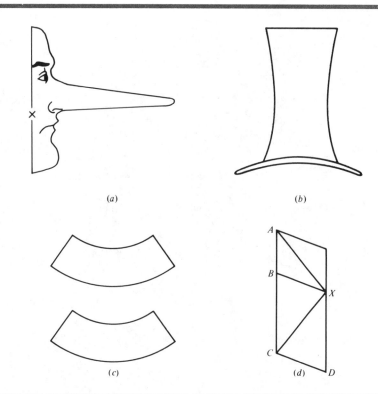

FIGURE 3.6
Common perceptual illusions.
(*Sources:* These illusions are found in almost all introductory psychology textbooks. For example, see Gregory A. Kimble and Norman Garmezy, *General Psychology,* 2d ed., Ronald, New York, 1963, pp. 324–325.)

Figure 3.7 brings out the role that learned set plays in perception even more strongly than Figure 3.6. The three men in Figure 3.7 are drawn exactly equal in height. Yet they are perceived to be of different heights because the viewer has learned that the cues found in the picture normally imply depth and distance. A lot of what a person "sees" in the world is a result of past experience and learning. Even though the past experience may not be relevant to the present situation, it is nevertheless used by the perceiver.

Perceptual Set in the Workplace. Perceptual set has many direct implications for organizational behavior. In organizational life, some employees have learned to perceive the world around them in the same way. For example, the single sentence "I cannot recommend this young man too highly" was reproduced and distributed to several managers in the same organization. Although this statement is ambiguous and unclear, without exception all the managers interpreted this to be a positive recommendation.[2] They had all learned to perceive this statement the same way—positive and favorable.

In most cases, however, learning leads to extreme individual differences. For example, the young woman–old woman illustration demonstrates that the same stimulus may be perceived two completely different ways (young and beautiful or

FIGURE 3.7
The role that learning plays in perception.

old and ugly) because of the way the individual is set to perceive. Numerous instances of this situation occur in a modern organization. Participants may perceive the same stimulus or situation in entirely different ways. A specific organizational example might be a poor output record in the production department of a manufacturing plant. The engineer perceives the solution to this problem as one of improved machine design. The personnel manager perceives the solution as one of more training and better wage incentives. The department head perceives the solution to be more effective organizing, planning, and controlling. On the other hand, the workers may perceive the low output with pleasure because it is a way of "getting back" at their supervisor, whom they dislike. For the purpose of this discussion, it is not important who is right or wrong in this example; rather, the point is that all the relevant personnel perceive the *same* situation in completely *different* ways.

Another common example is the differences in perception that occur between the union and management. Some industrial relations researchers believe that perceptual differences are a major explanation for industrial disputes. The same "facts" in a dispute are perceived quite differently by union members and by management. For example, union members may perceive that they are underpaid, whereas management perceives that they are overpaid for the amount of work they do. In reality, pay may have nothing to do with the ensuing dispute. Maybe it is a matter of the workers not having control over their own jobs and getting any recognition and they are reacting by perceiving that they are underpaid.

Motivation and Perception. Besides the learned aspects of perceptual set, motivation also has a vital impact on perceptual selectivity. The primary motives of sex and hunger could be used to demonstrate the role that motivation plays in perception.

In traditional American culture, the sex drive has been largely suppressed, with the result being an unfulfilled need for sex. Accordingly, any mention of sex or a visual stimulus dealing with sex is very attention-getting to the average American. The picture of a scantily clad or naked male or female is readily perceived. On the other hand, as nudity becomes increasingly commonplace in magazines, motion pictures, live entertainment, and fashions, the human anatomy slowly begins to lose its appeal as an attention getter. Analogously, however, if there is a great need for food in the culture, the mention, sight, or smell of food is given a great deal of attention.

The secondary motives also play an important role in developing perceptual set. A person who has a relatively high need for power, affiliation, or achievement will be more attentive to the relevant situational variables. An example is the worker who has a strong need for affiliation. When such a worker walks into the lunchroom, the table where several coworkers are sitting tends to be perceived, and the empty table or the one where a single person is sitting tends to get no attention. Although very simple, the lunchroom example points out that perception may have an important impact on motivation, and vice versa. This demonstrates once again the interrelatedness of these concepts.

Personality and Perception. Closely related to learning and motivation is the personality of the perceiving person, which affects what is attended to in the confronting situation. For example, senior-level executives often complain that the new young "hot shots" have trouble making the "tough" personnel decisions concerning terminating or reassigning people and paying attention to details and paperwork. The young managers, in turn, complain about the "old guard" resisting change and using rules and paperwork as ends in themselves. The senior- and junior-level executives' personalities largely explain these perceptions.

The growing generation gap recognized in recent years definitely contributes to differing perceptions. An example can be found in the perceptions of modern movies. Older people tend either to be disgusted by or to not understand some of the popular movies of recent years. Those in the thirty-five to forty-five age group tend to perceive these movies as "naughty but neat." Young, college-age people tend to perceive them as "where it's at." They tend to get neither uptight nor titillated. Of course, there are individual differences in all age categories, and the above example tends to stereotype (this is discussed later in the chapter) people by age. Yet it does show how personalities, values, and even age may affect the way people perceive the world around them.

PERCEPTUAL ORGANIZATION

The discussion of perceptual selectivity was concerned with the external and internal variables that gain an individual's attention. This section focuses on what takes place in the perceptual process once the information from the situation is received. This aspect of perception is commonly referred to as *perceptual organization.* An individual seldom perceives patches of color or light or sound. Instead, the person will perceive organized patterns of stimuli and identifiable whole objects. For example, when a college student is shown a football, the student does not normally perceive it as the color brown or as grain-leather in texture or as the odor of leather. Rather, the student perceives a football which has, in addition to the characteristics named, a potential for giving the perceiver fun and excitement as either a participant or a spectator. In other words, the person's perceptual process organizes the incoming information into a meaningful whole.

Figure-Ground

Figure-ground is usually considered to be the most basic form of perceptual organization. The figure-ground principle means simply that perceived objects stand out as separable from their general background. It can be effectively demonstrated as one is reading this paragraph. In terms of light-wave stimuli, the reader is receiving patches of irregularly shaped blacks and whites. Yet the reader does not perceive it this way. The reader perceives black shapes—letters, words, and sentences—printed against a white background. To say it another way, the reader perceptually organizes incoming stimuli into recognizable figures (words) that are seen against a ground (white page).

Another interesting figure-ground illustration is shown in Figure 3.8. At first glance, one probably perceives a jumble of black, irregular shapes against a white

FIGURE 3:8
Illustrations of figure-ground. (*Sources:* (a) Warner Brown and Howard Gilhousen, *College Psychology,* Prentice-Hall, Englewood Cliffs, N.J., 1949, p. 330; (b) Jerome Kagan and Ernest Havemann, *Psychology: An Introduction,* Harcourt, Brace, & World, New York, 1968, p. 166.)

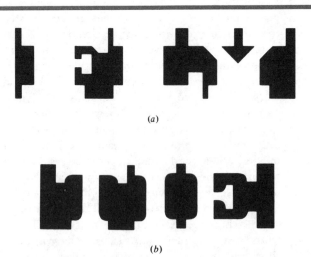

(a)

(b)

background. Only when the white letters are perceptually organized against a black background will the words FLY and TIE literally jump out with clarity. This illustration shows that perceptual selectivity will influence perceptual organization. The viewer is set to perceive black on white because of the black words (figures) throughout the book. However, in Figure 3.8 the reverse is true. White is the figure and black is the ground.

Perceptual Grouping

The grouping principle of perceptual organization states that there is a tendency to group several stimuli together into a recognizable pattern. This principle is very basic and seems to be largely inborn. There are certain underlying uniformities in grouping. When simple constellations of stimuli are presented to people, they will tend to group them together by closure, continuity, proximity, or similarity.

Closure. The closure principle of grouping is closely related to the gestalt school of psychology. A basic gestalt principle is that a person will sometimes perceive a whole when one does not actually exist. The person's perceptual process will close the gaps which are unfilled from sensory input. In the formal organization, participants may either see a whole where none exists or not be able to put the pieces together into a whole that does exist. An example of the first case is the department head who perceived complete agreement among the members of her department on a given project when, in fact, there was opposition from several members. The department head in this situation closed the existing gaps and perceived complete agreement when, in fact, it did not exist. An example of the other side of the coin is the adage of not being able to see the forest (whole) because of the trees (parts). High degrees of specialization have often resulted in functionally oriented managers' losing sight of the whole organization's objectives. Specialists may get so caught up in their own little area of interest and responsibility that they may lose sight of the overall goal. They cannot close their part together with the other parts to perceive the whole.

Continuity. Continuity is closely related to closure. Some psychologists do not even bother to make a distinction between the two grouping principles. However, there is a slight difference. Closure supplies *missing* stimuli, and the continuity principle says that a person will tend to perceive *continuous* lines or patterns. This type of continuity may lead to inflexible, or noncreative, thinking on the part of organizational participants. Only the obvious, continuous patterns or relationships will be perceived. For example, a new design for some productive process or product may be limited to obvious flows or continuous lines. New, innovative ideas or designs may not be perceived. Continuity can greatly influence the systems design of an organizational structure.

Proximity. The principle of proximity, or nearness, states that a group of stimuli that are close together will be perceived as a whole pattern of parts belonging together. For example, several employees in an organization may be identified as a single group because of physical proximity. Several workers who work on a particular machine may be perceived as a single whole. If the output is low and the supervisor reports a number of grievances from the group, management may perceive all the workers on the machine as one troublemaking group when, in fact, some of the workers are loyal, dedicated employees. Yet, the fact remains that often department or work groups are perceived as a single entity because of physical proximity.

Similarity. The principle of similarity states that the greater the similarity of the stimuli, the greater the tendency to perceive them as a common group. Similarity is conceptually related to proximity but in most cases is stronger than proximity. In an organization, all employees who wear white collars may be perceived as a common group, when, in reality, each worker is a unique individual. Similarity also applies to minorities and women. There is a tendency to perceive minority and women employees as a single group, the famous "they."

Perceptual Constancy

Constancy is one of the more sophisticated forms of perceptual organization. It gives a person a sense of stability in a changing world. Constancy permits the individual to have some constancy in a tremendously variable and highly complex world. Learning plays a much bigger role in the constancy phenomenon than in figure-ground or grouping phenomena.

The size, shape, color, brightness, and location of an object are fairly constant regardless of the information received by the senses. It should be pointed out that perceptual constancy results from *patterns* of cues. These patterns are for the most part learned, but each situation is different and there are interactions between the inborn and learned tendencies within the entire perceptual process.

If constancy were not at work, the world would be very chaotic and disorganized for the individual. An organizational example would be the worker who must select a piece of material or a tool of the correct size from a wide variety of materials and tools at varying distances from a work station. Without perceptual constancy, the sizes, shapes, and colors of objects would change as the worker moved about and would make the job almost impossible.

Perceptual Context

The highest, most sophisticated form of perceptual organization is context. It gives meaning and value to simple stimuli, objects, events, situations, and other persons in the environment. The principle of context can be simply demonstrated by doodles such as the one shown in Figure 3.9 (answer is given in reference no. 3). The visual stimuli by themselves are meaningless. Only when the doodle is placed in a verbal context does it take on meaning and value to the perceiver.

The organizational culture and structure provide the primary context in which workers and managers do their perceiving. Thus, a verbal order, a memo, a new policy, a suggestion, a raised eyebrow, or a pat on the back takes on special meaning and value when placed in the context of the work organization. Chapters 2, 19, and

FIGURE 3.9
Doodles illustrate the role that context plays in perception.

20 on culture and the international context and those in Part 5 on processes and structure form the major context in which organizational participants perceive.

Perceptual Defense

Closely related to context is perceptual defense. A person may build a defense (a block or a refusal to recognize) against stimuli or situational events in the context that are personally or culturally unacceptable or threatening. Accordingly, perceptual defense may play an influential role in understanding union-management or supervisor-subordinate relationships.

Although there is some conflicting evidence, most studies verify the existence of a perceptual defense mechanism. Two examples are classic studies which found barriers to perceiving personality-threatening words[4] and identification thresholds for critical, emotionally toned words.[5] In another study more directly relevant to organizational behavior, the researchers describe how people may react with a perceptual defense that is activated in them when they are confronted with a fact that is inconsistent with a preconceived notion.[6] In this study, college students were presented with the word "intelligent" as a characteristic of a factory worker. This was counter to their perception of factory workers, and they built defenses in the following ways:

1. *Denial.* A few of the subjects denied the existence of intelligence in factory workers.
2. *Modification and distortion.* This was one of the most frequent forms of defense. The pattern was to explain away the perceptual conflict by joining intelligence with some other characteristic, for example, "He is intelligent, but doesn't possess the initiative to rise above his group."
3. *Change in perception.* Many of the students changed their perception of the worker because of the intelligence characteristic. The change, however, was usually very subtle; for example, "He cracks jokes" became "He's witty."
4. *Recognition, but refusal to change.* Very few subjects explicitly recognized the conflict between their perception of the worker and the characteristic of intelligence that was confronting them. For example, one subject stated, "the traits seem to be conflicting . . . most factory workers I have heard about aren't too intelligent."[7]

The general conclusion to be drawn from this classic study is that people may learn to avoid perceiving certain conflicting, threatening, or unacceptable aspects of the context.

These and other relevant experiments have been summarized into three general explanations of perceptual defense:

1. Emotionally disturbing information has a higher threshold for recognition (that is, we do not perceive it readily) than neutral or nondisturbing information. This is why a chain of events may be seen differently by those who are not personally involved and by those who are involved; thus, warning signs of trouble are often not seen by those who will be most affected by the trouble.

2. Disturbing information and stimuli are likely to bring about substitute perceptions which are distorted to prevent recognition of the disturbing elements. In this way a manager can perceive that workers are happy, when actually they are disgruntled. Then when a grievance committee is formed or a strike takes place, the manager cannot perceive that these "happy" workers are participating willingly and concludes that it is because they have fallen victim to some agitator and that things in the shop are still basically fine.

3. Emotionally arousing information actually does arouse emotion, even though the emotion is distorted and directed elsewhere. Kicking the cat, snarling at the kids, cutting someone off for trying to pass you on the right while driving home, and browbeating an underling all offer a sense of relief and are good substitutes for perceiving that people "upstairs" think you are an idiot.[8]

Such findings as the above help explain why some people, especially supervisors and subordinates in an organization, have a "blind spot." They do not "see" or they consistently misinterpret certain events or situations. As the accompanying Application Example, Police Perceptions, indicates, certain groups such as the police must be very careful not to make such misinterpretations.

Application Example ‖➡

Police Perceptions

Training police to handle or quell a riot normally includes a session or two on the importance of accurately perceiving what is happening within an unruly crowd. This need for accurate perception has resulted from several incidents in which instigators of riots deliberately attempted to provoke police into acting in a violent manner. It has been shown in several riots that what the police perceived as a threat to their lives was really nothing more than a deliberate attempt to provoke them with harmless acts or objects. For example, crumpled paper has been mistaken for a rock in the fist of an angry rioter. The sound of a thrown light bulb breaking has been confused with a gun discharging. A protruding stick being carried by a protestor has been confused from a distance with the barrel of a rifle. All these possible misperceptions could lead, and in some cases have led, to violence and death. Training the police in accurate perception can be a life-or-death matter.

SOCIAL PERCEPTION

Although context and perceptual defense are closely related to social perception, this section gives recognition to social perception per se. The social aspects of perception are given detailed coverage because they play such an important role in organizational behavior. Social perception is directly concerned with how one individual perceives other individuals: how we get to know others.

Characteristics of Perceiver and Perceived

A summary of research findings on some specific characteristics of the perceiver and the perceived reveals a profile of the perceiver as follows:

1. Knowing oneself makes it easier to see others accurately.
2. One's own characteristics affect the characteristics one is likely to see in others.
3. People who accept themselves are more likely to be able to see favorable aspects of other people.
4. Accuracy in perceiving others is not a single skill.[9]

These four characteristics greatly influence how a person perceives others in the environmental situation.

There are also certain characteristics of the person being perceived which influence social perception. Research has shown that:

1. The status of the person perceived will greatly influence others' perception of the person.
2. The person being perceived is usually placed into categories to simplify the viewer's perceptual activities. Two common categories are status and role.
3. The visible traits of the person perceived will greatly influence others' perception of the person.[10]

These characteristics of the perceiver and the perceived suggest the extreme complexity of social perception. Organizational participants must realize that their perceptions of another person are greatly influenced by their own characteristics and the characteristics of the other person. For example, if a manager has high self-esteem and the other person is physically attractive and pleasant and comes from the home office, then the manager will likely perceive this other person in a positive, favorable manner. On the other hand, if the manager has low self-esteem and the other person is an arrogant, unattractive salesperson, the manager will likely perceive this other person in a negative, unfavorable manner. Such attributions that people make of others play a vital role in their social perceptions and resulting behavior.

Participants in formal organizations are constantly perceiving one another. Managers are perceiving workers, workers are perceiving managers, line personnel are perceiving staff personnel, staff personnel are perceiving the line personnel, superiors are perceiving subordinates, subordinates are perceiving superiors, and on and on. There are numerous complex factors which enter into such social perception, but the primary factors are found in the psychological processes and personality.

Attribution

Attribution refers simply to how a person explains the cause of another's or of his or her own behavior. It is the process by which people draw conclusions about the factors that influence one another's behavior. Applied to social perception, there are two general types of attributions that people make: *dispositional attributions* which ascribe a person's behavior to internal factors such as personality traits, motivation, or ability and *situational attributions* which attribute a person's behavior to external factors such as equipment or social influence from others.[11] In recent years, attribution theories have been playing an increasingly important role in work motivation, performance appraisal, and leadership,[12] but also are recognized to influence perceptions.

Attributions have been found to strongly affect evaluations of others' performance, to determine the manner in which supervisors behave toward subordinates, and to influence personal satisfaction with one's work.[13] These attribution theories of motivation will be covered in Chapter 6. Applied to social perception, attribution is the search for causes (attributes) in making interpretations of other persons or of oneself. For example, what the manager perceives as the cause of a subordinate's behavior will affect the manager's perception of, and resulting behavior toward, the subordinate. If the subordinate's outstanding performance is attributed to situational factors such as a new machine or engineering procedure, the perception and resulting treatment will be different from the perception and resulting treatment if the performance is attributed to dispositional factors such as ability and drive. The same is true of attributions made of one's own behavior. Perceptions and thus behaviors will vary depending on whether internal dispositional attributions or external, situational attributions are made. In other words, the type of causal attributions one makes greatly affects perception, and, as the later discussions of motivation and leadership will indicate, there is growing evidence that the attributional process and the form it takes seem to greatly affect the resulting organizational behavior.

Stereotyping

In addition to attribution, there are two other important areas of social perception that are especially relevant to the understanding of organizational behavior. These are the common errors or problems that creep into social perception called *stereotyping* and the *halo effect*.

The term *stereotype* refers to the tendency to perceive another person (hence social perception) as belonging to a *single* class or category. From attribution theory, a stereotype also involves general agreement on the attributed traits and the existence of a discrepancy between attributed traits and actual traits.

The word stereotype is derived from the typographer's word for a printing plate made from previously composed type. In 1922, Walter Lippmann applied the word to perception. Since then, stereotyping has become a frequently used term to describe perceptual errors. In particular, it is employed in analyzing prejudice. Not commonly acknowledged is the fact that stereotyping may attribute favorable or unfavorable traits to the person being perceived. Most often a person is put into a stereotype because the perceived knows only the overall category to which the person belongs. However, because each individual is unique, the real traits of the person will generally be quite different from those the stereotype would suggest.

Stereotyping greatly influences social perception in today's organizations. Common stereotyped groups include managers, supervisors, union members, minorities, women, white- and blue-collar workers, and all the various functional and staff specialists, for example, accountants, salespeople, computer programmers, and engineers. There is a consensus about the traits possessed by the members of these categories. Yet in reality there is often a discrepancy between the agreed-upon traits of each category and the actual traits of the members. In other words, not all engineers carry calculators and are coldly rational, nor are all personnel managers do-gooders who are trying to keep workers happy. On the contrary, there are individual differences and a great deal of variability among members of these groups. In spite of this, other organization members commonly make blanket perceptions and behave accordingly. For example, in one classic research study it was found that individuals will both perceive and be perceived according to whether they are identified with a union or a management group. "Thus, 74 percent of the subjects in the managerial group chose the word 'honest' as a description of Mr. A, *when he was identified as a manager.* The same managerial subjects, however, chose the word 'honest' to describe Mr. A only 50 percent of the time when he was identified as a representative of the union."[14] There are numerous other research studies and common, everyday examples which point out the stereotyping that occurs in organizational life.

The Halo Effect

The *halo effect* in social perception is very similar to stereotyping. Whereas in stereotyping the person is perceived according to a single category, under the halo effect the person is perceived on the basis of one trait. Halo is often discussed in performance appraisal when a rater makes an error in judging a person's total personality and/or performance on the basis of a single trait such as intelligence, appearance, dependability, or cooperativeness. Whatever the single trait is, it may override all other traits in forming the perception of the person.

A recent comprehensive review of the performance appraisal literature found that the halo effect was the dependent variable in over a third of the studies and was found to be a major problem affecting appraisal accuracy.[15] Examples of the halo effect are the extremely attractive woman secretary who is perceived by her male boss as being an intelligent, good performer, when, in fact, she is a poor typist and quite dense, and the good typist who is also very bright but who is perceived by her male boss as a "secretary," not as a potential manager with the ability to cope with important responsibilities. One classic research study noted three conditions under which the halo effect is most marked: (1) when the traits to be perceived are unclear in behavioral expressions, (2) when the traits are not frequently encountered by the perceiver, and (3) when the traits have moral implications.[16]

Many other research studies have pointed out how the halo effect can influence perception. For example, one study found that when two persons were described as having identical personalities except for one trait—the character qualities in one list included the trait *warm* and, in the other list, the trait *cold*—two completely different perceptions resulted.[17] In other words, one trait blinded the perceiver to all other traits in the perceptual process. Another study also documented the impact of the halo effect on employee perceptions in a company that was in receivership. Although the company paid relatively high wages and provided excellent working conditions and at least average supervision, the employees did not perceive these favorable factors. The insecurity produced an inverse halo effect so that insecurity dominated over the pay and positive conditions of the job.[18] The results of this study make the point that "when there's one important 'rotten' attitude, it can spoil the 'barrel' of attitudes."[19]

Like all the other aspects of the psychological process of perception discussed in this chapter, the halo effect has important implications for the study and eventual understanding of organizational behavior. Unfortunately, even though halo effect is one of the longest recognized and most pervasive problems associated with applications such as performance appraisal in the field of organizational behavior, attempts at solving it have not yet been very successful.[20] The "perceptual and cognitive differences among raters may affect their ratings as much as or more than the nature of the rating scale itself."[21]

IMPRESSION MANAGEMENT

Whereas social perception is concerned with how one individual perceives other individuals, *impression management* (sometimes called "self-presentation") is the process by which people attempt to manage or control the perceptions others form of them. There is often a tendency for people to try to present themselves in such a way as to impress others in a socially desirable way. Thus, impression management has considerable implications for areas such as the validity of performance appraisals (is the evaluator being manipulated into giving a positive rating?) and a pragmatic, political tool for one to climb the ladder of success in organizations.

The Process of Impression Management

As with other cognitive processes, impression management has many possible conceptual dimensions and has been researched in relation to aggression, attitude change, attributions, and social facilitation, among other things.[22] Most recently, however, two separate components of impression management have been identified—impression motivation and impression construction.[23] Especially in an employment situation, subordinates may be motivated to control how their boss perceives them. The degree of this motivation to impression-manage will depend on such factors as the relevance the impressions have to the individual's goals, the value of these goals, and the discrepancy between the image one would like others to hold and the image one believes others already hold.[24]

Impression construction, the other major process, is concerned with the specific type of impression people want to make and how they go about doing it.

Although some theorists limit the type of impression only to personal characteristics, others include such other things as attitudes, physical states, interests, or values. Using this broader approach, five factors have been identified as being especially relevant to the kinds of impressions people try to construct: the self-concept, desired and undesired identity images, role constraints, target's values, and current social image.[25] Although there is considerable research on how these five factors influence the type of impression that people try to make, there is still little known of how they select the way to manage others' perceptions of them. For example, do they directly tell their boss things such as "I'm really competitive and want to get ahead" or do they make indirect statements such as "I really like racquetball; it is really competitive."

Employee Impression Management Strategies

There are two basic strategies of impression management that employees can use. If employees are trying to minimize responsibility for some negative event or to stay out of trouble, they may employ a demotion-preventative strategy. On the other hand, if they are seeking to maximize responsibility for a positive outcome or to look better than they really are, then they can use a promotion-enhancing strategy.[26] The demotion-preventative strategy is characterized by the following:

1. *Accounts.* These are employees' attempts to excuse or justify their actions. Example excuses are not feeling well or not getting something done on time because of another higher priority assignment.
2. *Apologies.* When there is no logical way out, the employee may apologize to the boss for some negative event. Such an apology not only gives the impression that the individual is sorry, but also indicates that it will not happen again. The employee is big enough to face up to a problem and solve it.
3. *Disassociation.* When employees are indirectly associated with something that went wrong (for example, they are a member of a committee or work team that made a bad decision), they may secretly tell their boss that they fought for the right thing but were overruled. Employees using this approach try to remove themselves both from the group and from responsibility for the problem.[27]

The promotion-enhancing strategies involve the following:

1. *Entitlements.* Under this approach, employees feel that they have not been given credit for a positive outcome. They make sure that it is known through formal channels. Or, they may informally note to key people that they are pleased their suggestions or efforts worked out so well.
2. *Enhancements.* Here employees may have received credit, but they point out that they really did more and had a bigger impact than originally thought. For example, their effort or idea not only served a customer well or met a difficult deadline, but can be used in the future to greatly increase profits.
3. *Obstacle Disclosures.* In this strategy, employees identify either personal (health or family) or organization (lack of resources or cooperation) obstacles they had to overcome to accomplish an outcome. They are trying to create the perception that

because they obtained the positive outcome despite the big obstacles, they really deserve a lot of credit.

4. *Association.* Here, the employee makes sure to be seen with the right people at the right times. This creates the perception that the employee is well connected and is associated with successful projects.[28]

The above strategies help construct impressions or perceptions. The motivation on the part of employees may or may not be a deliberate attempt to enhance themselves in terms of political power, promotions, and monetary rewards. Managers should be aware of deliberate manipulation of perceptions when making evaluations of their people. By the same token, such impression management could be used to get ahead in an organization or keep good relations with customers.

Summary

Perception is an important mediating cognitive process. Through this complex process, persons make interpretations of stimulus situations they are faced with. Both selectivity and organization go into perceptual interpretations. Externally, selectivity is affected by intensity, size, contrast, repetition, motion, novelty, and familiarity. Internally, perceptual selectivity is influenced by the individual's motivation, learning, and personality. After the stimulus situation is filtered by the selective process, the incoming information is organized into a meaningful whole. Figure-ground is the most basic form of perceptual organization. Another basic form is the grouping of constellations of incoming stimuli by closure, continuity, proximity, and similarity. The constancy, context, and defensive aspects of perceptual organization are more complex. The social context in particular plays an important role in understanding human behavior in organizations. Controlling and constructing perceptions through impression management has also recently been recognized by the field of organizational behavior.

Questions for Discussion and Review

1. Do you agree with the opening observation that people are human information processors? Why?
2. How does sensation differ from perception?
3. Give some examples of the external factors that affect perceptual selectivity.
4. Explain how perceptual constancy works.
5. What does "stereotyping" mean? Why is it considered to be a perceptual problem?
6. What effect can the perceptual process have on organizational behavior?
7. What are some of the major strategies employees use in impression management?

References

1. *The Wall Street Journal,* Dec. 2, 1986, p. 1.
2. John Swanda, *Organizational Behavior,* Alfred, Sherman Oaks, Calif., 1979, p. 91.
3. The answer to the doodle in Fig. 3.9 is the start of a "rat race."
4. Jerome S. Bruner and Leo Postman, "Emotional Selectivity in Perception and Reaction," *Journal of Personality,* September 1947, pp. 69–77.
5. Elliott McGinnies, "Emotionality and Perceptual Defense," *Psychological Review,* September 1949, pp. 244–251.
6. Mason Haire and Willa Freeman Grunes, "Perceptual Defenses: Processes Protecting an Organized Perception of Another Personality," *Human Relations,* November 1950, pp. 403–412.
7. Ibid., pp. 407–411.
8. David J. Lawless, *Organizational Behavior,* Prentice-Hall, Englewood Cliffs, N.J., 1979, p. 85.
9. Sheldon S. Zalkind and Timothy W. Costello, "Perception: Some Recent Research and Implications for Administration," *Administrative Science Quarterly,* September 1962, pp. 227–229.
10. Ibid., p. 230.
11. Spencer A. Rathus, *Psychology,* 4th ed., Holt, Rinehart and Winston, Fort Worth, Tex., 1990, pp. 613–614.
12. For summaries of this literature, see James C. McElroy, "A Typology of Attribution Leadership Research," *Academy of Management Review,* July 1982, pp. 413–417; James C. McElroy and Charles B. Shrader, "Attribution Theories of Leadership and Network Analysis," *Journal of Management,* vol. 12, no. 3, 1986, pp. 351–362; and Christy L. DeVader, Allan G. Bateson, and Robert G. Lord, "Attribution Theory: A Meta-Analysis of Attributional Hypotheses," in Edwin A. Locke (ed.), *Generalizing from Laboratory to Field Settings,* Lexington (Heath), Lexington, Mass., 1986, pp. 63–81.
13. See Robert A. Baron, *Behavior in Organizations,* Allyn and Bacon, Boston, 1986, pp. 131–132, 190; and Joseph F. Porac, Gail Nottenburg, and James Eggert, "On Extending Weiner's Attributional Model to Organizational Contexts," *Journal of Applied Psychology,* February 1981, pp. 124–126.
14. Mason Haire, "Role-Perception in Labor-Management Relations: An Experimental Approach," *Industrial and Labor Relations Review,* January 1955, p. 208.
15. H. John Bernardin and Peter Villanova, "Performance Appraisal," in Locke, op. cit., pp. 45 and 53.
16. Jerome S. Bruner and Renato Tagiuri, "The Perception of People," in Gardner Lindzey (ed.), *Handbook of Social Psychology,* Addison-Wesley, Reading, Mass., 1954, p. 641.
17. S. E. Asch, "Forming Impressions of Personalities," *Journal of Abnormal and Social Psychology,* July 1946, pp. 258–290.
18. Byron A. Grove and Willard A. Kerr, "Specific Evidence on Origin of Halo Effect in Measurement of Employee Morale," *Journal of Social Psychology,* August 1951, pp. 165–170.
19. Timothy W. Costello and Sheldon S. Zalkind, *Psychology in Administration,* Prentice-Hall, Englewood Cliffs, N.J., 1963, p. 35.
20. Rick Jacobs and Steve W. J. Kozlowski, "A Closer Look at Halo Error in Performance Ratings," *Academy of Management Journal,* March 1985, pp. 201–212.
21. Berkeley Rice, "Rating People: Performance Review," *Current,* December 1985, p. 12.
22. For example, see R. F. Baumeister, "A Self-Presentational View of Social Phenomena," *Psychological Bulletin,* vol. 91, 1982, pp. 3–26; R. F. Baumeister (ed.), *Public Self and Private Self,* Springer-Verlag, New York, 1986; and B. R. Schlenker, *Impression Management: The Self-Concept, Social Identity, and Interpersonal Relations,* Brooks/Cole, Monterey, Cal., 1980.
23. Mark R. Leary and Robin M. Lowalski, "Impression Management: A Literature Review and Two-Component Model," *Psychological Bulletin,* vol. 107, no. 1, 1990, pp. 34–47.
24. Ibid., pp. 38–39.
25. Ibid., pp. 40–42.
26. Robert A. Giacalone, "Image Control: The Strategies of Impression Management," *Personnel,* May 1989, pp. 52–55.
27. Ibid., p. 54.
28. Ibid., pp. 54–55.

REAL CASE: IS PATRIOTISM FOR SALE?

There currently is a debate raging in the United States regarding the role of lobbyists in Washington. The reason for this debate is that many people perceive lobbyists as using "inside" information that they have acquired through their experience working for organizations such as the Office of the U.S. Trade Representative or the International Trade Commission. Since 1973, one-third of all former top officials from the Trade Representative office now work as lobbyists for the Japanese. Some observers of the Washington scene feel that by using this experience, these lobbyists have been able to influence Congress and the Administration into giving Japanese businesses special treatment. For example, a few years ago Japanese auto makers shipped light trucks to the United States but claimed that they were cars and thus were not subject to import duty. Working through its Washington lobbyists, the auto makers were able to get the Customs Department to allow the vehicles to be reclassified and thus avoid $500 million in duties. Then the lobbyists went to work to get the vehicles reclassified as light trucks so that they would not have to have all of the auto emission equipment required in cars.

Commenting on the manipulation of the American political and economic system by Japanese lobbyists, many business people are very upset. Lee Iacocca has remarked that, "If an American CIA agent quit one day and went to work for a foreign intelligence service the next, we'd call it treason. But when American trade officials . . . defect in droves to the Japanese, we don't even bat an eye."

The major problem in dealing with this issue is that the lobbyists are doing nothing that is illegal. As long as government officials refrain from lobbying for one year after they leave their job, they are free to trade on their knowledge and influence in Washington circles. There are efforts currently under way to extend this time period from the current one year to five years, thus greatly reducing the likelihood that people will take government jobs as a sabbatical during which they will gather experience and information to be used in their new job, lobbying. This has led one analyst to raise the issue: What are the demands of patriotism in a world where global economic rivalry has replaced the cold war? Many observers believe that Americans are too quick to sell their services to the highest bidder. There must be changes in the way business is being done. A report on the topic recently concluded:

> Americans who work to advance the causes of foreign governments or corporations have an obligation to be wary that their activities do not harm the national interest. A global economy is no excuse for continuing to tolerate a laissez-faire ethical climate in which all of Washington is available to the highest bidder.

1. What is Lee Iacocca's perception of Japanese lobbyists? Why?
2. Why would lobbyists disagree with the point of view espoused by this case?
3. Do you think the government should exercise more control of lobbyists for foreign companies or countries? What does your answer relate about your perception?

Case: Space Utilization

Sherman Adder, assistant plant manager for Frame Manufacturing Company, is chairperson of the ad hoc committee for space utilization. The committee is made up of the various department heads in the company. The plant manager of Frame has given Sherman the responsibility for seeing whether the various office, operations, and warehouse facilities of the company are being optimally utilized. The company is beset by rising costs and the need for more space. However, before okaying an expensive addition to the plant, the plant manager wants to be sure that the currently available space is being utilized properly.

Sherman opened up the first committee meeting by reiterating the charge of the committee. Then Sherman asked the members if they had any initial observations to make. The first to speak was the office manager. He stated, "Well, I know we are using every possible inch of room that we have available to us. But when I walk out into the plant I see a lot of open spaces. We have people piled on top of one another, but out in the plant there seems to be plenty of room." The production manager quickly replied, "We do not have a lot of space. You office people have the luxury facilities. My supervisors don't even have room for a desk and a file cabinet. I have repeatedly told the plant manager we need more space. After all, our operation determines whether this plant succeeds or fails, not you people in the front office pushing paper around." Sherman interrupted at this point and said, "Obviously we have different interpretations of the space utilization around here. Before further discussion I think it would be best if we have some objective facts to work with. I am going to ask the industrial engineer to provide us with some statistics on plant and office layouts before our next meeting. Today's meeting is adjourned."

1. What perceptual principles are evident in this case?
2. What concept was brought out when the production manager labeled the office personnel a bunch of "paper pushers"? Can you give other organizational examples of this concept?
3. Do you think that Sherman's approach to getting "objective facts" from statistics on plant and office layout will affect the perceptions of the office and production managers? How does such information affect perception in general?

**Case:
Same
Accident,
Different
Perceptions**

According to the police report, on July 9 at 1:27 P.M., bus number 3763 was involved in a minor noninjury accident. Upon arriving at the scene of the accident, police were unable to locate the driver of the bus. Since the bus was barely drivable, the passengers were transferred to a backup bus, and the damaged bus was returned to the city bus garage for repair.

The newly hired general manager, Aaron Moore, has been going over the police report and two additional reports. One of the additional reports was submitted by Jennifer Tye, the transportation director for the City Transit Authority (CTA), and the other came directly from the driver in the accident, Michael Meyer. According to Tye, although Mike has been an above-average driver for almost eight years, his performance has taken a drastic nosedive during the past fifteen months. Always one to join the other drivers for an after-work drink or two, Mike recently has been suspected of drinking on the job. Furthermore, according to Tye's report, Mike was seen having a beer in a tavern located less than two blocks from the CTA terminal at around 3 P.M. on the day of the accident. Tye's report concludes by citing two sections of the CTA Transportation Agreement. Section 18a specifically forbids the drinking of alcoholic beverages by any CTA employee while on duty. Section 26f prohibits drivers from leaving their bus unattended for any reason. Violation of either of the two sections results in automatic dismissal of the employee involved. Tye recommends immediate dismissal.

According to the driver, Michael Meyer, however, the facts are quite different. Mike claims that in attempting to miss a bicycle rider he swerved and struck a tree, causing minor damage to the bus. Mike had been talking with the dispatcher when he was forced to drop his phone receiver in order to miss the bicycle. Since the receiver broke open on impact, Mike was forced to walk four blocks to the nearest phone to report the accident. As soon as he reported the accident to the company, Mike also called the union to tell them about it. Mike reports that when he returned to the scene of the accident, his bus was gone. Uncertain of what to do and a little frightened, he decided to return to the CTA terminal. Since it was over a 5-mile walk and because his shift had already ended at 3 P.M. Mike stopped in for a quick beer just before getting back to the terminal.

1. Why are the two reports submitted by Jennifer and Mike so different? Did Jennifer and Mike have different perceptions of the same incident?
2. What additional information would you need if you were in Aaron Moore's position? How can he clarify his own perception of the incident?
3. Given the information presented above, how would you recommend resolving this problem?

4 Personality

Do successful managers have any common personality traits? Is there anything that distinguishes them from their less successful counterparts? In an effort to identify personality similarities among the most coveted managers, *Fortune* magazine asked a dozen executive search firms to give their top picks for chief executive officer (CEO) in ten different industries: aerospace and defense, communications, diversified manufacturing, energy equipment manufacturing, financial services, food and drugs, high technology, retailing and fashion, and travel. From the list of 150 names, further pruning was conducted until there were but three individuals for each industry. Finally, from each threesome one was chosen over the others. What were the major characteristics and personality traits of the winners? Here is the profile:

1. All were in their forties and considered ripe for plucking by other firms that were looking for chief executive officers.
2. They were action-oriented, able to institute and carry out change.
3. They had the ability to build a sense of shared values regarding where the enterprise should be heading.
4. They were self-confident and had the ability to take risks without undue worry.
5. They had excellent communication skills.
6. They had high integrity.
7. They had achieved a pattern of accomplishment in whatever jobs they undertook.
8. They had a commitment to what they were doing and were willing to pay the price to get there.
9. They had a vision that could be imparted to others.
10. They liked competitive sports.

These particular characteristics and personality traits were evident in the brief description that the executive recruiters gave of the ten winners. Some of these descriptions included the following:

- A driver, a strong, abilitious leader, grounded in all aspects of the industry.
- Bright, aggressive, goal-oriented. Leads by example. A workaholic who wins loyalty and results.

- Good strategic thinker. Personable, sensitive to people. Versatile.
- Charismatic, creative, gutsy. Has unbelievable energy and Boy Scout ethics.
- Keen mind, intuitive, but also strong numbers man. Inspirational leader.

Learning Objectives

- **Define** the overall meaning of personality.
- **Describe** personality development by use of the stage theories most relevant to organizational behavior.
- **Discuss** the major input that biological, cultural, and family determinants make to personality development.
- **Explain** the important role that socialization plays in personality development.

This chapter discusses the cognitive processes that are important to the understanding of organizational behavior. It takes a micro perspective from the *whole person*, personality standpoint. Organizational participants operate as a whole, not as a series of distinct parts. To make a very simple analogy, the various psychological processes may be thought of as the pieces of a jigsaw puzzle, and personality as the completed puzzle picture. As was recently noted, "events in the external environment (including the presence and behavior of others) strongly influence the way people behave at any particular point in time; yet people always bring something of themselves to the situation. We often refer to this 'something,' which represents the unique qualities of the individual, as *personality.*"[1]

The discussion of personality in this chapter is aimed at improving the understanding of the complexities of today's employees. Such understanding is vital to the study and analysis of organizational behavior, but it offers only a few *direct* applications of its content to the management of human resources. It attempts to be more education- than applications-oriented, and it serves as an important component of the second part of the book, which examines organizational behavior from an individual, micro perspective.

The first section of the chapter defines and clarifies the concept of personality. The next section is devoted to personality development and includes discussions of some well-known theories on stages of development formulated by Levinson, Hall, and Argyris. The third section breaks down the determinants of personality development into biological, cultural, family, social, and situational categories. Some of the more important research findings on these determinants of personality are included, and the socialization process is given detailed attention because it is especially relevant to organizational behavior.

THE MEANING OF PERSONALITY

Through the years there has not been universal agreement on the exact meaning of personality. Much of the controversy can be attributed to the fact that people in general and behavioral scientists define *personality* from different perspectives. Most people tend to equate personality with social success (good, popular, or "a lot of personality") and to describe personality by a single dominant characteristic (strong, weak, or polite). When it is realized that more than 4000 words can be used to describe personality this way, the definitional problem becomes staggering. Psychologists, on the other hand, take a different perspective. For example, the descriptive-adjective approach commonly used by most people plays only a small part. However, scholars cannot agree on a definition of personality because they operate from different theoretical bases. As long as there is disagreement on the theory of personality, there will be disagreement on its definition.

The word "personality" has an interesting derivation. It can be traced to the Latin words *per sona*, which translates as "to speak through." The Latin term was used to denote the masks worn by actors in ancient Greece and Rome. This Latin meaning is particularly relevant to the contemporary analysis of personality. Common usage of the word emphasizes the role which the person (actor) displays to the public. The academic definitions are concerned more directly with the person (actor) than with the role played. Probably the most meaningful approach would be to include both the person and the role.

In addition, some personality theorists emphasize the need to recognize the person-situation *interaction*, that is, the social learning aspects of personality. Such a social learning interpretation may be the most comprehensive and meaningful to the overall study of human/organizational behavior. Thus, a comprehensive discussion of personality should include the uniqueness of each situation (rather than the commonality assumed by the more traditional approaches to personality), and any measure of personality must attempt to assess the person-situation interaction. In summary, in this book "personality" will mean how people affect others and how they understand and view themselves, as well as their pattern of inner and outer measurable traits, and the person-situation interaction.

How people affect others depends primarily upon their external appearance (height, weight, facial features, color, and other physical aspects) and behavior (vulgar, friendly, courteous, and so on). A very large, friendly worker will have a different impact on other people from that of a very small, courteous manager. Obviously, all the ramifications of perception enter into these aspects of personality.

The Self-Concept: Self-Esteem and Self-Efficacy

People's attempts to understand themselves are called the *self-concept* in personality theory. The self is a unique product of many interacting parts and may be thought of as the personality viewed from within. This self is particularly relevant to the concepts of self-esteem and self-efficacy in the field of organizational behavior. People's *self-esteem* has to do with their self-perceived competence and self-image.[2] *Self-efficacy* is concerned with self-perceptions of how well a person can cope with situations as they arise.[3] Miner points out that self-esteem tends to be a generalized trait (it will be present in any situation), while self-efficacy is always situation-specific.[4] As he also notes, research supports that people with low self-esteem perform less well than those with high self-esteem, and that people with high self-efficacy (those who feel capable of performing well in a situation) persevere, and end up doing a good job.[5] Thus, there is a fairly well-established relationship in the research literature between self-efficacy and performance.[6]

Person-Situation Interaction

The pattern of measurable traits such as external appearance and behavior and the self-concept adds to the understanding of the human personality. The person-situation interaction dimension of personality provides further understanding. Each situation, of course, is different. The differences may seem to be very small on the surface, but when filtered by the person's cognitive mediating processes, they can lead to quite large, subjective differences and diverse behavioral outcomes. Thus, this last dimension suggests that people are not static, acting the same in all situations, but instead are ever-changing and flexible. For example, employees can change depending on the particular situation they are in interaction with. Even everyday work experience can change people. The sections in this chapter dealing with the socialization process and the situation are relevant to this important person-situation interaction.

In summary, the personality is a very diverse and complex psychological concept. It incorporates almost everything covered in this book, and more. As defined above, personality is the whole person and is concerned with external appearance and behavior, self, and situational interactions. Probably the best statement on personality was made many years ago by Kluckhohn and Murray, who said that, to some extent, a person's personality is like all other people's, like some other people's, and like no other people's.[7]

THE DEVELOPMENT OF PERSONALITY

Study of, and research on, the development of personality has traditionally been an important area for understanding human behavior. The developmental approach is actually a form of personality theory, but, in contrast to most personality theories, it is highly research-oriented. Modern developmental psychology does not get into the argument of heredity versus environment or of maturation versus learning. The human being consists of both physiological *and* psychological interacting parts. Therefore, heredity, environment, maturation, and learning *all* contribute to the human personality.

The study of personality development can be divided into two separate but closely allied approaches. One approach has attempted to identify specific physiological and psychological stages that occur in the development of the human personality. The other approach has tried to identify the important determinants of personality. The "stage" approach has been theoretical in nature, whereas the search for major determinants has been more empirically based.

There are many well-known stage theories of personality development. Most deal with psychological development rather than directly with personality development. As with most aspects of personality, there is little agreement among psychologists about the exact stages. In fact, a growing number of today's psychologists contend that there are *no* identifiable stages. Their argument is that personality development consists of a continuous process, and the sequence is based solely upon the learning opportunities available. The opposing view supports stages in personality development. Particularly relevant to the understanding of organizational behavior are the theories provided by Levinson, Hall, and Argyris.

Adult Life Stages

The work of Daniel Levinson on adult life stages has received considerable attention. At first, he believed that "the life structure evolves through a relatively orderly sequence throughout the adult years,"[8] and, unlike other stage theories that were event-oriented (for example, marriage, parenthood, or retirement), his was age-based. In particular, he believed there was little variability (a maximum of two or three years) in four identifiable stable periods:

1. Entering the adult world (ages twenty-two to twenty-eight)
2. Settling down (ages thirty-three to forty)
3. Entering middle adulthood (ages forty-five to fifty)
4. Culmination of middle adulthood (ages fifty-five to sixty)

He identified four transitional periods:

1. Age-thirty transition (ages twenty-eight to thirty-three)
2. Mid-life transition (ages forty to forty-five)
3. Age-fifty transition (ages fifty to fifty-five)
4. Late adult transition (ages sixty to sixty-five)

Like historically significant stage theories of personality such as those by Freud and Erikson, Levinson's theory of adult life stages had a lot of intuitive and popular appeal, but, as is also the case with previous stage theories, the research is quite mixed. For example, one study utilizing longitudinal data found no support for Levinson's hypothesis that there should be greater variability in work attitudes during transitional as compared with stable developmental periods or that the greatest variability occurs during the mid-life transition.[9] In other words, there may be such large individual differences among people that stage theories such as Levinson's don't really hold up. As a result, Levinson has reformulated his stages into what he now calls "eras" (early adult, mid-life, and late adult) and includes a transition-in period, a period of stability, and a transition-out period.[10] In contrast to his earlier work discussed above, in which mobility or stability characterized whole stages of development, this new approach examines the interplay of mobility and stability within each life stage.[11]

Hall has synthesized Levinson's theory and other adult stage theories (in particular the work of Erikson and Super) into an overall model for career stages. Figure 4.1 shows that there are four major career stages. During the first stage there is considerable *exploration*. The young employee is searching for an identity and undergoes considerable self-examination and role tryouts. This stage usually results in taking a number of different jobs and is, in general, a very unstable and relatively unproductive period in the person's career. In the second stage, *establishment*, the employee begins to settle down and indicates a need for intimacy. This is usually a growing, productive period in the employee's career. The third stage of *maintenance* occurs when the person levels off into a highly productive plateau and has a need for generativity (the concern to leave something to the next generation). This need often leads the person to assume a paternalistic or perhaps a mentor role with younger subordinates. As shown in Figure 4.1, the person may either have a growth spurt or become stagnant and decline during this third career stage. The final stage, *decline*, is

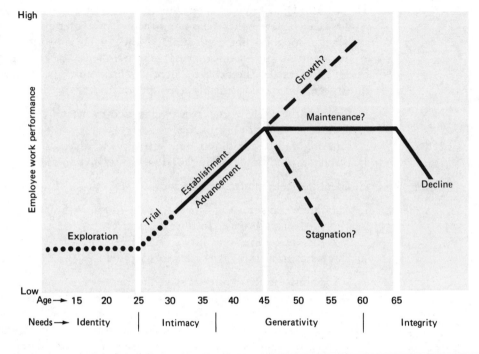

FIGURE 4.1
A career-stage model.
(*Source:* Adapted from Douglas T. Hall, *Careers in Organizations,* Goodyear, Santa Monica, Calif., 1976, p. 57.)

self-explanatory. The person indicates a need for integrity (that is, the person needs to feel satisfied with his or her life choices and overall career). With the recent changes in mandatory retirement laws (there is no longer an upper age limit for mandatory retirement), better medical treatment, and the expectations of society concerning "gray power," this last stage may undergo drastic changes in the years ahead.

There is recent evidence that the heretofore assumed direct, linear relationship between age and job satisfaction may not be true.[12] As Figure 4.2 shows, toward the end of employees' careers, there may be a downturn in their satisfaction. This decline would agree with the career stage model, shown in Figure 4.1, but may be happening at an earlier age. The decline may be the result of unmet expectations and the downsizing and "merger mania" that have left long-term employees feeling unwanted and with no sense of loyalty or belonging.

Immaturity to Maturity

In a departure from the strict stage approach, organizational behavior theorist Chris Argyris has identified specific dimensions of the human personality as it develops. Argyris proposes that the human personality, rather than going through precise stages, progresses along a continuum from immaturity as an infant to maturity as an

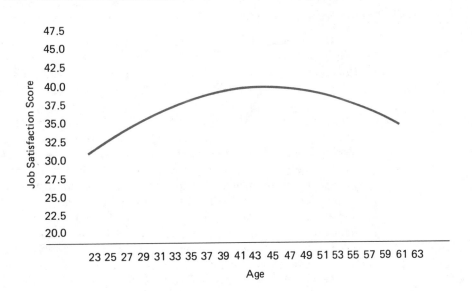

FIGURE 4.2
The relationship between age and job satisfaction. (*Source:* Adapted from Fred Luthans and Linda T. Thomas, "The Relationship between Age and Job Satisfaction," *Personnel Review*, vol. 18, no. 1, 1989, p. 25.

adult. However, at any age, people can have their degree of development plotted according to the seven dimensions shown in Table 4.1.

Argyris carefully points out that this model does not imply that all persons reach or strive for all dimensions on the mature end of the continuum. He further explains:

1. The seven dimensions represent only one aspect of the total personality. Much also depends upon the individual's perception, self-concept, and adaptation and adjustment.
2. The seven dimensions continually change in degree from the infant to the adult end of the continuum.
3. The model, being only a construct, cannot predict specific behavior. However, it does provide a method of describing and measuring the growth of any individual in the culture.

TABLE 4.1 The Immaturity-Maturity Continuum

Immaturity Characteristics	Maturity Characteristics
Passivity	Activity
Dependence	Independence
Few ways of behaving	Diverse behavior
Shallow interests	Deep interests
Short-time perspective	Long-time perspective
Subordinate position	Superordinate position
Lack of self-awareness	Self-awareness and control

Source: Adapted from Chris Argyris, *Personality and Organization*, Harper, New York, 1957, p. 50.

4. The seven dimensions are based upon latent characteristics of the personality, which may be quite different from the observable behavior.[13]

In contrast to the classic stage theories of Freud and Erikson, Argyris's immaturity-maturity model of personality is specifically directed to the study and analysis of organizational behavior. Argyris assumes that the personalities of organizational employees can be generally described by the mature end of the continuum. This being the case, in order to obtain full expression of employees' personalities, the formal organization should allow for activity rather than passivity, independence rather than dependence, long-time rather than short-time perspective, occupation of a position higher than that of peers, and expression of deep, important abilities.[14] Argyris argues that too often the exact opposite occurs. The mature organizational participant becomes frustrated and anxious and is in conflict with the modern formal organization. In other words, Argyris sees a *basic incongruity* between the needs of the mature personality and the nature of the formal organization. This incongruity premise is an important cornerstone for the entire conceptualization of person-organization structure interaction, which was discussed in relation to the organizational behavior framework used in this book. It is also particularly relevant to the analysis of frustration and conflict in Chapter 13 and stress in Chapter 14.

MAJOR DETERMINANTS OF PERSONALITY

What determines personality? Of all the complexities and unanswered questions in the study of human behavior, this question may be the most difficult. The problem lies in the fact that the cognitive and psychological processes, plus many other variables, *all* contribute to personality. However, for ease of study and analysis, the determinants of personality can perhaps best be grouped in five broad categories: biological, cultural, familial, social, and situational.

Biological Contributions

The study of the biological contributions to personality can be divided into several major approaches: heredity, managerial thinking, biofeedback, and physical characteristics.

The Role of Heredity. The impact of heredity on personality is a very active but still unsettled area of understanding. One problem is that geneticists face a major obstacle in gathering information scientifically on the human being. Animal scientists can conduct highly controlled breeding experiments, but geneticists studying human heredity cannot. Through research on animals, it has been clearly shown that both physical and psychological characteristics can be transmitted through heredity. However, in the case of humans, who cannot be subjected to the necessary controls, the evidence is much less conclusive. Studies of twins, which permit some control over the critical variables, have proved to be newsworthy. For example, the now famous "Jim twins," who were identical twins separated at birth, were both named Jim by their adoptive parents. When they were reunited for the first time at age thirty-nine, there were eerie similarities:

Both of their first wives were named Linda, their second wives Betty. One named his son James Alan, the other James Allan, and both had dogs named Toy. They both chain-smoked Salems, had served as sheriff's deputies, and both drove their Chevrolets from Ohio to the same three-block beach on Florida's Gulf Coast. Both chewed their fingernails to the nub, disliked baseball, were mediocre students, enjoyed stock car racing, and had basement workshops. They had both built circular benches around a tree in their respective yards. They had both inexplicably gained 10 pounds at about the same time in their lives and then lost it. They both felt they had suffered heart attacks but had not and they both started getting migraine headaches of about the same duration in the same period of their lives.[15]

There are other such publicized cases of similarities of twins raised apart which would support the position that heredity plays the major role in personality and behavior (that is, identical twins have the same genetic endowment, but if they are raised apart they have different environments, and thus similarities support the heredity position, while differences support the environment position). The recent highly publicized results of a long-term study of more than 350 pairs of twins conducted by psychologists at the University of Minnesota give unprecedented support to the influence of heredity.[16] Of particular relevance to the study of organizational behavior was the finding that the traits relating to leadership, traditionalism, and obedience to authority were most strongly determined by heredity. Other relevant traits that seemed to be mostly determined by heredity in this study were alienation, vulnerability or resistance to stress, and risk seeking. The study is not automatically accepted because of measurement problems and controls it used. There are also recent comprehensive meta-analyses of twin studies that indicate the impact that age and other developmental factors have on the results.[17] In other words, the heredity-versus-environment debate is still alive, and no definitive conclusions are yet possible.

Genetic Engineering and Intelligence. Despite the continuing debate on heredity versus environment, recent breakthroughs in genetics (for example, the discovery of the double-helix model of DNA) have opened up potential ways of altering and controlling behavior. This is called *genetic engineering.* Genetics experts feel that some aspects of the human personality are at least partly affected by heredity. In particular, the impact of heredity on intelligence has created much controversy. Geneticists have been joined by some educational psychologists, such as Arthur Jensen, in claiming that intelligence is largely inherited. This, of course, has implications for racial differences, which adds emotional fuel to the fire. For example, the Prime Minister of Japan created considerable controversy both here and abroad when he publicly stated a few years ago:

> So high is the level of education in our country that Japan's is an intelligent society. Our average score is much higher than those of countries like the U.S. There are many blacks, Puerto Ricans, and Mexicans in America. In consequence the average score over there is exceedingly low.[18]

Naturally, American minority members were incensed by this statement and demanded an apology. However, statistically the Japanese may have a higher average IQ score than Americans. For example, a study published by British psychologist Robert Lynn reported that Japan's mean national IQ is 111, compared with the American norm of 100.[19] The major issue of the controversy is how intelligence is measured. Until this is fully resolved, the controversy and emotional debates will continue. In the meantime, there seems little doubt that the role of heredity in behavior will receive increased attention in the coming years.

Managerial Thinking. After much research, some behavioral scientists are concluding that managers think differently from the general population. For example, England's Elliott Jaques concludes that unlike most people, executives can see a long way into the future, identify the steps necessary for some move that will take years to complete, envision the consequences of each step, and then take the measures to set everything in motion.[20] He notes that Japan's Konosuke Matsushita has laid down a 250-year plan for his giant company.[21] Other researchers conclude that senior managers have a greater capacity for differentiation (looking at things in different ways) and integration (pulling things together), and are flexible.[22]

Split-Brain Thinking. Split-brain (right versus left) psychology is closely related to managerial thinking, but it has less research backup. The split-brain fad was carried over to the management field when Henry Mintzberg wrote a widely read article entitled "Planning on the Left Side and Managing on the Right." He went so far as to declare, "Which hemisphere of one's brain is better developed may determine whether a person ought to be a planner or a manager."[23] This article and his recent book,[24] and others in the popular management and psychology literature, have generated considerable interest among industrial training and development personnel. Some workshops and training sessions are based on split-brain psychology.

Split-brain psychology is the subject of a controversy that can be traced back to the classic mind-body dualism debate in psychology: Are the mind and the body separate entities, or is the mind simply a function of the physical being? Work done on ESB (electrical stimulation of the brain) suggests that there are clearly identifiable portions of the physical brain that control "mind" functions such as emotion and aggression. There is also evidence to indicate that the right hemisphere of the brain may have functions such those listed in the right-hand column of Table 4.2 and that the left hemisphere may have the functions listed in the left-hand column of the table. But these areas are still open for further research.

As the discussion of the split brain indicates, there are more questions raised than answers provided.[25] Yet few would disagree with the idea that the brain certainly holds many unlocked secrets for the future, and some training experts, such as General Electric's Ned Herrmann, suggest that the future is already here. He feels that enough is known about the brain to design and deliver new learning and training systems.[26]

Biofeedback. Similar to the results of work on the brain have been some of the widely publicized and spectacular results of biofeedback training (BFT). Until recently, physiologists and psychologists felt that certain biological functions such as brain-wave patterns, gastric secretions, and fluctuations in blood pressure and skin

TABLE 4.2 Summary of Characteristics and Dimensions Attributed to the Left and Right Hemispheres of the Brain

Left Hemisphere (Right Side of Body)	Right Hemisphere (Left Side of Body)
Speech/verbal	Spatial/musical
Logical, mathematical	Holistic
Linear, detailed	Artistic, symbolic
Sequential	Simultaneous
Controlled	Emotional
Intellectual	Intuitive, creative
Dominant	Minor (quiet)
Worldly	Spiritual
Active	Receptive
Analytic	Synthetic, gestalt-oriented
Reading, writing, naming	Facial recognition
Sequential ordering	Simultaneous comprehension
Perception of significant order	Perception of abstract patterns
Complex motor sequences	Recognition of complex figures

Source: Adapted from Robert J. Trotter, "The Other Hemispheres," *Science News,* Apr. 3, 1976, p. 219.

temperature were beyond conscious control. Now a growing number of scientists believe that these involuntary functions can be consciously controlled through biofeedback. In BFT the individual learns the internal rhythms of a particular body process through electronic signals fed back from equipment that is wired to the body area (for example, skin, brain, or heart). From this biofeedback the person can learn to control the body process in question. A very simple example of biofeedback involves holding a thermometer between the index finger and the thumb. If the person watches the thermometer and concentrates and thinks very hard about the finger and the thumb getting warmer, the temperature may begin to rise.

It is now generally recognized that BFT has several medical applications. For example, it may be used to alleviate migraine headaches by diverting blood from the throbbing region to other parts of the body; cerebral palsy patients have learned to control muscle spasms by listening to clicks from a feedback machine wired to the body; people with dangerously irregular heart rhythms have learned to modify them by watching blinking lights that tell them when the heart is functioning properly; and, on the lighter side, a person can control an electric train through brain waves.[27] Such applications of biofeedback are now widely used by therapists and in clinics and hospitals across the United States.[28]

Physical Characteristics and Rate of Maturing. Another biologically based approach to the study of personality is to analyze the effects of physical characteristics and rate of maturing. Despite the tremendous potential offered by the study of genetics, the brain, and biofeedback, this approach has already proved to be a significant contributor to the study of personality. An individual's physical appearance, which is said to be a vital ingredient of the personality, is biologically determined. The fact that a person is tall or short, fat or skinny, handsome or ugly, or black or white will influence the person's effect on others, and this in turn will affect the self-concept.

There are entire theories of personality based upon body build. Sheldon's classic theory, which correlates certain body builds (endomorphic, mesomorphic, and ectomorphic) with specific personality traits, is an example. However, most modern psychologists do not go so far as Sheldon in emphasizing the importance of physical attributes. There are too many exceptions for such a theory to be meaningful. On the other hand, practically all would agree that physical characteristics have at least some influence on the personality.

This same reasoning is applied to the rate of maturation. A rapidly maturing boy or girl is exposed to different physical and social situations and activities from those to which a slowly maturing child is exposed. This differing rate of maturation will be reflected in the personality.

Cultural Contributions

Traditionally, cultural factors are usually considered to make a more significant contribution to personality than biological factors. The learning process plays an important role in personality development. Often, however, in discussions that stress either the cognitive or the reinforcement aspects of this process, nothing is mentioned about what is learned—the *content*. Yet, in terms of personality development, the content is probably as important as the process. Culture is the key concept in analyzing the content of learning because what a person learns has content. The

International Application Example

Gift-Giving in Western Europe

Culture is important in understanding not only Americans' personalities but those of other countries as well. Western Europe is a good example. The United States does considerable business there, so it is very helpful for American businesspeople to know how to act in this corner of the globe. For example, when doing business with Europeans, when is it acceptable to give a gift and how should it be done? The following are some useful guidelines for gift-giving in Western Europe:

1. Do not give a business gift at the first meeting. This is considered bad manners.
2. If you are going to send flowers to your dinner hostess, send them ahead rather than handing them to her upon your arrival. This gives her time to arrange and place them as she wants. It also prevents any embarrassment among the other guests who may show up at the same time you do and be empty-handed.
3. When sending flowers, be sure of your choice. In France, chrysanthemums are associated with mourning. In France and Germany, red roses are a gift only between lovers.
4. Good chocolates and liqueurs are excellent house gifts. If the occasion demands something more elaborate, small porcelain and silver gifts such as candlesticks or table lighters are good choices.
5. Never give perfume or men's cologne as a gift. This is considered too personal for a business gift to or from either sex.
6. Do not enclose your business card with the gift. This is considered crass. Instead write a note on a blank card.

prevailing culture dictates *what* a person will learn. As Chapter 2 pointed out, culture is the context in which everything else takes place. The accompanying International Application Example, Gift-Giving in Western Europe, provides an example of such a cultural context.

As indicated in the introductory comments of this book, culture has become a major concept in the study of organizational behavior. Chapters 2 and 19 are specifically devoted to it. Culture can also be used to better understand personality development. For example, the methods by which an infant is fed and is toilet-trained and the ways in which the person later makes the transition from adolescence to adulthood are all culturally determined. As indicated by the discussion of the stage theories, such cultural events contribute significantly to the personality. The culture largely determines attributes such as independence, aggression, competition, and cooperation.

For example, Western cultures generally reward a person for being independent and competitive, while Far Eastern cultures do not. It follows that a person reared in a Western culture has a different personality from that of a person reared in a Far Eastern culture. A person who is biologically of Western descent but is brought up in a Far Eastern culture will have a Far Eastern type of personality, and vice versa.

Despite the importance of the cultural contribution to personality, a linear relationship cannot be established between personality and a given culture. One problem in complex societies stems from the existence of numerous subcultures within a given culture. For example, the Protestant ethic may be a dominant value of Western culture. However, there are extreme value differences among socio-economic classes, ages, and geographic regions. The point is that it is wrong to assume that all workers or managers in Western societies possess the Protestant ethic. On the other hand, this does not rule out the fact that culture affects personality. The difficulty comes when broad generalizations are made. When analyzing organizational behavior, the *relevant* cultural impact must be recognized.

Contributions from the Family

Whereas the culture generally prescribes and limits what a person can be taught, it is the family, and later the social group, which selects, interprets, and dispenses the culture. Thus, the family probably has the most significant impact on early personality development; later, the socialization process takes over.

The parents play an especially important part in the identification process, which is important to the person's early development. Usually, the parent of the same sex as the child will serve as the model for the child's development. Also, a substantial amount of empirical evidence indicates that the overall home environment created by the parents, in addition to their direct influence, is critical to personality development. For example, children with a markedly institutional upbringing (orphans) and children reared in a cold, unstimulating home are much more likely to be socially and emotionally maladjusted than children raised by parents in a warm, loving, and stimulating environment. The key variable here does not seem to be the parents per se, but rather the type of atmosphere that is generated for the child.

Research Study on Parental Influence. A classic study by James Abegglen effectively points up the impact of the parents on the personalities of very successful executives.[29] He conducted a detailed case study of twenty executives who had risen from a lower-class childhood to hold top-ranking positions with business firms. Data were accumulated from interviews which at first focused on personal and job histories and then on the use of eight thematic apperception cards (pictures about which subjects tell a story or report what they see). It was found that fifteen of the twenty executives, while children, had had what Abegglen calls a "separation trauma" with their fathers. Two fathers had died during the childhood of the subjects, two subjects had lived with their mothers following a divorce, six of the fathers had been in severe business and financial difficulties, and in five cases the fathers had been seriously ill. The fathers were blamed by the sons for the hardships suffered by the family. They were described as inept, sometimes hostile, and usually inadequate. The mother, on the other hand, was generally viewed as being economically and morally stable but not "motherly" in the sense of being affectionate.

The results obtained by Abegglen indicate that a classic Freudian reaction formation had taken place. The normal positive identification process between father and son had been blocked. Instead, the son negatively identified with his father and strove to be the opposite from him. This negative identification seemed to be a major motivating force throughout the son's life. The high needs for achievement and the low needs for affiliation exhibited by the subjects can be traced back to the negative identification in childhood. Thus, the father and mother (who transmitted values that were conducive to upward striving) seemed to have had a great deal of influence on the personalities of this group of business executives.

The Abegglen study has potentially significant implications for the study of organizational behavior. For instance, the case histories of organizational participants might provide much insight into their behavior. Yet, as with most studies of this nature in the behavioral sciences, broad generalizations or grandiose conclusions are unwarranted. One organizational behavior expert, in evaluating the Abegglen study, cautions:

> Intriguing as Abegglen's findings are, it must be remembered that they were drawn from a small and highly select group. He has demonstrated that an early reaction-formation can lead to a lifelong pattern of achievement striving and upward mobility; but so can other kinds of psychological relationships. Sons who are disappointed in their fathers are not destined to corner the market in successful careers.[30]

Birth–Order Data. Siblings (brothers and sisters) also contribute to personality. So far, studies of birth order have produced some very interesting but inconclusive results. Studies by social psychologists have found that firstborn and only children have a stronger need to affiliate than children born later. The conclusion drawn from one such research study is that "firstborn children, at least in our society, are probably more anxious, more dependent on others, especially in anxious situations, and more inclined to go along with the group than are other children."[31] Other research evidence, although it is far from being conclusive, indicates that firstborns may be more serious, less carefree, and more likely to be a problem than later-borns.[32]

Staunch advocates of birth-order data claim it is possible to describe major personality characteristics solely on the basis of position in the family constellation. For example, one psychologist gives specific personality sketches for the oldest and youngest brothers of one or more brothers (OBB and YBB, respectively) and for the oldest and youngest brothers of sisters (OBS and YBS, respectively). These four types have equivalent female counterparts making a total of eight combinations. This approach even makes suggestions, based upon empirical data, as to the kind of worker each type will be. For example, the OBB is a good worker and independent; the YBB fakes independence and tends to be an irregular worker; the OBS, who is also said to be a "true ladies' man" who adores women, is a responsible worker, and the YBS, who is greatly loved by women, is not a very regular or systematic worker but is capable of great accomplishments.[33] On the surface, there seems to be a great deal of truth to these descriptions and possible implications for management. For example, if found to correlate with employment variables, birth order may take on added significance in the selection process. At the present time, however, birth-order data, like astrology charts, make a lot of surface sense but need much more scientific research before any definitive conclusions can be drawn.

The Socialization Process

Besides the biological, cultural, and family influences on personality, there is increasing recognition given to the role of other relevant persons, groups, and especially organizations, which greatly influence an individual's personality. This is commonly called the *socialization process*. It is especially relevant to organizational behavior because the process is not confined to early childhood; rather, it takes place throughout one's life. In particular, evidence is accumulating that socialization may be one of the best explanations for why employees behave the way they do in today's organizations. For example, Edgar Schein notes: "It is high time that some of our managerial knowledge and skill be focused on those forces in the organization environment which derive from the fact that organizations are social systems which do socialize their new members. If we do not learn to analyze and control the forces of organizational socialization, we are abdicating one of our primary managerial responsibilities."[34] A recent study found that the socialization tactics that organizations employ (providing information to newcomers, new recruits going through common learning experiences, and so forth) does have the intended impact. It was found that different patterns of socialization lead to different forms of newcomer adjustment to organizations.[35]

Socialization starts with the initial contact between a mother and her new infant. After infancy, other members of the immediate family (father, brothers, and sisters), close relatives and family friends, and then the social group (peers, school friends, and members of the work group) play influential roles. Of particular interest is Schein's idea that the organization itself also contributes to socialization.[36] He points out that the process includes only the learning of those values, norms, and behavior patterns which, from the organization's and the work group's points of view, are necessary for any new organization member to learn. The following are widely accepted characteristics of such organizational socialization of employees:

1. Change of attitudes, values, and behaviors
2. Continuity of socialization over time
3. Adjustment to new jobs, work groups, and organizational practices
4. Mutual influence between new recruits and their managers
5. Criticality of the early socialization period[37]

Accordingly, organization members must learn things like not to drive a Ford if they are working for Chevrolet, not to criticize the company in public, and not to wear the wrong kind of clothes or be seen in the wrong kind of place.[38] They must understand "who holds power and who does not, which informal networks of communication are reliable and which are unreliable, and what political maneuvers they are likely to encounter in their department or unit. In short, if they wish to survive and prosper in their new work home, they must soon come to 'know the ropes.'"[39]

Studies have indicated that socialization is important not only to new organization members but also in the superior-subordinate relationship and when people switch jobs (for example, when they move from a line to a staff position) or are promoted.[40] Van Maanen also suggests specific socialization strategies, such as formal or informal, individual or collective, sequential or nonsequential, and fixed or variable.[41] For example, a company may use a sequential socialization strategy to groom people for top management positions by first rotating them through a series of relevant functional specialties. Another organization, say, a government agency, may take someone with political power from the rank and file and make that person the head of the agency. This nonsequential strategy will result in different personal (that is, the personality will be affected) and organizational outcomes.

Specific techniques of socializing new employees would include the use of mentors or role models, orientation and training programs, reward systems and career planning.[42] Specific steps that can lead to successful organizational socialization would include the following:

1. Provide a challenging first job.
2. Provide relevant training.
3. Provide timely and consistent feedback.
4. Select a good first supervisor to be in charge of socialization.
5. Design a relaxed orientation program.
6. Place new recruits in work groups with high morale.[43]

Such deliberate socialization strategies have tremendous potential impact on human resources management and organizational effectiveness.

More Immediate Situational Considerations

The socialization process is obviously concerned with the situational impact on personality and thus falls in line with a social learning perspective. The cultural and

Long Hours and Hard Work

Are people today under more pressure than they were a decade ago? Recent evidence would support that they are. A survey of over a million workers at 171 large corporations has found that during the last five years the number of managers who report that they have too much work to do has jumped from 34 percent up to 46 percent. Among nonmanagers, the increase has been from 30 percent up to 39 percent. Moreover, a recent Gallup poll has found that at 201 large and small corporations, 25 percent of the employees, on average, suffer from anxiety or stress-related disorders.

There are two groups of companies where the situation seems to be the worst for employees. One is labor-intensive companies, such as food retailers, where profitability depends heavily on how hard the employees work. For example, a former store manager at a Food Lion in the supermarket chain complained: "I put in more and more and more time—a hundred hours a week—but no matter how many hours I worked or what I did, I could never satisfy the supervisors. I lived, ate, breathed, slept Food Lion. The hardest thing for me was to be a bitch. And I was a bitch. I had to be. They wanted 100 percent conditions, seven days a week, twenty-four hours a day. And there's no damn way you could do it." The other type of situation which is particularly bad is in those firms that are in the process of downsizing by reducing the number of employees and spreading their work around to the rest of the employees.

What can firms do to reduce this pressure situation? One of the most helpful approaches is to use work scheduling that allows people to pace themselves through the day. In this way, after working hard for a while employees can slack off and do work that is less tiring. This use of "downtime" has been found to be particularly helpful in reducing labor turnover. Another helpful approach is to give employees a chance to participate in decision making, especially on things that directly affect them. These methods will not totally reduce the competitive situation in most of today's organizations, but they are proving to be important ways of helping people learn to cope with the psychological and physical pressures of their job.

family impact is more concerned with the historical nature of personality development. Both the cultural/family and the socialization processes are important to personality, but it should also be recognized that the immediate situation may in the final analysis predominate. As the Application Example, Long Hours and Hard Work, shows, today's situation at work is becoming increasingly demanding and having an effect on employees' personality and behavior.

From a social learning perspective, as discussed in Chapter 1, it is the situation interacting with the human being, including the individual's personality, that is the vital antecedent to behavior. An example is the worker whose developmental history has shaped a personality which incorporates a high need for power and achievement. When placed in a highly bureaucratized work situation, this individual may become frustrated and behave apathetically and/or aggressively. Thus, on the surface this worker appears to be lazy and/or a troublemaker. Yet the developmental history would predict that the individual would be a very hard worker, striving to get ahead.

The countless potential combinations of the situation and the human being make it virtually impossible always to predict accurately, from the developmental history alone, the ways in which the personality will be behaviorally expressed. The interaction is too complex, and when the role of consequences is included, it becomes obvious that the developmental aspects of personality by themselves do not provide the answer of understanding, predicting, and controlling human behavior.

Research on the Immediate Situational Impact. The very dramatic, classic study by Stanley Milgram gives support to the important role that the immediate situation plays in the human personality.[44] He conducted a series of tightly controlled experimental studies that used almost 1000 adult subjects.[45] These subjects were not students, ranged from twenty to fifty years of age, and came from a wide variety of occupations (unskilled, skilled, white-collar, sales, business, and professional). Each experimental session consisted of a naive subject, an accomplice, and the experimenter. The experimenter explained that the subject would be part of a learning experiment to test the effect of punishment on memory. After a rigged drawing on roles to be played, the naive subject always became the "teacher" and the accomplice became the "learner" in the experiment. The learner (the experimenter's accomplice) was then taken to the next room and strapped into a sinister-looking "electric chair," which the subject could see through a glass partition. The experimenter carefully explained that the teacher (the naive subject) would administer increasing levels of shock to the learner whenever a mistake was made. The shock generator had clearly marked voltage levels that ran from 15 to 450 volts and printed descriptions that ranged from "Slight Shock" to "Danger: Severe Shock." To convince the naive subjects of the authenticity of the shock device, they were given a real shock from the 45-volt switch.

For control purposes, the accomplices' responses to the shocks were broadcast from a premade tape, and of course they did not actually receive any shocks. Starting with what the subject believed to be a 75-volt shock, the learner began to grunt and moan. As the succeeding shocks increased in voltage, the cries became louder and more desperate. The learner pleaded with the teacher to have mercy and stop the experiment. Whenever the teacher (subject) would hesitate to administer more shock, the experimenter would prod the teacher on by saying, "You have no other choice; you must go on!" Finally, the learner could give no more answers, and the naive subject was told by the experimenter to give the maximum-voltage shock. Contrary to common or expert opinion, almost two-thirds of the subjects went ahead and administered what they thought was a very dangerous, severe shock that might even lead to death. Milgram, who was obviously disturbed by his findings, stated:

> With numbing regularity good people were seen to knuckle under the demands of authority and perform actions that were callous and severe. Men who are in every-day life responsible and decent were seduced by the trappings of authority, by the control of their perceptions, and by the uncritical acceptance of the experimenter's definition of the situation, into performing harsh acts.[46]

Implications of the Milgram Study. Compared with the developmental aspects of personality, relatively little attention has been given to the situational impact. Yet Milgram's research suggests the very powerful role that the immediate situation can play in the human personality. In fact, he calls for a theory that would provide a definition and typology of situations. He believes that if such guidance were available, certain definable properties of situations could be transformed into psychological forces in the individual.[47] In other words, studying the determinants may be of as much value as studying case histories. To prove the point, Milgram put leading advocates of the case-history approach to the test. Forty psychiatrists from a prestigious medical school were asked to predict the behavior of the subjects in the shock experiment. The highly trained experts did a very poor job. They estimated that only about one-tenth of 1 percent of the subjects would administer the maximum-voltage shock, when in fact almost two-thirds did so.

The Milgram research certainly does not completely rule out the importance of the developmental aspects of personality. Rather, it demonstrates that the immediate situation may potentially have a very big impact on the behavioral expression of the personality, even to the point where it seems to override what one would predict on the basis of the developmental history. The experimenter in the Yale psychological laboratory where the studies were conducted produced a situation in which people violated their moral codes. They were obedient to scientific authority. When the setting was moved to a run-down commercial building under the guise of Research Associates of Bridgeport, the percenteage of those who obeyed to the end dropped to 48 percent.

The results of Milgram's studies produced a strong emotional reaction from both academicians and the public. Critics claim that Milgram was unethical, and they doubt that the subjects really believed that they were administering such a severe shock. Milgram answers the first charge by saying that every precaution was taken and that all subjects were carefully debriefed. He supported those who disobeyed and assured those who obeyed that their behavior was perfectly normal and that other subjects had shared their conflicts. Follow-up questionnaires found that almost everyone thought the experiment had been worthwhile and that only 1 percent of the subjects were sorry they had participated. As for the charge concerning the validity of the study, Milgram has data from direct observation, interviews, and questionnaires to support his claim that the subjects accepted the experiment at face value. He feels that not one subject suspected the deception.

In his book *Obedience to Authority* Milgram expounds on some of his original findings and discusses the follow-up on the modifications and variations. The following summarizes some of the finer points of, and variations in, obedience to authority:

1. Obedience decreases when the learner is in the same room as the teacher and decreases further when the teacher must touch the learner directly to administer the shock. The modern state, of course, is designed for impersonality; people can pull switches and drop bombs without ever seeing the victims.
2. Obedience drops sharply when the experimenter is absent. To commit acts they would otherwise consider immoral, people must have authority behind them.
3. Obedience drops when the subject is in a group of rebellious peers. Rebels awaken the subject to the possibility of disobedience and, in this case, to its benign results. The group offers social support for the decision to disobey.

4. By contrast, obedience increases when the subject is merely an accessory to the crime and does not actually have to pull the shock lever. In such a case, thirty-seven subjects out of forty stay in the experiment to the end.[48]

The findings of Milgram's study have implications for explaining the behavior during some of the highly publicized war atrocities (for example, at Auschwitz in World War II and My Lai in the Vietnam war). In fact, the studies are sometimes called the "Eichmann experiments," after the Nazi war criminal Adolf Eichmann. Some of the anxieties of Milgram and the implications of the study have also been captured in a fictionalized television drama, *The Tenth Level*. Besides the emotional impact the studies have on people, Milgram's work does have significant implications for understanding organizational behavior. Although this chapter has been concerned primarily with the impact of the situation on personality, in the broader sense the Milgram study reinforces the importance that the situation also has for overall human behavior. As stated by Milgram: "A situation exerts an important press on the individual. It exercises constraints and may provide push. In certain circumstances it is not so much the kind of person a man is, as the kind of situation in which he is placed, that determines his actions."[49] Once again, the person-situation interaction surfaces as an important, but often overlooked, dynamic in the understanding of human behavior.

Summary

Personality represents the "whole person" concept. It includes perception, learning, motivation, and more. Definitionally, people's external appearance and behavior, their inner awareness of self, and the person-situation interaction make up their personalities. Levinson's and Hall's stage theories of personality development have made significant contributions to areas such as career development, but Argyris's seven-dimension continuum of immaturity-maturity is also very relevant to the study of organizational behavior. Determining the inputs into personality may be the most complex and difficult task in the study of human behavior, but a comprehensive approach would have to include biological, cultural, family, socialization, and immediate situational factors.

Questions for Discussion and Review

1. Critically analyze the statement that "the various psychological processes can be thought of as pieces of a jigsaw puzzle, and personality as the completed puzzle picture."
2. What is the comprehensive definition of "personality"? Give brief examples of each of the major elements.
3. What are the various factors in the biological contributions to personality? The

cultural contributions? The family contributions? The socialization contributions? The immediate situational contributions?

4. How does the study of personality help an understanding of organizational behavior?

References

1. Don Hellriegel, John W. Slocum and Richard W. Woodman, *Organizational Behavior*, 5th ed., West, St. Paul, Minn., 1989, p. 37.
2. Abraham K. Korman, *The Psychology of Motivation*, Prentice-Hall, Englewood Cliffs, N.J., 1974, p. 227.
3. Albert Bandura, "Self-Efficacy Mechanism in Human Agency," *American Psychologist*, vol. 37, 1982, pp. 122–147.
4. John B. Miner, *Organizational Behavior*, Random House, New York, 1988, p. 84.
5. Ibid., pp. 84–85.
6. Edwin A. Locke and Gary P. Latham, *A Theory of Goal Setting and Task Performance*, Prentice-Hall, Englewood Cliffs, N.J., 1990, pp. 70–75.
7. Clyde Kluckhohn and H. A. Murray, "Personality Formation: The Determinants," in C. Kluckhohn and H. A. Murray (eds.), *Personality*, Knopf, New York, 1948, p. 35.
8. Daniel J. Levinson, *The Seasons of a Man's Life*, Knopf, New York, 1978, p. 49.
9. Richard E. Kopelman and Michael Glass, "Test of Daniel Levinson's Theory of Adult Male Life States," *National Academy of Management Proceedings*, 1979, pp. 79–83.
10. D. J. Levinson, "A Conception of Adult Development," *American Psychologist*, vol. 41, 1986, pp. 3–13.
11. Daniel C. Feldman, "Careers in Organizations: Recent Trends and Future Directions," *Journal of Management*, vol. 15, 1989, p. 142.
12. Fred Luthans and Linda T. Thomas, "The Relationship Between Age and Job Satisfaction," *Personnel Review*, vol. 18, no. 1, 1989, pp. 23–26.
13. Chris Argyris, *Personality and Organization*, Harper, New York, 1957, pp. 51–53.
14. Ibid., p. 53.
15. Kay Bartlett, "Twin Study: Influence of Genes Surprises Some," *Lincoln Journal and Star*, Oct. 4, 1981, p. 3F.
16. "Genes, Not Child-Rearing, Dictate Personality More," *Omaha World-Herald*, Dec. 3, 1986, p. 54.
17. Kathleen McCartney, Monica J. Harris, and Frank Bernieri, "Growing Up and Growing Apart: A Developmental Meta-Analysis of Twin Studies," *Psychological Bulletin*, vol. 107, no. 2, 1990, pp. 226–237.
18. "Nakasone's World-Class Blunder," *Time*, Oct. 6, 1986, p. 66.
19. Ibid.
20. Walter Kiechel, "How Executives Think," *Fortune*, Feb. 4, 1985, p. 127.
21. Ibid.
22. Ibid., p. 128.
23. Henry Mintzberg, "Planning on the Left Side and Managing on the Right," *Harvard Business Review*, July-August 1976, p. 49.
24. Henry Mintzberg, *Mintzberg on Management*, Free Press, New York, 1989, pp. 43–55.
25. For a recent critical review, see Terence Hines, "Left Brain/Right Brain Mythology and Implications for Management and Training," *Academy of Management Review*, October 1987, pp. 600–606.
26. Ned Herrmann, "The Creative Brain," *Training and Development Journal*, October 1981, pp. 10–16.
27. *Newsweek*, Oct. 14, 1974, pp. 76–77.
28. "Stress: Can We Cope?" *Time*, June 6, 1983, p. 53.
29. James C. Abegglen, "Personality Factors in Social Mobility: A Study of Occupationally Mobile Businessmen," *Genetic Psychology Monographs* August 1958, pp. 101–159.
30. Saul W. Gellerman, *Motivation and Productivity*, American Management Association, New York, 1963, p. 147.
31. Bernard Berelson and Gary A. Steiner, *Human Behavior*, Harcourt, Brace & World, New York, 1964, p. 74.
32. Ibid., p. 73.

33. Walter Toman, "Birth Order Rules All," *Psychology Today*, December 1970, pp. 46–49.
34. Edgar H. Schein, "Organizational Socialization and the Profession of Management," in David Kolb, Irwin Rubin, and James McIntyre (eds.), *Organizational Psychology: A Book of Readings*, Prentice-Hall, Englewood Cliffs, N.J., 1971, pp. 14–15.
35. Gareth R. Jones, "Socialization Tactics, Self-Efficiency, and Newcomers' Adjustments to Organizations," *Academy of Management Journal*, June 1986, pp. 262–279.
36. Schein, op. cit., p. 3.
37. Daniel C. Feldman and Hugh J. Arnold, *Managing Individual and Group Behavior in Organizations*, McGraw-Hill, New York, 1983, pp. 79–80.
38. Schein, op. cit.
39. Robert A. Baron, *Behavior in Organizations*, 2d ed., Allyn and Bacon, Boston, 1986, p. 65.
40. John Gabarro, "Socialization at the Top: How CEOs and Subordinates Evolve Interpersonal Contracts," *Organizational Dynamics*, Winter 1979, pp. 3–23.
41. John Van Maanen, "People Processing: Strategies of Organizational Socialization," *Organizational Dynamics*, Summer 1978, pp. 19–36.
42. Gregory B. Northcraft and Margaret A. Neale, *Organizational Behavior*, Dryden, Chicago, 1990, p. 475.
43. Feldman and Arnold, op. cit., pp. 83–86.
44. The Milgram study still receives considerable attention in psychology, see: Spencer A. Rathus, *Psychology*, 4th ed., Holt, Rinehart and Winston, Fort Worth, Tex., 1990, pp. 624–629, and David G. Myers, *Social Psychology*, 3rd ed., McGraw-Hill, 1990, pp. 208–217.
45. Stanley Milgram, "Some Conditions of Obedience and Disobedience to Authority," *Human Relations*, February 1965, pp. 57–76.
46. Ibid., p. 75.
47. Ibid.
48. See *Psychology Today*, June 1974, p. 77.
49. Milgram, op. cit., p. 72.

REAL CASE: LOOKING FOR AN EQUAL CHANCE

A recent investigation of the success of women in reaching the top levels of corporate America found a pretty bleak picture, now and for the future. What follows is the profile of those few who have made it to the top of their respective companies:

- Many successful women are married, but not all have a family. Nearly half of the women on the 1990 *Fortune* list of highly paid executives were childless. Those who do have children find that the demands of the job require them to carefully structure their home life so that everything runs smoothly. For example, Phyllis Swersky, executive vice president of AlCorp, has a live-in nanny, a live-in housekeeper, and a supportive husband, who all help manage house affairs and look after the three young children, ages four to eight. Notes Swersky, "I don't take care of the house. I don't cook. I don't do laundry. I don't market. I don't take my children to malls and museums. And I don't have close friends."
- Some women find that marriage and work cannot both be accommodated, so they remain single. Claudia Goldin, the first tenured economics professor at Harvard, falls into this category. Commenting on her choice, she says, "I'm at the top of my profession now, and it took a tremendous amount of concentration and focus in a brief period of time. If I were married and had kids, I wouldn't have had the energy."
- These women work extremely long hours. For example, Maria Monet, chief financial officer for the Ogden Corporation, reports that she works eleven-hour days and then works out for one and a half hours at a nearby health club. Swersky reports that she leaves home at 8 A.M. and does not return before 7 P.M.
- All of the women have chosen to work for companies where their expectations and

those of the employer are compatible. Kathryn Braun, senior vice president of Western Digital, has pointed out that in her industry there is no old boy network, so that there is less resistance to promoting women into senior-level positions.

- Women who want to get to the top have to take the same route as men: aim for line positions, not staff jobs like personnel and public relations. They also need to take risks and show that they can succeed. As Mary Rudie Barneby of the Dreyfus Corporation puts it, "You have to prove you're a leader. You have to show you're willing to steal second base."

1. How might Argyris's immaturity-maturity theory help explain why many women are not being promoted into top level management positions?
2. In what way can culture be a barrier to the upward mobility of women in business?
3. How did the brief sketch of the women in this case help illustrate how they blended their abilities with the culture of the company?

Case: Cheerleader versus Activist

Liz Schmit grew up in a Midwestern town of 25,000 people. She was the third generation of the Schmit family in this town. Her grandparents, who had come from Germany, were retired, but they took care of her and her younger brother whenever her mother and dad had to go someplace—like a wedding or a funeral. Neither of Liz's parents had attended college, but once her father took an IQ test and scored almost in the genius category. Her parents always encouraged her to do well in school and saved their money so that she could go to State University. Liz also worked during the summer to save money for college. She did very well academically in high school and was a varsity cheerleader. She went on to State University, joined a sorority, majored in English, graduated with honors, and took a job with Landis and Smith Advertising Agency. Liz, now thirty-seven years old, has been with L&S for fifteen years and has a good work record.

One of Liz's coworkers is Todd Long. Todd grew up in a suburb of Los Angeles. Both his parents had attended UCLA, and he saw his grandparents, who were retired military people, only a few times. While Todd was growing up, his parents were gone a lot. His mother arranged for baby-sitters while she got her degree at UCLA. It was always assumed that when Todd graduated from high school he too would go to UCLA. Todd did not participate in many extracurricular activities, but he graduated in the top 10 percent of his high school class. At UCLA, he majored in journalism and was very active in the student movement in the late 1960s. Upon graduation, he cut his hair and went to work for L&S. Todd, now forty-three, has been employed by L&S for fifteen years and has a very good work record.

The job of copy editor is now open, and Liz and Todd are the two top candidates. The head of L&S, Stacy McAdams, made it clear that "this job requires a good personality. The person will be in contact with all the people in the office, and we need someone who can get along well with others and still be able to coordinate the work and meet our critical deadlines."

1. On the basis of the brief sketches of these two people, what do you think their personalities are like? Use the determinants of personality and give an example of each determinant that can be found in the description of this situation.

2. Who do you think will get the job? You can discuss the male/female implications; however, solely on the basis of the personalities that you outlined in question 1, who do you think *would* get the job? Who do you think *should* get the job?
3. What did the boss mean when she said that a "good personality" is required? Is there such a thing? Do you feel that personality has much of an input into this type of staffing decision? Should it have an input? Why?
4. Do you think the socialization processes at L&S have completely overcome Liz's and Todd's biological, cultural, and family influences? Why or why not?

5

Micro Variables Applied: Job Attitudes, Satisfaction, and Commitment

■ They Just Don't Get Any Respect

How satisfied are workers with their jobs? Recent evidence indicates that, contrary to popular opinion, most people feel that they are appreciated by their boss and that their contributions are recognized. On the other hand, there still is a substantial minority who feel their organizations have a long way to go in providing the desired praise and support. For example, a recent survey of employees asked: How often does your boss recognize or praise your accomplishments and achievements? The results were as follows: (a) 11 percent said all of the time; (b) 50 percent said most of the time; (c) 28 percent said rarely; and (d) 10 percent said never. The survey found that managers who are free with criticism but frugal with compliments tend to have resentful employees. In these organizations morale is low, turnover is high, and profits are eroding. What is particularly interesting about this survey is the importance the respondents gave to being treated well. Twenty-seven percent of the respondents said that they would quit their current job if another firm with a reputation for giving recognition and praise offered them a similar position with the same salary and benefits. Simply put: Money is not the only way to retain people. Attitudes and job satisfaction are also important.

Similar results are being reported among older workers, who are now playing an increasingly larger role in the work force. Over the last five years, the number of people sixty-five years of age or older has jumped from 2.9 to 3.4 million and many of these individuals work for younger people. Their biggest complaint: Young managers do not respect their experience or judgment. And while older employees welcome the opportunity to supplement their retirement income, many do not like the conditions under which they work. Among many of them, attitudes and job satisfaction are not very high.

Learning Objectives

- **Examine** the emotional, informational, and behavioral components of attitudes.
- **Explain** how attitudes are formed, the functions they perform, and how they are changed.
- **Discuss** the meaning of job satisfaction of American employees.
- **Identify** the major sources and outcomes of job satisfaction.
- **Define** organizational commitment and explore its implications.

This chapter deals with the job attitudes and commitment of today's employees. The chapter begins by exploring the nature of attitudes from all dimensions. Next, the focus is on employee attitudes and satisfaction. Particular attention is given to how job satisfaction is measured and the outcomes. The last section is devoted to organizational commitment, its meaning and outcomes.

THE NATURE AND DIMENSIONS OF ATTITUDES

The term "attitude" frequently is used in describing people and explaining their behavior. For example: "He has a poor attitude." "I like her attitude." "Our workers turn out poor quality products because they have poor attitudes." More precisely, an *attitude* can be defined as a persistent tendency to feel and behave in a particular way toward some object. For example, George does not like working the night shift. He has a negative attitude toward his work assignment.

Attitudes are a complex cognitive process, but can be characterized three ways. First, they tend to persist unless something is done to change them. For example, if George is transferred to the day shift, his attitude may become positive. Second, attitudes can fall anywhere along a continuum from very favorable to very unfavorable. At the present time, George's attitude may be moderately unfavorable. If he is transferred to the day shift, his attitude may change to highly favorable. Third, attitudes are directed toward some object about which a person has feelings (sometimes called "affect") and beliefs. In George's case this is the work shift. The following sections discuss the various dimensions of attitudes, including the basic components, antecedents, functions, and, finally, how they can be changed.

Components of Attitudes

Attitudes can be broken down into three basic components: emotional, informational, and behavioral. The emotional component includes the person's feelings or affect about an object, i.e., positive, neutral, or negative. Thus, emotion is given the greatest attention in the organizational behavior literature in relation to job satisfaction.[1] In addition, the expression of emotions—either positive, like a customer service representative; negative, like a bill collector or police officer; or neutral, like an academic administrator or public servant—is also important to work behavior.

The informational component consists of the beliefs and information the individual has about the object. It makes no difference whether or not this information is empirically real or correct. A supervisor may believe that two weeks of training is necessary before a worker can operate a particular piece of equipment. In reality, the average worker may be able to operate the machine successfully after only four days of training. Yet the information the supervisor is using (that two weeks is necessary) is the key to his attitude about training.

The behavioral component consists of a person's tendencies to behave in a particular way toward an object. For example, the supervisor in the above paragraph may assign two weeks of machine training to all his new people.

It is important to remember that of the three components of attitudes, only the behavioral component can be directly observed. One cannot see another person's feelings (the emotional component) or the informational component. These two components can only be inferred. For example, when the supervisor assigns a new employee to two weeks of training on the equipment, it is only inferred that (1) the supervisor has strong feelings about the length of training required; and (2) the individual believes that this length of training is necessary. Yet, understanding the antecedents of work-related attitudes is important in the study of organizational behavior.

Antecedents of Work-Related Attitudes

Traditionally, the situational determinants of attitudes received the most attention. In particular, Salancik and Pfeffer noted that the social context provided information to the employee to form their feelings or affect (their job-related attitudes).[2] More recently, personality traits or dispositions have been receiving increasing attention as antecedents of work-related attitudes.[3] In particular, the disposition of positive affectivity (PA) and negative affectivity (NA) have been found to be important antecedents to attitudes about one's job. As explained by George,[4] NA reflects a personality disposition to experience negative emotional states; those with high NA tend to feel nervous, tense, anxious, worried, upset, and distressed. Accordingly, those with high NA are more likely to experience negative affective states—they are more likely to have a negative attitude toward themselves, others, and the world around them. Those with high PA have the opposite disposition and tend to have an overall sense of well-being, see themselves as pleasurably and effectively engaged, and tend to experience positive attitudes. Such PA and NA states are important in understanding job satisfaction and work stress.[5]

Functions of Attitudes

An understanding of the functions of attitudes is important to the study of organizational behavior for a number of reasons. One is that attitudes help predict work behavior. For example, if an attitude survey shows that workers are upset by a change in the work rules and the next week absenteeism begins to increase sharply, management may conclude that a negative attitude toward work rules led to an increase in worker absenteeism. Another reason why an understanding of attitudes is important is that attitudes help people adapt to their work environment. Katz has noted that attitudes serve four important functions in this process.[6]

The Adjustment Function. Attitudes often help people adjust to their work environment. When employees are well treated by the boss, they are likely to develop a positive attitude toward supervision and the organization. When employees are berated and given minimal salary increases, they are likely to develop a negative attitude toward supervision and the organization. These attitudes help employees adjust to their environment and are a basis for future behaviors. For example, if employees who are well treated are asked about supervision or the organization, they are likely to say good things. Just the reverse would probably be true for those berated and given minimal salary increases.

The Ego-Defensive Function. Besides helping employees adjust, attitudes also help them defend their self-images. For example, an older manager whose decisions are continually challenged by a younger subordinate manager may feel that the latter is brash, cocky, immature, and inexperienced. In truth, the younger subordinate may be right in challenging the decisions. The older manager may not be a very effective leader and may constantly make poor decisions. On the other hand, the older manager is not going to admit this, but will try to protect his ego by putting the blame on the other party. As a result, the older manager will have a negative attitude toward the younger one. The same is undoubtedly true for the younger manager, who will feel that the boss is not doing a good job. This attitude helps the younger person protect her ego. If the subordinate were to change this perception and believe that the boss was doing a good job, she would also have to stop criticizing the boss. Quite obviously this is something that the younger person does not want to do. So the attitude serves to justify the action and to defend the ego.

The Value-Expressive Function. Attitudes provide people with a basis for expressing their values. For example, a manager who believes strongly in the work ethic will tend to voice attitudes toward specific individuals or work practices as a means of reflecting this value. A supervisor who wants a subordinate to work harder might put it this way, "You've got to work harder. That's been the tradition of the company since it was founded. It helped get us where we are today, and everyone is expected to subscribe to this ethic." A company president who believes strongly in the need to support the United Way campaign might tell the top management, "Everyone in this firm from top to bottom ought to support United Way. It's a wonderful organization and it does a great deal of good for our community. I don't know where we'd be without it." In both these cases, attitudes serve as a basis for expressing one's central values.

The Knowledge Function. Attitudes help supply standards and frames of reference that allow people to organize and explain the world around them. For example, a union organizer may have a negative attitude toward management. This attitude may not be based in fact, but it does help the individual relate to management. As a result, everything that management says is regarded by the union organizer as nothing more than a pack of lies, a deliberate distortion of the truth, or an attempt to manipulate the workers. Regardless of how accurate a person's view of reality is, attitudes toward people, events, and objects help the individual make sense out of what is going on. Table 5.1 provides a further explanation and summarizes the functions of attitudes.

Changing Attitudes

Employee attitudes can be changed, and sometimes it is in the best interests of management to try to do so. For example, if employees believe that their employer does not take care of them, management would like to change this attitude. Sometimes attitude change is difficult to accomplish because of certain barriers. After these barriers are examined, some ways of overcoming them and effectively changing attitudes will be examined.

Barriers to Changing Attitudes. There are two basic barriers that can prevent people from changing their attitude. One is called prior commitments. This occurs

TABLE 5.1 Determinants of Attitude Formation, Arousal, and Change in Relation to Type of Function

Function	Origin and Dynamics	Arousal Condition	Change Condition
Adjustment	Utility of attitudinal object in need satisfaction; maximizing external rewards and minimizing punishments	1. Activation of needs 2. Salience of cues associated with need satisfaction	1. Need deprivation 2. Creation of new needs and new levels of aspiration 3. Shifting rewards and punishments 4. Emphasis on new and better paths for need satisfaction
Ego defense	Protection against internal conflicts and external changes	1. Posing of threats 2. Appeal to hatred and repressed impulses 3. Rise in frustrations 4. Use of authoritarian suggestion	1. Removal of threats 2. Catharsis 3. Development of self-insight
Value expression	Maintenance of self-identity; enhancing favorable self-image: self expression and self-determination	1. Salience of cues associated with values 2. Appeal to individual to reassert self-image 3. Ambiguities that threaten self-concept	1. Some degree of dissatisfaction with self 2. Greater appropriateness of new attitude for the self 3. Control of all environmental supports to undermine old values
Knowledge	Need for understanding, meaningful cognitive organization, consistency, and clarity	Reinstatement of cues associated with old problems or of old problems themselves	1. Ambiguity created by new information or by change in environment 2. More-meaningful information about problems

Source: Adapted from T. W. Costello and S. S. Zalkind, *Psychology in Administration,* Prentice-Hall, Englewood Cliffs, N.J., 1963, p. 274.

when people feel a commitment to a particular course of action and are unwilling to change. For example, the president of the company graduated from an Ivy League school and was personally instrumental in hiring the new head of the personnel department, who had graduated from the same school. Unfortunately, things are not working out well. The personnel manager is not very good. However, because the president played such a major role in hiring the personnel manager, the chief executive is unwilling to admit the mistake. Using the ego-defensive function of attitudes, the president distorts all negative information received about the personnel manager and continues to believe that everything is going well and the right selection decision was made.

A second barrier is a result of insufficient information. Sometimes people do not see any reason to change their attitude. The boss may not like a subordinate's negative attitude, but the latter may be quite pleased with his or her own behavior. Unless the boss can show the individual why a negative attitude is detrimental to career progress or salary raises or some other desirable personal objective, the subordinate may continue to have a negative attitude. This is particularly true when the attitude is a result of poor treatment by management. The worker will use the negative attitude to serve an adjustment function, i.e., "I can't respect a manager that treats me the way this one does."

Providing New Information. Fortunately, there are ways in which the barriers can be overcome and attitudes can be changed. One of these is by providing new information. Sometimes this information will change a person's beliefs and, in the process, his or her attitudes. In one classic study it was found that union workers had an antimanagement attitude. However, when some of the workers were promoted into the management ranks, their attitudes changed.[7] They became aware of what the company was doing to help the workers, and, over time, this new information resulted in a change in their beliefs about management and their attitude toward both the company and the union. They became more procompany and less prounion.

Use of Fear. A second way of changing attitudes is through the use of fear. Some researchers have found that fear can cause some people to change their attitudes. However, the degree of fear seems to be important to the final outcome. For example, if low levels of fear arousal are used, people often ignore them. The warnings are not strong enough to warrant attention. If moderate levels of fear arousal are used, people often become aware of the situation and will change their attitudes. However, if high degrees of fear arousal are used, people often reject the message because it is too threatening and thus not believable. They essentially dig in their heels and refuse to be persuaded. A good example is provided in the case of anti–cigarette smoking commercials. The Department of Health and Human Services found that when it ran ads using patients who were dying of cancer, the message was so threatening to smokers that they shut it out; they refused to listen. As a result, the commercials did not have the desired impact. Health officials found that moderate fear arousal commercials were the most effective ones.

Resolving Discrepancies. Another way in which attitudes can be changed is by resolving discrepancies between attitudes and behavior. For example, research shows that when job applicants have more than one offer of employment and are forced to choose, they often feel that their final choice may have been a mistake. However, this mild conflict or dissonance does not usually last very long. The theory of cognitive dissonance says that people will try to actively reduce the dissonance by attitude and behavior change.[8] Thus, when people take new jobs and begin working, they also start to have negative feeling toward the firms that were not chosen and positive ones toward the company that was chosen. The result may be that the new employees conclude they did indeed make the right choice.

Influence of Friends or Peers. Still another way in which attitude changes can come about is through persuasion from friends or peers. For example, if Joe Smith has been padding his expense account and finds out that his friends in sales have not, he is likely to change his own attitude. This assumes that Joe likes his coworkers and they have some persuasive control over him. On the other hand, if Joe believes that the other salespeople are all lazy and would pad their accounts if they only knew how, he is unlikely to change his attitude toward doing so.

Additionally, it is important to remember that when a particular matter is of personal interest to people, they are likely to reject extreme discrepancies between their current behavior and that of others. For example, if the other salespeople tell Joe that they never pad their expenses while he is padding his by several thousand dollars annually, Joe is unlikely to let them influence him. There are too many benefits to be achieved if he just keeps on doing what he has been doing.

The Coopting Approach. A final way in which attitude changes often take place is by coopting. This means taking people who are dissatisfied with a situation and getting them involved in improving things. For example, Nancy Jones feels that more needs to be done in improving employee benefits. As a result, the company appoints Nancy as a member of the employee benefits committee. By giving her the opportunity to participate in employee benefits decision making, the company increases the chances that Nancy's attitude will change. Once she begins realizing how these benefits are determined and how long and hard the committee works to ensure that the personnel are given the best benefits possible, she is likely to change her attitude.

JOB SATISFACTION

Employee attitudes are important to human resource management because they affect organizational behavior. In particular, attitudes relating to job satisfaction and organizational commitment are of major interest to the field of organizational behavior and the practice of human resource management. Whereas the discussion of attitudes so far has direct implications, job satisfaction focuses on employees' attitudes toward their job and organizational commitment focuses on their attitudes toward the overall organization. The more widely recognized job satisfaction is first discussed. The more recently recognized attitude of organizational commitment follows.

What Is Meant by Job Satisfaction?

Locke gives a comprehensive definition of job satisfaction as "a pleasurable or positive emotional state resulting from the appraisal of one's job or job experience."[9] Job satisfaction is a result of employees' perception of how well their job provides those things which are viewed as important. It is generally recognized in the organizational behavior field that job satisfaction is the most important and frequently studied attitude.[10]

There are three important dimensions to job satisfaction. First, job satisfaction is an emotional response to a job situation. As such, it cannot be seen; it can only be inferred. Second, job satisfaction is often determined by how well outcomes meet or exceed expectations. For example, if organizational participants feel that they are working much harder than others in the department but are receiving fewer rewards, they will probably have a negative attitude toward the work, the boss, and/or coworkers. They will be dissatisfied. On the other hand, if they feel they are being treated very well and are being paid equitably, they are likely to have a positive attitude toward the job. They will be job-satisfied. Third, job satisfaction represents several related attitudes. Smith, Kendall, and Hulin have suggested that there are five job dimensions that represent the most important characteristics of a job about which people have affective responses. These are:

1. *The work itself*—the extent to which the job provides the individual with interesting tasks, opportunities for learning, and the chance to accept responsibility
2. *Pay*—the amount of financial remuneration that is received and the degree to which this is viewed as equitable vis-à-vis others in the organization
3. *Promotion opportunities*—the chances for advancement in the hierarchy
4. *Supervision*—the abilities of the superior to provide technical assistance and behavioral support
5. *Co-workers*—the degree to which fellow workers are technically proficient and socially supportive[11]

Measuring Job Satisfaction

Since job satisfaction is an attitude, it cannot be directly observed and therefore must rely on the employees' self-reports. These surveys are receiving renewed interest in the practice of human resource management as seen in the accompanying Application Example. There are a number of ways of measuring job satisfaction. Some of the most common are rating scales, critical incidents, interviews, and action tendencies.

Rating Scales.   The most common approach for measuring job satisfaction is the use of rating scales. One of the most popular is the Minnesota Satisfaction Questionnaire (MSQ). Figure 5.1 illustrates a short form of the MSQ. This instrument provides a detailed picture of the specific satisfactions and dissatisfactions of employees.

**Application
Example**

⫸

Rediscovering the Benefits of Employee Surveys

Over the last couple of years, companies have found that there are many benefits in using employee surveys to discover how satisfied their employees are. A recent survey by A. Foster Higgens & Company, a human resources consulting firm in New Jersey, found that 97 percent of chief executive officers who were polled believe that employee surveys provide important information. At one hospital, for example, the administration implemented a benefits program without telling the employees what it was doing. Although the program was less costly than the previous one and was just as effective, the workers disagreed with the way the implementation took place. After a survey found that the employees deeply resented the change, the hospital was eventually forced to revert to the old program. This is in direct contrast to another hospital which did a survey of its employees before tinkering with the benefits package. As a result, the employees found that the newly proposed package was not as comprehensive as they thought and were dissatisfied with the proposal. That hospital is now developing a new plan.

In another case, the J. P. Morgan company conducted a survey to determine how satisfied the employees were with internal communications programs. While the results were positive, a senior-level official still praised the use of such surveys. "You often think you know what your colleagues want," he noted, "but until you ask them you aren't really sure." In still another case, Mobil Oil sensed unrest among its employees regarding relocation policies and other aspects of its career development program. The firm conducted a confidential survey and, as a result, has now revamped policies on child care, relocation, and performance appraisal.

Another popular rating scale is the Job Descriptive Index (JDI). This scale measures the dimensions identified by Smith, Kendall, and Hulin in the five points cited in the previous section. Figure 5.2 provides an example of the index. It has been widely used by organizational behavior researchers over the years and provides a broad picture of employee attitudes toward the major components of jobs.

Still another popular instrument is the Porter Need Satisfaction Questionnaire (NSQ), shown in Figure 5.3. It is typically used for management personnel only. The questions focus on particular problems and challenges faced by managers.

Rating scales offer a number of important advantages in measuring job satisfaction. One is that they are usually short and can be filled out quickly and easily. Another is that they tend to be worded in general language so that they can be used with employees in many different types of organizations. A third is that because they have been so widely used in research, there is usually normative data available so that the responses can be compared with those of employees in other organizations who have taken the test in previous years.

On the negative side, these instruments are based on the assumption that the personnel are willing to respond honestly and that they are able to describe their feelings accurately. Another problem is the underlying assumption that the questionnaire items are valid (they measure what they are supposed to measure) and reliable (they accurately and consistently measure). Validity and reliability were discussed in Chapter 2.

Ask Yourself: How satisfied am I with this aspect of my job?

Very Sat. means I am very satisfied with this aspect of my job.
Sat. means I am satisfied with this aspect of my job.
N means I can't decide whether I am satisfied or not with this aspect of my job.
Dissat. means I am dissatisfied with this aspect of my job.
Very Dissat. means I am very dissatisfied with this aspect of my job.

On my present job, this is how I feel about . . .	Very Dissat.	Dissat.	N	Sat.	Very Sat.
1. Being able to keep busy all the time	☐	☐	☐	☐	☐
2. The chance to work alone on the job	☐	☐	☐	☐	☐
3. The chance to do different things from time to time	☐	☐	☐	☐	☐
4. The chance to be "somebody" in the community	☐	☐	☐	☐	☐
5. The way my boss handles the staff	☐	☐	☐	☐	☐
6. The competence of my supervisor in making decisions	☐	☐	☐	☐	☐
7. Being able to do things that don't go against my conscience	☐	☐	☐	☐	☐
8. The way my job provides for steady employment	☐	☐	☐	☐	☐
9. The chance to do things for other people	☐	☐	☐	☐	☐
10. The chance to tell people what to do	☐	☐	☐	☐	☐
11. The chance to do something that makes use of my abilities	☐	☐	☐	☐	☐
12. The way company policies are put into practice	☐	☐	☐	☐	☐
13. My pay and the amount of work I do	☐	☐	☐	☐	☐
14. The chances for advancement on this job	☐	☐	☐	☐	☐
15. The freedom to use my own judgment	☐	☐	☐	☐	☐
16. The chance to try my own methods of doing the job	☐	☐	☐	☐	☐
17. The working conditions	☐	☐	☐	☐	☐
18. The way my coworkers get along with each other	☐	☐	☐	☐	☐
19. The praise I get for doing a good job	☐	☐	☐	☐	☐
20. The feeling of accomplishment I get from the job	☐	☐	☐	☐	☐
	Very Dissat.	Dissat.	N	Sat.	Very Sat.

FIGURE 5.1

The Minnesota Satisfaction Questionnaire.
(*Source:* D. J. Weiss, R. V. Dawis, G. W. England, and L. H. Lofquist, *Manual for the Minnesota Satisfaction Questionnaire*, Minnesota Studies in Vocational Rehabilitation, vol. 22, University of Minnesota Industrial Relations Center, Minneapolis, 1967. Reprinted by permission.

Critical Incidents. The critical incidents approach to the measurement of job satisfaction was popularized by Frederick Herzberg. He and his colleagues used this technique in their research on the two-factor theory of motivation covered in the next chapter.[12] Employees were asked to describe incidents on their job when they were particularly satisfied and dissatisfied. These incidents were then content-analyzed in determining which aspects were most closely related to positive and negative attitudes. Chapter 6, on motivation, will consider these research results as part of a detailed discussion of the two-factor theory.

One of the major benefits of the critical incidents approach is that it allows the respondents to say whatever they want. The individuals are not restricted by predetermined categories or events as on a structured questionnaire. On the other hand, the approach is time-consuming and there is the chance that both the responses and the interpretations will be biased. The respondents might tell the interviewer what they think the interviewer wants to hear or something that makes them look good

Think of your present work. What is it like most of the time? In the blank beside each word given below, write

<u>Y</u> for "Yes" if it describes your work
<u>N</u> for "No" if it does NOT describe it
<u>?</u> if you cannot decide

Think of the pay you get now. How well does each of the following words or phrases describe your present pay? In the blank beside each word, put

<u>Y</u> if it describes your pay
<u>N</u> if it does NOT describe it
<u>?</u> if you cannot decide

Think of the opportunities for promotion that you have now. How well does each of the following words or phrases describe this? In the blank beside each word, put

<u>Y</u> for "Yes" if it describes your opportunities for promotion
<u>N</u> for "No" if it does NOT describe them
<u>?</u> if you cannot decide

WORK ON PRESENT JOB

___ Routine
___ Satisfying
___ Good
___ Tiring

PRESENT PAY

___ Income adequate for normal expenses
___ Insecure
___ Less than I deserve
___ Well paid

OPPORTUNITIES FOR PROMOTION

___ Promotion on ability
___ Dead-end job
___ Unfair promotion policy
___ Regular promotions

Think of the kind of supervision that you get on your job. How well does each of the following words or phrases describe this? In the blank beside each word below, put

<u>Y</u> if it describes the supervision you get on your job
<u>N</u> if it does NOT describe it
<u>?</u> if you cannot decide

Think of the majority of the people that you work with now or the people you meet in connection with your work. How well does each of the following words or phrases describe these people? In the blank beside each word below, put

<u>Y</u> if it describes the people you work with
<u>N</u> if it does NOT describe them
<u>?</u> if you cannot decide

SUPERVISION

___ Impolite
___ Praises good work
___ Influential
___ Doesn't supervise enough

PEOPLE ON YOUR PRESENT JOB

___ Boring
___ Responsible
___ Intelligent
___ Talk too much

FIGURE 5.2
Sample of the Job Descriptive Index. (*Source:* Reprinted by permission of Dr. P. C. Smith, Copyright © 1975, 1985, Bowling Green University, Department of Psychology, Bowling Green, Ohio.)

FIGURE 5.3
Sample items from the Porter Need Satisfaction Questionnaire. (*Source:* L. W. Porter, "A Study of Perceived Need Satisfaction in Bottom and Middle Management Jobs," *Journal of Applied Psychology,* vol. 45, 1961, p. 3. Copyright © 1961 by the American Psychological Association. Reprinted by permission of the publisher and author.)

Instructions: Circle the number on the scale that represents the amount of the characteristic being rated. Low numbers represent low or minimum amounts, and high numbers represent high or maximum amounts.

1. The opportunity for personal growth and development in my management position.
   a. HOW MUCH IS THERE NOW?
      (Minimum) 1   2   3   4   5   6   7   (Maximum)
   b. HOW MUCH SHOULD THERE BE?
      (Minimum) 1   2   3   4   5   6   7   (Maximum)

2. The feeling of security in my management position.
   a. HOW MUCH IS THERE NOW?
      (Minimum) 1   2   3   4   5   6   7   (Maximum)
   b. HOW MUCH SHOULD THERE BE?
      (Minimum) 1   2   3   4   5   6   7   (Maximum)

such as, "I like it best when my supervisor gets out of my hair and lets me do the job my way. No one knows how to do this work better than I do."

Interviews. Another method of assessing job satisfaction is through the use of personal interviews. This approach allows for an in-depth exploration of job attitudes. If the respondent says something that the interviewer does not understand or would like to learn more about, the interviewer can follow up with additional questions. On the negative side, responses can be misinterpreted and thus lead to erroneous conclusions. A second problem is the possibility of interviewer bias. The way in which the individual asks the questions or the types of information the person chooses to record can affect the outcome. Finally, there is the cost factor. Interviews are a relatively time consuming and thus expensive way of gathering information.

Action Tendencies. Action tendencies are the inclinations people have to approach or to avoid certain things. By gathering information about how they feel like acting with respect to their jobs, the job satisfaction can be measured. Figure 5.4 provides some examples of action tendencies.

There are a number of advantages associated with this approach to measuring attitudes. One is that less self-insight is required by the respondent. Thus, the chance of self-bias is reduced. A second is that the approach provides greater opportunity for people to express their in-depth feelings than do many other, more surface job satisfaction instruments.

Job Satisfaction of American Employees

Are most workers dissatisfied with their jobs? Job attitude surveys generally reveal that they are not, although job satisfaction continues to be a major concern. Although surveys are reported all the time, the University of Michigan's Survey

FIGURE 5.4
Sample items for an action tendency schedule for job satisfaction.
(*Source:* Edwin A. Locke, "Nature and Causes of Job Satisfaction," in M. D. Dunnette (ed.), *Handbook of Industrial and Organizational Behavior,* Rand McNally, Chicago, 1976, p. 1336. Copyright © John Wiley & Sons, Inc. Used with permission.)

1. When you wake up in the morning, do you feel reluctant to go to work?
2. Do you ever feel reluctant to go home from work at night because of the enjoyment you are getting from the job?
3. Do you often feel like going to lunch at work sooner than you do?
4. Do you feel like taking a coffee break more often than you should?
5. Do you ever wish you could work at your job on evenings or weekends?
6. Are you sometimes reluctant to leave your job to go on a vacation?
7. When you are on vacation, do you ever look forward to getting back to work?
8. Do you ever wake up at night with the urge to go to work right then and there?
9. Do you ever wish holidays or weekends would get over with so that you could go back to work?
10. If you were starting over in your working career, would you lean toward taking the same type of job you have now?
11. Would you be tempted to recommend your present job to a friend with the same interests and education as yours?

Research Center and the National Opinion Research Center have found that workers in a wide range of jobs across a diverse set of organizations consistently report that they are generally satisfied with their jobs.

There are, however, some differences that can be discerned. For example, the results of a very large recent survey conducted by the Institute of Industrial Engineers covering a broad cross-section of organizations and job responsibilities concluded that American employees are working harder than they did ten years ago, but are less enthusiastic about it. They are also less motivated and less loyal to their companies. At the same time, however, their workmanship has improved as has their pride in the work they do.[13]

Young Workers. Young workers seem to be less satisfied with their jobs than their older counterparts. There are a number of reasons for this. One is that young workers come into the workplace with high expectations that may not be fulfilled, as jobs prove insufficiently challenging or meaningful. Another reason for dissatisfaction is that many young graduates of colleges and even high schools may be overqualified for their jobs. For example, the Bureau of Labor Statistics estimates that the number of college graduates exceeds job openings that require college degrees by about 1 million a year. As a result, some college graduates are taking lower-income, lower-status jobs, and this is leading to frustration and lack of job satisfaction on their part. One young person put it this way:

> I didn't go to school for four years to type. I'm bored; continuously humiliated. They sent me to Xerox school for three hours. . . . I realize that I sound cocky, but after you've been in the academic world, after you've had your own class [as a student teacher] and made your own plans, and someone tries to teach you to push a button—you get pretty mad. They even gave me a gold plated plaque to show I've learned how to use the machine.[14]

Another reason why young employees are dissatisfied with their jobs is that they do not have any authority or control over their work. The loss of control is becoming increasingly recognized as a major problem in leading to dissatisfaction and work stress.[15] Young people in particular find that they lose control over their lives in the workplace. They find that their bosses are in charge and they must respond to their directives. This situation is quite different from what they encountered at home and school, where they had some control over their lives.

Blue-Collar Workers. Many blue-collar workers do not believe that there is much opportunity for either themselves or their children. In fact, for the first time in decades, the children of many blue-collar workers are becoming blue-collar workers themselves. Today, about 50 percent of all blue-collar workers have high school diplomas; in 1960 this was but 25 percent. These workers are becoming better educated, but their opportunities are not improving.

Many blue-collar workers are particularly frustrated by the lack of respect accorded them. The popular press often portrays them in negative terms. For example, newspaper stories that report cases in which plumbers or electricians earn $50 an hour while the average person earns far less continue to appear and give the impression that many blue-collar people are overpaid for doing menial work.

Another problem is the increasing feeling among blue-collar workers that there are not enough of the good things of life to go around and they are failing to receive their fair share. In truth many blue-collar workers are barely able to scrape by because of low wages and the high cost of living.

Middle Managers. Many middle managers feel that their organizations are not doing enough for them. One of their major complaints in recent years has been the decline in organizational loyalty to the personnel. Years ago, middle managers used to believe that if they did a good job, they could expect the company to take care of them. This is no longer true. As companies continue to become "lean and mean" through downsizing, it is having a devastating effect on all employees, but especially on middle managers. The Fortune 500 industrial companies eliminated 3.2 million jobs in the eighties. Many of those jobs were held by middle managers, who had previously been very satisfied. Now in the nineties, where the trend continues, the great majority of remaining managers have been found in surveys to have low morale, to fear future cutbacks, and to distrust their top level management.[16] Here are some representative examples of the traumatic effect such cuts have on the middle managers affected:

- I was hurt. After thirty-four years with the company, I was surprised that it came down to an economic relationship between the two of us. I thought I was in a family kind of thing.
  —Married man, 57, nudged into early retirement by a big drug company.
- It was pretty traumatic. My self-worth was nil. It was the worst period of my life. Today you can't count on working for a company for twenty to thirty years. It's important to stay flexible.
  —Married man, 43, victim of cutbacks at a large minerals company.

- It was like some unseen hand that came down from on high. People are freaked out and anxious. I've never seen anything like it.
—Single woman, 30, who survived white-collar cutbacks at a major oil company.[17]

Even middle managers who have survived these cutbacks feel that they do not have much influence in the organization or, again, like the young workers, feel they have lost control over their lives. They are paid to do their work and not to ask a lot of questions. Middle managers continue to share the goals of top management, but they are becoming increasingly concerned, anxious, and dissatisfied.

Influences on Job Satisfaction

There are a number of factors that influence job satisfaction. The major ones can be summarized by recalling the dimensions identified earlier: pay, the work itself, promotions, supervision, the work group, and working conditions.

Pay. Wages are a significant factor in job satisfaction. Money not only helps people attain their basic needs but is instrumental in providing upper-level need satisfaction. Employees often see pay as a reflection of how management views their contribution to the organization. Fringe benefits are also important, but they are not as influential. One reason undoubtedly is that most employees do not even know how much they are receiving in benefits. Moreover, most tend to undervalue these benefits because they cannot see their practical value.[18] Chapters in the next part of the book will examine pay as a reinforcer.

The Work Itself. The content of the work itself is another major source of satisfaction. For example, research related to the job characteristics approach to job design, covered in Chapter 7, shows that feedback from the job itself and autonomy are two of the major job-related motivational factors. Some of the most important ingredients of a satisfying job uncovered by surveys include interesting and challenging work, work that is not boring, and a job that provides status.[19]

Promotions. Promotional opportunities seem to have a varying effect on job satisfaction. This is because promotions take a number of different forms and have a variety of accompanying rewards. For example, individuals who are promoted on the basis of seniority often experience job satisfaction but not as much as those who are promoted on the basis of performance. Additionally, a promotion with a 10 percent salary raise is typically not as satisfying as one with a 20 percent salary raise. This helps explain why executive promotions may be more satisfying than promotions that occur at the lower levels of organizations.

Supervision. Supervision is another moderately important source of job satisfaction. Chapter 11 discusses the impact of leadership style. For now, however, it can be said that there seem to be two dimensions of supervisory style that affect job satisfaction. One is employee-centeredness. This is measured by the degree to which a supervisor takes a personal interest in the employee's welfare. It commonly is manifested in ways such as checking to see how well the subordinate is doing, providing advice and assistance to the individual, and communicating with the worker on a personal as well as an official level. American employees generally complain that their supervisors don't do a very good job on these dimensions. For example, a recent large survey found that less than half of the respondents felt their bosses provided them regular feedback or tried to solve their problems.[20]

The other dimension is participation or influence, as illustrated by managers who allow their people to participate in decisions that affect their own jobs. In most cases, this approach leads to higher job satisfaction. For example, comprehensive meta-analysis concluded that participation does have a positive effect on job satisfaction. A participative climate created by the supervisor has a more substantial effect on workers' satisfaction than does participation in a specific decision.[21]

Work Group. The nature of the work group will have an effect on job satisfaction. Friendly, cooperative coworkers are a modest source of job satisfaction to individual employees. The work group serves as a source of support, comfort, advice, and assistance to the individual worker. A "good" work group makes the job more enjoyable. However, this factor is not essential to job satisfaction. On the other hand, if the reverse conditions exist—the people are difficult to get along with—this may have a negative effect on job satisfaction. For example, many women have low job satisfaction because they feel they are subject to male stereotyping that hinders their chances for promotion. This stereotyping seems to exist even among well-educated managers.[22]

Working Conditions. Working conditions are another factor that have a modest effect on job satisfaction. If the working conditions are good (clean, attractive surroundings, for instance), the personnel will find it easier to carry out their jobs. If the working conditions are poor (hot, noisy surroundings, for example), personnel will find it more difficult to get things done. In other words, the effect of working conditions on job satisfaction is similar to that of the work group. If things are good, there will not be a job satisfaction problem; if things are poor, there will be.

Most people do not give working conditions a great deal of thought unless they are extremely bad. Additionally, when there are complaints about working conditions, these sometimes are really nothing more than manifestations of other problems. For example, a manager may complain that his office has not been properly cleaned by the night crew, but his anger is actually a result of a meeting he had with the boss earlier in the day in which he was given a poor performance evaluation.

Outcomes of Job Satisfaction

To society as a whole as well as from an individual employee's standpoint, job satisfaction in and of itself is a desirable outcome. However, from a pragmatic management and organizational effectiveness perspective, it is important to know how, if at all, satisfaction relates to outcome variables. For instance, if job satisfaction is high, will the employees perform better and the organization be more effective? If job satisfaction is low, will there be performance problems and ineffectiveness? This question has been asked by both researchers and practitioners through the years. There are no simple answers. In examining the outcomes of job satisfaction, it is important to break down the analysis into a series of specific subtopics. The following examines the most important of these.

Satisfaction and Productivity. Are satisfied workers more productive than their less-satisfied counterparts? This "satisfaction-performance controversy" has raged over the years. Although most people assume a positive relationship, the preponderance of research evidence indicates that there is no strong linkage between satisfaction and productivity. For example, a comprehensive meta-analysis of the research literature found only a 0.17 average correlation between job satisfaction and productivity.[23] Satisfied workers will not necessarily be the highest producers. There are many possible mediating variables, the most important of which seems to be rewards. If people receive rewards they feel are equitable, they will be satisfied and this is likely to result in greater performance effort.[24] Also, there is considerable debate whether satisfaction leads to performance or performance leads to satisfaction. The chapters in the next part of the book will examine in detail these and other possible dimensions of the relationship.

Satisfaction and Turnover. Does high employee job satisfaction result in low turnover? Unlike that between satisfaction and productivity, research has uncovered a moderate relationship between satisfaction and turnover.[25] High job satisfaction will not, in and of itself, keep turnover low, but it does seem to help. On the other hand, if there is considerable job dissatisfaction, there is likely to be high turnover. One group of researchers found that for women eighteen to twenty-five, satisfaction was an excellent predictor of whether or not they changed jobs. On the other hand, as job tenure (length of time on the job) increased, there was less likelihood of their leaving.[26] Tenure has also been found to lessen the effects of dissatisfaction among male employees.[27]

There are other factors, such as commitment to the organization, that play a role in this relationship between satisfaction and turnover. Some people cannot see themselves working anywhere else, so they remain regardless of how dissatisfied they feel. Another factor is the general economy. When things in the economy are going well and there is little unemployment, typically there will be an increase in turnover because people will begin looking for better opportunities with other organizations. Even if they are satisfied, many people are willing to leave if the opportunities elsewhere promise to be better. On the other hand, if jobs are tough to get, dissatisfied employees will stay where they are. On an overall basis, however, it is accurate to say that job satisfaction is important in employee turnover. Although absolutely no turnover is not necessarily beneficial to the organization, a low turnover rate is usually desirable because of training costs and the drawbacks of inexperience.

Satisfaction and Absenteeism. Research has pretty well demonstrated an inverse relationship between satisfaction and absenteeism.[28] When satisfaction is high, absenteeism tends to be low; when satisfaction is low, absenteeism tends to be high. However, as with the other relationships with satisfaction, there are moderating variables such as the degree to which people feel that their jobs are important. For example, research among state government employees has found that those who believed that their work was important had lower absenteeism than did those who did not feel this way. Additionally, it is important to remember that while high job satisfaction will not necessarily result in low absenteeism, low job satisfaction is likely to bring about high absenteeism.[29]

Other Effects of Job Satisfaction. In addition to the above, there are a number of other effects brought about by high job satisfaction. Research reports that highly satisfied employees tend to have better mental and physical health, learn new job-related tasks more quickly, have fewer on-the-job accidents, and file fewer grievances. On the positive side, it has also been recently found that satisfied employees are more likely to exhibit prosocial "citizenship" type behaviors and activities such as helping coworkers, helping customers, and being more cooperative.[30] From an overall standpoint, then, most organizational behavior researchers as well as practicing managers would argue that job satisfaction is important to an organization. Some critics have argued, however, that this is pure conjecture because there is so much we do not know about the positive effects of satisfaction. On the other hand, when job satisfaction is low, there seem to be negative effects on the organization that have been documented. So if only from the standpoint of viewing job satisfaction as a minimum requirement or point of departure, it is of value to the organization's overall health and effectiveness and is deserving of study and application in the field of organizational behavior.

ORGANIZATIONAL COMMITMENT

The job satisfaction attitude has received the most attention over the years. Recently, the more global organizational commitment attitude has emerged out of the research literature as being important to understanding and predicting organizational behavior. Although a strong relationship between satisfaction and commitment has been found,[31] most studies treat them differently and, especially in light of the "downsizing syndrome" of modern organizations, commitment deserves special attention.

The Meaning of Organizational Commitment

As with other topics in organizational behavior, there are a wide variety of definitions and measures of organizational commitment. As an attitude, organizational commitment is most often defined as: (1) a strong desire to remain a member of a particular organization; (2) a willingness to exert high levels of effort on behalf of the organization; and (3) a definite belief in, and acceptance of, the values and goals of the organization.[32] In other words, this is an attitude about employees' loyalty to their organization and is an ongoing process through which organizational participants express their concern for the organization and its continued success and well being.[33] Using this definition, it is commonly measured by the Organizational Commitment Questionnaire shown in Figure 5.5.

FIGURE 5.5
Organizational
Commitment
Questionnaire
(OCQ).
(*Source:*
R. T. Mowday,
R. M. Steers, and
L. W. Porter, "The
Measure of
Organizational
Commitment,"
*Journal of Voca-
tional Behavior,*
vol. 14, 1979,
p. 228. Used with
permission.)

Listed below are a series of statements that represent possible feelings that individuals might have about the company or organization for which they work. With respect to your own feelings about the particular organization for which you are now working (company name) please indicate the degree of your agreement or disagreement with each statement by checking one of the seven alternatives below each statement.*

1. I am willing to put in a great deal of effort beyond that normally expected in order to help this organization be successful.
2. I talk up this organization to my friends as a great organization to work for.
3. I feel very little loyalty to this organization. (R)
4. I would accept almost any type of job assignment in order to keep working for this organization.
5. I find that my values and the organization's values are very similar.
6. I am proud to tell others that I am part of this organization.
7. I could just as well be working for a different organization as long as the type of work was similar. (R)
8. This organization really inspires the very best in me in the way of job performance.
9. It would take very little change in my present circumstances to cause me to leave this organization. (R)
10. I am extremely glad that I chose this organization to work for over others I was considering at the time I joined.
11. There's not too much to be gained by sticking with this organization indefinitely. (R)
12. Often, I find it difficult to agree with this organization's policies on important matters relating to its employees. (R)
13. I really care about the fate of this organization.
14. For me this is the best of all possible organizations for which to work.
15. Deciding to work for this organization was a definite mistake on my part. (R)

*Responses to each item are measured on a 7-point scale with scale point anchors labeled:
(1) strongly disagree; (2) moderately disagree; (3) slightly disagree; (4) neither disagree nor agree;
(5) slightly agree; (6) moderately agree; (7) strongly agree. An "R" denotes a negatively phrased and reverse scored item.

The organizational commitment attitude is determined by a number of personal (age, tenure in the organization, and dispositions such as positive or negative affectivity, or internal or external control attributions) and organizational (the job design and the leadership style of one's supervisor) variables.[34] Even nonorganizational factors such as the availability of alternatives after making the initial choice to join an organization will affect subsequent commitment.[35]

The Outcomes of Organizational Commitment

As is the case with job satisfaction, there are mixed outcomes of organizational commitment. Although early research seemed to support a positive relationship between organizational commitment and desirable outcomes such as low turnover, limited tardiness, low absenteeism, and enhanced job performance,[36] subsequent research has been less convincing. This may result from the different definitions and interpretations of commitment that are used.[37]

In general, however, most researchers would agree that the organizational commitment attitude as defined here is a somewhat better predictor than job satisfaction of outcome variables such as turnover, if not performance.[38] In fact, after reviewing the relevant literature, Locke and Latham conclude that the stronger causal relationship goes from satisfaction to commitment. "If this is true, it is an important breakthrough in the satisfaction-performance controversy in that it allows one to get, at last, from affect to performance."[39]

Summary

Attitude is a persistent tendency to feel and behave in a particular way toward some object. Attitudes are a complex cognitive process but have three basic characteristics: they persist unless changed in some way; they range along a continuum; and they are directed toward an object about which a person has feelings or affect and beliefs. Attitudes also have three components: emotional, informational, and behavioral. Both situational and personality traits or dispositions such as positive affectivity (PA) and negative affectivity (NA) are important antecedents to attitudes about one's job.

Attitudes often help employees to adapt to their work environment. There are four functions that attitudes have in this process: (1) they help people adjust to their environment; (2) they help people defend their self-image; (3) they provide people with a basis for expressing their values; and (4) they help supply standards and frames of reference that allow people to organize and explain the world around them.

It is sometimes difficult to change attitudes. One reason is prior commitments. A second is insufficient information on the part of the person. Research shows that some of the ways of bringing about attitude changes are providing new information, use of fear, resolving discrepancies between behavior and attitude, persuasion from friends or peers, and coopting.

Job satisfaction is a pleasurable or positive emotional state resulting from the appraisal of one's job or job experience. There are a number of ways of measuring job satisfaction. Some of these are rating scales, critical incidents, interviews, and action tendencies. Each was explained in the chapter.

Research generally shows over the years that most workers are satisfied with their jobs. However, there are some groups that are less satisfied than others. For example, a substantial percentage of young workers, blue-collar workers, and middle managers are not very satisfied. A number of factors influence job satisfaction. Some of the major ones are pay, the work itself, promotions, supervision, the work group, and working conditions. There are a number of outcomes of job satisfaction. For example, although the relationship with productivity is not clear, low job satisfaction tends to lead to both turnover and absenteeism, while high job satisfaction often results in fewer on-the-job accidents and work grievances and less time needed to learn new job-related tasks. Most recently, satisfied workers have been found to exhibit prosocial "citizenship" behaviors and activities.

Closely related to job satisfaction is the organizational commitment attitude. It involves the employees' loyalty to the organization and is determined by a number of personal, organizational, and nonorganizational variables. Like job satisfaction, it has mixed results, but, in general, is thought to have a somewhat stronger relationship with organizational outcomes such as performance, absenteeism, and turnover.

Questions for Discussion and Review

1. In your own words, what is an attitude? What are three characteristics of attitudes?
2. What are the three components of attitudes?
3. What is positive and negative affectivity and how does it influence the formation of attitudes?
4. Attitudes serve four important functions for individuals. What are these four functions?
5. What types of barriers prevent people from changing their attitudes? How can attitudes be changed?
6. What is meant by the term "job satisfaction"? How does it relate to attitudes?
7. Describe each of the following measures of job satisfaction: rating scales, critical incidents, interviews, action tendencies.
8. In general, how satisfied are young people with their jobs? Blue-collar workers? Middle managers? Explain.
9. What are some of the major factors that influence job satisfaction?
10. What are some of the important outcomes of job satisfaction?
11. What is organizational commitment and how does it relate to job satisfaction? Why may an understanding of organizational commitment be especially important in the years ahead?

References

1. Anat Rafaeli and Robert I. Sutton, "Expression of Emotion as Part of the Work Role," *Academy of Management Review,* January 1987, p. 23.
2. Gerald Salancik and Jeffrey Pfeffer, "A Social Information Processing Approach to Job Attitudes and Task Design," *Administrative Science Quarterly,* June 1978, pp. 224–253.
3. For example, see Barry Staw and Jerry Ross, "Stability in the Midst of Change: A Dispositional Approach to Job Attitudes," *Journal of Applied Psychology,* vol. 70, 1985, pp. 469–480.
4. Jennifer M. George, "Personality, Affect, and Behavior in Groups," *Journal of Applied Psychology,* vol. 75, no. 2, 1990, p. 108.
5. A. P. Brief, M. J. Burke, J. M. George, B. Robinson, and J. Webster, "Should Negative Affectivity Remain an Unmeasured Variable in the Study of

Job Stress?" *Journal of Applied Psychology,* vol. 73, 1988, pp. 193–198.
6. D. Katz, "The Functional Approach to the Study of Attitudes," *Journal of Opinion Quarterly,* Summer 1960, pp. 163–204.
7. S. Lieberman, "The Effect of Changes in Roles on the Attitudes of Role Occupants," *Human Relations,* November 1956, pp. 385–402.
8. Leon Festinger, *A Theory of Cognitive Dissonance,* Stanford University, Stanford, Calif., 1957.
9. E. A. Locke, "The Nature and Cause of Job Satisfaction," in M. D. Dunnette (ed.), *Handbook of Industrial and Organizational Psychology,* Rand McNally, Chicago, 1976, p. 1300.
10. Terence R. Mitchell and James R. Larson, Jr., *People in Organizations,* 3d ed., McGraw-Hill, New York, 1987, p. 146.

11. P. C. Smith, L. M. Kendall, and C. L. Hulin, *The Measure of Satisfaction in Work and Retirement*, Rand McNally, Chicago, 1969.

12. Frederick Herzberg, Bernard Mausner, and Barbara Bloch Snyderman, *The Motivation to Work*, 2d ed., Wiley, New York, 1959.

13. Institute of Industrial Engineers, Norcross, Ga., 1990.

14. *Work in America*, Report of the Secretary of Health, Education and Welfare, MIT Press, Cambridge, 1973, p. 45.

15. For example, see: M. Frankenhaeuser and B. Gardell, "Underload and Overload in Working Life," *Journal of Human Stress*, vol. 2, 1976, pp. 35–46, and M. Frankenhaeuser, U. Lundberg, M. Fredrikson, B. Melin, M. Tuomisto, and A. Myrsten, "Stress On and Off the Job as Related to Sex and Occupational Status in White Collar Workers," *Journal of Organizational Behavior*, vol. 1, 1989, pp. 321–346.

16. Ronald Henkoff, "Cost Cutting: How to Do It Right," *Fortune*, April 9, 1990, p. 40.

17. Bruce Nussbaum and others, "The End of Corporate Loyalty," *Business Week*, Aug. 4, 1986, p. 42.

18. Brenda Major and Ellen Konar, "An Investigation of Sex Differences in Pay Expectations and Their Possible Causes," *Academy of Management Journal*, December 1984, pp. 777–792.

19. Jane Ciabattari, "The Biggest Mistake Top Managers Make," *Working Woman*, October 1986, p. 48.

20. "Labor Letter," *The Wall Street Journal*, Dec. 22, 1987, p. 1.

21. Katharine I. Miller and Peter R. Monge, "Participation, Satisfaction, and Productivity: A Meta-Analytic Review," *Academy of Management Journal*, December 1986, p. 748.

22. Peter Dubno, "Attitudes toward Women Executives: A Longitudinal Approach," *Academy of Management Journal*, March 1985, pp. 235–239.

23. M. T. Iffaldano and P. M. Muchinsky, "Job Satisfaction and Job Performance: A Meta-Analysis," *Psychological Bulletin*, vol. 97, 1985, pp. 251–273.

24. P. M. Podsakoff and L. J. Williams, "The Relationship Between Job Performance and Job Satisfaction." In E. A. Locke (ed.), *Generalizing from Laboratory to Field Settings*, Lexington Books, Lexington, Mass., 1986.

25. For an example of a recent study that verifies the relationship between satisfaction and turnover see Thomas W. Lee and Richard T. Mowday, "Voluntarily Leaving an Organization: An Empirical Investigation of Steers and Mowday's Model of Turnover," *Academy of Management Journal*, December 1987, pp. 721–743.

26. Sookom Kim, Roger Roderick, and John Shea, *Dual Careers: A Longitudinal Study of the Labor Market Experience of Women*, vol. 2, U.S. Government Printing Office, Washington, D.C., 1973, pp. 55–56.

27. Herbert Parnes, Gilbert Nestel, and Paul Andrisani, *The Pre-Retirement Years: A Longitudinal Study of the Labor Market Experience of Men*, vol. 3, U.S. Government Printing Office, Washington, D.C., 1973, p. 37.

28. K. Dow Scott and G. Stephen Taylor, "An Examination of Conflicting Findings on the Relationship between Job Satisfaction and Absenteeism: A Meta-Analysis," *Academy of Management Journal*, September 1985, pp. 599–612.

29. C. W. Clegg, "Psychology of Employee Lateness, Absenteeism, and Turnover: A Methodological Critique and an Empirical Study," *Journal of Applied Psychology*, February 1983, pp. 88–101.

30. D. W. Organ, *Organizational Citizenship Behavior: The Good Soldier Syndrome*, Lexington Books, Lexington, Mass., 1987.

31. Edwin A. Locke and Gary P. Latham, *A Theory of Goal Setting and Task Performance*, Prentice-Hall, Englewood Cliffs, N.J., 1990, pp. 249–250.

32. R. T. Mowday, L. W. Porter and R. M. Steers, *Employee-Organization Linkages*, Academic Press, New York, 1982.

33. Gregory B. Northcraft and Margaret A. Neale, *Organizational Behavior*, Dryden, Chicago, 1990, p. 465.

34. For example, see Fred Luthans, Donald Baack, and Lew Taylor, "Organizational Commitment: Analysis of Antecedents," *Human Relations*, vol. 40, no. 4., 1987, pp. 219–236.

35. Northcraft and Neale, op. cit., p. 472.

36. R. T. Mowday, R. M. Steers, and L. W. Porter, "The Measurement of Organizational Commitment," *Journal of Vocational Behavior*, vol. 14, 1979, pp. 224–247.

37. Donna M. Randall, Donald B. Fedor, and Clinton

O. Longenecker, "The Behavioral Expression of Organizational Commitment," *Journal of Vocational Behavior*, vol. 36, 1990, pp. 210–224.
38. Lynn McMarlane Shore, George C. Thornton, and Lucy A. Newton, "Job Satisfaction and Organizational Commitment as Predictors of Behavioral Intentions and Employee Behavior," *Academy of Management Proceedings*, 1989, pp. 229–333.
39. Locke and Latham, op. cit., p. 250.

REAL CASE: SURPRISINGLY, POSITIVE ATTITUDES

Japanese production techniques are well-known and many organizations have adopted them in recent years. However, are Japanese workers more satisfied with their jobs than American workers? Surprisingly, recent evidence indicates that they are not. Drawing upon 106 United States and Japanese factories (a total of over 8,000 workers), researchers have recently found that there are differences in work attitudes between the two countries. Among their conclusions are the following:

Question	U.S. average	Japanese average
All in all, how satisfied are you with your job? (0 = not at all, 4 = very)	2.95	2.12
If a good friend of yours told you that he or she was interested in working at a job like yours at this company, what would you say? (0 = advise against it, 1 = would have second thoughts, 2 = would recommend it)	1.52	.909
Knowing what you know now, if you had to decide all over again whether to take the job you now have, what would you decide? (0 = would not take the job again, 1 = would have some second thoughts, 2 = would take job again)	1.67	.837
How much does your job measure up to the kind of job you wanted when you first took it? (0 = not what I wanted, 1 = somewhat, 2 = what I wanted)	1.20	.427

Simply put, American workers report higher levels of job satisfaction than do Japanese workers. This is certainly in direct contrast to what many people in this country have come to believe. How can this be explained? One explanation is that Americans have come to have low job expectations and aspirations and, as a result, are more easily satisfied with their jobs than the Japanese. A second possible reason is that Americans are more optimistic and upbeat than the Japanese, so they paint a rosier picture of things and thus report higher job satisfaction. A third explanation is that the facts speak for themselves and Americans simply are more satisfied.

1. How much more satisfied are American workers than Japanese workers?

2. Is there any linkage between job satisfaction and performance? What relevance does your answer have for American companies?
3. How, if at all, does organizational commitment relate to the Japanese versus American workers?

Case: Doing His Share

When Ralph Morgan joined the Beacher Corporation, he started out as an assembler on the line. Ralph remained in this position for five years. During this time there were two major strikes. The first lasted five weeks; the second went on for eighteen weeks. As a member of the union, Ralph was out of work during both of these periods, and in each case the strike fund ran out of money before a labor agreement was reached.

Last year Ralph was asked if he would like to apply for a supervisory job. The position paid $2500 more than he was making, and the chance for promotion up the line made it an attractive offer. Ralph accepted.

During the orientation period, Ralph found himself getting angry at the management representative. This guy seemed to believe that the union was too powerful and management personnel had to hold the line against any further loss of authority. Ralph did not say anything, but he felt the speaker was very ill informed and biased. Two developments have occurred over the last six months, however, that have led Ralph to change his attitude toward union-management relations at the company.

One was a run-in he had with a shop steward who accused Ralph of deliberately harassing one of the workers. Ralph could not believe his ears. "Harassing a worker? Get serious. All I did was tell him to get back to work," he explained to the steward. Nevertheless, a grievance was filed and withdrawn only after Ralph apologized to the individual whom he supposedly harassed. The other incident was a result of disciplinary action. One of the workers in his unit came late for the third day in a row and, as required by the labor contract, Ralph sent him home without pay. The union protested, claiming that the worker had really been late only twice. When Ralph went to the personnel office to get the worker's clock-in sheets, the one for the first day of tardiness was missing. The clerks in that office, who were union members, claimed that they did not know where it was.

In both of these cases, Ralph felt the union went out of its way to embarrass him. Earlier this week the manager from the orientation session called Ralph. "I've been thinking about bringing line supervisors into the orientation meetings to discuss the union's attitude toward management. Having been on the other side, would you be interested in giving them your opinion of what they should be prepared for and how they should respond?" Ralph said he would be delighted. "I think it's important to get these guys ready to take on the union and I'd like to do my share," he explained.

1. What was Ralph's attitude toward the union when he first became a supervisor? What barriers were there that initially prevented him from changing his attitude regarding the union?
2. Why did Ralph's attitude change? What factors accounted for this?
3. Are workers who are recruited for supervisory positions likely to go through the same attitude changes as Ralph?

**Case:
Measuring
Job
Satisfaction
in a Hospital**

Trudy Willworth is the training and development director of a large metropolitan hospital. She has been in her current position only two weeks, but she is already putting together a long-range plan of action designed to improve employee performance throughout the hospital.

One of the things that Trudy feels is important is job satisfaction. She is convinced that happy workers are productive workers. She also believes that the best way to determine whether people are satisfied in their jobs is to systematically measure their job satisfaction. Unfortunately, she is not sure how to go about doing this. She has talked to a number of colleagues inside the hospital and other personnel managers she met through the City Personnel Association. She has received a variety of suggestions. The two most common are (1) to have a job satisfaction questionnaire filled out by everyone and (2) to conduct interviews with a large portion of the hospital work force. Trudy is not sure which of these two approaches, if either, would be best.

Trudy is also thinking about how the results can be interpreted. If she finds that job satisfaction is low, what will this mean? Can it be used to explain absenteeism, tardiness, or low productivity? She is not sure. This is why she has been thinking about holding off on gathering this information and, instead, devoting herself to other important training issues. Unfortunately, earlier this morning Trudy received a memo from the head administrator. "I am looking forward to the results of your job satisfaction survey," he wrote. "Please send me a copy as soon as it is available. If possible, I would like to report the findings to the board of trustees at next month's meeting." Trudy is not sure what to do but is certain about one thing: there is no turning back now. She has to measure job satisfaction and write up the results for the administrator.

1. Is Trudy right in thinking that satisfied workers are productive workers?
2. Should she use a rating scale approach or interviews to measure satisfaction? Why?
3. If the results show that job satisfaction is low, would this help explain the tardiness and absenteeism that is higher than normal? Why or why not?

INTEGRATIVE CONTEMPORARY CASE FOR PART 2

The New Work
Ethic: You
Cannot Work
Too Hard or
Too Long*

Sometime in the last decade an 11th commandment—Achieve excellence in your work—crept into the set of grand precepts by which we are to live our lives. For the mass of baby-boomers struggling to make their mark, the new creed was particularly useful. "With the world so competitive, how do you distinguish yourself without excellence?" was one Silicon Valley boomer's view until recently. Corporate chiefs eager to get their companies lean and productive found this workism a godsend, producing as it did a crop of purposeful, gung-ho lieutenants willing to fly anywhere and work all night, a splendid example to the rest of the troops.

But now many hard chargers have begun to have second thoughts. Has something gone awry? That be-the-best ethic has been warped into a dictate more like, You cannot work too hard or too long. A new corporate style dubbed the "high commitment" model has sprung up, suggesting ominously that your life should revolve around work and not much else. And top management doesn't sound as if it's slacking off in its demands.

"Nobody ever got up on a desk and said, 'Work harder,'" says a former executive at Bankers Trust. "But somebody would call an occasional meeting at 8 A.M. Then it became the regular 8 o'clock meeting. So there was the occasional 7 A.M. meeting. And the dinner meetings. It just kept spreading." At many companies the kind of punishing hours once reserved for crises have become the standard drill. A whole generation of managers has grown up who never had a 40-hour workweek; it appears that some never will. Or will they? With their personal and family lives in smithereens or a state of perpetual postponement, what seems a substantial contingent of the formerly ambitious have begun harboring seditious thoughts about the work ethic and the all-importance of a dazzling career. Exhaustion and disillusion are setting in.

Why does the job seem so demanding? It isn't just long hours or clumsy direction from above, though there's plenty of that. All sorts of pressure, from the stress of participatory management techniques to the hyperkinesia of two-career marriages to the dismay of finding your workload increasing as you near 50, just when you thought you could adopt a more dignified pace, are working together to squeeze the oomph from heretofore steely-eyed achievers.

It isn't just the drones at the water cooler who are thinking anew about the burden of hard work, either. It is senior executives and ambitious yuppies—men and women who have been running flat out for years—who have been keeping such thoughts bottled up inside for fear of appearing weak or uncommitted. "It's a very dangerous topic," says management consultant Robert Paulson, director of McKinsey & Co.'s Los Angeles office. "You'll be on an airplane and two guys sitting together are diving into their briefcases while the plane is still taking off. But dinner comes and some wine gets passed around, and the subject comes up. It's very accessible, right under the surface."

*Source: Brian O'Reilly, "Is Your Company Asking Too Much?" *Fortune*, March 12, 1990, pp. 39–41, 43, 46, copyright 1990, Time, Inc. All rights reserved. Reprinted by permission from TIME.

Pierre Mornell, a San Francisco Bay Area psychiatrist, addresses groups of two dozen top IBM executives on balancing work and personal life during two-week-long advanced management courses in Armonk, New York. Managers are usually stone-faced initially. "There's a tremendous resistance to get into these personal issues," Mornell says. Eventually the managers' concerns rise to the surface. "By the end of one session, everyone was talking. Many came up to me privately and said they were very troubled by 14-hour days and six-day weeks."

Some of the heavy-laden have already bailed out. Understandably, they are the people most willing to talk about how the pressure got to them. For 18 months prior to the introduction of Steve Jobs's Next computer, Cathy Cook was responsible for fielding questions from hordes of reporters eager to learn about the secret machine. At times she would work from 7:30 in the morning to 11:30 at night, come home, and find 100 phone calls on the answering machine to review before the next day. "I was working so hard I didn't even realize it," says Cook. "People would tell me to slow down and I didn't understand what they were saying." Her boyfriend got fed up with her long hours and took off. She says that when she got word on the morning of a big Next media event that her mother was seriously ill, "I had about five minutes to be upset before the phone started ringing again. You get so far into it, you don't even realize your life has gotten away from you completely."

Last year Cook started teaching part time at a college in San Jose, in addition to her work for Next. "It didn't let me slacken the pace," she says. "But a light bulb went on. I saw there could be another aspect to my life." In September she enrolled at Harvard's Kennedy School of Government. She will return to Silicon Valley eventually, but vows to keep her life in balance.

Tom Klein, 38, spent four years as a McKinsey consultant in the early 1980s, then decided to chuck the high pressure and constant travel to join Klein Bros., his family's food-processing business in Northern California. His record suggests it wasn't because he was lazy. An honors student and a Stanford MBA, he says he has always worked hard. But at McKinsey he had to race off and meet with clients whenever they wanted. "I got tired of jumping up every time the boss said 'Let's go,'" he explains.

And his new job? "The worries are greater, but the pace is a little easier." When he's in the office he works just as hard as he ever did, but the hours are a lot more reasonable—8 to 5:30, "and *never* on weekends." He finds he's more productive too. Klein has expanded sales of the company's nuts, raisins, and grains into overseas markets and acquired a 500-acre winery in California's Sonoma County that makes acclaimed wines under the Rodney Strong label.

Still, it wasn't easy to leave McKinsey, Klein says. The internal debate over whether to go off to work for his family's little-known firm made him wrestle with his ego. "It forced me to ask just who I am without a prestigious job title."

A flourishing personal life more than makes up for the loss, he finds. An avid golfer and fly fisherman, he has dropped his handicap from 12 to six since he left and has fished in many of the great fly-casting streams around the world.

He urges friends to get more balance in their lives, even if they don't have a prospering family business to retreat to: "It sounds corny, but you really only get to pass through this life once. This is not a practice run."

Not everyone shares Klein's view, of course. Interviews with more than 70 managers, consultants, psychologists, and CEOs make it clear that work is still an important source of self-esteem. There is no general movement toward the anticorporate radicalism of the 1960s. For now, millions of ambitious people are out there still eager to work incredibly hard for their companies.

Bonnie Stedt, for example, an executive vice president at American Express Travel Related Services Co. Stedt, 46, works 12-hour days, Saturday mornings, and Sunday evenings. She doesn't expect others to work that hard and has no illusions about having it all. "Of course I've missed things," she says. "Friends try to call for three weeks and can't reach me." She is single and admits she is lonely occasionally. But she says her work, as head of human resources, is enormously satisfying. "I have one of the best jobs in the company, with total freedom to do my job. I don't feel victimized."

What few CEOs seem to appreciate is that not all the troops in the barracks are Bonnie Stedts. Discontent is brewing, and there may be bigger trouble ahead. According to a FORTUNE poll, 77% of CEOs believe U.S. corporations will have to push their managers harder than ever in order to compete internationally. Only 9% believe that restructuring and getting leaner has resulted in pushing managers *too* hard. If we want to compete against the Japanese, goes this line of thought, don't we have to work the same kind of hours they do?

Most CEOs appear to appreciate, intellectually at least, that companies must encourage creativity, develop better incentives, and bestow more autonomy on managers. When push comes to shove, however, they shove. Says Arnold B. McKinnon, CEO of Norfolk Southern: "Over the last ten years or so, many companies have pushed and now they just need to keep people working as hard. You just naturally have to work harder and get rid of those people who don't."

Perhaps, but some untoward consequences are beginning to show. The pool of highly talented people in large corporations willing to take on more work appears to be shrinking. Korn/Ferry International, the big executive search firm, surveyed 700 senior executives at FORTUNE 500 companies last year and found only 47% want more responsibility than they already have. When the question was first asked ten years ago, 58% were hungry for more chores. Says Lester Korn, the firm's chairman: "A lot of people don't want the pressure."

"The best are leading the move away from overwork," argues Robert Kelley, a business professor at Carnegie Mellon University and an expert on corporate restructuring. "It used to be that 60-hour workweeks gave you warrior status, but the trend is reversing. People are saying that 60-hour weeks mean something is wrong with the system or with the person."

In case you wonder how your father seemed to work long and hard without having his life become so crazy, rest assured that he was not necessarily made of sterner stuff than you. The problem is not longer hours so much as the amount of stress and effort packed into them. A Harvard MBA was comparing time on the job with his father, who had worked as a high-powered lawyer, and was about to conclude that the world hadn't really changed much—until the father asked incredulously, "You mean you *don't* take a nap every day after lunch?"

It would be comforting to think that the rising demands of corporate and professional life were only temporary, or that they flowed from some easily dammable source. But the reasons you don't get to curl up on the sofa in the afternoon are many and seem fairly intractable.

The role of the executive has changed significantly. When baby-boomers were growing up and their dads wore fedoras, the job of a corporate executive was often relatively stable and narrowly focused. "Institutions had a clear sense of what they did, and they did it efficiently," says Robert Shapiro, head of NutraSweet. "If you made widgets, you did it again and again. You wanted conformance to norms, and you set up systems to detect deviations, and the executive was part of that process."

This approach no longer works in the face of global competition, rapid innovation, and considerable uncertainty. "Many of us don't know if what we're doing will be valid tomorrow," Shapiro says. Effective managers nowadays don't get to execute clear-cut orders from on high; rather, each manager has to understand the company's overall strategy and then improvise. Says Shapiro: "We're demanding a lot more."

When the strategy is missing, the demands on an executive grow intolerable. At one company a manager was told the goal for the year was market share. The next year it was improved profit margins, then new accounts, and then in the fourth year, cost cutting. "He got top evaluations every year, but he didn't make it to the fifth year," says Bob Swain, co-founder of Swain & Swain, an outplacement firm in New York City. "He couldn't bring himself to fire up the troops and head off in another direction. He quit."

More participatory management, while an improvement, often takes more time. A boss barking orders into the phone in the old days wasn't fun for the underlings, but it was fast. Now subordinates have lots of autonomy, but the boss has to spend hours providing general direction, guiding group decision-making, and wandering around to keep an eye on things. Says Chrisopher York, a former top Citicorp officer and now vice president at AmBase, a financial services company: "That increases the level of ambiguity and stress a manager has to live with."

Even if you survived the latest round of cutbacks, you can't breathe easy. To the contrary. The vast restructurings under way at large companies have piled on the work for those who have kept their jobs. Kim Cameron, a University of Michigan business professor who studied downsizings at 30 auto-related industrial companies in the upper Midwest, concludes that most restructurings are done badly, with little thought given to rebalancing the workload among the survivors. About two-thirds of the downsizings he studied were botched, he says: The wrong jobs were eliminated, or blanket offers of early retirement prompted invaluable managers to leave.

When Cameron asked 2,000 managers at the companies about their workloads after layoffs, 47% of respondents said they were working "a great deal" more than two years earlier. Says Cameron: "There's a general approach of throwing a hand grenade at a bunch of employees, and whoever survives has to do all the work there was before." Worse, since the survivors often don't know how to do the departeds' work, morale and productivity plummet.

"It's a rare corporation that asks about the impact of restructuring on individuals," says William Bridges, a San Francisco area consultant who helps companies eliminate layers of management. "The CEOs say, 'We'll restructure because the company will function better,' but nobody asks about exhaustion." Too often, Bridges observes, the top brass declare managers will "work smarter" but don't offer any guidance on how to do that. Instead, says Bridges, " 'work smarter' is usually a euphemism for 'work harder next week.' "

Technology may make you more productive, but it doesn't necessarily help you work less. Lawyers at big-name firms such as Cravath Swaine & Moore in New York City have always worked some of the most horrendous hours anywhere. Now at Cravath they work more than ever—an average 2,300 billable hours a year, up from around 2,000 in 1960. One culprit appears to be office technology.

Says Sam Butler, presiding partner at Cravath: "We used to type up drafts of contracts on seven-page carbons, and by 9:30 at night you had to give them to the typing pool. Then you went home." But since the arrival of computers, lawyers can print out flawless contracts as late as they want. And now there are facsimile machines. Says Butler: "We can print out a contract, fax it to London, and wait around until 3 A.M. when they've finished reviewing it, and we can start working on it again."

Few corporations are sensitive to the stresses their managers are under, says Marilyn Puder-York, a psychologist counseling executives on Wall Street. "Developing the proper balance is such a fine line and requires so much wisdom. I don't know if enough senior managers have experienced enough trauma in their own personal lives to be that wise."

The danger is that corporations, especially those anxious about foreign competition or possible takeover, are asking more and more of employees just as workers are becoming less and less willing to give. Since customer service and innovativeness are increasingly important competitive weapons, it doesn't pay to create a sullen, dispirited, or burned-out work force. Some ways for corporations to turn down the heat:

■ **For starters, don't presume you're another Lee Iacocca, inspiring workers to joyous and extraordinary effort by the force of your dazzling personality.** Carol Orsborn, co-owner of a San Francisco public relations firm, found herself disabused of this illusion in a way that wound up making her company far more productive. "I thought I was an inspirational leader," she says.

"Whenever I gave a speech on the goals of the company, I noticed everyone worked harder." One day, though, the workers rebelled and presented her with a list of demands for change. Says Orsborn: "I wasn't inspiring them. It turned out they were afraid of getting fired."

Orsborn and her husband, Dan, realized they were driving themselves and their employees too hard, so they told everyone to cut back to a 40-hour week. They got rid of half their clients, sold their Porsches, moved into a smaller house, and half expected to be out of business in a few months. "Business boomed," Orsborn says. The clients they disposed of were the most exhausting ones—"the ones that were driving us by fear." Employee turnover dropped sharply, workers felt less frightened about making mistakes, "and we discovered you could have creative ideas while you were gardening." Despite the shorter hours, revenues shot back to their former level in months.

■ **If you have to restructure, solicit employees' ideas on how to go about it.** Workers are far less resentful of the added workload that often follows if they feel they had some say in what tasks they would inherit. "People will work hard if they have a choice," says Michigan professor Cameron. The auto companies he studied that failed to improve efficiency three years after layoffs had piled new duties on their managers and given them no choice. "The managers' attitude was, 'I'm working as fast as I can. I'm not going to spend more time making the company innovative.'"

■ **Don't let work turn into an endurance contest.** An executive at Xerox used to work all day in New York, fly all night to London and put in a full day, then fly back to New York and work all day. One joker pulling such stunts can force everyone else to do the same and drag the entire organization down. "People can't sustain the effort," says a venture capitalist, who saw the phenomenon in corporate life. "It leads to chaos, and then everybody gets addicted to the adrenaline that comes when you're battling chaos."

Aside from a few macho fools, most workers would be delighted to end such displays of extraordinary commitment but fear looking as if they don't care about their work. "It's like two aging gunslingers squaring off to go at it," says Paulson at McKinsey. "Both of them would be happy to go off and have an ice cream soda together, but neither one wants to be the first to blink." Sometimes blinking works. Robin Juarez, a NutraSweet executive, declined to go along with a company practice of commencing business trips to Latin America on Sundays. A single mother at the time, she didn't feel right leaving her children on weekends. "There was a collective sigh of relief," says Juarez. "Even my boss said, 'Okay, we won't travel on Sunday.'"

■ **Be flexible.** The inability to pursue a sane family life is what makes most workers feel the job is too demanding. Women are the most vulnerable. Even in two-career families, women handle about 70% of the child rearing. Don't demand that all work be done at the office; reward good workers with computers and telecommunications devices so they can work at home. Charles Rodgers, vice president of Work/Family Directions, a Boston-based consulting company, says, "A lot of people want flexible hours, not shorter hours."

Is your company working you too hard? Odds are that it will let you work yourself silly if you choose. Wittingly or unwittingly, the brass will set up contests between managers to see who produces the most or works the longest. The company may spur contestants on by giving money or titles to the winners, but it will not tell you to stop working. Apple Computer is more sensitive than most companies to the stress that comes with overwork—it offers massage on the premises, sponsors an equestrian club, and gives aikido lessons to help workers blow off steam. But the manager at Apple who came to work a couple of days after she gave birth last year was not sent home. The hard job of not working so hard is up to you.

How to kick back without getting kicked out? You may have to approach deceleration gradually and strategically, says Puder-York, the Wall Street psychologist. One way to break the pattern of unbridled overwork is to join philanthropic or professional organizations that have been blessed by the company. Getting a seat on the National Footwear Council won't be seen by your superiors as running away from work, she says. "You get to tell your boss you have a board meeting to attend, and that it is business-related." It could also provide some badly needed socialization in a more relaxed setting than work. Building up a network of contacts at other companies in your industry may boost your sense of security too; if nothing else, you've got people to call if you lose your current job.

Take up exercise on your lunch hour. Unless your boss is prepared to confess that he doesn't care if you drop dead at your desk, he can hardly argue with your pursuit of fitness. Heading off to the gym sends a message that you're putting your own needs ahead of the company's, at least for an hour or so, and helps you establish some personal time in your day. Once it's clear that you are not available to hop every moment the boss gets a brainstorm, you could use the time for other needs—seeing your kids at lunch, for instance.

Thinking of quitting the corporate scene altogether but not quite ready to open an inn in Vermont? Consider becoming a consultant to your current employer. More and more companies are comfortable negotiating consulting contracts with employees, says Nella Barkley, head of Crystal-Barkley, a New York firm that counsels executives on career advancement. A consulting contract offers erstwhile corporate apparatchiks a steady income and a lot of flexibility, she says; they can decide how much of the time freed up they want to use going after new clients. Companies can reduce overhead costs but still engage experienced help easily during peak demand periods. "It's a super alternative," says Barkley. "My experience coaching people who do it is that their egos get a big boost. They feel in charge of their lives, and they're loaded with queries from the full-timers still on the job."

It's often tough to recognize that you're overworking. Anything less than full effort seems immoral—"There's no ethic more ethical than the work ethic," observes economist John Kenneth Galbraith. You probably believe that you can handle overwork better than most. Says Leonard Greenhalgh, a psychologist teaching at Dartmouth's Amos Tuck School of Business: "A typical reaction is, 'A normal person can't do all this, but I'm so talented I can.'"

It is easy to forget that hard work is not inherently good or moral, but only as noble as what you're striving to achieve. Working so hard that you're a dismal parent is wrong. Working hard so you can be filthy rich is merely greedy. Working overtime because your boss is too dim to let you do meaningful, efficient work is foolish, unless you are paid handsomely for the aggravation.

In case you need to kick yourself in the pants in order to slow down, try taking the simple and unnerving tombstone test: Ask yourself what you want to be known for after you've shuffled off to the Big Office in the Sky. If it's for winning an extra fraction of a point of market share for the pillowcase division in the third quarter of 1990, well, knock yourself out. If it's to lead a great company that employs thousands, gives customers something they need, and provides shareholders with wealth for retirement, you're onto something noble. But consider that in driving yourself and others, less may be more. And if the urge is rising to become one of the great Boy Scout leaders of southwestern Iowa or the most earnest jazz clarinetist ever to screech out a tune, go do it. Making yourself a better person—more diverse in your interests, more reflective, perhaps even more loving—may well make you a better manager. But don't wait for your boss to get excited about the idea. Just get started. And remember that the only people who are pushed too hard are those who let themselves be pushed.

1. How do your perceptions of the world of work compare to what you read and the examples in this case? Do you agree that the workplace is getting tougher in terms of longer hours and more pressure? Why is this the case?

2. The case notes that "it doesn't pay to create a sullen, dispirited, or burned-out work force." Do you agree or disagree and why? What solutions are offered? Which do you like the most and least?

3. How can the study of perception, personality and attitudes/job satisfaction help you to understand the situation described in the case and provide solutions for more effective human resource management now and in the future?

EXPERIENTIAL EXERCISES FOR PART 2

EXERCISE: SELF-PERCEPTION AND DEVELOPMENT OF THE SELF-CONCEPT

Goals:

1. To enable the students to consider their own self-concepts and to compare this with how they feel they are perceived by others
2. To explore how the self-concept in personality is formed largely on the basis of feedback received from others (the reality that we "mirror ourselves in others")
3. To stimulate student thinking about how management of human resources may involve perception and personality

Implementation:

1. The students take out a sheet of paper and fold it in half from top to bottom.
2. The students write "How I See Myself" and "How I Think Others See Me."
3. The students write down five one-word descriptions (adjectives) under each designation which, in their opinion, best describe how they perceive themselves and how others perceive them.
4. The students then share their two lists with their classmates (in dyads and triads, or the whole class) and discuss briefly. Each person may communicate what he or she is most proud of.
5. The instructor may participate in the exercise by sharing his or her list of adjectives.

EXERCISE: HE WORKS, SHE WORKS

Objective:

To increase your awareness of common stereotypes that exist in many organizations about male and female characteristics.

Instructions:

1. Complete the "He Works, She Works" worksheet shown at the top of the next page. In the appropriate spaces, write what you think the stereotyped responses would be. Do not spend too much time considering any one item. Rather, respond quickly and let your first impression or thought guide your answer.
2. Compare your individual responses with those on the "He Works, She Works" answer sheet provided by your instructor.
3. Compare your individual responses with those of other class members or participants. It is interesting to identify and discuss the most frequently used stereotypes.

He Works, She Works (Worksheet)

The family picture is on *his* desk: *(e.g., He's a solid, responsible family man.)*	The family picture is on *her* desk: *(e.g., Her family will come before her career.)*
His desk is cluttered:	*Her* desk is cluttered:
He's talking with coworkers:	*She's* talking with coworkers:
He's not at his desk:	*She's* not at her desk:
He's not in the office:	*She's* not in the office:
He's having lunch with the boss:	*She's* having lunch with the boss:
The boss criticized *him:*	The boss criticized *her:*
He got an unfair deal:	*She* got an unfair deal:
He's getting married:	*She's* getting married:
He's going on a business trip:	*She's* going on a business trip:
He's leaving for a better job:	*She's* leaving for a better job:

PART **3**

THE HEART OF ORGANIZATIONAL BEHAVIOR: MOTIVATION, LEARNING, AND LEADERSHIP

6

Motivation Theory: Needs and Processes

■ Keeping Money in Perspective

How important is money as a motivator? The answer is mixed, but recently it has been used as an incentive in unique applications. For example, some firms are beginning to use monetary bonuses to encourage minority hiring, environmental protection, and improvement of customer satisfaction. At Colgate-Palmolive, executives' bonuses are contingent on hiring or promoting at least one woman or minority member. At Conoco, environmental protection is a major component of incentive compensation for all top managers. A management committee sets environmental goals and bonuses are given based on how well these are met. The management committee then determines what realistic continuous environmental improvements are achievable.

At Xerox, customer satisfaction as measured by consumer surveys is the major criterion for bonuses. As one manager recently put it, "An executive of a profitable unit might get no bonus if customers said his unit performed inadequately." Chemical Bank's Consumer Banking Group has a similar approach, except that instead of waiting until the end of the year, the group gets feedback from customers on a monthly basis and uses a composite of these results to determine executive bonuses. At Aluminum Corporation of America—besides providing monetary incentives for equal opportunity, environmental protection, and customer service—a hefty chunk of upper management bonuses is based on continual improvement in safety records.

These monetary bonus systems have one thing in common: They are designed to improve company performance in areas which are not measurable in financial terms. However, this does not mean that "pay for performance" bonuses are being abandoned. An increasing number of companies are using incentive payment plans to help bolster productivity and performance. In fact, there is recent evidence that bonuses, stock options, and other long-term incentives are being used by more companies than ever. Unfortunately, there may not be a direct relationship between the use of monetary incentives and such bottom-line measures as return on investment or profit. Why? Because bonuses may not be tied to performance, but instead are based on the bonuses that competitive firms offer their top people. With such nonperformance bonuses, there may be no incentive for managers to improve performance because they will gain or lose nothing as a result. The lesson to be learned is that the use of money as an incentive should be directly linked to specific performance. Otherwise, money becomes just another perk and may not serve to motivate the manager to improve performance.

Learning Objectives

- **Define** the motivation process.
- **Identify** the primary, general, and secondary motives.
- **Discuss** the Maslow, Herzberg, and Alderfer content theories of work motivation.
- **Explain** the Vroom, Porter-Lawler, equity, and attribution process theories of work motivation.

Motivation is a basic psychological process. Few would deny that it is the most important focus in the micro approach to organizational behavior. Many people equate the causes of behavior with motivation. Chapter 1 and the four preceding chapters emphasized that the causes of behavior are much broader and more complex than can be explained by motivation alone. However, motivation should never be underrated. Along with perception, personality, attitudes, and learning, it is presented here as a very important process in understanding behavior. Nevertheless, it must be remembered that motivation should not be thought of as the only explanation of behavior. It interacts with and acts in conjunction with other mediating processes and the environment. It must also be remembered that, like the other mediating processes, motivation cannot be seen. All that can be seen is behavior. Motivation is a hypothetical construct that is used to help explain behavior; it should not be equated with behavior. In fact, while recognizing the "central role of motivation," many of today's organizational behavior theorists "think it is important for the field to reemphasize behavior."[1]

This chapter presents motivation as a basic psychological process. The more applied aspects of motivation are covered in the next chapter on job design and goal setting. The first section of this chapter clarifies the meaning of motivation by defining the relationship between its various parts. The need-drive-incentive cycle is defined and analyzed. The next section is devoted to an overview of the various types of needs or motives: primary, general, and secondary. The motives within the general and secondary categories are given major attention, and a summary of supporting research findings on these motives is included. The last half of the chapter presents the content and process theories of, and approaches to, work motivation.

THE MEANING OF MOTIVATION

Today, virtually all people—practitioners and scholars—have their own definition of motivation. Usually one or more of the following words are included in the definition: "desires," "wants," "wishes," "aims," "goals," "needs," "drives," "motives," and "incentives." Technically, the term *motivation* can be traced to the Latin word *movere*, which means "to move." This meaning is evident in the

FIGURE 6.1
The basic motivation process.

following comprehensive definition: Motivation is a process that starts with a physiological or psychological deficiency or need that activates behavior or a drive that is aimed at a goal or incentive. Thus, the key to understanding the process of motivation lies in the meaning of, and relationship between, needs, drives, and incentives.

Figure 6.1 graphically depicts the motivation process. Needs set up drives aimed at incentives; this is what the basic process of motivation is all about. In a systems sense, motivation consists of theses three interacting and interdependent elements:

1. *Needs.* Needs are created whenever there is a physiological or psychological imbalance. For example, a need exists when cells in the body are deprived of food and water or when the personality is deprived of other people who serve as friends or companions. Although psychological needs may be based on a deficiency, sometimes they are not. For example, an individual with a strong need to get ahead may have a history of consistent success.

2. *Drives.* With a few exceptions,[2] drives or motives (the two terms are often used interchangeably) are set up to alleviate needs. A physiological drive can be simply defined as a deficiency with direction. Physiological and psychological drives are action-oriented and provide an energizing thrust toward reaching an incentive. They are at the very heart of the motivational process. The examples of the needs for food and water are translated into the hunger and thirst drives, and the need for friends becomes a drive for affiliation.

3. *Incentives.* At the end of the motivation cycle is the incentive defined as anything that will alleviate a need and reduce a drive. Thus, attaining an incentive will tend to restore physiological or psychological balance and will reduce or cut off the drive. Eating food, drinking water, and obtaining friends will tend to restore the balance and reduce the corresponding drives. Food, water, and friends are the incentives in these examples.

PRIMARY MOTIVES

Psychologists do not totally agree on how to classify the various human motives, but they would acknowledge that some motives are unlearned and physiologically based. Such motives are variously called *physiological, biological, unlearned,* or *primary.* The last term is used here because it is more comprehensive than the others. The use of the term *primary* does not imply that this group of motives always takes precedence over the general and secondary motives. Although the precedence of primary motives is implied in some motivation theories, there are many situations in which general and secondary motives predominate over primary motives. Common examples are celibacy among priests and fasting for a religious, social, or political cause. In both cases, learned secondary motives are stronger than unlearned primary motives.

Two criteria must be met in order for a motive to be included in the primary classification: It must be *unlearned,* and it must be *physiologically based.* Thus defined, the most commonly recognized primary motives include hunger, thirst, sleep, avoidance of pain, sex, and maternal concern. Because people have the same basic physiological make-up, they will all have essentially the same primary needs. This is not true of the learned secondary needs.

GENERAL MOTIVES

A separate classification for general motives is not always given. Yet such a category seems necessary because there are a number of motives which lie in the gray area between the primary and secondary classifications. To be included in the general category, a motive must be unlearned but not physiologically based. While the primary needs seek to reduce the tension or stimulation, these general needs induce the person to increase the amount of stimulation. Thus, these needs are sometimes called "stimulus motives."[3] Although not all psychologists would agree, the motives of curiosity, manipulation, activity, and affection seem best to meet the criteria for this classification. An understanding of these general motives is important to the study of human behavior—especially in organizations. General motives are more relevant to organizational behavior than primary motives.

The Curiosity, Manipulation, and Activity Motives

Early psychologists noted that the animals used in their experiments seemed to have an unlearned drive to explore, to manipulate objects, or just to be active. This was especially true of monkeys that were placed in an unfamiliar or novel situation. These observations and speculations about the existence of curiosity, manipulation, and activity motives in monkeys were later substantiated through experimentation. In this case, psychologists feel completely confident in generalizing the results of animal experiments to humans. It is generally recognized that human curiosity, manipulation, and activity drives are quite intense; anyone who has reared or been around small children will quickly support this generalization.

Although these drives often get the small child into trouble, curiosity, manipulation, and activity, when carried forward to adulthood, can be very beneficial. If these motives were stifled or inhibited, the total society might become very stagnant. The same is true on an organizational level. If employees are not allowed to express their curiosity, manipulation, and activity motives, they may not be motivated. For example, sticking an employee behind a machine or a desk for eight hours a day may stifle these general motives.

The Affection Motive

Love or affection is a very complex form of general drive. Part of the complexity stems from the fact that in many ways love resembles the primary drives and in other ways it is similar to the secondary drives. In particular, the affection motive is closely associated with the primary sex motive, on the one hand, and with the secondary affiliation motive, on the other. For this reason, affection is sometimes placed in all three categories of motives, and some psychologists do not even recognize it as a separate motive.

Affection merits specific attention because of its growing importance to the modern world. There seems to be a great deal of truth to the adages, "Love makes the world go round" and "Love conquers all." In a world where we suffer from interpersonal, intraindividual, and national conflict and where quality of life and human rights are becoming increasingly important to modern society, the affection motive takes on added importance in the study of human behavior.

SECONDARY MOTIVES

Whereas the general drives seem relatively more important than the primary ones to the study of human behavior in organizations, the secondary drives are unquestionably the most important. As a human society develops economically and becomes more complex, the primary drives, and to a lesser degree the general drives, give way to the learned secondary drives in motivating behavior. With some glaring exceptions that have yet to be eradicated, the motives of hunger and thirst are not dominant among people living in the economically developed Western world. This situation is obviously subject to change; for example, the "population bomb" or the "greenhouse effect" may alter certain human needs. But for now, the learned secondary motives dominate.

Secondary motives are closely tied to the learning concepts that will be discussed in Chapter 8. In particular, the learning principle of reinforcement is conceptually and practically related to motivation. The relationship is obvious when reinforcement is divided into primary and secondary categories and is portrayed as incentives. Although some discussions regard reinforcement as simply a consequence serving to increase the *motivation* to perform the behavior again,[4] they are treated separately in this book. Once again, however, it should be emphasized that although the various behavioral concepts can be separated for study and analysis, in reality concepts like reinforcement and motivation do not operate as separate entities in producing human behavior. The interactive effects are always present.

A motive must be learned in order to be included in the *secondary* classification. Numerous important human motives meet this criterion. Some of the more important ones are power, achievement, and affiliation, or, as they are commonly referred to today, *n Pow*, *n Ach*, and *n Aff*. In addition, especially in reference to organizational behavior, security and status are important secondary motives. Table 6.1 gives examples of each of these important secondary needs.

The Power Motive

The power motive is discussed first because it has been formally recognized and studied for a relatively long time. The leading advocate of the power motive was the pioneering behavioral scientist Alfred Adler. Adler officially broke his close ties with Sigmund Freud and proposed an opposing theoretical position. Whereas Freud

TABLE 6.1 Examples of Key Secondary Needs

Need for Achievement
- Doing better than competitors
- Attaining or surpassing a difficult goal
- Solving a complex problem
- Carrying out a challenging assignment successfully
- Developing a better way to do something

Need for Power
- Influencing people to change their attitudes or behavior
- Controlling people and activities
- Being in a position of authority over others
- Gaining control over information and resources
- Defeating an opponent or enemy

Need for Affiliation
- Being liked by many people
- Being accepted as part of a group or team
- Working with people who are friendly and cooperative
- Maintaining harmonious relationships and avoiding conflicts
- Participating in pleasant social activities

Need for Security
- Having a secure job
- Being protected against loss of income or economic disaster
- Having protection against illness and disability
- Being protected against physical harm or hazardous conditions
- Avoiding tasks or decisions with a risk of failure and blame

Need for Status
- Having the right car and wearing the right clothes
- Working for the right company in the right job
- Having a degree from Harvard or Stanford
- Living in the right neighborhood and belonging to the country club
- Having executive privileges

Source: Adapted from Gary Yukl, *Skills for Managers and Leaders,* Prentice-Hall, Englewood Cliffs, N.J., 1990, p. 41. The examples of need for status were not covered by Yukl.

stressed the impact of the past and of sexual, unconscious motivation, Adler substituted the future and a person's overwhelming drive for superiority or power.

To explain the power need—the need to manipulate others or the drive for superiority over others—Adler developed the concepts of *inferiority complex* and *compensation.* He felt that every small child experiences a sense of inferiority. When this feeling of inferiority is combined with what he sensed as an innate need for superiority, the two rule all behavior. The person's lifestyle is characterized by striving to compensate for feelings of inferiority, which are combined with the innate drive for power.

Although modern psychologists do not generally accept the tenet that the power drive is inborn and so dominant, in recent years it has prompted renewed interest. The quest for power is readily observable in modern American society. The politician is probably the best example, and political scandals make a fascinating study of the striving for, and use of, power in government and politics. However, in addition to politicians, anyone in a responsible position in business, government, unions, education, or the military may also exhibit a considerable need for power. The power motive has significant implications for organizational leadership and for the informal, political aspects of organizations. Chapter 15 will examine in detail the dynamics of power. It has emerged as one of the most important dynamics in the study of organizational behavior.

The Achievement Motive

Whereas the power motive has been recognized and discussed for a long time, only very recently has there been any research activity. The opposite is true of the achievement motive. Although it does not have as long a history as the other motives, more is known about achievement than about any other motive because of the tremendous amount of research that has been devoted to it. The Thematic Apperception Test (TAT) has proved to be a very effective tool in researching achievement. The TAT can effectively identify and measure the achievement motive. The test works in the following manner: One picture in the TAT shows a young man plowing a field; the sun is about to sink in the west. The person taking the test is supposed to tell a story about what he or she sees in the picture. The story will project the person's major motives. For example, the test taker may say that the man in the picture is sorry the sun is going down because he still has more land to plow and he wants to get the crops planted before it rains. Such a response indicates high achievement. A low achiever might say that the man is happy the sun is finally going down so that he can go into the house, relax, and have a cool drink. The research approach to achievement has become so effective that it is often cited by psychologists as a prototype of how knowledge and understanding can be gained in the behavioral sciences.

David C. McClelland, a Harvard psychologist, is most closely associated with study of the achievement motive, and, as Chapter 15 will indicate, he is now doing considerable research on power as well. McClelland thoroughly investigated and wrote about all aspects of *n Ach* (achievement). Out of this extensive research has emerged a clear profile of the characteristics of the high achiever. Very simply, the achievement motive can be expressed as a desire to perform in terms of a standard of excellence or to be successful in competitive situations. The specific characteristics of a high achiever can be summarized in the following sections.

Moderate Risk Taking. Taking moderate risks is probably the single most descriptive characteristic of the person possessing high *n Ach*. On the surface it would seem that a high achiever would take high risks. However, once again research gives a different answer from the commonsense one. The ring-toss game can be used to demonstrate risk-taking behavior. It has been shown that when ring tossers are told that they may stand anywhere they want to when they toss the rings at the peg, low and high achievers behave quite differently. Low achievers tend either to stand very close and just drop the rings over the peg or to stand very far away and wildly throw the rings at the peg. In contrast, high achievers almost always carefully calculate the exact distance from the peg that will challenge their own abilities. People with high *n Ach* will not stand too close because it would be no test of their ability simply to drop the rings over the peg. By the same token, they will not stand ridiculously far away because luck and not skill would then determine whether the rings landed on the peg. In other words, low achievers take either a high or low risk, and high achievers take a moderate risk. This seems to hold true both for the simple children's game and for important adult decisions and activities.

Need for Immediate Feedback. Closely connected to high achievers' taking moderate risks is their desire for immediate feedback. People with high *n Ach* prefer activities which provide immediate and precise feedback information on how they are progressing toward a goal. Some hobbies and vocations offer such feedback, and others do not. High achievers generally prefer hobbies such as woodworking or mechanics, which provide prompt, exact feedback, and they shy away from the coin-collecting type of hobby, which takes years to develop. Likewise, high achievers tend to gravitate toward, or at least to be more satisfied in, jobs or careers, such as sales or certain management positions, in which they are frequently evaluated by specific performance criteria. On the other end of the scale, high *n Ach* persons are generally not to be found, or tend to be frustrated, in research and development or teaching vocations, where feedback on performance is very imprecise, vague, and long-range.

Satisfaction with Accomplishment. High achievers find accomplishing a task intrinsically satisfying in and of itself, or they do not expect or necessarily want the accompanying material rewards. A good illustration of this characteristic involves money, but not for the usual reasons of wanting money for its own sake or for the material benefits that it can buy. Rather, high *n Ach* people look at money as a form of feedback or measurement of how they are doing. Given the choice between a simple task with a good payoff for accomplishment, and a more difficult task with a lesser payoff, other things being equal, high achievers generally choose the latter.

Preoccupation with the Task. Once high achievers select a goal, they tend to be totally preoccupied with the task until it is successfully completed. They cannot stand to leave a job half finished and are not satisfied with themselves until they have given their maximum effort. This type of dedicated commitment is often reflected in their outward personalities, which frequently have a negative effect on those who come into contact with them. High achievers often strike others as being unfriendly and as "loners." They may be very quiet and may seldom brag about their accomplishments. They tend to be very realistic about their abilities and do not allow other people to get in the way of their goal accomplishments. Obviously, with this type of approach, high achievers do not always get along well with other people. Typically, high achievers make excellent salespersons but seldom good sales managers.

The accompanying Application Example, High Achievers in Action, gives the strategies entrepreneurs use to start new businesses. Almost all such entrepreneurs have a relatively high need for achievement.

The Affiliation Motive

Affiliation plays a very complex but vital role in human behavior. Sometimes affiliation is equated with social motives and/or group dynamics. As presented here, the affiliation motive is neither as broad as is implied by the definition of social motives nor as comprehensive or complex as is implied by the definition of group dynamics. The study of affiliation is further complicated by the fact that some behavioral scientists believe that it is an unlearned motive. Going as far back as the Hawthorne studies, the importance of the affiliation motive in the behavior of organizational participants has been very clear. Employees, especially rank-and-file employees, have a very intense need to belong to, and be accepted by, the group. This affiliation motive is an important part of group dynamics, which is the subject of Chapter 12.

Application Example
||||➡

High Achievers in Action

One of the best examples of high achievers are entrepreneurs who start and manage their own businesses. While many of these owner-managers do not stay in business more than five years, a large percentage are very successful and manage to keep their enterprises afloat for an indefinite period. How do successful entrepreneurs operate? By sidestepping the potential pitfalls and problems before they even open the doors of their new venture. Prior to starting, they take steps to ensure that the enterprise is able to survive the first two years—the most critical period for most small business ventures. Some of the strategic steps they take include the following:

1. Draw up a five-year plan. This assures entrepreneurs that they will have goals to aim for during the first sixty months of operation. The plan often has both annual and quarterly forecasts.
2. Raise more money than is needed. One of the biggest problems is running out of capital. To ensure that this does not happen, successful entrepreneurs allow for a margin of error by starting out with more money than they estimate will be needed. Then, if sales are not generated as quickly as forecasted, the new company has enough capital to tide it over.
3. Test the market. Successful entrepreneurs look over their market and ensure that there is sufficient demand for their goods or services. If the demand is weak, they look for different geographic locales. If the demand is strong, they look for specific target markets they can further exploit.
4. Don't take no for an answer. If the bank turns down an application for a loan, successful entrepreneurs find out why. If there is something wrong with their financial plan, they fix it. If their projected costs of operations are too high, they figure out ways of reducing them. They then return to the bank and get the loan—or find another financial institution that is willing to give them the loan.

The Security Motive

Security is a very intense motive in a fast-paced, highly technological society such as is found in modern America. The typical American can be insecure in a number of areas of everyday living—for example, being liable for payments on a car or house, keeping a lover's or a spouse's affections, staying in school, getting into graduate school, or obtaining and/or keeping a good job. Job insecurity, in particular, has a great effect on organizational behavior. For example, the Chapter 5 discussion of organizational commitment indicated that, because of the "downsizing" mania of the last several years, most employees at all levels are feeling very insecure about their jobs. On the surface, security appears to be much simpler than other secondary motives, for it is based largely on fear and is avoidance-oriented. Very briefly, it can be said that people have a learned security motive to protect themselves from the contingencies of life and actively try to avoid situations which would prevent them from satisfying their primary, general, and secondary motives.

In reality, security is much more complex than it appears on the surface. There is the simple, conscious security motive described above, but there also seems to be another type of security motive that is much more complicated and difficult to identify. This latter form of security is largely unconscious but may greatly influence the behavior of many people. The simple, conscious security motive is typically taken care of by insurance programs, personal savings plans, and other fringe benefits at the place of employment. An innovative company such as the Washington, D.C.–based insurance company Consumers United Group never lays off its employees and has a minimum annual salary of $18,000 designed to give a family a secure, decent living.[5] On the other hand, the more complex, unconscious security motive is not so easily fulfilled but may have a greater and more intense impact on human behavior. Although much attention has been given to the simple security motive, much more understanding is needed concerning the role of the unconscious, complex security motive.

The Status Motive

Along with security, the status or prestige motive is especially relevant to a dynamic society. The modern affluent person is often pictured as a status seeker. Such a person is accused of being more concerned with the material symbols of status—the right clothes, the right car, the right address, and a swimming pool or the latest computer software—than with the more basic, human-oriented values in life. Although the symbols of status are considered a unique by-product of modern society, the fact is that status has been in existence since there have been two or more persons on the earth.

Status can be simply defined as the *relative* ranking that a person holds in a group, organization, or society. Under this definition, any time two or more persons are together, a status hierarchy will evolve, even if both have equal status. The symbols of status attempt to represent only the relative ranking of the person in the status hierarchy. The definition also corrects the common misconception that "status" means "high status." Everyone has status, but it may be high or low, depending on how the relative positions are ranked.

How are status positions determined? Why is one person ranked higher or lower than another? In the final analysis, status determination depends upon the prevailing cultural values and societal roles. Status-determining factors generally have quite different meanings, depending on the values of the particular culture. An example of the impact of cultural values on status is the personal qualities of people. In some cultures, the older persons are, the higher their status. However, in other cultures, once a person reaches a certain age, the status goes downhill. It must be remembered that such cultural values are highly volatile and change with the times and circumstances. There are also many subcultures in a given society which may have values different from the prevailing values of society at large and correspondingly different statuses.

WORK–MOTIVATION APPROACHES

So far, motivation has been presented as a basic psychological process consisting of primary, general, and secondary motives and drives such as the *n Pow, n Aff,* and *n Ach* motives. In order to understand organizational behavior, these basic motives must be recognized and studied. However, these serve as only background and foundation for the more directly relevant work-motivation approaches.

Figure 6.2 graphically summarizes the various theoretical streams for work motivation. In particular, the figure shows four major approaches. The content models go as far back as the turn of the century, when pioneering scientific managers such as Frederick W. Taylor, Frank Gilbreth, and Henry L. Gantt proposed sophisticated wage incentive models to motivate workers. Next came the human relations movement, and then the content models of Maslow, Herzberg, and Alderfer. More recent developments have come from process models. Most work has been done on expectancy-based process models, but recently, equity and attribution theories have received attention. These process models are cognitively based; other cognitive models exist in psychology, but equity and attribution are the ones that have had the greatest influence on work motivation so far. Figure 6.2 purposely shows that at present there is a lack of integration or synthesis of the various models. In addition to this need for integration, a comprehensive assessment of the status of work-motivation theory also noted the need for contingency models and group/

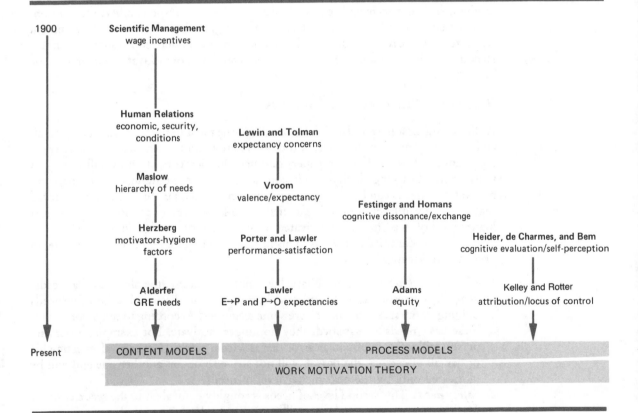

FIGURE 6.2
The theoretical development of work motivation.

social processes.[6] At present, however, a group of content models can be identified and a group of process models can be identified, but an overall theory of work motivation does not exist.

THE CONTENT THEORIES OF WORK MOTIVATION

The content theories of work motivation attempt to determine what it is that motivates people at work. The content theorists are concerned with identifying the needs/drives that people have and how these needs/drives are prioritized. They are concerned with the types of incentives or goals that people strive to attain in order to be satisfied and perform well. The content theories are referred to as "static" because they incorporate only one or a few points in time and are either past- or present-time oriented. Therefore, they do not necessarily predict work motivation or behavior, but are still important to understanding what motivates people at work.[7]

At first, money was felt to be the only incentive (scientific management), and then a little later it was felt that incentives include working conditions, security, and perhaps a democratic style of supervision (human relations). More recently, the content of motivation has been deemed to be the so-called "higher-level" needs or motives, such as esteem and self-actualization (Maslow); responsibility, recognition, achievement, and advancement (Herzberg); and growth and personal development (Alderfer). A thorough study of the major content models contributes to understanding and leads to some of the application techniques of motivation covered in the next chapter.

Maslow's Hierarchy of Needs

Although the first part of the chapter discussed the most important primary, general, and secondary needs of humans, it did not relate them to a theoretical framework. Abraham Maslow, in a classic paper, outlined the elements of an overall theory of motivation.[8] Drawing chiefly on his clinical experience, he thought that a person's motivational needs can be arranged in a hierarchical manner. In essence, he believed that once a given level of need is satisfied, it no longer serves to motivate. The next higher level of need has to be activated in order to motivate the individual.

Maslow identified five levels in his need hierarchy (see Figure 6.3). They are, in brief, the following:

1. *Physiological needs.* The most basic level in the hierarchy, the physiological needs, generally corresponds to the unlearned primary needs discussed earlier. The needs of hunger, thirst, sleep, and sex are some examples. According to the theory, once these basic needs are satisfied, they no longer motivate. For example, a starving person will strive to obtain a carrot that is within reach. However, after eating his or her fill of carrots, the person will not strive to obtain another one and will be motivated only by the next higher level of needs.
2. *Safety needs.* This second level of needs is roughly equivalent to the security need. Maslow stressed emotional as well as physical safety. The whole organism may become a safety-seeking mechanism. Yet, as is true of the physiological needs, once these safety needs are satisfied, they no longer motivate.

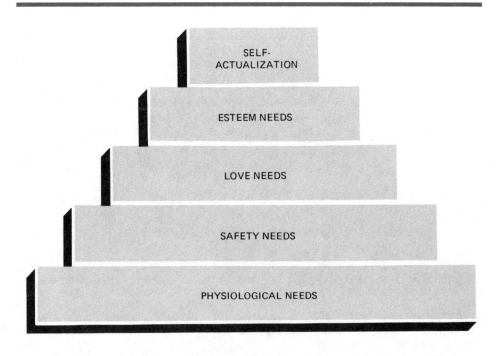

FIGURE 6.3
Maslow's hierarchy of needs.

3. *Love needs.* This third, or intermediate, level of needs loosely corresponds to the affection and affiliation needs. Like Freud, Maslow seems guilty of poor choice of wording to identify his levels. His use of the word "love" has many misleading connotations, such as sex, which is actually a physiological need. Perhaps a more appropriate word describing this level would be "belongingness" or "social."

4. *Esteem needs.* The esteem level represents the higher needs of humans. The needs for power, achievement, and status can be considered to be part of this level. Maslow carefully pointed out that the esteem level contains both self-esteem and esteem from others.

5. *Needs for self-actualization.* This level represents the culmination of all the lower, intermediate, and higher needs of humans. People who have become self-actualized are self-fulfilled and have realized all their potential. Self-actualization is closely related to the self-concept discussed in Chapter 4. In effect, self-actualization is the person's motivation to transform perception of self into reality.

Maslow did not intend that his need hierarchy be directly applied to work motivation. In fact, he did not delve into the motivating aspects of humans in organizations until about twenty years after he originally proposed his theory. Despite this lack of intent on Maslow's part, others, such as Douglas McGregor, in his widely read book *The Human Side of Enterprise,* popularized the Maslow theory in management literature. The need hierarchy has had a tremendous impact on the modern management approach to motivation.

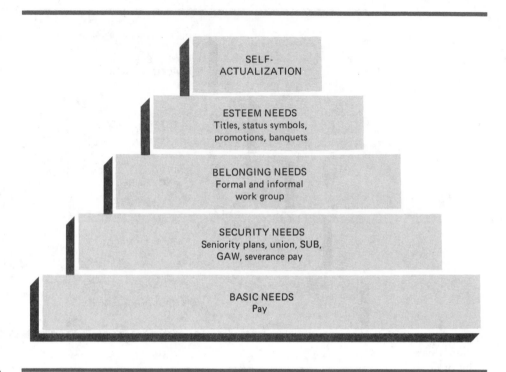

FIGURE 6.4
A hierarchy of
work motivation.

In a very rough manner, Maslow's need hierarchy theory can be converted into the content model of work motivation shown in Figure 6.4. If Maslow's estimates are applied to an organization example, the lower-level needs of personnel would be generally satisfied (85 percent of the basic needs and 70 percent of the security needs), but only 50 percent of the belongingness needs, 40 percent of the esteem needs, and a mere 10 percent of the self-actualization needs would be met.

On the surface, the content model shown in Figure 6.4 and the estimated percentages given by Maslow seem logical and applicable to the motivation of humans in today's organizations. Maslow's need hierarchy has often been uncritically accepted by writers of management textbooks and by practitioners. Unfortunately, the limited research that has been conducted lends little empirical support to the theory. About a decade after publishing his original paper, Maslow did attempt to clarify his position by saying that gratifying the self-actualizing need of growth-motivated individuals can actually increase rather than decrease this need. He also hedged on some of his other original ideas, for example, that higher needs may emerge after lower needs that have been unfulfilled or suppressed for a long period are satisfied. He stressed that human behavior is multidetermined and multimotivated.

Most research findings indicate that Maslow's is not the final answer in work motivation. Yet the model does make a significant contribution in terms of making management aware of the diverse needs of humans at work. As one recent comprehensive analysis concluded, "indeed, the general ideas behind Maslow's theory seem to be supported, such as the distinction between deficiency needs and growth needs."[9] However, the number and names of the levels are not so important, nor, as the studies show, is the hierarchical concept. What is important is the fact that humans in the workplace have diverse motives, some of which are "high-level." In other words, such needs as esteem and self-actualization are important to the content of work motivation. The exact nature of these needs and how they relate to motivation are not clear. To try to overcome some of the problems of the Maslow hierarchy, Alderfer has more recently proposed the ERG model, which contains three groups of needs. This model will be covered after the discussion of Herzberg's two-factor theory.

Herzberg's Two—Factor Theory of Motivation

Herzberg extended the work of Maslow and developed a specific content theory of work motivation. He conducted a widely reported motivational study on about 200 accountants and engineers employed by firms in and around Pittsburgh, Pennsylvania. He used the critical incident method of obtaining data for analysis. The professional subjects in the study were essentially asked two questions: (1) When did you feel particularly good about your job—what turned you on; and (2) when did you feel exceptionally bad about your job—what turned you off?

Responses obtained from this critical incident method were interesting and fairly consistent. Reported good feelings were generally associated with job experiences and job content. An example was the accounting supervisor who felt good about being given the job of installing new computer equipment. He took pride in his work and was gratified to know that the new equipment made a big difference in the overall functioning of his department. Reported bad feelings, on the other hand, were generally associated with the surrounding or peripheral aspects of the job—the job context. An example of these feelings was related by an engineer whose first job was to keep tabulation sheets and manage the office when the boss was gone. It turned out that his boss was always too busy to train him and became annoyed when he tried to ask questions. The engineer said that he was frustrated in this job context and that he felt like a flunky in a dead-end job. Tabulating these reported good and bad feelings, Herzberg concluded that job satisfiers are related to job content and that job dissatisfiers are allied to job context. Herzberg labeled satisfiers *motivators*, and he called the dissatisfiers *hygiene factors*. Taken together, they became known as Herzberg's *two-factor theory of motivation*.

Relation to Maslow. Herzberg's theory is closely related to Maslow's need hierarchy. The hygiene factors are preventive and environmental in nature, and they are roughly equivalent to Maslow's lower-level needs (see Table 6.2). These hygiene factors prevent dissatisfaction, but they do not lead to satisfaction. In effect, they bring motivation up to a theoretical zero level and are a necessary "floor" to prevent dissatisfaction, and they serve as a takeoff point for motivation. By themselves, the hygiene factors do not motivate. Only the motivators (see Table 6.2) motivate humans on the job. They are roughly equivalent to Maslow's higher-level needs. According to the Herzberg theory, an individual must have a job with a challenging content in order to be truly motivated.

TABLE 6.2 Herzberg's Two-Factor Theory

Hygiene Factors	Motivators
Company policy and administration	Achievement
Supervision, technical	Recognition
Salary	Work itself
Interpersonal relations, supervisor	Responsibility
Working conditions	Advancement

Contribution to Work Motivation. Herzberg's two-factor theory cast a new light on the content of work motivation. Up to this point, management had generally concentrated on the hygiene factors. When faced with a morale problem, the typical solution was higher pay, more fringe benefits, and better working conditions. However, as has been pointed out, this simplistic solution did not really work. Management are often perplexed because they are paying high wages and salaries, have an excellent fringe-benefit package, and provide great working conditions, but their employees are still not motivated. Herzberg's theory offers an explanation for this problem. By concentrating only on the hygiene factors, management are not motivating their personnel.

There are probably very few workers or managers who do not feel that they deserved the raise they received. On the other hand, there are many dissatisfied workers and managers who feel they did not get a large-enough raise. This simple observation points out that the hygiene factors seem to be important in preventing dissatisfaction but do not lead to satisfaction. Herzberg would be the first to say that the hygiene factors are absolutely necessary to maintain the human resources of an organization. However, as in the Maslow sense, once "the belly is full" of hygiene factors, which is the case in most modern organizations, dangling any more in front of employees will not motivate them. According to Herzberg's theory, only a challenging job which has the opportunities for achievement, recognition, responsibility, advancement, and growth will motivate personnel.

Critical Analysis of Herzberg's Theory. Although Herzberg's two-factor theory became very popular as a textbook explanation of work motivation and was widely accepted by practitioners, it also is true that from an academic perspective the theory oversimplifies the complexities of work motivation. When researchers deviate from the critical incident methodology used by Herzberg, they do not get the two factors. There seem to be job factors that lead to both satisfaction and dissatisfaction. These findings indicate that a strict interpretation of the two-factor theory is not warranted.

In spite of the obvious limitations, few would question that Herzberg contributed substantially to the study of work motivation. He extended Maslow's need hierarchy concept and made it more applicable to work motivation. Herzberg also drew attention to the importance of job content factors in work motivation, which previously had been badly neglected and often totally overlooked. The job design technique of job enrichment is also one of Herzberg's contributions. Job enrichment is covered in detail in the next chapter. Overall, Herzberg added much to the better understanding of job content factors and satisfaction, but, like his predecessors, he fell short of a comprehensive theory of work motivation. His model describes only some of the content of work motivation; it does not adequately describe the complex motivation process of organizational participants.

Alderfer's ERG Theory

An extension of the Herzberg and, especially, the Maslow content theories of work motivation comes from the work of Clayton Alderfer. He formulated a need category model that was more in line with the existing empirical evidence. Like Maslow and Herzberg, he does feel that there is value in categorizing needs and that there is a basic distinction between lower-order needs and higher-order needs.

Alderfer identified three groups of core needs: existence, relatedness, and growth (hence ERG theory). The *existence needs* are concerned with survival (physiological well-being). The *relatedness needs* stress the importance of interpersonal, social relationships. The *growth needs* are concerned with the individual's intrinsic desire for personal development. Figure 6.5 shows how these groups of needs are related to the Maslow and Herzberg categories. Obviously, they are very close, but the ERG needs do not have strict lines of demarcation.

Alderfer is suggesting more of a continuum of needs than hierarchical levels or two factors of prepotency needs. Unlike Maslow and Herzberg, he does not contend that a lower-level need has to be fulfilled before a higher-level need is motivating or that deprivation is the only way to activate a need. For example, under ERG theory the person's background or cultural environment may dictate that the relatedness

FIGURE 6.5
The relationship between Alderfer's ERG needs, Maslow's five-level hierarchy, and Herzberg's two-factor theory.

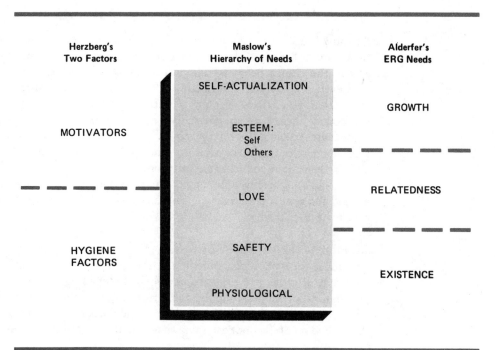

Herzberg's Two Factors	Maslow's Hierarchy of Needs	Alderfer's ERG Needs
	SELF-ACTUALIZATION	GROWTH
MOTIVATORS	ESTEEM: Self Others	
	LOVE	RELATEDNESS
HYGIENE FACTORS	SAFETY	EXISTENCE
	PHYSIOLOGICAL	

needs will take precedence over unfulfilled existence needs and that the more the growth needs are satisfied, the more they will increase in intensity.

There has not been a great deal of research on ERG theory. Although there is some evidence to counter the theory's predictive value, most contemporary analyses of work motivation tend to support Alderfer's theory over Maslow's and Herzberg's. Overall, the ERG theory seems to take some of the strong points of the earlier content theories but is less restrictive and limiting. The fact remains, however, that the content theories in general lack explanatory power over the complexities of work motivation and, with the possible exception of the implications for job design of Herzberg's work, do not readily translate to the actual practice of human resources management.

THE PROCESS THEORIES OF WORK MOTIVATION

The content models attempt to identify what motivates people at work (for example, self-actualization, responsibility, and growth); they try to specify correlates of motivated behavior. The process theories, on the other hand, are more concerned with the cognitive antecedents that go into motivation or effort and, more important, with the way they relate to one another. As Figure 6.2 shows, the expectancy models make the most significant contribution to understanding the complex processes involved in work motivation. After these are examined, equity and attribution theories will also be presented and analyzed as major process models of work motivation.

Vroom's Expectancy Theory of Motivation

As shown in Figure 6.2, the expectancy theory of work motivation has its roots in the cognitive concepts of pioneering psychologists Kurt Lewin and Edward Tolman and in the choice behavior and utility concepts from classical economic theory. However, the first to formulate an expectancy theory directly aimed at work motivation was Victor Vroom. Contrary to most critics, Vroom proposed his expectancy theory as an alternative to the content models, which he felt were inadequate explanations of the complex process of work motivation. At least in academic circles, his theory has become a popular explanation for work motivation and has generated considerable research.

Figure 6.6 briefly summarizes the Vroom model. As shown, the model is built around the concepts of valence, instrumentality, and expectancy and is commonly called the *VIE theory*.

Meaning of the Variables. By *valence*, Vroom means the strength of an individual's preference for a particular outcome. Other terms that might be used include *value, incentive, attitude,* and *expected utility*. In order for the valence to be positive, the person must prefer attaining the outcome to not attaining it. A valence of zero occurs when the individual is indifferent toward the outcome; the valence is negative when the individual prefers not attaining the outcome to attaining it. Another major input

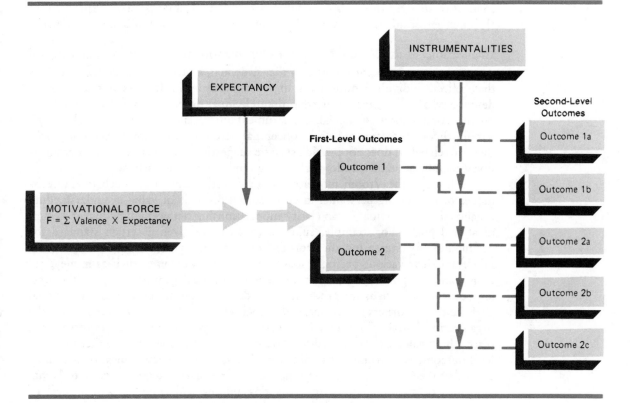

FIGURE 6.6
The Vroom expectancy, or VIE, theory of work motivation.

into the valence is the *instrumentality* of the first-level outcome in obtaining a desired second-level outcome. For example, the person would be motivated toward superior performance because of the desire to be promoted. The superior performance (first-level outcome) is seen as being instrumental in obtaining promotion (second-level outcome).

Another major variable in the Vroom motivational process is *expectancy*. Although psychological theorists all agree that expectancies are mental or cognitive states, there is little agreement about the nature of these states.[10] Although at first glance the expectancy concept may seem to be the same as the instrumentality input into valence, it is actually quite different. Expectancy relates efforts to first-level outcomes (see Figure 6.6), while instrumentality relates first-level outcomes and second-level outcomes. In other words, expectancy in Vroom's theory is the probability (ranging from 0 to 1) that a particular action or effort will lead to a particular *first-level* outcome. *Instrumentality* refers to the degree to which a first-level outcome will lead to a desired *second-level* outcome. In summary, the strength of the motivation to perform a certain act will depend on the algebraic sum of the products of the valences for the outcomes (which include instrumentality) times the expectancies.

Implications of the Vroom Model for Organizational Behavior. Vroom's theory departs from the content theories in that it depicts a process of cognitive variables that reflects individual differences in work motivation. It does not attempt to describe what the content is or what the individual differences are. Everyone has a unique combination of valences, instrumentalities, and expectancies. Thus, the Vroom theory indicates only the conceptual determinants of motivation and how they are related. It does not provide specific suggestions on what motivates organizational members, as the Maslow, Herzberg, and Alderfer models do.

Although the Vroom model does not directly contribute much to the techniques of motivating personnel in an organization, it is of value in understanding organizational behavior. It can clarify the relationship between individual and organizational goals. For example, suppose workers are given a certain standard for production. By measuring the workers' output, management can determine how important their various personal goals (second-level outcomes such as money, security, and recognition) are; the instrumentality of the organizational goal (the first-level outcomes, such as the production standard) for the attainment of the personal goals; and the workers' expectancies that their effort and ability will accomplish the organizational goal. If output is below standard, it may be that the workers do not place a high value on the second-level outcomes; or they may not see that the first-level outcome is instrumental in obtaining the second-level outcomes; or they may think that their efforts will not accomplish the first-level outcome. Vroom feels that any one, or a combination, of these possibilities will result in a low level of motivation to produce. The model is designed to help management understand and anaylze workers' motivation and identify some of the relevant variables; it does not provide specific solutions to motivational problems. Besides the application problem, the model also assumes, as earlier economic theory did, that people are rational and logically calculating. Such an assumption may be unrealistic.

Importance of the Vroom Model. Probably the major reason why Vroom's model has emerged as an important modern theory of work motivation and has generated so much research is that it does not take a simplistic approach. The content theories oversimplify human motivation. Yet the content theories remain extremely popular with practicing managers because the concepts are easy to understand and to apply to their own situations. On the other hand, the VIE theory recognizes the complexities of work motivation, but it is relatively difficult to understand and apply. Thus, from a theoretical standpoint, the VIE model seems to help managers appreciate the complexities of motivation, but it does not give them much practical help in solving their motivational problems.

In some ways Vroom's expectancy model is like marginal analysis in economics. Businesspeople do not actually calculate the point where marginal cost equals marginal revenue, but it is still a useful concept for a theory of the firm. The expectancy model attempts only to mirror the complex motivational process; it does not attempt to describe how motivational decisions are actually made or to solve actual motivational problems facing a manager.

The Porter-Lawler Model

Comments in Chapter 5 on job satisfaction referred to the controversy over the relationship between satisfaction and performance that has existed since the human relations movement. The content theories implicitly assume that satisfaction leads to improved performance and that dissatisfaction detracts from performance. The Herzberg model is really a theory of job satisfaction, but still it does not deal with the relationship between satisfaction and performance. The Vroom model also largely avoids the relationship between satisfaction and performance. Although satisfactions make an input into Vroom's concept of valence and although the outcomes have performance implications, it was not until Porter and Lawler refined and extended Vroom's model (for example, the relationships are expressed diagrammatically rather than mathematically, there are more variables, and the cognitive process of perception plays a central role) that the relationship between satisfaction and performance was dealt with directly by a motivation model.

Porter and Lawler start with the premise that motivation (effort or force) does not equal satisfaction and/or performance. Motivation, satisfaction, and performance are all separate variables and relate in ways different from what was traditionally assumed. Figure 6.7 depicts the multivariable model used to explain the complex relationship that exists between motivation, performance, and satisfaction. As shown in the model, boxes 1, 2, and 3 are basically the same as the Vroom equation. It is important, however, that Porter and Lawler point out that effort (force or motivation) does not directly lead to performance. It is mediated by abilities/traits and role perceptions. More important in the Porter-Lawler model is what happens after the performance. The rewards that follow and how these are perceived will determine satisfaction. In other words, the Porter-Lawler model suggests—and this is a significant turn of events from traditional thinking—that performance leads to satisfaction.

A recent comprehensive review of research verifies the importance of rewards in the relationship between performance and satisfaction. Specifically it was concluded that performance and satisfaction will be more strongly related when rewards are made contingent upon performance than when they are not.[11]

Implications for Practice. Although the Porter-Lawler model is more applications-oriented than the Vroom model, it is still quite complex and has proved to be a difficult way to bridge the gap to actual management practice. To Porter and Lawler's credit, they have been very conscious of putting their theory and research into practice. They recommend that practicing managers go beyond traditional attitude measurement and attempt to measure variables such as the values of possible rewards, the perceptions of effort-reward probabilities, and role perceptions. These variables, of course, can help managers better understand what goes into employee effort and performance. Giving attention to the consequences of performance, Porter

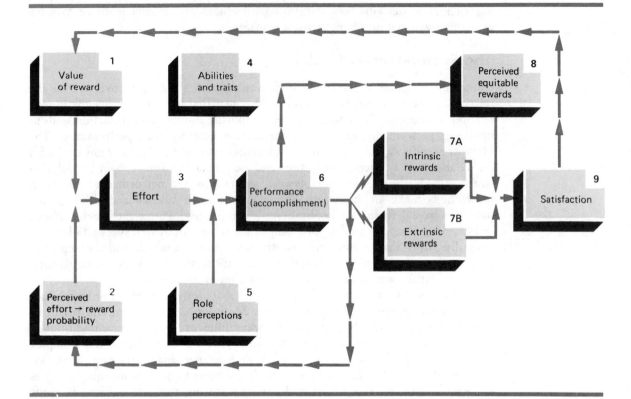

FIGURE 6.7
The Porter-Lawler motivation model.
(*Source:* Lyman W. Porter and Edward E. Lawler III, *Managerial Attitudes and Performance,*
Irwin, Homewood, Ill., 1968, p. 165. Used with permission.)

and Lawler also recommend that organizations critically reevaluate their current reward policies. They stress that management should make a concentrated effort to measure how closely levels of satisfaction are related to levels of performance. These types of recommendations have been verified by research.

Contributions to Work Motivation. The Porter and Lawler model has definitely made a significant contribution to the better understanding of work motivation and the relationship between performance and satisfaction, but, to date, it has not had much impact on the actual practice of human resources management. Yet the expectancy models provide certain guidelines that can be followed by human resources management. For example, on the front end (the relationship between motivation and performance), it has been suggested that the following barriers must be overcome:

1. Doubts about ability, skill, or knowledge
2. The physical or practical possibility of the job

3. The interdependence of the job with other people or activities
4. Ambiguity surrounding the job requirements[12]

In addition, on the back end (the relationship between performance and satisfaction), guidelines such as the following have been suggested:

1. Determine what rewards each employee values
2. Define desired performance
3. Make desired performance attainable
4. Link valued rewards to performance[13]

The last point above is getting recognition in the management compensation plans of many big companies, as indicated by the accompanying Application Example.

Application Example

Linking Manager's Rewards with Unit Performance

Linking rewards to performance has received attention in top management, as well as in low-level employee ranks. Traditionally, top management bonuses and profit sharing have been tied into overall company performance. However, with the increased diversity and autonomy of large companies, a manager in one division may be performing very well while the overall company profits are down. This high-performing manager may not be rewarded. Now, companies such as Westinghouse (with twenty-three units ranging from broadcasting to nuclear power) have moved to link rewards to unit, rather than overall company, performance results. As the head of compensation for Westinghouse noted, "we can't have one [incentive] formula that applies to everyone because each business is different. Some are in tough growth markets, and others are in stable, cash-cow markets." Thus, companies such as Westinghouse are dropping their bonus and stock-option incentives based on overall corporate profits and instead tying rewards more to unit profit centers.

In addition to these guidelines, by recognizing the reward implications in the Porter-Lawler model, especially the intrinsic-extrinsic distinction, there has been a move away from a strictly cognitive view of work motivation and toward more of an operant, environmentally based view of motivation. Chapters 8 and 9 will discuss this view in detail.

Equity Theory of Work Motivation

Equity theory has been around just as long as the expectancy theories of work motivation. However, only recently has equity as a process of motivation received widespread attention in the organizational behavior field. As Figure 6.2 indicates, its roots can be traced back to cognitive dissonance theory and exchange theory. As a theory of work motivation, credit for equity theory is usually given to J. Stacy Adams. Simply put, the theory argues that a major input into job performance and satisfaction is the degree of equity (or inequity) that people perceive in their work situation. In other words, it is another cognitively based motivation theory, and Adams depicts a specific process of how this motivation occurs.

Inequity occurs when a person perceives that the ratio of his or her outcomes to inputs and the ratio of a relevant other's outcomes to inputs are unequal. Schematically this is represented as follows:

$$\frac{\text{Person's outcomes}}{\text{Person's inputs}} < \frac{\text{other's outcomes}}{\text{other's inputs}}$$

$$\frac{\text{Person's outcomes}}{\text{Person's inputs}} > \frac{\text{other's outcomes}}{\text{other's inputs}}$$

Equity occurs when

$$\frac{\text{Person's outcomes}}{\text{Person's inputs}} = \frac{\text{other's outcomes}}{\text{other's inputs}}$$

Both the inputs and the outputs of person and other are based upon the person's perceptions. Age, sex, education, social status, organizational position, qualifications, and how hard the person works are examples of perceived input variables. Outcomes consist primarily of rewards such as pay, status, promotion, and intrinsic interest in the job. In essence, the ratio is based upon the person's *perception* of what the person is giving (inputs) and receiving (outcomes) versus the ratio of what the relevant other is giving and receiving. This cognition may or may not be the same as someone else's observation of the ratios or the same as the actual situation.

If the person's perceived ratio is not equal to the other's, he or she will strive to restore the ratio to equity. This "striving" to restore equity is used as the explanation of work motivation. The strength of this motivation is in direct proportion to the perceived inequity that exists. Adams suggests that such motivation may be expressed in several forms. To restore equity, the person may alter the inputs or outcomes, cognitively distort the inputs or outcomes, leave the field, act on the other, or change the other.

It is important to note that inequity does not come about only when the person feels cheated. For example, Adams has studied the impact that perceived overpayment has on equity. His findings suggest that workers prefer equitable payment to overpayment. Workers on a piece-rate incentive system who feel overpaid will reduce their productivity in order to restore equity. More likely, however, is the case of people who feel underpaid (outcome) or overworked (input) in relation to others in the workplace. In the latter case, there would be motivation to restore equity in a way that may be dysfunctional from an organizational standpoint. For example, the owner of an appliance store in Oakland, California, allowed his employees to set their own wages. Interestingly, none of the employees took an increase in pay, and one serviceman actually settled on lower pay because he did not want to work as hard as the others.[14]

To date, research that has specifically tested the validity of Adams' equity theory has been fairly supportive. A comprehensive review found considerable laboratory research support for the "equity norm" (persons review the inputs and outcomes of themselves and others, and if inequity is perceived, they strive to restore equity) but only limited support from more relevant field studies.[15] One line of recent field research on equity theory uses baseball players. One study of players who played out their option year, and thus felt they were inequitably paid, performed as the theory would predict.[16] Their performance decreased in three of four categories (not batting average) during the option year, and when they were signed to a new contract, the performance was restored. However, a more recent study using the same type of sample, only larger, found the opposite to what equity theory would predict.[17] Mainly, performance improved during the option year. The reason, of course, was that the players wanted to look especially good, even though they felt they were inequitably paid, in order to be in a stronger bargaining position for a new contract. In other words, there are no easy answers or 100 percent predictive power when applying a cognitive process theory such as equity. Another critique suggests that the time lag effects of inequity have also been overlooked.[18]

The work on equity theory goes beyond expectancy theory as a cognitive explanation of work motivation and serves as a point of departure for attribution theory and locus of control explanations.

Attribution Theory

Chapter 3, on perception, discussed the important role of attributions in the cognitive processes of individuals. Recently, the attributions that people make have emerged as important explanations of work motivation. Unlike the other motivation theories, attribution theory is more a theory of the relationship between personal perception and interpersonal behavior than a theory of individual motivation. There are an increasing variety of attribution theories. A recent analysis of these theories, however, concludes that all of them share the following common assumptions:

1. We seek to make sense of our world.
2. We often attribute people's actions either to internal or external causes.
3. We do so in fairly logical ways.[19]

Attribution theorist Harold Kelley stresses that attribution theory is concerned mainly with the cognitive processes by which an individual interprets behavior as being caused by (or attributed to) certain parts of the relevant environment. It is concerned with the "why" questions of motivation and behavior. Since most causes, attributes, and "whys" are not directly observable, the theory says that people must depend upon cognitions, particularly perception. The attribution theorist assumes that humans are rational and are motivated to identify and understand the causal structure of their relevant environment. It is this search for attributes that characterizes attribution theory.

Although attribution theory has its roots in all the pioneering cognitive theorists' work (for example, that of Lewin and Festinger), in de Charmes' ideas on cognitive evaluation, and in Bem's notion of "self-perception," the theory's initiator is generally recognized to be Fritz Heider. Heider believed that both internal forces (personal attributes such as ability, effort, and fatigue) and external forces (environmental attributes such as rules and the weather) combine additively to determine behavior. He stressed that it is the *perceived*, not the actual, determinants that are important to behavior. People will behave differently if they perceive internal attributes from the way they will behave if they perceive external attributes. It is this concept of differential ascriptions that has very important implications for work motivation.

Locus of Control Attributions. Using *locus of control*, work behavior may be explained by whether employees perceive their outcomes as controlled internally or externally. Employees who perceive internal control feel that they personally can influence their outcomes through their own ability, skills, or effort. Employees who perceive external control feel that their outcomes are beyond their own control; they feel that external forces control their outcomes. What is important is that this perceived locus of control may have a differential impact on their performance and satisfaction. For example, studies by Rotter and his colleagues suggest that skill versus chance environments differentially affect behavior.[20] In addition, a number of studies have been conducted in recent years to test the attribution-theory–locus-of-control model in work settings. One study found that internally controlled employees are generally more satisfied with their jobs, are more likely to be in managerial positions, and are more satisfied with a participatory management style than employees who perceive external control.[21] Other studies have found that internally controlled managers are better performers,[22] are more considerate of subordinates,[23] tend not to burn out,[24] and follow a more strategic style of executive action.[25] In addition, the attribution process has been shown to play a role in coalition formation in the political process of organizations. In particular, coalition members made stronger internal attributions, such as ability and desire, and nonmembers made stronger external attributions, such as luck.[26]

The implication of these studies is that internally controlled managers are better than externally controlled managers. However, such generalizations are not yet warranted because there is some contradictory evidence. For example, one study concluded that the ideal manager may have an external orientation because the results indicated that externally controlled managers were perceived as initiating more structure and consideration than internally controlled managers.[27] In addition to the implications for managerial behavior and performance, attribution theory has been shown to have relevance in explaining goal-setting behavior,[28] leadership behavior,[29] and poor employee performance.[30] A review article concludes that locus of control is related to the performance and satisfaction of organization members and may moderate the relationship between motivation and incentives.[31]

In addition, attributions are related to *organizational symbolism*, which in effect says that in order to understand organizations one must recognize their symbolic nature.[32] Much of organization is based on attributions rather than physical or observed realities under this view. For example, research has found that symbols are a salient source of information used by people in forming their impressions of psychological climate.[33]

Other Attributions. Attribution theory seems to hold a great deal of promise for the better understanding of organizational behavior. However, for the future, other dimensions besides the internal and external locus of control will have to be accounted for and studied. One social psychologist, for example, suggests that a stability (fixed or variable) dimension must also be recognized.[34] Experienced employees will probably have a stable internal attribution about their abilities, but an unstable internal attribution concerning effort. By the same token, these employees may have a stable external attribution about task difficulty but an unstable external attribution about luck.

Besides the stability dimension, other researchers suggest that dimensions such as consensus (do others act this way in a situation?), consistency (does this person act this way in this situation at other times?), and distinctiveness (does this person act differently in other situations?) will affect the type of attributions that are made.[35] For example, if there is high consensus, consistency, and distinctiveness, then attributions to external causes are made, but if there is low consensus and distinctiveness and high consistency, then attributions to internal causes are made. Thus, in trying to understand the poor performance of a subordinate, if there seems to be high consensus (others are also performing poorly on the task), high consistency (this poor performer does not do well on this task at any time or in any place), and high distinctiveness (this subordinate has done well on other tasks), then the supervisor would make an external attribution, that is, that this subordinate is having bad luck or something is wrong that is beyond the control of the subordinate. By the same token, if in analyzing this same poor performer it is determined that there is low consensus (others are performing well on this task), low distinctiveness (this subordinate does poorly on other tasks as well), and high consistency (this poor performer does not do well on this task at any time or in any place), then the supervisor would make an internal attribution, that is, that the subordinate just doesn't have the ability or necessary motivation to perform well. There is some empirical evidence from research on the attributions made by nursing supervisors that supports these theoretical propositions.[36]

Attribution Errors. Recently, social psychologists have given attention to two potent biases when people make attributions. The first is called the *fundamental attribution error*. Research has found that people tend to ignore powerful situational forces when explaining others' behavior.[37] People tend to attribute *others'* behavior to personal factors (for example, intelligence, ability, motivation, attitudes, or personality), even when it is very clear that the situation or circumstances caused the person to behave the way he or she did.

Another attribution bias that has emerged from the research is that people tend to present themselves favorably. This *self-serving bias* has been found in study after study; people readily accept credit when told they have succeeded (attributing the success to their ability and effort), yet often attribute failure to such external, situational factors as bad luck or the problem's inherent "impossibility."[38] For example, in explaining their victories, athletes commonly credit themselves, but are more likely to attribute losses to something else—bad breaks, poor officiating, or the other team's superior effort.[39]

When something goes wrong in the workplace, there is a tendency for the boss to blame the inability or poor attitude of the subordinates, but the situation is blamed as far as he or she is concerned. The reverse is true of the subordinates. They blame the situation for their difficulties, but make a personal attribution in terms of their boss. By the same token, if something goes well, the boss makes personal attributions for him- or herself and situational attributions for subordinates, and the subordinates make personal attributions for themselves but situational attributions for the boss. In other words, it is typical to have conflicting attributional biases between superiors and subordinates in organizations. As a way of creating more productive relationships, researchers suggest that efforts must be made to reduce divergent perceptions and perspectives between the parties through increased interpersonal interaction, open-communication channels and workshops, and team-building sessions devoted to reducing attributional errors.[40]

The Role of Self-Efficacy in Attributions. Closely related to the attribution errors is the recently popular concept of self-efficacy (discussed in Chapters 4 and 14). Taking off from the self-serving bias, self-efficacy (how effective people think they, themselves, are) will affect the attributions people make. If individuals have high self-efficacy, they will tend to make positive internal attributions about their successes and attribute setbacks as situational, a fluke, or to think "I need a new approach."[41] By the same token, attributions also affect a person's self-efficacy. If people make internal attributions for their successful performance, this will enhance their self-efficacy beliefs.[42]

These various dimensions of attribution theory recognize the complexity of human behavior, and this must be part of a theory that attempts to *explain* and *understand* organizational behavior. As has recently been pointed out, it should not be restrictive. Theoretical, information processing, and situational factors all affect the attribution models of organizational behavior.[43] Despite this complexity, and unlike some of its predecessors in the cognitive approaches to motivation discussed earlier, it does seem to have more potential for application and relevance, instead of being a purely academic exercise in theory building.

Summary

Motivation is a basic psychological process. The comprehensive understanding of motivation lies in the need-drive-incentive sequence, or cycle. The basic process involves needs, which set drives in motion to accomplish incentives (anything which alleviates a need and reduces a drive). The drives or motives may be classified into *primary, general,* and *secondary* categories. The primary motives are unlearned and physiologically based. Common primary motives are hunger, thirst, sleep, avoidance of pain, sex, and maternal concern. The general or stimulus motives are also unlearned but are not physiologically based. Curiosity, manipulation, activity, and affection are examples of general motives. Secondary motives are learned and are most relevant to the study of organizational behavior. The needs for power, achievement, affiliation, security, and status are major motivating forces in the behavior of organizational participants.

When the theories of motivation are specifically focused on work motivation, there are several popular approaches. The Maslow, Herzberg, and Alderfer models attempt to identify specific content factors in the individual (in the case of Maslow and Alderfer) or in the job environment (in the case of Herzberg) that motivate employees. Although such a content approach has surface logic, is easy to under-sand, and can be readily translated into practice, the research evidence points out some definite limitations. There is very little research support for these models' theoretical basis and predictability. The trade-off for simplicity sacrifices true under-standing of the complexity of work motivation. On the positive side, however, the content models have given emphasis to important content factors that were largely ignored by the human relationists. In addition, the Alderfer model allows more flexibility, and the Herzberg model is useful as an explanation for job satisfaction and as a point of departure for job design covered in the next chapter.

The process theories provide a much sounder theoretical explanation of work motivation. The expectancy model of Vroom and the extensions and refinements provided by Porter and Lawler help explain the important cognitive variables and how they relate to one another in the complex process of work motivation. The Porter-Lawler model also gives specific attention to the important relationship between performance and satisfaction. Porter and Lawler propose that performance leads to satisfaction, instead of the human relations assumption of the reverse. A growing research literature is somewhat supportive of these expectancy models, but conceptual and methodological problems remain. Unlike the content models, these expectancy models are relatively complex and difficult to translate into actual prac-tice, and consequently they have generally failed to meet the goals of prediction and control of organizational behavior. More recently, in academic circles, equity theory and especially attribution theory have received increased attention. These were presented for the better understanding of work motivation. Both process theories—the equity model, which is based upon perceived input-outcome ratios, and attribu-tion theory, which ascribes internal, external, and other causes to behavior—lend increased understanding to the complex cognitive process of work motivation but have the same limitation as the expectancy models for prediction and control in the practice of human resources management. Attribution theory can make potentially important contributions to the cognitive development of work-motivation theory and may be able to overcome some of the application limitations of the process theories of work motivation and bring us closer to the goals of prediction and control.

Questions for Discussion and Review

1. Briefly define the three classifications of motives. What are some examples of each?
2. What are the characteristics of high achievers?
3. How is status defined? What are some determinants of status?
4. What implications does the security motive have for modern human resources management?
5. In your own words, briefly explain Maslow's theory of motivation. Relate it to work motivation and Alderfer's ERG model.

6. What is the major criticism of Herzberg's two-factor theory of motivation? Do you think it has made a contribution to the better understanding of motivation in the workplace? Defend your answer.

7. In Vroom's model, what are valence, expectancy, and force? How do these variables relate to one another and to work motivation? Give realistic examples.

8. In your own words, briefly explain the Porter-Lawler model of motivation. How do performance and satisfaction relate to each other?

9. Briefly give an example of an inequity that a manager of a small business might experience. How would the manager strive to attain equity in the situation you describe?

10. What is attribution theory? How can analysis of locus of control be applied to workers and managers?

11. What has surfaced as two important attribution errors or biases? Give an example of each.

References

1. Martin G. Evans, "Organizational Behavior: The Central Role of Motivation," *Journal of Management*, vol. 12, no. 2, 1986, p. 203.

2. The most frequently cited exception is the need for oxygen. A deficiency of oxygen in the body does not automatically set up a corresponding drive. This is a fear of high-altitude pilots. Unless their gauges show an oxygen leak or the increased intake of carbon dioxide sets up a drive, they may die of oxygen deficiency without a drive ever being set up to correct the situation. The same is true of the relatively frequent deaths of teenagers parked in "lovers' lanes." Carbon monoxide leaks into the parked automobile, and they die from oxygen deficiency without its ever setting up a drive (to open the car door).

3. Spencer A. Rathus, *Psychology*, 4th ed., Holt, Rinehart and Winston, Fort Worth, Tex., 1990, p. 312.

4. Ronald E. Riggio, *Introduction to Industrial/Organizational Psychology*, Scott Foresman/Little, Brown, Glenview, Ill., 1990, p. 175.

5. "Labor Letter," *The Wall Street Journal*, Mar. 31, 1987, p. 1.

6. Terrence R. Mitchell, "Motivation: New Directions for Theory, Research, and Practice," *Academy of Management Review*, January 1982, p. 86.

7. James L. Bowditch and Anthony F. Buono, *A Primer on Organizational Behavior*, 2d ed., Wiley, New York, 1990, p. 54.

8. A. H. Maslow, "A Theory of Human Motivation," *Psychological Review*, July 1943, pp. 370–396.

9. Robert A. Baron, *Behavior in Organizations*, 2d ed., Allyn and Bacon, Boston, 1986, p. 78.

10. Anthony Dickinson, "Expectancy Theory in Animal Conditioning." In Stephen B. Klein and Robert R. Mowrer (eds.), *Contemporary Learning Theories*, Erlbaum, Hillsdale, N.J., 1989, p. 280.

11. Philip M. Podsakoff and Larry Williams, "The Relationship between Job Performance and Job Satisfaction," in Edwin Locke (ed.), *Generalizing from Laboratory to Field Settings*, Lexington Books, Lexington, Mass., 1986, p. 244. Also see: Edwin A. Locke and Gary P. Latham, *A Theory of Goal Setting and Task Performance*, Prentice-Hall, Englewood Cliffs, N.J., 1990, pp. 265–267.

12. James M. McFillen and Philip M. Podsakoff, "A Coordinated Approach to Motivation Can Increase Productivity," *Personnel Administrator*, July 1983, p. 46.

13. Robert A. Baron, *Behavior in Organizations*, Allyn and Bacon, Boston, 1983, p. 137.

14. Robert E. Callahan, C. Patrick Fleenor, and Harry R. Knudson, *Understanding Organizational Behavior*, Merrill, Columbus, Ohio, 1986, pp. 108–109.

15. Michael R. Carrell and John E. Dittrich, "Equity Theory: The Recent Literature, Methodological Considerations, and New Directions," *Academy of Management Review*, April 1978, pp. 202–210

16. Robert G. Lord and Jeffrey A. Hohenfeld, "Longitudinal Field Assessment of Equity Effects on the Performance of Major League Baseball Players," *Journal of Applied Psychology*, February 1979, pp. 19–26.

17. Dennis Duchon and Arthur G. Jago, "Equity and Performance of Major League Baseball Players: An Extension of Lord and Hohenfeld," *Journal of Applied Psychology*, December 1981, pp. 728–732.

18. Richard A. Cosier and Dan R. Dalton, "Equity Theory and Time: A Reformulation," *Academy of Management Review*, April 1983, pp. 311–319.

19. David G. Myers, *Social Psychology*, 2d ed., McGraw-Hill, New York, 1990, p. 71.

20. Julian B. Rotter, Shephard Liverant, and Douglas P. Crowne, "The Growth and Extinction of Expectancies in Chance-Controlled and Skilled Tasks," *The Journal of Psychology*, July 1961, pp. 161–177.

21. Terence R. Mitchell, Charles M. Smyser, and Stan E. Weed, "Locus of Control: Supervision and Work Satisfaction," *Academy of Management Journal*, September 1975, pp. 623–631.

22. Carl R. Anderson, Don Hellriegel, and John W. Slocum, Jr., "Managerial Response to Environmentally Induced Stress," *Academy of Management Journal*, June 1977, pp. 260–272. The higher performance of internally-controlled managers was verified by the use of student subjects in a study by Carl R. Anderson and Craig Eric Schneier, "Locus of Control, Leader Behavior and Leader Performance among Management Students," *Academy of Management Journal*, December 1978, pp. 690–698.

23. Margaret W. Pryer and M. K. Distenfano, "Perceptions of Leadership, Job Satisfaction, and Internal-External Control across Three Nursing Levels," *Nursing Research*, November–December 1971, pp. 534–537.

24. Eli Glogow, "Research Note: Burnout and Locus of Control," *Public Personnel Management*, Spring 1986, p. 79.

25. Danny Miller, Manfred F. R. Kets DeVries, and Jean-Marie Toulouse, "Top Executive Locus of Control and Its Relationship to Strategy-Making, Structure, and Environment," *Academy of Management Journal*, June 1982, pp. 237–253.

26. John A. Pearce and Angelo S. DeNisi, "Attribution Theory and Strategic Decision Making: An Application to Coalition Formation," *Academy of Management Journal*, March 1983, pp. 119–128.

27. Douglas E. Durand and Walter R. Nord, "Perceived Leader Behavior as a Function of Personality Characteristics of Supervisors and Subordinates," *Academy of Management Journal*, September 1976, pp. 427–428.

28. Dennis L. Dossett and Carl I. Greenberg, "Goal Setting and Performance Evaluation: An Attributional Analysis," *Academy of Management Journal*, December 1981, pp. 767–779.

29. Bobby J. Calder, "An Attribution Theory of Leadership," in Barry Staw and Gerald Salancik (eds.), *New Directions in Organizational Behavior*, St. Clare Press, Chicago, 1977, pp. 179–204; and James C. McElroy, "A Typology of Attribution Leadership Research," *Academy of Management Review*, July 1982, pp. 413–417; and Gregory Dobbins, "Effects of Gender on Leaders' Responses to Poor Performers: An Attributional Interpretation," *Academy of Management Journal*, September 1985, pp. 587–598; James C. McElroy and Charles B. Shrader, "Attribution Theories of Leadership and Network Analysis," *Journal of Management*, vol. 12, no. 3, 1986, pp. 351–362.

30. Terence R. Mitchell and Robert E. Wood, "Supervisors' Responses to Subordinate Poor Performance: A Test of an Attribution Model," *Organizational Behavior and Human Performance*, February 1980, pp. 123–138.

31. Paul E. Spector, "Behavior in Organizations as a Function of Employees' Locus of Control," *Psychological Bulletin*, May 1982, pp. 482–497.

32. Peter J. Frost, "Special Issue on Organizational Symbolism," *Journal of Management*, vol. 11, no. 2, 1985, pp. 5–9.

33. Suzyn Ornstein, "Organizational Symbols: A Study of Their Meanings and Influences on Perceived Psychological Climate," *Organizational Behavior and Human Decision Processes*, October 1986, pp. 207–229.

34. Bernard Weiner, *Theories of Motivation*, Rand McNally, Chicago, 1972, Chap. 5.

35. Harold H. Kelley, "The Process of Causal Attribution," *American Psychologist*, February 1973, pp. 107–128.

36. Mitchell and Wood, op. cit.

37. Myers, op. cit., pp. 74–77.

38. Ibid., p. 82.

39. B. Mullen and C. A. Riordan, "Self-Serving Attributions for Performance in Naturalistic Settings," *Journal of Applied Social Psychology*, vol. 18, 1988, pp. 3–22.

40. Bowditch and Buono, op. cit., p. 90.

41. Myers, op. cit., p. 95.

42. Raymond A. Katzell and Donna E. Thompson, "Work Motivation," *American Psychologist*, February 1990, pp. 145–146.

43. Robert G. Lord and Jonathan E. Smith, "Theoretical, Information Processing, and Situational Factors Affecting Attribution Theory Models of Organizational Behavior," *Academy of Management Review*, January 1983, pp. 50–60.

REAL CASE: KEEPING THEM MOTIVATED

There is wide variety in the ways today's organizations attempt to motivate their top-level managers. One of the most interesting is that used by Phillips–Van Heusen, famous for its manufacture of shirts, sweaters, and casual shoes. The company has designed an incentive plan for its eleven senior executives that is tied directly to earnings per share growth. If earnings grow at a 35 percent compound annual rate for 1988–1992, each executive stands to make $1 million. Half of this amount is spread over the four years of the plan. Every time the company meets its annual growth rate, the executives get $125,000 each. If the company meets the goal for all four consecutive years, each individual gets an additional $500,000. The latter is particularly important given that the executives made the first year goal but missed the second. They are now trying to get back on track and keep heading toward the compounded growth rate of 35 percent.

Another common use of financial incentives is to keep people from moving to other companies. One of the most typical is to give them payments that cannot be touched for five to ten years or until they reach near retirement age. An example is a stock option worth ten to twenty times the person's annual salary. In such cases executives are reluctant to leave, and the longer they stay the less likely it is that they will ever move to another company. The company has their services for life.

Another common way that companies try to motivate their executives is the use of recognition. Superstars, in particular, want more than money. They want to be recognized, sometimes through money, for their achievement. For example, a computer whiz decided to leave his bank and move to a competitor. His current employer offered an increase in salary and bonus, but also offered a move up the hierarchy to where he would report to the vice chairman instead of a lower-level manager. Result: The computer expert decided to stay with the company.

Another typical way of motivating people to stay with a company is to give them more challenge. In the case of Kenichi Ohmae, McKinsey & Company's well known consultant in Japan, the firm structured his work assignments so that he could handle more counseling and fewer traditional product-market studies. He was also given more time to work on writing books and to take strong, and controversial, stands on trade issues and protectionism. Notes Mr. Ohmae, "I appreciate the firm and the colleagues who have allowed me to do these things. They've allowed me to explore these mind-stretching exercises." He plans to stay with the firm until his retirement—in 2003.

1. What particular needs does money satisfy? Incorporate Maslow's need hierarchy into your answer.

2. Is the need for recognition and challenge more important than that of money? Explain.
3. How could equity theory be used to help explain the best way to motivate a successful manager? Give an example.

Case: **Star** **Salesperson**	While growing up, Jerry Slate was always rewarded by his parents for showing independence. When he started school, he was successful both inside and outside the classroom. He was always striving to be things like traffic patroller and lunchroom monitor in grade school. Yet his mother worried about him because he never got along well with other children his own age. When confronted with this, Jerry would reply, "Well, I don't need them. Besides, they can't do things as well as I can. I don't have time to help them; I'm too busy improving myself." Jerry went on to do very well in both high school and college. He was always at or near the top of his class academically and was a very good long-distance runner for the track teams in high school and college. In college he shied away from joining a fraternity and lived in an apartment by himself. Upon graduation he went to work for a large insurance company and soon became one of the top salespersons. Jerry is very proud of the fact that he was one of the top five salespersons in six out of the eight years he has been with the company.

At the home office of the insurance company, the executive committee in charge of making major personnel appointments was discussing the upcoming vacancy of the sales manager's job for the Midwestern region. The personnel manager gave the following report: "As you know, the Midwestern region is lagging far behind our other regions as far as sales go. We need a highly motivated person to take that situation over and turn it around. After an extensive screening process, I am recommending that Jerry Slate be offered this position. As you know, Jerry has an outstanding record with the company and is highly motivated. I think he is the person for the job."

1. Do you agree with the personnel manager? Why or why not?
2. Considering Jerry's background, what motives discussed in the chapter would appear to be very intense in Jerry? What motives would appear to be very low? Give specific evidence from the case for each motive.
3. What type of motivation is desirable for people in sales positions? What type of motivation is desirable for people in managerial positions?

Case: **What Do** **They Want?**	Mike Riverer is vice president of manufacturing and operations of a medium-size pharmaceutical firm in the Midwest. Mike has a Ph.D. in chemistry but has not been directly involved in research and new-product development for twenty years. He is from the "school of hard knocks" when it comes to managing operations, and he runs a "tight ship." The company does not have a turnover problem, but it is obvious to Mike and other key management personnel that the hourly people are only putting

in their eight hours a day. They are not working anywhere near their full potential. Mike is very upset with the situation because, with rising costs, the only way that the company can continue to prosper is to increase the productivity of its hourly people.

Mike called in his personnel manager and laid it on the line. "What is it with our people, anyway? Your wage surveys show that we pay near the top in this region, our conditions are tremendous, and our fringes choke a horse. Yet these people still are not motivated. What in the world do they want?" The personnel manager replied, "I have told you and the president time after time that money, conditions, and benefits are not enough. Employees also need other things to motivate them. Also, I have been conducting some random confidential interviews with some of our hourly people, and they tell me that they are very discouraged because, no matter now hard they work, they get the same pay and opportunities for advancement as their co-workers who are just scraping by." Mike then replied, "Okay, you are the motivation expert; what do we do about it? We *have* to increase their performance."

1. Explain the "motivation problem" in this organization in terms of the content models of Maslow, Alderfer, and Herzberg. What are the "other things" that the personnel manager is referring to in speaking of things besides money, conditions, and fringe benefits that are needed to motivate employees?
2. Explain the motivation of the employees in this company in terms of one or more of the process models. On the basis of the responses during the confidential interviews, what would you guess are some of the expectancies, valences, inequities, and attributions of the employees in this company? How about Mike? Do you think he is internally or externally controlled?
3. How would you respond to Mike's last question and statement if you were the personnel manager in this company?

**Case:
Tom, Dick,
and Harry**

You are in charge of a small department and have three subordinates—Tom, Dick, and Harry. The key to the success of your department is to keep these employees as motivated as possible. Here is a brief summary profile on each of these subordinates.

Tom is the type of employee who is hard to figure out. His absenteeism record is much higher than average. He greatly enjoys his family (a wife and three small children) and thinks they should be central to his life. The best way to describe Tom is to say that he is kind of a throwback to the hippie generation and believes deeply in the values of that culture. As a result, the things that the company can offer him really inspire him very little. He feels that the job is simply a means of financing his family's basic needs and little else. Overall, Tom does an adequate job and is very conscientious, but all attempts to get him to do more have failed. He has charm and is friendly, but he is just not "gung-ho" for the company. He is pretty much allowed to "do his own thing" as long as he meets the minimal standards of performance.

Dick is in many respects opposite from Tom. Like Tom, he is a likable guy, but unlike Tom, Dick responds well to the company's rules and compensation schemes and has a high degree of personal loyalty to the company. The problem with Dick is that he will not do very much independently. He does well with what is assigned to him, but he is not very creative or even dependable when he is on his own. He also is a relatively shy person who is not very assertive when dealing with people outside the department. This hurts his performance to some degree because he cannot immediately sell himself or the department to other departments in the company or to top management.

   Harry, on the other hand, is a very assertive person. He will work for money and would readily change jobs for more money. He really works hard for the company but expects the company also to work for him. In his present job, he feels no qualms about working a sixty-hour week, if the money is there. Even though he has a family and is supporting his mother, he once quit a job cold when his employer didn't give him a raise on the premise that he was already making too much. He is quite a driver. A manager at his last place of employment indicated that, while Harry did do an excellent job for the company, his personality was so strong that they were glad to get rid of him. His former boss noted that Harry just seemed to be pushing all the time. If it wasn't for more money, it was for better fringe benefits; he never seemed satisfied.

1. Can you explain Tom's, Dick's, and Harry's motivation by one or more of the work-motivation models discussed in this chapter?
2. Using Alderfer's ERG theory, what group of core needs seems to dominate each of these three subordinates?
3. Using the attribution-theory approach, what type of locus control do you feel guides each of these three employees in his present job?

7

Motivation Applied: Job Design and Goal Setting

■ A Quality Rose Among the Thorns

In 1987, General Motors' Buick Division was turning out LeSabres that had 180 defects per 100 cars. By comparison, Japanese autos such as Honda had only 130 defects per 100 cars and were considered far superior in terms of overall quality. Today, however, this has changed dramatically, and many experts give credit to changes in job design and the implementation of techniques such as goal setting by the Buick Division. First, the company spent $400 million to change its LeSabre plant in Flint, Michigan, into a state-of-the-art factory. Using just-in-time inventory, the company cut inventory expenses sharply. Suppliers were required to provide higher-quality parts and to be on time with their deliveries. Those who were not were dumped—for failure to meet quality goals—and new suppliers were found. The firm also eliminated production-line inspectors and cut the number of supervisors in the plant by 50 percent. Quality assurance was pushed down to the worker level, and workers were given the authority to stop production if they saw a problem that warranted halting the line.

These changes began bringing about an increase in overall quality. In 1988, defects per 100 cars on the LeSabre had dropped to 155 and, by 1990, they were down to 82 per 100. This meant that the LeSabre was the sixth-best car out of 120 domestic and foreign models, based on problems owners reported during the first part of the model year. Buick is now turning its attention to its other lines in an attempt to use job design and goal-setting techniques to help them become more reliable. Going into the 1990s, Buick builds the highest quality cars of any domestic auto maker. Its goal is to extend this success so that in the near future it is building the highest-quality cars in the world. Only time will tell if these lofty goals are attained, but so far in the 1990s Buick is certainly a success story in a beleaguered American auto industry.

Learning Objectives

- **Discuss** the background of job design as an applied area of work motivation.
- **Define** the job enrichment and job characteristics approach to job design.
- **Present** the quality of work life (QWL) and sociotechnical approach to job design.
- **Explain** goal setting theory and guidelines from research.
- **Describe** the application of goal setting to overall systems performance.

The preceding chapter was devoted to the basic motivational process and the various theoretical approaches to work motivation. In this chapter the more applied areas of motivation are examined: job design and goal setting. In recent years, relatively more research has been generated in these two areas than elsewhere in the field of organizational behavior. It is becoming increasingly clear that appropriately designing jobs can have a positive impact on both employee satisfaction and quality of performance. The same is true of goal setting, which has been held up as a prototypical model for how theory should or can lead to application. The purpose of this chapter is to give some of the background, review the related research, and spell out some of the specific applications for these important areas of the field of organizational behavior.

JOB DESIGN

Job design has emerged as an important application area for work motivation and the study of organizational behavior. In particular, job design is based on an extensive and still-growing theoretical base, it has had considerable research attention in recent years, and it is being widely applied to the actual practice of management.

Initially, the field of organizational behavior paid attention only to job enrichment approaches to job design. Now, with *quality of work life* (QWL) becoming a major societal issue in this country and throughout the world, job design has taken a broader perspective. Figure 7.1 summarizes the various dimensions of a comprehensive look at job design. Job enrichment still dominates the job design literature on organizational behavior, but from the perspective of job characteristics rather than Herzberg's motivators. Goal setting is beginning to be linked to the design of jobs, and the sociotechnical approach to job design is most closely associated with QWL. Job engineering, job enlargement, and job rotation are considered to have historical significance for job design, but they are not in the current mainstream of job design research or application.

Background on Job Design

Job design concerns and approaches are usually considered to have begun with the scientific management movement at the turn of the century. Pioneering scientific managers such as Frederick W. Taylor and Frank Gilbreth systematically examined jobs with techniques such as time and motion analysis. Their goal was to maximize human efficiency in jobs. Taylor suggested that task design might be the most prominent single element in scientific management.

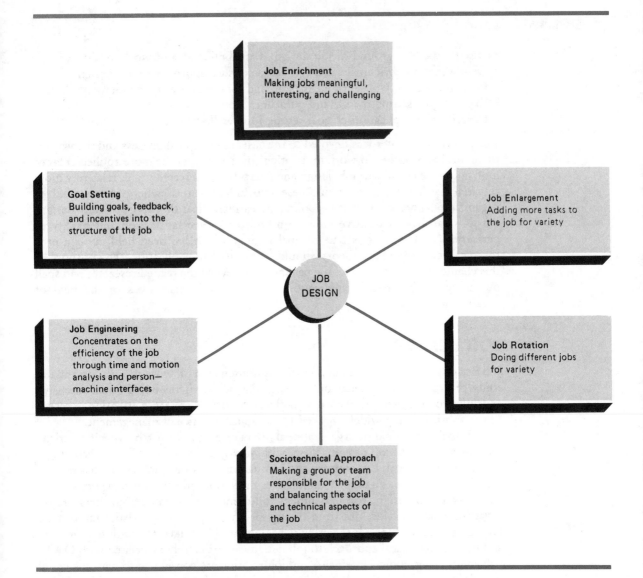

FIGURE 7.1
Various approaches to job design.
(*Source:* Adapted from Don Hellriegel, John W. Slocum, and Richard W. Woodman, *Organizational Behavior,*
4th ed., West, St. Paul, Minn., 1986, p. 363.)

The scientific management approach evolved into what is now generally called *job engineering.* This industrial engineering approach is concerned with product, process, and tool design; plant layout; standard operating procedures; work measurement and standards; worker methods; and human-machine interactions. It has been the dominant form of job design analysis since the turn of the century; it went hand in hand with automation in the previous generation, and it has been closely associated with cybernation (automatic feedback control mechanisms) and sophisticated computer applications involving artificial intelligence (AI) and expert systems. These computer systems have had a positive impact by reducing task and work-flow uncertainty.[1] At first blue-collar production jobs, but then white-collar jobs as well, became highly specialized (the employee did one or a very few tasks) and standardized (the employee did the task the same way every time).

The often cited example of the employee on the assembly line putting a nut on a bolt as the product moves by on the conveyor belt became quite common in manufacturing plants across the country. The same types of specialized jobs became common in banks, offices, hospitals, schools, and every other kind of organizational setting. The general consensus was that these highly specialized, standardized jobs were very efficient and led to a high degree of control over workers. Up to recent times, few people questioned the engineering approach to job design. Top management could readily determine and see immediate cost savings from job engineering. But side effects on quality, absenteeism, and turnover were generally ignored.

Starting in the 1950s, some practicing managers around the country, such as the founder of IBM, Thomas Watson, became concerned about the impact of job engineering approaches to work and began implementing job enlargement and rotation programs. Essentially, the job enlargement programs horizontally loaded the job (expanded the number of operations performed by the worker, that is, made the job less specialized), and the job rotation programs reduced boredom by switching people around to various jobs. Then, starting in the late 1960s, there began to be increasing concern with employee dissatisfaction and declining productivity. These problems were felt to be largely the result of so-called "blue-collar blues" and "white-collar woes."

Attention in the work place has since shifted away from the boredom problems and now focuses on the significant challenges facing today's employees. Starting in the 1990s, there have been some dramatic changes. Because of the downsizing of organizations in the 1980s and the increase of advanced technology, jobs have suddenly become much more demanding and employees must think in different ways and adapt to unpredictable changes. For example, in manufacturing, assembly-line methods are being replaced by flexible, "customized" production. This new manufacturing approach requires workers to deal with an ever-increasing line of products. Similar job changes have occurred in the white-collar service industry. For example, bank tellers must not only demonstrate facility with computers but also be marketers—rather than just number crunchers and clerks.[2]

For both academicians and practitioners, job design takes on special importance in today's human resource management. It is essential to design jobs so that stress (covered in Chapter 14) can be reduced, motivation can be enhanced, and satisfaction of employees (covered in Chapter 5) and their performance can be so improved that organizations can effectively compete in the global marketplace.

Job Enrichment

Job enrichment represents an extension of the earlier, more simplified job rotation and job enlargement techniques of job design. Since it is a direct outgrowth of Herzberg's two-factor theory of motivation, the assumption is that in order to motivate personnel, the job must be designed to provide opportunities for achievement, recognition, responsibility, advancement, and growth. The technique entails "enriching" the job so that these factors are included. In particular, *job enrichment* is concerned with designing jobs that include a greater variety of work content; require a higher level of knowledge and skill; give workers more autonomy and responsibility in terms of planning, directing, and controlling their own performance; and provide the opportunity for personal growth and a meaningful work experience. As opposed to job enlargement, which horizontally loads the job, job enrichment *vertically* loads the job; for example, there are not necessarily more tasks to perform, but more responsibililty and autonomy. Table 7.1 gives some specific examples of job enrichment.

As with the other application techniques discussed in this book, job enrichment is not a panacea for all job design problems facing modern management. After noting that there are documented cases where this approach to job design did not work, Miner concluded that the biggest problem is that traditional job enrichment has little to say about when and why the failures can be expected to occur.[3] Job enrichment is a valuable motivational technique, but management must use it selectively and give proper recognition to the complex human and situational variables. The newer job characteristics models of job enrichment are beginning to do this.

The Job Characteristics Approach to Task Design

To meet some of the limitations of the Herzberg approach to job enrichment (which he prefers to call *orthodox job enrichment*, or OJE), a group of researchers began to concentrate on the relationship between certain job characteristics or the job scope

TABLE 7.1 Examples of Job Enrichment

Old Situation	Situation after Job Enrichment
Each employee was rotated among all machines.	Each employee is assigned to only two machines.
When machine failure occurred, operator called on maintenance group.	Each operator is given training in maintenance; each conducts preventive and corrective maintenance on the two machines for which he or she is responsible.
Operator changed the slicing blade (the most important component of the machine) following a rigid rule contained in a manual.	Operator is given authority to decide when to replace the blade, based on his or her own judgment.
Supervisor monitored operator and corrected unsatisfactory performance.	A performance feedback system has been developed that provides daily information on operators' work quality directly to them.
Individuals performed a specialized task on units passing by them.	Three- to five-person teams build an entire unit.
Supervisor decided who should do what.	The team decides who should do what.
Inspectors and supervisor tested output and corrected performance.	The team conducts its own quality audits.

Source: Adapted from Ross A. Webber, *Management*, rev. ed., Irwin, Homewood, Ill., 1979, p. 82. These examples were provided to Weber by Davis R. Sirota, Wharton School, University of Pennsylvania.

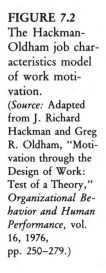

FIGURE 7.2
The Hackman-Oldham job characteristics model of work motivation.
(*Source:* Adapted from J. Richard Hackman and Greg R. Oldham, "Motivation through the Design of Work: Test of a Theory," *Organizational Behavior and Human Performance,* vol. 16, 1976, pp. 250–279.)

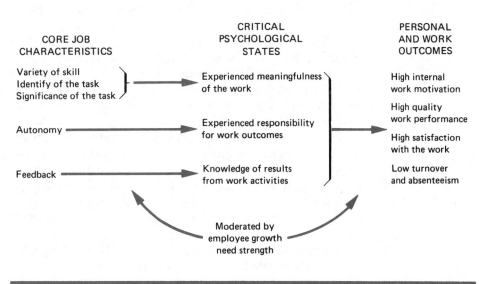

and employee motivation. J. Richard Hackman and Greg Oldham developed the most widely recognized model of job characteristics, shown in Figure 7.2. This model recognized that certain job characteristics contribute to certain psychological states and that the strength of employees' need for growth has an important moderating effect. Table 7.2 summarizes what is meant by each of the job characteristics and psychological states.

TABLE 7.2 The Dimensions in the Hackman-Oldham Model

Core Job Dimensions

1. *Variety of skill.* This refers to the degree to which the job requires the person to do different things and involves the use of a number of different skills, abilities, and talents.
2. *Identity of the task.* This involves a complete module of work; the person can do the job from beginning to end with a visible outcome.
3. *Significance of the task.* This is concerned with the importance of the job. Does it have a significant impact on others—both internal and external to the organization?
4. *Autonomy.* This refers to the amount of freedom, independence, and discretion the person has in areas such as scheduling the work, making decisions, and determining how to do the job.
5. *Feedback.* This involves the degree to which the job provides the person with clear and direct information about job outcomes and performance.

Critical Psychological States

1. *Experienced meaningfulness.* This is concerned with the extent to which the person experiences the work as important, valuable, and worthwhile.
2. *Experienced responsibility.* This is concerned with the degree to which the individual feels personally responsible or accountable for the results of the work.
3. *Knowledge of results.* This involves the degree to which the person understands on a regular basis how effectively he or she is performing in the job.

Source: Adapted from David A. Nadler, J. Richard Hackman, and Edward E. Lawler, *Managing Organizational Behavior,* Little, Brown, Boston, 1979, pp. 81–82.

In essence, the model says that certain job characteristics lead to critical psychological states. That is, skill variety, task identity, and task significance lead to experienced meaningfulness; autonomy leads to the feeling of responsibility; and feedback leads to knowledge of results. The more these three psychological states are present, the more employees will feel good about themselves when they perform well. Hackman states: "The model postulates that internal rewards are obtained by an individual when he *learns* (knowledge of results) that he *personally* (experienced responsibility) has performed well on a task that he *cares* about (experienced meaningfulness)."[4] Hackman then goes on to point out that these internal rewards are reinforcing to employees, causing them to perform well. If they don't perform well, they will try harder in order to get the internal rewards that good performance brings. He concludes: "The net result is a self-perpetuating cycle of positive work motivation powered by self-generated rewards. This cycle is predicted to continue until one or more of the three psychological states is no longer present, or until the individual no longer values the internal rewards that derive from good performance."[5]

An example of an enriched job according to the Hackman-Oldham job characteristics model would be that of a surgeon. Surgeons must draw on a wide variety of skills and abilities; usually surgeons can readily identify the task because they handle patients from beginning to end (that is, they play a role in the diagnosis, perform the operation, and are responsible for postoperative care and follow-up); the job has life-and-death significance; there is a great deal of autonomy, since surgeons have the final word on all decisions concerning patients; and there is clear, direct feedback on whether the operation was successful. At the other extreme would be traditional blue-collar or white-collar jobs. All five core job dimensions would be low or nonexistent in the latter jobs.

There are several ways that the Hackman-Oldham model can be used to diagnose the degree of task scope that a job possesses. For instance, a manager could simply assess a particular job by clinically analyzing it according to the five core dimensions, as was done in the example of the surgeon's job, discussed above. Others have suggested a specific checklist, which would include such items as the use of inspectors or checkers, labor pools, or narrow spans of control, to help pinpoint deficiencies in the core dimentions.[6] More systematically, Hackman and Oldham have developed a questionnaire, the Job Diagnostic Survey (JDS), to analyze jobs. The questions on this survey yield a quantitative score that can be used to calculate an overall measure of job enrichment, or what is increasingly called *job scope*—to differentiate it from Herzberg-type job enrichment. The formula for this motivating potential score (MPS) is the following:

$$MPS = \left[\frac{\text{skill variety} + \text{task identity} + \text{task significance}}{3}\right] \times \text{autonomy} \times \text{feedback}$$

Notice that the job characteristics of skill variety, task identity, and task significance are combined and divided by 3, while the characteristics of autonomy and feedback stand alone. Also, since skill variety, task identity, and task significance are additive, any one or even two of these characteristics could be completely missing and the person could still experience meaningfulness, but if either autonomy or feedback were missing, the job would offer no motivating potential (MPS = 0) because of the multiplicative relationships.

The JDS is a widely used instrument to measure task characteristics or task scope, but the research on the impact that the motivating potential of a job has on job satisfaction and performance is not that clear. Most of the support for the model comes from Hackman and his colleagues, who claim that people on enriched jobs (according to their characteristics as measured by the JDS) are definitely more motivated and satisfied and, although the evidence is not as strong, may have better attendance and performance effectiveness records.[7] In a recent study, and one of the very few that has looked at the long-term impact, some fairly encouraging results were found. Using about a thousand tellers from thirty-eight banks of a large holding company, the following results were obtained from the job redesign intervention:

1. Perceptions of changed job characteristics increased quickly and held at that level for an extended period. Thus, employees perceive meaningful changes that have been introduced into their jobs and tend to recognize those changes over time.
2. Satisfaction and commitment attitudes increased quickly, but then diminished back to their initial levels.
3. Performance did not increase initially, but did increase significantly over the longer time period. The implication here is that managers and researchers need to be more patient in their evaluation of work redesign interventions.[8]

In addition to this large longitudinal study, a meta-analysis of about 200 studies of the job characteristics model found general support for its structure and for its effects on motivation and satisfaction and performance outcomes.[9]

Guidelines for Redesigning Jobs

To redesign jobs, specific guidelines such as those found in Figure 7.3 are offered. Such easily implementable guidelines make the job design area popular and practical for more effective human resource management. An example would be the recent application in a large department store.[10] In a training session format, the sales employees' jobs were redesigned in the following manner:

1. *Skill variety:* The salespeople were asked to try to think of and use
   a. different selling approaches
   b. new merchandise displays
   c. better ways of recording sales and keeping records
2. *Task identity:* The salespeople were asked to
   a. keep a personal record of daily sales volume in dollars
   b. keep a record of number of sales/customers
   c. mark off a display area that you consider yours—keep it complete and orderly
3. *Task significance:* The salespeople were reminded that
   a. selling a product was the basic overall objective of the store
   b. the appearance of the display area was important to selling
   c. they are "the store" to customers; they were told that courtesy and pleasantness help to build the store's reputation and set the stage for future sales

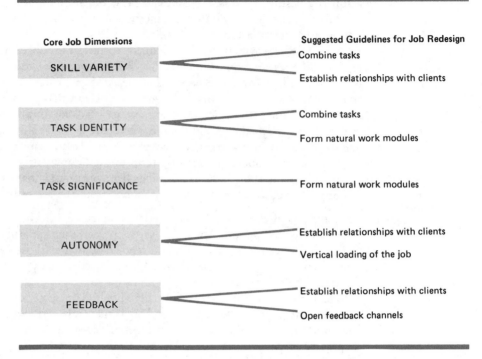

FIGURE 7.3
Specific guidelines for redesigning jobs for the more effective practice of human resources management. (*Source:* Adapted from J. Richard Hackman, Greg R. Oldham, Robert Janson, and Kenneth A. Purdy, "A New Strategy for Job Enrichment," *California Management Review,* Summer 1975, pp. 57–71.

4. *Autonomy:* The salespeople were
   a. encouraged to develop and use their own unique approach and sales pitch
   b. allowed freedom to select their own break and lunch times
   c. encouraged to make suggestions for changes in all phases of the policy and operations
5. *Feedback from the job itself:* Salespeople were
   a. encouraged to keep personal records of their own sales volume
   b. encouraged to keep a sales/customer ratio
   c. reminded that establishing a good rapport with customers is also a success; they were told that if the potential customer leaves with a good feeling about the store and its employees, the salesperson has been successful
6. *Feedback from agents:* Salespeople were encouraged to
   a. observe and help each other with techniques of selling
   b. seek out information from their boss and relevant departments on all phases of their jobs
   c. invite customer reactions and thoughts concerning merchandise, service, and so forth

Both the salespeople's functional (conversing with customers, showing merchandise, handling returns, and so forth) and dysfunctional (socializing with coworkers or visitors, idly standing around, being gone for no legitimate reason) performance behaviors moved in the desired directions and a subanalysis also indicated they were more satisfied. A control group of salespeople, with everything else the same except they did not have their jobs redesigned, showed no change in their performance behaviors. Thus, there is some evidence that the job characteristics approach can be practically applied with desirable performance and satisfaction results. Such well-known companies as 3M, AT&T, Xerox, and Motorola are among those that have actually implemented job design changes in accordance with the job characteristics model.[11]

A Social Information Processing Approach

A social information processing approach (SIPA) to work motivation in general[12] and task design in particular[13] has emerged in recent years. As Salancik and Pfeffer explain it, the basic premise of SIPA is that "individuals, as adaptive organisms, adapt attitudes, behaviors, and beliefs to their social context and to the reality of their own past and present behavior and situation."[14] Thus, according to SIPA, there are three major causes of a jobholder's perceptions, attitudes, and actual behavior:

1. The jobholder's cognitive evaluation of the real task environment
2. The jobholder's past actions, including reinforcement history and learning
3. The information that the immediate social context provides

Salancik and Pfeffer give the third point above the most weight. They suggest that social information or social cues are much more dominant in how jobholders view their tasks than the real task environment or past actions are.

The SIPA model of job design is quite complex. As explained by Moorhead and Griffin, it suggests that through a variety of processes, commitment (discussed in Chapter 5), rationalization (self-interpretation of behavior), and information saliency (or importance) are defined. These processes include the following:

1. *Choice:* The freedom to choose different behaviors
2. *Revocability:* The ability to change behaviors
3. *Publicness:* The degree of visibility to others
4. *Explicitness:* The ability to be clear and obvious
5. *Social norms and expectations:* The knowledge of what others expect from someone
6. External priming: The receiving of cues from others.[15]

These attributional processes combine with social information (from others and the organizational environment) to form and influence the jobholder's perceptions, attitudes, and behaviors.

The SIPA model of job design has generated considerable research over the last several years.[16] As with the job characteristics approach, results have been mixed.[17] Some studies do support the notion that social cues, such as negative versus positive coworker comments, may be more important to the way employees perceive their tasks than characteristics such as whether the job is enriched or unenriched. In other words, as in other areas of organizational behavior, the importance of the social environment is becoming recognized in the job design area. However, most recently, research suggests that an integrated approach to job design that includes both objective job characteristics and social information may be the most effective.[18]

QUALITY OF WORK LIFE AND SOCIOTECHNICAL DESIGN

So far, the discussion of job design has revolved mainly around job characteristics, job enrichment, and social information processing. The concern for quality of work life (QWL) and the accompanying sociotechnical approach to job design take a more macro perspective.

Unlike the job enrichment and social information processing approaches, QWL is not based on a particular theory, nor does it advocate a particular technique for application. Instead, QWL is more concerned with the overall climate of work. One analysis of QWL described it as "(1) a concern about the impact of work on people as well as on organizational effectiveness, and (2) the idea of participation in organizational problem solving and decision making."[19] The recognized purpose is to change the climate at work so that the human-technological-organizational interface leads to a better quality of work life. Although how this is actually accomplished and exactly what is meant by a better *quality* of work life are still unclear, there are a number of analyses and applications of the closely associated sociotechnical approach to job design.

Unlike the more general concept of QWL, the sociotechnical approach to job design (which is sometimes even equated with QWL) has a systems theoretical base. In particular, the sociotechnical approach to job design is concerned with the interface and harmony between personal, social, and technological functioning.[20] In application, this translates into the redesign of technological work processes and the formation of autonomous, self-regulating work groups or teams. A few widely publicized projects have used this approach.

The Volvo Project

The sociotechnical approach to job design has an international flavor, and although the Swedish automaker Saab pioneered the use of autonomous work groups to work on automobile subassembly, the more widely publicized example is that of a Volvo automobile plant in Sweden. When Pehr Gyllenhammar took over as the head of Volvo, Sweden's largest employer, he was convinced that the very serious turnover and absenteeism problems were symptomatic of the values of the employees. Hand in hand with the emerging values of society as a whole, the Volvo employees were demanding more meaningful work—better pay and security, but also participation in the decision-making process and self-regulation. But the technological work process for making automobiles (that is, the assembly lines) did not allow such values to be expressed, and the results were turnover, absenteeism, and low-quality performance.

Under Gyllenhammar's leadership, which took a sociotechnical approach, technological changes were made to reflect more of a natural module of work rather than a continuous work flow, and autonomous work groups were formed. These groups consisted of five to twelve workers who elected their own supervisors and scheduled, assigned, and inspected their own work. Group rather than individual piece rates were used, and all group members made the same amount, except the elected supervisor.

This sociotechnical approach (changing the technological process and utilizing autonomous, self-regulating work groups) was at first applied on a piecemeal basis around the company. Then the new Kalmar assembly plant was completely redesigned along the lines of a sociotechnical approach. On the technological side, the conventional continuous assembly line was changed so that the work remains stationary. A special carrier was developed to transport the car to the various work groups. On the social side, about twenty-five groups made up of about twenty members each perform work on the various modules of an automobile (electrical system, instrumentation, steering and controls, interior, and so forth). These work teams organize any way they want, and they contract with management to deliver a certain number of products per day, for example, brake systems installed or interiors finished. The workers have almost complete control over their own work, scheduling the pace of work and break times. Also important, these teams inspect their own work, and feedback is given to each group via a TV screen at the work station.

In line with more general quality of work-life objectives, a more humane work climate was designed for this Volvo plant. The plant layout is set up to be very light and airy and have a low noise level. There are carpeted "coffee corners," where the groups take their breaks, and there are well-equipped changing rooms.

After this approach to job design was installed at Volvo, turnover and absenteeism were reduced, and quality of work life was reportedly improved. To date, however, no systematic analysis has demonstrated that causal inferences can be made. However, the Volvo top management feel that their new approach to job design has been successful. The latest update from those at the scene is that there have been "false starts, errors, outright failures and, periodically, brilliant breakthroughs."[21] Objectively, the fact is that Kalmar, where QWL is used, has the lowest assembly costs of all Volvo plants.

Self-Managed Teams

Although the Volvo project is the most famous historically, a few companies in the United States also tried a sociotechnical approach to job design. Probably the most widely reported example was that of the General Foods plant in Topeka, Kansas, which produces Gaines pet food. Similar to the Kalmar Volvo plant, this Topeka plant was technologically designed to be compatible with autonomous work groups. The groups were set up in basically the same way as those at the Volvo plant. They had shared responsibility and worked for a coach rather than a supervisor. Status symbols such as parking privileges were abolished.

Initially, the reports on this General Foods project were very favorable. The employees themselves expressed very positive attitudes toward this new approach to work, and management reported that after implementing the project, 35 percent fewer employees were needed to run the plant, quality rejects dipped 92 percent below the industry norm, annual savings of $600,000 resulted from the reduction of variable manufacturing costs, and turnover dropped below the company average.[22] However, more recent reports do not paint such a rosy picture.[23] Some former employees at the Topeka plant indicate that the approach has steadily eroded. Apparently, some managers at the plant are openly hostile to the project because it

Power to the People

One of the lessons that American management has learned about increasing efficiency is that downsizing is not enough. Anyone can come into a company and reduce the number of workers, come up with a lean structure, and reduce short-run costs. However, getting the employees to do the work over the long run, and do it well, is sometimes another story. Quite often, those who remain after downsizing are concerned that they too will be let go. As a result, they do not try very hard. Instead of getting greater productivity, the firm ends up with less. For some companies in the nineties, a new rule is being followed: Eliminate work, not the workers. This means cutting out wasteful procedures and revising operating methods while giving the workers more authority to handle those matters that directly affect productivity. A good example is found in the case of Kodak.

For six years, Kodak had tried to cut costs, but this approach had been both difficult and slow. Then the company introduced a supplemental method. It began by empowering its operating personnel and making them responsible for more of what happened in the factory. For example, at its precision components manufacturing division, assembly workers who make X-ray cassettes and spools, canisters, and cartons for Kodak film now arrange their own hours, keep track of their productivity, and fix their machines. People who used to run punch presses for eight hours a day now coach fellow team members in how to use statistical process controls. These empowered workers also meet with suppliers, interview prospective recruits, and help manage just-in-time inventory. Result: The Kodak team has been able to cut production time for X-ray cassettes by nearly 67 percent with an operation more efficient than ever. By giving the personnel control over their operations and allowing them to do things their own way, Kodak is managing to create a more profitable company for the 1990s.

has undermined their power, authority, and decision-making flexiblity. The project became a media event, and some of the results need tempering.

Volvo and the Topeka General Foods plant are historically important, but the nineties have ushered in a new form of QWL called "self-managed teams" (sometimes called "autonomous work teams" if they direct themselves or "semi-autonomous work teams" if they still have a supervisor to serve as a coach or facilitator). A decade ago, besides the highly-publicized Volvo and General Foods examples, self-managed teams were only being used in a very few innovative companies such as Procter and Gamble, Digital Equipment, and TRW. However, now, because of the influence of the Japanese and the need to become more competitive, more and more companies are turning to this approach to QWL.

A recent survey of Fortune 1000 companies found that while only 7 percent of their work force is currently organized in self-managed teams, half the firms indicated they will be using them more in the years ahead.[24] There are many success stories from well-known companies such as General Mills, Federal Express, and 3M on how their teams have greatly contributed to cost savings and improved productivity.[25] The Application Example, Power to the People, gives details on the successful team approach at Kodak. However, along with the successes are some new problems. One such problem is increased stress and conflict. Here are how these problems are explained at Corning Glass, which has about 3000 teams currently in operation:

> "People problems are the issue," says Sherri Hadrich, a 29-year old kiln operator. For instance, some teams have felt pulled down by one lazy member. "If there's conflict," she says, "we're expected to resolve it," instead of turning to a supervisor. "If someone isn't feeling well or pulling their weight, we can't let it go on or it'll just be a bigger problem," she adds, noting how it's difficult to confront a co-worker. (A new training course focuses on how to get along with teammates.)[26]

Besides the popular press testimonials of the successes and failures of self-managed teams and QWL in general, there is a need for more systematic evaluations before any broad conclusions can be drawn. But with the increasing use by companies to meet competitive pressures as well as societal support for the general improvement of QWL, there is no question but that the sociotechnical approach should and will play an increasingly important role in job design in particular and in the field of organizational behavior in general.

GOAL SETTING

Goal setting is often given as an example of how the field of organizational behavior should progress from a sound theoretical foundation to sophisticated research to the actual application of more effective management practice. There has been considerable theoretical development of goal setting, coming mainly from the cognitively based work of Edwin Locke and his colleagues. To test the theory, there has been considerable research in both laboratory and field settings on the various facets of goal setting. Finally, and important to an applied field such as organizational behavior, goal setting has become an effective tool for the practice of human resources management and an overall performance system approach.

Theoretical Background of Goal Setting

A 1968 paper by Locke is usually considered to be the seminal work on a theory of goal setting.[27] He gives considerable credit to Ryan[28] for stimulating his thinking on the role that intention plays in human behavior, and he also suggests that goal-setting theory really goes back to scientific management at the turn of the century. He credits its first exponent, Frederick W. Taylor, with being the "father of employee motivation theory,"[29] and he says that Taylor's use "of tasks was a forerunner of modern day goal setting."[30]

Although Locke argues that expectancy theories of work motivation originally ignored goal setting and were nothing more than "cognitive hedonism,"[31] his theoretical formulation for goal setting is very similar. He basically accepts the purposefulness of behavior, which comes out of Tolman's cognitive theorizing (see Chapter 1), and the importance of values or valence and consequences. Thus, as in the expectancy theories of work motivation (see Chapter 6), *values and value judgments,* which he defines as the things the individual acts upon to gain and/or to keep, are important cognitive determinants of behavior. He then goes on to say that emotions or desires are the way the person experiences these values. In addition to values, *intentions* or *goals* play an important role as cognitive determinants of behavior. It is here, of course, where Locke's theory of goal setting goes beyond expectancy theories of work motivation. He feels that people strive to attain goals in order to satisfy their emotions and desires. Goals provide a directional nature to people's behavior and guide their thoughts and actions to one outcome rather than another. The individual then responds and performs according to these intentions or goals, even if the goals are not attained. Consequences, feedback, or reinforcement are the result of these responses. Figure 7.4 summarizes the goal-setting theory. Reviews of the literature generally provide considerable support for the theory.[32] A survey of scholars in the field of organizational behavior was conducted to rate fifteen major work-motivation theories on the criteria of scientific validity and practical usefulness. Goal-setting theory was ranked first in validity and second in practical usefulnes.[33]

As previously noted, except for the concept of intentions or goals, Locke's theory is very similar to the other process theories (most notably the Porter-Lawler expectancy model) of work motivation and more recently has been explained in terms of attribution theory, discussed in the last chapter.[34] To Locke's credit, he does carefully point out that goal setting is not the only, or necessarily the most important, concept of work motivation. He notes that the concepts of need and value are the more fundamental concepts of work motivation and are, along with the person's knowledge and premises, what determine goals.

Unlike many other theorists, Locke is continually refining and developing his theory. Recently he has given attention to the role that commitment plays in the theory. He recognized from the beginning that if there is no commitment to goals, goal setting will not work. However, to clarify some of the confusion surrounding its use, Locke and his colleagues define commitment as "one's attachment to or determination to reach a goal, regardless of the goal's origin" and developed a cognitive model to explain the process.[35]

Locke is an ardent supporter of the cognitive interpretation of behavior and is an outspoken critic of other theories, for he says that goal setting is really the underlying explanation for the other theories—whether that be Vroom's VIE theory, Maslow's or Herzberg's motivation theories, or—especially—operant-based behaviorism.[36] He is also critical of more recent *control theory*,[37] and feels that it—like earlier theories—can be interpreted in terms of goal theory. A brief summary of

FIGURE 7.4
Locke's goal-setting theory of work motivation.

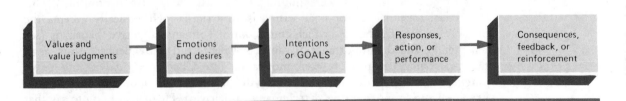

| Values and value judgments | Emotions and desires | Intentions or GOALS | Responses, action, or performance | Consequences, feedback, or reinforcement |

control theory appears in Figure 7.5. Locke and Latham then translate this control theory into goal theory as follows: "The input is feedback from previous performance, the reference signal is the goal, the comparator is the individual's conscious judgment, and the effector or response is his or her subsequent action which works to reduce the discrepancy between the goal and performance."[38] This, of course, is logical, but by the same token, control theory or the other theories could also be used to explain goal-setting theory.

Although Locke is critical of operant-based behaviorism as being too mechanistic, he is supportive of Bandura's expanded social-learning theory (explained in Chapters 1 and 8) and more recent social-cognitive theory[39] (how people come to understand what others are like and explain others' behavior) as being compatible with goal-setting theory. In particular, he feels that social-cognitive theory not only includes goal setting but adds the important dimensions of role-modeling, with significant effects on goal choice and goal commitment and self efficacy (covered in Chapters 4, 6, and 14)—which affects goal choice, goal commitment, and response to feedback.[40]

Research on the Impact of Goal Setting

Locke's theory has generated considerable research. In particular, a series of laboratory studies by Locke and his colleagues and a series of field studies by Gary Latham and his colleagues have been carried out to test the linkage between goal setting and performance.[41]

1. *Specific goals* are better than vague or general goals such as "do your best." In other words, giving a salesperson a specific quota or a worker an exact number of units to produce should be preferable to setting a goal such as "try as hard as you can" or "try to do better than last year."

FIGURE 7.5
Control theory.

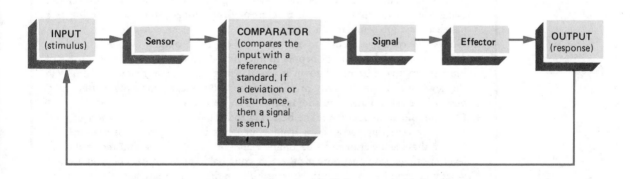

2. *Difficult, challenging goals* are better than relatively easy, mundane goals. However, these goals must be reachable and not so hard to attain that they would be frustrating.

3. *"Owned" and accepted goals* arrived at through participation seem preferable to assigned goals. Although the research is not as clear here as in the first two guidelines,[42] there is evidence that people who set their goals through a participative process, and who thus own their own goals, will perform better than those who are told what their goals are going to be. As the accompanying Application Example demonstrates, personal goals can lead individuals to career success.

4. *Objective, timely feedback about progress toward goals* is preferable to no feedback. Although researchers are still trying to understand the exact effect of feedback (discussed further in Chapter 9), it is probably fair to say that feedback is a necessary but not sufficient condition for successful application of goal setting.

Application Example ⫸

Making Personal Goal Setting Pay Off

Can personal goal setting really help get things done? The answer seems to be yes. Goals not only help people perform better, but can also be an important means of improving career opportunities and getting top dollar. For example, some goals that seem to have particular value to those interested in building a reputation as an expert in their career include the following:

1. *Get something published in your area of expertise.* Examples are writing an article or, even better, a book. Publications help one's expertise and are a good credential to have. The best publisher to use is one that currently markets to those in related career fields. Hence, the publication is likely to be read by relevant others, and the author's reputation will spread. Another good outlet is the local newspaper, which often publishes business-related articles. Many papers have a business section that caters specifically to those interested in picking up the latest information and tips.

2. *Be a lecturer or panelist.* This is another good way to get publicity, and there are many opportunities. Three common ones are guest teaching at a local university, being a luncheon speaker at a local club or professional group, and serving as a panelist for a job seminar at a local college.

3. *Get media coverage.* Work to get on radio or TV programs. Quite often local programmers are looking for people to interview or to discuss some recent topic of interest. If you can become known as a local expert in some area that is continually in the news, such as productivity problems or how to manage people more effectively, you will be asked back time and again.

4. *Use professional associations.* The best way to become known as an expert in your area is by receiving recognition from your peers in professional associations. By joining these associations and becoming active first at the local- and then national-level meetings, you ensure that others in your field get to know who you are and what you stand for. As a result, your visibility in the marketplace increases and so do your chances of being tapped for more important, higher-paying jobs either in your company or with the competition.

To give some idea of the tremendous backup for these "core findings," Locke and Latham recently concluded the following:

> Goal-setting theory is based on the results of some 393 findings on the goal difficulty and difficulty versus do best aspects of the theory alone. The success rate or partial success rate of these studies, regardless of study quality, is over 90 percent. The core findings of the theory are based on data from close to forty thousand subjects in eight countries; eighty-eight different tasks; numerous types of performance measures; laboratory and field settings; experimental and correlational designs; time spans ranging from one minute to three years; studies of assigned, self-set, and participatively-set goals; and data from the group and organizational as well as individual level of analysis.[43]

Although the practical guidelines from goal-setting theory and research are as sound as any in the entire field of organizational behavior, it must be remembered that, as with any complex phenomenon, there still appear to be many important moderating variables in the relationship between goal setting and performance, and there are some contradictory findings.[44] For example, a study by Latham and Saari found that a supportive management style had an important moderating effect and that, contrary to the results of previous studies, specific goals did not lead to better performance than a generalized goal such as "do your best."[45] However, another study did find a highly significant relationship between goal level and performance.[46] Another recent analysis indicated there are also some unexplored areas, such as the distinction between quantity and quality goals,[47] and task complexity,[48] that limit the application of goal setting.

There are also some practical limitations in goal setting. For example, setting difficult goals increases the level of risk managers and employees are willing to take and this may be counterproductive.[49] Also, difficult goals may lead to stress, put a perceptual ceiling on performance, cause the employees to ignore nongoal areas, and encourage short-range thinking, dishonesty, or cheating.[50] However, Locke and Latham do provide specific guidelines of how these potential pitfalls can be overcome by better communication, rewards, and setting examples.[51] On balance, there has been impressive support for the positive impact of setting specific, difficult goals that are accepted and of providing feedback on progress toward goals.

The Application of Goal Setting to Organizational System Performance

A logical extension of goal setting is the traditionally used management-by-objectives, or MBO, approach to planning, control, personnel appraisal, and overall system performance. This approach has been around for over thirty years and thus preceded the theory and research on goal setting per se. MBO is usually attributed to Peter Drucker, who coined the term and suggested that a systematic approach to setting of objectives and appraising by results would lead to improved organizational performance and employee satisfaction. Today, the terminology MBO may no longer be used. Instead, MBO has evolved into an overall systems performance approach using goal setting and appraisal by results. For example, Locke and Latham

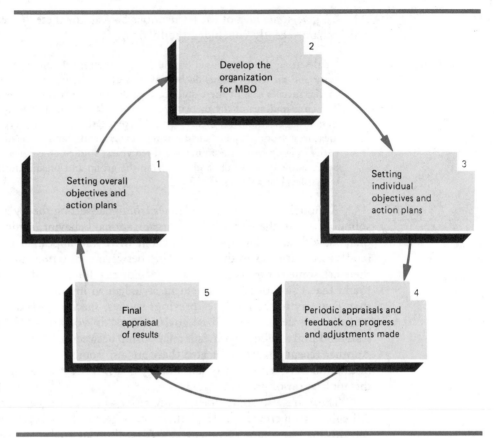

FIGURE 7.6
The application of
goal setting to
system perfor-
mance.

recently noted that "MBO can be viewed as goal setting applied to the macro or
organizational level."[52]

The application of goal setting and appraisal by results of overall organizational
systems generally follows the series of systematic steps outlined in Figure 7.6. As
shown, once the overall objectives have been set and the organization is developed to
the point of accommodating the performance system, individual objectives are set.
These individual objectives are determined by each superior-subordinate pair, starting at the top and going down as far as the system is to be implemented. The scenario
for this process would be something like the following: The boss would contact each
of his or her subordinates and say:

> As you know, we have completed our system performance improvement orientation
> and development program, and it is now time to set individual objectives. I would
> like you to develop by next Tuesday a proposed set of objectives for your area of
> responsibility. Remember that your set of objectives should be in line with the orga-
> nization's overall objectives, which you have a copy of, and they should be able to
> contribute to the objectives that you interact with, namely, my objectives, the other
> units' objectives on your same level, and your subordinates' objectives. Your objec-

tives should be stated in quantifiable, measurable terms and should have a target date. I will also have some suggestions that I think should be given top priority for your area of responsibility. We will sit down and have an open give-and-take session until we reach a *mutually* agreeable set of objectives for your area of responsibility.

In line with the goal-setting research, these objectives should be specific, difficult, and accepted. Like the overall objectives, this set of individual objectives should also be accompanied by action plans developed to spell out how the objectives are to be accomplished.

Although the goal-setting dimension is most closely associated with this approach to system performance, as shown in Figure 7.6, feedback and appraisal by results also play an important role. Individuals will be given feedback and will be appraised on the basis of how they perform in accordance with the objectives that are set. This feedback and appraisal process takes place on both a periodic (at least every quarter in most systems) and an annual basis. The appraisal sessions attempt to be diagnostic rather than purely evaluative. This means simply that the subordinate's superior assesses the reasons why objectives were either attained or not attained, rather than giving punishments or rewards for failure or success in meeting objectives.

Periodic reviews are conducted in order to provide feedback and evaluate progress toward the attainment of objectives. They give the opportunity to make the necessary changes in objectives. Every organization is operating in such a dynamic environment that objectives set at the beginning of the period (usually the fiscal year) may be rendered obsolete in a few months because of changing conditions. Priorities and conditions are constantly changing; these must be monitored in the periodic review sessions, and the needed changes must be made. Constant revision of the individual objectives and, to a lesser degree, of the overall objectives makes a living system that is adaptable to change. At the annual review session, an overall diagnosis and evaluation is made according to results attained, and the system starts over again.

The research results on MBO-type performance systems have been mixed.[53] The most recent comprehensive analyses conclude that these overall goal-setting systems have a slightly positive effect on employee satisfaction, but a much larger, but still modest, effect on productivity.[54]

Summary

This chapter dealt with two of the most important application areas that have emerged in the field of organizational behavior and human resources management. The first part examined job design. Although the concern for designing jobs goes back to the scientific management movement at the turn of the century, the recent concern for the quality of work life (QWL) has led to renewed interest in, and research on, job design. The older job engineering and job enlargement and rotation approaches have given way to a job enrichment approach. Based primarily on the work of Herzberg, job enrichment has been popular (at least in the literature) but may be overly simplistic.

The more recent approach to job design tries to determine the important job characteristics that relate to psychological or motivational states that in turn relate to employee satisfaction and performance. Characteristics such as skill variety, task identity, task significance, autonomy, and feedback do seem to be related to employee satisfaction and quality of work. But the way employees perceive these characteristics and the importance of moderating variables such as growth-need strength are being shown to have an important impact on the relationship between job scope and job satisfaction and employee performance. Alternative models are beginning to account for these effects and also to recognize the impact of more macrooriented variables such as organization structure and technology. More in line with this macro perspective and incorporating QWL concerns is the societechnical approach to job design. Sociotechnical projects at Volvo in Sweden and at General Foods and other companies in this country have important historical significance. Most recently, self-managed teams are having a surge of interest as companies try to use Japanese-style management approaches to meet their competitive problems. These traditional (Volvo and General Foods) and modern applications of self-managed teams have reportedly been very successful. Yet, as is true of the other techniques discussed in this book, more systematic research is needed for the future.

The last half of the chapter dealt with the applications-oriented areas of goal setting in general and an MBO-type performance system approach in particular. Basing his approach on a cognitive perspective, Locke has developed a goal-setting theory of motivation. This theory emphasizes the important relationship between goals and performance. Laboratory and field studies have generally verified this relationship. In particular, the most effective performance seems to result when specific, difficult goals are accepted and when feedback on progress and results is provided. An extension and systematic application of the goal-setting approach is MBO, which has evolved into a total performance system approach with a positive, but modest impact on satisfaction and productivity.

Questions for Discussion and Review

1. Compare and contrast the engineering versus the enrichment approach to job design.
2. What are the core job characteristics in the Hackman-Oldham model? How do you calculate the motivating potential of a job? How would a professor's job and a janitor's job measure up on these characteristics? Be specific in your answer.
3. Describe the sociotechnical project at Volvo. Would you rather work there or at the typical automobile plant in this country? Why?
4. Considering that former employees at the General Foods plant indicate there may be some problems with sociotechnical design, what do you think the future holds for this type of approach? Do you think QWL will and should be legislated? Why?
5. In your own words, describe the theory behind goal setting. What has the research generally found in testing this theory?
6. Summarize the five basic steps of an overall performance systems approach using goal-setting. What have been the research findings on this approach?

References

1. Don Hellriegel, John W. Slocum, Jr., and Richard W. Woodman, *Organizational Behavior*, 5th ed., West, St. Paul, 1989, p. 334.
2. Alecia Swasy and Carol Hymowitz, "The Workplace Revolution," *The Wall Street Journal*, Feb. 9, 1990, p. R6.
3. John B. Miner, *Organizational Behavior*, Random House, New York, 1988, p. 201.
4. J. Richard Hackman, "Work Design," in J. Richard Hackman and J. Lloyd Suttle (eds.), *Improving Life at Work*, Goodyear, Santa Monica, Calif., 1977, p. 129.
5. Ibid., p. 130.
6. David Whitsett, "Where Are Your Enriched Jobs?," *Harvard Business Review*, January–February 1975, pp. 74–80.
7. J. Richard Hackman, Greg R. Oldham, Robert Janson, and Kenneth Purdy, "A New Strategy for Job Enrichment," *California Management Review*, Summer 1975, pp. 55–71.
8. Ricky W. Griffin, "Work Redesign Effects on Employee Attitudes and Behaviors: A Long-Term Field Experiment," *Academy of Management Best Paper Proceedings*, 1989, pp. 216–217.
9. Y. Fried and G. R. Ferris, "The Validity of the Job Characteristics Model: A Review and Meta-Analysis," *Personnel Psychology*, vol. 40, 1987, pp. 287–322.
10. Fred Luthans, Barbara Kemmerer, Robert Paul, and Lew Taylor, "The Impact of a Job Redesign Intervention on Sales-persons' Observed Performance Behaviors," *Group and Organization Studies*, March 1987, pp. 55–72.
11. Gregory Moorhead and Ricky W. Griffin, *Organizational Behavior*, 2d ed., Houghton Mifflin, Boston, 1989, p. 238.
12. Terence R. Mitchell, "Motivation: New Directions for Theory, Research and Practice," *Academy of Management Review*, January 1982, p. 80.
13. Gerald Salancik and Jeffrey Pfeffer, "A Social Information Processing Approach to Job Attitudes and Task Design," *Administrative Science Quarterly*, June 1978, pp. 224–253.
14. Ibid., p. 226.
15. Moorhead and Griffin, op cit., p. 245. For those wishing a more technical discussion see Robert S. Wyer, Jr., and Thomas K. Srull, *Memory and Cognition in Its Social Context*, Erlbaum, Hillsdale, N.J., 1989, Chap. 2, "A General Model of Social Information Processing," pp. 13–32.
16. See Gary J. Blau and Ralph Katerberg, "Toward Enhancing Research with the Social Information Processing Approach to Job Design," *Academy of Management Review*, October 1982, pp. 543–550; William H. Glick, G. Douglas Jenkins, and Nina Gupta, "Method versus Substance: How Strong Are Underlying Relationships between Job Characteristics and Attitudinal Outcomes?" *Academy of Management Journal*, September 1986, pp. 441–464; and Joe G. Thomas, "Sources of Social Information," *Human Relations*, vol. 39, no. 9, 1986, pp. 855–870.
17. Joe Thomas and Ricky W. Griffin, "The Social Information Processing Model of Task Design: A Review of the Literature," *Academy of Management Review*, October 1983, pp. 672–682.
18. Ricky W. Griffin, Thomas S. Bateman, Sandy J. Wayne, and Thomas C. Head, "Objective and Social Factors as Determinants of Task Perceptions and Responses: An Integrated Perspective and Empirical Investigation," *Academy of Management Journal*, September 1987, pp. 501–523; Donald J. Campbell, "Task Complexity: A Review and Analysis," *Academy of Management Review*, January 1988, pp. 40–52.
19. David A. Nadler and Edward E. Lawler III, "Quality of Work Life: Perspectives and Directions," *Organizational Dynamics*, Winter 1983, p. 26.
20. Raymond A. Katzell and Donna E. Thompson, "Work Motivation: Theory and Practice," *American Psychologist*, February 1990, p. 145.
21. Berth Jönsson and Alden G. Lank, "Volvo: A Report on the Workshop on Production Technology and Quality of Working Life," *Human Resources Management*, Winter 1985, p. 463.
22. Richard E. Walton, "How to Counter Alienation in the Plant," *Harvard Business Review*, November–December 1972, p. 77.
23. "Stonewalling Plant Democracy," *Business Week*, Mar. 28, 1977, pp. 78–81, and Lyle Yorks and David Whitsett, "Hawthorne, Topeka, and the Issue of Science versus Advocacy in Organizational Behavior," *Academy of Management Review*, January 1985, pp. 24–26.
24. Brian Dumaine, "Who Needs a Boss?," *Fortune*, May 7, 1990, p. 52.

25. Ibid., pp. 52–53.

26. Swasy and Hymowitz, op. cit., p. R8.

27. Edwin A. Locke, "Toward a Theory of Task Motivation and Incentives," *Organizational Behavior and Human Performance*, May 1968, pp. 157–189.

28. T. A. Ryan and P. C. Smith, *Principles of Industrial Psychology*, Ronald, New York, 1954; and T. A. Ryan, *International Behavior*, Ronald, New York, 1970.

29. Edwin A. Locke, "The Ubiquity of the Technique of Goal Setting in Theories of and Approaches to Employee Motivation," *Academy of Management Review*, July 1978, p. 600.

30. Edwin A. Locke, "The Ideas of Frederick W. Taylor: An Evaluation," *Academy of Management Review*, January 1982, p. 16.

31. Edwin A. Locke, "Personnel Attitudes and Motivation," *Annual Review of Psychology*, vol 26, 1975, pp. 457–480, 596–598.

32. A. J. Mento, R. P. Steele, and R. J. Karren, "A Meta-Analytic Study of the Effects of Goal Setting on Task Performance: 1966–1984," *Organizational Behavior and Human Decision Processes*, vol. 39, 1987, pp. 52–83.

33. C. Lee and P. C. Earley, "Comparative Peer Evaluations of Organizational Behavior Theories," College of Business Administration, Northeastern University, 1988. This study is reported in Edwin A. Locke and Gary P. Latham, *A Theory of Goal Setting and Task Performance*, Prentice-Hall, Englewood Cliffs, N.J., 1990, p. 46.

34. Edwin A. Locke, "Personnel Attitudes and Motivation," pp. 457–480, 596–598.

35. Edwin A. Locke, Gary P. Latham, and Miriam Erez, "The Determinants of Goal Commitment," *Academy of Management Review*, January 1988, p. 24.

36. See Edwin A. Locke, "The Myths of Behavior Mod in Organizations," *Academy of Management Review*, October 1977, pp. 543–553; and Edwin A. Locke, "Resolved: Attitudes and Cognitive Processes are Necessary Elements in Motivational Models," in Barbara Karmel (ed.), *Point and Counterpoint in Organizational Behavior*, Dryden Press, Hinsdale, Ill., 1980, pp. 19–42.

37. See: M. A. Campion and R. G. Lord, "A Control System Conceptualization of the Goal-Setting and Changing Process," *Organizational Behavior and Human Performance*, vol. 30, 1982, pp. 265–287;

R. G. Lord and P. J. Hanges, "A Control System Model of Organizational Motivation: Theoretical Development and Applied Implications," *Behavioral Science*, vol. 32, pp. 161–178; and M. E. Hyland, "Motivational Control Theory: An Integrative Framework," *Journal of Personality and Social Psychology*, vol. 55, 1988, pp. 642–651.

38. Edwin A. Locke and Gary P. Latham, *A Theory of Goal Setting and Task Performance*, Prentice-Hall, Englewood Cliffs, N.J., 1990, p. 19.

39. Albert Bandura, *Social Foundations of Thought and Action*, Prentice-Hall, Englewood Cliffs, N.J., 1986.

40. Locke and Latham, *A Theory of Goal Setting*, pp. 23–24.

41. Locke, "Toward a Theory of Task Motivation and Incentives," summarizes the laboratory studies; and Gary P. Latham and Gary A. Yukl, "A Review of the Research on the Application of Goal Setting in Organizations," *Academy of Management Journal*, December 1975, pp. 824–845, summarizes the field studies. Comprehensive summaries of this research can be found in Edwin A. Locke, Karylle A. Shaw, Lise M. Saari, and Gary P. Latham, "Goal Setting and Task Performance: 1969–1980," *Psychological Bulletin*, July 1981, pp. 125–152; Gary P. Latham and Thomas W. Lee, "Goal Setting," in Edwin A. Locke (ed.), *Generalizing from Laboratory to Field Settings*, Lexington Books, Lexington, Mass., 1986, pp. 101–117; and Mark E. Tubbs, "Goal Setting: A Meta-Analytic Examination of the Empirical Evidence," *Journal of Applied Psychology*, vol. 71, no. 3, 1986, pp. 474–483.

42. For example, see Gary P. Latham and Gary A. Yukl, "The Effects of Assigned and Participative Goal Setting on Performance and Job Satisfaction," *Journal of Applied Psychology*, April 1976, pp. 166–171; Katherine I. Miller and Peter Monge, "Participation, Satisfaction, and Productivity: A Meta-Analytic Review," *Academy of Management Journal*, December 1986, pp. 727–753.

43. Locke and Latham, *A Theory of Goal Setting*, p. 62.

44. See Richard D. Arvey, H. Dudley Dewhirst, and Edward M. Brown, "A Longitudinal Study of the Impact of Changes in Goal Setting on Employee Satisfaction," *Personnel Psychology*, Autumn 1978, pp. 595–608; John R. Hollenbeck and

Arthur P. Brief, "The Effects of Individual Differences and Goal Origin on Goal Setting and Performance," *Organizational Behavior and Human Decision Processes,* vol. 40, 1987, pp. 392–414.

45. Gary P. Latham and Lise M. Saari, "Importance of Supportive Relationships in Goal Setting," *Journal of Applied Psychology,* April 1979, pp. 151–156.

46. Howard Garland, "Goal Level and Task Performance: A Compelling Replication of Some Compelling Results," *Journal of Applied Psychology,* April 1982, pp. 245–248.

47. James T. Austin and Philip Bobko, "Goal Setting Theory: Unexplored Areas and Future Research Needs," *Journal of Occupational Psychology,* vol. 58, no. 4., 1985, pp. 289–308.

48. Donald J. Campbell, "Task Complexity: A Review and Analysis," *Academy of Management Review,* January 1988, pp. 40–52.

49. E. A. Locke and G. P. Latham, *Goal Setting: A Motivational Technique That Really Works,* Prentice-Hall, Englewood Cliffs, N.J., 1984, pp. 171–172.

50. Ibid.

51. Ibid.

52. Locke and Latham, *A Theory of Goal Setting and Task Performance,* p. 15.

53. For example, see J. M. Ivancevich, "Changes in Performance in a Management by Objectives Program," *Administrative Science Quarterly,* vol. 19, 1974, pp. 563–574; Jan P. Muczyk, "A Controlled Field Experiment Measuring the Impact of MBO on Performance Data," *Journal of Management Studies,* October 1978, pp. 318–329; and Kenneth R. Thompson, Fred Luthans, and Will Terpening, "The Effects of MBO on Performance and Satisfaction in a Public Sector Organization," *Journal of Management,* Spring 1981, pp. 53–69.

54. Locke and Latham, *A Theory of Goal Setting and Task Performance,* p. 244. Also see: Raymond A. Katzell and Donna E. Thompson, "Work Motivation: Theory and Practice," *American Psychologist,* Feb. 1990, pp. 149–150.

REAL CASE: MADE BY HAND

One of the major problems for most car makers is auto quality. Each year, quality improves and those who were ahead one year often find themselves falling behind the next. It is a never-ending struggle in which some car firms are able to win the annual battle, but all realize that the war continues and must be waged again and again.

In this industry of "dog eat dog," there is one firm that seems to maintain consistent quality, year after year: Rolls-Royce. The firm claims that approximately 60 percent of all models built since its founding in 1904 are roadworthy. No one disputes the claim. At the same time, the company has not had to engage in a never-ending race to couple advanced technology to the auto line. If anything, Rolls has resisted the introduction of high tech and still managed to turn out one of the world's highest-quality cars. (Some would say, *the* highest-quality car.) One sheet-metal worker who solders six radiator shells a week has noted: "Every so often, someone comes up with the bright idea of bringing in welding machines. But we always come back to hand-molding." And this is not the only area in which handcrafting occurs. Most of the car is made by hand and, in those cases where technology is employed, machine tools are often fifty or more years old. However, this does not stop Rolls from turning out approximately 3200 high-quality automobiles each year. Employing a laborious assembly process, the firm manages to keep its 80,000 parts flowing in sync with the personnel. As a result, the right parts are always at hand and the work is done correctly the first time.

Handcrafting at Rolls-Royce takes a variety of forms. For example, the body shell of each Rolls is cleaned and treated for four days before paint is applied. Some of the hydraulic components are assembled in oil to prevent contamination by dirt. At the same time, the firm is careful to keep the car up-to-date in terms of technological innovation, yet it refuses to hurry the process. For example, Rolls added antiskid brakes five years after most of the other luxury makers did so, because it wanted to refine the system and ensure that the car would not lose its ultrasensitive brake pedal. The latest cars also contain such major innovations as a microprocessor-controlled suspension system, which took the firm four years to develop. Rolls also encourages feedback from the customer regarding ways to improve the car. Thanks to such suggestions the company has developed wood-veneer covers that slide over sun visors when not in use. In the planning stage are additions of slots to steady glasses in the picnic tables that drop from the rear of the front seats.

So while Rolls-Royce is certainly not a giant auto manufacturer (annual sales: $456 million), the company knows that it can continue to maintain its market niche through careful handcrafting and high quality. This combination of old-time quality and the careful introduction of advanced technology appears likely to keep the Rolls reputation intact.

1. Does the company use job enrichment in its auto production? Explain.
2. Does Rolls' approach to building cars incorporate any of the critical psychological states in the job characteristics model?
3. Will Rolls need to change its process and incorporate sociotechnological developments? Explain.

Case: The Rubber Chicken Award	Kelly Sellers is really fed up with his department's performance. He knows that his people have a very boring job, and the way the technological process is set up leaves little latitude for what he has learned about vertically loading the job through job enrichment. Yet he is convinced that there must be some way to make it more interesting to do a dull job. "At least I want to find out for my people and improve their performance," he thinks.

The employees in Kelly's department are involved in the assembly of small hair dryer motors. There are twenty-five to thirty steps in the assembly process, depending upon the motor that is being assembled. The process is very simple, and currently each worker completes only one or two steps of the operation. Each employee has his or her own assigned workstation and stays at that particular place for the entire day. Kelly has decided to try a couple of things to improve performance. First, he has decided to organize the department into work groups. The members of each group would be able to move the workstations around as they desired. He has decided to allow each group to divide the tasks up as they see fit. Next, Kelly has decided to post each group's performance on a daily basis and to reward the group with the highest performance by giving them a "rubber chicken" award that they can display at their workbenches. The production manager, after checking with engineering, has reluctantly agreed to Kelly's proposal on a trial basis.

1. Do you think Kelly's approach to job redesign will work? Rate the core job dimensions from the Hackman-Oldham model of Kelly's employees before and after he redesigned their jobs. What could he do to improve these dimensions even more?

2. How do you explain the fact that Kelly feels he is restricted by the technological process but has still redesigned the work? Is this an example of sociotechnical job redesign?
3. What will happen if this experiment does not work out and the production manager forces Kelly to return to the former task design?

Case: Specific Goals for Human Service

Jackie Jordan is the regional manager of a state human services agency that provides job training and rehabilitation programs for deaf persons. Her duties include supervising counselors as well as developing special programs. One of the difficulties that Jackie has had was with a project supervisor, Kathleen O'Shean. Kathleen is the coordinator of a three-year federal grant for a special project for the deaf. Kathleen has direct responsibility for the funds and the goals of the project. The federal agency that made the grant made continuance of the three-year grant conditional upon some "demonstrated progress" toward fulfilling the purpose of the grant. Jackie's problem with Kathleen was directly related to this proviso. She repeatedly requested that Kathleen develop some concrete goals for the grant project. Jackie wanted these goals written in a specific, observable, and measurable fashion. Kathleen continually gave Jackie very vague, nonmeasurable platitudes. Jackie, in turn, kept requesting greater clarification, but Kathleen's response was that the work that was being done was meaningful enough and took all her time. To take away from the work itself by writing these specific goals would only defeat the purpose of the grant. Jackie finally gave up and didn't push the issue further. One year later the grant was not renewed by the federal government because the program lacked "demonstrated progress."

1. Do you think Jackie was right in requesting more specific goals from Kathleen? Why or why not?
2. Do you think the federal government would have been satisfied with the goal-setting approach that Jackie was pushing as a way to demonstrate progress?
3. Would you have handled the situation differently if you were Jackie? How?

Learning Theory: Reinforcement and Punishment

■ Positive Discipline: Punishing Workers with a Day Off

Disciplining employees has been a continuing problem. Traditionally, companies have relied on progressive discipline, giving an oral reprimand, then a written reprimand, then a suspension and/or docking pay, and then termination. This approach treats problem employees worse and worse and expects them to get better and better. It just has not been working very well. Today, a growing number of firms such as AT&T, General Electric, Tampa Electric, Martin Marietta, and Union Carbide have gone 180 degrees and have tried what has become known as positive discipline. Here's how it works:

1. When employees break a rule or do poor-quality work or are chronically absent or tardy, they first get an oral "reminder" of the deficiency and how to correct it instead of the traditional reprimand.
2. The second infraction draws a written reminder pointing out the problem and how to correct it.
3. Next comes a paid day off. Often called a "decision making leave day," this represents a radical departure from traditional discipline. At this point, disciplined employees are usually required to agree in writing (or orally in some union shops) to be on their best behavior for the following year.
4. If employees still do not shape up after the paid day off, then they are terminated.

This radical approach seems to work. One manager at Tampa Electric initially thought it was ridiculous, until he tried it. He said, "It sounded like a reward for bad behavior, like a gimmick from some consultant." Then he tried it on a lazy mechanic. "We gave him a day off to decide if he wanted his job, and we sure got his attention. He turned around on his own." As a young construction worker with Martin Marietta who was positively disciplined commented: "It got me to change my attitude. I was embarrassed in front of everyone when they told me I had the day off. I didn't want that to happen again." Since his "day off" this worker received two promotions and a 50 percent raise in pay.

Learning Objectives

- **Define** the types and theories of learning with special attention given to classical and operant approaches.
- **Explain** social learning theory with special attention given to modeling processes and applications.
- **Discuss** reinforcement and the law of effect.
- **Analyze** organizational reward systems with special attention given to feedback and money.
- **Relate** the techniques of administering reinforcement.
- **Present** the meaning of punishment and the ways to administer it.

Along with motivation, learning has occupied a central role in the micro perspective of organizational behavior. Whereas motivation has been a more popular construct over the years in the field of organizational behavior, learning has been more dominant in the field of psychology. Learning has been given secondary attention in the study of organizational behavior. However, few organization behavior theorists and researchers would challenge the statement that learning is involved in almost everything that everyone does. Learning definitely affects human behavior in organizations. There is little organizational behavior that is not either directly or indirectly affected by learning. For example, a worker's skill, a manager's attitude, a supervisor's motivation, and a secretary's mode of dress are all learned.

The purpose of this chapter is to present an overview of the learning process and some of the basic principles which will contribute to the better understanding, prediction, and control of organizational behavior and which will serve as a foundation for the application techniques discussed in the next chapter. The first section distinguishes between the various types of learning and summarizes the major theoretical approaches. The next section is concerned with the reinforcement principle and its application. Included are discussions of the law of effect, types of reinforcement, and organizational reward systems. The third section deals with techniques of administering reinforcement. The last section is devoted to the effect of punishment on learning and behavior.

TYPES AND THEORIES OF LEARNING

Learning is a term frequently used by a great number of people in a wide variety of contexts. Yet, despite its diverse use, academicians have generally recognized one, or at most two, ways in which behavior can be acquired or changed. Starting with the early behaviorists (for example, John B. Watson and later B. F. Skinner), the most common explanation of learning has been *direct,* noncognitively mediated, classical and operant conditioning. Most of the learning principles that have been developed over the years and the discussion in this chapter and the next are greatly influenced by this approach to learning. However, recognition of the interactive nature of human behavior and the role of cognitive contingencies that fall under the social learning theory described in Chapter 1 implies other explanations of learning. In particular, learning can also be explained by cognitively or noncognitively mediated vicarious or *modeling* processes and/or by cognitively or noncognitively mediated *self-control* processes. These three types of learning—direct, modeling, and self-control—suggest that there are different theoretical bases for learning, and these will be drawn upon in the following sections.

The most basic purpose of any theory is to better explain the phenomenon in question. When theories become perfected, they have universal application and should enable prediction and control. Thus, a perfected theory of learning would have to be able to explain all aspects of learning (how, when, and why), have universal application (for example, to children, college students, managers, and workers), and predict and control learning situations. To date, no such theory of learning exists. Although there is general agreement on some principles of learning, there is still disagreement on the theory behind it. This does not mean that no attempts have been made to develop a theory of learning. In fact, the opposite is true. The most widely recognized theoretical approaches follow the behavioristic and cognitive approaches discussed in Chapter 1 and the newly emerging social learning theory. An understanding of these three learning theories is important to the study of organizational behavior.

Connectionist, Behavioristic Theories of Learning

The dominant and most researched theory comes out of the behaviorist school of thought in psychology. Most of the principles of learning discussed in this chapter and the applications discussed in the next chapter are based on operant, or Skinnerian, behaviorism.

The classical behaviorists, such as Pavlov and Watson, attributed learning to the association or connection between stimulus and response (S-R). The operant behaviorists, in particular Skinner, give more attention to the role that consequences play in learning, or the R-S (response-stimulus) connection. The emphasis on the connection (S-R or R-S) has led some to label these the *connectionist* theories of learning. The S-R deals with classical or respondent conditioning, and the R-S deals with instrumental or operant conditioning. An understanding of these conditioning processes is vital to the study of learning and serves as a point of departure for understanding and modifying organizational behavior.

Classical Conditioning. Pavlov's classical conditioning experiment using dogs as subjects is undoubtedly the single most famous study ever conducted in the behavioral sciences. A simple surgical procedure permitted Pavlov to measure accurately the amount of saliva secreted by a dog. When he presented meat powder (unconditioned stimulus) to the dog in the experiment, Pavlov noticed a great deal of salivation (unconditioned reponse). On the other hand, when he merely rang a bell (neutral stimulus), the dog had no salivation. The next step taken by Pavlov was to accompany the meat with the ringing of the bell. After doing this several times, Pavlov rang the bell without presenting the meat. This time, the dog salivated to the bell alone. The dog had become classically conditioned to salivate (conditioned response) to the sound of the bell (conditioned stimulus). The classical experiment was a major breakthrough and has had a lasting impact on the understanding of learning.

Pavlov went beyond the simple conditioning of his dogs to salivate to the sound of the bell. He next paired a black square with the bell. After a number of trials with this pairing, the dogs salivated to the black square alone. The original conditioned stimulus (bell) had become a reinforcing unconditioned stimulus for the new conditioned stimulus (black square). When the dogs responded to the black square, they became what is known as *second-order-conditioned*. Pavlov was able to obtain no higher than third-order conditioning with his dogs.

Most behaviorists would argue that humans are capable of being conditioned higher than the third order. The exact number is not important, but the potential implications of higher-order conditioning for human learning and behavior should be recognized. For example, higher-order conditioning can explain how learning can be transferred to stimuli other than those used in the original conditioning. The existence of higher-order conditioning shows the difficulty of tracing the exact cause of a certain behavior. Another important implication concerns the principle of reinforcement. Higher-order conditioning implies that reinforcement can be acquired. A conditioned stimulus becomes reinforcing under higher-order conditioning. It substantiates, and perhaps offers a plausible explanation for, the secondary rewards such as money which play an important role in organizational behavior.

Despite the theoretical possibility of the widespread applicability of classical conditioning, most modern theorists agree that it represents only a very small part of total human learning. Skinner in particular felt that classical conditioning explains only respondent (reflexive) behaviors. These are the involuntary responses that are elicited by a stimulus. Skinner felt that the more complex, but common, human behaviors cannot be explained by classical conditioning alone. He felt that most human behavior affects, or operates on, the environment. The latter type of behavior is learned through operant conditioning.

Operant Conditioning. Operant conditioning is concerned primarily with learning that occurs as a *consequence* of behavior. It is not concerned with the eliciting causes of behavior, as classical or respondent conditioning is. The specific differences between classical and operant conditioning may be summarized as follows:

1. In classical conditioning, a change in the stimulus (unconditioned stimulus to conditioned stimulus) will elicit a particular response. In operant conditioning, one particular response out of many possible ones occurs in a given stimulus situation. The stimulus situation serves as a cue in operant conditioning. It does not elicit the response but serves as a cue for a person to emit the response. The critical aspect of operant conditioning is what happens as a consequence of the response. The strength and frequency of classically conditioned behaviors are determined mainly by the frequency of the eliciting stimulus (the environmental event that precedes the behavior). The strength and frequency of operantly conditioned behaviors are determined mainly by the consquences (the environmental event that follows the behavior).

2. During the classical conditioning process, the unconditioned stimulus, serving as a reward, is presented every time. In operant conditioning, the reward is presented only if the organism gives the correct response. The organism must operate on the environment in order to receive a reward. The response is instrumental in obtaining the reward. Table 8.1 gives some examples of classical (S-R) and operant (R-S) conditioning.

Operant conditioning has a much greater impact on human learning than classical conditioning. Operant conditioning also explains, at least in a very simple sense, much of organizational behavior. For example, it might be said that employees work eight hours a day, five days a week, in order to feed, clothe, and shelter themselves and their families. Working (conditioned response) is instrumental only in obtaining the food, clothing, and shelter. Some significant insights can be directly gained from this kind of analysis. The consequences of organizational behavior can change the environmental situation and largely affect subsequent employee behaviors. Although some organizations are concerned with trying to unlearn their managers' behaviors, as indicated in the accompanying Application Example, most are concerned with the analysis of the consequences of organizational behavior to help accomplish the goals of prediction and control. Some organizational behavior researchers are currently using the operant framework to analyze the effectiveness of managers at work.[1] In addition, the next chapter will discuss in detail most of these aspects of operant conditioning and the applications of operant conditioning to organizational behavior.

Cognitive Theories of Learning

Edward Tolman was portrayed in the introductory chapter as a pioneering cognitive theorist. He felt that learning consists of a *relationship between cognitive environ-*

TABLE 8.1 Examples of Classical and Operant Conditioning

	Classical Connection	
	(S) Stimulus ——————————→	(R) Response
The individual:	is stuck by a pin is tapped below the kneecap is shocked by an electric current is surprised by a loud sound	flinches flexes lower leg jumps/screams jumps/screams
	Operant Connection	
	(R) Response ——————————→	(S) Stimulus
The individual:	works talks to others enters a restaurant enters a library works hard	is paid meets more people obtains food finds a book receives praise and a promotion

Application Example ⟶

Unlearning

While reinforcement is the key to learning, there are a number of firms that are now providing their managers with training programs that try to get them to "unlearn" or undo previous learning. In particular, these companies want to teach their managers that sometimes the old cliché "If at first you don't suceed, try, try again" may not be a good one. Sometimes it is important to know when to quit trying and move on to something else. This is particularly true when a manager faces a "no win" situation in which managers end up wasting their time. For example, many managers fail to realize that some projects will not come to fruition and it is best to terminate them early. Once it becomes obvious that the undertaking is going to take a lot more time or money than the firm can or should wisely invest, it is time to drop this project and go on to another one. Managers who fail to realize this often endanger their own careers in the process. They are viewed as "win at all costs" types and are soon tabbed as too hard-headed for further promotion.

What kinds of guidelines should managers follow in learning when to push forward and when to back off? Some of the most important are these:

1. *Set realistic, but not perfectionistic, work standards.* If too much time is exhausted on one project, other more lucrative ones may suffer as a result.
2. *It is often better to perform consistently well than to have a perfect score.* Managers who strive for perfect scores often contribute less to the organization than do those who consistently do a better-than-average job.
3. *Remember that planning is important.* Managers who figure out what needs to be done in their department and then match the tasks with personnel abilities often achieve outstanding results. It is not necessary to spend countless hours in the planning process; a few hours a week is often more than enough.
4. *Sometimes it is impossible to prevent things from going wrong.* All managers have problems with their projects. These are to be expected. The important thing is to accept problems as inevitable and learn from them so that they are not repeated in the future.
5. *Keep the door open for improvement.* Many companies provide advice and assistance in the form of coaching, counseling, mentoring, and outside consulting. Successful managers learn to accept this help and profit from it. Those who do not often find their career opportunities stymied or end up leaving the firm because they are unable to be team players. They put their ego ahead of the company's welfare.

---

mental cues and expectation. He developed and tested this theory through controlled experimentation. He was one of the first to use the now famous white rat in psychological experiments. He found that a rat could learn to run through an intricate maze, with purpose and direction, toward a goal (food). Tolman observed that at each choice point in the maze, expectations were established. In other words, the rat learned to *expect* that certain cognitive cues associated with the choice point might eventually lead to food. If the rat actually received the food, the association between the cue and the expectancy was strengthened, and learning occurred. In contrast to the S-R and R-S learning in the classical and operant approaches, Tolman's approach could be depicted as S-S (stimulus-stimulus).

Tolman's experiments called into question some of the operant learning assumptions. For example, in his famous place-learning experiments he trained a rat to turn right in a "T" maze in order to obtain food. Then he started the rat from the opposite part of the maze; according to operant theory, the rat should have turned right because of past conditioning. But in Tolman's experiments the rat instead turned toward where the food had been placed. Tolman concluded that the rat's behavior was purposive, that is, that the rat formed a cognitive map to figure out how to get to the food. In other words, Tolman said that reinforcing consequences were not a precondition for learning to take place. One stimulus leads to another stimulus, or S-S, rather than the classical S-R or the operant R-S explanation.

Tolman also conducted latent learning and transposition experiments to demonstrate that reinforcement is not needed for learning to occur. However, in time the behavioristic theorists were able to negate Tolman's results. By using more controlled experimental procedures, they were able to verify their predictions. For example, when there were perfectly sterile conditions in the place-learning experiments (for example, when a bubble was placed over the maze and the runways were carefully scrubbed), the rat turned right as conditioned instead of purposively going toward the food.

Even though most of Tolman's experiments have been discredited, he made a significant contribution to the development of learning theory. He forced behaviorists to develop more complex explanations of behavior, and he pinpointed the need to consider cognitions as having at least a possible mediating role between the stimulus environment and the behavior. The theory building has served as a transition and an integrating mechanism leading toward social learning theory, which will be covered in the next section.

Besides being the forerunner of modern social learning theory, Tolman's S-S cognitive theory also had a great impact on the early human relations movement. Industrial training programs in the 1940s and 1950s drew heavily on Tolman's ideas. Programs were designed to strengthen the relationship between cognitive cues (supervisory, organizational, and job procedures) and worker expectations (incentive payments for good performance). The theory was that the worker would learn to be more productive by building an association between taking orders or following directions and expectancies of monetary reward for this effort.

Today, the cognitive sciences focus more on the structures and processes of human competence (e.g., the role of memory and information processing) rather than on the acquisition and transition processes that have dominated learning theory explanations.[2] In organizational behavior, the cognitive approach has mainly applied to motivation theories and techniques as discussed in the preceding two chapters. Expectations, attributions and locus of control, and goal setting (which are in the forefront of modern work motivation) are all cognitive concepts and represent the purposefulness of organizational behavior. Many researchers are currently concerned about the relationship or connection between cognitions and organizational behavior.[3]

Social Learning Theory

Chapter 1 introduced social learning theory. It was said that social learning theory combines and integrates both behaviorist and cognitive concepts and emphasizes the interactive nature of cognitive, behavioral, and environmental determinants. This social learning approach was used as the basis for developing the conceptual framework for this book.

It is important to recognize that social learning theory is a *behavioral* theory and draws heavily from the principles of classical and operant conditioning. But equally important is the fact that social learning theory goes beyond classical and operant theory by recognizing that there is more to learning than direct learning via antecedent stimuli and contingent consequences. Social learning theory posits that learning can also take place via vicarious or modeling and self-control processes. Thus, social learning theory agrees with classical and operant conditioning processes but says they are too limiting.

Modeling Processes. The vicarious or modeling processes essentially involve observational learning. "Modeling in accordance with social learning theory can account for certain behavior acquisition phenomena that cannot be easily fitted into either operant or respondent conditioning."[4]

Many years ago, Miller and Dollard suggested that learning need not result from discrete stimulus-response or response-consequence connections. Instead, learning can take place through imitating others. Albert Bandura is most closely associated with the modern view of modeling as an explanation of learning. He states:

> Although behavior can be shaped into new patterns to some extent by rewarding and punishing consequences learning would be exceedingly laborious and hazardous if it proceeded solely on this basis. . . . [It] is difficult to imagine a socialization process in which the language, mores, vocational activities, familial customs and educational, religious and political practices of a culture are taught to each new member by selective reinforcement of fortuitous behavior, without benefit of models who exemplify the cultural patterns in their own behavior. Most of the behaviors that people display are learned either deliberately or inadvertently, through the influence of example.[5]

Bandura has done considerable research that demonstrates that people can learn from others.[6] This learning takes place in two steps. First, the person observes how others act and then acquires a mental picture of the act and its consequences (rewards and punishers). Second, the person acts out the acquired image and if the consequences are positive, he or she will tend to do it again. If the consequences are negative, the person will tend not to do it again. This, of course, is where there is a tie-in with operant theory. But because there is cognitive, symbolic representation of the modeled activities instead of discrete response-consequence connections in the acquisition of new behavior, modeling goes beyond the operant explanation. In particular, Bandura concludes that modeling involves interrelated subprocesses such as *attention, retention,* and *motoric reproduction,* as well as reinforcement. Others emphasize that a primary basis of vicarious learning is a cognitively held "script" on the part of the observer of a model.[7] This script is a procedural knowledge or cognitive structure or framework for understanding and doing behaviors.

Modeling Applications. There is a growing literature that suggests that modeling can be effectively applied to the field of organizational behavior.[8] A specific modeling strategy could be used to improve human performance in today's organizations.[9] Such a strategy might include the following steps:

1. Precisely identify the goal or target behavior that will lead to performance improvement.
2. Select the appropriate model and modeling medium (for example, a live demonstration, a training film, or a videotape).
3. Make sure the employee is capable of meeting the technical skill requirements of the target behavior.
4. Structure a favorable learning environment which increases the probability of attention and reproduction and which enhances motivation to learn and improve.
5. Model the target behavior and carry out supporting activities, such as role playing. Clearly demonstrate the positive consequences of the modeled target behavior.
6. Positively reinforce reproduction of the target behavior both in training and back on the job.
7. Once it is reproduced, maintain and strengthen the target behavior, first with a continuous schedule of reinforcement and later with an intermittent schedule.[10]

A number of studies show that such modeling procedures have had a very favorable impact on industrial training programs.[11] For example, in one study, forty first-line supervisors who received modeling training in nine interpersonal skill areas (for example, orienting a new employee, reducing absenteeism, and overcoming resistance to change) were judged to be significantly more effective than a group of matched supervisors who did not receive the training.[12]

REINFORCEMENT: THE KEY TO LEARNING

Reinforcement plays a central role in the learning process. Most learning experts agree that reinforcement is the single most important principle of learning. Yet there is much controversy over its theoretical explanation. The first major theoretical treatment given to reinforcement in learning and the theory that still dominates today is Thorndike's classic law of effect.

The Law of Effect

In Thorndike's own words, the law of effect is simply stated thus: "Of several responses made to the same situation, those which are accompanied or closely followed by satisfaction (reinforcement) . . . will be more likely to recur; those which are accompanied or closely followed by discomfort (punishment) . . . will be less likely to occur."[13] From a strictly empirical standpoint, most behavioral scientists, even those with a cognitive orientation, generally accept the validity of this law.

It has been demonstrated time after time in highly controlled learning experiments and is directly observable in everyday learning experiences. Desirable or reinforcing consequences will increase the strength of a response and increase its probability of being repeated in the future. Undesirable or punishing consequences will decrease the strength of a response and decrease its probability of being repeated in the future.

Although there is wide acceptance of the law of effect, there are occasions when a person's cognitive rationalizations may neutralize it. For example, people with inaccurate self-efficacy beliefs may not be affected by the consequences of their actions. In the workplace, this is a real problem for managers. Those with inaccurate self-efficacy beliefs who experience performance failures time after time will not learn from their mistakes nor respond to the manager on how to correct the problem. They have high self-efficacy (they believe that their behaviors are appropriate to successfully accomplish the task) and they are wrong.[14] In addition to this type of cognitive processing that may neutralize the law of effect, there is some disagreement when it is carried a step further and used as an overall theory or an absolute requirement for learning.

As the discussion of cognitive learning theory indicated, Tolman and other critics of the requirement of reinforcement use such concepts as that of latent learning to make their point. For example, in latent learning experiments it was shown that rats that were reinforced after successful trials in running a maze showed fewer errors than rats that were not reinforced. However, once the rat was reinforced after a number of nonreinforced trials, there were very few errors. In other words, even though the nonreinforced rats were not as efficient, when they finally were reinforced, they were more efficient. The explanation offered was that learning indeed takes place during the nonreinforcement trials and that the reinforcement only makes it worthwhile. Like the researchers who conducted the place-learning experiments, the behaviorists were eventually able to show that, under highly controlled experimental conditions, such latent, nonreinforced learning did not occur.

Despite the theoretical controversy, few would argue against the importance of reinforcement to the learning process. Theoretical attempts besides the law of effect have generally failed to explain reinforcement fully. However, as with the failure to develop a generally accepted overall theory of learning, the lack of an accepted theory of reinforcement does not detract from its extreme importance.

Definition of Reinforcement

The term *reinforcement* is conceptually related to the psychological process of motivation, which was covered in the preceding chapters. There is a temptation to equate reinforcement with motivation. Although this is sometimes deliberately or nondeliberately done,[15] this book treats them separately. Motivation is a basic psychological process and is broader and more complex than is implied by the learning principle of reinforcement as used here. In addition, the need states that are so central to motivation are cognitive in nature; they are unobservable inner states. Reinforcement, on the other hand, is environmentally based. Reinforcers under a behavioristic perspective are external, environmental events that are consequences of behavior. In general terms, motivation is an internal explanation of behavior, and reinforcement is an external explanation of behavior. Thus, the perspectives and explanation of behavior as being due to motivation and reinforcement are quite different.

An often cited circular definition of reinforcement says that it is anything the person finds rewarding. This definition is of little value because the words "reinforcing" and "rewarding" are used interchangeably, but neither one is operationally defined. A more operational definition can be arrived at by reverting back to the law of effect. Under this law, reinforcement can be defined as anything that both increases the strength of response and tends to induce repetitions of the behavior that preceded the reinforcement.

A reward, on the other hand, is simply something that the person who presents it deems to be desirable. A reward is given by a person who thinks it is desirable. Reinforcement is functionally defined. Something is reinforcing only if it strengthens the response preceding it and induces repetitions of the response. For example, a manager may ostensibly reward an employee who found an error in a report by publicly praising the employee. Yet, upon examination it is found that the employee is embarrassed and harassed by coworkers, and error-finding behavior decreases in the future. In this example, the "reward" is *not* reinforcing. Even though there is this technical difference between a reward and a reinforcer, the terms are often used interchangeably and will be in this book.

To better understand reinforcers it is necessary, besides clearing up the differences between reinforcers and rewards, to make the distinctions between positive and negative reinforcers.

Positive and Negative Reinforcers

There is much confusion surrounding the terms *positive reinforcement* and *negative reinforcement* and the terms *negative reinforcement* and *punishment*. First of all, it must be understood that reinforcement, positive or negative, strengthens the response and increases the probability of repetition. But the positive and negative reinforcers accomplish this impact on behavior in completely different ways. Positive reinforcement strengthens and increases behavior by the *presentation* of a desirable consequence. Negative reinforcement strengthens and increases behavior by the *termination* or *withdrawal* of an undesirable consequence. Figure 8.1 briefly summarizes the differences between positive and negative reinforcement and punishment. Giving praise to an employee for the successful completion of a task could be an example of *positive* reinforcement (if this does in fact strengthen and subsequently increase this task behavior). On the other hand, a worker is *negatively* reinforced for getting busy when the supervisor walks through the area. Getting busy terminates being "chewed out" by the supervisor.

Negative reinforcement is more complex than positive reinforcement, but it should not be equated with punishment. In fact, they have an opposite effect on behavior. Negative reinforcement strengthens and increases behavior, while punishment weakens and decreases behavior. However, both are considered to be forms of negative control of behavior. Negative reinforcement is really a form of social blackmail because the person will behave in a certain way or be punished. A

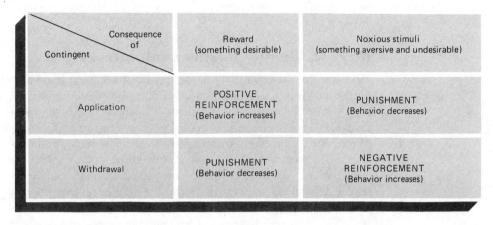

FIGURE 8.1
Summary of the operational definitions of positive and negative reinforcement and punishment.

discussion of escape and avoidance learning will help clarify this aspect of negative reinforcement.

Escape–Avoidance Learning: A Special Case of Negative Reinforcement

A learning phenomenon which demonstrates the impact of negative reinforcement is escape-avoidance learning. It goes a step beyond simple conditioning by using negative reinforcement. A simple escape learning experiment involves shocking a rat in a Skinner box. Only pressing the bar will terminate the shock. The rat must learn to press the bar to escape the pain from the shock. Once escape is learned, avoidance can also be learned. In the Skinner box, a light may be timed to go on a few seconds before the shock is administered. The rat can learn to avoid the shock altogether by running over to press the bar whenever the bulb lights up.

Humans learn escape-avoidance in much the same way. For example, workers may learn to escape a boring job with no challenge by organizing into informal groups or by playing games during working hours. When the quitting whistle blows, the aversive situation stops, and the employees return to being very active, serious-minded individuals. In another situation a worker may learn to avoid an unpleasant confrontation with a supervisor by knowing the time of day when the supervisor makes rounds. The worker is either conveniently gone or too busy to have any interaction with the supervisor, thus avoiding a punishing situation. People come to work on time to *avoid* being reprimanded by the boss. Supervisors get their reports in on time to *avoid* being punished by the boss. Middle managers conform to established policies to *avoid* being punished by top managers, and top managers try to look good on the balance sheet to *avoid* getting into trouble with the board of directors. In other words, organizational participants are exhibiting many avoidance behaviors and are under negative control. A major goal for human resource management would be somehow to turn this situation around so that organizational participants would perform appropriate behaviors because they are *positively* reinforced for doing so.

Ways to Identify Positive Reinforcers

Since some of the commonly used organizational rewards are not necessarily positive reinforcers, it is vitally important that objective measures be used whenever possible to tell whether a reward is in fact a positive reinforcer. Several techniques are available to help determine potential positive reinforcers. The most accurate method of identifying positive reinforcers, but often the most difficult to implement, is to empirically analyze each individual's history of reinforcement. Knowledge of what a particular person likes and dislikes, gained through experience, can help in this regard. However, in cases where there is little or no experience with the individual, several self-reporting techniques can be used.

The most straightforward technique is simply to ask what the person finds to be rewarding. Although the person may not always tell the truth, it is nonetheless a logical point of departure for identifying potential reinforcers. Table 8.2 gives examples of questions that employees could be asked to help identify potential reinforcers. Employees could fill out such a form when they are hired, or every year or so, to help the manager find specific rewards for each employee.

Organizational Reward Systems

The technique discussed above can be used to help identify organizational rewards. Although reinforcers are highly individualized, research and experience have shown that there are several rewards that most organizational participants find positively reinforcing. These can be classified as *contrived* and *natural* rewards. Contrived rewards are brought in from outside the work environment and generally involve

TABLE 8.2 Questions That Could Be Asked in an Employee Reinforcer Survey

Employee Reinforcer Survey
1. In my free time my favorite activity is _____
2. I would like to visit _____
3. My favorite sports activity is _____
4. My favorite hobby is _____
5. Something that I really want to buy is _____
6. If I had $50 to spend on myself right now, I would _____
7. My job would be more rewarding if _____
8. If my manager would _____ I would enjoy working here.
9. I would work harder if _____
10. The place that I most like to shop is _____

Source: Adapted from Lawrence M. Miller, *Behavior Management*, Wiley, New York, 1978, p. 149.

costs for the organization over and above the existing situation. Examples would include the consumables, manipulatables, visual and auditory reinforcers, and tokens listed in Table 8.3. Natural rewards, as Table 8.3 shows, are already part of the work environment. The two most widely used and effective rewards are feedback about performance (natural) and money (contrived).

Feedback as a Reinforcer. The literature on the impact that feedback has on organizational participants was discussed in Chapter 7. There is little question that despite the tremendous amount of data being generated by computerized information systems in modern organizations, individuals still receive very little, if any, feedback about their performance. People generally have an intense desire to know *how* they are doing, especially if they have some degree of achievement motivation (see Chapter 6). It is generally accepted that feedback enhances individual performance.[16] A recent comprehensive review (thirty laboratory and forty-two field experiments) concluded that objective feedback had a positive effect.[17] In general, feedback should be as *positive*, *immediate*, *graphic*, and *specific*—i.e., the acronym PIGS—as possible to be effective.[18]

Despite the recognized importance, there is some disagreement as to whether feedback per se is automatically reinforcing or simplistic.[19] For example, after reviewing the existing research literature on feedback, one researcher concluded that its

TABLE 8.3 Classifications On-The-Job Rewards

Contrived On-The-Job Rewards				Natural Rewards	
Consumables	**Manipulatables**	**Visual and auditory**	**Tokens**	**Social**	**Premack**
Coffee-break treats	Desk accessories	Office with a window	Money	Friendly greetings	Jobs with more responsibility
Free lunches	Wall plaques	Piped-in music	Stocks	Informal recognition	Job rotation
Food baskets	Company car	Redecoration of work environment	Stock options	Formal acknowledgment of achievement	Early time off with pay
Easter hams	Watches	Company literature	Movie passes	Feedback about performance	Work on personal project on company time
Christmas turkeys	Trophies	Private office	Trading stamps (green stamps)	Solicitations of suggestions	Use of company machinery or facilities for personal projects
Dinners for the family on the company	Commendations	Popular speakers or lecturers	Paid-up insurance policies	Solicitations of advice	
Company picnics	Rings/tie pins	Book club discussions	Dinner and theater tickets	Compliment on work progress	Use of company recreation facilities
After-work wine and cheese parties	Appliances and furniture for the home		Vacation trips	Recognition in house organ	Special assignments
	Home shop tools		Coupons redeemable at local stores	Pat on the back	
	Garden tools		Profit sharing	Smile	
	Clothing			Verbal or nonverbal recognition or praise	
	Club privileges				

Source: Fred Luthans and Robert Kreitner, *Organizational Behavior Modification and Beyond*, Scott, Foresman, Glenview, Ill., 1985, p. 127.

impact is contingent upon factors such as the nature of the feedback information, the process of using feedback, individual differences among the recipients of the feedback, and the nature of the task.[20] One study, for instance, found that self-generated feedback with goal setting had a much more powerful effect on technical/engineering employees than externally generated feedback with goal setting.[21] Also, another study found subjects rated specific feedback more positively than they rated nonspecific feedback, and preferred feedback that suggested an external cause of poor performance to feedback that suggested an internal cause.[22] And the source of the feedback seems important as well. Not only are the amount and the frequency of feedback generated by a source important, but also the consistency and usefulness of the information generated, as a study found. Individuals viewed feedback from formal organizations least positively, from coworkers next, then from supervisors and tasks, and the best was self-generated feedback.[23]

Despite these qualifications and contingencies, a general guideline regarding feedback about performance is that it can be an effective positive reinforcer. For example, a supervisor faced with the problem of people taking unscheduled breaks successfully used feedback to reinforce them for staying on the job. Specifically, the supervisor calculated the exact cost for each worker in the unit (in terms of lost group piece-rate pay) every time any one of them took an unscheduled break. This information regarding the relatively significant amount of lost pay when any one of them took an unscheduled break was fed back to the employees of the unit. After this feedback, staying on the job increased in frequency, and taking unscheduled breaks dramatically decreased. The feedback pointed out the contingency that staying on the job meant more money. At least in this case, money proved to be a more reinforcing consequence than the competing contingencies of enjoying social rewards with friends in the rest room and withdrawing from the boring job. The feedback in this case clarified the monetary contingency.

Money as a Reinforcer. Despite the tendency in recent years to downgrade the importance of money as an organizational reward, there is ample evidence that money can be positively reinforcing for most people. The downgrading of money is partly the result of the motivation theories of Maslow and Herzberg, plus the publicity given to surveys which consistently place wages and salaries near the middle of the list of employment factors that are important to workers and managers.

There are also recent studies indicating that a salary increase, no matter how large, merely intensifies the belief that the employee deserves more.[24] The idea here is that once the money covers the basic needs, people use it to get ahead, which is always just out of reach. Although money was probably overemphasized in classical management theory and motivation techniques, the pendulum now seems to have swung too far in the opposite direction. Money remains a very important but admittedly complex potential reinforcer. The Application Example, It's Big League Bucks, helps explain this statement.

In terms of Maslow's hierarchy, money is often equated only with the most basic level of needs. It is viewed in the material sense of buying food, clothing, and shelter. Yet money has a symbolic as well as an economic material meaning. It can

It's Big League Bucks

Is money important to individuals who make large annual salaries? If the major leagues are any indication, it certainly is. Every year, there are ballplayers who have played out their option and become free agents so that they can negotiate with other teams and, in the process, greatly increase their earning power. Thirty years ago, only a handful of players made $100,000 for the season. Today, the major stars make millions. Moreover, those who have been around for more than ten years and are still major drawing cards, such as Carlton Fisk of the Chicago White Sox, have found that their current season income is often more than what they made during the first ten years of their career. What pushes these salaries so high? The economic concepts of supply and demand and the large TV contracts are two factors. However, the following salaries of ten players going into the 1991 season seem hard to explain under any conditions:

Player	Team	Average Salary (per year for next few years in most cases)
Clemens	Boston Red Sox	$5,380,250
Gooden	New York Mets	$5,150,000
Canseco	Oakland Athletics	4,700,000
Strawberry	Los Angeles Dodgers	4,050,000
Mattingly	New York Yankees	3,860,000
Clark	San Francisco Giants	3,750,000
Mitchell	San Francisco Giants	3,750,000
Winfield	California Angels	3,750,000
Dawson	Chicago Cubs	3,700,000
Stewart	Oakland Athletics	3,500,000

In addition to the salaries spelled out in their multiyear contracts, some players are also eligible for performance bonuses based on factors such as batting averages, home runs, runs batted in, games pitched, games won, or being on the All Star team.

provide power and status and can be a means to measure achievement. In the latter sense, money can be used as an effective positive reinforcement intervention strategy.

Accepting the importance of money as a possible reinforcer does not mean that the traditional techniques for dispensing it are adequate. Starting with the scientific management movement at the turn of the century, numerous monetary incentive techniques have been developed.

The standard base-pay technique provides for minimum compensation for a particular job. Pay by the hour for workers and the base salary for managers are examples. The technique does not reward above-average performance or penalize below-average performance, and it is controlled largely by the job rather than by the person performing the job. A variable-pay technique, however, attempts to reward according to individual or group differences and is thus more human- than job-controlled. Seniority variable-pay plans recognize age and length-of-service differentials, and merit-pay and individual- or group-incentive plans attempt to reward contingently on the basis of performance.

Managers have been rewarded by incentive pay and bonus plans based on performance for years. For example, at USX, cash bonuses may run up to 85 percent of an executive's base salary. There is considerable evidence that this approach is becoming more popular.[25] Also, work groups and whole departments are receiving monetary rewards. For example, DuPont's Fibers Department has moved to a variable pay program providing bonuses when earning objectives are exceeded.[26] Besides managers and groups, lower-level employees are also now being rewarded by monetary incentives. For example, at the food products company Borden, some 28,000 workers at 180 different plants can get bonuses ranging from $250 to $800 each, depending on specific behaviors relating to attendance, safety, quality, and quantity.[27] At the other extreme are scientists and engineers in high-tech firms who make such significant contributions as inventing a new product or developing a new software program that cannot be adequately rewarded by the typical merit pay plan. The majority of high-tech firms now have pay plans in place to reward such innovations and thus help retain their best people. For example, IBM has a Corporate Award (they recently awarded $150,000 each to two of its scientists who won Nobel Prizes) and Outstanding Innovation Awards (these are given for important inventions or scientific discoveries and range from $2,500 to $25,000.)[28]

Incentive plans involve piece rates, bonuses, or profit sharing. A third technique, supplementary pay, has nothing to do with the job or performance per se. The extensive fringe-benefit package received by employees in most modern organizations is an example. These supplements can be very costly to organizations. The U.S. Chamber of Commerce recently reported that employee benefits on average represented one-third of payroll costs and about $10,000 per employee.[29]

Analyses of the role of money are usually couched in cognitive terms. However, from these cognitive explanations it is very clear that the real key in assessing the use of money as a reinforcer is not necessarily whether it satisfies inner needs but rather how it is administered. In order for money to be effective in the organizational reward system, it must be administered contingently on the employee's exhibiting critical performance behavior. Some of the new monetary incentive systems in industry are beginning to recognize this. For example, at Borden, they used to peg monetary incentives to return on equity. However, as one senior executive at the firm pointed out, this technical (we would say noncontingent) financial target was "too difficult for the hourly employee to understand."[30] Now, they have successfully moved to the more contingent pay for specific performance behaviors.

Unfortunately, about the only reinforcing function that pay often has in organizations is to reinforce employees for walking up to the pay window or for opening an envelope every two weeks or every month. With the exception of such companies as Borden and other very specific, piece-rate incentive systems and commissions paid to salespersons, pay is generally not contingent on the performance of critical behaviors.[31] One experimental study clearly demonstrated that money contingently administered can have a positive effect on employee behavior. A contingently administered monetary bonus plan significantly improved the punctuality of workers in a Mexican division of a large U.S. corporation.[32] It should be pointed out, however, that the mere fact that money was valued by the Mexican workers in this study does not mean that it would have the same impact on all workers. For example, in a study of managers in the Social Security Administration, merit pay seemingly had no effect on organizational performance.[33]

In a society with an inflationary economy and nonmaterialistic social values, money may be much less likely to be a potential reinforcer for critical job behaviors. Money certainly cannot be automatically dismissed as a positive reinforcer, but, because of its complexity, it may also turn out to be a reward but not a reinforcer. Only objective measurement will determine whether in fact money is an effective positive reinforcer for the critical behavior in question.

Natural Reinforcers. Besides obvious rewards such as money, which most organizations tend to depend upon, a host of overlooked natural reinforcers are available.[34] Potentially very powerful, these are the rewards that exist in the natural occurrence of events[35] and have been deliberately used to successfully enhance employee performance at companies such as Blue Cross and Blue Shield of Massachusetts.[36] Table 8.3 categorizes natural reinforcers.

Social rewards such as recognition, attention, and praise tend to be very reinforcing for most people. In addition, few people become satiated with social rewards. However, similar to contrived rewards, social rewards must be administered on a contingent basis. For example, a pat on the back or verbal praise that is randomly given (as under the old human relations approach) may have more of a punishing, "boomerang" effect than a positive reinforcement effect. But genuine social rewards, contingently administered for performance of the target behavior, can be a very effective positive reinforcer for most employees. The added benefit of such a strategy, in contrast to the use of contrived rewards, is that the cost of social rewards to the organization is absolutely nothing.

In Table 8.3, Premack rewards refer to the work of psychologist David Premack.[37] Simply stated, the Premack principle is that high-probability behaviors can be used to reinforce low-probability behaviors. For example, if there are two tasks, A and B, and the person prefers task A to task B, the Premack principle says that the person should perform task B first and then task A. In this sequence, task A serves as a contingent reinforcer for completing task B, and the person will perform better on both tasks than if the sequence were reversed. In common practice, people often tend to do the task they like best first and to put off the less pleasant task. This common sequence of doing things is in direct violation of the Premack principle and can contribute to ineffective performance.

Applied to organizational reward systems, the Premack principle would suggest that a natural reinforcer could always be found. Certain job activities could always be used to reinforce other job activities. No matter how much employees dislike their jobs, there are going to be some things they like to do better than others. Premack sequencing would allow the more-desired activities to reinforce the less-desired activities. This principle was supported in a study of employees who improved their quality performance in a fast food restaurant.[38] The Premack rewards listed in Table 8.3 can be used to reinforce the less desirable activities on a job.

TECHNIQUES OF ADMINISTERING REINFORCEMENT

The preceding discussion was concerned primarily with the theoretical basis, categories, and content of reinforcement. The importance of the role of reinforcement in the study of organizational behavior cannot be overemphasized. It plays a central role in human resources management areas such as training, appraisal, adaptation to change, and performance. Modification of certain specific aspects of organizational behavior, such as tardiness or participation, and overall organization development also depend upon reinforcement. Reinforcement will increase the strength of desired organizational behavior and the probability of its being repeated. How reinforcement is administered is also important. For example, during the acquisition phase of classical conditioning experiments, every conditioned response is reinforced. This seldom occurs in reality. Human behavior in organizations or everyday life is generally reinforced on an intermittent or random basis. The exact pattern and timing of the reinforcement have a tremendous impact on the resulting behavior. In other words, how the reward is administered can greatly influence the specific organizational behavior that takes place. The four major techniques of administering rewards are fixed ratio, fixed interval, variable ratio, and variable interval schedules.

Fixed Ratio Schedules

If a schedule is administered on a ratio basis, reinforcement is given after a certain *number* of responses. If the schedule is a fixed ratio, the exact number of responses is specified. A fixed ratio that reinforces after every response is designated as 1:1. The 1:1 fixed ratio is generally used in basic conditioning experiments, and almost every type of learning situation must begin with this schedule. However, as learning progresses, it is more effective to shift to a fixed ratio of 2:1, 4:1, 8:1, and even 20:1.

Administering rewards under a fixed ratio schedule tends to produce a high rate of response that is characterized as vigorous and steady. The person soon determines that reinforcement is based on the number of responses and performs the responses as quickly as possible in order to receive the reward. A common example of how the fixed ratio schedule is applied to industrial organizations is the piece-rate incentive system. Production workers are paid on the basis of how many pieces they produce (number of responses). Other things being equal, the worker's performance responses should be energetic and steady. In reality, of course, other things are not always equal, and a piece-rate incentive system may not lead to this type of behavior. Nevertheless, knowledge of the effects of the various methods of administering rewards would be extremely valuable in analyzing employee-incentive systems.

Fixed Interval Schedules

A second common way to administer rewards is on a fixed interval basis. Under this schedule, reinforcement is given after a specified period of *time*, which is measured from the last reinforced response. The length of time that can be used by this schedule varies a great deal. In the beginning of practically any learning situation, a very short interval is required. However, as learning progresses, the interval can be stretched out.

Behavior resulting from a fixed interval method of reinforcing is quite different from that exhibited as a result of a fixed ratio schedule. Whereas under a fixed ratio schedule there is a steady, vigorous response pattern, under a fixed interval schedule there is an uneven pattern that varies from a very slow, unenergetic response immediately following reinforcement to a very fast, vigorous response immediately preceding reinforcement. This type of behavior pattern can be explained by the fact that the person figures out that another reward will not immediately follow the last one. Therefore, the person may as well relax a little until it is time to be rewarded again. A common example of administering rewards on a fixed interval schedule is the payment of employees by the hour, week, or month. Monetary reinforcement comes at the end of a period of time. In practice, however, even though people are paid by the hour, they receive their reward only weekly, biweekly, or monthly. This time interval is generally too long to be an effective schedule of reinforcement for the work-related behavior.

Variable or Intermittent Schedules

Both ratio and interval schedules can be administered on a variable or intermittent basis. This means that the reinforcement is given in an irregular or unsystematic manner. In variable ratio, the reward is given after a number of responses, but the exact number is randomly varied. When the variable ratio is expressed as some number—say, 1:50—this means that on the *average* the organism is reinforced after fifty responses. However, in reality, the ratio may randomly vary from 1:1 to 1:100. In other words, each response has a chance of being reinforced regardless of the number of reinforced or nonreinforced responses that have preceded it.

The variable interval schedule works basically the same as the variable ratio schedule except that a reward is given after a randomly distributed length of time rather than after a number of responses. A fifty-minute variable interval schedule means that on the *average*, the individual is reinforced after fifty minutes, but the actual reinforcement may be given anywhere from every few seconds to every two or three hours.

Behavior under Variable Schedules. Both variable ratio and variable interval schedules tend to produce stable, vigorous behavior. The behavior under variable schedules is similar to that produced by a fixed ratio schedule. Under a variable schedule, the person has no idea when the reward is coming, and so the behavior tends to be steady and strong. It logically follows that variable schedules are very resistant to extinction. A good example is the behavior of those playing slot machines in gambling casinos that pay off on a variable-ratio schedule. As one psychologist observed:

> Players can be seen popping coins into their maws and pulling their "arms" with barely a pause. I have seen players who do not even stop to pick up their winnings. Instead, they continue to smoothly pop in the coins, whether from their original sack or from the winnings tray.[39]

Variable schedules are not very effective in highly controlled learning experiments and are seldom used. On the other hand, they are the way in which many real-life, everyday learning situations are reinforced. Although primary reinforcers for humans are administered on a relatively fixed basis (for example, food is given three times a day at mealtimes, and most organization compensation plans are on either a fixed ratio or a fixed interval basis), most of the other human behavior that takes place is reinforced in a highly variable manner. For example, practically all social rewards are administered on a variable basis. Attention, approval, and affection are generally given as rewards in a very random fashion.

Administration of Reinforcement in Human Resources Management

The fixed ratio and fixed interval schedules and the variable ratio and variable interval schedules are not the only methods of administering rewards. Many other possible combinations exist. However, these four schedules are the way most employees in today's organizations are reinforced. Much of the learning and resulting behavior of every worker, supervisor, salesperson, engineer, and executive is determined by when and how they are reinforced. Even the automobile industry learned, the hard way, that customers' buying behavior in recent years has been greatly affected by schedules of reinforcement.

The automobile companies depended on cash rebates and cut-rate financing to stimulate the sales of their new cars. These programs were *randomly* offered; that is, there was a variable interval schedule of reinforcement. Under such a schedule, behavior is very resistant to extinction. Thus, what happened was that long-run sales were not stimulated by a one-shot rebate program; instead, customers did not buy after the rebate expired, and sales declined. As explained by one industry analyst: "The auto industry's on-again, off-again pattern of rebates over the past two years has conditioned the customer to wait—almost indefinitely—for some giveaway."[40] Under this variable schedule of reinforcement, when the expensive giveaways stopped coming, it took a long time to convince car buyers, as it did Skinner's pigeons, that there wasn't any point in continuing to wait.

Besides this real example of consumer behavior, there is growing research literature on the impact that continuous versus variable schedules have on employee behavior. The problem is, however, that job simulation studies conducted with student subjects in laboratory settings have different results from those of studies using actual workers in a field setting. The laboratory studies found that variable schedules led to better performance.[41] This verified what the operant learning theorists had been saying over the years. However, a couple of studies conducted on tree-planting crews found that continuous schedules of reinforcement actually led to better performance.[42] Both the laboratory and, especially, the field studies had definite methodological problems that prevent any definitive conclusions. A follow-up study of the tree-planting crews did try to eliminate some of the problems and still found that the employees as a whole performed better on a continuous schedule of reinforcement.[43] Yet, despite this overall finding, the researchers recognize that some limitations still remain and that there are individual differences. For example, inexperienced subjects worked better on a variable schedule.

Although the research results on the application of schedules are still not very clear and cannot be generalized for monetary schedules,[44] there are some guidelines that can be given for effective human resource management. For example, rewards should be given as soon after the desired response as possible, not two weeks or a month later, as in the case of most of today's employees' paychecks. In addition, ratio schedules are generally more desirable than interval schedules because they tend to produce steady, strong responses, but as the discussion of the research indicated, specific guidance on the use of continuous versus variable schedules cannot yet be given. Although some types of employees may work better under continuous schedules, variable schedules may be better for other types of employees and certainly are more resistant to extinction. Understanding and then applying what is known about the administration of reinforcement can be of great assistance to modern human resource managers. In fact, one of the most important functions of all managers may well be the way they administer reinforcement to their people. The next chapter carries this discussion further by giving specific attention to behavioral-change strategies for modern human resource management.

THE EFFECT OF PUNISHMENT

Punishment is one of the most used but least understood and badly administered aspects of learning. Whether in rearing children or dealing with subordinates in a complex organization, parents and supervisors often revert to punishment instead of positive reinforcement in order to modify or control behavior. Punishment is commonly thought to be the reverse of reinforcement but equally effective in altering behavior. However, this simple analogy with reinforcement may not be warranted. The reason is that punishment is a very complex phenomenon and must be carefully defined and used.

The Definition of Punishment

The meaning of *punishment* was mentioned earlier. To reiterate, punishment is anything which weakens behavior and tends to decrease its subsequent frequency. Punishment usually consists of the *application* of an undesirable or noxious consequence, but it can also be defined as the *withdrawal* of a desirable consequence.[45] Thus, taking away certain organizational privileges from a manager who has a poor performance record could be thought of as punishment.

Regardless of the distinction between punishment as the application of an undesirable consequence and the withdrawal of a desirable consequence in order for punishment to occur, there must be a weakening of, and a decrease in, the behavior which preceded it. Just because a supervisor gives a "tongue-lashing" to a subordinate and thinks this is a punishment, it is not necessarily that unless the behavior that preceded the tongue-lashing weakens and decreases. In many cases when supervisors think they are punishing employees, they are in fact reinforcing them because they are giving attention, and attention tends to be very reinforcing. This explains the common complaint that supervisors often make: "I call Joe in, give him heck for goofing up, and he goes right back out and goofs up again." What is happening is that the supervisor thinks Joe is being punished, when operationally what is obviously happening is that the supervisor is reinforcing Joe's undesirable behavior by giving him attention and recognition.

Administering Punishment

Opinions on administering punishment range all the way from the one extreme of dire warnings never to use it to the other extreme that it is the only effective way to modify behavior. As yet, research has not been able to support either view completely. However, there is little doubt that the use of punishment tends to cause many undesirable side effects. Neither children nor adults like to be punished. The punished behavior tends to be only temporarily suppressed rather than permanently changed, and the punished person tends to get anxious or "uptight" and resentful of the punisher. Thus, the use of punishment as a strategy to control behavior is a "lose-lose" approach. Unless the punishment is severe, the behavior will reappear very quickly, but the more severe the punishment, the bigger the side effects such as "hate" and "revenge."

To minimize the problems with using punishment, persons administering it must always provide an acceptable alternative to the behavior that is being punished. If they do not, the undesirable behavior will tend to reappear and will cause fear and anxiety in the person being punished. The punishment must always be administered as close in time to the undesirable behavior as possible. Calling subordinates into the office to give them a reprimand for breaking a rule the week before is not effective. All the reprimand tends to do at this time is to punish them for getting caught. It has little effect on the rule-breaking behavior.

Attention must also be exercised so that what is intended as punishment does not in fact act as a reward for the recipient. A supervisor who shouts a reprimand at a worker may be rewarding this individual's position as the informal leader of a work-restricting group. The same is true of the example, given in the last section, of punishment turning into rewarding attention. It is very easy for supervisors or managers to use punishment, but it is very difficult for them to effectively administer punishment so as to modify or change undesirable behavior. There is, however, recent evidence that, like reinforcement, vicarious punishment can be effectively used in a work setting.[46]

A rule of thumb for human resource managers should be: Always attempt to reinforce instead of punish in order to change behavior. Furthermore, the use of a reinforcement strategy is usually more effective in accelerating desirable behaviors than the use of punishment is for decelerating undesirable behaviors because no bad side effects accompany reinforcement. As one comprehensive analysis of punishment concluded, "in order to succeed, (punishment) must be used in an orderly, rational manner—not, as is too often the case, as a handy outlet for a manager's anger or frustration. If used with skill, and concern for human dignity, it can be useful."[47] Perhaps the best practical advice is the old red-hot-stove rule of discipline—it gives advance warning, and is immediate, consistent, and impersonal. In addition, most modern approaches stress that discipline should be contingently applied (a crew of nineteen-year-old high school dropouts should be treated differently from a $100,000 per year professional) and progressive.[48] The next chapter will get into these behavioral-change strategies in more depth and will apply them more directly to human resource management.

Summary

Learning is a major psychological process that has been largely neglected in the study of organizational behavior. It has not been generally recognized that there are different types of learning and different theoretical explanations of learning (operant, cognitive, and social). Despite the controversy surrounding learning theory, there are many accepted principles of learning that are derived largely from experimentation and the analysis of operant conditioning. Reinforcement is probably the single most important concept in the learning process and is most relevant to the study of organizational behavior. On the basis of the classic law of effect, *reinforcement* can be operationally defined as anything which increases the strength of response and which tends to induce repetitions of the behavior that preceded the reinforcement. Within the organizational reward system, both contrived and natural rewards are important to employee behavior and performance. Reinforcers may be positive or negative. They may be administered on a fixed ratio or fixed interval basis or on a variable ratio or variable interval basis. The effective administration of reinforcement and punishment may be one of the most critical challenges facing modern human resource management.

Questions for Discussion and Review

1. Do you agree with the statement that learning is involved in almost everything that everyone does? Explain.
2. What are the major dimensions of operant, cognitive, and social learning theories?
3. What is the difference between classical and operant conditioning?
4. What is the difference between positive and negative reinforcement? What is the difference between negative reinforcement and punishment?
5. What is the difference between contrived and natural rewards? What role does money play in the organizational reward system? What could be done to make it more effective?
6. Why is the administration of reinforcement so vitally important to learning and management practice?
7. Make arguments for and against punishment.

References

1. For example, see Judith L. Komaki, "Toward Effective Supervision: An Operant Analysis and Comparison of Managers at Work," *Journal of Applied Psychologoy,* vol. 71, no. 2, 1986, pp. 270–279.

2. Robert Glaser, "The Reemergence of Learning

Theory Within Instructional Research," *American Psychologist*, Jan. 1990, p. 29.

3. For example, see Dennis A. Gioia and Henry P. Sims, Jr., "Cognition-Behavior Connections: Attribution and Verbal Behavior in Leader-Subordinate Interactions," *Organizational Behavior and Human Decision Processes*, vol. 37, 1986, pp. 197–229.

4. Thomas C. Mawhinney, "Learning," in Dennis W. Organ and Thomas Bateman, *Organizational Behavior*, 3d ed., Business Publications, Plano, Tex., 1986, pp. 90–91.

5. Albert Bandura, "Social Learning Theory," in J. T. Spence, R. C. Carson, and J. W. Thibaut (eds.), *Behavioral Approaches to Therapy*, General Learning, Morristown, N.J., 1976, p. 5.

6. See Albert Bandura, *Social Foundations of Thought and Action: A Social-Cognitive View*, Prentice-Hall, Englewood Cliffs, N.J., 1986, for a summary of this research.

7. Dennis A. Gioia and Charles C. Manz, "Linking Cognition and Behavior: A Script Processing Interpretation of Vicarious Learning," *Academy of Management Review*, July 1985, pp. 527–539.

8. Charles C. Manz and Henry P. Sims, Jr., "Vicarious Learning: The Influence of Modeling on Organizational Behavior," *Academy of Management Review*, January 1981, pp. 105–113; and Henry P. Sims and Charles C. Manz, "Modeling Influences on Employee Behavior," *Personnel Journal*, January 1982, pp. 58–65.

9. Kenneth E. Hultman, "Behavior Modeling for Results," *Training and Development Journal*, December 1986, p. 60.

10. Fred Luthans and Robert Kreitner, *Organizational Behavior Modification and Beyond*, Scott, Foresman, Glenview, Ill., 1985, p. 157.

11. Robert F. Burnaska, "The Effects of Behavior Modeling Training upon Managers' Behaviors and Employees' Perceptions," *Personnel Psychology*, Autumn 1976, pp. 329–335: Allen I. Kraut, "Developing Managerial Skills via Modelling Techniques: Some Positive Research Findings—A Symposium." *Personnel Psychology*, vol. 29, 1976, pp. 325–328: Gary P. Latham and Lise M. Saari, "Application of Social-Learning Theory to Training Supervisors through Behavioral Modeling," *Journal of Applied Psychology*, June 1979, pp. 239–246; and Phillip J. Decker, "The Enhancement of Behavior Modeling Training of Super-

visory Skills by the Inclusion of Retention Processes," *Personnel Psychology*, Summer 1982, pp. 323–332.

12. Latham and Saari, op. cit.

13. Edward L. Thorndike, *Animal Intelligence*, Macmillan, New York, 1911, p. 244.

14. Gregory B. Northcraft and Margaret A. Neale, *Organizational Behavior*, Dryden, Chicago, 1990, p. 162.

15. For example, see Ronald E. Riggio, *Introduction to Industrial/Organizational Psychology*, Scott, Foresman/Little, Brown, Glenview, Ill., 1990, p. 175.

16. D. M. Prue and J. A. Fairbank, "Performance Feedback in Organizational Behavior Management: A Review," *Journal of Organizational Behavior Management*, Spring 1981, pp. 1–16.

17. Richard E. Kopelman, "Objective Feedback," in Edwin A. Locke (ed.), *Generalizing from Laboratory to Field Settings*, Lexington Books, Lexington, Mass., 1986, pp. 119–145.

18. Fred Luthans, Richard M. Hodgetts, and Stuart A. Rosenkrantz, *Real Managers*, Ballinger, Cambridge, Mass., 1988, pp. 141–142.

19. Daniel R. Ilgen, Cynthia D. Fisher, and M. Susan Taylor, "Consequences of Individual Feedback on Behavior in Organizations," *Journal of Applied Psychology*, August 1979, pp. 349–371; and Edwin A. Locke and Gary P. Latham, *A Theory of Goal Setting and Task Performance*, Prentice-Hall, Englewood Cliffs, N.J., 1990, pp. 185–189.

20. David A. Nadler, "The Effects of Feedback on Task Group Behavior: A Review of the Experimental Research," *Organizational Behavior and Human Performance*, June 1979, pp. 309–338.

21. John M. Ivancevich and J. Timothy McMahon, "The Effects of Goal Setting, External Feedback, and Self-Generated Feedback on Outcome Variables: A Field Experiment," *Academy of Management Journal*, June 1982, pp. 359–372.

22. Robert C. Linden and Terence R. Mitchell, "Reactions to Feedback: The Role of Attributions," *Academy of Management Journal*, June 1985, pp. 291–308.

23. David M. Herold, Robert C. Linden, and Marya L. Leatherwood, "Using Multiple Attributes to Assess Sources of Performance Feedback," *Academy of Management Journal*, December 1987, pp. 826–835.

24. "Labor Letter," *The Wall Street Journal,* Jan. 20, 1987, p. 1.
25. Sally Solo, "Stop Whining and Get Back to Work," *Fortune,* March 12, 1990, p. 50.
26. Robert P. McNutt, "Achievement Pays Off at DuPont," *Personnel,* June 1990, pp. 5–10.
27. "All Pulling Together, To Get the Carrot," *The Wall Street Journal,* Apr. 30, 1990, p. B1.
28. Luis R. Gomez-Mejia, David B. Balkin, and George T. Milkovich, "Rethinking Rewards for Technical Employees," *Organizational Dynamics,* Spring 1990, p. 67.
29. *Nation's Business,* March 1990, p. 12.
30. "All Pulling Together," op. cit.
31. See Raymond A. Katzell and Donna E. Thompson, "Work Motivation," *American Psychologist,* Feb. 1990, pp. 148–149.
32. Jaime A. Hermann, Ana I. deMontes, Benjamin Dominguez, Francisco deMontes, and B. L. Hopkins, "Effects of Bonuses for Punctuality on the Tardiness of Industrial Workers," *Journal of Applied Behavioral Analysis,* Winter 1973, pp. 563–570.
33. Jone L. Pearce, William B. Stevenson, and James L. Perry, "Managerial Compensation Based on Organizational Performance: A Time Series Analysis of the Effects of Merit Pay," *Academy of Management Journal,* June 1985, pp. 261–278.
34. William H. Wagel, "Make Their Day—The Noncash Way," *Personnel,* May 1990, pp. 41–44.
35. Luthans and Kreitner, op. cit.
36. Arlene Saffron, "Rekindling the Spirit at Blue Cross/Blue Shield," *Personnel,* May 1990, pp. 46–48.
37. David Premack, "Reinforcement Theory," in David Levine (ed.), *Nebraska Symposium on Motivation,* University of Nebraska Press, Lincoln, 1965, pp. 123–180.
38. Dianne H. B. Welsh, Daniel J. Bernstein, and Fred Luthans, "Application of the Premack Principle of Reinforcement: Analysis of the Impact on Quality Performance of Service Employees," *Jour-*

nal of Organizational Behavior Management, in press.
39. Spencer A. Rathus, *Psychology,* 4th ed., Holt, Rinehart and Winston, Fort Worth, 1990, p. 207.
40. Robert L. Simison, "Why Are Auto Sales Strictly for the Birds? Just Ask Any Pigeon," *The Wall Street Journal,* Dec. 15, 1982, p. 1.
41. Gary A. Yukl, Kenneth N. Wexley, and J. D. Seymore, "Effectiveness of Pay Incentives under Variable Ratio and Continuous Schedules of Reinforcement," *Organizational Behavior and Human Performance,* October 1975, pp. 227–243.
42. Gary A. Yukl and Gary P. Latham, "Consequences of Reinforcement Schedules and Incentive Magnitudes for Employee Performance: Problems Encountered in an Industrial Setting," *Journal of Applied Psychology,* June 1975, pp. 294–298; and G. A. Yukl, G. P. Latham, and E. D. Pursell, "The Effectiveness of Performance Incentives under Continuous and Variable Ratio Schedules of Reinforcement," *Personnel Psychology,* vol. 29, 1976, pp. 221–231.
43. Gary P. Latham and Dennis L. Dossett, "Designing Incentive Plans for Unionized Employees: A Comparison of Continuous and Variable Ratio Reinforcement Schedules," *Personnel Psychology,* Spring 1978, pp. 47–61.
44. Thomas C. Mawhinney, "Reinforcement Schedule Stretching Effects," in Edwin A. Locke (ed.), *Generalizing from Laboratory to Field Settings,* Lexington Books, Lexington, Mass., 1986, pp. 181–186.
45. Robert S. Feldman, *Understanding Psychology,* 2d ed., McGraw-Hill, New York, 1990, pp. 169–170.
46. Mel E. Schnake, "Vicarious Punishment in a Work Setting," *Journal of Applied Psychology,* vol. 71, no. 2, 1986, pp. 343–345.
47. Robert A. Baron, *Behavior in Organizations,* Allyn and Bacon, Boston, 1986, p. 51.
48. Walter Kiechel, "How to Discipline in the Modern Age," *Fortune,* May 7, 1990, pp. 179–180.

**REAL CASE:
THANKS FOR
THE FAVOR**

In late 1990 Michael Milken, the junk bond king, was sentenced to ten years in jail after pleading guilty to violating federal securities laws. One of the crimes that he was not charged with, but which was presented to the judge by the prosecution in an effort to supply a guilty conviction, related to the Wickes Company, a California retailer. The heart of the story rests with the 10 percent convertible preferred issue on which Wickes was paying $15 million in annual dividends. The president of Wickes realized that if he could get this preferred issue converted into common stock, the company would save the $15 million in dividends. However, the stock price was too low and none of the holders of the preferred issue were willing to convert to common stock. There were only two ways to get rid of this $15 million annual burden. One was to wait another two years, at which time the stock, by previous agreement, could be converted at the option of the company. The other way was if the stock closed above $6 a share for twenty trading days out of any consecutive thirty. The company decided that this latter course was the best one to pursue. Working with Michael Milken's brokerage, Drexel Burnham, Wickes made an offer to buy the National Gypsum Company. Its own stock then rose above $6 a share, because investors felt that—with National Gypsum—Wickes would be a more valuable holding. The stock closed above $6 a share for nineteen of twenty-eight trading days. However, on the twenty-ninth day it fell below $6. The company had only one more day to get the price above $6.

Milken's company was legally forbidden from trading in Wickes stock, since it was helping with the National Gypsum takeover and was now regarded as an insider in the deal. However, this did not prevent Milken from urging his people to find clients to buy Wickes. At the same time, he had one of his associates call Ivan Boesky, another convicted inside trader who had done a great deal of business with Drexel, and ask him "as a favor" to buy the stock. Within twenty minutes of the close of the stock exhange, Milken's people were able to get 1.6 million shares purchased. However, this was only enough to stabilize the price at $6. They then called the broker on the trading floor of the New York Stock Exchange and learned that, in order to get the price to $6 ⅛ by the close, they would have to buy another 300,000 shares. This was done immediately and the stock closed at $6 ⅛. Five days later, Wickes exercised its option and called in the preferred stock and replaced it with common stock. In the process, the company saved itself $15 million in dividends for the next two years. Those who helped push the stock over $6 then began disposing of their holdings. Within three weeks, they were out of the stock. The total cost to those who helped out was about $500,000 including brokerage fees. In turn, Wickes saved a total of $30 million. Drexel, which over a three-and-a-half-year period earned $118 million in investment banking fees from Wickes, was able to keep its client happy.

1. Was money a reinforcer in this case?
2. Later research found that Boesky's firm lost about $400,000 for doing this favor for Milken. Why then was it willing to help Milken?
3. When the judge sentenced Milken to ten years in prison, the harshest sentence ever given to anyone for violating federal security laws, how was she using learning theory to send a message?

Case: Contrasting Styles

Henry Adams has been a production supervisor for eight years. He came up through the ranks and is known as a tough but hardworking supervisor. Jerry Wake has been a production supervisor for about the same length of time and also came up through the ranks. Jerry is known as a nice, hardworking guy. Over the past several years these two supervisors' sections have been head and shoulders above the other six sections on hard measures of performance (number of units produced). This is true despite the almost opposite approaches the two have taken in handling their workers. Henry explained his approach as follows:

> The only way to handle workers is to come down hard on them whenever they make a mistake. In fact, I call them together every once in a while and give them heck whether they deserve it or not, just to keep them on their toes. If they are doing a good job, I tell them that's what they're getting paid for. By taking this approach, all I have to do is walk through my area, and people start working like mad.

Jerry explained his approach as follows:

> I don't believe in that human relations stuff of being nice to workers. But I do believe that a worker deserves some recognition and attention from me if he or she does a good job. If people make a mistake, I don't jump on them. I feel that we are all entitled to make some errors. On the other hand, I always do point out what the mistake was and what they should have done, and as soon as they do it right I let them know it. Obviously, I don't have time to give attention to everyone doing things right, but I deliberately try to get around to people doing a good job every once in a while.

Although Henry's section is still right at the top along with Jerry's section in units produced, personnel records show that there has been 3 times as much turnover is Henry's section than in Jerry's section, and the quality-control records show that Henry's section has met quality standards only twice in the last six years, while Jerry's has missed attaining quality standards only once in the last six years.

1. Both these supervisors have similar backgrounds. On the basis of learning, how can you explain their opposite approaches to handling people?
2. What are some of the examples of punishment, positive reinforcement, and negative reinforcement found in this case? What schedule of reinforcement is Jerry using? If Jerry is using a reinforcement approach, how do you explain this statement: "I don't believe in that human relations stuff of being nice to workers"?
3. How do you explain the performance, turnover, and quality results in these two sections of the production department?

**Case:
Volunteers
Can't Be
Punished**

Ann-Marie Jackson is head of a volunteer agency in a large city. She is in charge of a volunteer staff of over twenty-five people. Weekly, she holds a meeting with this group in order to keep them informed and teach them the specifics of any new laws or changes in state and federal policies and procedures that might affect their work, and she discusses priorities and assignments for the group. This meeting is also a time when members can share some of the problems and concerns for what they are personally doing and what the agency as a whole is doing. The meeting is scheduled to begin at 9 A.M. sharp every Monday. Lately, the volunteers have been filtering in every five minutes or so until almost 10 A.M. Ann-Marie has felt she has to delay the start of the meetings until all the people arrive. The last few weeks the meetings haven't started until 10 A.M. In fact, at 9 A.M., nobody has shown up. Ann-Marie cannot understand what has happened. She feels it is important to start the meetings at 9 A.M. so that they can be over before the whole morning is gone. On the other hand, she feels that her hands are tied because, after all, the people are volunteers and she can't push them or make them get to the meetings on time.

1. What advice would you give Ann-Marie? In terms of reinforcement theory, explain what is happening here and what Ann-Marie needs to do to get the meetings started on time.
2. What learning theories (operant, cognitive, and/or social) could be applied to Ann-Marie's efforts to teach her volunteers the impact of new laws and changes in state and federal policies and procedures?
3. How could someone like Ann-Marie use modeling to train her staff to do a more effective job?

9 Learning Applied: Organizational Behavior Modification

■ Things Are Just Going to Have to Change

One of the best examples of applied learning concepts is provided by the U.S. Constitution, which allows voters to decide whom to send to Washington and whom to recall. In recent years, some critics have argued that the learning phase of this process is overrated. For example, in the latest congressional elections incumbents outspent their opponents by a ratio of 19:1 and 97 percent were returned to Washington. On the other hand, many observers believe that the country is on the threshold of major changes in government representation. People are becoming fed up with a Congress that seems ineffective in dealing with major problems and which seems to lack the willpower to bring the deficit under control. Will the years ahead see big changes in the congressional makeup? It will, if a recent poll among chief executive officers (CEOs) of companies is reflective of attitudes in the general population.

When these CEOs were asked how much confidence they have in the federal government's ability to identify and deal with the major problems America will face in the decade ahead, 62 percent said that they had less confidence today than they did ten years ago. Most of them (56 percent) believe that more power should be shifted from the federal government to the state and local levels.

The brunt of their concern, however, was directed toward Congress. By an almost 2:1 ratio, the CEOs believe that Congress has become less responsive to business's concerns; and among those who feel that Congress has become more responsive or who perceive no change in responsiveness, there is agreement that more needs to be done. In particular, CEOs point to the fact that other governments are helping their national businesses compete on a worldwide basis while the U. S. government sits on the sidelines.

What can be done to modify the behavior of Congress and get it in step with the times? One of the major ideas that is beginning to gain favor around the country is to limit the terms of office of legislators. The CEOs also favor this idea with 37 percent of them saying that it would help improve the performance of the federal government. Other popular CEO suggestions include giving the president a line-item veto and reforming the budgeting process by passing a balanced budget amendment. These ideas are also popular with many citizens and may indeed be useful in helping Washington deal more effectively with national problems. In any event, one thing is certain: During the years ahead, many politicians are going to find that if they do not modify their behavior, the electorate is going to modify it for them—by getting someone else to do the job.

Learning Objectives

- **Identify** the five steps of O.B. Mod.: identify, measure, analyze, intervene, and evaluate.
- **Discuss** the experience of using O.B. Mod. in manufacturing and nonmanufacturing applications.
- **Explain** behavioral self-management.
- **Present** the applications of behavioral self-management.
- **Analyze** O.B. Mod. as a method of improving human performance in today's organizations.

Chapter 1 introduced the environment-based behavioristic approach to organizational behavior. This approach emphasizes the important role that the environment plays in organizational behavior; in particular, the importance of environmental consequences in the prediction and control of organizational behavior. Chapter 8 added some depth of understanding to this approach by explaining behavioral learning concepts, especially reinforcement. With the exception of Chapter 8, the motivation chapters in this part are presented mainly from an internal, cognitive perspective.

This chapter is devoted specifically to an applied, behavioral approach to the practice of human resources management. Employee behaviors and their direct impact on performance effectiveness are the focus of attention. The concepts and techniques presented in this chapter are not proposed as an alternative to the more traditional and widely accepted methods of human resource management presented in the other chapters. Instead, the suggested behavioral approach in this chapter is meant to supplement and to be used in combination with the other approaches.

O.B. Mod. has its roots in modern behaviorism. Modern behaviorism stems from the significant distinction that B. F. Skinner made between respondent or reflexive behaviors, which are the result of classical conditioning, and operant behaviors, which are the result of operant conditioning (see Chapter 8 for a detailed discussion of the difference). In today's complex organizations, very few of the behaviors of participants are the result of classical conditioning; the mechanistic S-R type of behaviorism is of little value for analyzing or changing organizational behaviors. Operant conditioning is a much better basis for the pragmatic analysis and change of organizational behavior. Most recently a social learning approach as outlined in Chapters 1 and 8 has been suggested as the most comprehensive theoretical base for the understanding of organizational behavior in general and for application areas such as O.B. Mod.

This chapter builds on and applies the material given in Chapters 1 and 8. The chapter is devoted to a fairly detailed explanation and analysis of this approach to human resources management. All the steps of O.B. Mod. (identification, measurement, analysis, intervention, and evaluation) are given attention, but relatively more attention is given to the intervention strategies that can be used to change employee behaviors. The last part of the chapter reports in detail on some actual experiences with, and research findings on, the application of O.B. Mod. in practicing organizations.

THE STEPS OF O.B. MOD.

As a specific approach to human resource management, O.B. Mod. can be portrayed as a five-step problem-solving model. Figure 9.1 shows this model. O.B. Mod. can be used in a step-by-step process to actually change performance-related employee behaviors in today's organizations. Again, the reader should remember that O.B. Mod. is only one technique; there are others, such as job design and goal setting, discussed in Chapter 7, and the techniques discussed in other chapters of the book The following sections discuss the various steps of O.B. Mod.

Step 1: Identification of Critical Behaviors

In this first step the critical behaviors that make a significant impact on performance (making or selling widgets or providing a service to clients or customers) are identified. In every organization, regardless of type or level, numerous behaviors are occurring all the time. Some of these behaviors have a significant impact on performance, and some do not. The goal of the first step of O.B. Mod. is to identify the critical behaviors—the 5 to 10 percent of the behaviors that may account for up to 70 or 80 percent of the performance in the area in question.

Methods of Identifying Critical Behaviors. The process of identifying critical behaviors can be carried out in a couple of ways. One approach is to have the person closest to the job in question—the immediate supervisor or the actual jobholder—determine the critical behaviors. This goes hand in hand with using O.B. Mod. as a problem-solving approach for the individual manager. Its advantages are that the person who knows the job best can most accurately identify the critical behaviors, and, because that person is participating, he or she may be more committed to carrying the O.B. Mod. process to its successful completion.

Another approach to identifying critical behaviors would be to conduct a systematic *behavioral audit*. The audit would use internal staff specialists and/or outside consultants. The audit would systematically analyze each job in question, in the manner that jobs are analyzed using job analysis techniques commonly employed in personnel administration. The advantages of the personal approach (where the

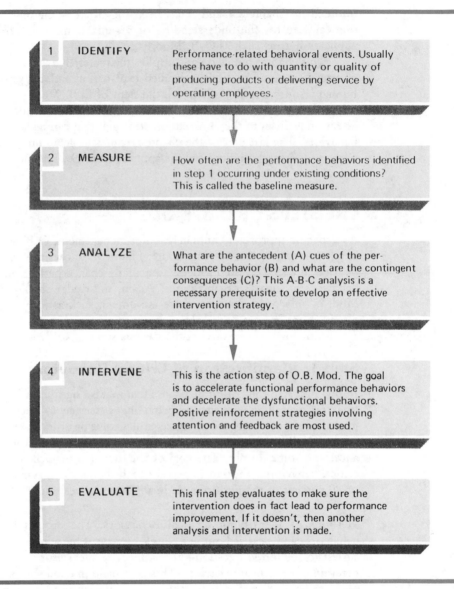

FIGURE 9.1
Steps of O.B.
Mod.

jobholder and/or the immediate supervisor makes a vital input into the audit) can be realized by the audit. In addition, the advantages of staff expertise and consistency can be gained.

Guidelines for Identifying Critical Behaviors. Regardless of the method used, there are certain guidelines that can be helpful in identifying critical behaviors. First, only direct performance behaviors are included. An employee's "bad attitude" and someone's "goofing off" all the time are unacceptable. Only direct performance behaviors such as absenteeism or attendance, tardiness or promptness, or complaints or constructive comments are identified. Specifically, doing or not doing a particular task or procedure that leads to quantity and/or quality outcomes play the major role in O.B. Mod. Something like goofing off is not acceptable because it is not operationally measurable. It could be broken down into measurable behaviors such as not being at the work station, being tardy when returning from breaks, spending time at the water cooler, disrupting coworkers, and even flirting with employees of the opposite sex. However, for a behavior to be identified as a critical behavior appropriate for O.B. Mod., there must be a positive answer to the questions (1) can it be measured? and (2) does it have a direct impact on a performance outcome?

Another helpful guideline for identifying such behaviors is to work backward from an obvious performance deficiency. Just as not all behaviors contribute to performance (for example, complaining behavior may have nothing to do with performance), not all performance problems can be traced to behaviors. For example, the cause of poor performance of a production unit in a manufacturing organization may be faulty machinery, poorly trained workers (they do not know the proper procedures), or unrealistically high production standards. Each of these possible causes is not, at least directly, a behavioral problem. The same is true of the person who does not have the ability to produce at an acceptable level. This is a selection problem, not a behavioral problem.

After noting the possibility of performance problems that are not behaviorally related, it should be emphasized that in general such problems are the exception rather than the rule. Most organizations do not have problems with their technology or the ability or training of their people, but they have many behaviorally related performance problems. Functional behaviors (those which contribute to performance goals) need to be strengthened and accelerated in frequency, and dysfunctional behaviors (those which detract from, or are detrimental to, performance goals) need to be weakened and decelerated in frequency. As in the initial step of any problem-solving process, these behaviors must be properly identified, or the subsequent steps of O.B. Mod. become meaningless for attaining the overall goal of performance improvement.

Step 2: Measurement of the Behaviors

After the performance behaviors have been identified in step 1, they are measured. A baseline frequency is obtained by determining (either by observing and counting or by extracting from existing records) the number of times that the identified behavior is occurring under present conditions. Often this baseline frequency is in and of itself very revealing. Sometimes it is discovered that the behavior identified in step 1 is occurring much less or much more frequently than anticipated. The baseline measure may indicate that the problem is much smaller or much bigger than was thought to be the case. In some instances, the baseline measure may cause the "problem" to be dropped because its low (or high) frequency is now deemed not to need change. For example, attendance may have been identified in step 1 as a critical behavior that needed to be improved. The supervisor reports that the people "never seem to be here." The baseline measure, however, reveals that on average there is 96 percent attendance, which is deemed to be acceptable. In this example, the baseline measure rules out attendance as being a problem. The reverse, of course, could also have occurred. Attendance may have been a much bigger problem than anticipated.

The purpose of the baseline measure is to provide objective frequency data on the critical behavior. A baseline frequency count is an operational definition of the strength of the behavior under existing conditions. Such precise measurement is the hallmark of any scientific endeavor, and it separates O.B. Mod. from more subjective human resource management approaches, such as participation. Although the baseline is established before the intervention to see what happens to the behavior as a result of the intervention, it is important to realize that measures are taken after the intervention as well. Busy managers may feel that they do not have time to record behavioral frequencies objectively, but, at least initially, they should record them in order to use the O.B. Mod. approach effectively.

With some behaviors, such as attendance or complaints, it may be feasible to record every occurrence. However, with many other behaviors recording every frequency would be so time-consuming that it would be practically impossible. With behaviors of the latter type, time-sampling techniques have been used successfully by industrial engineers for years. An example of a time-sampling approach would be to randomly select a time during each working hour to observe the behavior. As in any sampling procedure, if the times are in fact random, confident generalizations can be made to the whole day.

Questionnaire and interview data were criticized in Chapter 2 as being highly reactive. However, the mere presence of an observer (recorder) may also badly distort the behaviors being measured. For this reason, it is important that observational data be gathered as unobtrusively (unnoticed) as possible. Advocating the use of unobtrusive observational measures does not mean that hidden observers or hidden audio and/or video equipment should be used. Obviously, such practices get into ethical and legal problems. With possibly a few exceptions (for example, security), such hidden or deceptive approaches cannot be justified. On the other hand, straightforward observational techniques that use common sense can minimize the reactive effects on those being measured. The recorder should be completely open to any questions that the person being observed may have. Most employees in modern organizations are not sensitive to being measured because industrial engineers and human resource specialists have been doing it for years. There have certainly been abuses of this in the past, but lessons have been learned and the abuses can be eliminated.

Many data on typical behaviors (for example, absenteeism and quantity and quality of output) are already being gathered by other techniques. All that managers using the O.B. Mod. approach have to do is retrieve these data; they do not have to intrusively intervene. Finally, self-reporting procedures can be employed to gather data. Having people reinforced for honestly and accurately keeping records on their own targeted behaviors will eliminate the need for outside measurement.

Step 3: Functional Analysis of the Behavior

Once the performance behavior has been identified and a baseline measure has been obtained, a functional analysis is performed. As Chapters 1 and 8 brought out, both the antecedent and the consequent environments are vital to the understanding, prediction, and control of human behavior in organizations. In Table 9.1 a simple operant-based A-B-C functional analysis is shown. Remember that in an operant approach, cognitive mediating processes do not play a role. Such an omission may detract from the comprehensive understanding of organizational behavior and the analysis of modeling and self-control processes, but for pragmatic application, an A-B-C functional analysis is sufficient.[1] A four-term S-O-B-C (stimulus-organism-behavior-consequence) functional analysis, which accounts for cognitive mediating processes (the O) and covert (unobservable) as well as overt contingencies, is more appropriate for the broader-based social learning approach and is more applicable to a behavioral self-management approach.[2] In the A-B-C functional analysis, A is the antecedent cue, B is the performance behavior identified in step 1, and C is the contingent consequence. Table 9.1 identifies some of the A's, B's, and C's for attendance and absenteeism. A review of absenteeism found work unit size, worker responsibility, and organizational scheduling three potential antecedent influences

TABLE 9.1 An Example of Functional Analysis

Functional Analysis of Attendance Behaviors

A → Antecedent cues	B → Behaviors	C Consequences
Awareness of any consequence	Going to bed on time	Reward programs
Advertising	Setting the alarm	Contingent time-off
Meetings	Waking up	Gifts and prizes
Memorandums	Getting dressed	Preferred jobs
Orientation	Getting children off	Social
Bulletin board	to school	Attention
Observation of any consequence	Leaving home	Recognition
Social status and pressure	Getting a baby-sitter	Praise
Temporal cues	Driving to work	Feedback
Special events	Reporting to work	Data on attendance
Weather		

Functional Analysis of Absenteeism Behaviors

A → Antecedent cues	B → Behaviors	C Consequences
Illness/accident	Getting up late	Discipline programs
Hangover	Sleeping in	Verbal reprimands
Lack of transportation	Staying home	Written reprimands
Traffic	Drinking	Pay docks
No day-care facilities	Fishing/hunting	Layoffs
Family problems	Working at home	Dismissals
Company policies	Visiting	Social consequences from
Group personal norms	Caring for sick child	coworkers
Seniority/age		Escape from, and avoidance of working
Awareness/observation of any consequence		Nothing

Source: Fred Luthans and Mark Martinko, "An Organizational Behavior Modification Analysis of Absenteeism," *Human Resources Management,* Fall 1976, p. 15.

that could be used to improve employee attendance and feedback, rewards, and punishers as effective attendance control procedures.[3]

This functional analysis step of O.B. Mod. brings out the problem-solving nature of the technique. Both the antecedent cues that emit the behavior, and sometimes control it, and the consequences that are currently maintaining the behavior must be identified and understood before an effective intervention strategy can be developed. The accompanying Application Example gives the functional analysis of a production supervisor's problem of his workers taking unscheduled breaks.

Application Example

Functional Analysis in Action

In an actual case of an O.B. Mod. application, a production supervisor in a large manufacturing firm identified unscheduled breaks as a critical behavior affecting the performance of his department. It seemed that workers were frequently wandering off the job, and when they were not tending their machines, time was lost—and irrecoverable production. When a baseline measure of this critical behavior was obtained, the supervisor was proved to be right. The data indicated that unscheduled breaks (defined as leaving the job for reasons other than to take a scheduled break or to obtain materials) were occurring in the department on a relatively frequent basis. The functional analysis was performed to determine the antecedent(s) and consequence(s) of the unscheduled-break behavior.

It was found that the clock served as the antecedent cue for the critical behavior. The workers in this department started work at 8 A.M., they had their first scheduled break at 10 A.M., and they had lunch at noon. They started again at 1 P.M., had a break at 3 P.M., and quit at 5 P.M. The functional analysis revealed that almost precisely at 9 A.M., 11 A.M., 2 P.M., and 4 P.M., the workers were leaving their jobs and going to the rest room. In other words, the clock served as a cue for them to take an unscheduled break midway between starting time and the first scheduled break, between the first scheduled break and lunch, between lunch and the scheduled afternoon break, and between the afternoon break and quitting time. The clock did not *cause* the behavior; it served only as a cue to emit the behavior. On the other hand, the behavior was under stimulus control of the clock because the clock dicated when the behavior would occur. The consequence, however, was what was maintaining the behavior. The critical behavior was a function of its consequences. The functional analysis revealed that the consequence of the unscheduled-break behavior was escaping from a dull, boring task (that is, the unscheduled-break behavior was being negatively reinforced) and/or meeting with coworkers and friends to socialize and have a cigarette (that is, the unscheduled-break behavior was being positively reinforced). Through such a functional analysis the antecedents and consequences are identified so that an effective intervention strategy can be developed.

The functional analysis pinpoints one of the most significant practical problems of using an O.B. Mod. approach to change critical performance behaviors. Only the *contingent* consequences have an impact on subsequent behavior. The functional analysis often reveals that there are many competing contingencies for every organizational behavior. For example, a supervisor may be administering what he or she believes to be contingent punishment for an undesirable behavior. In many cases, the persons who are supposedly being punished will allow their coworkers' rewards to be the contingent consequence, and their undesirable behavior will increase in subsequent frequency. In other words, the supervisor's punishment is not contingent; it has no impact on the subordinates' subsequent behavior. The functional analysis must make sure that the *contingent* consequences are identified, and the analyst must not be deluded by the consequences that on the surface appear to be affecting the critical behavior.

Step 4: Development of an Intervention Strategy

The first three steps in an O.B. Mod. approach are preliminary to the action step, the intervention. The goal of the intervention is to strengthen and accelerate functional performance behaviors and/or weaken and decelerate dysfunctional behaviors. There are several strategies that can be used, but the main ones are positive reinforcement and punishment–positive reinforcement.

A Positive Reinforcement Strategy. The last chapter devoted considerable attention to the concept of reinforcement. A *positive reinforcer* was defined as a consequence which strengthens the behavior and increases its subsequent frequency. It was also brought out that negative reinforcement (the termination or withdrawal of an undesirable consequence) has the same impact on behavior; that is, it strengthens and increases subsequent frequency. Yet positive and not negative reinforcement is recommended as an effective intervention strategy for O.B. Mod. The reason is that positive reinforcement represents a form of positive control of behavior, while negative reinforcement and punishment represent forms of negative control of behavior. As Chapter 8 pointed out, negative reinforcement is actually a type of "blackmail" control of behavior; the person behaves in a certain way in order not to be punished. Most organizations today control participants in this manner. People come to work in order not to be fired, and they look busy when the supervisor walks by in order not to be punished. Under positive control, the person behaves in a certain way in order to receive the desired consequence. Under positive control, people come to work in order to be recognized for making a contribution to their department's goal of perfect attendance, or they keep busy whether the supervisor is around or not in order to receive incentive pay or because they get self-reinforcement from doing a good job. Positive control through a positive reinforcement intervention strategy is much more effective and long-lasting than negative control. It creates a much healthier and more productive organizational climate.

A positive reinforcer used as an O.B. Mod. intervention strategy could be anything, as long as it increases the performance behavior. Most often money is thought of as the logical, or sometimes the only, positive reinforcer available to managers using this approach. However, as the last chapter pointed out, money is potentially a very powerful reinforcer, but often turns out to be ineffective because it is not contingently administered as a consequence of the behavior being managed. Besides money, positive reinforcers that are also very powerful, readily available to all behavioral managers, and costs nothing are the social reinforcers (attention and recognition) and performance feedback. These reinforcers (money, attention, recognition, and feedback) can and, as will be demonstrated later in the chapter, have been effectively used as an O.B. Mod strategy.

A Punishment–Positive Reinforcement Strategy. There is little debate that a positive reinforcement strategy is the most effective intervention for O.B. Mod. Yet realistically it is recognized that in some cases the use of punishment to weaken and decelerate undesirable behaviors cannot be avoided. This would be true in the case of something like unsafe behaviors that need to be immediately decreased. However, as was pointed out in Chapter 8, so many negative side effects accompany the use of punishment that it should be avoided if at all possible. Punished behavior tends to be only temporarily suppressed; for example, if a supervisor reprimands a subordinate for some dysfunctional behavior, the behavior will decrease in the presence of the supervisor but will surface again when the supervisor is absent. In addition, a punished person becomes very anxious and uptight; reliance on punishment may have a disastrous impact on employee satisfaction and create unnecessary stress.

Perhaps the biggest problem with the use of punishment, however, is that it is very difficult for a supervisor to switch roles from punisher to positive reinforcer. Some supervisors and managers rely on punishment so much in dealing with their subordinates that it is almost impossible for them to administer positive reinforcement effectively. This is a bad situation for the management of human resources because the use of positive reinforcement is a much more effective way of changing employee behavior. If punishment is deemed to be necessary, the desirable alternative behavior (for example, safe behavior) should be positively reinforced at the first opportunity. Use of this combination strategy will cause the alternative desirable behavior to begin to replace the undesirable behavior in the person's behavioral repertoire. Punishment should never be used alone as an O.B. Mod. intervention. If punishment is absolutely necessary, it should always be used in combination with positive reinforcement.

Step 5: Evaluation to Ensure Performance Improvement

A glaring weakness of most human resource management programs is the absence of any systematic, built-in evaluation.[4] A comprehensive analysis of the evaluation of human resources programs concluded that the typical approach is "to review a program with one or two vice presidents at the corporate office, various managers in the field, and perhaps a group of prospective trainees. It continues to be used until someone in a position of authority decides that the program has outlived its usefulness. All of this is done on the basis of opinion and judgment."[5] Such haphazard evaluations have resulted in the termination of some effective programs and the perpetuation of some ineffective ones. In either case, there are severe credibility problems, and today all programs dealing with people, whether they are government welfare programs or human resource management programs, are under the pressure of accountability. Human resource managers no longer have the luxury of just trying something new and different and hoping they can improve performance. Today there is pressure for everything that is tried to be *proved* to have value. As in the case of the validity of selection and appraisal techniques, which are currently under scrutiny, systematic evaluations of human resources management techniques should have been done all along.

O.B. Mod. attempts to meet the credibility and accountability problems head-on by including evaluation as an actual part of the process. In this last step of the approach, the need for four levels of evaluation (reaction, learning, behavioral change, and performance improvement) is stressed. The *reaction level* refers simply to whether the people using the approach and those having it used on them like it. If O.B. Mod. is well received and there is a positive reaction to it, there is a better chance of its being used effectively. In addition, reaction evaluations are helpful because (1) positive reactions help ensure organizational support, (2) they can provide information for planning future programs, (3) favorable reactions can enhance the other levels of evaluation (learning, behavioral change, and performance improvement), and (4) they can provide useful comparative data between units and across time.[6]

The second level of evaluation is learning. This is especially important when first implementing an O.B. Mod. approach. Do the people using the approach understand the theoretical background and underlying assumptions and the meaning of, and reasons for, the steps in the model? If they do not, the model will again tend to be used ineffectively. The third level is aimed at *behavioral change*. Are behaviors actually being changed? The charting of behaviors gives objective data for this level of evaluation. The fourth and final level, *performance improvement*, is the most important. The major purpose of O.B. Mod. is not just to receive a favorable reaction, learn the concepts, and change behaviors. These dimensions are important mainly because they contribute to the overriding purpose, which is to improve performance. "Hard" measures (for example, data on quantity and quality, turnover, absenteeism, customer complaints, employee grievances, length of patient stay, number of clients served, and rate of return on investment) and scientific methodology as discussed in Chapter 2 are used whenever possible to evaluate systematically the impact of O.B. Mod. on performance.

EXPERIENCE WITH THE APPLICATION OF O.B. MOD.

There is a body of research that evaluates the effectiveness of O.B. Mod. when applied in manufacturing as well as in nonprofit and service-oriented organizations. In addition to the direct application of O.B. Mod. as described in this chapter, considerable basic research has been conducted on operant and social learning variables in experimental psychology. For many years and in very recent times, a number of studies have assessed the application of closely related behavioral management techniques. The *Handbook of Organizational Behavior Management* summarizes these findings as follows:[7]

1. *Employee productivity.* Most applications by far have focused on this area. The considerable number of research studies clearly indicate that employee productivity or task completion is positively affected by behavioral management tech-

niques. After reviewing a number of field studies, it was concluded that the improvement of either quantity or quality of employee output cuts across virtually all organizational settings and all intervention techniques.[8]

2. *Absenteeism and tardiness.* This is probably the second biggest area of application. Studies that have examined this area have used some combination of rewards (for example, small monetary bonuses or lottery incentive systems) for attendance or promptness and/or punishers for absenteeism or tardiness. One extensive search of this literature found very positive results.[9] The six most sound methodological studies reported an 18 to 50 percent reduction in the absence rate and a 90 percent reduction in the frequency of tardiness. One study found a positive, causal impact that an O.B. Mod. program had on the attendance of employees in a bank.[10]

3. *Safety and accident prevention.* Most organizations, especially manufacturing firms and others in which dangerous equipment is used, are very concerned about safety. However, since accidents occur at such a relatively low frequency, most studies have focused on reducing identifiable safety hazards or increasing safe behaviors (for example, wearing earplugs, the utilization of which went from 35 to 95 percent, according to one study;[11] wearing hard hats; or keeping the safety guard in place on dangerous equipment). A review article indicates the considerable success that behavioral management techniques have had in these areas.[12] Some actual company examples are Boston Gas, where employees without accidents are eligible for lottery drawings; Virginia Electric & Power Co., where employees can win from $50 to $1000 for safe work habits; Southern New England Telecommunications, which gives gift coupons to employees without accidents; and Turner Corp., a New York–based engineering and construction firm, where employees can earn company stock if they meet safety goals. All of these companies report improved accident rates.[13]

4. *Sales Performance.* Sales managers and trainers have traditionally relied on internal motivation techniques to get their salespeople to improve their performance. For example, one behavioral management consultant tells about a company that gave its sales personnel a typical high-powered, multimedia training program which supposedly taught them effective selling skills. However, when the enthusiastic trainees finished the program and actually tried the things presented to them in the program, they received little if any feedback or reinforcement. Within a few weeks the enthusiasm began to wane, and, most important, actual sales performance began to decline.[14] In other words, even though these salespeople had probably acquired effective selling skills during their training, the environment did not support the use of these skills. An O.B. Mod. approach, in which important selling behaviors such as customer approach, suggestive statements, and closing statements are identified, measured, analyzed, intervened in, and evaluated, would be an alternative to the motivation-skill-teaching approach. A comprehensive review of the behavioral approach to sales in restaurants, retail stores, wholesale establishments, and telephone operations found considerable success.[15] By using a combination of antecedent and consequence intervention strategies, dramatic improvements were shown in areas such as wine and dessert sales, average customer transactions, customer assistance, sales forecasting, sales-call frequency, sales of telephone services, and airline reservations. A recent study

of fast-food restaurants also found that antecedent prompts ("can I get you some fries with that") significantly increased consumer purchases.[16] The successful application of O.B. Mod. to the selling, absent-from-the-work-station, and idle-time behaviors of clerks in a large retail store is reported in detail later in the chapter.

Although the above results are not exhaustive and do not always reflect the exact O.B. Mod. model outlined in this chapter, they are representative of the growing application of this behavioral approach to human resources management. In addition, recent comprehensive reviews generally support the above findings.[17] The following sections summarize the research on direct applications of O.B. Mod. as conducted by the author of this text and his colleagues.

Manufacturing Applications of O.B. Mod.

To date, most of the direct applications of O.B. Mod. have been in manufacturing firms of all sizes.

The First Application.   The initial study was conducted almost twenty years ago in a medium-size light manufacturing firm located in a large city. Two groups (experimental and control) of nine production-type supervisors were used in the study. The experimental group received training, essentially on the five steps, discussed earlier in this chapter, of the O.B. Mod. approach. The results showed that O.B. Mod. had a definite positive impact on reaction, behavioral change, and performance. Learning was not evaluated in this study. Questionnaires administered to the trained supervisors indicated that they liked the O.B. Mod. approach, and the supervisors indicated that their subordinates seemed to react positively. On the charts kept by each trainee (step 2) it was clearly shown that in all cases they were able to change critical behaviors. Examples of behavioral changes accomplished by the supervisors included decreasing the number of complaints, reducing the group scrap rate, decreasing the number of overlooked defective pieces, and reducing the assembly reject rate.[18] The most important result of the study, however, was the significant impact that the O.B. Mod. approach had on the performance of the supervisor's departments. By use of a pretest-posttest control group experimental design, it was found that the experimental group's departments (those in which the supervisors used O.B. Mod.) outperformed the control group's departments. Figure 9.2 shows the results. Statistical analysis revealed that the department production rates of supervisors who used O.B. Mod. increased significantly more than the department production rates of the control supervisors (those who were not using O.B. Mod.).[19]

The Second Study.   A replication in a larger plant obtained results almost identical to those of the original study on all levels of evaluation (including learning). The following summarizes some typical cases of behavioral change that occurred in the production area of the larger manufacturing firm:

1. *Use of idle time.* One supervisor had a worker with a lot of idle time. Instead of using this time productively by helping others, the worker would pretend to look busy and stretch out the day. After getting a baseline measure and doing a

FIGURE 9.2
Performance results of experimental (those who used the O.B. Mod. approach) and control groups. (*Source:* Robert Ottemann and Fred Luthans, "An Experimental Analysis of the Effectiveness of an Organizational Behavior Modification Program in Industry," *Academy of Management Proceedings*, 1975, p. 141.)

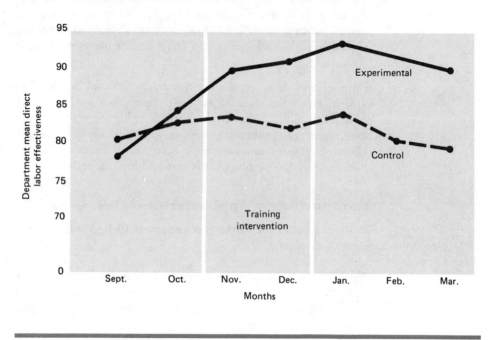

functional analysis, the supervisor intervened by giving the worker social rein-forcers (attention, praise, and recognition) contingent upon the worker's helping out at other jobs during idle time. Eventually the supervisor also reinforced the worker through assigning more responsibility. This approach dramatically in-creased the worker's productive use of idle time.

2. *Low performer.* A production worker in one of the supervisor's departments was producing way below standard (80.3 percent of standard on a six-month base-line). The low performance was not deemed to be an ability, technical, training, or standards problem. After the functional analysis, the supervisor used an intervention of feedback and social reinforcers to increase the types of behaviors that would lead to higher output. This intervention resulted in a 93 percent of standard performance level, with no decrease in quality.

3. *Group quality.* One supervisor had a problem with the quality of work in his department. The baseline measure verified this problem. After the functional analysis, the supervisor used feedback and social reinforcers on the group as a whole. Shortly after the use of this intervention strategy, the group attained the quality standard for the first time in three years.

4. *Group attendance.* Another supervisor felt that he had an attendance problem in his department. The baseline measure revealed 92 percent attendance, which was not as big a problem as he had thought. However, he established the goal of 100 percent. After he used daily feedback and social reinforcers on the group, 100 percent attendance was attained very rapidly. An interesting anecdote told by the

supervisor was that one of his workers was riding to work from a small town in a car pool early one morning when they hit a deer. The car was disabled by the accident. Coworkers who worked in other departments in the plant and were also riding in the car pool called relatives and went back home for the day. This worker, however, did not want to spoil the 100 percent attendance record, so she hitchhiked to work by herself and made it on time.

5. *Problem with another department.* One supervisor felt that the performance of his department was being adversely affected by the unrecoverable time of truck-lift operators who were not directly under his supervision. After obtaining baseline data and making a functional analysis, the supervisor decided to use feedback and social reinforcers with the informal group leader and the supervisor of the truck-lift operators. This intervention substantially reduced the unrecoverable time affecting the operational performance of his department.

The five examples above are only representative of the types of behavior that the supervisors using an O.B. Mod. approach were able to change. Cumulatively, such individual behavioral projects were able to improve the overall performance of these supervisors' departments in both the original study and the follow-up.

Application to an Entire Small Manufacturing Plant. Next, the O.B. Mod. approach was extended beyond the first-line supervisory level of application to a total small manufacturing plant with all levels of management and to a very large multiplant manufacturing firm. In the small manufacturing plant, O.B. Mod. was implemented in three major phases.[20] The first phase was primarily educational and consisted of training all three levels of management (first the owner/manager, then the four department heads, and finally the eight supervisors) in the O.B. Mod. approach, basically following the five-step model discussed in this chapter. The second stage involved simulation/experiential exercises. At first, the participants analyzed case studies and developed intervention strategies. Then, once both the participants and the researchers/trainers had developed confidence in the participants' skills, the participants applied the O.B. Mod. approach to their own work areas in a manner similar to that already described in the first study. The third and final phase involved the development of a total organizational performance management system. In this phase, all levels of management collaborated to identify key behaviors and performance indices. An organization-wide feedback system was then developed on the basis of key behaviors and performance measures. In addition, programs for specific problem areas were developed.

The results of this comprehensive, *total organization* application indicated that there were significant improvements in both quantity and quality of performance. In fact, *record* performance was attained. Statistical analyses demonstrated the significance of these changes, and simple inspection of the graphic representation of the data shown in Figure 9.3 shows the impact that the O.B. Mod. approach had in this company. The left-hand portion of the graph depicts the average levels and variability of both quantity and quality prior to the intervention. The next segment of the graph displays the effects of a type of contingent time-off (Friday afternoon was given off for reaching a stated level of performance during the week) intervention

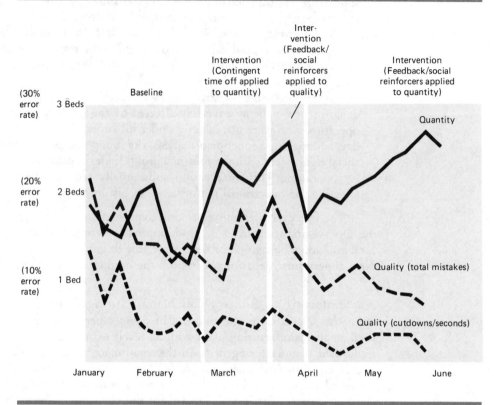

FIGURE 9.3
The impact of O.B. Mod. on the total performance improvement of a small factory.
(*Source:* Fred Luthans and Jason Schweizer, "How Behavior Modification Techniques Can Improve Total Organizational Performance," *Management Review,* September 1979, p. 49.)

strategy on quantity when no consequences were being applied to quality. As evidenced by the changes illustrated, quantity improved with the application of the contingent time-off consequences, while the quality level, for which consequences were not changed, remained about the same. The third segment demonstrates that the contingent application of social reinforcers had a positive impact on quality, while the quantity levels remained about the same. Finally, the last segment demonstrates improved levels of both quality and quantity under the control of the feedback system and contingent social reinforcement.

Whereas the first study used a control group design, the multiple-baseline design was deemed to be more appropriate for the evaluation where the total organization was being affected by the O.B. Mod. approach. Such designs give considerable weight to the conclusion that the O.B. Mod. approach did indeed cause the total performance of this organization to improve.

Application to a Very Large Multiplant Firm. Still another study of the application of O.B. Mod. was conducted in eleven major product areas in two plants of a very large labor-intensive firm.[21] One hundred and thirty-five production supervisors were trained in and then implemented an O.B. Mod. approach. Specifically, these supervisors first made a detailed analysis audit that identified objective, measurable employee behaviors in their respective departments that contributed to quality and/or quantity performance. These included behaviors such as performing a particular operation more efficiently or delivering a certain piece of material in a more timely manner. The supervisors then quantitatively measured and charted the frequency of occurrence of these identified behaviors. This was followed by an analysis of the antecedents and consequences of the critical behavior (that is, an A-B-C functional analysis). The intervention step consisted of providing performance feedback and social reinforcement (attention and recognition) for progress and attainment. Finally, an evaluation of the results was made to determine the exact impact on performance.

The results are summarized in Table 9.2. The O.B. Mod. approach had a positive impact on all product areas in which it was applied. The impact had wide variation, but it should be noted that although there was only a 2 percent gain in product 2, this still translated to an annualized value of nearly $900,000 in this company, and the 1.4 percent gain in product 6 equated to an annualized value of about $750,000. The projected annual values of the gains in other product areas were estimated for this company as follows: product 1, +$259,000; product 3, +$510,000; product 4, +$371,000; and product 5, an impressive +$2.276 million. Although information for computing the actual dollar values of the improvements in products 7 through 11 was not available, they were judged to be very similar in magnitude to the others. Besides this tremendous impact on value added performance (several million dollars in this company), it is important to note that in no case did the O.B. Mod. approach have a negative impact.

It should be noted that this study did not contain the rigorous methodology of the other manufacturing applications. Thus, the results in this case cannot lead to the same causal conclusions concerning the impact of O.B. Mod. Yet there is still

TABLE 9.2 The Impact of O.B. Mod. on the Quantity and Quality of Performance in a Large Production Operation

Product	Group	Quality Improvement, Percent	Quantity Improvement, Percent
1	B	50	
2	A		2
3	A	15	
4	A	23	
	C	64	
5	A	35	
	C	51	
6	A		1.4
7	B		16
8	B		16
9	B	42	
10	B	39	
11	B		52

Source: Adapted from Fred Luthans, Walter S. Maciag, and Stuart A. Rosenkrantz, "O.B. Mod.: Meeting the Productivity Challenge with Human Resource Management," *Personnel*, March–April 1983, p. 31. Groups A and B are two shifts in one plant and group C is at another plant in the same company.

considerable evidence that O.B. Mod. did lead to the improved performance. For instance, when examined closely, the performance changes following the staggered starting dates of the program support the conclusion that the effects were indeed caused by the O.B. Mod. approach rather than some other factor. This is a simplified version of the multiple-baseline design from which causal conclusions can be drawn. In every product area tracked in this part of the analysis, the start of the O.B. Mod. program was followed almost immediately by a clear improvement in the quality or quantity of performance.

Contingent Time Off in a Manufacturing   A contingent time-off (CTO) program was tried in a unit of a fairly large high-technology firm.[22] Most organizations in recent times have not had the luxury of using monetary reward systems to increase the performance of their employees. A potentially powerful, but largely overlooked, alternative is the use of contingent time off. This usually involves employees' attaining "earned time" (that is, leisure time or time off from the job) once both quantity and quality performance standards are met. In other words, CTO focuses on performance results, not hours worked. Time off, not just the pay, becomes the reward. Labor costs do not decrease under a CTO program, but performance may substantially increase at no additional cost to the employer.

Using an O.B. Mod. approach, it was determined by a combined team of in-house staff members and researchers that quantity and quality of performance were a problem in this high-technology manufacturing plant, which consisted of noninterdependent work groups that assembled different products. Measurement revealed that one representative group was producing an average of 160 units per day with about 10 percent rejects. Functional analysis revealed that this group could probably produce more than this with better quality, if there were reinforcing consequences for doing so. Since this firm did not have funds available for monetary incentives, a CTO intervention was applied. The contingency contract was: *If* the group produced 200 units with three additional good units for every defective unit, *then* they could leave work for the rest of that day. Within a week of the time the CTO intervention was implemented, the group was producing more than 200 units with an average of 1.5 percent rejects. These employees, who had formerly *put in* an eight-hour day, were now *working* an average of 6 hours per day, and, more important, they increased their performance by 25 percent with better quality at no additional cost to the company.

Except for some minor problems with parts availability, the employees obviously reacted very favorably to the CTO plan, and, of course, management was very happy with record performance with no additional labor costs. It was a "win-win" strategy. However, there is an interesting but disturbing postscript to this success story. After things had been going along very well (for example, there were plans to implement CTO in all independent work units in the plant), there was an unanticipated changeover in top management. Unfortunately, the new general manager reviewed the CTO plan and concluded: "If employees can produce 200 units in six hours, then they were goldbricking before. Given that we pay them for an eight-hour day, they should be able to produce at least 240 units." The manager then proceeded to terminate the CTO plan and told the group to "get with it." As would be predicted from a behavioral perspective, production immediately dropped in this group to 140 units, 20 units below the original productivity rate. The contingency contract was broken, and the employees were punished for being productive. The lesson to be learned here, of course, is that there must be a strong commitment on the part of management to carry through and support contingency contracts, such as the CTO plan, if the desired results are to be achieved and then maintained. Behavior is a function of its consequences; if reinforced, it will increase; if punished, it will decrease. Not living up to contingency contracts can have disastrous results.

Nonmanufacturing Applications: Health and Service Industries

The studies discussed above do provide considerable evidence that an O.B. Mod. approach can have a positive impact on employee performance, at least in relatively structured environments such as are found in most manufacturing plants. But what about less-structured, nonmanufacturing organizations? Research indicates that similar results are possible in these organizations as well.

In a large hospital application, eleven supervisors from medical service, business, and operations units were given O.B. Mod. training in eight sessions over a two-month period.[23] During the O.B. Mod. training these hospital supervisors learned the principles of O.B. Mod. and used the five-step approach; that is, they identified, measured, functionally analyzed, and intervened to change key performance behaviors of their subordinates, and then they evaluated the results in their respective areas of responsibility. The results of this program are shown in Table 9.3. Although the researchers were unable to employ an experimental design in this study (and therefore cause-and-effect conclusions are not warranted), the simple before-and-after analysis provides a rather convincing argument that the O.B. Mod. approach was effective in modifying a broad range of performance-related behaviors in a hospital setting. The O.B. Mod. approach seemed to affect both the quality and the quantity performance measures. Moreover, the data indicate that each of the O.B. Mod.–trained supervisors was successful in applying the intervention, despite the wide variety of situations encountered.

In another nonmanufacturing organization, a somewhat different type of O.B. Mod. application was tried.[24] Instead of training supervisors to use an O.B. Mod. approach, the researchers themselves carried out the steps normally handled by the supervisors. An experiment (an A-B-A compared with a control group, that is, a true experimental design) was conducted in a major metropolitan department store. Critical performance behaviors of eighty-two retail clerks from sixteen randomly selected departments were identified. These behaviors included selling, stock work, idle behaviors, absenteeism from the workstation, and miscellaneous. Next, the baseline measure of these behaviors was obtained by observational and work-sampling techniques. A detailed analysis was then conducted to determine the appropriate performance goals for these behaviors. For example, on the basis of job descriptions, organizational goals and policies, direct observations, and role playing, it was determined that (1) salespersons, except when they had an excused absence, should be present in the department, within 3 feet of displayed merchandise, during

TABLE 9.3 Performance Measures before and after an O.B. Mod. Training Program in a Large Hospital

Unit	Measure	Pre-intervention	Post-intervention	Percent Change
Emergency room clerks	Registration errors (per day)	19.16	4.58	76.1
Hardware engineer group, HIS	Average time to repair (minutes)	92.53	33.25	61.4
Medical records file clerks	Errors in filing (per person per audit)	2.87	0.078	97.3
Medical records	Complaints	8.0	1.0	875.0
Transcriptionists	Average errors	2.07	1.4	33.0
	Average output	2258.0	2303.33	2.0
Heart station	EKG procedures accomplished (average)	1263.0	1398.97	11.0
	Overdue procedures	7.0*	4.0	42.8
Eye clinic	Daily patient throughput	19.0	23.0	21.0
	Daily patient teaching documentation	1.0	2.8	180.0
	Protocols produced	0.0	2.0	200.0
Pharmacy technicians	Drug output (doses)	348.8	422.1	21.0
	Posting errors	3.67	1.48	59.7
	Product waste (percent)	5.8	4.35	25.0
Radiology technicians	Average patient throughput (procedural)	3849.5	4049.0	5.0
	Retake rate (percent)	11.2	9.95	11.2
Patient accounting	Average monthly billings	2561.0	3424.5	33.7
Admitting office	Time to admit (minutes)	43.73	13.57	68.97
	Average cost	$15.05	$11.73	22.0
Data center operations	Systems log-on (time)	1.54	1.43	13.4

*Estimate. All averages are arithmetic means.
Source: Adapted from Charles A. Snyder and Fred Luthans, "Using O.B. Mod. to Increase Hospital Productivity," *Personnel Administrator,* August 1982, p. 72.

assigned working hours; (2) when customers came to the department, they should be offered assistance or acknowledged and promised immediate aid within five seconds; and (3) the display shelf should be filled to at least 70 percent capacity.

The intervention consisted of contingently applying time off with pay or equivalent cash and an opportunity to compete for a free vacation for two for attaining the performance goals. Observationally gathered behavioral data were collected before, during, and after this intervention. For computational and graphic presentation, the selling, stock work, and miscellaneous behaviors were collapsed into a single category, called *aggregate retailing behavior,* and absence from the workstation and idle time were also combined for this purpose. Figure 9.4 shows the results. The baseline frequencies of these behaviors were not significantly different, but immediately on the first day of the intervention the aggregate retailing behavior of the experimental group dramatically increased and there was a huge decline in the average incidence of absence from the workstation and idleness. As shown, this frequency maintained itself even after the intervention was withdrawn. This suggests that other, more natural reinforcers in the environment and perhaps self-reinforcement had taken over.

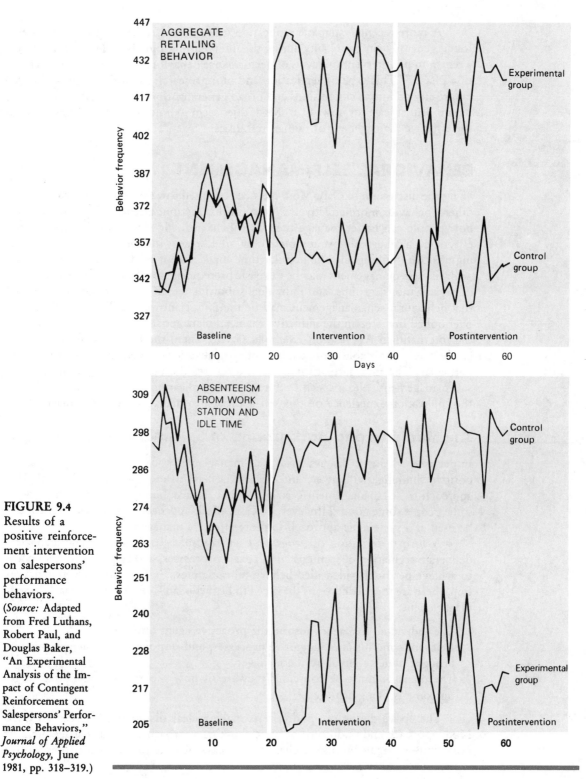

FIGURE 9.4 Results of a positive reinforcement intervention on salespersons' performance behaviors. (*Source:* Adapted from Fred Luthans, Robert Paul, and Douglas Baker, "An Experimental Analysis of the Impact of Contingent Reinforcement on Salespersons' Performance Behaviors," *Journal of Applied Psychology,* June 1981, pp. 318–319.)

A more recent systematic replication using tighter controls in the field setting found generally similar results during the intervention, but also a reversal (there was a return to preintervention levels of performance behaviors) during the postintervention phase.[25] This type of replication and more research in more settings is needed before any definitive conclusions and broad generalizations about O.B. Mod. can be drawn. But at least for now, O.B. Mod. does seem to hold considerable potential for the effective management of human resources.

BEHAVIORAL SELF-MANAGEMENT

So far the discussion of O.B. Mod. has been oriented toward how people can manage others' behavior more effectively. Now, in this section, attention is shifted toward how people can better manage their own behavior. How to manage oneself more effectively has been almost completely ignored, except for some accolades concerning positive thinking and the popular time-management guidelines. But in the final analysis, self-management may be the basic prerequisite for the effective management of organizations, groups, and individual subordinates; in fact, it has been suggested that behavioral self-management may be the important missing link, or at least the overlooked first step in the inductive chain, in managerial effectiveness.[26] As seen in the International Application Example, Giving Them the Power, self-management can be a very profitable approach for both organizations in general and employees in particular. The first part of this section discusses the meaning and background of self-management. Next, specific strategies for application are presented, and finally the application experience on this self-approach to management is summarized.

The Meaning and Background of Self-Management

In the past, whenever discussions of self-management took place, the importance of positive thinking, willpower, and perhaps self-motivation was brought out. This approach to self-management certainly didn't do any harm, and it may have done some people some good. However, an O.B. Mod. approach to self-management can be used as a systematic approach to more effective management.

A formal definition of *behavioral self-control* is as follows: "The manager's deliberate regulation of stimulus cues, covert processses, and response consequences to achieve personally identified behavioral outcomes."[27] In addition to this definition, there are three conditions that need to be met in an O.B. Mod. approach to self-management:

1. The individual manager must be the proactive agent of change.
2. Relevant stimulus cues, cognitive processes, and response consequences must be brought under control by the manager.
3. The manager must be consciously aware of how a personally identified target outcome is being achieved.[28]

The above definitions and criteria make a clear distinction between an O.B. Mod. approach and traditional positive-thinking approaches to self-management, or even time-management approaches. In the case of time management, prescriptive

Giving Them the Power

Who builds the best quality cars in the world? Many people think it is Toyota, which has proven over and over that no matter how good the quality of this year's model, next year's will be even better. How does it manage this feat? One way is through its use of self-management techniques that ensure that everyone is devoted to quality.

Each assembler on a Toyota auto line is trained to think of him- or herself as a quality-control inspector. Rather than totally relying on other people to ensure that each auto meets quality standards, the assembler is empowered to take personal action. If a piece has not been installed correctly when it reaches his or her station, the assembler has the authority to refuse it. The individual's first act is to tug a rope that turns on a warning light. If the problem is not corrected by the time the next piece comes down, the worker is empowered to stop the line. At the same time, the individual is given authority to identify problems that are occurring on the line and to see that management learns about these problems and does something about them. In particular, workers focus on eliminating what the company calls the three D's of work: dangerous, dirty, and demanding.

Nor do Toyota's self-management ideas end at the blue-collar level. The company also trains its white-collar people to identify and solve problems. These people are given lectures and instruction on how to spot problems, and how to rework solutions until they find one that is suitable to the situation. By instilling this self-management process into its white-collar personnel, Toyota is ensuring that these people can be given international assignments and they will have a worldwide cadre of independent-minded team players who are all working in unison.

Are these approaches really paying off? According to recent reports, Toyota now has the highest operating margins of all major auto producers in the world, and it is introducing new entries into all price niches from the Corolla that sells in the $10,000 range to the Lexus in the mid-$40,000 range. Apparently, the company's self-management ideas are proving to be very profitable.

guidelines are offered (for example, delegate more, reduce paperwork, and establish goals), but no suggestions as to exactly *how* to accomplish these objectives or how to deal with other-imposed or self-imposed environmental antecedents and consequences are given. There is considerable theoretical and research backup for an O.B. Mod. approach to self-management.

The last chapter indicated that behavioral self-control is a vital part of social learning theory, along with modeling and cognitive mediating processes. As was pointed out, it is important to recognize that the social learning approach is a behavioral theory and depends heavily upon classical and operant principles. Thus, behavioral self-management fits into the O.B. Mod. framework.

To B. F. Skinner, the notion of self-control was no different from other forms of operant behavioral control. In the strict (Skinnerian) operant interpretation, behavior is deemed to be under the control of the stimulus environment (that is, the antecedent, discriminant stimulus) and of the contingent consequences, irrespective of whether these are manipulated by individuals themselves or by others in the environment. In other words, under the operant view, behavioral self-control depends on the individual's ability to manage the stimulus environment and the contingent consequences. However, just as social learning theory accepts the operant principles but goes beyond them, so does the approach to self-management suggested here.

To review again, the social learning approach encompasses the operant premise of the importance of the antecedent and consequent environment; in addition, however, it recognizes and gives attention to the role of cognitive mediating processes—thoughts, feelings, and self-evaluative behavior—and it recognizes that the antecedents and consequences can be covert (inner and unobservable) as well as overt (external and observable). This extension from the operant to the social learning view is also represented by a move from the three-term antecedent-behavior-consequence functional analysis (A-B-C) to a four-term stimulus-organism-behavior-consequence functional analysis (S-O-B-C). In other words, behavioral self-management falls within an expanded O.B. Mod. framework and depends on the S-O-B-C functional analysis.

Strategies for Behavioral Self-Management

Besides the S-O-B-C functional analysis, which is used to help identify and more effectively manage the environmental contingencies and the cognitive mediating processes, there are two other major strategies for effective behavioral self-management; these are discussed below.

Stimulus Management. This strategy is concerned with the antecedent or stimulus side and can be either covert or overt. Stimulus management involves the gradual removal of, or only selective exposure to, stimuli that evoke behaviors whose frequency the manager is trying to decrease or wants to eliminate altogether. At the same time, or alternatively, the manager would deliberately introduce new cuing stimuli or rearrange existing stimuli in order to evoke behavior that he or she wants to create or whose frequency is to be increased.

For example, managers who want to decrease the amount of time spent in idle chitchat with subordinates could have their secretaries screen all visits and apply certain criteria before a subordinate is allowed into the office. This method of stimulus management—the removal or selective exposure of the stimulus (visiting subordinates)—will decrease the amount of unproductive time spent chatting with subordinates. This same strategy could also be used by managers who want to increase informal interactions with subordinates. They could schedule weekly appointments with each subordinate or have their coffee breaks and those of their subordinates scheduled together. The introduction of the new stimulus (having subordinates come up to the office) or the rearrangement of the existing stimuli (scheduling the coffee breaks to coincide) would evoke more informal interactions with subordinates.

Consequence Management. This second major strategy concentrates on the consequence side of the self-behavior. It involves the contingent application of new reinforcers or the rearrangement of existing ones to increase the behavior in subsequent frequency, or the application of punishers to decrease it. This strategy is basically the same as the intervention strategies for O.B. Mod. discussed so far, except that the self-reinforcers and punishers can be covert as well as overt.

An example of a self-reinforcement strategy would be that of managers who want to limit their weekly staff meetings to an hour. When they are able to do this, they could reinforce themselves by having a cup of coffee (overt) or by simply congratulating themselves and feeling good about it (covert). If they do not keep the meeting time to an hour, they could punish themselves by staying after work for the amount of time over an hour (overt) or simply by admonishing themselves and feeling bad about it (covert).

Analogous to the point made in this chapter and the last one, that positive reinforcers tend to be more effective than punishers, it is also generally found, at least in clinical applications, that self-reinforcement is a more effective strategy than self-punishment. The problem with self-punishment, besides people's tendency only to suppress rather than change the behavior, is that if a punishment is too aversive, the person just won't use it. Thus, the dilemma for a self-punishment strategy is to find a punisher that will in fact decrease the behavior but, at the same time, will not be so aversive that the person will avoid using it.

Other Strategies. There are slight variations in the two main strategies discussed above, in addition to several other possibilities.[29] A variation of stimulus management—or, more accurately, a part of stimulus management—is the goal-setting procedure discussed in Chapter 7. Self-goal setting can serve as both a cuing stimulus and feedback, and accomplishment of progress and attainment of self-goals can be the reinforcers. The same is true of a self-recording strategy. In a feedforward-feedback sense, self-recording can serve both as a reminder and as a cue for the behavior ("I have to record every hour" or "I have to record every occurrence," for example) and also reinforces it ("I can see the progress I am making from the records I am keeping"). Some psychologists believe that self-observation is a necessary first step in any program of self-change. Finally, the rehearsal and modeling techniques that were discussed in Chapter 8 could be used in self-control. This can be found in the following example: "A salesperson could rehearse a sales presentation both covertly and overtly and thereby refine it. Then through intentionally imagining the desirable consequences of a successful sale, feelings of confidence could be reinforced."[30]

Applications of Self-Management

Although the research on and application of behavioral self-management are just getting under way, a number of line and staff managers in a wide variety of positions such as advertising, retailing, manufacturing, and public service have applied it in the hope of increasing their effectiveness.[31] For example, one assistant manager in a retail store determined that one of the major problems detracting from her effectiveness was her overdependence on her boss. With the help of the researcher, she systematically applied self-management to try to reduce this behavior.

She first used the S-O-B-C model to functionally analyze and identify the relevant environmental and cognitive variables. She then set up a combination stimulus and consequence management strategy to decrease her visits with (that is, her dependence on) her boss. This strategy consisted mainly of self-recording. She maintained a record of the number of times she resisted going to see her boss when she normally would have, and she also kept track of the number of times she did visit with her boss and what was discussed. The index card she carried and the notebook record she kept served to cue the appropriate behavior—to resist visiting her boss and take her own action—and the feedback served to reinforce the appropriate behavior and punish the inappropriate behavior.

Using a reversal design to evaluate the intervention, it was concluded that this approach did indeed have its intended effect on the targeted behavior. Figure 9.5 shows the results. Both the boss and this assistant manager were pleased with the results. Once the study was over, the assistant manager reported that she would go back to using self-management to control this behavior and would try to use the approach with other dysfunctional behaviors as well.

Another example is that of an advertising manager who systematically applied self-management to three critical behaviors that were targeted for analysis and change: not processing enough paperwork, leaving the office without telling anyone, and failing to fill out a daily expense form. In other words, the more important-

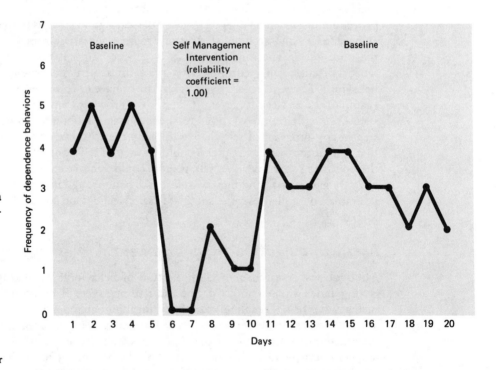

FIGURE 9.5
A reversal design to analyze the effects of self-management on a manager's dependence behaviors. (*Source:* Fred Luthans and Tim R. V. Davis, "Behavioral Self-Management: The Missing Link in Managerial Effectiveness," *Organizational Dynamics*, Summer 1979, p. 53.)

sounding but highly unrealistic, and in some cases nonexistent, management activities such as strategic planning or matrix management were not the problems facing this manager. He had problems with too much paperwork, keeping his staff informed of his whereabouts, and meeting bureaucratic requirements such as filling out his expense vouchers. Behavioral self-management is especially adaptable to these mundane, yet cumulatively very important, activities that contribute to managerial effectiveness.

After carefully analyzing the paperwork process in S-O-B-C terms, the manager, in conjunction with the researcher, set up a combination stimulus and consequence strategy to reduce the number of unprocessed paperwork items at the end of each day. In particular, the inflows of paperwork items were categorized, and the behaviors to be performed by both the manager and his secretary were cognitively clarified. For example, the secretary now screened out some of the items according to certain criteria and presented other items in consolidated form. The manager, instead of vacillating over each item and then putting it on ever-higher piles on his desk, now acted immediately, noted an action step, or put the item in his out box. He also employed a self-monitoring strategy whereby he recorded each item by category, noted what action was taken, and transferred these data in summary form to a wall-chart display. This self-monitoring provided both feedforward (cuing stimulus) and feedback (reinforcement from progress). Figure 9.6 shows the significant results. The numbers along the upper graph represent the total number of incoming paperwork items. Obviously, the number of unprocessed items on the desk during the baseline period (an average of 9.4) was greatly reduced when self-management was applied (an average of only 0.22).

The same type of approach (that is, S-O-B-C functional analysis and stimulus and consequence management strategies to change the targeted behavior in the desired direction) was applied to the problem of leaving the office without informing the staff and to the problem of filling out expense vouchers. Figure 9.6 shows that these dysfunctional behaviors also dramatically improved after the self-management approach. The use of the multiple-baseline design lends considerable support to the conclusion that the self-management was responsible for the improvement in the dysfunctional behaviors. The manager was able to exercise self-control over his dysfunctional behaviors, and the result was that he was a more effective manager.

O.B. MOD. IN PERSPECTIVE

The analysis of the manufacturing and nonmanufacturing applications and behavioral self-management indicates that O.B. Mod. can and does work to improve performance in today's organizations. Yet some of the theories that O.B. Mod. is based upon and specific behavior modification applications made in mental hospitals, clinics, classrooms, and especially prisons still generate emotional criticism and controversy. Surprisingly, this concern has not really carried over to the applications in human resource management. To be sure, there are some criticisms of an O.B. Mod. approach in terms of theoretical orientation and its usefulness to practice,[32] but generally the ethics of the approach have not been unduly criticized. Nevertheless,

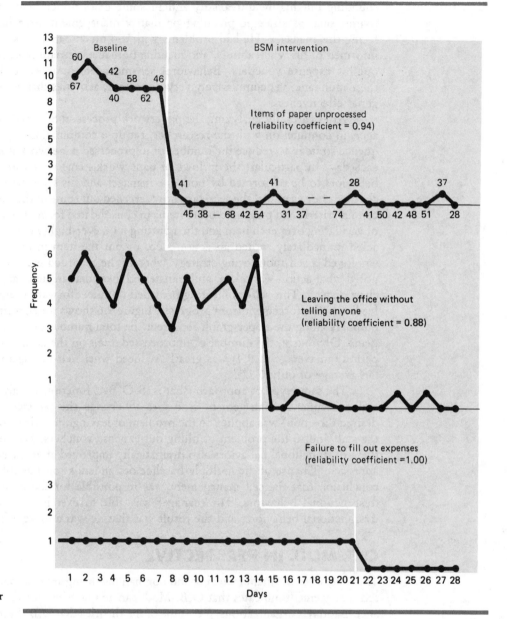

FIGURE 9.6
A multiple-baseline design to analyze the effects of self-management of dysfunctional behaviors.
(*Source:* Fred Luthans and Tim R. V. Davis, "Behavioral Self-Management: The Missing Link in Managerial Effectiveness," *Organizational Dynamics,* Summer 1979, p. 56.)

there are probably many managers and potential managers who still feel uneasy about using an O.B. Mod. approach. Although they may agree that it works, they still feel it is somehow wrong. Such concerns must by fully aired and constructively analyzed if O.B. Mod. is to continue to be a viable human resource management approach now and in the future.

Summary

This chapter presented an O.B. Mod. approach to human resource management. The model consists of identifying critical performance-related behaviors, obtaining a baseline measure, functionally analyzing the antecedents and the consequences of the critical behaviors, intervening by using a positive reinforcement strategy to accelerate functional performance-related behaviors and punishment (followed by positive reinforcement) to decelerate dysfunctional behaviors, and evaluating to ensure performance improvement. This is an applied, behavioral approach to management rather than just an internal, motivational approach. O.B. Mod. represents only one, but potentially a very powerful, approach to human resource management. It was given detailed attention in order to provide the reader with an in-depth understanding of an applied approach, but it should be recognized that the techniques covered in the other chapters are also important to effective human resource management in today's organizations.

Questions for Discussion and Review

1. What are some methods that can be used to identify important performance behaviors in O.B. Mod.? What are some simple guidelines that can be used?
2. Why is positive reinforcement a more effective intervention strategy than punishment?
3. Briefly summarize the procedures and results of at least one manufacturing and one nonmanufacturing study reported in the chapter. How would you go about implementing and evaluating an O.B. Mod. approach in an organization you are familiar with? Be specific in your answer.
4. What are the definition and criteria of behavioral self-management? How does it differ from traditional positive-thinking approaches to self-control? How does it differ from time management?
5. Identify and give an example of stimulus and consequence management in self-management.

References

1. See Fred Luthans, "Resolved: Functional Analysis Is the Best Technique for Diagnostic Evaluation of Organizational Behavior," in Barbara Karmel (ed.), *Point and Counterpoint in Organizational Behavior*, Dryden, Hinsdale, Ill., 1980, pp. 48–60.
2. See Tim R. V. Davis and Fred Luthans, "Leadership Reexamined: A Behavioral Approach," *Academy of Management Review*, April 1979, pp. 237–248; Fred Luthans and Tim R. V. Davis,

"Operationalizing a Behavioral Approach to Leadership," in E. G. Miller (ed.), *Proceedings of the Midwest Academy of Management*, 1979, University of Michigan Press, Ann Arbor, pp. 144–155; and Tim R. V. Davis and Fred Luthans, "A Social Learning Approach to Organizational Behavior," *Academy of Management Review*, April 1980, pp. 281–290.
3. V. Mark Durand, "Employee Absenteeism: A Selective Review of Antecedents and Conse-

quences," *Journal of Organizational Behavior Management*, Spring/Summer 1985, p. 157.

4. See Ellen Ernst Kossek, "Why Many HR Programs Fail," *Personnel*, May 1990, p. 52.

5. Kenneth N. Wexley and Gary P. Latham, *Developing and Training Human Resources*, Scott, Foresman, Glenview, Ill., 1981, p. 78.

6. Ibid., pp. 81–84.

7. See Lee W. Frederiksen (ed.), *Handbook of Organizational Behavior Management*, Interscience-Wiley, New York, 1982, pp. 12–14; these findings are summarized in Fred Luthans and Robert Kreitner, *Organizational Behavior Modification and Beyond*, Scott, Foresman, Glenview, Ill., 1985, chap. 8.

8. Frederiksen, op. cit., p. 14.

9. R. W. Kempen, "Absenteeism and Tardiness," in Frederiksen, op. cit., p. 372.

10. Fred Luthans and Terry L. Maris, "Evaluating Personnel Programs through the Reversal Technique, *Personnel Journal*, October 1979, pp. 696–697.

11. Dov Zohar and Nahum Fussfeld, "A Systems Approach to Organizational Behavior Modification: Theoretical Considerations and Empirical Evidence," *International Review of Applied Psychology*, October 1981, pp. 491–505.

12. Beth Sulzer-Azaroff, "Behavioral Approaches to Occupational Health and Safety," in Frederiksen, op. cit., pp. 505–538.

13. "Labor Letter," *The Wall Street Journal*, Jan. 27, 1987, p. 1.

14. Thomas K. Connellan, *How to Improve Human Performance*, Harper & Row, New York, 1978, pp. 170–174.

15. Robert Mirman, "Performance Management in Sales Organizations," in Frederiksen, op. cit., pp. 427–475.

16. Mark J. Martinko, J. Dennis White, and Barbara Hassell, "An Operant Analysis of Prompting in a Sales Environment," *Journal of Organizational Behavior Management*, vol. 10, no. 1, 1989, pp. 93–107.

17. See Kirk O'Hara, C. Merle Johnson, and Terry A. Beehr, "Organizational Behavior Management in the Private Sector: A Review of Empirical Research and Recommendations for Further Investigation," *Academy of Management Review*, October 1985, pp. 848–864; Gerald A. Merwin, John A. Thompson, and Eleanor E. Sanford, "A Methodology and Content Review of Organiza-

tional Behavior Management in the Private Sector 1978–1986," *Journal of Organizational Behavior Management*, vol. 10, no. 1, 1989, pp. 39–57; and Frank Andrasik, "Organizational Behavior Modification in Business Settings: A Methodological and Content Review," *Journal of Organizational Behavior Management*, vol. 10, no. 1, 1989, pp. 59–77.

18. These examples are reported in detail, including the charts, in Luthans and Kreitner, op. cit.

19. Robert Ottemann and Fred Luthans, "An Experimental Analysis of the Effectiveness of an Organizational Behavior Modification Program in Industry," *Academy of Management Proceedings*, 1975, pp. 140–142.

20. Fred Luthans and Jason Schweizer, "How Behavior Modification Techniques Can Improve Total Organizational Performance," *Management Review*, September 1979, pp. 43–50.

21. Fred Luthans, Walter S. Maciag, and Stuart A. Rosenkrantz, "O.B. Mod.: Meeting the Productivity Challenge with Human Resource Management," *Personnel*, March–April 1983, pp. 28–36.

22. Diane L. Lockwood and Fred Luthans, "Contingent Time Off: A Nonfinancial Incentive for Improving Productivity," *Management Review*, July 1984, pp. 48–52.

23. Charles A. Snyder and Fred Luthans, "Using O.B. Mod. to Increase Hospital Productivity," *Personnel Administrator*, August 1982, pp. 67–73.

24. Fred Luthans, Robert Paul, and Douglas Baker, "An Experimental Analysis of the Impact of Contingent Reinforcement on Salespersons' Performance Behaviors," *Journal of Applied Psychology*, June 1981, pp. 314–323.

25. Fred Luthans, Robert Paul, and Lew Taylor, "The Impact of Contingent Reinforcement on Retail Salespersons' Performance Behaviors: A Replicated Field Experiment," *Journal of Organizational Behavior Management*, Spring/Summer 1985, pp. 25–35.

26. Luthans and Davis, "Behavioral Self-Management," pp. 42–60. Also see Charles C. Manz, *The Art of Self-Leadership*, Prentice-Hall, Englewood Cliffs, N.J., 1983; and Charles C. Manz, "Self-Leadership: Toward an Expanded Theory of Self-Influence Processes in Organizations," *Academy of Management Review*, July 1986, pp. 585–608.

27. Luthans and Davis, "Behavioral Self-Management," p. 43.

28. Ibid.

29. For a comprehensive treatment of various self-control techniques see Spencer A. Rathus, *Psychology*, 4th ed., Holt, Rinehart and Winston, Fort Worth, 1990, pp. 540–543.

30. Charles C. Manz and Henry P. Sims, "Self-Management as a Substitute for Leadership: A Social Learning Perspective," *Academy of Management Review*, July 1980, pp. 364–365.

31. The examples and discussion in this section are drawn from Luthans and Davis, "Behavioral Self-Management," pp. 51–59.

32. For example, see M. Hammer, "The Application of Behavior Conditioning Procedures to the Problems of Quality Control: Comment," *Academy of Management Journal*, December 1971, pp. 529–532; Fred Fry, "Operant Conditioning and O.B. Mod.: Of Mice and Men," *Personnel*, July–August 1974, pp. 17–24; W. F. Whyte, "Skinnerian Theory in Organizations," *Psychology Today*, April 1972, pp. 66–68; Edwin A. Locke, "The Myths of Behavior Mod in Organizations," *Academy of Management Review*, October 1977, pp. 543–553; Patricia Cain Smith, "Resolved: Functional Analysis Is the Best Technique for Diagnostic Evaluation of Organizational Behavior," in Karmel, op. cit., pp. 60–81; Don Hellriegel, John Slocum, and Richard W. Woodman, *Organizational Behavior*, 5th ed., West, St. Paul, Minn. 1989, pp. 133–135.

REAL CASE: FORGET THE RAISE, HOW ABOUT A NICE BONUS?

Most white-collar workers get an annual raise. However, there is a current trend in some firms toward eliminating the annual raise and in its place giving people one-time bonuses. For example, a person making $30,000 could expect to get a $1500 raise if the company gave an across-the-board 5 percent salary increase. Under a one-time bonus approach, however, the individual would get $1500, but this would leave the base pay at $30,000. General Electric has used this approach with some of its salaried personnel. So has Bell Atlantic.

What are reasons for substituting a bonus system for an annual raise? One reason is that the company can now establish a clear contingency between performance and pay. If the manager performs well, the firm can give a bonus. If the manager does not perform well, no bonus is given. A second, less-talked-about reason is that many insurance and retirement benefit programs are tied directly to the individual's base pay. If the base pay remains steady, so do the accompanying expenses.

Most industry analysts believe that employees will fight attempts to substitute bonuses for annual raises. However, from the standpoint of modifying organizational behavior and getting people to conform to company performance goals, there may be merit in a bonus system. In fact, one consulting group recently reported that currently only about 7 percent of the firms they surveyed were using the bonus system, but another 20 to 30 percent of these firms were considering the idea.

1. What type of O.B. Mod. intervention strategy is a bonus system?
2. Why would personnel prefer an annual raise rather than a bonus?
3. How could a company evaluate the usefulness of the two approaches in deciding which was more effective?

Case: Up the Piece Rate

Larry Ames has successfully completed a company training program in O.B. Mod. He likes the approach and has started using it on the workers in his department. Following the O.B. Mod. model, he has identified several performance behaviors, measured and analyzed them, and used a positive reinforcement-extinction intervention strategy. His evaluation has showed a significant improvement in the performance of his department. Over coffee one day he commented to one of the other supervisors, "This contingent reinforcement approach really works. Before, the goody-goody people up in personnel were always telling us to try to understand and be nice to our workers. Frankly, I couldn't buy that. In the first place, I don't think there is anybody who can really *understand* my people—I certainly can't. More important, though, is that under this approach I am only nice *contingently*—contingent upon good performance. That makes a lot more sense, and my evaluation proves that it works." The other supervisor commented, "You are being reinforced for using the reinforcement technique on your people." Larry said, "Sure I am. Just like the trainer said: 'Behavior that is reinforced will strengthen and repeat itself.' I'm so reinforced that I am starting to use it on my wife and kids at home, and you know what? It works there, too."

The next week Larry was called into the department head's office and was told, "Larry, as you know, your department has shown a substantial increase in performance since you completed the O.B. Mod. program. I have sent our industrial engineer down there to analyze your standards. I have received her report, and it looks like we will have to adjust your rates upward by 10 percent. Otherwise, we are going to have to pay too much incentive pay. I'm sure you can use some of the things you learned in that O.B. Mod. program to break the news to your people. Good luck, and keep up the good work."

1. Do you think Larry's boss, the department head, attended the O.B. Mod. program? Analyze the department head's action in terms of O.B. Mod.
2. What do you think will be Larry's reaction now and in the future? How do you think Larry's people will react?
3. Given the 10 percent increase in standards, is there any way that Larry could still use the O.B. Mod. approach with his people? With his boss? How?

Case:
A Tardiness
Problem

You have been getting a lot of complaints recently from your boss about the consistent tardiness of your work group. The time-sheet records indicate that your people's average start-up time is about ten minutes late. While you have never been concerned about the tardiness problem, your boss is really getting upset. He points out that the tardiness reduces the amount of production time and delays the start-up of the assembly line. You realize that the tardiness is a type of avoidance behavior—it delays the start of a very boring job. Your work group is very cohesive, and each of the members will follow what the group wants to do. One of the leaders of the group seems to spend a lot of time getting the group into trouble. You want the group to come in on time, but you don't really want a confrontation on the issue because, frankly, you don't think it is important enough to risk getting everyone upset with you. You decide to use an O.B. Mod. approach.

1. Trace through the five steps in the O.B. Mod. model to show how it could be applied to this tardiness problem. Make sure you are specific in identifying the critical performance behaviors and the antecedents and consequences of the functional analysis.
2. Do you think the approach you have suggested in your answer to question 1 will really work? Why or why not?

Leadership Theory: Background and Processes

■ The Flight Is Over

When the airline industry was deregulated over a decade ago, competition increased and many small carriers wound up being sold to larger ones. This industry shakeup has resulted in a smaller number of large, major competitors. One of the key players in the industry was Frank Lorenzo, who many thought might provide the leadership needed to bring Continental and Eastern Airlines back to profitability.

Lorenzo began his airline venture when he and a partner put up $25,000 in 1969 to form Jet Capital. In 1970, they were called in to help ailing Texas International Airlines, and Jet Capital took control. In 1980, Lorenzo started nonunion New York Airlines and created Texas Air. The next year, he took over Continental Airlines. In 1986, Texas Air acquired Eastern, People Express, and Frontier airlines. With this type of track record, it appeared that Lorenzo was the type of leader needed in the airline industry. Unfortunately, this proved to be wrong.

Far from being a first-rate visionary leader, Lorenzo's real strengths were his financial knowledge and skills. He knew and cared more about cost-cutting than about negotiating a labor contract with unions. In fact, soon after he assumed control of Continental, Lorenzo took the company into bankruptcy so that he would not have to honor the union contract. In 1989, he faced a major showdown with Eastern unions and again chose the bankruptcy route. However, this time his luck ran out. The unions held the line and sued to prevent him from selling away the most lucrative parts of Eastern. Then in 1990, the bankruptcy judge threw him out of Eastern and appointed a trustee to run the airline, which then went out of business. By late 1990, Lorenzo had agreed to sell Jet Capital, which controlled Continental, to SAS Airlines and agreed to stay out of the airline business for seven years.

In retrospect, Lorenzo had many of the traits and characteristics of an effective leader. He was a good negotiator and he was able to influence people to follow his ideas. However, when things got tough, he proved highly inflexible and arbitrary. He eventually lost the confidence and trust that people initially had in him, and from then on it was downhill. People began to refuse to travel on his airlines because they did not know if the companies would be flying the next day. The stockholders demanded that he improve performance and start turning things around. Eventually, the critics prevailed. Lorenzo could not get the job done and the board of directors stepped in and started making some of the critical decisions. He left Continental in very bad shape after almost a decade of crisis management in which people made decisions on an almost day-to-day basis. As one observer put it, "There is no infrastructure," something that every effective leader would have ensured was in place. When the history of the airline industry after deregulation is written, Lorenzo will be given prominent attention, but it is unlikely to be very flattering.

Learning Objectives

- **Define** leadership.
- **Present** the background and classic studies of leadership.
- **Discuss** the established theories of leadership including the trait, group and exchange, contingency, and path-goal approaches.
- **Identify** some other emerging theoretical frameworks for leadership such as social learning, substitutes for leadership, charismatic, and transformational processes.

This chapter on leadership theory and the next on leadership application is an appropriate conclusion to this central part or heart of the book. Leadership is the focus and conduit of most of the other areas of organizational behavior. The first half of the chapter deals with the definition and classical background. The last half then presents the major theoretical perspectives of leadership. Particular attention is devoted to both the established and emerging theories of leadership.

WHAT IS LEADERSHIP?

Leadership has probably been written about, formally researched, and informally discussed more than any other single topic. For example, it has even been humorously proposed that leadership succession depends on birthdays. The discovery was made while developing a list of birth dates of famous people. It seems that the heads of some large corporations often shared the same birthday as their successor. For instance, Edward G. Jefferson and his predecessor at Du Pont Corporation, Irving S. Shapiro, share a July 15 birthday. Although astrologers would suggest that companies need leaders with the same "sun signs" that influence their styles, the companies vigorously deny considering the calendar in making leadership appointments.[1]

Throughout history, it has been recognized that the difference between success and failure, whether in a war, a business, a protest movement, or a basketball game, can be attributed largely to leadership. The intensity of today's concern about leadership is pointed out by recent observations such as the following:

> Business in America has lost its way, adrift in a sea of managerial mediocrity, desperately needing leadership to face worldwide economic competition. Once the dominant innovator in technology, marketing, and manufacturing, American business has lost ground to foreign competition.[2]

Yet, despite all the attention given to it and its recognized importance, leadership still remains pretty much of a "black box," or unexplainable concept. It is known to exist and to have a tremendous influence on human performance, but its inner workings and specific dimensions cannot be precisely spelled out. Despite these inherent difficulties there are still many attempts over the years to define leadership. Unfortunately, almost everyone who studies or writes about leadership defines it differently. About the only commonality is the role that influence plays in leadership.

In recent years, many theorists and practitioners emphasize the difference between managers and leaders. For example, Bennis recently noted that, "To survive in the twenty-first century, we are going to need a new generation of leaders—leaders, not managers. The distinction is an important one. Leaders conquer the context—the volatile, turbulent, ambiguous surroundings that sometimes seem to conspire against us and will surely suffocate us if we let them—while managers surrender to it."[3] He then goes on to point out his thoughts on some specific differences between leaders and managers, as shown in Table 10.1. Obviously, these are not scientifically derived differences, but it is probably true that an individual can be a leader without being a manager and a manager without being a leader.

Although many specific definitions could be cited, most would depend on the theoretical orientation taken. Besides influence, leadership has been defined in terms of group processes, personality, compliance, particular behaviors, persuasion, power, goal achievement, interaction, role differentiation, initiation of structure, and

TABLE 10.1 Some Characteristics of Managers Versus Leaders in the Twenty-first Century

Manager Characteristics	Leader Characteristics
Administers	Innovates
A copy	An Original
Maintains	Develops
Focuses on systems and structure	Focuses on people
Relies on control	Inspires trust
Short-range view	Long-range perspective
Asks how and when	Asks what and why
Eye on the bottom line	Eye on the horizon
Imitates	Originates
Accepts the status quo	Challenges the status quo
Classic good soldier	Own person
Does things right	Does the right thing

Source: Adapted from Warren G. Bennis, "Managing the Dream: Leadership in the 21st Century," *Journal of Organizational Change Management*, vol. 2, no. 1, 1989, p. 7.

combinations of two or more of these.[4] The specific definition is not important. What is important is to interpret leadership in terms of the specific theoretical framework and to realize that leadership, however defined, does make a difference.

THE BACKGROUND AND CLASSIC STUDIES ON LEADERSHIP

Unlike many other topics in the field of organizational behavior, there are a number of studies and a considerable body of knowledge on leadership. A review of the better-known classic studies can help set the stage for the established and emerging theories of leadership.

The Iowa Leadership Studies

A series of pioneering leadership studies conducted in the late 1930s by Ronald Lippitt and Ralph K. White under the general direction of Kurt Lewin at the University of Iowa have had a lasting impact. Lewin is recognized as the father of group dynamics and as an important cognitive theorist. In the initial studies, hobby clubs for ten-year-old boys were formed. Each club was submitted to three different styles of leadership—authoritarian, democratic, and laissez faire. The authoritarian leader was very directive and allowed no participation. This leader tended to give individual attention when praising and criticizing but tried to be friendly or impersonal rather than openly hostile. The democratic leader encouraged group discussion and decision making. He tried to be "objective" in his praise or criticism and to be one of the group in spirit. The laissez faire leader gave complete freedom to the group; he essentially provided no leadership.

Under experimental conditions, the three leadership styles were manipulated to show their effects on variables such as satisfaction and frustration/aggression. Some of the results were clear-cut and others were not. One definite finding was the boys' overwhelming preference for the democratic leader. In individual interviews, nineteen of the twenty boys stated they liked the democratic leader better than the authoritarian leader. The boys also chose the laissez faire leader over the autocratic one in seven out of ten cases. For most of the boys, even confusion and disorder were preferable to strictness and rigidity.

Unfortunately, the effects that styles of leadership had on productivity were not directly examined. The experiments were designed primarily to examine patterns of aggressive behavior. However, an important by-product was the insight that was gained into the productive behavior of a group. For example, the researchers found that the boys subjected to the autocratic leaders reacted in one of two ways: either aggressively or apathetically. Both the aggressive and apathetic behaviors were deemed to be reactions to the frustration caused by the autocratic leader. The researchers also pointed out that the apathetic groups exhibited outbursts of aggression when the autocratic leader left the room or when a transition was made to a freer leadership atmosphere. The laissez faire leadership climate actually produced the greatest number of aggressive acts from the group. The democratically led group fell between the one extremely aggressive group and the four apathetic groups under the autocratic leaders.

Sweeping generalizations on the basis of the Lippitt and White studies are dangerous. Preadolescent boys making masks and carving soap are a long way from adults working in a complex, formal organization. Furthermore, from the viewpoint of modern behavioral science research methodology, many of the variables were not controlled. Nevertheless, these leadership studies have extremely important historical significance. They were the pioneering attempts to determine, experimentally, what effects styles of leadership have on a group. Like the Hawthorne studies, the Iowa studies are too often automatically discounted or at least deemphasized because they were experimentally crude. The values of the studies were that they were the first to analyze leadership from the standpoint of scientific methodology, and, more important, they showed that different styles of leadership can produce different, complex reactions from the same or similar groups.

The Ohio State Leadership Studies

In 1945, the Bureau of Business Research at Ohio State University initiated a series of studies on leadership. An interdisciplinary team of researchers from psychology, sociology, and economics developed and used the Leader Behavior Description Questionnaire (LBDQ) to analyze leadership in numerous types of groups and situations. Studies were made of Air Force commanders and members of bomber crews; officers, noncommissioned personnel, and civilian administrators in the Navy Department; manufacturing supervisors; executives of regional cooperatives; college administrators; teachers, principals, and school superintendents; and leaders of various student and civilian groups.

The Ohio State studies started with the premise that no satisfactory definition of leadership existed. They also recognized that previous work had too often assumed that *leadership* was synonymous with *good leadership*. The Ohio State group was determined to study leadership, regardless of definition or of whether it was effective or ineffective.

In the first step, the LBDQ was administered in a wide variety of situations. In order to examine how the leader was described, the answers to the questionnaire were then subjected to factor analysis. The outcome was amazingly consistent. The same two dimensions of leadership continually emerged from the questionnaire data. They were *consideration* and *initiating structure*. These two factors were found in a wide variety of studies encompassing many kinds of leadership positions and contexts. The researchers carefully emphasize that the studies show only *how* leaders carry out their leadership function. Initiating structure and consideration are very similar to the time-honored military commander's functions of mission and concern with the welfare of the troops. In simple terms, the Ohio State factors are task or goal orientation (initiating structure) and recognition of individual needs and relationships (consideration). The two dimensions are separate and distinct from each other.

The Ohio State studies certainly have value for the study of leadership. They were the first to point out and emphasize the importance of *both* task and human dimensions in assessing leadership. This two-dimensional approach lessened the gap between the strict task orientation of the scientific management movement and the human relations emphasis, which had been popular up to that time. However, on the other side of the coin, the rush for empirical data on leadership led to a great dependence on questionnaires in the Ohio State studies to generate data about leadership behaviors, and this may not have been justified. For example, Schriesheim and Kerr concluded after a review of the existing literature that "the Ohio State scales cannot be considered sufficiently valid to warrant their continued uncritical usage in leadership research."[5] In addition to the validity question is the almost unchallenged belief that these indirect questionnaire methods are in fact measuring leadership *behaviors* instead of simply measuring the questionnaire respondent's behavior and/or perceptions of, and attitudes toward, leadership. A multiple measures approach, especially observation techniques, seems needed and has been used in recent years. The discussion later in the chapter will further explain this need for a behavioral emphasis in leadership studies and its accompanying observation measurement techniques.

The Early Michigan Leadership Studies

At about the same time that the Ohio State studies were being conducted, a group of researchers from the Survey Research Center at the University of Michigan began their studies of leadership. In the original study at the Prudential Insurance Company, twelve high-low productivity pairs were selected for examination. Each pair represented a high-producing section and a low-producing section, with other variables, such as type of work, conditions, and methods, being the same in each pair. Nondirective interviews were conducted with the 24 section supervisors and 419 clerical workers. Results showed that supervisors of high-producing sections were significantly more likely to be general rather than close in their supervisory styles and be employee-centered (have a genuine concern for their people). The low-producing section supervisors had essentially opposite characteristics and techniques. They were found to be close, production-centered supervisors. Another important, but sometimes overlooked, finding was that employee satisfaction was *not* directly related to productivity.

The general, employee-centered supervisor, described above, became the standard-bearer for the traditional human relations approach to leadership. The results of the Prudential studies were always cited when human relations advocates were challenged to prove their theories. The studies have been followed up with hundreds of similar studies in a wide variety of industrial, hospital, governmental, and other organizations. Thousands of employees, performing unskilled to highly professional and scientific tasks, have been analyzed. Rensis Likert, the one-time director of the Institute for Social Research of the University of Michigan, presented the results of the years of similar research in his books and became best known for his "System 4" leadership style, which is covered in the next chapter.

ESTABLISHED THEORIES OF LEADERSHIP

The Iowa, Ohio State, and Michigan studies are three of the historically most important leadership studies for the study of organizational behavior. Unfortunately, they are still heavily depended upon, and leadership research has not surged ahead from this relatively auspicious beginning. Before analyzing the current status of leadership research, it is important to look at the theoretical development that has occurred through the years.

There are several distinct theoretical bases for leadership. At first, leaders were felt to be born, not made. This so-called "great man" theory of leadership implied that some individuals are born with certain traits that allow them to emerge out of any situation or period of history to become leaders. This evolved into what is now known as the *trait theory* of leadership. The trait approach is concerned mainly with identifying the personality traits of the leader. Dissatisfied with this approach, and stimulated by research such as the Ohio State studies, researchers switched their emphasis from the individual leader to the group being led. In the group approach, leadership is viewed more in terms of the leader's behavior and how such behavior affects and is affected by the group of followers.

In addition to the leader and the group, the situation began to receive increased attention in leadership theory. The situational approach was initially called *Zeitgeist* (a German word meaning "spirit of the times"); the leader is viewed as a product of the times and the situation. The person with the particular qualities or traits that a situation requires will emerge as the leader. The International Application Example: Yeltsin Speaks illustrates a current example of such a leader. This view has much historical support as a theoretical basis for leadership and serves as the basis for situational—and now, contingency—theories of leadership. Fiedler's contingency theory which suggests that leadership styles must fit or match the situation in order to be effective is the best known. A more recent situational or contingency theory takes some of the expectancy concepts of motivation that were discussed in Chapter 6 and applies them to leadership and situations. Called the path-goal theory of leadership, it is an attempt to synthesize motivational and leadership concepts. The following sections examine these established trait, group, contingency, and path-goal theories of leadership.

Trait Theories of Leadership

The scientific analysis of leadership started off by concentrating on leaders themselves. The vital question that this theoretical approach attempted to answer was, what characteristics or traits make a person a leader? The earliest trait theories, which can be traced back to the ancient Greeks and Romans, concluded that leaders are born, not made. The "great man" theory of leadership said that a person is born either with or without the necessary traits for leadership. Famous figures in history—for example, Napoleon—were said to have had the "natural" leadership abilities to rise out of any situation and become great leaders.

Eventually, the "great man" theory gave way to a more realistic trait approach to leadership. Under the influence of the behavioristic school of psychological

Yeltsin Speaks

Mikhail Gorbachev was the best-known leader in the Soviet Union in recent years but Boris Yeltsin became regarded by many as the most effective. An early ally of Gorbachev, Yeltsin resigned from the Soviet Politburo in 1987 and broke with the Communist Party in 1989. At the time, it appeared that any hopes he had of playing a role in Soviet history were at an end. However, if nothing else, Yeltsin was an effective leader. Once in opposition, he quickly earned a reputation as a combative advocate of a faster road to democracy. For the next three years, he cleverly baited Gorbachev for failing to act decisively. As a result, he became identified as a man with both vision and boldness. In May 1990, over the opposition of Gorbachev, he was elected chairman of the Russian Federation's 252-member Supreme Soviet after a campaign in which he pledged to hold Russian law "juridically higher" than Soviet law—a statement that, in essence, amounted to a declaration of independence.

Once in power, Yeltsin wasted no time setting up a tough and independent-minded government. He attracted some of the best young, talented technocrats in the Soviet system. One Western diplomat who was familiar with the Yeltsin team noted, "These guys look like the student council at Berkeley in the Sixties—young, tough, and radical. This is the kind of government perestroika needs." The team is made up of such members as Boris Fyodorov, a 32-year old finance minister, who is an expert on international banking. Another is Grigori Yavlinsky, 38, an economist and deputy prime minister who echoes the feelings of many Russians when he says, "Our goal is to get out of the bottomless pit we find ourselves in. In the entire history of human existence, no one has thought of anything more efficient than the free market. By mastering it, we will free ourselves from the abyss and gain the capacity to draw on the achievements of world civilization."

Yeltsin supported these ideas and believed that the republics that make up the USSR should be given the bulk of all power. Only defense, railways, foreign policy, shipping, civil aviation, and energy should be in the hands of the central government. Obviously, Gorbachev and many other members of the Communist Party opposed such action and intended to keep power centralized. Only time will tell what the eventual outcome will be for the Soviet Union, but certainly, Yeltsin must be regarded as an effective leader.

thought, researchers accepted the fact that leadership traits are not completely inborn but can also be acquired through learning and experience. Attention turned to the search for universal traits possessed by leaders. The results of this voluminous research effort were generally very disappointing. Only intelligence seemed to hold up with any degree of consistency. When these findings are combined with those of studies on physical traits, the conclusion seems to be that leaders are bigger and brighter than those being led, but not too much so.

When the trait approach is applied to organizational leadership, the result is even cloudier. One of the biggest problems is that all managers think they know what the qualities of a successful leader are. Obviously, almost any adjective can be used to describe a successful leader. Recognizing these semantic limitations and realizing that there is no cause-and-effect relationship between observed traits and successful leadership, there is some evidence to suggest that empathy or interpersonal sensitivity and self-confidence are desirable leadership traits.[6]

In general, research findings do not agree on which traits are generally found in leaders or even on which ones are more important than others. Similar to the trait theories of personality, the trait approach to leadership has provided some descriptive insight but has little analytical or predictive value. The trait approach is still alive, but now the emphasis has shifted away from personality traits and toward job-related skills. Katz has identified the technical, conceptual, and human skills needed for effective management.[7] Yukl includes skills such as creativity, organization, persuasiveness, diplomacy and tactfulness, knowledge of the task, and the ability to speak well.[8] These skills are important and can be used both to select leaders and in training and development.

Group and Exchange Theories of Leadership

The group theories of leadership have their roots in social psychology. Classic exchange theory, in particular, serves as an important basis for this approach. Discussed in Chapters 6 and 12, this means simply that the leader provides more benefits/rewards than burdens/costs for followers. There must be a positive exchange between the leaders and followers in order for group goals to be accomplished. Chester Barnard applied such an analysis to managers and subordinates in an organizational setting more than a half-century ago. More recently, this social exchange view of leadership has been summarized as follows:

> Exchange theories propose that group members make contributions at a cost to themselves and receive benefits at a cost to the group or other members. Interaction continues because members find the social exchange mutually rewarding.[9]

The above quotation emphasizes that leadership is an exchange process between the leader and followers. Social psychological research can be used to support this notion of exchange. In addition, the original Ohio State studies and follow-up studies through the years, especially the dimension of giving consideration to followers, give support to the group perspective of leadership.

Followers' Impact on Leaders. A few important research studies indicate that followers/subordinates may actually affect leaders as much as leaders affect followers/subordinates. For example, one study found that when subordinates were not performing very well, the leaders tended to emphasize initiating structure, but when subordinates were doing a good job, leaders increased their emphasis on consideration.[10] In a laboratory study it was found that group productivity had a greater impact on leadership style than leadership style had on group productivity,[11] and in another study it was found that in newly formed groups, leaders may adjust their supportive behavior in response to the level of group cohesion and arousal already present.[12] In other words, such studies seem to indicate that subordinates affect leaders and their behaviors as much as leaders and their behaviors affect subordinates. Some practicing managers, such as the vice president of Saga Corporation, feel that subordinates lack followership skills, and there is growing evidence that the newer generation of managers is increasingly reluctant to accept a followership role.[13] Moreover, it is probably not wise to ignore followership. Most managers feel that subordinates have an obligation to follow and support their leader. As the CEO of Commerce Union Corporation noted, "Part of a subordinate's responsibility is to make the boss look good."[14]

The Vertical Dyad Linkage Model. Relevant to the exchange view of leadership is the vertical dyad linkage (VDL) approach,[15] more recently called leader-member exchange (LMX).[16] The VDL or LMX theory says that leaders treat individual subordinates differently. In particular, leaders and subordinates develop dyadic (two-person) relationships which affect the behavior of both leaders and subordinates. For example, subordinates who are committed and who expend a lot of effort for the unit are rewarded with more of the leader's positional resources (for example, information, confidence, and concern) than those who do not display these behaviors.

Over time, the leader will develop an "in-group" of subordinates and an "out-group" of subordinates and treat them accordingly. Thus, for the same leader, research has shown that in-group subordinates report fewer difficulties in dealing with the leader and perceive the leader as being more responsive to their needs than out-group subordinates do.[17] Also, leaders spend more time "leading" members of the in-group (that is, they do not depend on formal authority to influence them), and they tend to "supervise" those in the out-group (that is, they depend on formal roles and authority to influence them).[18] Finally, there is evidence that subordinates in the in-group (those who report a high-quality relationship with their leader) assume greater job responsibility, contribute more to their units, and are rated as higher performers than those reporting a low-quality relationship.[19]

This exchange theory has been around for some time now, and although it is not without criticism,[20] in general the research continues to be relatively supportive. However, at present, VDL or LMX seems to be more descriptive of the typical process of role making by leaders, rather than prescribing the pattern of downward exchange relations optimal for leadership effectiveness.[21]

Contingency Theory of Leadership

After the trait approach proved to fall short of being an adequate overall theory of leadership, attention turned to the situational aspects of leadership. Social psychologists began the search for situational variables that affect leadership roles, skills, and behavior and on followers' performance and satisfaction. Numerous situational variables were identified, but no overall theory pulled it all together until Fred Fiedler proposed a widely recognized situation-based or contingency theory for leadership effectiveness.

Fiedler's Contingency Model of Leadership Effectiveness. To test the hypothesis he had formulated from previous research findings, Fiedler developed what he called a *contingency model of leadership effectiveness*. This model contained the relationship between leadership style and the favorableness of the situation. Situational favorableness was described by Fiedler in terms of three empirically derived dimensions:

1. The *leader-member relationship*, which is the most critical variable in determining the situation's favorableness.
2. The *degree of task structure*, which is the second most important input into the favorableness of the situation.
3. The *leader's position power* obtained through formal authority, which is the third most critical dimension of the situation.[22]

Situations are favorable to the leader if all three of the above dimensions are high. In other words, if the leader is generally accepted by followers (high first dimension), if the task is very structured and everything is "spelled out" (high second dimension), and if a great deal of authority and power is formally attributed to the leader's position (high third dimension), the situation is very favorable. If the opposite exists (if the three dimensions are low), the situation will be very unfavorable for the leader. Fiedler was convinced that the favorableness of the situation in combination with the leadership style determines effectiveness.

Through the analysis of research findings, Fiedler was able to discover that under very favorable *and* very unfavorable situations, the task-directed, or "hard-nosed," type of leader was most effective. However when the situation was only moderately favorable or unfavorable (the intermediate range of favorableness), the human relations, or lenient, type of leader was most effective. Figure 10.1 summarizes this relationship between leadership style and the favorableness of the situation.

Why is the task-directed leader successful in very favorable situations? Fiedler offered the following explanation:

> In the very favorable conditions in which the leader has power, informal backing, and a relatively well-structured task, the group is ready to be directed, and the group expects to be told what to do. Consider the captain of an airliner in its final landing approach. We would hardly want him to turn to his crew for a discussion on how to land.[23]

As an example of why the task-oriented leader is successful in a highly unfavorable situation, Fiedler cited

> . . . the disliked chairman of a volunteer committee which is asked to plan the office picnic on a beautiful Sunday. If the leader asks too many questions about what the group ought to do or how he should proceed, he is likely to be told that "we ought to go home."[24]

The leader who makes a wrong decision in this highly unfavorable type of situation is probably better off than the leader who makes no decision at all. Figure 10.1 shows that the human relations leader is effective in the intermediate range of favorableness. An example of such situations is the typical committee or a unit which is staffed by professionals. In these situations, the leader may not be wholly accepted by the other members of the group, the task may be generally vague and not completely structured, and little authority and power may be granted to the leader. Under such

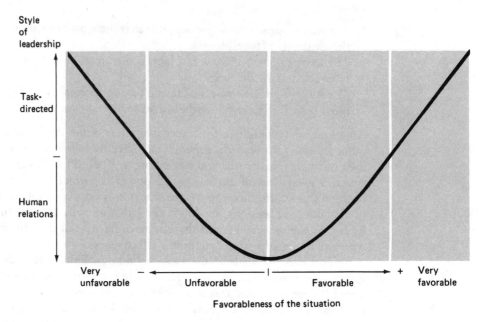

FIGURE 10.1
Fiedler's contingency model of leadership.
(*Source:* Adapted from Fred E. Fiedler, *A Theory of Leadership Effectiveness*, McGraw-Hill, New York, 1967, pp. 142–148.)

a relatively unfavorable, but not extremely unfavorable, situation, the model predicts that a human relations, lenient type of leader will be most effective.

Research Support for the Contingency Model. As is true of any widely publicized theoretical development, Fiedler's model has stimulated a great deal of research. Not surprisingly, the results are mixed and a controversy has been generated. Fiedler and in particular his students have provided almost all the support for the model over the years. For example, to defend the validity of his theory, he cites thirty studies in a wide variety of teams and organizations (Navy teams, chemical research teams, shop departments, supermarkets, heavy machinery plant departments, engineering groups, hospital wards, public health teams, and others) and concludes that "the theory is highly predictive and that the relations obtained in the validation studies are almost identical to those obtained in the original studies."[25] With one exception, which Fiedler explains away, he maintains that the model correctly predicted the correlations that should exist between the leader's style and performance in relation to the identified favorableness of the situation. As predicted, his studies show that in very unfavorable and very favorable situations, the task-oriented leader performs best. In a moderately favorable and moderately unfavorable situation, the human relations–oriented leader is more effective. Although Fiedler recognizes that there is increasing criticism of his conslusions, he still maintains that "methodologically sound validation studies have on the whole provided substantial support for the theory,"[26] and some comprehensive reviews support this contention,[27] but others do not.

Critical Analysis of the Contingency Model. Although there is probably not as much criticism of Fiedler's work as there is, for example, of Herzberg's motivation theory, a growing number of leadership researchers do not wholly agree with Fiedler's interpretations or conclusions. For example, Graen and his colleagues initially raised some criticisms of the procedures and statistical analysis of the studies used to support the validity of the model.[28] Schriesheim and his colleagues have been especially critical of the reliability and validity of Fiedler's measurement instrument.[29] Fiedler[30] and his colleagues[31] have answered these criticisms to their satisfaction, but most summaries remain critical. For example, Yukl recently concluded—after reviewing the research—that the model has serious conceptual deficiencies limiting its utility for explaining leadership effectiveness, deficiencies such as its narrow focus on a single leader trait, ambiguity about what is really measured, and the absence of explanatory processes.[32]

Applications of Fiedler's Work. In addition to the conceptual and methodological questions, there is also the criticism of Fiedler's extension of the model to the actual practice of human resources management. On the basis of the model, Fiedler suggests that management would be better off engineering positions so that the requirements fit the leader instead of using the more traditional technique of selecting and developing leaders to fit into existing jobs.[33] With this in mind, Fiedler and his colleagues then developed a self-programmed training manual (called *Leader Match*), which includes a series of questionnaires that identify the person's leadership style and the situational dimensions of his or her job (task structure, leader-member relations, and position power).[34] Then the trainee is given a series of short problems with several alternative solutions.

Under Fiedler's leadership effectiveness training, the trainee is taught (on the basis of feedback compatible with the contingency model) ways to diagnose the situation so as to change it and optimize the leader style–leader situation match. Some of the suggested ways to modify leader-member relations are spending more (or less) informal time with subordinates and suggesting or effecting transfers of particular subordiantes into or out of the unit. To decrease task structure, the leader may ask for new or unusual problems; to increase task structure, the leader may ask for more instructions and prepare a detailed plan. To raise position power, the leader could become an expert on the job, or to lower position power, the leader could call on subordinates to participate in planning and decision making.[35]

Most of the support for this Leader Match training has come from Fiedler and his students/colleagues. After a review of five studies conducted in civilian organizations and seven conducted in military settings, Fiedler concluded that all twelve studies yielded statistically significant results supporting Leader Match training.[36] He claims that these studies also support "the contested point that leaders are able to modify their leadership situations to a degree sufficient to increase their effectiveness."[37] Other, more recent research is critical of Leader Match as not being very consistent with what the contingency model should predict.[38]

Overall, there seems little question that Fiedler has provided one of the major breakthroughs for leadership theory and practice. Although much of the criticism is justified, there are several reasons why Fiedler's model has made a contribution:

1. It was the first highly visible leadership theory to present the contingency approach.
2. It emphasized the importance of both the situation and the leader's characteristics in determining leader effectiveness.
3. It stimulated a great deal of research, including tests of its predictions and attempts to improve on the model, and inspired the formulation of alternative contingency theories.
4. It led to the development of the Leader Match program that applies the model to actual leadership situations.[39]

At the very least, Fiedler has done and continues to do considerable empirical research, and in recent years he has proposed a new contingency theory.[40]

In the Cognitive Resource Theory, Fiedler identifies the situations under which a leader's cognitive resources such as intelligence, experience, and technical expertise relate to group performance. For example, under stressful situations, effective performance is more related to the leader's experience than to his or her intelligence. Although Fiedler has reported studies that support his theory,[41] because of the newness, not enough research has yet accumulated to draw any meaningful conclusions about the validity of the theory.

Path–Goal Leadership Theory

The other widely recognized theoretical development from a contingency approach, is the path-goal theory derived from the expectancy framework of motivation theory. Although Georgopoulos and his colleagues at the University of Michigan's Institute for Social Research used path-goal concepts and terminology many years ago in analyzing the impact of leadership on performance, the modern development is usually attributed to Martin Evans and Robert House, who wrote separate papers on the subject.[42] In essence, the path-goal theory attempts to explain the impact that leader behavior has on subordinate motivation, satisfaction, and performance. The House version of the theory incorporates four major types or styles of leadership.[43] Briefly summarized, these are:

1. *Directive leadership:* This style is similar to that of the Lippitt and White authoritarian leader. Subordinates know exactly what is expected of them, and the leader gives specific directions. There is no participation by subordinates.
2. *Supportive leadership:* The leader is friendly and approachable and shows a genuine concern for subordinates.
3. *Participative leadership:* The leader asks for and uses suggestions from subordinates but still makes the decisions.
4. *Achievement-oriented leadership:* The leader sets challenging goals for subordinates and shows confidence that they will attain these goals and perform well.

This path-goal theory—and here is how it differs in one respect from Fiedler's contingency model—suggests that these various styles can be and actually are used by the same leader in different situations.[44] Two of the situational factors that have been identified are the personal characteristics of subordinates and the environmental pressures and demands facing subordinates. With respect to the first situational factor, the theory asserts:

> Leader behavior will be acceptable to subordinates to the extent that the subordinates see such behavior as either an immediate source of satisfaction or as instrumental to future satisfaction.[45]

And with respect to the second situational factor, the theory states:

> Leader behavior will be motivational (e.g., will increase subordinate effort) to the extent that (1) it makes satisfaction of subordinate needs contingent on effective performance, and (2) it complements the environment of subordinates by providing the coaching, guidance, support, and rewards which are necessary for effective performance and which may otherwise be lacking in subordinates or in their environment.[46]

Using one of the four styles contingent upon the situational factors as outlined above, the leader attempts to influence subordinates' perceptions and motivate them, which in turn leads to their role clarity, goal expectancies, satisfaction, and performance. This is specifically accomplished by the leader as follows:

1. Recognizing and/or arousing subordinates' needs for outcomes over which the leader has some control
2. Increasing personal payoffs to subordinates for work-goal attainment
3. Making the path to those payoffs easier to travel by coaching and direction
4. Helping subordinates clarify expectancies
5. Reducing frustrating barriers
6. Increasing the opportunities for personal satisfaction contingent on effective performance[47]

In other words, by doing the above the leader attempts to make the path to subordinates' goals as smooth as possible. But to accomplish this path-goal facilitation, the leader must use the appropriate style contingent on the situational variables present. Figure 10.2 summarizes this path-goal approach.

As is true of the expectancy theory of motivation, there has been a surge of research on the path-goal theory of leadership. So far, most of the research has concentrated on only parts of the theory rather than on the entire theory. For example, a sampling of the research findings indicates the following:

1. Studies of seven organizations have found that *leader directiveness* is (*a*) positively related to satisfactions and expectancies of subordinates engaged in ambiguous tasks and (*b*) negatively related to satisfactions and expectancies of subordinates engaged in clear tasks.
2. Studies involving ten different samples of employees found that *supportive leadership* will have its most positive effect on satisfaction for subordinates who work on stressful, frustrating, or dissatisfying tasks.
3. In a major study in an industrial manufacturing organization, it was found that in nonrepetitive ego-involving tasks, employees were more satisfied under *participative leaders* than under nonparticipative leaders.

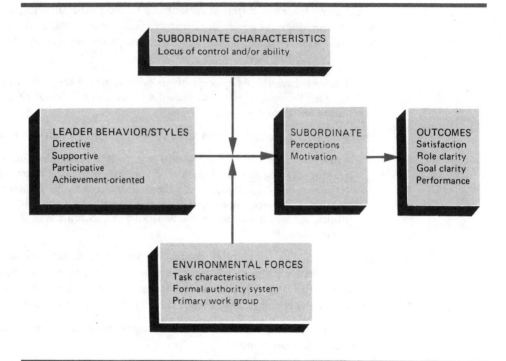

FIGURE 10.2
A summary of
path-goal
relationships.

4. In three separate organizations it was found that for subordinates performing ambiguous nonrepetitive tasks, the higher the *achievement orientation of the leader,* the more subordinates were confident that their efforts would pay off in effective performance.[48]

The more recent reviews of the research on the path-goal theory are not as supportive as the above. For example, Schriesheim and DeNisi note that only a couple of hypotheses have really been drawn from the theory, which means that it may be incapable of generating meaningful predictions.[49] Another note of pessimism offered by these reviewers is that only one of the two hypotheses has received consistent empirical support. Research has generally substantiated the hypothesis that the higher the task structure (repetitiveness) of the jobs performed by subordinates, the higher the relationship between supportive leader behavior/style and subordinate satisfaction. On the other hand, the second hypothesis—that the higher the task structure, the lower the correlation between instrumental (directive) leader behavior and subordinate satisfaction—has received, at best, mixed research support. Schriesheim and DeNisi then report results of their own research, which indicates that the path-goal theory is capable of producing meaningful and testable predictions beyond the two task structure hypotheses.[50] Also, a recent comprehensive review of forty-eight studies demonstrated that the mixed results of the individual studies, when cumulated, were transformed into support for continued testing of path-goal theory.[51]

Overall, the path-goal theory, like the other established theories presented in this chapter, seems to need more research, but it certainly warrants further attention in the coming years. One recent analysis concluded that leaders will be perceived most favorably by their subordinates, and succeed in exerting most influence over them, when they behave in ways that closely match (1) the needs and values of subordinates and 2) the requirements of a specific work situation.[52] In other words, the path-goal theory, like the expectancy theory in work motivation, may help better explain the complexities of the leadership process.

EMERGING THEORETICAL FRAMEWORKS FOR LEADERSHIP

Despite a relative degree of acceptance of the contingency and path-goal theories of leadership and the great (at least relative to other areas in organizational behavior) amount of research that has been conducted, few would disagree today that leadership is still in trouble. Leadership is currently being attacked on all fronts—in terms of theories relating to it, research methods for studying it, and applications.[53] For example, John Miner was very critical of leadership theory and then proposed that it be dropped altogether,[54] and Schriesheim and Kerr are quite critical of the methods used in leadership research.[55] The time seems ripe for alternative theories, research methods, and applications for leadership studies.

Besides the established trait, group, contingency, and path-goal theories of leadership, a number of other theories have emerged in recent years. These include the charismatic, transformational, social learning, and substitutes theories of leadership. An overview of each of these provides better understanding of the complex leadership process.

Charismatic Leadership Theories

Charismatic leadership is a throwback to the old conception of leaders as being those who "by the force of their personal abilities are capable of having profound and extraordinary effects on followers."[56] Although the charismatic concept or charisma goes as far back as the ancient Greeks and is cited in the Bible, its modern development is attributed to the work of Robert House.[57] Based on the analysis of political and religious leaders, House suggests that charismatic leaders are characterized by self-confidence and confidence in subordinates, high expectations for subordinates, ideological vision, and the use of personal example. Followers of charismatic leaders identify with the leader and the mission of the leader, exhibit extreme loyalty to and confidence in the leader, emulate the leader's values and behavior, and derive self-esteem from their relationship with the leader.[58] More recently, Bass extended the profile of charismatic leaders by including business leaders such as Lee Iacocca or even someone like George Varga, discussed in the International Application Example: Charismatic Capitalist. In particular, he notes that charismatic leaders have superior debating and persuasive skills and technical expertise, and foster attitudinal, behavioral, and emotional changes in their followers.[59]

Because of the effects that charismatic leaders have on followers, the theory

Charismatic Capitalist

If charismatic leaders have technical expertise, and are able to foster attitudinal, behavioral, and emotional changes in their followers, George Varga is a charismatic leader. Varga is head of the Tungsram plant near Budapest, Hungary. This nearly hundred-year-old plant is now being run by General Electric under an arrangement that gives the company a controlling stake in the firm. This is quite a challenge given that when the plant was run by the communist government in Hungary, it produced outmoded products that were not competitive in the international market and at the same time served as a major employer in the local area. The chief financial officer of the company today has described Tungsram's past by saying, "The company was run like a production-and-employment machine." No longer.

Today Varga is turning the company into a state-of-the-art light bulb manufacturer. The old company was producing high quality incandescent bulbs, but the problem was that this is the low-margin end of the lighting business and they were rapidly losing ground to a whole family of costlier, high-tech, energy-efficient products: compact fluorescent bulbs for homes and offices, high pressure sodium lamps used in street lighting, and miniature spotlights that lend sparkle to shop windows displaying jewelry or antiques. Worse yet, the factory was not expected to make a profit. So when Varga explained to his employees the importance of controlling inventory, they asked; Why? When he told them that the company must turn a profit, they asked: What is profit? When he explained, they asked: Why?

Yet this has not upset Varga. He was brought in from GE's Netherlands operation where he was head of a European plastics business branch, so he knows how to lead an international work force. He has surrounded himself with seasoned GE executives who have experience in improving plant operations, and has refused to bring on board young managers with a reputation for cockiness or arrogance. He explained his approach this way: "We didn't want the young tigers. We need people with the sensitivity to perform a cultural marriage. We have the ideal team to sell our ideas to the Hungarians." Working with this basic cadre of managers and infusing new technology and equipment into the plant, Varga hopes to lead the firm to new heights of profitability. His goal: $30 million in earnings by 1995 coupled with a 12 percent share of the European market. If he is the charismatic leader that GE is counting on, these goals will become a reality.

predicts that charismatic leaders will produce in followers performance beyond expectations as well as strong commitment to the leader and his/her mission. House and his colleagues provide beginning support for charismatic theory,[60] but as with the other leadership theories, more research is needed. Also, extensions of the theory are being proposed. For example, Conger and Kanungo treat charisma as an attributional phenomenon and propose that it varies with the situation.[61] Leader traits that foster charismatic attributions include self-confidence, impression-management skills, social sensitivity, and empathy. Situations that promote charismatic leadership include a crisis requiring dramatic change, or followers who are very dissatisfied with the status quo. Bass also suggested that charismatic leadership is really just one component of another, broader-based emerging theory of transformational leadership.[62]

Transformational Leadership Theory

Identifying charismatic characteristics of leaders can become very important as organizations transform traditional ways of being led to meet the challenge of dramatic change. It is this transformation process that has led to the transformational theory.

Burns identified two types of political leadership: transactional and transformational.[63] The more traditional transactional leadership involves an exchange relationship between leaders and followers, but transformational leadership is based more on leaders' shifting the values, beliefs, and needs of their followers. Table 10.2 summarizes the characteristics and approaches of transactional versus transformational leaders. Based on his research findings, Bass concludes that in many instances (such as relying on passive management by exception), transactional leadership is a prescription for mediocrity and that transformational leadership leads to superior performance in organizations facing demands for renewal and change. He suggests that fostering transformational leadership through policies of recruitment, selection, promotion, training, and development will pay off in the health, well-being, and effective performance of today's organizations.[64]

Most of the research on transformational leadership to date has relied on Bass's questionnaire, which has received some criticism,[65] or qualitative research that simply describes leaders through interviews. An example of the latter were the interviews with top executives of major companies conducted by Tichy and Devanna. They found that effective transformational leaders share the following characteristics:

1. They identify themselves as change agents.
2. They are courageous.
3. They believe in people.

TABLE 10.2 Characteristics and Approaches of Transactional Versus Transformational Leaders

Transactional Leaders

1. *Contingent Reward:* Contracts exchange of rewards for effort, promises rewards for good performance, recognizes accomplishments.
2. *Management by Exception* (active): Watches and searches for deviations from rules and standards, takes corrective action.
3. *Management by Exception* (passive): Intervenes only if standards are not met.
4. *Laissez-Faire:* Abdicates responsibilities, avoids making decisions.

Transformational Leaders

1. *Charisma:* Provides vision and sense of mission, instills pride, gains respect and trust.
2. *Inspiration:* Communicates high expectations, uses symbols to focus efforts, expresses important purposes in simple ways.
3. *Intellectual Stimulation:* Promotes intelligence, rationality, and careful problem solving.
4. *Individual Consideration:* Gives personal attention, treats each employee individually, coaches, advises.

Source: Bernard M. Bass, "From Transactional to Transformational Leadership: Learning to Share the Vision," *Organizational Dynamics*, Winter 1990, p. 22.

4. They are value-driven.
5. They are lifelong learners.
6. They have the ability to deal with complexity, ambiguity, and uncertainty.
7. They are visionaries.[66]

In addition to the charismatic and transformational theories, social learning and a substitutes approach have also emerged to meet the challenge of understanding the complexities and alternatives to leadership.

A Social Learning Approach

Just as social learning theory was shown in Chapter 1 to provide the basis for an overall conceptual framework for organizational behavior,[67] social learning theory can provide a model for the continuous, reciprocal interaction between the leader (including his or her cognitions), the environment (including subordinates/followers and macro variables), and the behavior itself.[68] These interactions are shown in Figure 10.3. This would seem to be a comprehensive and viable theoretical foundation for understanding leadership.[69]

Any of the other theoretical approaches, standing alone, seem too limiting. For example, the one-sided, cognitively based trait theories suggest that leaders are causal determinants that influence subordinates independent of subordinates' behaviors or the situation. The contingency theories are a step in the right direction, but even they for the most part have a unidirectional conception of interaction, in which leaders and situations somehow combine to determine leadership behavior. Even those leadership theories which claim to take a bidirectional approach (either in the exchange sense between the leader and the subordinate group or in the contingency sense between the leader and the situation) actually retain a unidirectional view of leadership behavior. In these theories, the causal input into the leader's behavior is the result of the interdependent exchange, but the behavior itself is ignored as a leadership determinant.

As far as leadership application for the social learning approach is concerned, the four-term contingency S-O-B-C (situation-organism-behavior-consequence) model introduced in Chapter 9 can be used by leaders to perform a functional analysis. Unlike the more limited A-B-C (antecedent-behavior-consequence) functional analysis used in O.B. Mod. (see Chapter 9), the variables in the S-O-B-C functional analysis can be either overt (observable), as in the operant view, or covert (unobservable), as recognized in the social learning view, and, of course, recognition is given to the role of cognitive mediating processes by the insertion of the O. The successful application of this S-O-B-C functional analysis to human resources management "depends upon the leader's ability to bring into awareness the overt or covert antecedent cues and contingent consequences that regulate the leader's and subordinate's performance behavior."[70] More specifically, in this leadership application, the subordinates are actively involved in the process, and together with the leader they concentrate on their own and one another's *behaviors*, the environmental contingencies (both antecedent and consequent), and their mediating cognitions. Some examples of this approach would be the following:

FIGURE 10.3
A social learning approach to leadership. (*Source:* Adapted from Albert Bandura, *Social Learning Theory*, Prentice-Hall, Englewood Cliffs, N.J., 1977; and Fred Luthans, "Leadership: A Proposal for a Social Learning Theory Base and Observational and Funcational Analysis Techniques to Measure Leader Behavior," in James G. Hunt and Lars L. Larson [eds.], *Crosscurrents in Leadership*, Southern Illinois University Press, Carbondale, 1979, p. 205.)

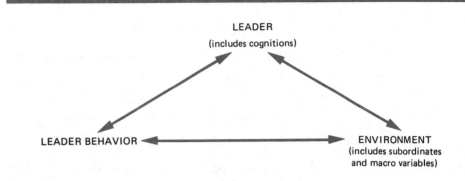

1. The leader becomes acquainted with the macro and micro variables that control his or her own behavior.
2. The leader works with the subordinate to discover the personalized set of behavioral contingencies that regulate the subordinate's behavior.
3. The leader and the subordinate jointly attempt to discover ways in which they can manage their individual behavior to produce more mutually reinforcing and organizationally productive outcomes.[71]

In such an approach, the leader and the subordinate have a negotiable, interactive relationship and are consciously aware of how they can modify (influence) each other's behavior by giving or holding back desired rewards.

Although work has been done on the theoretical development of a social learning approach to leadership, research and application are just getting under way.[72] Only time will tell whether it will hold up as a viable, researchable approach to leadership. However, because of its growing importance as a theoretical foundation for the fields of psychology and organizational behavior as a whole and because it recognizes the interactive nature of all the variables of previous theories, a social learning approach to leadership would seem to have potential for the future.

Substitutes for Leadership

Because of dissatisfaction with the progress of leadership theory and research in explaining and predicting the effects of leader behavior on performance outcomes, some of the basic assumptions about the importance of leadership per se are being challenged. In particular, Kerr and Jermier propose that there may be certain "substitutes" for leadership that make leader behavior unnecessary and redundant and "neutralizers" which prevent the leader from behaving in a certain way or which counteract the behavior.[73] These substitutes or neutralizers can be found in subordinate, task, and organization characteristics. Figure 10.4 gives specific examples of possible substitutes and neutralizers according to supportive/relationship leadership and instrumental/task leadership.

As shown, subordinate experience, ability, and training may substitute for instrumental/task leadership. For example, craftspersons or professionals such as

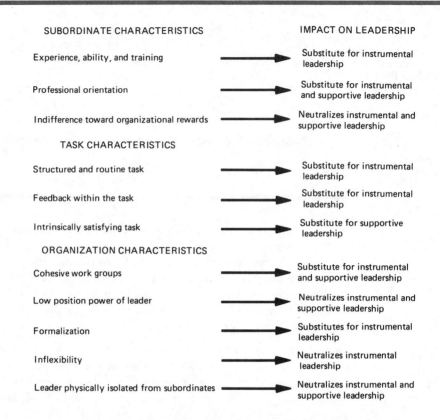

FIGURE 10.4
Substitutes and neutralizers for leadership.
(*Source:* Adapted from Steven Kerr and John M. Jermier, "Substitutes for Leadership: Their Meaning and Measurement," *Organizational Behavior and Human Performance,* Dec. 1978, pp. 375–403.)

accountants or engineers may have so much experience, ability, and training that they do not need instrumental/task leadership to perform well and be satisfied. Those subordinates who don't particularly care about organizational rewards (for example, professors or musicians) will neutralize both supportive/relationship and instrumental/task leadership attempts. Tasks that are highly structured and automatically provide feedback substitute for instrumental/task leadership, and those which are intrinsically satisfying (for example, teaching) do not need supportive/relationship leadership. There are also a number of organizational characteristics that substitute for or neutralize leadership.

There has been further analysis of the leader substitutes concept,[74] and Kerr and Jermier have provided some empirical support from field studies of police officers.[75] They found that substitutes such as feedback from the task being performed had more impact on certain job-related activities than leader behaviors did. Other studies have also been interpreted (post hoc) to support organizational characteristics such as formalization as leader substitutes.[76] More recent direct tests have yielded mixed results. One study using hospital personnel with a wide variety of skills and backgrounds and in a wide variety of professions found several potential substitutes to predict subordinate satisfaction and commitment, but only one of the single substitutes (organizational formalization) rendered leadership impossible and/or unnecessary.[77] A follow-up study found that worker professionalism was an important moderator variable. It also found that professionals differed from non-professionals in that intrinsically satisfying work tasks and importance placed on organizational rewards were strong substitutes for leaders' support.[78]

Overall, the substitutes notion puts leadership back into proper perspective and may help explain the relatively poor track record of leadership research. In particular, the leadership situation (subordinate, task, or organization) may replace or counteract the leader's behavior in affecting subordinate satisfaction and performance. It has recently been noted that "the idea of leadership substitutes and neutralizers helps to account for the largely mixed results of research on most leadership theories. Studies of leadership that ignore the effect of neutralizers and substitutes may fail to uncover hypothesized relationships because the particular leadership process is irrelevant, rather than because the theory is invalid."[79]

In other words, some things are beyond leaders' control; leaders do not have mystical powers over people. The situation does play a role. By the same token, leaders can have a considerable impact. The substitutes idea does not negate leadership; it just puts a more realistic boundary on what leadership is capable of achieving from subordinates. Some styles of leadership are more effective than others. The next chapter examines leadership styles.

Summary

This chapter presented and analyzed various theoretical aspects of leadership. The classic research studies on leadership set the stage for the theoretical development of leadership. The trait theories concentrate on the leaders themselves but, with the possible exception of intelligence and empathy/interpersonal sensitivity and self-confidence, really do not come up with any agreed-upon traits of leaders. In recent times the trait approach has surfaced in terms of managerial skills and abilities identified for selection and training/development purposes.

The group and exchange theories emphasize the importance of followers, and although the vertical dyad linkage (VDL or LMX) model is still quite popular and is generating considerable research, the group/exchange theories in general are recognized to be only partial theories. Today, the widely recognized theories of leadership are situationally based. In particular, Fiedler's contingency model makes a significant contribution to leadership theory and potentially to the practice of human resources management. The path-goal approach is also an important contribution to leadership theory. It incorporates expectancy motivation concepts.

All the established theories of leadership continue to provide understanding and a foundation for the practice of leadership in today's organizations. However, in recent years a number of alternative theories have emerged to supplement and, in some cases, help better understand the various processes of leadership. In particular, the charismatic, transformational, social learning, and substitutes approaches have received attention in recent years. Charismatic leaders (characterized as having qualities beyond the usual appointed leader) get extraordinary commitment and performance from followers. The charismatic leaders, however, as a group are only considered to be a subsection of the larger group of transformational leaders characterized by charisma, inspiration, and intellectual and individualized stimulation. These transformational leaders are felt to be especially suited to today's organizations as they experience dramatic change. The social-learning theory of leadership incorporates the leader, the situation, and the behavior itself. This social-learning approach emphasizes the importance of behavior and the continuous, interacting nature of all the variables in leadership. Finally, the substitutes approach recognizes that certain subordinate, task, and organizational characteristics may substitute for or neutralize the impact that leader behavior has on subordinate performance and satisfaction.

Questions for Discussion And Review

1. Briefly summarize the findings of the three classical leadership studies.
2. How do the group theories differ from the trait theories of leadership?
3. What are the three critical situational variables identified by Fiedler? If these are very favorable, what is the most effective style to use?
4. In simple terms, what is the path-goal theory of leadership? What is the leader's function in this conceptualization?
5. What are the major differences between traditional transactional leaders and emerging transformational leaders? Can you clarify these differences in how today's organizations are led?
6. What are the three variables in the social learning approach to leadership? How do they relate to one another? How can this approach be applied to the practice of human resources management?
7. What is meant by *substitutes* for, and *neutralizers* of, leadership? Give some subordinate, task, and organizational examples of these substitutes and neutralizers.

References

1. Andrea Rothman, "Maybe Your Skills Aren't Holding You Back; Maybe It's a Birthday," *The Wall Street Journal*, Mar. 19, 1987, p. 35.
2. Abraham Zaleznik, "The Leadership Gap," *Academy of Management Executive*, February 1990, p. 9.
3. Warren G. Bennis, "Managing The Dream: Leadership in the 21st Century," *Journal of Organizational Change Management*, vol. 2, no. 1, 1989, p. 7.
4. Bernard M. Bass, *Bass and Stogdill's Handbook of Leadership*, 3d ed., Free Press, New York, 1990, p. 11.
5. Chester A. Schriesheim and Steven Kerr, "Theo-

ries and Measures of Leadership: A Critical Appraisal of Current and Future Directions," in James G. Hunt and Lars L. Larson (eds.), *Leadership: The Cutting Edge*, Southern Illinois University Press, Carbondale, 1977, p. 22.
6. H. Joseph Reitz, *Behavior in Organizations*, 3d ed., Irwin, Homewood, Ill., 1987, p. 469.
7. Robert Katz, "Skills of an Effective Administrator," *Harvard Business Review*, September–October 1974, pp. 90–101.
8. Gary A. Yukl, *Leadership in Organizations*, Prentice-Hall, Englewood Cliffs, N.J., 1981, p. 70.
9. Bass, op. cit., p. 48.
10. Charles N. Greene, "The Reciprocal Nature of

Influence between Leader and Subordinate," *Journal of Applied Psychology*, vol. 60, 1975, pp. 187–193.

11. J. C. Barrow, "Worker Performance and Task Complexity as Causal Determinants of Leader Behavior Style and Flexibility," *Journal of Applied Psychology*, vol. 61, 1976, pp. 433–440.

12. Charles N. Greene and Chester A. Schriesheim, "Leader-Group Interactions: A Longitudinal Field Investigation," *Journal of Applied Psychology*, February 1980, pp. 50–59.

13. Keith Davis and John Newstrom, *Human Behavior at Work: Organizational Behavior*, 7th ed., McGraw-Hill, New York, 1985, pp. 160 and 182; Ann Howard and James A. Wilson, "Leadership in a Declining Work Ethic," *California Management Review*, Summer 1982, pp. 33–46.

14. Larry Reibstein, "Follow the Leader: Workers Face Dilemma When Boss Is Sinking," *The Wall Street Journal*, Mar. 10, 1987, p. 29.

15. F. Dansereau, Jr., G. Graen, and W. J. Haga, "A Vertical Dyad Linkage Approach to Leadership within Formal Organizations: A Longitudinal Investigation of the Role Making Process," *Organizational Behavior and Human Performance*, February 1975, pp. 46–78.

16. G. Graen, M. Novak, and P. Sommerkamp, "The Effects of Leader-Member Exchange and Job Design and Productivity and Satisfaction: Testing a Duel Attachment Model," *Organizational Behavior and Human Performance*, vol. 30, 1982, pp. 109–131.

17. Dansereau, Graen, and Haga, op. cit.

18. Fred Dansereau, Jr., Joseph A. Alutto, Steven E. Markham, and MacDonald Dumas, "Multi-plexed Supervision and Leadership: An Application of Within and Between Analysis," in James G. Hunt, Uma Sekaran, and Chester A. Schriesheim (eds.), *Leadership: Beyond Establishment Views*, Southern Illinois University Press, Carbondale, 1982, pp. 81–103.

19. Robert C. Liden and George Graen, "Generalizability of the Vertical Dyad Linkage Model of Leadership," *Academy of Management Journal*, September 1980, pp. 451–465.

20. Robert P. Vecchio, "A Further Test of Leadership Effects Due to Between-Group Variation and Within-Group Variation," *Journal of Applied Psychology*, April 1982, pp. 200–208; Richard M. Dienesch and Robert C. Liden, "Leader-Member Exchange Model of Leadership: A Critique and Further Development," *Academy of Management Review*, July 1986, pp. 618–634.

21. Gary Yukl, "Managerial Leadership: A Review of Theory and Research," *Journal of Management*, vol. 15, no. 2, 1989, p. 266.

22. Fred E. Fiedler, *A Theory of Leadership Effectiveness*, McGraw-Hill, New York, 1967, pp. 13–144.

23. Ibid., p. 147.

24. Ibid.

25. Fred Fiedler and Martin M. Chemers, *Leadership and Effective Management*, Scott, Foresman, Glenview, Ill., 1974, p. 83.

26. Fred E. Fiedler and Linda Mahar, "The Effectiveness of Contingency Model Training: A Review of the Validation of Leader Match," *Personnel Psychology*, Spring 1979, p. 46.

27. Michael J. Strube and Joseph E. Garcia, "A Meta-Analytic Investigation of Fiedler's Contingency Model of Leadership Effectiveness," *Psychological Bulletin*, September 1981, pp. 307–321.

28. George Graen, D. Alvares, J. B. Orris, and J. A. Martella, "Contingency Model of Leadership Effectiveness: Antecedent and Evidential Results," *Psychological Bulletin*, October 1970, pp. 285–296; George Graen, James B. Orris, and Kenneth M. Alvares, "Contingency Model of Leadership Effectiveness: An Evaluation," *Organizational Behavior and Human Performance*, June 1973, pp. 339–355.

29. Schriesheim and Kerr, op. cit.; and Chester A. Schriesheim, Brendan D. Bannister, and William H. Money, "Psychometric Properties of the LPC Scale: An Extension of Rice's Review," *Academy of Management Review*, April 1979, pp. 287–290.

30. Fred E. Fiedler, "A Rejoinder to Schriesheim and Kerr's Premature Obituary of the Contingency Model," in Hunt and Larson, op. cit., pp. 45–51.

31. Robert W. Rice, "Reliability and Validity of the LPC Scale: A Reply," *Academy of Management Review*, April 1979, pp. 291–294.

32. Yukl, op. cit., p. 266.

33. Fred E. Fiedler, "Engineer the Job to Fit the Manager," *Harvard Business Review*, September–October 1965, pp. 115–122.

34. Fred E. Fiedler, Martin M. Chemers, and Linda Mahar, *Improving Leadership Effectiveness: The Leader Match Concept*, Wiley, New York, 1976.

35. Ibid., pp. 154–158.

36. Fiedler and Mahar, op. cit.

37. Ibid., p. 61.

38. Arthur G. Jago and James W. Ragan, "The Trouble with Leader Match Is That It Doesn't Match Fiedler's Contingency Model," *Journal of Applied Psychology*, vol. 71, no. 4, 1986, pp. 555–559.

39. Ronald E. Riggio, *Introduction to Industrial/ Organizational Psychology*, Scott, Foresman/ Little, Brown, Glenview, Ill., 1990, p. 293.

40. F. E. Fiedler, "The Contribution of Cognitive Resources to Leadership Performance," *Journal of Applied Social Psychology*, vol. 16, 1986, pp. 532–548; F. E. Fiedler and J. E. Garcia, *New Approaches to Leadership: Cognitive Resources and Organizational Performance*, Wiley, New York, 1987.

41. Ibid.

42. Basil S. Georgopoulos, Gerald M. Mahoney, and Nyle W. Jones, "A Path-Goal Approach to Productivity," *Journal of Applied Psychology*, December 1957, pp. 345–353; Martin G. Evans, "The Effect of Supervisory Behavior on the Path-Goal Relationship," *Organizational Behavior and Human Performance*, May 1970, pp. 277–298; and Robert J. House, "A Path-Goal Theory of Leader Effectiveness," *Administrative Science Quarterly*, September 1971, pp. 321–338.

43. Robert J. House and Terence R. Mitchell, "Path-Goal Theory of Leadership," *Journal of Contemporary Business*, Autumn 1974, pp. 81–97.

44. Ibid.

45. Ibid., in Steers and Porter, op. cit., p. 386.

46. Alan C. Filley, Robert J. House, and Steven Kerr, *Managerial Process and Organizational Behavior*, 2d ed., Scott, Foresman, Glenview, Ill., 1976, p. 254.

47. House and Mitchell, op. cit., in Steers and Porter, op. cit., pp. 385–386.

48. Filley, House, and Kerr, op. cit., pp. 256–260.

49. Chester A. Schriesheim and Angelo DeNisi, "Task Dimensions as Moderators of the Effects of Instrumental Leadership: A Two Sample Applicated Test of Path-Goal Leadership Theory," *Journal of Applied Psychology*, October 1981, pp. 589–597. Also see Schriesheim and Kerr, op. cit.

50. Ibid., pp. 103–105.

51. Julie Indvik, "Path-Goal Theory of Leadership: A Meta-Analysis," *Academy of Management Best Papers Proceedings*, 1986, pp. 189–192.

52. Robert A. Baron, *Behavior in Organizations*, 2d ed., Allyn and Bacon, Boston, 1986, p. 292.

53. Representative of the critical analysis of modern leadership theory and research would be Korman, op. cit., pp. 189–195; Charles N. Greene, "Disenchantment with Leadership Research: Some Causes, Recommendations, and Alternative Directions," in Hunt and Larson (eds.), *Leadership: The Cutting Edge*, pp. 57–67; Schriesheim and Kerr, op. cit.; Barbara Karmel, "Leadership: A Challenge to Traditional Research Methods and Assumptions," *Academy of Management Review*, July 1978, pp. 475–482; and James S. Phillips and Robert G. Lord, "Notes on the Practical and Theoretical Consequences of Implicit Leadership Theories for the Future of Leadership Measurement," *Journal of Management*, vol. 12, no. 1, 1986, pp. 31–41.

54. John B. Miner, "The Uncertain Future of the Leadership Concept: An Overview," in James G. Hunt and Lars L. Larson (eds.), *Leadership Frontiers*, Kent State University, Comparative Administration Resources Institute, Kent, Ohio, 1975, pp. 197–208.

55. Schriesheim and Kerr, op. cit.

56. R. J. House and J. L. Baetz, "Leadership: Some Empirical Generalizations and New Research Directions," in B. M. Staw (ed.), *Research in Organizational Behavior*, vol. 1, JAI Press, Greenwich, Conn., 1979, p. 399.

57. Robert J. House, "A 1976 Theory of Charismatic Leadership," in Hunt and Larson (eds.), *Leadership: The Cutting Edge*, pp. 189–207.

58. Ibid.

59. Bernard M. Bass, *Leadership and Performance Beyond Expectations*, Free Press, New York, 1985, pp. 54–61.

60. R. J. House, J. Woycke, and E. M. Fodor, "Charismatic and Non Charismatic Leaders: Differences in Behavior and Effectiveness," in J. A. Conger and R. M. Kanungo (eds.), *Charismatic Leadership: The Elusive Factor in Organizational Effectiveness*, Jossey-Bass, San Francisco, pp. 98–121; Robert J. House, William D. Spangler, and James Woycke, "Personality and Charisma in the U.S. Presidency: A Psychological Theory of Leadership Effectiveness," *Academy of Management Best Paper Proceedings*, 1990, pp. 216–219.

61. J. A. Conger and R. Kanungo, "Toward a Behavioral Theory of Charismatic Leadership in Organizational Settings," *Academy of Management Review*, vol. 12, 1987, pp. 637–647; J. A. Conger and R. N. Kanungo, "Behavioral Dimensions of zational Settings," *Academy of Management*

Charismatic Leadership," in J. A. Conger and R. M. Kanungo (eds.), *Charismatic Leadership: The Elusive Factor in Organizational Effectiveness*, Jossey-Bass, San Francisco, pp. 78–97.

62. Bass, *Bass & Stogdill's Handbook*, p. 221.

63. J. M. Burns, *Leadership*, Harper & Row, New York, 1978.

64. Bernard M. Bass, "From Transactional to Transformational Leadership: Learning to Share the Vision," *Organizational Dynamics*, Winter 1990, pp. 19–31.

65. Yukl, op. cit., pp. 272–273.

66. Noel M. Tichy and Mary Anne Devanna, *The Transformational Leader*, Wiley, New York, 1986; and Noel M. Tichy and Mary Anne Devanna, "The Transformational Leader," *Training and Development Journal*, July 1986, pp. 30–32.

67. See Tim R. V. Davis and Fred Luthans, "A Social Learning Approach to Organizational Behavior," *Academy of Management Review*, April 1980, pp. 281–290.

68. See Fred Luthans, "Leadership: A Proposal for a Social Learning Theory Base and Observational and Functional Analysis Techniques to Measure Leader Behavior," in Hunt and Larson (eds.), *Crosscurrents in Leadership*, pp. 201–208; Fred Luthans and Tim R. V. Davis, "Operationalizing a Behavioral Approach to Leadership," *Proceedings of the Midwest Academy of Management*, 1979, pp. 144–155; and Tim R. V. Davis and Fred Luthans, "Leadership Reexamined: A Behavioral Approach," *Academy of Management Review*, April 1979, pp. 237–248.

69. See Luthans, op. cit., for an expanded discussion.

70. Davis and Luthans, "Leadership Reexamined," p. 244.

71. Ibid., p. 245.

72. See Fred Luthans and Tim R. V. Davis, "Behavioral Self-Management: The Missing Link in Managerial Effectiveness," *Organizational Dynamics*, Summer 1979, pp. 42–60; and Tim R. V. Davis and Fred Luthans, "Defining and Researching Leadership as a Behavioral Construct: An Idiographic Approach," *Journal of Applied Behavioral Science*, vol. 20, no. 3, 1984, pp. 237–251.

73. Steven Kerr and John M. Jermier, "Substitutes of Leadership: Their Meaning and Measurement," *Organizational Behavior and Human Performance*, December 1978, pp. 375–403. Also see Steven Kerr, "Substitutes for Leadership: Some Implications for Organization Design," *Organization and Administrative Sciences*, vol. 8, no. 1, 1977, p. 135; and Jon P. Howell, Peter Dorfman, and Steven Kerr, "Moderator Variables in Leadership Research," *Academy of Management Review*, vol. 11, no. 1, 1986, pp. 88–102.

74. J. Jermier and L. Berkes, "Leader Behavior in a Police Command Bureaucracy: A Closer Look at the Quasi-Military Model," *Administrative Science Quarterly*, March 1979, pp. 1–23; and S. Kerr and J. W. Slocum, Jr., "Controlling the Performances of People in Organizations," in P. C. Nystrom and W. H. Starbuck (eds.), *Handbook of Organizational Design*, Oxford, New York, 1981, pp. 116–134.

75. Kerr and Jermier, op. cit.

76. Robert H. Miles and M. M. Petty, "Leader Effectiveness in Small Bureaucracies," *Academy of Management Journal*, June 1977, pp. 238–250.

77. Jon P. Howell and Peter W. Dorfman, "Substitutes for Leadership: Test of a Construct," *Academy of Management Journal*, December 1981, pp. 714–728.

78. Jon P. Howell and Peter W. Dorfman, "Leadership and Substitutes for Leadership among Professionals and Nonprofessional Workers," *Journal of Applied Behavioral Science*, vol. 22, no. 1, 1986, pp. 29–46.

79. Robert P. Vecchio, *Organizational Behavior*, Dryden, Chicago, 1988, p. 309.

REAL CASE: PRESIDENTIAL LEADERSHIP

One of the most interesting looks at leadership can be found in presidential styles. Ronald Reagan, for example, was popular with some people and unpopular with others, but all agree on one basic fact: he had a leadership style that was interesting and in some ways unique. Close observers have concluded that some of the basic approaches that exemplified Reagan's style were the following:

1. He always put a great deal of emphasis on being able to communicate well. In fact, when his speech writers would hand him their material, the president would go over it and change some of their examples to ones he liked better and felt were more appropriate to his audience.
2. He always tried to convey an upbeat message. If things were not going well, his emphasis would be on how they could be improved.
3. He identified his major goals and continued moving toward them during his terms in office. He did not change his mind in midstream and begin shifting toward different major objectives. This consistency of behavior made it easier for him to keep his programs heading in a consistent direction.
4. He repeated his national goals over and over again so everyone knew what he wanted done. In particular, those who supported him were able to line up behind him. Having heard the message often enough, they became part of his cheering squad—something every effective leader needs.
5. He tried to compromise on those issues where he realized he would be unable to achieve all he was seeking. For example, if he wanted $100 million for a program and could get only 70 percent of this, he would take it and then work on getting the other 30 percent the next fiscal year. He did not get himself caught up in an "all or nothing" strategy.
6. He focused on the major issues without getting bogged down in the day-to-day decision making. This was left for others who were more skilled than he at implementation.
7. During Cabinet meetings he encouraged people to speak their minds; if they disagreed with the majority, they should say so. In this way, Reagan was able to get input on both sides of the issue under discussion.
8. He believed that the most important thing a leader could do was surround himself with the best possible talent. Then he could delegate authority and let these people carry out the overall policy that had been agreed upon.

In the years ahead, a great deal of additional research is likely to be conducted regarding Ronald Reagan's leadership style. However, for the time being at least, most experts believe that his approach to leadership worked pretty well for him.

1. How can Fiedler's contingency model of leadership be used to explain the success of President Reagan's style?
2. How can the path-goal theory of leadership be used in explaining the President's approach? Cite an example in your answer.
3. Was Reagan a charismatic leader? Support your answer?

**Case:
He Sure
Looked
Good**

Mannion Inc. started looking for a new corporate president almost eighteen months ago. The process was slow; for a while, it appeared that none of the applicants would make the final list. However, after interviewing over thirty executives from both inside and outside the company, the selection committee recommended that five people be considered for the position. In its report to the board of directors, the committee said that each of the five finalists was "equal to the task and any one of them can provide us the leadership needed for the twenty-first century."

The board reviewed the list and unanimously agreed that there were two individuals who warranted initial consideration. If either was deemed superior to the other after the interviews, this person would be offered the job and the second would be kept as a backup. Only if both individuals proved unacceptable or could not be hired would the board move on and consider the remaining three candidates.

The first person to be interviewed was Mark Schlaiffer. Mark, forty-four, has worked for a major competitor for fourteen years. He currently is senior production vice president and is considered to be one of the most effective managers in the industry. Based on a strategic plan he developed, his company was able to cut costs by 22 percent and emerge as one of the low cost producers in the world. It is likely that Mark will be made president of his company if he remains.

The other person was Margaret Hutchins, forty-five, vice president of operations at a large high-tech company. Although Mannion Inc. is not in the high-tech business, Margaret's success in nurturing and developing research and development projects is well-known in the industry and she is considered a first-rate leader. Much of the success of her company is attributed, by insiders as well as industry analysts, to Margaret's skills and abilities. She has been offered the presidency of three companies over the last five years, and in each case she has declined. However, she has indicated that she would take the job at Mannion if it were offered.

Yesterday, the board met and made its decision. The offer was made to Mark. In explaining why they chose him, there were five reasons that seemed to outweigh the others. They were these:

- He is distinguished looking; he has a "presidential" look.
- He is tall (6'6") and this helps him convey an image of power and authority.
- He is affable and friendly.
- He is a good public speaker.
- He is extremely intelligent.

There were also many positive comments made about Margaret, including her fine operating performance. However, the board was unanimous in deciding to make the first offer to Mark. If he did not accept, they planned to invite in two more individuals and then choose between them and Margaret in deciding whom next to offer the job.

1. On what basis did the company make its choice?
2. Based on your answer to the above question, did the board make a mistake?
3. What recommendations would you make to them based on their decision and the comments supporting it?

Case:
The Missing
Ingredient

When Cecil Schmidt took over the helm of Rugersby Insurance, a large brokerage firm in the northeast, he knew that things were in bad shape. The industry had been suffering massive losses and most insurers had come to realize that their rates were too low. Premiums had to be raised and the price-cutting strategies of earlier years had to be abandoned if the firm was to survive.

Cecil was brought in with the mandate to "straighten things out and get our profitability up." It took him almost three years to get things turned around. First, he stopped all hiring except for replacements and encouraged voluntary retirement.

Second, all nonessential personnel were let go and their work was redistributed to others. Third, all marginally profitable accounts were dropped and the focus of attention was placed on the money makers. Fourth, in-house operating and maintenance costs were cut to the bone.

As a result of these efficiency and marketing-related measures, monthly losses dropped from $30,000 to under $2,000 within three months. A year after he assumed the helm, Cecil was able to tell the board that the company was operating at its breakeven point. The next year profits were in excess of $200,000; for the three years following, they doubled every year. Rugersby was now in the top half of the industry in terms of profitability for a firm its size. Cecil attributed a great deal of this success to his draconian measures of cost cutting and heavy emphasis on efficiency.

Unfortunately, a year ago, profits started to decline. There appear to be two major reasons for this. One is that the company's revenues have increased 207 percent since Cecil has come on board, while the number of personnel has declined by 24 percent. Many people feel that they are overworked and have begun looking for positions elsewhere. To make matters worse, the company has been having trouble hiring new people. A second reason is that overall efficiency is declining. Many of the cost-cutting steps taken by Cecil appear to have been short-run. For example, managers used to take the overnight flight from New York to San Francisco. Since they were in first class, they would be well fed, see a movie, and sleep. When they arrived in San Francisco the next morning, they were ready to begin work. Now that they must travel coach, the managers take a day flight and this means that they lose one day of work going out and another coming back. When Cecil asked them to fly at night, they told him that they cannot sleep in coach because it is too uncomfortable. As a result, they have to fly out during the day in order to ensure that they got a good night's sleep and are prepared for work the next day; the same is true for the return flight.

Earlier this week the board of directors of Rugersby met and decided to ask for Cecil's resignation. The chairman summed up the feelings of the committee by saying, "Cecil has done a good job, but it's time for a change. If we don't do something, we'll be back where we were when Cecil arrived. We want to bring in someone who is less cost-focused and more people-oriented. We think that this is the missing ingredient that is causing our problems."

1. Why are Cecil's cost-cutting efforts now losing their effectiveness?
2. Is the board correct in its assessment of the situation? Why or why not?
3. What leadership lessons can be learned from this case? Cite and describe two.

11

Leadership Applied: Styles and Performance

■ An International MBA

How do you develop leaders? One way is through university education by means of undergraduate and MBA programs. Recently, the Amos Tuck School at Dartmouth has been attempting to expand this idea through a joint-MBA program in Japan. The students, for the most part, are nominated by their company to attend the two-year program and the curriculum is basically the same as that back in the United States, except that some courses are taught by Tuck professors and others by Japanese professors.

Will an MBA from a United States university really be of any value to the Japanese? The answer is probably yes, if these students hope someday to hold international management positions. One of the major reasons for this is that Japanese education does not prepare students for all of the challenges they will face in the international arena. One particular gap is their ability to look at the big picture, think strategically, and conceptualize. Japanese students are taught to handle the computational side of problems, but they do not learn how to integrate these data into the overall scheme of things. They are good at micro-level problem solving, but have trouble handling macro-level issues. The international MBA teaches them to deal with both types of problems.

Another interesting finding from the Tuck program was the way in which the Japanese divide homework among themselves and then share the results. This is in direct contrast to American MBA students who tend to work more individually and take personal responsibility for the results. During their program, the Japanese students began to learn something that international managers must know: The ability to personally make a decision and stand by it is critical to effective leadership.

Another benefit the students derive from the program is learning how to ask critical questions. Japanese students are not taught to question their professors or ask them to repeat something that is unclear. Nor are the Japanese expected to participate in class discussions back home. One Japanese student explained it this way. "In our universities, there were 400 in the class; people slept and picked up notes from the guy in the front row to memorize for the exam. Then you could pass." In the Tuck program, the professor calls on the students and asks specific questions. The student is also encouraged to challenge the professor's comments, offer additional facts that might result in a new way of analyzing the problem, and assume some of the responsibility for helping improve the learning environment.

Finally, the Japanese learn to evaluate their instructors, something that they would never do in Japan. Surprisingly, perhaps, to the Japanese professors, the American instructors are rated much higher because of their ability to relate to the students and to get them involved in the course.

Will the MBA be their ticket to the top? Maybe not, since the degree is not highly regarded by most Japanese firms. On the other hand, the graduates now indicate that they believe the MBA is their passport to job change. Some are looking for better positions. Several have also reported that their companies are "stingy." These developments indicate that many of the students are beginning to exhibit individual leadership ability and may well find that the MBA will be extremely helpful in their international management careers.

Learning Objectives

- **Relate** the style implications from the classic studies and modern theories of leadership.
- **Present** the widely recognized styles of leadership, including those from the managerial grid, life cycle, Likert's systems, and the Vroom and Yetton model.
- **Discuss** the latest findings on women and leadership.
- **Examine** the impact that styles and activities have on the success and effectiveness of leaders.

The last chapter presented the background and the established and emerging theoretical frameworks for leadership. Analogous to the earlier treatment of motivation and learning in this part of the book, this chapter serves as the follow-up application of leadership theories. This leadership application chapter mainly deals with the various leadership styles that managers can use to more effectively manage their people and their organizations.

At first, the style implications from the classic studies and theories of the last chapter are examined. Then, the main part of the chapter presents and analyzes the widely recognized styles of leadership. The last part of the chapter initially pays special attention to women leaders in today's organizations, then gives the results of an extensive study that focused on the activities of those leaders/managers who were successful and those that were effective.

LEADERSHIP STYLES

The classic leadership studies and the various leadership theories discussed in the last chapter all have have direct implications for what style the manager or supervisor uses in human resources management. The word "style" is roughly equivalent to the

International Application Example

Japanese versus Korean Leadership Styles

When America's productivity began to slide in comparison with Japan's, American management professors and practitioners looked toward Japanese management for answers. It was found that Japanese management gave extra attention to human resources management. Since then, American managers have adopted many of the Japanese practices. Quality circles and lifetime employment come quickly to mind. Recently, however, another success story is gaining America's attention. South Korea, not Japan, has been winning the competitive battle in many areas. Korean-run businesses such as Lucky-Goldstar, Samsung, Hyundai, and Daewoo have had much success. They have posed a new threat to American business leadership. Thus, Americans are now looking toward the Koreans as well as the Japanese style for the answers.

In some ways the Koreans are similar to the Japanese. For instance, Korean managers espouse teamwork, employee participation, minimal hierarchies, and emphasis on the employee's personal needs. However, when the Koreans come to run their operations in the United States, they are more flexible than the Japanese. As a result, Koreans have adjusted better to American ways. For instance, although managers in Korea sit in open-air offices, Korean managers in America separate themselves with lightly tinted glass. Also, Americans are not asked to sing a company song or to take exercise breaks. Thomas G. Dimmick, a manager with the Korean firm Samsung, comments on the inflexibility of the Japanese: "The Japanese are from a homogeneous society, so they are less accepting of anything that is not Japanese. Korea is a land of division, so the people are willing to listen and not get their feet stuck in concrete."

The Korean-run plants in the United States have experienced considerable success. The average American worker at a Korean-run plant produces more goods compared with American-owned companies. However, American workers at Japanese-run plants still produced the most. Yet, management experts predict that the gap between Japanese and Korean plants will narrow. After all, Korean managers tend to work more hours than their Japanese or American counterparts. The diligence of the Koreans should pay off in the long run. If the Korean-run plants continue to succeed, Korean management may replace Japanese management as a model for managerial leadership.

---

way in which the leader influences followers. The accompanying International Application Example indicates that this style may be influenced by culture, as seen in the differences between Japanese and Korean managers.

Style Implications of the Classic Studies and the Modern Theories

Chapter 2 discussed the major historical contributions to the study of organizational behavior. Most of this discussion had indirect or direct implications for leadership style. For example, the Hawthorne studies were interpreted in terms of their implications for supervisory style. Also relevant is the classic work done by Douglas McGregor, in which his Theory X represents the old, authoritarian style of leadership and his Theory Y represents the enlightened, humanistic style. The studies discussed at the beginning of the last chapter are directly concerned with style. The Iowa studies analyzed the impact of autocratic, democratic, and laissez faire styles, and the studies conducted by the Michigan group found the employee-centered supervisor to be more effective than the production-centered supervisor. The Ohio State studies indentified consideration (a supportive type of style) and initiating structure (a directive type of style) as being the major functions of leadership. The trait and group theories have indirect implications for style, and the human relations and task-directed styles play an important role in Fiedler's contingency theory. The path-goal conceptualization depends heavily upon directive, supportive, participative, and achievement-oriented styles of leadership.

The same is true of the charismatic and transformational leaders. They have an inspirational style with vision and "do the right thing" for their people. Table 11.1 summarizes the charismatic leader style according to three major types of behavior, with illustrative actions. An example of such a style in recent times would be Paul O'Neil of ALCOA. He espoused a clear vision for his firm anchored on quality, safety, and innovation. He made his vision compelling and central to the company, set high expectations for his management team and employees throughout the organization, and provided continuous support and energy for his vision through meetings, task forces, video tapes, and extensive personal contact.[1]

A rough approximation of the various styles derived from the studies and theories discussed so far can be incorporated into the continuum shown in Table 11.2. For ease of presentation, the styles listed may be substituted for the expressions "boss-centered" and "subordinate-centered" used by Tannenbaum and Schmidt in their classic leadership continuum shown in Figure 11.1. The verbal descriptions and the relationship between authority and freedom found in Figure 11.1 give a rough representation of the characteristics of the various styles of leadership. This depiction

TABLE 11.1 Charismatic Leadership Styles

Types of Charismatic Leadership Styles	Meaning	Examples
Envisioning	Creating a picture of the future—or a desired future state—with which people can identify and which can generate excitement	Articulating a compelling vision Setting high expectations
Energizing	Directing the generation of energy, the motivation to act, among members of the organization	Demonstrating personal excitement and confidence Seeking, finding, and using success
Enabling	Psychologically helping people act or perform in the face of challenging goals	Expressing personal support Empathizing

Source: Adapted from David A. Nadler and Michael L. Tushman, "Beyond the Charismatic Leader: Leadership and Organizational Change," *California Management Review,* Winter 1990, pp. 82–83.

TABLE 11.2 Summary Continuum of Leadership Styles Drawn from the Classic Studies and Theories of Leadership

Boss-centered	Subordinate-centered
Theory X ⟵————————————————⟶	Theory Y
Autocratic ⟵————————————————⟶	Democratic
Production-centered ⟵————————————⟶	Employee-centered
Close ⟵————————————————————⟶	General
Initiating structure ⟵———————————⟶	Consideration
Task-directed ⟵————————————————⟶	Human relations
Directive ⟵————————————————————⟶	Supportive
Directive ⟵————————————————————⟶	Participative

can serve as background for a more detailed examination of the specific application of styles to the practice of human resources management.

One thing is certain: leadership style can make a difference. For example, a survey found that senior executives view their companies' leadership styles as pragmatic rather than conceptual, and conservative rather than risk taking. Importantly, these same executives felt that to meet their current and future challenges, the styles should be the other way around.[2] As Bennis has recently noted, "Never before has American business faced so many challenges, and never before have there been so

FIGURE 11.1
A continuum of leadership behavior. (*Source*: Robert Tannenbaum and Warren H. Schmidt, "How to Choose a Leadership Pattern," *Harvard Business Review*, March–April 1958, p. 96. Used with permission.)

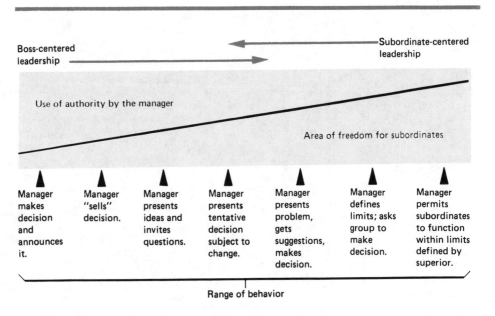

many choices in how to face those challenges. We must look now at what it is going to take not just to regain global leadership, but simply to stay a player in the game."[3] The following sections examine the widely-recognized leadership styles available to today's managers to meet these challenges.

Managerial Grid Styles

One very popular approach to identifying leadership styles of practicing managers is Blake and Mouton's managerial grid. Figure 11.2 shows that the two dimensions of the grid are concern for people along the vertical axis and concern for production along the horizontal axis. These two dimensions are equivalent to the consideration and initiating structure functions identified by the Ohio State studies and the employee-centered and production-centered styles used in the Michigan studies.

The five basic styles identified in the grid represent varying combinations of concern for people and production. The 1,1 manager has minimum concern for people and production; this style is sometimes called the "impoverished" style. The

FIGURE 11.2
The managerial grid.
(*Source*: Robert R. Blake and Jane S. Mouton, "Managerial Facades," *Advanced Management Journal*, July 1966, p. 31. Used with permission.)

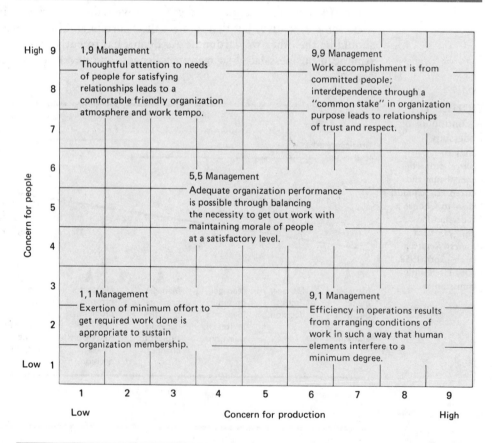

opposite is the 9,9 manager. This individual has maximum concern for both people and production. The implication is that the 9,9 is the best style of leadership, and Blake and Mouton have stated in no uncertain terms: "There should be no question about which leadership style is the most effective. It's that of the manager whom we call, in the terminology of the Managerial Grid, a 9,9 team builder." [4] Blake and Mouton provided empirical evidence that their interactive notion of leadership style (that is, concern for people interacting with concern for production) has more predictive validity than additive situational approaches.[5] The 5,5 manager is the "middle-of-the-roader," and the other two styles represent the extreme concerns for people (1,9, "country club" manager) and production (9,1, "task" manager). A manager's position on the grid can be determined by a questionnaire developed by Blake and Mouton and can play an important role in organization development (OD). Chapter 21 will discuss this grid approach to OD and will analyze the research findings. The International Application Example, Balancing People and Profits, offers an example of the managerial grid approach to international negotiations.

International Application Example

Balancing People and Profits

One of the most interesting examples of current leadership practices is provided by those individuals in the international arena who are negotiating business deals. Quite often, they fit into one of two groups: business people from other countries who are seeking opportunities to invest, and national leaders who are seeking to attract investment. Each would like to enter into a contract that enhances his or her position, and this is where effective leadership enters the picture.

Take the case of the Soviet Union. Going into the 1990s, Gorbachev was working furiously to attract American capital. Major U.S. leaders such as Don Kendall of PepsiCo, Dwayne Andreas of Archer Daniels Midland, Bill Esrey of United Telecommunications, and Den Derr of Chevron all went to the Soviet Union in an effort to find out what the country had to offer and where the government would allow them to invest. Given that the Soviet Union was in major need of investment capital, it would seem that anything these business leaders wanted to do would be acceptable. However, this was not true. On the one hand, Gorbachev talked about the need for investment, while on the other he offered no immediate promise of return on investment. The picture is no different in other countries seeking to attract investors. Leaders on both sides of the negotiating table are finding that they must balance a concern for people with a concern for work.

In the case of the Soviet Union, they must find investment that will help improve the lifestyle of the country (concern for people) while also ensuring that the investors have the freedom needed to operate efficiently and to repatriate their profits (concern for work). American leaders need to convince the leaders of the Soviet Union that their country will not be highly attractive unless a definition of property ownership rights is clarified, control of operations is ensured, and the ruble is convertible into dollars or other desirable foreign currency (concern for work) while also illustrating that such investment will help improve the standard of living in the country (concern for people). Quite obviously, both sides are learning that a 9,9 leadership style is not restricted to the confines of one's own organization.

Hersey and Blanchard's Life-Cycle, or Situational, Approach

Another popular approach to management training and development is the *life-cycle* (later termed the *situational*) approach to leadership.[6] It is an extension of the managerial grid approach. Following the original Ohio State studies and the grid approach. Hersey and Blanchard's approach identifies two major styles:

1. *Task style:* The leader organizes and defines roles for subordinates; the leader explains the tasks that each subordinate is to do and when, where, and how the subordinate is to do them.
2. *Relationship style:* The leader has close, personal relationships with the members of the group, and there is open communication and psychological and emotional support.

Taking the lead from some of Fiedler's work on situational variables, Hersey and Blanchard incorporated the maturity of the followers into their model. The level of maturity is defined by three criteria:

1. Degree of achievement motivation
2. Willingness to take on responsibility
3. Amount of education and/or experience

Although they recognize that there may be other important situational variables, Hersey and Blanchard focus only on this maturity level of subordinates in their model.

Figure 11.3 summarizes the situational approach. The key for leadership effectiveness in this model is to match up the situation with the appropriate style. The following summarizes the four basic styles:

1. *Telling style:* This is a high-task, low-relationship style and is effective when followers are at a very low level of maturity.
2. *Selling style:* This is a high-task, high-relationship style and is effective when followers are on the low side of maturity.
3. *Participating style:* This is a low-task, high-relationship style and is effective when followers are on the high side of maturity.
4. *Delegating style:* This is a low-task, low-relationship style and is effective when followers are at a very high level of maturity.

Like the grid approach, Hersey and Blanchard's approach includes a questionnaire instrument which presents twelve situations that generally depict the various levels of maturity of the group; respondents answer how they would handle each situation. These responses follow the four styles. How closely respondents match the situation with the appropriate style will determine their effectiveness score.

The theoretical rationale is generally criticized as being "weak, because Hersey and Blanchard have neglected to provide a coherent, explicit rationale for the hypothesized relationships."[7] They also, by their own admission, highly oversimplify the situation by giving only surface recognition to follower maturity. Also, as in the grid approach, there is a noted absence of any empirical tests of the model.

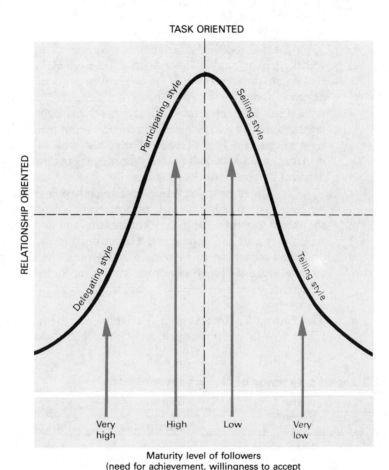

FIGURE 11.3
Hersey and
Blanchard's situational leadership
model.
(*Source*: Adapted
from Paul Hersey
and Kenneth H.
Blanchard, *Management of Organizational Behavior:
Utilizing Human
Resources*, 3d ed.,
Prentice-Hall,
Englewood Cliffs,
N.J., 1977, p. 170.)

One review of all facets of the approach was particularly critical of the instrument that Hersey and Blanchard used to measure leader effectiveness,[8] and a recent empirical test did not find support for the underlying assumptions or predictions.[9] Overall, as is true of the other style approaches, this situational approach seems to be of some value in training and development work in that it can point out the need for flexibility and take into consideration the different variables affecting leaders, but this type of approach has limited utility for identifying leadership effectiveness.

Likert's Four Systems of Management

The grid and situational approaches are both highly descriptive and at this time lack empirically validated research backup. In contrast, Rensis Likert proposed four basic systems or styles of organizational leadership that evolved from the many years of research by the Michigan group. Table 11.3 summarizes these four styles, called *systems of management leadership.*

The manager who operates under a system 1 approach is very authoritarian and actually tries to exploit subordinates. The system 2 manager is also authoritarian but in a paternalistic manner. This benevolent autocrat keeps strict control and never delegates authority to subordinates, but he or she "pats them on the head" and "does it for their best interests." The system 3 manager uses a consultative style. This manager asks for and receives participative input from subordinates but maintains the right to make the final decision. The system 4 manager uses a democratic style. This manager gives some direction to subordinates but provides for total participation and decision by consensus and majority.

To give empirical research backup on which style is most effective, Likert and his colleagues asked thousands of managers to describe, on an expanded version of the format shown in Table 11.3, the highest- and lowest-producing departments with which they had had experience. Quite consistently, the high-producing units were described according to systems 3 and 4, and the low-producing units fell under systems 1 and 2. These responses were given irrespective of the manager's field of experience or of whether the manager was in a line or staff position.[10]

The Impact of Intervening Variables and Time. An important refinement of Likert's work is the recognition of three broad classes of variables that affect the

TABLE 11.3 Likert's Systems of Management Leadership

Leadership Variable	System 1 (Exploitive Autocratic)	System 2 (Benevolent Autocratic)	System 3 (Participative)	System 4 (Democratic)
Confidence and trust in subordinates	Manager has no confidence or trust in subordinates.	Manager has condescending confidence and trust, such as a master has in a servant.	Manager has substantial but not complete confidence and trust; still wishes to keep control of decisions.	Manager has complete confidence and trust in subordinates in all matters.
Subordinates' feeling of freedom	Subordinates do not feel at all free to discuss things about the job with their superior.	Subordinates do not feel very free to discuss things about the job with their superior.	Subordinates feel rather free to discuss things about the job with their superior.	Subordinates feel completely free to discuss things about the job with their superior.
Superiors seeking involvement with subordinates	Manager seldom gets ideas and opinions of subordinates in solving job problems.	Manager sometimes gets ideas and opinions of subordinates in solving job problems.	Manager usually gets ideas and opinions and usually tries to make constructive use of them.	Manager always asks subordinates for opinions and always tries to make constructive use of them.

Source: Adapted from Rensis Likert, *The Human Organization,* McGraw-Hill, New York, 1967, p. 4. Used with permission.

relationship between leadership and performance in a complex organization.[11] Briefly summarized, these are:

1. *Causal variables:*   These are the independent variables that determine the course of developments and results of an organization. They include only those variables which are under the control of management; for example, economic conditions are *not* causal variables in this sense. Examples would be organization structure and management's policies and decisions and their leadership styles, skills, and behavior.
2. *Intervening variables:*   These reflect the internal climate of the organization. Performance goals, loyalties, attitudes, perceptions, and motivations are some important intervening variables. They affect interpersonal relations, communication, and decision making in the organization.
3. *End-result variables:*   These are the dependent variables, the outcomes of the organization. Examples would be productivity, service, costs, quality, and earnings.

Likert points out that there is not a direct cause-and-effect relationship between, for example, leadership style (a causal variable) and earnings (an end-result variable). The intervening variables must also be taken into consideration. For example, moving to a system 1 style of management may lead to an improvement in profits but a deterioration of the intervening variables (that is, attitudes, loyalty, and motivation decline). In time, these intervening variables may lead to a decrease in profits. Thus, although on the surface it appeared that system 1 was increasing profits, because of the impact on the intervening variables, in the long run system 1 may lead to a decrease in profits. The same can be said for the application of a system 4 style. In the short run, profits may dip, but because of the impact on intervening variables, there may be an increase in profit over time. Obviously, the time lag between intervention and the impact on end-result variables becomes extremely important to Likert's scheme. On the basis of some research evidence, Likert concludes: "Changes in the causal variables toward System 4 apparently require an appreciable period of time before the impact of the change is fully manifest in corresponding improvement in end-result variables."[12]

An Example of Time Lag. Likert's "time lag" helps explain the following relatively common sequence of events. A system 1 manager takes over an operation and immediately gets good performance results. In the meantime, however, the intervening variables are declining. Because of the good results, the system 1 manager is promoted. A system 4 manager now takes over the operation. Because of the time lag, the intervening variables, which were affected by the system 1 manager, now start to affect performance. Under the system 4 manager, performance starts to decline, but the intervening variables start to improve. However, top management see that when the system 4 manager took over, performance started to decline. The system 4 manager is replaced by a system 1 manager to "tighten up" the operation. The intervening variables affected by the system 4 manager now start to affect performance, and the cycle repeats itself. Figure 11.4 depicts this situation. In other

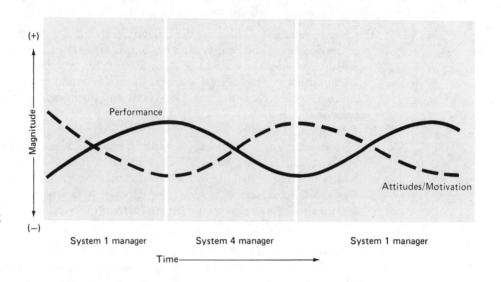

FIGURE 11.4
A hypothetical example depicting Likert's time lag impact of intervening variables on performance.

words, the cause-and-effect relationships that appear on the surface may be very misleading because of the time lag impact of the intervening variables. As in the example, top management evaluations often credit the wrong manager (the system 1 manager in this case) for improving performance and unjustly blame the wrong manager (the system 4 manager in the example) for poor performance. Some organizations may be guilty of this never-ending cycle of rewarding and punishing the wrong managers because of the time lag effect of intervening variables.

Analysis of Likert's Approach. One of the major criticisms of Likert's work concerns its overdependence on survey questionnaire measures for gathering data to develop the theory and application of system 4 management. Sole dependence on Likert scale (continuums of dimensions as shown in Table 11.3) questionnaire responses is not enough. As has been pointed out a number of times in this book, there is increasing criticism of data gathered only by questionnaires and interviews. Multiple measures of behaviorally oriented variables in organizations are needed. More use of archival information (existing records kept by every organization for other uses, for example, government reports, personnel records, and performance data) and data gathered through observation are needed.

Although ethical standards must always be maintained, subject awareness must be minimized to increase the reliability and validity of data that are gathered for research purposes. Both questionnaires and interviews have a great deal of subject awareness or intrusiveness. Archival analysis and some naturalistic observational techniques minimize subject awareness and are called *unobtrusive measures.*[13] Not only Likert's work but also much of the other research reported in this book is based upon indirect questionnaire measures. What is needed is to supplement these measures with other measures such as observations and archival data. As Chapter 2 pointed out, the use of multiple measures increases tremendously the chance of getting better, more accurate, and more valid data.

Another problem inherent in Likert's scheme besides the real and potential measurement problems is the implication of the universality of the system 4 approach. Although Likert points out that "differences in the kind of work, in the traditions of the industry, and in the skills and values of the employees of a particular company will require quite different procedures and ways to apply appropriately the basic principles of system 4 management,"[14] he still implies that system 4 will *always* be more effective than system 1. Proponents of situational/contingency leadership theories and their research findings would, of course, counter this generalization.

Convincing arguments can be made for directive, rather than system 4, styles of leadership. This position has been stated as follows:

> The inescapable fact is that many, many organizations who are less than "excellent" in the caliber of their people and support systems simply can't afford to have their managers be participative without a commensurate dose of direction. That is, in the vast majority of actual leadership situations democratic behaviors must be tempered with a measure of direction or follow-up to assure that organizational goals are accomplished efficiently and effectively.[15]

This position on leadership effectiveness was essentially ignored by Likert.

Vroom–Yetton Leadership Model

The Blake and Mouton, Hersey and Blanchard, and Likert approaches to leadership are all directly or by implication prescriptive. In addition, they try in varying degrees to take into consideration the situation (Blake and Mouton and Likert in passing, and Hersey and Blanchard as a vital part of their approach). But none of these approaches spell out exactly *how* a manager should act or what decision should be made in a given situation. Vroom and Yetton attempted to provide a specific, normative model (how decisions "ought" to be made in given situations) that a leader could actually use in making effective decisions.[16]

The Vroom-Yetton model was first developed several years ago and has since been modified. The model contains five leadership styles, seven situation dimensions, fourteen problem types, and seven decision rules. The leadership styles consist of variations on autocratic, consultative, and group styles, and the situational dimensions are of two general types: (1) the way in which problems affect the quality and acceptance of a decision and (2) the way in which the problems affect the degree of participation. The seven situational dimensions are stated in the form of "yes"–"no" questions, and the answers can quickly diagnose the situation for the leader.

Vroom and Yetton use a decision tree to relate the situation to the appropriate leadership style. Figure 11.5 shows the approach. The seven situational questions are listed at the top. Starting at the left, the manager would answer each question above the box in the decision tree until it led to the appropriate style. In this way the manager could determine the appropriate style on the basis of the given situation. Vroom and Yetton also point out that the fourteen problem types (the combinations of the seven situational variables, listed as 1 through 14 in the decision tree) could

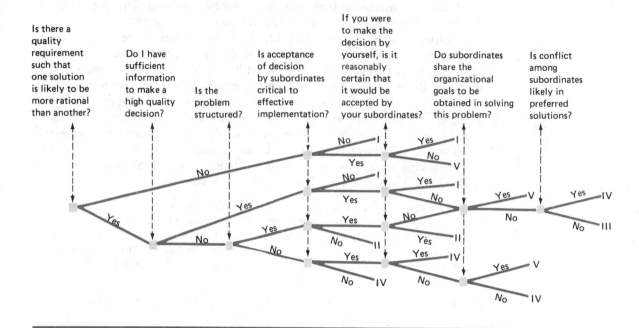

FIGURE 11.5
The Vroom-Yetton normative leadership model.
(*Source:* Adapted from Victor H. Vroom, "A New Look at Managerial Decision Making," *Organizational Dynamics*, Spring 1973, pp. 67, 70.)

actually have more than one acceptable leadership style. In order to be acceptable, the style must meet the criteria of seven decision rules that protect quality and acceptance. If more than one style remains after the test of both quality and acceptance (and many do), the third most important aspect of a decision—the amount of time—is used to determine the single style that ought to be used in the given situation. The styles shown at the ends of the various branches on the decision tree reflect the single best style that should be used in light of the way the situation was diagnosed by answers to the questions at the top.

Several studies have tested the Vroom-Yetton model.[17] Most of this research has been done by Vroom and his colleagues, and they do provide some evidence that the model is valid. However, more recent critiques that have closely examined the methodology used in these studies have led to questions about the validity of the model.[18]

Although the potential problem that support of the Vroom-Yetton model may be attributed to chance alone may be discounted,[19] there may be a problem with the dependence on the self-report data. For example, managers going through training and development programs are simply asked to recall a problem they have encountered and to indicate which of the five styles in the model they used to solve the problem. In addition, managers are given standardized problem cases and are asked which style from the model could best be used to solve each case. Such methods, of course, have a number of internal validity problems (experimenter effect and social desirability effect) and external validity problems (the use of standardized cases in a training situation may not generalize to the real world). In addition to the validity problems of the model, it may also have limited utility for two major reasons: "*First,* it is not as parsimonious as other models of leader decision process choice. *Second*, it deals with only one aspect of leader behavior, that of selecting different decision processes for different problem situations."[20] Vroom answers this criticism by reanalyzing his data and concludes that the relative complexity of his model is justified for predictive purposes.[21] Also, a revision of the model by Vroom and Jago that replaces the yes-no with five-point scales and adds new attributes dealing with time, information, and motivation contains research that indicates greater accuracy of prediction.[22] The most recent test found evidence of the validity of the Vroom-Yetton model with manager data but not subordinate data.[23]

Overall, the Vroom-Yetton model has much surface logic, and it does give precise answers to practicing managers. However, as in the case of the other approaches, more research is needed. On the positive side, its attempt to bridge the gap from theory to practice may be a step in the right direction, and it can serve as a prototype for the actual practice of contingency management.

WOMEN AND LEADERSHIP

In the past couple of decades, there has been considerable interest, both in research and in practice, in women in a leadership role. However, because the societal situation is changing so rapidly, earlier research on women leadership may no longer be relevant. After a recent comprehensive analysis of all aspects of women leaders, Bass concludes the following:

> Despite the many continuing handicaps to movement into positions of leadership owing to socialization, status, conflict, and stereotyping, progress is being made. . . . Characteristics that are usually linked to masculinity are still demanded for effective management. Nevertheless, most differences in male and female leaders tend to be accounted for by other controllable or modifiable factors.[24]

Bass is mainly summarizing the research literature, but a key part of his statement is the initial words, "Despite the many continuing handicaps to movement into positions of leadership." This may drastically understate the still bleak situation of women in leadership roles. Although the U.S. Department of Labor says that going into the 1990s women make up 40 percent of the broad category of managers and administrators, only a minuscule number of women are in the top jobs of America's major corporations. In fact, *Fortune* recently found only nineteen women out of 4,000 officers and directors of the 500 largest firms. Table 11.4 identifies these nineteen top level managers. Importantly, this less than one-half of one percent was about the same number as existed in 1978 and not many more are in the zone for promotion to these top jobs any time soon. The *Fortune* analysis concludes by considering the question, "When will women in decent numbers finally make it into

TABLE 11.4 Top-Level Women Executives Found in Fortune 500 Firms in 1990

Name	Age	Company	Title	1989 Cash Compensation	Family Status
Rosetta Bailey	55	Citizens Federal Bank	Senior vice president	$123,272	Married, two children
Jill Barad	39	Mattel	Division president	$504,923	Married, two children
Ilene Beal	44	BayBanks	Executive vice president	$163,020	Single, no children
Cathleen Black	46	Gannett	Executive vice president	$600,000	Married, one child
Kathryn Braun	39	Western Digital	Senior vice president	$255,365	Married, one stepchild
Jean Carrick	43	Delta Woodside Industries	Corporate controller	$76,342	Divorced, no children
Patricia Dawley	52	Anchor Savings Bank	Executive vice president, secretary	$139,500	Divorced, no children
Katharine Graham	73	Washington Post	Chairman, chief executive officer	$739,874	Widowed, four children
Jane Greer	51	Delta Woodside Industries	Vice president	$166,898	Divorced, no children
Bernice Lavin	64	Alberto-Culver	Vice president, secretary, treasurer	$513,746	Married, three children
Nina McLemore	45	Liz Claiborne	Senior vice president	$600,000	Married, no children
Debbie Miede	34	Downey Savings & Loan	Senior vice president	$140,892	Married, three children
Maria Monet	40	Ogden	Chief financial officer	$733,617	Married, no children
Hazel O'Leary	53	Northern States Power	Senior vice president	$174,170	Widowed, one child
Carole St. Mark	43	Pitney Bowes	Division president	$376,946	Divorced, no children
Mary Sammons	43	Fred Meyer	Senior vice president	$253,847	Married, one child
Marion Sandler	59	Golden West Financial	President, chief executive officer	$665,357	Married, two children
Irene Adams Staskin	60	Kelly Services	Senior vice president	$214,500	Married, two children
Faye Widenmann	41	Pinnacle West Capital	Vice president, secretary	$82,889	Divorced, no children

Adapted from Jaclyn Fierman, "Why Women Still Don't Hit the Top," *Fortune*, July 30, 1990, p. 46.

the highest ranks of corporate America? The short answer: not in this millennium."[25]

This so-called "glass ceiling" is a sober reality. It alone should be enough to stimulate further research and interest in women and leadership. As far as the differences between male and female leadership styles, three distinct points of view have emerged:

1. *No differences:* Women who pursue the nontraditional career of manager reject the feminine stereotype and have needs, values, and leadership styles similar to those of men who pursue managerial careers.
2. *Stereotypical differences:* Female and male managers differ in ways predicted by stereotypes, as a result of early socialization experiences that reinforce masculinity in males and femininity in females.
3. *Nonstereotypical differences:* Female and male managers differ in ways opposite to stereotypes, because women managers have to be exceptional to compensate for early socialization experiences that are different from those of men.[26]

Powell conducted a comprehensive review of the research literature to determine the level of support for each of the above three positions in terms of behavior, motivation, commitment, and subordinates' responses. The results are shown in Table 11.5.[27] He then concludes the following:

TABLE 11.5 Sex Differences Found in the Research

Type of Difference	Research Results Between Men and Women
Behavior	
Task orientation	*No difference.*
People orientation	*No difference.*
Effectiveness ratings	*Stereotypical difference* in evaluations of managers in laboratory studies: Males favored. *No difference* in evaluations of actual managers.
Response to poor performer	*Stereotypical difference:* Males use norm of equity, whereas females use norm of equality.
Influence strategies	*Stereotypical difference:* Males use a wider range of strategies, more positive strategies, and less negative strategies. This difference diminishes when women managers have high self-confidence.
Motivation	*No difference* in some studies.
	Nonstereotypical difference in other studies: Female motivational profile is closer to that associated with successful managers.
Commitment	*Inconsistent evidence* regarding difference.
Subordinates' responses	*Stereotypical difference* in responses to managers in laboratory studies: Managers using style that matches sex role stereotype are favored.
	No difference in responses to actual managers.

Adapted from Gary N. Powell, "One More Time: Do Female and Male Managers Differ?" *Academy of Management Executive*, August 1990, p. 69.

There is little reason to believe that either women or men make superior managers, or that women and men are different types of managers. Instead, there are likely to be excellent, average, and poor managerial performers within each sex. Success in today's highly competitive marketplace calls for organizations to make best use of the talent available to them. To do this, they need to identify, develop, encourage, and promote the most effective managers, regardless of sex.[28]

FROM LEADERSHIP STYLES TO MANAGERIAL ACTIVITIES

So far, in the discussion of leadership, the various theories in the last chapter and the styles in this chapter have been analyzed. In recent years, there has been increasing interest in translating these theories and styles into the actual day-to-day behaviors of managers. The author and his colleagues conducted a comprehensive study to answer three such questions: (1) What do managers do? (2) What do successful managers do? and (3) What do effective managers do?[29] Answers to these questions can provide insights and specific descriptions of the daily activities of successful (those promoted relatively rapidly in their organizations) and effective (those with satisfied and committed subordinates and high-performing units) managers or leaders.

What Do Managers Do?

The so-called "Real Managers Study" first used trained observers to freely observe and record in detail the behaviors and activities of forty-four managers from all levels and types of midwest organizations (retail stores, hospitals, corporate headquarters, a railroad, government agencies, insurance companies, a newspaper office, financial institutions, and manufacturing plants). The voluminous data gathered from the free observation logs were then reduced through the Delphi technique (described in Chapter 17) into twelve categories with observable behavioral descriptors, as shown in Table 11.6. These empirically-derived behavioral descriptors were then conceptually collapsed into the four managerial activities shown in Figure 11.6. Briefly summarized, these activities are as follows:

1. *Communication:* This activity consists of exchanging routine information and processing paperwork. Its observed behaviors include answering procedural questions, receiving and disseminating requested information, conveying the results of meetings, giving or receiving routine information over the phone, processing mail, reading reports, writing reports/memos/letters, routine financial reporting and bookkeeping, and general desk work.

2. *Traditional Management:* This activity consists of planning, decision making, and controlling. Its observed behaviors include setting goals and objectives, defining tasks needed to accomplish goals, scheduling employees, assigning tasks, providing routine instructions, defining problems, handling day-to-day operational crises, deciding what to do, developing new procedures, inspecting work, walking around inspecting the work, monitoring performance data, and doing preventive maintenance.

3. *Human Resource Management:* This activity contains the most behavioral categories: motivating/reinforcing, disciplining/punishing, managing conflict, staffing, and training/developing. Because it was not generally permitted to be observed, the disciplining/punishing category was subsequently dropped from the analysis. The observed behaviors for this activity include allocating formal rewards, asking for input, conveying appreciation, giving credit where due, listening to suggestions, giving positive feedback, group support, resolving conflict between subordinates, appealing to higher authorities or third parties to resolve a dispute, developing job descriptions, reviewing applications, interviewing applicants, filling in where needed, orienting employees, arranging for training, clarifying roles, coaching, mentoring, and walking subordinates through a task.

4. *Networking:* This activity consists of socializing/politicking and interacting with outsiders. The observed behaviors associated with this activity include nonwork-related "chit chat"; informal joking around; discussing rumors, hearsay, and the grapevine; complaining, griping, and putting others down; politicking and gamesmanship; dealing with customers, suppliers, and vendors; attending external meetings; and doing/attending community service events.

The above empirically answers the question of what managers really do. They include some of the classic activities identified by pioneering theorists such as Henri

TABLE 11.6 Managerial Activities and Behavioral Descriptors Derived from Free Observation of Real Managers

1. Planning/Coordinating
  a. setting goals & objectives
  b. defining tasks needed to accomplish goals
  c. scheduling employees, timetables
  d. assigning tasks and providing routine instructions
  e. coordinating activities of each subordinate to keep work running smoothly
  f. organizing the work

2. Staffing
  a. developing job descriptions for position openings
  b. reviewing applications
  c. interviewing applicants
  d. hiring
  e. contacting applicants to inform them of being hired or not
  f. "filling in" where needed

3. Training/Developing
  a. orienting employees, arranging for training seminars, etc.
  b. clarifying roles, duties, job descriptions
  c. coaching, mentoring, walking subordinates through task
  d. helping subordinates with personal development plans

4. Decision Making/Problem Solving
  a. defining problems
  b. choosing between 2 or more alternatives or strategies
  c. handling day-to-day operational crises as they arise
  d. weighing the trade-offs; cost benefit analyses
  e. actually deciding what to do
  f. developing new procedures to increase efficiency

5. Processing Paperwork
  a. processing mail
  b. reading reports, in-box
  c. writing reports, memos, letters, etc.
  d. routine financial reporting and bookkeeping
  e. general desk work

6. Exchanging Routine Information
  a. answering routine procedural questions
  b. receiving and disseminating requested information
  c. conveying results of meetings
  d. giving or receiving routine information over the phone
  e. staff meetings of an informational nature (status update, new company policies, etc.)

7. Monitoring/Controlling Performance
  a. inspecting work
  b. walking around and checking things out, touring
  c. monitoring performance data (e.g., computer printouts, production, financial reports)
  d. preventive maintenance

8. Motivating/Reinforcing
  a. allocating formal organizational rewards
  b. asking for input, participation
  c. conveying appreciation, compliments
  d. giving credit where due
  e. listening to suggestions
  f. giving positive performance feedback
  g. increasing job challenge
  h. delegating responsibility & authority
  i. letting subordinates determine how to do their own work
  j. sticking up for the group to superiors and others, backing a subordinate

9. Disciplining/Punishing
  a. enforcing rules and policies
  b. nonverbal glaring, harassment
  c. demotion, firing, layoff
  d. any formal organizational reprimand or notice
  e. "chewing out" a subordinate, criticizing
  f. giving negative performance feedback

10. Interacting with Outsiders
  a. public relations
  b. customers
  c. contacts with suppliers, vendors
  d. external meetings
  e. community-service activities

11. Managing Conflict
  a. managing interpersonal conflict between subordinates or others
  b. appealing to higher authority to resolve a dispute
  c. appealing to third-party negotiators
  d. trying to get cooperation or consensus between conflicting parties
  e. attempting to resolve conflicts between subordinate and self

12. Socializing/Politicking
  a. nonwork related chit chat (e.g., family or personal matters)
  b. informal "joking around," B.S.
  c. discussing rumors, hearsay, grapevine
  d. complaining, griping, putting others down
  e. politicking, gamesmanship

Source: Adapted from Fred Luthans and Diane Lee Lockwood, "Toward an Observation System for Measuring Leader Behavior in Natural Settings," in J. G. Hunt, D. Hosking, C. Schriesheim, and R. Stewart (eds.), *Leaders and Managers*, Pergamon Press, New York, 1984, p. 122.

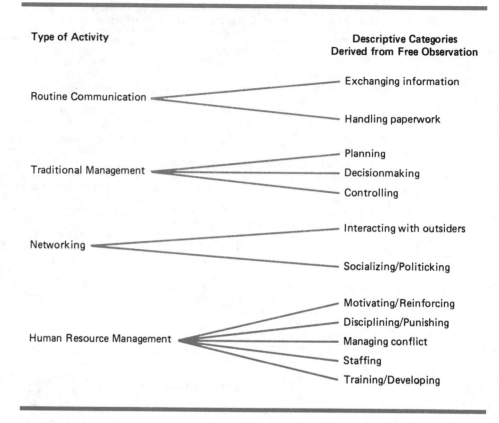

FIGURE 11.6
Conceptual categories of real managers' activities.
(*Source*: Fred Luthans, Richard M. Hodgetts, and Stuart A. Rosenkrantz, *Real Managers*, Ballinger, Cambridge, Mass., 1988, p. 12.

Fayol[30] (the traditional activities), as well as more recent views by modern leadership theorists such as Henry Mintzberg[31] (the communication activities) and John Kotter[32] (the networking activities). As a whole, however, especially with the inclusion of human resource management activities, this view of real managers' activities is more comprehensive than previous studies of management work.

After the nature of managerial activities was determined through the free observation of the 44 managers, the next phase of the study was to determine the relative frequency of these activities. Data on another sample of 248 real managers (not the 44 used in the initial portion of this study but from similar organizations) were gathered. Trained participant observers filled out a checklist based on the managerial activities shown in Table 11.6 at a random time, once every hour, over a two-week period. As shown in Figure 11.7, the managers were found to spend about a third of their time and effort in communication activities, a third in traditional management activities, a fifth in human resource management activities, and a fifth in networking activities. This relative-frequency analysis—based on observational data of a large sample—provides a fairly confident answer to the question of what real managers do.

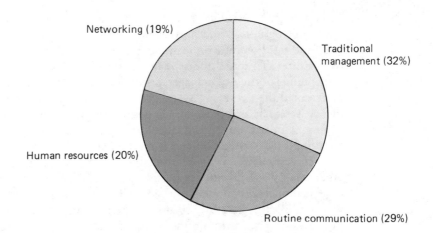

FIGURE 11.7
Relative distribution of real managers' activities.
(*Source*: Fred Luthans, Richard M. Hodgetts, and Stuart A. Rosenkrantz, *Real Managers*, Ballinger, Cambridge, Mass., 1988, p. 27.)

What Do Successful Real Managers Do?

Important though it is to get an empirical answer to the basic question of what managers do, of even greater interest is determining what successful and effective managers do. Success was defined in terms of the speed of promotion within an organization. A success index on the sample in the study was calculated by dividing the managers' levels in their respective organizations by their tenure (length of service) there. Thus, a manager at the fourth level of management who has been with the organization for five years would be rated more successful than a manager at the third level who had been at that level for twenty-five years. Obviously, there are some potential problems with such a measure of success, but for the large sample of managers, this was an objective and useful measure.

To answer the question of what successful managers do, several types of analyses were conducted. In all of these analyses, the importance of networking in real managers' success was very apparent. Of the four major activities, only networking had a statistically significant relationship with success.[33] Overall, it was clear that networking made the biggest relative contribution to manager success and, importantly, human resources management activities made the least relative contribution.

What does this mean? It means that in this study of real managers, using speed of promotion as the measure of success, it was found that successful managers spend relatively more time and effort socializing, politicking, and interacting with outsiders than did their less successful counterparts. Perhaps equally important, the successful managers did not give relatively as much time or attention to the traditional management activities of planning, decision making, and controlling or to the human resources management activities of motivating/reinforcing, staffing, training/developing, and managing conflict. In other words, for the real managers in this study, networking seems to be the key to success (as defined by rapid promotion).

What Do Effective Real Managers Do?

Although the operational measure of success used in the study was empirical and direct, the definition and measurement of effectiveness was more indirect and elusive. The vast literature on managerial effectiveness offers little agreement on criteria or measures. To overcome as many of the obstacles and disagreements as possible, for a sample of the real managers, the study used a combined effectiveness index that represented the two major—and generally agreed upon—criteria of both leadership theory/research and practice: (1) getting the job done through high quantity and quality standards of performance, and (2) getting the job done through people, requiring their satisfaction and commitment.

In particular, an organizational effectiveness questionnaire[34] that measures the unit's quality and quantity of performance, a job satisfaction questionnaire[35], and an organizational commitment questionnaire[36] were used. This multiple-measure index was employed in the study to answer the most important question of what effective managers do. It was found that communication and human resources management activities made by far the largest relative contribution to the managers' effectiveness, and that the traditional management activities, and especially the networking activities, made by far the least relative contribution. In other words, if effectiveness is defined as the perceived quantity and quality of the performance of a manager's unit and his or her subordinates' satisfaction and commitment, then the biggest relative contribution to leadership effectiveness comes from the human-oriented activities—communication and human resource management.

Another intriguing finding from this part of the study was that the least relative contribution to the managers' measured effectiveness came from the networking activity. This, of course, is in stark contrast to the results of the successful manager analysis. Networking activity had by far the strongest relative relationship to success, but the weakest to effectiveness. On the other hand, human resources management activities had a strong relationship to effectiveness (second only to also human-oriented communication activities), but had the weakest relative relationship to success. In other words, the successful managers in this study did not do the same activities as the effective managers (in fact, they did almost the opposite). These contrasting profiles may have significant implications for understanding the current performance problems facing today's organizations.

Implications of the Real Managers Study

The Real Managers Study is obviously bound by the definitions that were used, and, of course, one could question the generalizability of the findings and conclusions to all managers. Yet, despite these limitations, there seem to be a number of important implications for the application of leadership in today's organizations. Probably the major implication stems from the significant difference between the activities of successful and effective managers. The most obvious implication from this finding is that more attention may need to be given to formal reward systems so that effective managers are promoted. Organizations need to tie formal rewards (especially promotions) to performance, in order to move ahead and meet the challenges that lie ahead. This can be accomplished most pragmatically in the short run by performance-based appraisal and reward systems and in the long run by developing cultural values that support and reward effective performance, not just successful socializing and politicking. An important goal to meet the challenges of the years ahead might be as simple as making effective managers successful.

Besides the implications for performance-based appraisal and reward systems and organizational culture, much can be learned from the effective managers in the study. In particular, it is important to note the relative importance that they gave to the human-oriented activities of communication and human resource management. The effective managers' day-to-day activities revolved around their people—keeping them informed, answering questions, getting and giving information, processing information, giving feedback and recognition, resolving conflicts, and conducting training and development. In other words, these effective managers provide some answers to how to meet the challenges that lie ahead. Human-oriented leadership skills and techniques may be of considerable value in meeting the challenges of global competition, of information, and of quality service.

LEADERSHIP SKILLS AND TECHNIQUES FOR THE FUTURE

As organizations head into the new millennium, leaders need to recognize that training their people should become a top priority. The Japanese, of course, have placed a high priority on training all along and it is a major reason for their tremendous success. Recently, however, premier American corporations have also become committed to the importance of training. For example, all employees at the highly successful Quad Graphics firm spend considerable time every week in training sessions—on their own time—to improve themselves and make their company more competitive. A major component of the Motorola "quality revolution" was that spending on employee training went to $100 million per year, with 40 percent directly devoted to the skills and procedures needed to produce a no-defect product or to provide timely, error-free, courteous service to internal and external customers. Old job-rotation training programs have also come to life at companies such as McDonnell Douglas, where they follow the adage that there is no training experience better than "walking a mile in the other person's shoes." The same goes for cross-training and the newer "pay for knowledge" approaches that an increasing number of U.S. firms are beginning to implement.

Besides training, job redesign is another important technique leaders need to implement. Covered in Chapter 7, this approach attempts to manage the job rather than the extremely complex person that holds the job. From enriching the job by building in more responsibility, the more recent approach is to concentrate on the characteristics of identity, variety, significance, autonomy, and feedback identified by Hackman and his colleagues and covered in Chapter 7. Importantly, there has been a stream of research to support the concept that when employees perceive these characteristics in their job, they do high quality work. Leaders need to give special attention to the autonomy and feedback characteristics of their people's jobs. Autonomy involves empowering their subordinates to make decisions and solve their own problems. In other words, giving them more control over their own job. Feedback can be built into some jobs, but leaders also must provide specific, immediate performance feedback to their people.

Finally, the behavioral management approach, covered in Chapter 9, could be effectively used by leaders to meet the challenges ahead. The organizational behavior modification (O.B. Mod.) techniques based on the principles of operant conditioning and social learning theory were shown in Chapter 9 to have dramatic results on human performance in organizations. Importantly, O.B. Mod. interventions have used mainly nonfinancial rewards—feedback systems and contingent recognition/attention in both manufacturing and service organizations.

The intent of this discussion is not to give an exhaustive list of leadership skills and techniques. All the theories and styles discussed in this chapter and the last chapter, plus the techniques discussed in the motivation and learning chapters, are relevant and can be effective. Obviously, there are many other leadership skills and techniques. However, the chapters in this part of the book on the theories and applications of motivation, learning, and leadership provide the heart of what organizational behavior is all about and what it can contribute to meeting the challenges of today and tomorrow.

Summary

There are many style implications in both the classic leadership studies and the modern theories. Blake and Mouton's managerial grid, Hersey and Blanchard's situational model, and Likert's four systems focus attention directly on leadership styles. Each of these is of value in relation to the actual practice of human resources management. The grid is valuable mainly because it allows managers to describe their styles. Hersey and Blanchard's approach shows how well managers can match the appropriate style with the maturity level of the group being led, and Likert's work has implications for organizational effectiveness. Likert's recognition of intervening variables and their time lag effects has significant implications for practice. Finally, the Vroom-Yetton model attempts to prescribe exactly what style to use in a given situation. However, all these approaches to style need more and better research in order to make meaningful contributions to the actual practice of human resources management in the future.

In recent times, there has been considerable interest and concern about women and leadership. The research generally suggests that there is little difference between men and women managers in terms of their style or effectiveness. However, the cold facts are that women have not, are not, and probably will not in the foreseeable future break through the glass ceiling into top level leadership positions in organizations. There is still a need to establish true equal opportunity for top leadership positions.

The last part of the chapter provides answers from an extensive observational study to the question of what managers do in their day-to-day activities and what successful and effective managers do. It was found that the managers spend about a third of their time and effort in communication activities, a third in traditional management activities, a fifth in human resources management activities, and a fifth in networking activities. The analysis of successful managers (those rapidly promoted) found that networking made the biggest relative contribution to their rise and human resources management activities the least. In contrast, however, the analysis of effective managers (those with satisfied and committed subordinates and high-performing units) found that communication and human resources management activities made the largest relative contribution and networking the least. This difference between successful and effective managers has considerable implications for how one gets ahead in an organization (networking involves socializing/politicking and interacting with outsiders) and the reward systems of organizations (the effective managers may not be promoted as fast as the politically savvy ones). In short, leaders, both the successful and the effective ones, have considerable challenges ahead. A commitment to training, as well as job design and behavioral management skills as discussed in the chapters in this part of the book, may help meet these challenges.

Questions for Discussion and Review

1. What are some styles of charismatic leadership? What do they mean? Give an example.
2. Briefly identify the major styles from Blake and Mouton's grid, from Hersey and Blanchard's situational model, and from Likert's four systems. Which are more effective or less effective?
3. What is the current status of women in a leadership role? What is meant by the "glass ceiling"? Is it a reality?
4. Based on the "Real Managers" study, briefly summarize the answers to the following: What do managers do? What do successful managers do? What do effective managers do?

References

1. David A. Nadler and Michael L. Tushman, "Beyond the Charismatic Leader: Leadership and Organizational Change," *California Management Review*, Winter 1990, p. 83.
2. "Changing Perspectives," *The Wall Street Journal*, Nov. 25, 1986, p. 1.
3. Warren G. Bennis, "Managing the Dream: Leadership in the 21st Century," *Journal of Organizational Change Management*, vol. 2, no. 1, 1989, p. 6.
4. Robert Blake and Jane S. Mouton, "Should You Teach There's Only One Best Way to Manage?" *Training HRD*, April 1978, p. 24.
5. Robert Blake and Jane S. Mouton, "Management by Grid Principles or Situationalism: Which?" *Group and Organization Studies*, December 1981, pp. 439–455.
6. Paul Hersey and Kenneth H. Blanchard, *Management of Organizational Behavior*, 4th ed., Prentice-Hall, Englewood Cliffs, N.J., 1982.
7. Gary A. Yukl, *Leadership in Organizations*, Prentice-Hall, Englewood Cliffs, N.J., 1981, pp. 143–144.
8. Claude L. Graeff, "The Situational Leadership Theory: A Critical View," *Academy of Management Review*, April 1983, pp. 285–291.
9. Warren Blank, John R. Weitzel, and Stephen G. Green, "A Test of the Situational Leadership Theory," *Personnel Psychology*, vol. 43, 1990, pp. 579–597.
10. Rensis Likert, *The Human Organization*, McGraw-Hill, New York, 1967, pp. 3, 11.
11. Ibid., pp. 26, 29.
12. Ibid., pp. 80–81.

13. Eugene J. Webb, Donald T. Campbell, Richard D. Schwartz, and Lee Sechrest, *Unobtrusive Measures: Nonreactive Research in the Social Sciences*, Rand McNally, Chicago, 1966.

14. Likert, *The Human Organization*, p. 192.

15. Jan P. Muczyk and Bernard C. Reimann, "The Case for Directive Leadership," *The Academy of Management Executive*, November 1987, p. 309.

16. Victor H. Vroom and Philip W. Yetton, *Leadership and Decision-Making*, University of Pittsburgh Press, Pittsburgh, 1973, chap. 3.

17. For example, see Thomas E. Hill and Neal Schmitt, "Individual Differences in Leadership Decision Making," *Organizational Behavior and Human Performance*, August 1977, pp. 353–367; Victor Vroom and Arthur G. Jago, "A Test of Spuriousness in Descriptive Models of Participative Leader Behavior," *Journal of Applied Psychology*, April 1978, pp. 151–162; and Charles Margerison and Richard Glube, "Leadership Decision-Making: An Empirical Test of the Vroom-Yetton Model," *Journal of Management Studies*, February 1979, pp. 45–55.

18. R. H. George Field, "A Critique of the Vroom-Yetton Model of Leadership Behavior," *Academy of Management Review*, April 1979, pp. 249–257; and Larry E. Pate and D. C. Heiman, "A Test of the Vroom-Yetton Decision Model in Seven Field Settings," *Personnel Review*, vol. 16, no. 2, 1987, pp. 22–26.

19. William C. Wedley and R. H. George Field, "The Vroom-Yetton Model: Are Feasible Set Choices Due to Chance?" *Proceedings of the Academy of Management*, New York, 1982, pp. 146–150.

20. Field, op. cit., p. 256.

21. Arthur G. Jago and Victor H. Vroom, "An Evaluation of Two Alternatives to the Vroom-Yetton Normative Model," *Academy of Management Journal*, June 1980, pp. 347–355.

22. Arthur G. Jago, Jennifer T. Ettling, and Victor H. Vroom, "Validating a Revision to the Vroom/Yetton Model: First Evidence," *Proceedings of the Academy of Management*, 1985, pp. 220–223. For a complete discussion of the new model see V. H. Vroom and A. G. Jago, *The New Leadership: Managing Participation in Organizations*, Prentice-Hall, Englewood Cliffs, N.J., 1987.

23. Richard H. G. Field and Robert J. House, "A Test of the Vroom-Yetton Model Using Manager and Subordinate Reports," *Journal of Applied Psychology*, vol. 75, no. 3, 1990, pp. 362–366.

24. Bernard M. Bass, *Bass & Stodgill's Handbook of Leadership*, Free Press, New York, 1990, p. 737.

25. Jaclyn Fierman, "Why Women Still Don't Hit the Top," *Fortune*, July 30, 1990, p. 40.

26. Gary Powell, "One More Time: Do Female and Male Managers Differ?" *Academy of Management Executive*, August 1990, p. 69.

27. Also see Alice H. Eagly and Blair T. Johnson, "Gender and Leadership Style: A Meta-Analysis," *Psychological Bulletin*, September 1990, pp. 233–236.

28. Powell, op. cit., p. 74.

29. The following sections are drawn from Fred Luthans, Richard M. Hodgetts, and Stuart A. Rosenkrantz, *Real Managers*, Ballinger, Cambridge, Mass., 1988; and Fred Luthans, "Successful vs. Effective Real Managers," *Academy of Management Executive*, May 1988, pp. 127–132. The very extensive study took place over a four-year period.

30. See Henri Fayol, *General and Industrial Management* (trans. Constance Storrs), Pitman, London, 1949.

31. See Henry Mintzberg, *The Nature of Managerial Work*, Harper & Row, New York, 1973, and Henry Mintzberg, "The Manager's Job: Folklore and Fact," *Harvard Business Reviw*, July–August, 1975, pp. 49–61.

32. See John Kotter, *The General Managers*, Free Press, New York, 1982, and John Kotter, "What Do Effective General Managers Really Do?" *Harvard Business Review*, November–December 1982, pp. 156–167.

33. Fred Luthans, Stuart Rosenkrantz, and Harry Hennessey, "What Do Successful Managers Really Do?" *Journal of Applied Behavioral Science*, August 1985, pp. 255–270.

34. Paul E. Mott, *The Characteristics of Effective Organizations*, Harper & Row, New York, 1972.

35. P. C. Smith, L. M. Kendall, and C. L. Hulin, *The Measurement of Satisfaction in Work and Retirement*, Rand-McNally, Chicago, 1969.

36. Richard T. Mowday, L. W. Porter, and Richard M. Steers, *Employee-Organizational Linkages: The Psychology of Commitment, Absenteeism, and Turnover*, Academic Press, New York, 1982.

**REAL CASE:
LEADING
THEM
INTO THE
21st
CENTURY**

Robert Horton, chairman of British Petroleum (BP), has one of the toughest jobs in the oil industry. BP gets 80 percent of its oil production from two giant but aging fields: Prudhoe Bay in Alaska and the Forties field in the North Sea. These fields were discovered and developed over twenty years ago and their output is now declining at the rate of about ten percent annually. Horton at present faces two major challenges: (1) find new sources of energy and (2) trim expenses so that the company is operating as leanly and productively as possible. Can Horton do it? One observer has noted the following:

> Meeting the challenges will require formidable leadership talent, which Horton appears to have plenty of. In the 1980s, he was the company's top troubleshooter. First, he hacked the refining and chemical division into profitability, earning the moniker Horton the Hatchet. In 1986, he went to Cleveland to restructure Standard Oil of Ohio, cutting middle management and overseeing BP's acquisition of the 45 percent of Sohio it didn't already own.
>
> At the same time, Horton has a knack for carrying out the unpleasantness of restructuring while stirring up a minimum of resentment. For example, while he was in Cleveland, he joined the Cleveland Orchestra board of directors and, at the same time, cut the company's contribution to charity by almost $4 million. At BP, he is cutting payroll and reassigning people. In the process, eighty standing committees and six of the eleven managerial levels in the structure have been eliminated. He has also empowered his people down the line so that they now can make expenditures of more than two-and-a-half times (on average) what they used to without getting prior approval; and spending authorizations that required a dozen signatures now need but two or three. Horton has also organized the corporate staff into teams, reporting directly to him, to the chief executive officer, or to one of the four division heads; and information services, a huge central facility in most companies, has been broken up and decentralized within the four divisions.
>
> Will Horton's leadership style prove effective in ensuring BP's future? Some employees think that a lot of things are being done but they probably will not make much difference in the long run. Others agree with the employee who said, "People here are not as cynical as I expected. They're saying, 'Okay, I'll give it a try.'"

1. Is Robert Horton a Theory X or a Theory Y manager? Defend your reasoning.
2. In terms of the managerial grid (see Figure 11.2), how would you describe Robert Horton?
3. How do you think Horton spends his day in terms of managerial activities? Use Figure 11.7 as a point of reference.

**Case:
If It Is Good
Enough for
Us, It Is
Good
Enough for
Them**

Jesse White is a training specialist for the personnel department of a large company. His boss, Rose O'Brien, called him in one day and said that she had just come back from an executive committee meeting. She had been given the charge of developing a leadership training program for all middle management personnel in the firm. She told Jesse that he would be in charge of the project. Jesse wanted to know what the objectives of the program were supposed to be. Rose replied that the top management of the company were concerned that the styles they were using now and had used in the past were not being used by the middle managers. For example, the executive vice president was concerned that the younger lower/middle managers were too idealistic about how to treat people. The others had all agreed with this observation. Then the vice president for finance added that it was their styles that had taken this company to the top of the industry, and if it was good enough for them, it should be good enough for the middle managers. Rose then said, "I have to follow orders so what I would like you to do is first get a good understanding of the modern theoretical basis for leadership. Then find out what styles of leadership the president and the vice presidents are using in their present jobs. Based upon the theory and what you find out about their present styles, design a program that I can present to the executive committee for middle management leadership training."

1. Do you agree with the approach outlined by Rose to set up the training program? If you were Jesse, what would be some important theoretical considerations that would go into your program? What techniques would you use to determine the top managers' present styles?
2. On the basis of the comments of the executive vice president and the vice president for finance, what styles do you feel you would find for the top managers? For the middle managers? How would you be able to justify a program that was different from the styles of the top managers?
3. Using the Blake and Mouton, Hersey and Blanchard, or Likert approach to style, describe some of the details and implications of your leadership program.

Case:
The Puppet

Rex Justice is a long-term employee of the Carfax Corporation, and for the last several years he has been a supervisor in the financial section of the firm. He is very loyal to Carfax and works hard to follow the company policies and procedures and the orders of the managers above him. In fact, upper-level management think very highly of him; they can always count on Rex to meet any sort of demand that the company places on him. He is valued and well liked by all the top managers. His employees in the financial section have the opposite opinion of Rex. They feel that he is too concerned with pleasing the upper-level brass and not nearly concerned enough with the needs and concerns of the employees in his department. For example, they feel that Rex never really pushes hard enough for a more substantial slice of the budget. Relative to other departments in the company, they feel thay are underpaid and overworked. Also, whenever one of them goes to Rex with a new idea or suggestion for improvement he always seems to have five reasons why it can't be done. There is considerable dissatisfaction in the department, and everyone thinks that Rex is just a puppet for management. Performance has begun to suffer because of his style and leadership. Upper-level management seem to be oblivious to the situation in the finance section.

1. How would you explain Rex's leadership style in terms of one or more of the theories discussed in the chapter?
2. What advice would you give Rex to improve his leadership style?
3. Could a leadership training program be set up to help Rex? What would it consist of?

INTEGRATIVE CONTEMPORARY CASE FOR PART 3

Farewell
Fast Track

If you're a fast-tracker aiming to nab the top job one day, you know you should model your career after that of the current boss, right? Well, guess again. At Du Pont Co., Edgar S. Woolard, Jr.'s dash up the ladder took him through a dizzying 20 jobs in 32 years. The longest he spent in any one position was three years; the shortest, five months. But the 56-year-old chief executive's successor—whoever he or she is—isn't likely to be someone who zipped through so many posts.

That's because there are a lot fewer promotions to go around. In 1985, the chemicals giant led the parade of big companies making deep cuts in work forces. With employment now slashed by 12,000 to 145,000, the $36 billion company has a flatter organization chart and shorter chains of command. In a

HOW TO KEEP MANAGERS MOTIVATED

The steady pruning of middle management presents many companies with a problem. Fewer layers mean fewer promotions for promising young managers. A more sluggish economy means less money for raises. So how can companies keep people happy, hard-working, and creative now that the traditional career ladder has lost many of its rungs?

Offer lateral movement. It used to be a way to ease managers out. Now it's a way to round them out with fresh challenges. But handle with care: Make it clear that sideways moves aren't a dead end by offering them both to stars and to journeymen.

Turn over more responsibility. Offer managers more to do—more people to supervise, more areas to influence. Greater control can be more meaningful than a loftier title or even more pay.

Tie raises to performance, not seniority. Reduce the number of pay grades to get maximum flexibility in giving raises. That makes it easier to reward people for results, even without an upgrade in title. And broader pay bands pose fewer obstacles to people who want to move across divisions. Don't worry if younger top performers take home more than the seasoned folks who have simply logged the hours.

Let managers just say 'no'. Don't penalize those who turn down transfers or promotions, especially with today's family-cherishing managers. They may feel they're not

ready or may want to learn all they can in a current post. Reverse the Peter Principle.

Offer offshore moves. An overseas assignment gives managers a chance to try something new. And their experience will be a plus for increasingly global companies. At Du Pont, for example, where almost half of sales are foreign, a stint overseas is becoming essential for promotion to top management.

Provide mid-career breaks. Send promising executives to management development programs at business schools. They can help prepare someone with a specialized background —in science, for example—for general management responsibilities. People will feel rewarded, and the company will get a more skilled employee.

Give more power. Offer autonomy. Make managers feel like owners—and they'll perform better than if they feel like bureaucrats who have to ask permission at every step. Harness their entrepreneurial impulses before those impulses make them decide to try it on their own.

Source: Reprinted from Dec. 10, 1990 issue of *Business Week* by special permission, copyright © by McGraw-Hill, Inc.

late-September steamlining, Du Pont even eliminated its executive committee, a group of top managers who ruled the company for decades. The group also was the pool from which Du Pont drew its CEOs. With the changes have come less upward mobility and smaller raises. The result: concern among Du Pont's top managers over how to motivate their stars now that the traditional incentives and rewards have grown scarce.

So Many Boomers. Welcome to the Slow Track. Throughout Corporate America, companies are advancing managers less often even as they are demanding more of them. The thinning of middle-management ranks nationwide has been profound. U.S. companies have eliminated nearly one of every four such positions since 1980, estimates Ross A. Webber, a management professor at the University of Pennsylvania's Wharton School. "In the heyday of expansions in the late 1960s and early 1970s, fast-trackers were being promoted every 18 to 24 months," Webber says. "The length of time has at least doubled."

Pay prospects have dimmed, too. Middle managers starting a career in 1975 could have expected to nearly triple their salary in 10 years, says Ira T. Kay, a managing director at Hay Group Inc., a management consultancy. Today's tyro managers will be lucky to double their pay by 2000. Worse, the slots and raises are dwindling just as the number of aspirants jockeying for them is ballooning. At a median age of 33, the 81 million baby boomers are beginning to clog the ranks of management.

Most companies haven't yet figured out how to keep their hard-chargers energized as reality sets in. Nearly 70% of the respondents to a recent survey of 700 managers complained that they were dissatisfied both with their responsibilities and attainments, according to the survey's sponsors, recruiting firm Korn/Ferry International and the University of California at Los Angeles. "There is a grudging awareness and acknowledgment that there is a slowing down, that organizations are flatter, and that there are fewer levels to go to," says Harold E. Johnson, a Korn/Ferry managing vice-president. "The younger managers I see are not very happy about it." Such attitudes, Johnson says, are making companies worry about how to keep their hotshots "tuned in and turned on."

That's likely to become an even more pressing concern as the U.S. economy slips into recession. The management ladder is losing still more rungs as companies ranging from investment banks to computer makers, broadcasters, and airlines take the ax to their work forces. And as austerity settles in, raises and bonuses are being further squeezed.

Fear Strikes Out. In an era of layoffs, fear becomes a powerful motivator. But it's not a particularly useful one. Fear stifles innovation and risk-taking while prompting inertia, caution, and buck-passing. "People have to figure out creative ways to do their jobs differently and better" in tough economic times, says John W. Himes, vice-president for human resources at Du Pont. "You really need them not to be sitting around worrying about losing their jobs."

The 1990s promise to be a time when American companies will place heavier demands than ever on their managers—and that means the problem of how to keep valuable talents motivated will pose one of the most important management challenges of the decade. It's one that's already preoccupying companies such as General Electric, PepsiCo, Merck, Hewlett-Packard, Hyatt, and Hughes Aircraft. Along with Du Pont, these companies are exploring a broad array of techniques to help managers adjust to life in the slow lane. In the face of defense cutbacks, Hughes, for example, has eliminated 14,000 jobs, or 17% of its total, and wiped out two middle-management layers since 1985. Now, it's encouraging managers it can no longer promote so quickly to consider lateral moves instead. An electrical engineer, for example, might switch to quality control.

And at Hyatt Corp., the sheer number of promising young managers means that each must wait longer before getting the chance to run a hotel. So the company is encouraging staffers to start new businesses. Other companies are offering transfers overseas to provide variety. Some allow staffers to shoulder more responsibility or grant them more autonomy. Some let managers go on sabbatical to study. And some are tinkering with pay scales, making them less rigid and tying compensation to performance rather than title.

In their most successful forms, these efforts do more than keep up-and-comers temporarily content: They yield broader benefits for the corporation down the line. A transfer abroad, for example, can offer a young manager a change. But it also creates an executive with international experience that an employer is likely to find valuable in an increasingly global business world.

Similarly, the Slow Track eliminates some of the problems lurking behind the old fast-track system. The era of rapid promotions created a cadre of executives whose experience was often shallow. Their brief tenures in any one job gave them little knowledge of follow-through and helped foster a short-term focus. "You would put a lot of initiatives in place, but then you would be transferred before you saw the result," Woolard recalls. "You were robbed of

Experiments in Motivation

GE	Hewlett-Packard	Merck
Cut the number of pay grades and broadened them dramatically to allow more latitude in raises. Also trimmed management layers from 10 to 4	Set up a technical track to let scientists advance without taking on management tasks. Now, technicians don't have to manage people to move up	Offers variety in career development. For example, scientists can attend law school and become patent attorneys. Encourages movement abroad

PepsiCo	TRW	Intel
Encourages lateral movement across divisions. Also broadening jobs, so a Taco Bell benefits-plan manager, for instance, can take on recruiting and planning, too	Offers 'technical fellowships' to engineers, who get generous research budgets and broad latitude to work on projects. Spurs teamwork by sharing Pentagon bonuses	Experimenting with job-sharing, putting as many as three managers on teams so fewer people can do more work. Even the chief executive and chairman share jobs

the pleasure of the success—or of the learning experience if it didn't work out."

'Retrogression.' Getting up-and-comers to accept the realities of diminished career expectations won't be easy, though. Donald C. Hambrick, a professor of management at Columbia University business school, notes that the thinning of middle management has spawned a serious morale problem among the survivors, who find that their jobs have broadened—downward. "The remaining middle manager is stuck not only with the work he was originally doing but the stuff his fired subordinates were doing," Hambrick says. "You've got career retrogression, where 45-year-olds find themselves doing things they did when they were in their 30s."

Even when jobs are broadened in the best sense to make up for the lack of traditional advancement, employers face stiff morale challenges. For starters, managers will have to be persuaded to ignore the time-honored cultural signposts they've used to gauge their standing in the career race. Their employers must make it clear that longer tenures and overseas moves aren't the kisses of death they once were.

And ultimately, there's the risk that the very best and brightest simply won't accept the Slow Track, but will choose to look elsewhere for the rewards their present employers can't offer. The slower pace at Du Pont worries some managers, who say they'll look outside the company if they start to feel bogged down. "My loyalty to Du Pont is not what it was," says one 13-year veteran.

To make such defections a little less likely, Du Pont is trying to reward managers with more autonomy. Five years ago, Kurt M. Landgraf found the hassles of starting new projects daunting: Proposals had to survive four levels of review. As a result, he says, Du Pont lost out on the opportunity to license some promising drugs in Europe.

Now, the 44-year-old division director feels free to take some chances. Two years ago, his request for $5 million to start a new generic-drug venture needed approval from only one manager above him. Just named executive vice-president of the newly formed Du Pont Merck Pharmaceutical Co. joint venture, he happily intends to stay in his post long enough to see the venture fly or fail.

The longer leashes are good for the company, too. Productivity among researchers has risen dramatically in Du Pont's $1.7 billion electronics business, which makes materials used in electronic gear, says Donald B. Rogers, a vice-president in charge of the R&D unit. Back when the unit had as many as 16 research managers, experimenters had to devote much time to bureaucratic busywork, such as filing weekly reports on projects. Rogers now has only two research managers in his group.

More Work. Now that researchers are freed of such time-wasters, more work gets done—and some of it is more venturesome, too. Earlier this year, for example, Du Pont introduced its Riston coated film, which is used in printed circuit boards, less than six weeks after customers asked for it. A few years ago, it would have spent six months in exhaustive internal testing and review. It's a smash product, too. "We broke a lot of historic protocols," Rogers says.

Du Pont and other companies are also hoping to use lateral moves as a motivating technique. Pay and title may stay the same, but a new challenge gets managerial juices flowing. At PepsiCo Inc., a lateral move used to be the equivalent of a death warrant. Now, it's standard for 6 of every 10 management-track staffers. For example, prized executives often bounce from the Kentucky Fried Chicken unit to Frito-Lay and overseas. The symbolism of such moves has changed, says Andrew S. Grove, chief executive of Intel Corp.: "The world accepts more career diversity than it used to. You can zigzag your way up and down and still hold up your head at the neighborhood store."

Bigger Pictures. Such zigzagging should help broaden U.S. managers, who have too often risen along narrow paths—advancing, say, up the marketing ranks—before getting more general management experience. "They then have a limited understanding of the business, because they've spent their entire careers in one function," says Edward E. Lawler, professor of management at the University of Southern California.

By contrast, Lawler says, the Japanese typically give their younger managers broad experience first and wind up with senior managers who know their businesses and companies far better. So at Du Pont, promising engineers who join the company now commonly go through a six-year initiation period, working in three different areas before settling in one department.

Academics are encouraged by another tool: the offshore move. Merck & Co., for instance, shipped a personnel director from the U.S. to Norway to give him breadth of experience. He got no new title and not much more money, but some worthwhile diversity on his resumé. "He did it for the experience," says Steven M. Darien, vice-president for human resources at Merck. Adventure isn't the only selling point: At Du Pont, where nearly half the sales are foreign, overseas tours are becoming *de rigueur* for eventual moves up.

New Balance. Du Pont is also sending some promising executives on academic sabbatical. Phyllis K. Allen, a 41-year-old molecular biologist who came to Du Pont when it acquired her nuclear-medicine company, took a three-month executive-development program at Massachusetts Institute of Technology's Sloan School of Management. The program gave Allen, a scientist who is destined for broad management responsibilities, her first formal education in such general management skills as financial planning. And for its $30,000 investment, Du Pont has won her renewed loyalty. "It was a tremendous commitment to me as an individual," she says.

For all the worry, there are plenty of managers who aren't alarmed by the Slow Track. Those who get their job satisfaction more out of what they do than what they're called aren't complaining. "I'm looking for the experience. I don't get a lot of ego gratification out of title," says Susan M. Stalnecker, comptroller of Du Pont's $1.8 billion agricultural-products unit. "Some of my white male counterparts really are a lot more hung up on advancing than I am." And as a mother of 6-year-old twins, the 37-year-old says that a more sensible pace sounds good: "I'm a wife and mother, and my job comes third."

Such priorities don't seem to have hurt her. Over the past 14 years,

Stalnecker rose from a modest corporate-finance staff slot through several management posts. She went part-time for three years to tend to her family before heading off to London in 1987. There, she soon rose to become treasurer and a director of a unit of Conoco, Du Pont's oil-and-gas arm. Now back in the company's hometown of Wilmington, Del., she would gladly stay in her ag-products post for years. "The notion of being bored? I can't even relate to that," she says. "On balance, people are happier with a system that develops them without the necessity of constantly moving up in order to be perceived as growing."

Academics and personnel managers argue that men and women alike want to strike a better balance among outside interests, family, and career. "With so many dual-career couples and so many mothers in the work force, there is just a practical need for additional flexibility," says Art F. Strohmer, Jr., director for executive staffing and development at Merck. These days, business students aren't just willing to settle for a slower climb: Some demand it. Says University of Southern California business administration professor Warren Bennis: "There's a feeling among the younger people, even at the business school at USC, that work is overrated."

The Slow Track lets companies accommodate that feeling. Some veterans admit that they regret spending more time in the office than today's younger managers. And some now say they won't penalize someone who refuses a career move for domestic reasons. "When I started working, if you turned down a promotion, you could forget about your career," says Landgraf, the Du Pont pharmaceuticals executive. "Now, it's widely accepted that people can and do turn down promotions and relocations."

Personal Growth. Still, work is inescapably the first priority for many. To help its managers thread their way through the new career maze, Du Pont offers more than the standard annual performance evaluations. Executives in Stalnecker's 120-person division have frequent informal talks with managers to set personal growth goals and chart out a path to reach them. "In the past, these were oriented to: 'What job am I getting next?'" says Stalnecker. "Now, it's more: 'How can I be developed as a person?'" Suggestions might include inhouse management training or outside volunteer work with United Way. Managers also size up the development efforts that their supervisors are making for them.

As management ladders change, experimentation is continuing at many companies. At Intel, CEO Grove recently let a valued but tired 16-year veteran turn his job over to another manager, take a pay cut, and report to his successor. After a one-year break-in period, the veteran will switch to an even less demanding post. But the new job will be "something that will charge up his juices again," Grove says.

Grove also now has executives sharing jobs: He shares the president's role, dubbed the "Executive Office," with Chairman Gordon E. Moore and Executive Vice-President Craig R. Barrett, for instance. Grove focuses on management issues and product strategy, while Moore concentrates on financial matters and Barrett on operations. Such team approaches are needed, Grove says, because more work is being done nowadays by fewer people.

Science-driven companies are also exploring different ways to advance their people. Technical whizzes disinclined to management at some companies now have so-called science or technical ladders they can climb without taking on supervisory chores. Merck gives its top scientists free rein in research, so long as their work shows promise of a new drug. Hewlett-Packard Co. has just set up a technical track to pay R&D project managers based on the scope of their research work instead of management chores. And in October, TRW Inc.'s space and defense business named its first 19 "technical fellows," who will receive generous research budgets and broad latitude to pursue projects unfettered by frequent reviews or reports.

To adjust to the leaner styles, companies are also changing longtime pay practices. Since General Electric Chief Executive John F. Welch, Jr., compressed 10 layers of management into 4, the company has replaced its longstanding 29-tier pay scale with a 5-level scheme. Pay grades 8 through 11, for example, have been compressed into a single band ranging from $33,000 to $74,000. The broader bands make lateral movement easier. A finance manager at the old level 9 who wanted to try marketing would have been stymied if the post he coveted was a level 8. With the wider bands, the manager can try a new area but avoid taking a step down.

Experimenting with wage scales can be risky, though. Two years ago, Du Pont's $6 billion-a-year fibers business tied raises to the unit's profits. With the business now in a slump, management scrapped the program in October rather than risk the morale problems that might come if the division's staffers got lower raises than their counterparts elsewhere at Du Pont.

Hard Feelings. Still, tinkering with salaries is easy compared with changing managers' attitudes. Those who define themselves solely by the rungs they've climbed are bound to have problems, says Michael J. Driver, a management organization professor at USC. Such linear-minded folks, as Driver describes them, are tough to reeducate. "This problem is going to create a lot of dissatisfaction, frustration, and internal political fighting," Driver says.

The medicine can go down especially hard for managers who rose at fierce clips in their early days. Seventeen years ago, Norman Hatter, Jr., handed his boss a four-page list of the jobs he planned to have as he rose at Du Pont. Ticking off promotions every two years or so, the brash young engineer ultimately aimed for a vice-presidency, a level only a half-dozen down from chairman at the title-stingy company. Since then, Hatter has moved through nine jobs, but the last three have kept him at the director's level, a step down from vice-president. At 48, Hatter still has time to make his goal, but he vows that his next move will have to bring him closer to that brass ring. "It has to lead somewhere," he insists.

For now, though, the Slow Track is becoming so commonplace that frustrated managers may not have many options: Job-hoppers are likely to find the same slog at their new employers. That's why Harvard business school professor Rosabeth Moss Kanter predicts a surge of entrepreneurialism as dissatisfied managers strike out on their own. But the majority will stay within the corporate ranks. And their employers will have to find more ways to make the pace tolerable for rising stars with less room to rise.

1. Do you agree that employees are on the "Slow Track" in organizations in the 1990s? Provide evidence and specific examples for your answer.
2. From the case, identify and evaluate the suggestions and specific company examples of how to manage those on the "Slow Track." Which one(s) do you feel will be most effective?
3. What implications does the "Slow Track" have for both the theory and application of motivation, learning, and leadership? Which theories lead to the best understanding of the current situation? Which application techniques would be most effective?

EXPERIENTIAL EXERCISES FOR PART 3

EXERCISE: Motivation questionaire

Goals:
1. To experience firsthand the concepts of one of the work-motiviation theories—in this case, the popular Maslow hierarchy of needs
2. To get personal feedback on your opinions of the use of motivational techniques in human resources management

Implementation:
The following questions have seven possible responses:

1. Please mark one of the seven responses by circling the number that corresponds to the response that fits your opinion. For example, if you "strongly agree," circle the number "+3."
2. Complete every item. You have about ten minutes to do so.

	Strongly Agree	Agree	Slightly Agree	Don't Know	Slightly Disagree	Disagree	Strongly Disagree
	+3	+2	+1	0	−1	−2	−3
1. Special wage increases should be given to employees who do their jobs very well.	+3	+2	+1	0	−1	−2	−3
2. Better job descriptions would be helpful so that employees will know exactly what is expected of them.	+3	+2	+1	0	−1	−2	−3
3. Employees need to be reminded that their jobs are dependent on the company's ability to compete effectively.	+3	+2	+1	0	−1	−2	−3
4. Supervisors should give a good deal of attention to the physical working conditions of their employees.	+3	+2	+1	0	−1	−2	−3
5. Supervisors ought to work hard to develop a friendly working atmosphere among their people.	+3	+2	+1	0	−1	−2	−3
6. Individual recognition for above-standard performance means a lot to employees.	+3	+2	+1	0	−1	−2	−3
7. Indifferent supervision can often bruise feelings.	+3	+2	+1	0	−1	−2	−3
8. Employees want to feel that their real skills and capacities are put to use on their jobs.	+3	+2	+1	0	−1	−2	−3
9. The company retirement benefits and stock programs are important factors in keeping employees on their jobs.	+3	+2	+1	0	−1	−2	−3

	Strongly Agree	Agree	Slightly Agree	Don't Know	Slightly Disagree	Disagree	Strongly Disagree
	+3	+2	+1	0	−1	−2	−3
10. Almost every job can be made more stimulating and challenging.	+3	+2	+1	0	−1	−2	−3
11. Many employees want to give their best in everything they do.	+3	+2	+1	0	−1	−2	−3
12. Management could show more interest in the employees by sponsoring social events after hours.	+3	+2	+1	0	−1	−2	−3
13. Pride in one's work is actually an important reward.	+3	+2	+1	0	−1	−2	−3
14. Employees want to be able to think of themselves as "the best" at their own jobs.	+3	+2	+1	0	−1	−2	−3
15. The quality of the relationships in the informal work group is quite important.	+3	+2	+1	0	−1	−2	−3
16. Individual incentive bonuses would improve the performance of employees.	+3	+2	+1	0	−1	−2	−3
17. Visibility with upper management is important to employees.	+3	+2	+1	0	−1	−2	−3
18. Employees generally like to schedule their own work and to make job-related decisions with a minimum of supervision.	+3	+2	+1	0	−1	−2	−3
19. Job security is important to employees.	+3	+2	+1	0	−1	−2	−3
20. Having good equipment to work with is important to employees.	+3	+2	+1	0	−1	−2	−3

Scoring:

1. Transfer the numbers you circled in the questionnaire to the appropriate places in the spaces below.

Statement no.	Score	Statement No.	Score
10	——	2	——
11	——	3	——
13	——	9	——
18	——	19	——
Total	——	Total	——
(Self-actualization needs)		(Safety needs)	

Statement no.	Score	Statement no.	Score
6	____	1	____
8	____	4	____
14	____	16	____
17	____	20	____
Total	____	Total	____
(Esteem needs)		(Basic needs)	

Statement no.	Score
5	____
7	____
12	____
15	____
Total	____
(Belongingness needs)	

2. Record your total scores in the following chart by marking an "X" in each row next to the number of your total score for that area of needs motivation.

	−12	−10	−8	−6	−4	−2	0	+2	+4	+6	+8	+10	+12
Self-actualization													
Esteem													
Belongingness													
Safety													
Basic													

Low use / High use

By examining the chart you can see the relative strength you attach to each of the needs in Maslow's hierarchy. There are no right answers here, but most work-motivation theorists imply that most people are concerned mainly with the upper-level needs (that is, belongingness, esteem, and self-actualization).

EXERCISE: Job design survey

Goals:

1. To experience firsthand the job characteristics approach to job design, in this case through the Hackman-Oldham Job Diagnostic Survey (JDS)

2. To get personal feedback on the motivating potential of your present or past job and to identify and compare its critical characteristics

Implementation:

1. Please describe your present job (or a job you have held in the past) as objectively as you can. Circle the number that best reflects the job.

   a. How much *variety* is there in your job? That is, to what extent does the job require you to do many things at work, using a variety of your skills and talents?

   1----------2----------3----------4----------5----------6----------7

Very little; the job requires me to do the same routine things over and over again.	Moderate variety.	Very much; the job requires me to do many different things, using a number of different skills and talents.

   b. To what extent does your job involve doing a *"whole"* and *identifiable piece of work?* That is, is the job a complete piece of work that has an obvious beginning and end, or is it only a small part of the overall piece of work, which is finished by other people or by machines?

   1----------2----------3----------4----------5----------6----------7

My job is only a tiny part of the overall piece of work; the results of my activities cannot be seen in the final product or service.	My job is a moderate-sized "chunk" of the overall piece of work; my own contribution can be seen in the final outcome.	My job involves doing the whole piece of work, from start to finish; the results of my activities are easily seen in the final product or service.

   c. In general, *how significant or important* is your job? That is, are the results of your work likely to significantly affect the lives or well-being of other people?

   1----------2----------3----------4----------5----------6----------7

Not very significant; the outcomes of my work are *not* likely to have important effects on other people.	Moderately significant.	Highly significant; the outcomes of my work can affect other people in very important ways.

   d. How much *autonomy* is there in your job? That is, to what extent does your job permit you to decide on *your own* how to go about doing the work?

   1----------2----------3----------4----------5----------6----------7

Very little; the job gives me almost no personal "say" about how and when the work is done.	Moderate autonomy; many things are standardized and not under my control, but I can make some decisions about the work.	Very much; the job gives me almost complete responsibility for deciding how and when the work is done.

   e. To what extent does doing the *job itself* provide you with information about your work performance? That is, does the actual *work itself* provide clues about how well you are doing—aside from any feedback coworkers or supervisors may provide?

1----------2----------3----------4----------5----------6----------7

Very little; the job itself is set up so that I could work forever without finding out how well I am doing.

Moderately; sometimes doing the job provides feedback to me; sometimes it does not.

Very much; the job is set up so that I get almost constant feedback as I work about how well I am doing.

2. The five questions above measure your perceived skill variety, task identity, task significance, autonomy, and feedback in your job. The complete JDS uses several questions to measure these dimensions. But to get some idea of the motivating potential, use your scores (1 to 7) for each job dimension and calculate as follows:

$$\text{MPS} = \frac{\text{skill variety} + \text{task identity} + \text{task significance}}{3} \times \text{autonomy} \times \text{feedback}$$

Next, plot your job design profile and MPS score on the graphs below. These show the national averages for all jobs. Analyze how you compare and suggest ways to redesign your job.

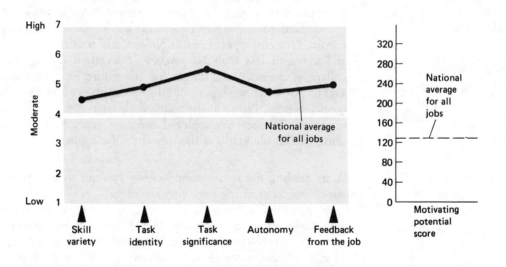

EXERCISE: Role playing and O.B. Mod.

Goal: To experience the application of the O.B. Mod. approach to human resources management

Implementation: This role-playing situation involves two people: Casey, the supervisor of claims processing in a large insurance firm, and Frances, an employee in the department. One person will be selected to play the role of Casey, and another will play Frances. The information on, and background for, each of the participants follow. When the participants have carefully read their roles, the supervisor, Casey, will be asked to conduct a performance-related discussion with Frances. Those who are not playing one of the roles should carefully observe the conversation between Casey and Frances and provide the information requested below. The observers should not necessarily read the roles of Casey and Frances.

1. List those words, phrases, or sentences that Casey used that seem particularly reinforcing.
2. List any words, phrases, or sentences used by Casey that may have been punishing.
3. List any suggestions that you have for improving Casey's future conversations with employees.
4. Using the steps of O.B. Mod. (identify, measure, analyze, intervene, and evaluate), how would you (or your group) improve the human performance in this claims department? Be as specific as you can for each step. You may have to fabricate some of the examples.

Role-playing situation for Casey:

After reading the information below, you are to conduct a performance-related discussion with Frances in order to reward increased productivity.

You are the supervisor of twenty people in the claims processing department of a large insurance company. Several weeks ago, you established standards for claims processing and measured each employee's work output. One employee, Frances Nelson, had particularly low output figures and averaged less than 80 percent of standard during the baseline data collection period. Your target for rewarding Frances was an 85 percent average for a one-week period. During the first two weeks, Frances failed to meet this goal. Now, in the third week after you have decided to use this approach, Frances has achieved the new goal. Frances's performance is illustrated in the graph at the top of the facing page.

Role-playing situation for Frances:

After reading the information below, you are to be interviewed by your supervisor concerning your performance.

You are Frances Nelson, an employee in the claims processing division of a large insurance company. Recently, your supervisor, Casey Parks, instituted a new system of measuring performance in the department. Most of the other employees have already discussed their performance with Casey, but for some reason Casey has not yet talked with you. Now this morning, Casey wanted to have a talk about your performance. You are somewhat anxious about what Casey will have to say. You know that you are not the best employee in the department, but you do make your best effort. You hope that Casey will recognize this and not be too hard on you.

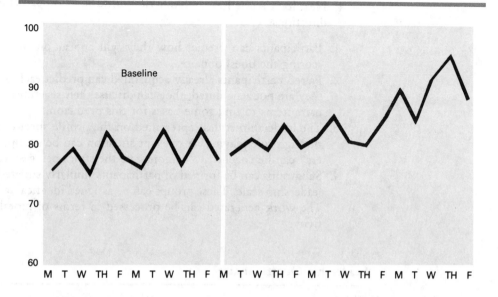

EXERCISE: Leadership questionnaire

Goal:

To evaluate oneself in terms of the leadership dimensions of task orientation and people orientation

Implementation:

1. Without prior discussion, fill out the Leadership Questionnaire below. Do *not* read the rest of this until you have completed the test.
2. In order to locate yourself on the Leadership Style Profile Sheet, you will score your own questionnaire on the dimensions of task orientation (T) and people orientation (P).
3. The scoring is as follows:
   a. Circle the item number for items 8, 12, 17, 18, 19, 30, 34, and 35.
   b. Write the number 1 in front of a *circled item number* if you responded S (seldom) or N (never) to that item.
   c. Also write a number 1 in front of *item numbers not circled* if you responded A (always) or F (frequently).
   d. Circle the number 1's which you have written in front of the following items: 3, 5, 8, 10, 15, 18, 19, 22, 24, 26, 28, 30, 32, 34, and 35.
   e. *Count the circled number 1's.* This is your score for the level of your concern for people. Record the score in the blank following the letter P at the end of the questionnaire.
   f. *Count the uncircled number 1's.* This is your score for your concern for the task. Record this number in the blank following the letter T.

4. Next look at the Leadership Style Profile Sheet on p. 341 and follow the directions.

Variations:

1. Participants can predict how they will appear on the profile prior to scoring the questionnaire.
2. Paired participants already acquainted can predict each other's scores. If they are not acquainted, they can discuss their reactions to the questionnaire items to find some bases for this predicion.
3. The leadership styles represented on the profile sheet can be illustrated through role playing. A relevant situation can be set up, and the "leaders" can be coached to demonstrate the styles being studied.
4. Subgroups can be formed of participants similarly situated on the shared leadership scale. These groups can be assigned identical tasks to perform. The work generated can be processed in terms of morale and productivity.

Leadership Questionnaire

Name_____   Group_____

Directions: The following items describe aspects of leadership behavior. Respond to each item according to the way you would most likely act if you were the leader of a work group. Circle whether you would most likely behave in the described way: always (A), frequently (F), occasionally (O), seldom (S), or never (N). Once the test is completed, go back to numbers 2 and 3 under implementation.

A F O S N	1. I would most likely act as the spokesperson of the group.
A F O S N	2. I would encourage overtime work.
A F O S N	3. I would allow members complete freedom in their work.
A F O S N	4. I would encourage the use of uniform procedures.
A F O S N	5. I would permit the members to use their own judgment in solving problems.
A F O S N	6. I would stress being ahead of competing groups.
A F O S N	7. I would speak as a representative of the group.
A F O S N	8. I would needle members for greater effort.
A F O S N	9. I would try out my ideas in the group.
A F O S N	10. I would let the members do their work the way they think best.
A F O S N	11. I would be working hard for a promotion.
A F O S N	12. I would tolerate postponement and uncertainty.
A F O S N	13. I would speak for the group if there were visitors present.
A F O S N	14. I would keep the work moving at a rapid pace.
A F O S N	15. I would turn the members loose on a job and let them go to it.
A F O S N	16. I would settle conflicts when they occur in the group.
A F O S N	17. I would get swamped by details.
A F O S N	18. I would represent the group at outside meetings.
A F O S N	19. I would be reluctant to allow the members any freedom of action.
A F O S N	20. I would decide what should be done and how it should be done.
A F O S N	21. I would push for increased production.
A F O S N	22. I would let some members have authority which I could keep.
A F O S N	23. Things would usually turn out as I had predicted.
A F O S N	24. I would allow the group a high degree of initiative.
A F O S N	25. I would assign group members to particular tasks.

A F O S N	26.	I would be willing to make changes.
A F O S N	27.	I would ask the members to work harder.
A F O S N	28.	I would trust the group members to exercise good judgment.
A F O S N	29.	I would schedule the work to be done.
A F O S N	30.	I would refuse to explain my actions.
A F O S N	31.	I would persuade others that my ideas are to their advantage.
A F O S N	32.	I would permit the group to set its own pace.
A F O S N	33.	I would urge the group to beat its previous record.
A F O S N	34.	I would act without consulting the group.
A F O S N	35.	I would ask that group members follow standard rules and regulations.

T _____   P _____

T-P Leadership Style Profile Sheet

Name_____   Group_____

Directions: To determine your style of leadership, mark your score on the concern for task dimension (T) on the left-hand arrow below. Next, move to the right-hand arrow and mark your score on the concern for people dimension (P). Draw a straight line that intersects the P and T scores. The point at which that line crosses the shared leadership arrow indicates your score on that dimension.

Shared leadership results from balancing concern for task and concern for people

AUTOCRATIC LEADERSHIP

High productivity

SHARED LEADERSHIP

High morale and productivity

LAISSEZ FAIRE LEADERSHIP

High morale

T: Concern for task   20   15   10   5

High   Medium   Low

P: Concern for people   15   10   5

PART **4**

THE DYNAMICS OF ORGANIZATIONAL BEHAVIOR: GROUPS, INTERACTIVE BEHAVIOR, CONFLICT, STRESS, POWER, AND POLITICS

12 Group Dynamics

■ It's Just in Time

One of the primary reasons for the creation of formal groups is to increase overall productivity. And no one provides a better example of this than Toyota with its just-in-time (JIT) inventory system. Although more than two-and-a-half times larger than its rival, Honda Motors, Toyota may be more efficient because of its unparalleled mastery of JIT.

The concept is not new. Detroit auto makers have been using JIT for over a decade and so have their competitors. However, while most of these manufacturers have limited the use of JIT to certain areas of operations, Toyota uses the concept throughout the entire production process. In a traditional mass production operation, parts and finished cars are turned out in large batches, then pushed down to the dealer level, where they are sold. In Toyota's Japanese operations, cars are not produced until orders come in from customers. In making this system work, Toyota dealers use on-line computers to order cars directly from the factory. The system operation is similar to an airline reservation system. Each car order reserves a portion of the factory capacity; and because the system is so well designed, customers can get built-to-order cars in seven to ten days. At the same time, the factory can balance production and stay in touch with changing demand. Results: Auto dealers carry very little inventory; the factory carries a minimum of parts, since it is producing "to order" rather than for inventory.

Formal and informal interaction between groups at Toyota is so effective that the company is able to produce fifty-nine passenger-car models. Ford Motor, which sells one-third more cars than Toyota, produces only forty-six passenger-car models. Moreover, careful coordination of activities allows Toyota to assemble a car in thirteen work hours, in contrast to nineteen and twenty-two hours respectively for Honda and Nissan; at GM, it takes even longer. What is even more impressive is that J. D. Power and Associates, the automotive research and consulting firm, reports that for 1990 Toyota's high-volume family cars (Corolla, Camry, and Cressida) all rank tops in their class for assembly quality.

The company also makes effective use of committees. Toyota recently reorganized product development so that a council headed by the president is now responsible for long-range product strategy. This reorganization was designed to help the firm respond to market changes. The head of the company's Tokyo Design Center explained the reasoning this way: "We have learned that universal mass production is not enough. In the twenty-first century, you personalize things more to make them more reflective of individual needs." In the auto industry, the winners are likely to be those companies able to target narrow customer niches with specific models. Thanks to the use of carefully created formal groups, Toyota is likely to continue excelling in this area.

Learning Objectives

- **Identify** the various types of groups.
- **Discuss** the implications that research on groups has for the practice of management.
- **Analyze** the positive and negative attributes of committees.
- **Explain** the dynamics of informal groups.

Parts 2 and 3 were devoted chiefly to the micro variables and mainstream applications of organizational behavior. This part is more concerned with the dynamic nature of organizational behavior. This chapter approaches organizational behavior dynamics from the perspective of the group, informal roles, and informal organization. The first section examines the way groups are formed, the various types of groups, some of the dynamics and functions of groups, and the findings of research on groups. The second section discusses the committee as a particular, practical case of group dynamics. The positive and negative attributes of committees are analyzed, and special attention is devoted to the "groupthink" problem. The last section focuses on the dynamics of informal roles and organization. Managerial roles and the implications of the informal organization are stressed.

THE NATURE OF GROUPS

Chapter 2 introduced the group as an important unit of sociological analysis which contributes much to the understanding of organizational behavior. This is especially true when the dynamics of the group are analyzed. Group dynamics are concerned with the interactions and forces among group members in a social situation. When the concept is applied to the study of organizational behavior, the focus is on the dynamics of members of formal or informal groups in the organization.

Just as there is no one definition of the word *group*, there is no universal agreement on what is meant by *group dynamics*. Although Kurt Lewin popularized the term in the 1930s, through the years different connotations have been attached to it. One normative view is that group dynamics describe *how* a group *should* be organized and conducted. Democratic leadership, member participation, and overall cooperation are stressed. This view of group dynamics was given attention in Chapters 10 and 11. Another view of group dynamics is that it consists of a set of *techniques*. Here, role playing, brainstorming, buzz groups, leaderless groups, group therapy, sensitivity training, team building, transactional analysis, and the

Johari window are equated with group dynamics. Some of these techniques are covered in the next chapter and in Chapter 21, on organization development. A third view is the closest to Lewin's original conception. Group dynamics are viewed from the perspective of the internal nature of groups, how they form, their structure and processes, and how they function and affect individual members, other groups, and the organization. The following sections are devoted to this third view of group dynamics. A modern, comprehensive definition of a *group* that will be used as a point of departure for the rest of the chapter is the following: "A group is a collection of individuals in which there is (1) interaction among members, (2) perception of group membership, (3) shared norms and values, and (4) fate interdependence (what happens to one group member affects other group members and what happens to the group as a whole affects the individual members)."[1]

The Dynamics of Group Formation

Why do individuals form into groups? Before discussing some very practical reasons, it would be beneficial to examine briefly some of the classic theories of group formation or why people affiliate with one another. The most basic theory explaining affiliation is propinquity. This interesting word means simply that individuals affiliate with one another because of spatial or geographical proximity. The theory would predict that students sitting next to one another in class, for example, are more likely to form into a group than students sitting at opposite ends of the room. In an organization, employees who work in the same area of the plant or office or managers with offices close to one another would more probably form into groups than those who are not physically located together. There is some research evidence to support the propinquity theory, and on the surface it has a great deal of merit for explaining group formation. The drawback is that it is not analytical and does not begin to explain some of the complexities of group formation. Some theoretical and practical reasons need to be explored.

Theories of Group Formation. A more comprehensive theory of group formation than mere propinquity comes from the theory based on activities, interactions, and sentiments.[2] These three elements are directly related to one another. The more activities persons share, the more numerous will be their interactions and the stronger will be their sentiments (how much the other persons are liked or disliked); the more interactions among persons, the more will be their shared activities and sentiments; and the more sentiments persons have for one another, the more will be their shared activities and interactions. This theory lends a great deal to the understanding of group formation and process. The major element is *interaction*. Persons in a group interact with one another, not in just the physical propinquity sense, but also to accomplish many group goals such as cooperation and problem solving.

There are many other theories that attempt to explain group formation. Most often they are only partial theories, but they are generally additive in nature. One of the more comprehensive is a *balance theory* of group formation.[3] The theory states that persons are attracted to one another on the basis of similar attitudes toward commonly relevant objects and goals. Figure 12.1 shows this balance theory. Indi-

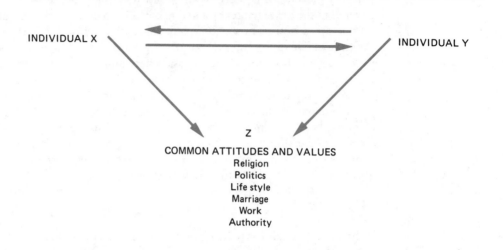

FIGURE 12.1
A balance theory
of group
formation.

vidual X will interact and form a relationship/group with individual Y because of common attitudes and values (Z). Once this relationship is formed, the participants strive to maintain a symmetrical balance between the attraction and the common attitudes. If an imbalance occurs, an attempt is made to restore the balance. If the balance cannot be restored, the relationship dissolves. Both propinquity and interaction play a role in balance theory.

Still another theoretical approach to group formation receiving considerable attention is *exchange theory*.[4] Similar to its functioning as a work-motivation theory, discussed in Chapter 6, exchange theory of groups is based upon reward-cost outcomes of interaction. A minimum positive level (rewards greater than costs) of an outcome must exist in order for attraction or affiliation to take place. Rewards from interactions gratify needs, while costs incur anxiety, frustration, embarrassment, or fatigue. Propinquity, interaction, and common attitudes all have roles in exhange theory.

Practicalities of Group Formation. Besides the theoretical explanations for group formation, there are some very practical reasons for joining and/or forming a group. For instance, employees in an organization may form a group for economic, security, or social reasons. Economically, workers may form a group to work on a project that is paid for on a group-incentive plan or may form a union to demand higher wages. For security, joining a group provides the individual with a united front in combating indiscriminant, unilateral treatment. The adage that there is strength in numbers applies in this case. The most important practical reason why individuals join or form groups is, however, that groups tend to satisfy the very intense social needs of most people. Workers, in particular, generally have a very strong desire for affiliation. This need is met by belonging to a group. Research going as far back as the Hawthorne studies has found the affiliation motive to have a major impact on human behavior in organizations. Chapter 6 also discussed this motive.

Types of Groups

There are numerous types of groups. The theories of group formation that were just discussed are based partly upon the attraction between two persons—the simple dyad group. Of course, in the real world groups are usually much more complex than the dyad. There are small and large groups, primary and secondary groups, coalitions, membership and reference groups, in- and out-groups, and formal and informal groups. Each type has different characteristics and different effects on its members.

Primary Groups. Often the terms *small group* and *primary group* are used interchangeably. Technically, there is a difference. A small group has to meet only the criterion of small size. Usually, no attempt is made to assign precise numbers, but the accepted criterion is that the group must be small enough for face-to-face interaction and communication to occur. In addition to being small, a primary group must have a feeling of comradeship, loyalty, and a common sense of values among its members. Thus, all primary groups are small groups, but not all small groups are primary groups.

Two examples of a primary group are the family and the peer group. Initially, the primary group was limited to a socializing group, but then a broader conception was given impetus by the results of the Hawthorne studies. Work groups definitely have primary group qualities. Research findings point out the tremendous impact that the primary group has on individual behavior, regardless of context or environmental conditions. An increasing number of companies such as General Mills, Federal Express, Chaparral Steel, and 3M have begun to use the power of primary groups by organizing employees into self-managed teams. These teams range between three and thirty members, consist of blue-collar workers, white-collar workers, or both, and arrange schedules, set goals, suggest improvements, hire and fire team members and managers, and even devise strategy.[5]

Coalitions. In addition to primary groups, coalitions are very relevant to organizations. The concept of a coalition has been used in organizational analysis through the years. Although the concept is used in different ways by different theorists, a recent comprehensive review of the coalition literature suggests that the following characteristics of a coalition be included:

1. Interacting group of individuals
2. Deliberately constructed by the members for a specific purpose
3. Independent of the formal organization's structure
4. Lacking a formal internal structure
5. Mutual perception of membership
6. Issue-oriented to advance the purposes of the members
7. External forms
8. Concerted member action, act as a group[6]

Although the above have common characteristics with other types of groups, coalitions are separate, usually very powerful, and often effective entities in organizations.

recent study found that employees in a large bureaucractic organization formed into coalitions to overcome petty conflicts and ineffective management in order to get the job done.[7]

Other Types of Groups. Besides primary groups and coalitions, there are also other classifications of groups that are important to the study of organizational behavior. Two important distinctions are between membership and reference groups, and between in-groups and out-groups. These differences can be summarized by noting that membership groups are those to which the individual actually belongs. An example would be membership in a craft union. Reference groups are those to which an individual would like to belong—those he or she identifies with. An example would be a prestigious social group. In-groups are those who have or share the dominant values, and out-groups are those on the outside looking in. All these types of groups have relevance to the study of organizational behavior, but the formal and informal types are most directly applicable.

There are many formally designated groups and committees in the modern organization. The functional departments (finance, marketing, operations, and personnel) are examples, as are standing committees such as the finance committee, grievance committee, or executive committee. Committees as a type of formal group are given detailed attention later in the chapter. Self-managed teams, as discussed under primary groups, are also being effectively applied in a variety of work situations. A recent review of work teams notes that successful applications include advice and involvement (as in quality control circles and committees); production and service (as in assembly groups and sales teams); projects and development (as in engineering and research groups); and action and negotiation (as in sports teams and combat units).[8]

Informal groups form for political, friendship, or common interest reasons. For political purposes, the informal group may form to attempt to get its share of rewards and/or limited resources. Friendship groups may form on the job and carry on outside the workplace. Common interests in sports or ways to get back at management can also bind members into an informal group. The dynamics of these informal groups are examined in more detail in the last part of the chapter.

Implications from Research on Group Dynamics

Starting with the Hawthorne studies, there has been an abundance of significant research on groups that has implications for organizational behavior and management. Besides the Hawthorne studies, there are numerous research studies on group dynamics which indirectly contribute to the better understanding of organizational behavior. Table 12.1 summarizes the research findings on the functions that groups can serve for both the organization as a whole and the individual organizational participant.

In addition to the somewhat general conclusions shown in Table 12.1, there are a number of studies in social psychology which seem to have particular relevance to organizational behavior. The work of social psychologist Stanley Schachter seems especially important for the application of group dynamics research to human resources management.

TABLE 12.1 Summary of Research on the Impact That Groups Have on Organizational and Individual Effectiveness

The Impact of Groups on Organizational Effectiveness	The Impact of Groups on Individual Employee Effectiveness
1. Accomplishing tasks that could not be done by employees themselves	1. Aiding in learning about the organization and its environment
2. Bringing a number of skills and talents to bear on complex difficult tasks	2. Aiding in learning about oneself
3. Providing a vehicle for decision making that permits multiple and conflicting views to be aired and considered	3. Providing help in gaining new skills
4. Providing an efficient means for organizational control of employee behavior	4. Obtaining valued rewards that are not accessible by oneself
5. Facilitating changes in organizational policies or procedures	5. Satisfying important personal needs, especially needs for social acceptance and affiliation
6. Increasing organizational stability by transmiting shared beliefs and values to new employees	

Source: Adapted from David A. Nadler, J. Richard Hackman, and Edward E. Lawler, *Managing Organizational Behavior*, Little, Brown, Boston, 1979, p. 102

The Schachter Study. In a classic study[9] Schachter and his associates tested the effect that group cohesiveness and induction (or influence) had on productivity under highly controlled conditions. *Cohesiveness* was defined as the average resultant force acting on members in a group. Through the manipulations of cohesiveness and induction, the following experimental groups were created:

1. High cohesive, positive induction (Hi Co, + Ind)
2. Low cohesive, positive induction (Lo Co, + Ind)
3. High cohesive, negative induction (Hi Co, − Ind)
4. Low cohesive, negative induction (Lo Co, − Ind)

The independent variables in the experiment were cohesiveness and induction, and the dependent variable was productivity. Figure 12.2 summarizes the results. Although Schachter's experiment did not obtain a statistically significant difference in productivity between the high and low cohesive groups that were positively induced, a follow-up study which used a more difficult task did.[10]

Implications of the Schachter Study. The results of Schachter's study contain some very interesting implications for the study of organizational behavior. The "pitchfork" productivity curves in Figure 12.2 imply that highly cohesive groups have very powerful dynamics, both positive and negative, for human resources management. On the other hand, the low cohesive groups are not so powerful. However, of even more importance to human resources management is the variable of induction. Performance depends largely on how the high or low cohesive group is induced.

At least for illustrative purposes, leadership may be substituted for induction. If this is done, the key variable for the subjects' performance in the Schachter experiment becomes leadership. A highly cohesive group that is given positive leadership will have the highest possible productivity. On the other side of the coin,

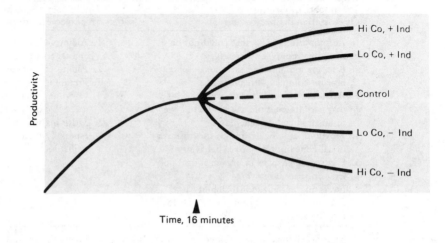

FIGURE 12.2
The "pitchfork"
results from the
Schachter study.

a highly cohesive group that is given poor leadership will have the lowest possible productivity. A highly cohesive group is analogous to a time bomb in the hands of management. The direction in which the highly cohesive group goes, breaking production records or severely restricting output, depends on how it is led. The low cohesive group is much safer in the hands of management. Leadership will not have a serious negative or positive impact on this group. However, the implication is that if management wishes to maximize productivity, it must build a cohesive group and give it proper leadership.

This discussion does not imply that subjects doing a simple task in a laboratory setting can be made equivalent to managing human resources in the modern, complex organization. This, of course, cannot and should not be attempted. On the other hand, there are some interesting insights and points of departure for organizational behavior analysis that can come out of laboratory investigations such as Schachter's. For instance, the results of Schachter's study can be applied in retrospect to the work of Frederick W. Taylor or to the Hawthorne studies. Taylor accounted only for the Hi Co, − Ind productivity curve when he advocated "breaking up the group." If his scientific management methods could be considered + Ind, the best productivity he could obtain would be that of Lo Co, + Ind.

In other words, in light of the Schachter study, Taylor's methods could yield only second-best productivity. In the Hawthorne studies, both the relay room operatives and the bank wirers were highly cohesive work groups. As was brought out in Chapter 2, a possible explanation of why one highly cohesive work group (the relay room workers) produced at a very high level and the other highly cohesive group (the bank wirers) produced at a very low rate is the type of induction (supervision) that was applied. Both leadership and group dynamics factors, such as cohesiveness, can have an important impact on group performance in organizations. Table 12.2 briefly summarizes some of the major factors that can increase and decrease group cohesiveness.

TABLE 12.2 Factors That Increase and Decrease Group Cohesiveness

Factors That Increase Group Cohesiveness	Factors That Decrease Group Cohesiveness
Agreement on group goals	Disagreement on goals
Frequency of interaction	Large group size
Personal attractiveness	Unpleasant experiences
Intergroup competition	Intragroup competition
Favorable evaluation	Domination by one or more members

Source: Adapted from Andrew D. Szilagyi, Jr., and Marc J. Wallace, Jr., *Organizational Behavior and Performance,* 5th ed., Scott, Foresman/Little, Brown, Glenview, Ill., 1990, pp. 282–283.

The Group's Contribution to Employee Satisfaction and Performance. Besides the work coming out of social psychology, more specific focus on the impact that groups have on employee behavior, especially the contribution to satisfaction and performance, has also received attention. A summary of the way to utilize groups to enhance satisfaction and performance would be the following:

1. Organizing work around intact groups
2. Having groups charged with selection, training, and rewarding of members
3. Using groups to enforce strong norms for behavior, with group involvement in off-the-job as well as on-the-job behavior
4. Distributing resources on a group rather than an individual basis
5. Allowing and perhaps even promoting intergroup rivalry so as to build within-group solidarity[11]

A review of the research literature also determined three factors that seem to play the major role in determining group effectiveness: (1) task interdependence (how closely group members work together); (2) outcome interdependence (whether, and how, group performance is rewarded); and (3) potency (members' belief that the group can be effective).[12]

COMMITTEE ORGANIZATION

No discussion of group dynamics within the context of organizational behavior would be complete without a thorough analysis of committee organization. The committee is the most important type of formally designated group found in today's organizations. Unfortunately, these committees are often described as follows:

A camel is a horse designed by a committee.
The best committee is a five-person committee with four members absent.
In a committee, minutes are taken but hours are wasted.
A committee is a collection of the unfit appointed by the unwilling to perform the unnecessary.

These remarks are jokes, but they represent the widespread negativism attached to the committee form of organization.

Despite the attacks, all indications are that the use and perceived value of committees in organizations are still increasing. Most committees seem to serve as a focal point for the exchange of different viewpoints and information, but some are making major decisions. The Application Example, Agreeing to Greater Productivity, illustrates an issue that was recently resolved between Chrysler management and union committees. There is considerable evidence that the use of committees is directly related to the size of the organization. With today's organizations becoming increasingly large and complex, the committee form of organization will undoubtedly become more important and more widely used in the future.

Agreeing to Greater Productivity

When committees work together toward a common objective, the benefits can be rewarding for both sides. A recent agreement between Chrysler and United Auto Workers provides a good example. Chrysler has been having a difficult time, but there are a few product lines that have been big money makers. One is the mini-van, which provides about $2,000 profit per unit. Chrysler would like to turn out as many of these vans as possible, and in the latest agreement with the union group, the St. Louis mini-van plant will be using a three-shift, or near-continuous, operation.

By running three seven-hour shifts instead of two eight-hour shifts six days a week, Chrysler will be able to increase its current 108 hours of weekly production to 126. This means that the company will be able to make an additional 50,000 mini-vans a year. One reason why the union agreed to go along with the request is that the only alternative was to retool the existing plant for mini-van assembly. This would cost approximately $500 million. Since the firm is currently strapped for capital, the only way it could pay for this retooling would be to cut back in other areas and to lay off personnel. Because the union did not want this to happen, it agreed to a round-the-clock type of operation.

Will union-management committees at Chrysler agree to this arrangement at other plants? Such an arrangement is unlikely. The union is convinced that it would eventually lead to big layoffs of its people. On the other hand, continued cooperation between the two committees is likely to be necessary, since round-the-clock operations are bound to create other problems. One such problem is that the line cannot be run hour after hour. Painting booths must be stopped daily for maintenance and filter changes in order to keep a high level of quality; any major breakdown will cut deeply into overall capacity. There are bound to be such occurrences when equipment is run on a continuous basis. While both Chrysler and the union committees may have come out ahead thanks to their willingness to cooperate, there will be a need to continue this process if future problems are to be surmounted.

The Nature and Functions of Committees

There are many definitions of a *committee*. Most stress the idea that committees consist of groups that are formed to accomplish specific objectives. They can be conducted in either a formal manner (for example, the finance committee) or an informal manner (for example, the weekly staff meeting). Most often, committees have specified duties and authority. Some committees meet on an ad hoc basis to solve some specialized problem and then disband. Committees may be referred to as *teams, commissions, boards, groups,* or *task forces.*

Committees are found in all types of organizations. There is a myriad of committees in government, educational, religious, and business organizations. For example, the board of directors is a type of committee present in all corporate forms of organization. Other prevalent types in business are the finance, executive, operations, bonus, audit, and grievance committees. Although they are more frequent at the top of the pyramid, there is usually some type of formal committee on every level of the organization.

Committees perform many different functions. They may act in a service, advisory, coordinating, informational, or final decision-making capacity. In the decision-making function, a committee acts in a line capacity and is usually termed a *plural-executive committee.* Many companies have moved to the plural-executive concept rather than a single executive head. Union Carbide is typical of this trend. The company's major policies evolve from the office of the president. This office is composed of the president and three executive vice presidents. This foursome serves as the central point of management authority in the company. This type of group management is becoming increasingly common.

Positive Attributes of Committees

Committee action has many advantages over individual action. Perhaps the greatest attribute of the committee group is the combined and integrated judgment which it can offer. The old adage says that two heads are better than one. To speak optimistically, committee members bring with them a wide range of experience, knowledge, ability, and personality characteristics. This agglomeration lends itself to the tremendous amount of diverse knowledge that is required to solve modern organizational problems. As the head of the National Bank of Greece recently noted, "Management is about problem solving, and the committee meeting is an instrument designed to solve problems. But effective meetings don't just happen," he says. "They happen only when there is an effective person chairing the meeting."[13]

Today's organizations also need an averaging of personalities and a source of creative ideas. The committee form of organization can contribute a great deal to these requirements, as is pointed out in Chapter 17's presentation of the group decision-making techniques of Delphi and the Nominal Group Technique (NGT). The interacting group may also inhibit individual creativity, but at least at some point the interactive, group dynamics effects as found in a committee can be beneficial to group problem solving.

Committees can be a very effective organizational device to help reduce conflict and promote coordination between departments and specialized subunits. Through committee discussion, each member can empathize with the others' purposes and problems. In effect, committees foster horizontal communication. An example is the interdepartmental meeting at which each member receives information and insights about the others' departments. The production department is informed of delivery dates being promised by sales, and sales get a firsthand look at the problems it may be creating for production scheduling and inventory. As Chapter 16 points out, the committee is about the only formalized vehicle for horizontal communication in most traditional forms of organization structure.

From a human standpoint, the biggest advantage of committees may be the increased motivation and commitment derived from participation. By being involved in the analysis and solution of committee problems, individual members will more readily accept and try to implement what has been decided. A committee can also be instrumental in human development and growth. Group members, especially the young and inexperienced, can take advantage of observing and learning from other members with much experience or with different viewpoints and knowledge. A committee provides the opportunity for personal development that individuals would never receive on their own.

Negative Attributes of Committees

The above discussion points out some definite advantages of committees, but the Application Example, Committees May Not Be the Answer, gives some of the problems that are inherent. Traditionally, management theorists have stressed the negative aspects. The classical theorist Luther Gulick wanted to limit the use of committees to abnormal situations because he thought they were too dilatory, irresponsible, and time-consuming for normal administration. The classical theorist Urwick was an even harsher critic. He listed no less than fourteen faults of committees, the main ones being that committees are often irresponsible, are apt to be bad employers, and are costly. Thus, the classicists tended to emphasize the negative, but in the more modern view, committees have both positive and negative attributes.

One very practical disadvantage is that committees are indeed time-consuming and costly. Anyone who has participated in committee meetings can appreciate the satirical definition, cited earlier, that a committee takes minutes but wastes hours. The nature of a committee is that everyone has an equal chance to speak out, but this takes a great deal of time, and time costs money. A $60,000-per-year manager costs about $30 per hour. Therefore, a five-person committee of this caliber costs the organization $150 per hour. Added to this figure may be transportation, lodging, and staff backup costs.

Most often, cost is discussed with regard to committee versus individual action. Taking another approach, it can be argued that committees are actually less expensive when compared with a series of repetitious conferences. In terms of work hours, a committee meeting at which a manager meets with five others for one hour represents six work hours. On the other hand, if the same executive meets for one hour with each of the five people individually, the expended time turns out to be ten work hours. Assume that the executive makes $60,000 ($30 per hour) per year and that the five others average $24,000 ($14 per hour). For the one-hour committee meeting the cost would be about $100, but for the five individual conferences the total cost would be about $220, over twice as much. The point of this elementary cost analysis is that one cannot automatically condemn all committees as being excessively expensive. The nature and purpose must be considered when assessing cost. Furthermore, it is difficult, if not impossible, to quantify for cost purposes the advantages of a committee in terms of member motivation and quality of decision or problem solution.

From an organizational standpoint, there are some potential problems inherent in committees. The most obvious is divided responsibility. This is saying that in a committee, there is group or corporate but no individual responsibility or account-

Committees May Not Be the Answer

Most modern management theorists espouse the benefits of getting together in committees to make decisions. It allows individuals to give their input and increases motivation and commitment. However, committees may not be appropriate for all decision-making situations. For example, holding committee meetings may simply be a facade for managers' own insecurities. Afraid to take responsibility for a decision, a manager may call a meeting to make a decision. In doing so, the manager can use the committee as a scapegoat for poor decisions.

Norman Sigband, a management communications professor, uses an example of a meeting he observed at a small plastics manufacturing firm. A committee consisting of a division manager, six department heads, and the heads of three sections was asked to discuss the replacement of an injured secretary. The group spent fifty minutes deciding whether a new person should be hired or a replacement acquired through a temporary service. As a result, the committee ran out of time to discuss the installation of a new fluorescent lighting system. This decision would have affected several departments and required an investment of $28,000. The secretarial decision, on the other hand, affected only one department and should have been made by the division manager. A side effect of such unnecessary meetings is a decline in committee attendance. When asked to address petty issues, members may become apathetic and skip meetings. Thus, when a really important issue needs to be addressed, relevant members may be absent. To overcome such problems, Sigband offers six suggestions for making committee meetings as productive as possible:

1. Only hold meetings for which there is a verifiable need.
2. Decide on an overall purpose and series of objectives each time.
3. Invite only people who can make a definite contribution.
4. Distribute an agenda and necessary handouts to each invitee prior to the session.
5. Make all mechanical arrangements ahead of time (room, projectors, seating, transparencies, etc.).
6. Begin and end every meeting on schedule.

ability. Thus, critics argue, the committee in reality turns out to have no responsibility or accountability. In fact, individuals may use the committee as a shield to avoid personal responsibility for bad decisions or mistakes. One solution to this problem is to make all committee members responsible, and another is to hold the chairperson responsible. Both approaches have many obvious difficulties. For example, if the entire committee is held responsible for a wrong decision, what about the individual members who voted against the majority? Holding them accountable for the committee's decision could have disastrous effects on their morale, but holding only those who voted for a particular decision responsible would create an inhibiting effect that would destroy the value of committee action.

Besides being time-consuming and costly and having divided responsibility, committees may reach decisions that are products of excessive compromise, logrolling, and one-person or minority domination. The comment that the camel is a horse designed by a committee underscores this limitation. It represents the reverse of the advantages of integrated group judgment and the pooling of specialized knowledge.

Where unanimity is either formally required or an informal group norm, the difficulties are compounded. The final decision may be so extremely watered down or "compromised to death" that the horse actually does turn out to be a camel. The strength of committee action comes through a synthesis and integration of divergent viewpoints, not through a compromise representing the least common denominator. One way to avoid the problem is to limit the committee to serving as a forum for the exchange of information and ideas. Another possibility is to let the chairperson have the final decision-making prerogative. Yet these solutions are not always satisfactory because when the committee is charged with making a decision, considerable social skill and a willingness to cooperate fully must exist if good-quality decisions are to evolve.

"Groupthink": A Major Problem with Committees and Groups

A dysfunction of highly cohesive groups and committees that has received a lot of attention recently has been called "groupthink" by Irving Janis. He defines it as "a deterioration of mental efficiency, reality testing, and moral judgment that results from in-group pressures."[14] Essentially, groupthink results from the pressures on individual members to conform and reach consensus. Committees that are suffering from groupthink are so bent on reaching consensus that there is no realistic appraisal of alternative courses of action in a decision, and deviant, minority, or unpopular views are suppressed.

Janis has concluded that a number of historic fiascos by government policy-making groups (for example, Britain's do-nothing policy toward Hitler prior to World War II, the unpreparedness of U.S. forces at Pearl Harbor, the Bay of Pigs invasion of Cuba, and the escalation of the Vietnam war) can be attributed to groupthink. The Watergate affair during the Nixon administration and the Iran-contra affair during the Reagan administration are also examples. The decision process by which NASA launched the space shuttle Challenger on its fateful mission can be analyzed in terms of the characteristics of groupthink. For example, conformity pressures were in evidence when NASA officials complained to the contractors about delays. Other symptoms of groupthink shown in Table 12.3—illusions of invulnerability and unanimity and mindguarding—were played out in the Challenger disaster by management's treatment and exclusion of input by the engineers.[15]

Although historically notorious news events can be used to dramatically point out the pitfalls of groupthink, it can commonly occur in committees in business firms or hospitals or any other type of organization. To date, there has been at least some partial support of the groupthink model when applied to areas such as leader behavior and decision making.[16] In general, committees should recognize and then avoid if possible the symptoms of groupthink identified in Table 12.3. For example, the first symptom leads to the so-called "risky shift phenomenon" of groups. Contrary to popular belief, research going back many years has shown that a group may make more risky decisions than the individual members would on their own.[17] This conclusion, of course, must be tempered by the values attached to the outcomes, but most of the research over the years finds that groups take more risks than individuals acting alone.

TABLE 12.3 Symptoms of Groupthink

1. There is the illusion of *invulnerability*. There is excessive optimism and risk taking.
2. There are *rationalizations* by the members of the group to discount warnings.
3. There is an unquestioned belief in the group's *inherent morality*. The group ignores questionable ethical or moral issues or stances.
4. Those who oppose the group are *stereotyped* as evil, weak, or stupid.
5. There is *direct pressure* on any member who questions the stereotypes. Loyal members don't question the direction in which the group seems to be heading.
6. There is *self-censorship* of any deviation from the apparent group consensus.
7. There is the *illusion of unanimity*. Silence is interpreted as consent.
8. There are *self-appointed mindguards* who protect the group from adverse information.

Source: Adapted from Irving L. Janis, *Victims of Groupthink*, Houghton Mifflin, Boston, 1972, pp. 197–198.

Such symptoms as this risky shift phenomenon and the others found in Table 12.3 should make groups take notice and be very careful that they do not slip into groupthink. To help overcome the potentially disastrous effects of groupthink, free expression of minority and unpopular viewpoints should be encouraged and legitimatized. Companies such as General Electric, Bausch and Laub, Apple Computer, Ford, Johnson and Johnson, and United Parcel Service are known for not only tolerating, but formally encouraging, conflict and debate during committee meetings.

Although many studies show that successful companies advocate such open conflict and healthy debate among group members, other studies point to the value of consensus. This apparent contradiction may be resolved by recognizing the following:

> Consensus may be preferred for smaller, non-diversified, privately held firms competing in the same industry while larger firms dealing with complex issues of diversification may benefit from the dissent raised in open discussions. Larger firms in uncertain environments need dissent while smaller firms in more simple and stable markets can rely on consensus.[18]

THE DYNAMICS OF INFORMAL GROUPS

Informal groups play a significant role in the dynamics of organizational behavior. The major difference between formal and informal groups is that the formal group has officially prescribed goals and relationships, whereas the informal one does not. Despite this distinction, it is a mistake to think of formal and informal groups as two distinctly separate entities. The two types of groups coexist and are inseparable. Every formal organization has informal groups, and every informal organization eventually evolves some semblance of formal groups.

Norms and Roles in Informal Groups

With the exception of a single social act such as extending a hand upon meeting, the smallest units of analysis in group dynamics are norms and roles. Many behavioral scientists make a point of distinguishing between the two units, but conceptually they are very similar. *Norms* are the "oughts" of behavior. They are prescriptions for acceptable behavior determined by the group. Norms will be strongly enforced by work groups if they:

1. Aid in group survival and provision of benefits
2. Simplify or make predictable the behavior expected of group members
3. Help the group to avoid embarrassing interpersonal problems
4. Express the central values or goals of the group and clarify what is distinctive about the group's identity[19]

A role consists of a pattern of norms; the use of the term in organizations is directly related to its theatrical use. A role is a position that can be acted out by an individual. The content of a given role is prescribed by the prevailing norms. Probably *role* can best be defined as a position that has expectations evolving from established norms.

Informal Managerial Roles

Informal roles vary widely and are highly volatile. Table 12.4 summarizes some of the general informal roles that today's employees often assume. These role descriptions are not intended to be stereotypes or to imply that each organizational participant has only one role. The same person may have one role in one situation (a member of a middle management work group) and another role in another situation (the informal leader of the dissident group on a new project).

TABLE 12.4 Informal Roles of Employees

Task-oriented employees: Those who have the role of "getting the job done" and are known as those who "deliver the goods"

Technique-oriented employees: the masters of procedure and method

People-oriented employees: those who have the role of patron saint and good samaritan to people in need

Nay-sayers: those who counterbalance the "yes" persons and who have thick skins and can find fault with anything

Yes-sayers: those who counterbalance the nay-sayers; the "yes" persons who circumvent opposition

Rule enforcers: the "people of the book," those who are stereotype bureaucrats

Rule evaders: the "operators," those who know how to get the job done "irrespective"

Rule blinkers: the people who are not against the rules but don't take them seriously

Involved employees: those who are fully immersed in their work and the activities of the organization

Detached employees: slackers who either "go along for the ride" or "call it quits" at the end of regular hours

Regulars: those who are "in," who accept the values of the group and are accepted by the group

Deviants: those who depart from the values of the group—the "mavericks"

Isolates: the true "lone wolves," who are further from the group than the deviants

Newcomers: those who know little and must be taken care of by others; people who are "seen but not heard"

Old-timers: those who have been around a long time and "know the ropes"

Climbers: those who are expected to "get ahead," not necessarily on the basis of ability but on the basis of potential

Stickers: those who are expected to stay put, who are satisfied with life and their position in it

Cosmopolitans: those who see themselves as members of a broader professional, cultural, or political community

Locals: those who are rooted to the organization and local community.

Source: Adapted from Bertram M. Gross, *Organizations and Their Managing*, Free Press, New York, 1968, pp. 242–248.

On the basis of observational studies of managerial work, Henry Mintzberg has proposed that managers perform the three types of roles shown in Figure 12.3. The *interpersonal roles* arise directly from formal authority and refer to the relationship between the manager and others. By virtue of the formal position, the manager has a *figurehead role* as a symbol of the organization. Most of the time spent as a figurehead is on ceremonial duties such as greeting a touring class of students or taking an important customer to lunch. The second interpersonal role is called the *leader role*. In this role the manager uses his or her influence to motivate and encourage subordinates to accomplish organizational objectives. In the third type of interpersonal role the manager undertakes a *liaison role*. This role recognizes that managers often spend more time interacting with others outside their unit (with peers in other units or those completely outside the organization) than they do working with their own superiors and subordinates.

Besides the interpersonal roles flowing from formal authority, Figure 12.3 shows that managers also have important *informational roles*. Most observational studies find that managers spend a great deal of time giving and receiving information. As *monitor*, the manager is continually scanning the environment and probing subordinates, bosses, and outside contacts for information; as *disseminator*, the manager distributes information to key internal people; and as *spokesperson*, the manager provides information to outsiders.

In the *decisional role*, the manager acts upon the information. In the *entrepreneurial role* in Mintzberg's scheme, the manager initiates the development of a

FIGURE 12.3
Mintzberg's managerial roles. (*Source:* Adapted from Henry Mintzberg, "The Manager's Job: Folklore and Fact," *Harvard Business Review*, July–August 1975, pp. 49–61.

FORMAL AUTHORITY
AND STATUS

INTERPERSONAL ROLES
Figurehead
Leader
Liaison

INFORMATIONAL ROLES
Monitor
Disseminator
Spokesperson

DECISIONAL ROLES
Entrepreneur
Disturbance handler
Resource allocator
Negotiator

project and assembles the necessary resources. The *disturbance handler*, on the other hand, instead of being proactive like the entrepreneur, is reactive to the problems and pressures of the situation. The disturbance handler has a crisis management type of role; for example, the employees are about to strike, or a major subcontractor is threatening to pull out. As *resource allocator* the manager decides who gets what in his or her department. Finally, the *negotiator* decisional role recognizes the time managers spend at all levels in the give-and-take of negotiating with subordinates, bosses, and outsiders. For example, a production manager may have to negotiate a grievance settlement with the union business agent, or a supervisor in a welfare department may have to negotiate certain benefit payments that one of the counselors wants to give a client.

These informal managerial roles suggested by Mintzberg get much closer to describing what managers really do than the formally described and prescribed functions of managers. Mintzberg's work has definitely shed some light on the nature of managerial work, but as he recently stated in a retrospective commentary about the ten roles: "we remain grossly ignorant about the fundamental content of the manager's job and have barely addressed the major issues and dilemmas in its practice."[20] More recent observational studies have found the Mintzberg type of activities with some variations. One study of a small sample of general managers found networking and setting informal agendas to be important activities;[21] and a large comprehensive observational study found traditional management (activities of decision making, planning, and controlling), communication, networking, and human resources management activities were what managers really do day-to-day[22] (see Chapter 11's discussion of this "Real Managers" study).

A recent study asked 1,412 managers to rate the importance of various managerial activities to their jobs and found the following to be most important:

- Managing individual performance
- Instructing subordinates
- Planning and allocating resources
- Coordinating interdependent groups
- Managing group performance
- Monitoring the business environment
- Representing one's staff[23]

The researchers found that the relative importance of these activities varies with the level of management. For example, the first two were relatively more important to first-line supervisors; activities involved with linking groups was most important to middle managers; outside activities such as monitoring the business environment were most important to executive-level management; and an "ambassador" role of representing one's staff was important to all levels.[24]

Informal Organization Structures

Besides the informal roles that managers perform, the overall informal organization structure has important dynamics for the study of organizational behavior. The classic Milo study conducted by Melville Dalton remains the best illustration of the power of the informal organization.[25] Figure 12.4a represents the formal organiza-

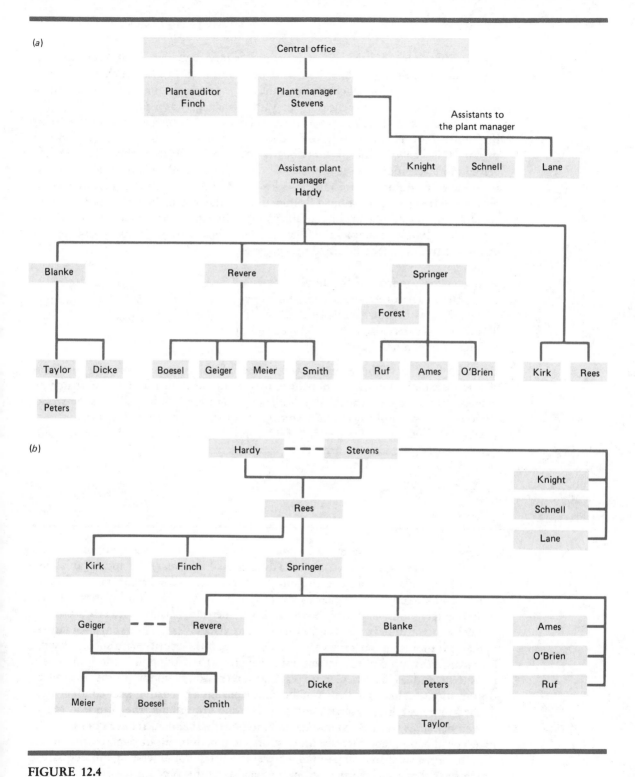

FIGURE 12.4
(*a*) A simplified formal organization chart of Milo. (*b*) An informal organization chart of Milo.
(*Source:* Adapted from Melville Dalton, *Men Who Manage,* Wiley, New York, 1959, pp. 21–22.)

tion at Milo. Through the use of intimates, interviews, diaries, observation, and socializing, Dalton was able to construct the informal organization chart shown in Figure 12.4*b*. This informal chart shows the actual power, as opposed to the formally designated power and influence, of the various managers at Milo.

Like the formal organization structures discussed in the next part of the book, the informal organization has both functions and dysfunctions. In contrast to formal organization analysis, the dysfunctional aspects of informal organization have received more attention than the functional ones. For example, conflicting objectives, restriction of output, conformity, blocking of ambition, inertia, and resistance to change are frequently mentioned dysfunctions of the informal organization.[26] More recently, however, organizational analysis has begun to recognize the functional aspects as well. For example, the following list suggests some practical benefits that can be derived from the informal organization:

1. Makes for a more effective total system.
2. Lightens the workload on management.
3. Fills in gaps in a manager's abilities.
4. Provides a safety valve for employee emotions.
5. Improves communication.[27]

Because of the inevitability and power of the informal organization, the functions should be exploited in the attainment of objectives rather than futilely combated by management. As a recent analysis of leadership points out, "informal social networks exert an immense influence which sometimes overrides the formal hierarchy. . . . Leadership goes beyond a person's formal position into realms of informal, hidden, or unauthorized influence."[28]

Summary

Groups represent an important dynamic input into organizational behavior. Group formation, types, and processes and the dynamics of informal roles and organization are all of particular relevance to the study of organizational behavior. Group formation can be theoretically explained by propinquity; as a relationship between activities, interactions, and sentiments; as a symmetrical balance between attraction and common attitudes; and as a reward-cost exchange. Participants in an organization also form into groups for very practical economic, security, and social reasons. Many different types of formal and informal groups are found in modern organizations. Committees in particular are playing an increasingly important role in modern organizations. Although they can be time-consuming, costly, and conducive to divided responsibility, excessive compromise, and groupthink, they can lead to improved decisions through combined and integrated judgment, reduce conflict, facilitate coordination, and increase motivation and commitment through participation.

Informal roles are being found increasingly useful for describing the true nature of managerial work. Informal structure coexists with every formal structure. The informal structure is not formally designated, but rather is determined by the various group-status positions and roles. Traditionally, only the dysfunctional aspects of informal organization have been emphasized. More recently, the functional aspects have also been recognized. Management in the future must be able to understand and, when possible, take advantage of group dynamics and informal roles and organization.

Questions for Discussion and Review

1. Briefly discuss the major theoretical explanations for group formation. Which explanation do you think is most relevant to the study of organizational behavior? Defend your choice.
2. What implications does the Schachter study have for the study of organizational behavior?
3. How can the disadvantages of committees be overcome?
4. What are some of the major symptoms of groupthink? Can you give an example from your own experience where this may have happened?
5. Summarize some of the informal managerial roles suggested by Mintzberg. Do you think that these roles are descriptive of what managers really do? Why or why not?
6. What are some functions of the informal organization? What are some of the dysfunctions?

References

1. Robert S. Feldman, *Understanding Psychology*, 2d ed., McGraw-Hill, New York, 1990, pp. 688–689.
2. George C. Homans, *The Human Group*, Harcourt, Brace & World, New York, 1950, pp. 43–44.
3. Theodore M. Newcomb, *The Acquaintance Process*, Holt, New York, 1961.
4. John W. Thibaut and Harold H. Kelley, *The Social Psychology of Groups*, Wiley, New York, 1959.
5. Brian Dumaine, "Who Needs a Boss," *Fortune*, May 7, 1990, p. 52.
6. William B. Stevenson, Jone L. Pearce, and Lyman Porter, "The Concept of 'Coalition' in Organization Theory and Research," *Academy of Management Review*, April 1985, pp. 261–262.
7. Nancy C. Morey and Fred Luthans, "The Use of Dyadic Alliances in Informal Organization: An Ethnographic Study," *Human Relations* (in press).
8. Eric Sundstrom, Kenneth P. De Meuse, and David Futrell, "Work Teams: Applications and Effectiveness," *American Psychologist*, February 1990, p. 120.
9. Stanley Schachter, Norris Ellertson, Dorothy McBride, and Doris Gregory, "An Experimental Study of Cohesiveness and Productivity," *Human Relations*, August 1951, pp. 229–239.
10. Leonard Berkowitz, "Group Standards, Cohesiveness, and Productivity," *Human Relations*, vol. 7, no. 4, 1954, pp. 509–519.
11. Barry W. Staw, "Organizational Psychology and the Pursuit of the Happy/Productive Worker,"

California Management Review, Summer 1986, p. 49.

12. Gregory P. Shea and Richard A. Guzzo, "Group Effectiveness: What Really Matters?" *Sloan Management Review*, Spring 1987, p. 25.

13. Cited in Thomas R. Horton, "In Praise of a Managerial Whipping Boy," *Management Review*, October 1990, p. 32.

14. Irving L. Janis, *Victims of Groupthink*, Houghton Mifflin, Boston, 1972, p. 9.

15. David G. Myers, *Social Psychology,* 3d ed., McGraw-Hill, New York, 1990, p. 297.

16. Carrie R. Leana, "A Partial Test of Janis' Groupthink Model: Effects of Group Cohesiveness and Leader Behavior on Defective Decision Making," *Journal of Management*, vol. 11, no. 1, 1985, pp. 5–17.

17. The original research on risky shift goes back to a master's thesis by J. A. F. Stoner, "A Comparison of Individual and Group Decisions Involving Risk," Massachusetts Institute of Technology, Sloan School of Industrial Management, Cambridge, Mass., 1961.

18. Richard A. Cosier and Charles R. Schwenk, "Agreement and Thinking Alike: Ingredients for Poor Decisions," *Academy of Management Executive*, February 1990, p. 70.

19. Don Hellriegel, John W. Slocum, Jr., and Richard W. Woodman, *Organizational Behavior*, 5th ed., West, St. Paul, 1989, p. 216.

20. Henry Mintzberg, "Retrospective Commentary on 'The Manager's Job: Folklore and Fact,'" *Harvard Business Review*, March–April, 1990, p. 170.

21. John Kotter, *General Managers*, Free Press, New York, 1982.

22. Fred Luthans, Richard M. Hodgetts, and Stuart A. Rosenkrantz, *Real Managaers*, Ballinger, Cambridge, Mass., 1988.

23. Allen I. Kraut, Patricia R. Pedigo, D. Douglas McKenna, and Marvin D. Dunnette, "The Role of the Manager: What's Really Important in Different Management Jobs," *Academy of Management Executive*, November 1989, p. 286.

24. Ibid., pp. 287–290.

25. Melville Dalton, *Men Who Manage*, Wiley, New York, 1959.

26. Ross Webber, *Management*, 2d ed., Irwin, Homewood, Ill., 1979, p. 118.

27. Keith Davis and John W. Newstrom, *Human Behavior at Work*, 7th ed., McGraw-Hill, New York, 1985, p. 311.

28. Louis B. Barnes and Mark P. Kriger, "The Hidden Side of Organizational Leadership," *Sloan Management Review*, Fall 1986, p. 15.

REAL CASE: THE MARIO BROTHERS STRIKE AGAIN	To many adults, the name Mario Brothers has no meaning; but among U.S. school children in a recent poll, Mario was more popular than Mickey Mouse. And well he might be, given that Nintendo has sold over 40 million copies of Super Mario Brothers, making it the all-time best-selling series of computer games. This is not to say that the competition is sitting on its hands: In fact, some of them have done a very good job of offering competitive products. For example, NEC unveiled a console that generated images superior to those offered by Nintendo and that looked like a sure winner. Unfortunately, so many young people were hooked on Nintendo's offerings that NEC was able to garner less than 10 percent of the U.S. market.

How does Nintendo manage to dominate the video game market? One way is by creating high cohesion among its employees and contractors and making this pay off in the form of high productivity and profit. For example, at Nintendo's research and development (R&D) center, groups of scruffy young engineers huddle in front of video screens and test and play video games. Sometimes the head of the R&D lab organizes his 200 people into rival teams that compete against each other. Result: The engineers learn more and more about how the games work, what is effective, and what needs improvement. They love the work and there is plenty of overtime pay for those who do not want to break away and go home.

Yet Nintendo does not restrict video game development efforts only to its R&D people. Ninety percent of the games come from outside contractors who assume the risk of developing and marketing the new titles. If a game is deemed worthy of being added to Nintendo's product line, the developer pays Nintendo to manufacture the cartridges, bears the cost of marketing and advertising, and agrees not to supply the game for other makes of machine. In turn, the individual is paid a royalty on each unit, and this can mean big dollars. Four years ago, Koichi Nakamura developed *Dragonquest,* which sold more than 10 million copies. Today, Nakamura is a millionaire and his contract company continues to work closely with Nintendo. He is only one of what are affectionately called "a brat pack of self-made millionaires," and like Nintendo, Nakamura knows how to treat his people in order to maintain high cohesion. He recently took his twenty-person staff to Hawaii for a surfing vacation.

Nintendo has found that the development of these games is so enjoyable and motivating that the personnel seem to thrive on the work. And the future promises even more interesting challenges. The firm is now working to develop more games for grownups, is introducing a new-generation game console that will produce more lavish video images than do current machines, and is looking into creating nationwide tournaments in which customers compete from their living rooms using Nintendos and TVs hooked to phone lines. But the company is not going to abandon its interest in the youth market. Nintendo recently gave $3 million to MIT for studies on how children learn. Obviously, the company wants its customers to be as hooked on video games as are its developers and contractors.

1. How has Nintendo managed to create high cohesion among its R&D employees?
2. How high is the cohesion and induction among the personnel who work for contractors such as Koichi Nakamura? Explain.
3. Do you think informal groups play any role in the success of Nintendo and the contractor firms? Why?

Case: The Schoolboy Rookie

Kent Sikes is a junior at State University. He has taken a summer job in the biggest factory in his hometown. He was told to report to the warehouse supervisor the first day at work. The supervisor assigned him to a small group of men who were responsible for loading and unloading the boxcars that supplied the materials and carried away the finished goods of the factory.

After two weeks on the job, Kent was amazed at how little work the men in his crew accomplished. It seemed that they were forever standing around and talking or, in some cases, even going off to hide when there was work to be done. Kent often found himself alone unloading a boxcar while the other members of the crew were off messing around someplace else. When Kent complained to his coworkers, they made it very plain that if he did not like it, he could quit, but if he complained to the supervisor, he would be sorry. Although Kent has been deliberately excluded from any of the crew's activities such as taking breaks together or having a Friday afternoon beer after work at the tavern across the street, yesterday he went up to one of the older members of the crew and said, "What gives with you guys, anyway? I am just trying to do my job. The money is good and I just don't give a hang about this place. I will be leaving to go back to school in a few weeks, and I wish I could have just trying to do my job. The money is good and I just don't give a hang about this place. I will be leaving to go back to school in a few weeks, and I wish I could have gotten to know you all better, but frankly I am sure glad I'm not like you guys." The older worker replied, "Son, if you'd been here as long as I have, you would be just like us."

1. Using some of the theories, explain the possible reasons for the group formation of this work crew. What types of groups exist in this case?
2. Place this work group in the Schachter study. What role does the supervisor play in the performance of this group?
3. What are the major informal roles of the crew members and Kent? What status position does Kent have with the group? Why?
4. Why hasn't Kent been accepted by the group? Do you agree with the older worker's last statement in the case? Why or why not?

Case: The Blue-Ribbon Committee	Mayor Sam Small is nearing completion of his first term in office. He feels his record has been pretty good, except for the controversial issue of housing. He has been able to avoid doing anything about housing so far and feels very strongly that this issue must not come to a head before the next election. The voters are too evenly divided on the issue, and he would lose a substantial number of votes no matter what stand he took. Yet with pressure increasing from both sides, he had to do something. After much distress and vacillation, he has finally come upon what he thinks is an ideal solution to his dilemma. He has appointed a committee to study the problem and make some recommendations. To make sure that the committee's work will not be completed before the election comes up, it was important to pick the right people. Specifically, Sam has selected his "blue-ribbon" committee from a wide cross section of the community so that, in Sam's words, "all concerned parties will be represented." He has made the committee very large, and the members range from Ph.Ds in urban planning to real estate agents to local ward committeepersons to minority group leaders. He has taken particular care in selecting people who have widely divergent, outspoken, public views on the housing issue.

1. Do you think Sam's strategy of using this committee to delay taking a stand on the housing issue until after the election will work? Why or why not?
2. What are some of the important dynamics of this committee? Do you think the committee will arrive at a good solution to the housing problems facing this city?
3. Do you think this committee will suffer from groupthink?
4. What types of informal roles is Sam exhibiting? Do you think he is an effective manager? Do you think he is an effective politician? Is there a difference?

13 Interactive Behavior and Conflict

■ Let's Do It Jointly

In the mid-1980s, Japan announced that it was going to build the FS-X jet fighter. The country's objective was to free itself from dependence on American weapons designs and to provide a basis for developing a commercial aircraft industry in Japan. However, the United States government objected and the Japanese eventually agreed to a "co-development" plan under which the aircraft's design would be based on the F-16 fighter built by General Dynamics. Under this arrangement, Mitsubishi Heavy Industries would work with technology from General Dynamics and build the planes in Japan. The plan looked fine on paper and the group proceeded toward the objective. Since then, unfortunately, there have been many problems.

The first big snag developed when Congress objected to the use of American-developed military technology as a springboard for building a commercial aircraft industry that would compete with American industry. Mistrust began to develop between the two parties. However, renegotiations eventually resolved some of the difficulties. It was now agreed that Japan would develop its own flight-control software for the aircraft, thus keeping some key American technologies out of Japanese hands.

However, a new problem arose when it became evident that the cost of building the FS-X was going to be a lot higher than anyone had originally thought. The original price for development had been placed at $1.25 billion but will probably be $2.5 billion or more. This means that the cost per plane is going to be in the range of $64 million, more than twice what it would have been had the plane been purchased outright from an aircraft manufacturer.

To make things even worse, there is now discussion in both Washington and Tokyo regarding canceling the project. The Americans feel that costs are out of hand; the Japanese wonder why they need a fighter aircraft since any threat from outsiders has declined markedly in recent years. However, it is likely that the project will continue, because both sides already have so much invested in it and the Japanese government will lose face if it pulls out now. On the other hand, there is not likely to be another joint venture like this for a long time because of the wide gulf of mistrust that has built up between both sides.

- **Discuss** intraindividual conflict due to frustration, goals, and roles.
- **Analyze** interpersonal conflict.
- **Identify** the dimensions of transactional analysis and the Johari window.
- **Define** the strategies of interpersonal conflict resolution.
- **Explain** intergroup behavior and conflict.
- **Relate** the dimensions of organizational conflict.

Interactive behavior can occur at the individual, interpersonal, group, or organizational level. It often results in conflict at all these levels. Although such conflict, especially intraindividual conflict, is very closely related to stress (discussed in Chapter 14), conflict is given separate treatment here because of the emphasis on interactive behavior. Thus, this chapter first analyzes intraindividual conflict stemming from frustration, goals, and roles. Next, interpersonal dynamics and the resulting conflict are examined from the perspective of transactional analysis and the Johari window. The last two sections are concerned with intergroup behavior and conflict and organizational conflict. Potential strategies for conflict resolution at each of these levels of analysis of interactive behavior (that is, individual, interpersonal, group, and organizational) are presented.

INTRAINDIVIDUAL CONFLICT

A smooth progression of the need-drive-goal motivational cycle (discussed in Chapter 6) and fulfillment of one's role expectations do not always occur in reality. Within every individual there are usually (1) a number of competing needs and roles, (2) a variety of different ways that drives and roles can be expressed, (3) many types of barriers which can occur between the drive and the goal, and (4) both positive and negative aspects attached to desired goals. These complicate the human adaptation process and often result in conflict. Intraindividual forms of conflict can be analyzed in terms of the frustration model, goals, and roles.

Conflict Due to Frustration

Frustration occurs when a motivated drive is blocked before a person reaches a desired goal. Figure 13.1 illustrates what happens. The barrier may be either overt (outward, or physical) or covert (inward, or mental-sociopsychological). An example of a frustrating situation might be that of a thirsty person who comes up against a stuck door and is prevented from reaching a water fountain. Figure 13.2 illustrates this simple frustrating situation. Frustration normally triggers defense mechanisms in the person. Traditionally, psychologists felt that frustration always leads to the defense mechanism of aggression. On becoming frustrated, it was thought that a person will react by physically or symbolically attacking the barrier. In the example in Figure 13.2, the person would react by kicking and/or cursing the jammed door.

More recently, aggression has come to be viewed as only one possible reaction. Frustration may lead to any of the defense mechanisms used by the human organism.

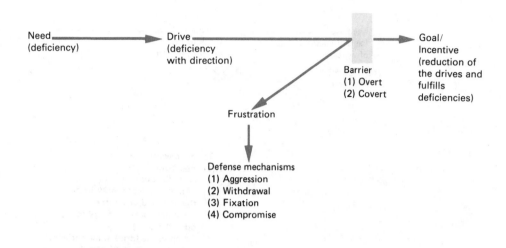

FIGURE 13.1
A simple model
of frustration.

Although there are many such mechanisms, they can be summarized into four broad categories: aggression, withdrawal, fixation, and compromise. In the illustration of Figure 13.2, backing away from the door and pouting would be an example of withdrawal; pretending the door is not jammed and continually trying to open it would be an example of fixation; and substituting a new goal (a cup of coffee already in the room) or a new direction (climbing out the window) would be an example of compromise.

Although the thirsty person frustrated by the stuck door is a very uncomplicated example, the same frustration model can be used to analyze more complex behavior. One example might be an African-American who comes from a disadvantaged educational and economic background but who still has intense needs for pride and dignity. A goal that may fulfill the individual's needs is meaningful employment. The drive set up to alleviate the need and accomplish the goal would be to search for a good job. The African-American in this example who meets barriers (prejudice, discrimination, lack of education, and nonqualification) may become frustrated. Possible reactions to this frustration may be aggression (riot or hate), withdrawal (apathy and unemployment), fixation (pretending the barriers do not exist and continuing to search unsuccessfully for a good job), or compromise (finding expression of pride and dignity in something other than a good job, such as in a militant group).

The frustration model can be useful in the analysis not only of behavior in general but also of specific aspects of on-the-job behavior. Table 13.1 summarizes some behavioral reactions to frustration that may occur in the formal organization. These examples generally imply that there is a negative impact on the individual's performance and on the organization as a result of frustration. Some of this frustration may actually be translated into real costs to the organization. For example, a survey of forty-seven corporations found that one-third of the employees reported

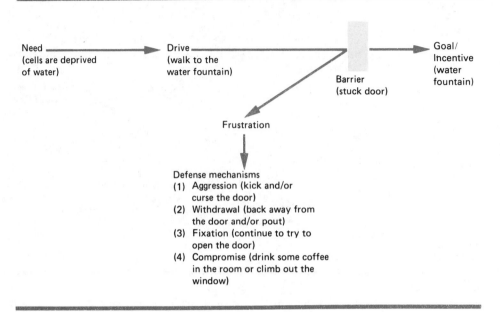

FIGURE 13.2
A simple example
of frustration.

stealing company property and that nearly two-thirds reported taking long lunch breaks, misusing sick leave, or using alcohol or drugs while at work.[1] A congressional report estimated that lost productivity and health problems caused by drugs are costing U.S. business at least $70 billion a year, and the National Institute on Drug Abuse believes one in every ten workers uses drugs to the degree that it interferes with job performance.[2]

Although these problems may not all be the result of frustration, even stealing, which is costing American business an estimated $5 to $10 billion per year, can be considered a form of displaced aggression resulting from on-the-job frustration. Thus, although the evidence indicates the dysfunctional nature of frustration, it should not be automatically assumed.

In some cases frustration may actually result in a positive impact on individual performance and organizational goals. An example is the worker or manager who has high needs for competence and achievement and who has a self-concept that includes confidence in being able to do a job well. A person of this type who is frustrated on the job may react in a traditional defensive manner, but the frustration may result in improved performance. The person may try harder to overcome the barrier or may overcompensate, or the new direction or goal sought may be more compatible with the organization's goals. In addition, it should be remembered that defense mechanisms per se are not bad for the individual. They play an important role in the psychological adjustment process and are "unhealthy" only when they dominate the individual's personality. Also those who have successfully overcome frustration in the past by learning that it is possible to surmount barriers or find substitute goals are more tolerant of frustration than those who have never experienced it, or those who have experienced excesses in frustration.[3] However, in general, a major goal of

TABLE 13.1 Examples of Reactions to Frustration

Adjustive Reactions	Psychological Process	Illustration
Compensation	Individual devotes himself to a pursuit with increased vigor to make up for some feeling of real or imagined inadequacy	Zealous, hard-working president of the Twenty-Five-Year Club who has never advanced very far in the company hierarchy
Displacement	Redirecting pent-up emotions toward persons, ideas, or objects other than the primary source of the emotion	Roughly rejecting a simple request from a subordinate after receiving a rebuff from the boss
Fantasy	Daydreaming or other forms of imaginative activity provide an escape from reality and imagined satisfactions	An employee daydream of the day in the staff meeting when he corrects the boss's mistakes and is publicly acknowledged as the real leader of the industry
Negativism	Active or passive resistance, operating unconsciously	The manager who, having been unsuccessful in getting out of a committee assignment, picks apart every suggestion that anyone makes in the meetings
Projection	Individual protects himself from awareness of his own undesirable traits or unacceptable feelings by attributing them to others	Unsuccessful person who, deep down, would like to block the rise of others in the organization and who continually feels that others are out to "get him"
Rationalization	Justifying inconsistent or undesirable behavior, beliefs, statements, and motivations by providing acceptable explanations for them	Padding the expense account because "everybody does it"
Regression	Individual returns to an earlier and less mature level of adjustment in the face of frustration	A manager, having been blocked in some administrative pursuit, busies himself with clerical duties or technical details more appropriate for his subordinates
Resignation, apathy, and boredom	Breaking psychological contact with the environment, withholding any sense of emotional or personal involvement	Employee who, receiving no reward, praise, or encouragement, no longer cares whether or not he does a good job
Flight or withdrawal	Leaving the field in which frustration, anxiety, or conflict is experienced, either physically or psychologically	The salesman's big order falls through and he takes the rest of the day off; constant rebuff or rejection by superiors and colleagues pushes an older worker toward being a loner and ignoring what friendly gestures are made

Source: Adapted from Timothy W. Costello and Sheldon S. Zalkind, *Psychology in Administration: A Research Orientation*, Prentice-Hall, Englewood Cliffs, N.J., 1963, pp. 148–149.

management should be to eliminate the barriers (imagined, real, or potential) that are or will be frustrating to employees.

Goal Conflict

Another common source of conflict for an individual is a goal which has both positive and negative features, or two or more competing goals. Whereas in frustration a single motive is blocked before the goal is reached, in goal conflict two or more motives block one another. For ease of analysis, three separate types of goal conflict are generally identified:

1. *Approach-approach* conflict, where the individual is motivated to approach two or more positive but mutually exclusive goals.
2. *Approach-avoidance* conflict, where the individual is motivated to approach a goal and at the same time is motivated to avoid it. The single goal contains both positive and negative characteristics for the individual.
3. *Avoidance-avoidance* conflict, where the individual is motivated to avoid two or more negative but mutually exclusive goals.

To varying degrees, each of these forms of goal conflict exists in the modern organization.

Approach-Approach Conflict. This type of goal conflict probably has the least impact on organizational behavior. Although conflict may arise about making a choice between two positive goals, they are preferable to two negative goals or a goal with both negative and positive characteristics. For example, if both personal and organizational goals are attractive to organizational participants, they will usually make a choice rather quickly and thus eliminate their conflict. A more specific example would be the new college graduate who is faced with two excellent job opportunities or the executive who has the choice between two very attractive offices in which to work. Such situations often cause the person some anxiety but are quickly resolved, and the person, unlike the donkey in the fable, does not "starve between two haystacks."

Approach-approach conflict can be analyzed in terms of the well-known theory of cognitive dissonance.[4] In simple terms, dissonance is the state of psychological discomfort or conflict created in people when they are faced with two or more goals or alternatives to a decision. Although these alternatives occur together, they do not belong or fit together. The theory states that the person experiencing dissonance will be highly motivated to reduce or eliminate it and will actively avoid situations and information which would be likely to increase it. For example, the young person faced with two equally attractive job opportunities would experience dissonance. According to this theory, the young person would actively try to reduce the dissonance. The individual may cognitively rationalize that one job is really better than the other one and, once the choice is made, be sincerely convinced that it was the right choice and actively avoid any evidence or argument to the contrary.

Approach-Avoidance Conflict. This type of goal conflict is most relevant to the analysis of organizational behavior. Normally, organizational goals have both positive and negative aspects for organization participants. Accordingly, the organizational goal may arouse a great deal of conflict within a person and may actually cause the person to vacillate anxiously at the point where approach equals avoidance.

Figure 13.3 shows some possible gradients for approach and avoidance. X represents the point of maximum conflict, where the organism may come to a complete stop and vacillate. In order for the organism to progress beyond X, there must be a shift in the gradients so that there is a greater strength of response for approach than for avoidance. The slopes of the gradients shown in Figure 13.3 approximate those obtained from animals who are first trained to approach food at the end of a runway and then are shocked while feeding there. As shown, the pull or effort toward a positive goal is stronger the nearer the goal, but not as strong as the tendency to get away from a negative goal. The slope of the avoidance from the negative goal is steeper than the slope of the approach to reach the positive goal.

The approach-avoidance gradients for humans will not always resemble those found in Figure 13.3. The slopes may be different for different people and different goals. In general, however, it is safe to assume that the positive aspects of a given organizational goal are stronger and more salient at a distance (in time and/or space) than the negative aspects. On the other hand, as a person gets nearer to the goal, the negative aspects become more pronounced, and at some point the individual may hesitate or fail to progress any further. For example, managers engaged in long-range planning typically are very confident of a goal (a strategic plan) they have developed for the future. Yet, as the time gets near to commit resources and implement the plan, the negative consequences seem to appeaer much greater than they did in the

FIGURE 13.3
Gradients of approach-avoidance conflict.

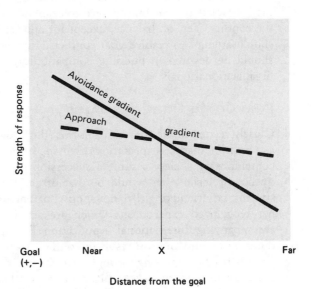

developing stage. Managers in such a situation may reach the point where approach equals avoidance. The result is a great deal of internal conflict and stress, which may cause indecision, ulcers, or even depression. Such conflict and its aftermath are very common among decision makers and people in responsible positions in modern, complex organizations. On the other hand, the approach-avoidance type of conflict can often be resolved in the same manner as cognitive dissonance, or the gradients may be shifted by the individual so that either the positive or the negative aspects clearly predominate.

Avoidance-Avoidance Conflict. Analogous to approach-approach conflict, this type of conflict does not have a great deal of impact on organizational behavior. Avoidance-avoidance conflict is usually easily resolved. A person faced with two negative goals may not choose either of them and may simply leave the situation. If this can be done, the conflict is quickly resolved. In some situations, however, the person is unable to leave. This would be true of persons in nonvoluntary organizations, such as inmates in a prison, patients in a hospital, or members of the armed services. To a lesser extent, most personnel in modern organizations are also restricted from leaving, for example, workers who detest their supervisor and have too much pride to be unemployed. Such workers cannot easily resolve their avoidance-avoidance conflict in a time when jobs are very scarce. This can lead to very dissatisfied workers who feel they have no escape.

Goal Conflict in Perspective. All three types of goal conflict might in certain instances benefit the organization. Approach-approach conflict can be mildly distressing for a person but represent the best of two worlds. Approach-avoidance conflict arising over organizational goals may force very careful planning and forecasting of exact positive and negative outcomes. Even avoidance-avoidance conflict may stimulate the person involved to examine and try to solve the problems causing the conflict. Yet, on balance, except for approach-approach conflicts, management should attempt to resolve goal conflicts. In particular, a major management effort should be devoted to building compatibility, not conflict, between personal and organizational goals.

Role Conflict and Ambiguity

Closely related to the concept of norms (the "oughts" of behavior), *role* was defined as a position that has expectations evolving from established norms. Persons living in contemporary society assume a succession of roles throughout life. A typical sequence of social roles would be that of child, son or daughter, teenager, college student, boyfriend or girlfriend, spouse, parent, and grandparent. Each of these roles has recognized expectations which are acted out like a role in a play. As the accompanying International Application Example shows, sometimes these roles differ by culture and can result in conflict.

Besides progressing through a succession of roles such as those just mentioned, the adult in modern society fills numerous other roles at the same time. It is not uncommon for the adult middle-class male to be simultaneously playing the roles of

**International
Application
Example**

Cultural Conflict

Japan's direct investment in the United States has increased dramatically in the last few years. This investment has not only brought new plants, technologies, and jobs to America but also has resulted in some conflict. The Japanese-run companies in the United States are an example of how cultural conflict can erupt. For instance, large Japanese companies are known for their lifetime employment policies, which purportedly produce corporate loyalty. Employees often stay in a Japanese company throughout their entire career. American workers, on the other hand, may work for several companies in the course of their career. Asa Jonishi, senior director of Japan's Kyocera Corporation, says, "Most Americans are very, very individualistic—you could almost say egotistic; they are quite different from the way we would like our people to be." Two other important cultural differences are trade unions and assertive women. In U.S. industry, both are common. The Japanese, on the other hand, have had little experience with either. As a result, Japanese companies are becoming experienced with lawsuits. For example, former female employees of Sumitomo Corporation of America filed a sex-discrimination suit that alleged that Sumitomo restricted women to clerical positions. Sumitomo settled the suit by promising to increase the number of women in sales and management positions. In another case, the AFL-CIO won a dispute with Toyota and its Japanese contractor. To end the negative publicity of the unions' campaign, Toyota and its contractor agreed to hire union workers to build their new plant.

It should be noted that some of the Japanese cultural values have been readily accepted in the American workplace. For instance, consensus management, which the Japanese are noted for, is being accepted in industries where autocratic leaders once existed. Pat Park, assistant general manager of Haseko, says, "There are many times when I'm the janitor here, picking up rubbish. But there are also many times the major decisions are made because I say so. There's more equity in Japanese companies." Thus, not all cultural differences lead to conflict. As all companies continue to transcend national borders, cultural differences may begin to narrow. However, culture still has a pervasive, but sometimes conflicting, influence on organizational behavior.

husband, father, provider, son (to elderly parents), worker or manager, student (in a night program), coach of a Little League baseball team, church member, member of a social club, bridge partner, poker club member, officer of a community group, and weekend golfer. Although all the roles which individuals bring into the organization are relevant to their behavior, in the study of organizational behavior the organizational role is the most important. Roles such as assembly line worker, clerk, supervisor, salesperson, engineer, systems analyst, department head, vice president, and chairperson of the board often carry conflicting demands and expectations.

There are three types of role conflict.[5] One type is the conflict between the *person and the role*. There may be conflict between the person's personality and the expectations of the role. For example, a production worker and member of the union is appointed to a supervisory position. This new supervisor may not really believe in keeping close control over the workers and it goes against the individual's personality to be "hard nosed," but that is what the head of production expects. A second type is *intrarole* conflict created by contradictory expectations about how a given role should be played. Should a new supervisor be autocratic or democratic in dealing with the workers? Finally, *interrole* conflict results from the differing requirements of two or more roles that must be played at the same time. Work roles and nonwork roles are often in such conflict. For example, one successful woman working for a computer company said that she often worked from 7:30 A.M. to 11:30 P.M. Her boyfriend got fed up with her long hours and left. When she got word that her mother was seriously ill, she remembered, "I had about five minutes to be upset before the phone started ringing again. You get so far into it, you don't even realize your life has gotten away from you completely."[6]

The first-line supervisor and the fast-climbing executive obviously represent the extreme cases of organizational role conflict. Yet to varying degrees, depending on the individual and the situation, people in every other position in the modern organization also experience one or all three types of conflict. Staff engineers are not sure of their real authority. The clerk in the front office does not know whether to respond to a union organizing drive. The examples are endless. The question is not whether role conflict and ambiguity exist—they do, and they seem inevitable. Rather, the key becomes a matter of determining how role conflict can be resolved or managed.

INTERPERSONAL CONFLICT

Besides the intraindividual aspects of conflict, the interpersonal aspects of conflict are also an important dynamic of interactive behavior. The interrole conflict discussed in the last section certainly has interpersonal implications, and so do intergroup and organizational conflict, discussed in the next sections. But this section is specifically concerned with analyzing the conflict that can result when two or more persons are interacting with one another. Two popular ways to analyze this interpersonal conflict are through transactional analysis and the Johari window.

Transactional Analysis

Eric Berne is usually credited with having started the transactional analysis (TA) movement with his best-selling book *Games People Play*; Thomas Harris's book *I'm OK—You're OK* further popularized TA. TA is still popular today and has a wide appeal. In many respects it is a fad and is sometimes confused with the equally popular transcendental meditation (TM) movement. However, TA has been able to transcend the fad stage because it is based on well-developed psychoanalytic theory. A major reason for its popularity, and where Freud and other pioneering psychoanalytic theorists failed, is that it uses very understandable, everyday, relevant terminology. Everyone can readily relate to the concepts and practice of TA. The following sections give attention to the three major areas of transactional analysis: ego states, transactions, and strokes and games.

Ego States. The ego plays a central role in the Freudian psychoanalytic model. In the structure of the human personality, the ego represents reality, and it rationally attempts to keep the impulsive id and the conscience of the superego in check. The ego is a hypothetical construct because it is not observable; it is used to help explain the complex dynamics of the human personality. TA uses this psychoanalytic theory as a background for identifying three important ego states: child, adult, and parent. These three ego states are roughly equivalent to the Freudian concepts of id (child), ego (adult), and superego (parent). A more detailed look at the three ego states is necessary to understand TA:

1. *Child (C) ego state.* This is the state in which the person acts like an impulsive child. This "child" state could be characterized by being either submissive and conforming (the dutiful child) or insubordinate, emotional, joyful, or rebellious (the "little brat"). In either case, the child state is characterized by very immature behavior. An example would be the employee who, when unfairly reprimanded by the boss, responds by saying, "You know best. Whatever you say." Another example would be the computer programmer who tells a coworker, "My boss makes me so mad sometimes I could scream" and then proceeds to burst into tears. Both examples illustrate immature, childlike behaviors.

2. *Adult (A) ego state.* In this state the person acts like a mature adult. In the adult state people attack problems in a "cool-headed," rational manner. They gather relevant information, carefully analyze it, generate alternatives, and make logical choices. In the adult state people do not act impulsively or in a domineering way. In dealings with other people, the adult state is characterized by fairness and objectivity. An example would be the sales manager who, when presented with a relatively high expense account by a subordinate, replies, "Well, this appears high, but we will have to look at the reasons for it. It may be that our other salespersons' expenses are too low to do the kind of job that needs to be done."

3. *Parent (P) ego state.* In this state people act like domineering parents. Individuals can be either overly protective and loving or stern and critical. The parent state is also illustrated by those who establish standards and rules for others. They tend to talk down to people and to treat others like children. An example would be the supervisor who comes up to a group of workers and says, "Okay, you guys, stop fooling around and get to work. You have to earn your keep around here."

Transactions between Ego States. It should be pointed out that people generally exhibit all three ego states, but one state may dominate the other two. The strong implication is, of course, that the adult state is far superior to the child or parent state, at least for effective interpersonal relations. However, the TA authors generally stress that all three ego states are necessary to a healthy personality. More important than the ego state per se is how one ego state matches or conflicts with another ego state in interpersonal interaction. The transactions between ego states are at the heart of TA and can be classified into the following:

1. *Complementary transactions.* Figure 13.4 shows three possible complementary transactions. As shown, transactions are complementary if the message sent or the behavior exhibited by one person's ego state receives the appropriate and expected response from the other person's ego state. For example, suppose that the two people interacting in Figure 13.4 are a boss and an immediate subordinate. In

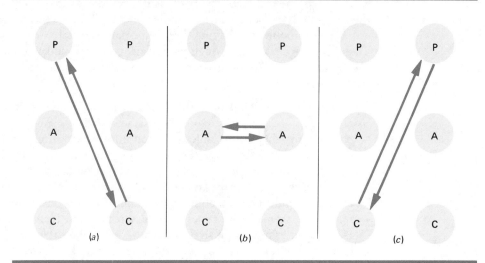

FIGURE 13.4
Complementary
transactions.

Figure 13.4*a*, the boss says, "Joe, I want you to be more careful in filling out a report on even the smallest accident. OSHA requirements are getting really tough, and we have to do better." The subordinate in Figure 13.4*a* replies, "Gee, boss, I really don't have time to fill out those dumb reports, but if you think I should, I will." In Figure 13.4*b*, the superior and subordinate both interact in an adult manner. For example, the boss says, "Joe, I would like your input on a report I am writing on how to improve the efficiency of the department." Joe responds by saying, "You bet, Jack. I have been gathering a lot of cost data over the past couple of months, and as soon as I analyze it, I would like to sit down with you and discuss it." In Figure 13.4*c*, the subordinate is in the parent state, and the boss is in the child state. Although rarer than the other two cases, an example might be the following dialogue:

Joe: Jack, I wish you would give more attention to maintenance around here. I can't do my job well unless you give me the proper support.

Boss: For heaven's sake! What do you want from me? You guys drive me up a wall. I can't take it anymore.

Once again it should be pointed out that although the adult-to-adult complementary transactions are probably most effective for organizational interpersonal relations, communication and understanding can also occur in the parent-child complementary transactions.

2. *Crossed transactions.* A crossed transaction occurs when the message sent or the behavior exhibited by one person's ego state is reacted to by an incompatible, unexpected ego state on the part of the other person. There are many more possible crossed transactions than there are complementary transactions. Figure 13.5 shows one crossed transaction that would typically occur in an organizational setting. As shown, the boss treats the subordinate like a child, but the

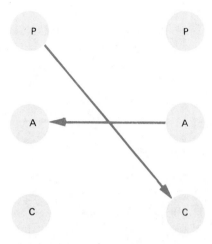

FIGURE 13.5
Crossed
transactions.

subordinate attempts to respond on an adult basis. The dialogue in this example might be as follows:

Boss: I have told you over and over that I want those reports in on time. You are going to have to meet my deadlines or look for another job.

Subordinate: I did not realize that the timing of the reports was so critical. I will have to reorder my priorities.

Crossed transactions are the source of much interpersonal conflict in an organization. The result can be hurt feelings and frustrations on the part of the parties involved and possible dysfunctional consequences for the organization.

3. *Ulterior transactions.* The most complex are the ulterior transactions. These can be very subtle, but, like the crossed transactions, they are generally very damaging to interpersonal relations. As shown in Figure 13.6, the ulterior transactions always involve at least two ego states on the part of one person. The individual may say one thing (for example, project an adult state, as indicated in Figure 13.6) but mean quite another (for example, the parent state, as shown by the dashed line in Figure 13.6). Although there are many other possibilities besides the one shown in Figure 13.6, an example is this typical one in organizations, where the boss says, "My door is always open; come in so that we can air your problems and reach a rational solution together" (adult state), when what he or she really means is, "Don't come whining to me with your troubles. Find an answer yourself. That is what you're getting paid for" (parent state). Obviously, these ulterior transactions are the most difficult to identify and deal with in transactional analysis.

Strokes and Games in TA. The three ego states and the three types of transactions are the basic elements of TA. In addition, however, there are other concepts and

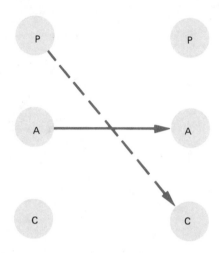

FIGURE 13.6
Ulterior
transactions.

dynamics inherent in the TA approach. Two of the more important are strokes and games:

1. *The concept of strokes.* TA experts feel that everyone has to have strokes. Using the common definition of the word, this means simply that beginning in infancy and continuing throughout their lives, people need cuddling, affection, recognition, and praise. Not everyone is turned on by the same strokes. (In the vernacular of TA this is stated as "different strokes for different folks.") But everyone needs them. It may be a simply "Good morning" or a pat on the back every once in a while. If people do not get such positive strokes, they will seek out negative strokes. The latter case may be the outgrowth of childhood experiences. People in this case tend to discount any attempts to give them positive strokes. Obviously, this TA concept of strokes is very closely related to the learning concept of reinforcement. For example, positive strokes could be thought of as social reinforcers.

2. *The games people play.* TA is also concerned with the ways that people structure their time. These games are a set or pattern of transactions that have surface logic but hidden meanings and attempt to draw in an unsuspecting participant. The outcome of games is almost always a win-lose proposition. Straightforward as well as devious people commonly play games. Games that are frequently played in organizations are summarized in Table 13.2. The games summarized in the table are only representative examples of the games people play in organizations. Anyone who has spent some time working can readily identify with many of these and other games that people play in organizational life. Most are dysfunctional for productive interpersonal relations and detract from organizational effectiveness. The goal should be to create an organizational climate that does not need or tolerate game playing.

TABLE 13.2 Games People Play in Organizations

Name of Game	Brief Description of Game
1. Now I've Got You, You S.O.B. (N.I.G.Y.Y.S.O.B.)	One employee gets back at another by luring her into what appears to be a natural work relationship. Actually the situation is rigged so that the other will fail. When the inevitable mistake is made, the game player pounces on the associate and publicly embarrasses her.
2. Poor Me	The person depicts himself to the boss as helpless. Criticisms for inadequate performance are avoided because the boss truly feels sorry for the individual, who may actually begin to feel sorry for himself.
3. Blemish	The boss appears to be objectively evaluating an employee's total performance. In reality, the boss is looking for some minor error. When the error is found, the employee is berated for the poor performance, the inference being that the whole project/task is inadequate.
4. Hero	The boss consistently sets up situations in which employees fail. At some point, the boss steps in to save the day miraculously.
5. King of the Hill	The boss sets up situations in which employees end up in direct competition with her. At the end, she steps in and demonstrates her competence and superiority while publicly embarrassing her employees.
6. Cops and Robbers	An employee continuously walks a fine line between acceptable and unacceptable behavior. The boss wastes unnecessary time desperately trying to catch the employee, while the employee stays one step ahead and laughs to himself through the day.
7. Prosecutor	The employee carefully carries around a copy of the union contract or organization regulations and investigates management practices. This employee dares the boss to act in an arbitrary manner. Once he does, the employee files a grievance and attempts to embarrass the boss.
8. If It Weren't for You. . . .	The employee discusses her problems openly but carefully works the conversation around so that she can rationalize her failure by blaming the boss for everything that goes wrong.
9. Yes, but. . . .	The boss responds with "Yes, but. . . ." to every good answer or idea that the subordinate may have. By doing this, the boss can maintain a superior position and keep subordinates in their place. It represents a form of pseudoparticipation; that is, the boss asks for participation but answers every suggestion with "Yes, but. . . ."

Source: Adapted from Fred Luthans and Mark J. Martinko, *The Practice of Supervision and Management,* McGraw-Hill, New York, 1979, pp. 386–387, which in turn is adapted from the literature on transactional analysis.

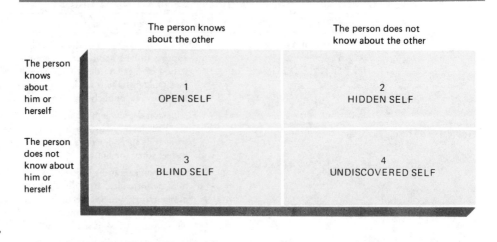

FIGURE 13.7
The Johari
window.
(*Source:* Adapted
from Joseph Luft,
"The Johari Win-
dow," *Human
Relations Training
News,* vol. 5, no. 1,
1961, pp. 6–7.)

The Johari Window

Besides transactional analysis, the other popular framework for analyzing the dynamics of interpersonal behavior is the Johari window. Developed by Joseph Luft
and Harry Ingham (thus the name *Johari*), this model is particularly useful in
analyzing interpersonal conflict. As Figure 13.7 shows, the model helps identify
several interpersonal styles, shows the characteristics and results of these styles, and
suggests ways of interpreting the conflicts that may develop between the self and
others.

In simple terms, the self can be thought of as "me," and others can be thought
of as "you" in a two-person interaction. There are certain things that the person
knows about himself or herself and certain things that are not known. The same is
true of others. There are certain things the person knows about the other and certain
things that are not known. The following summarizes the four cells in the Johari
window:

1. *Open self.* In this form of interaction the person knows about himself or herself
   and about the other. There would generally be openness and compatibility and
   little reason to be defensive. This type of interpersonal relationship would tend to
   lead to little, if any, interpersonal conflict.
2. *Hidden self.* In this situation the person understands himself or herself but does
   not know about the other person. The result is that the person remains hidden
   from the other because of the fear of how the other might react. The person may
   keep his or her true feelings or attitudes secret and will not open up to the other.
   There is potential interpersonal conflict in this situation.
3. *Blind self.* In this situation the person knows about the other but not about
   himself or herself. The person may be unintentionally irritating to the other. The
   other could tell the person but may be fearful of hurting the person's feelings. As
   in the hidden self, there is potential interpersonal conflict in this situation.
4. *Undiscovered self.* This is potentially the most explosive situation. The person
   does not know about himself or herself and does not know about the other. In

other words, there is much misunderstanding, and interpersonal conflict is almost sure to result.

The Johari window only points out possible interpersonal styles. It does not necessarily describe, but rather helps analyze, possible interpersonal conflict situations.

One way of decreasing the hidden self and increasing the open self is through the processes of self-disclosure. By becoming more trustful of others and disclosing information about themselves, people may reduce the potential for conflict. On the other hand, such self-disclosure is a risk for the individual, and the outcome must be worth the cost. To decrease the blind self and at the same time increase the open self, the other must give feedback, and the person must use it.

Strategies for Interpersonal Conflict Resolution

Besides the conflict resolution strategies inherent in the discussion of transactional analysis (for example, getting on an adult-to-adult level of transaction or quitting game playing), the Johari window (for example, moving to the open self or providing self-disclosure and feedback), and some simple ways of dealing with crises such as are found in the accompanying Application Example, there are three other basic strat-

Application Example

Dealing with Crises

A manager at a small cosmetics company learned that his firm had just been acquired by a large international conglomerate. His staff wanted to know how this would affect the firm's current plans for the new fiscal year. When he asked his boss, he was told, "Don't worry about anything. It's going to be business as usual." The manager had a difficult time accepting this. So did his staff, many of whom were convinced that their jobs were in jeopardy.

This situation is common in industry these days, and the worst part for many managers is that they will not know for several months how everything is going to turn out. In the interim, they need a strategy for dealing with the resulting conflict. What can they do? Psychologists who have studied these situations have concluded that there are two phases to crisis management: (*a*) emotion and (*b*) reason and action. By mentally "walking through" these two phases, psychologists contend, it is possible to get oneself prepared for managing in a crisis. The emotional phase is typically characterized by negative responses. Some managers feel panic brought on by the dismay and confusion caused by the crisis. Most feel some degree of anger, which is then followed by feelings of guilt. However, these feelings are then typically replaced by a take-charge attitude. The manager begins looking for ways of straightening out the situation. This is when the second phase begins. The reason and action phase is characterized by an assessment of the facts, followed by effective decision making. This entails examining the situation and setting goals, assessing ways of straightening things out, rebuilding confidence among the subordinates, and developing effective two-way communication. At this point the situation is usually well under control.

Whenever there is a setback or disaster, managers are likely to go through these two phases. The better that managers understand their emotional reactions to the crisis, the more effectively they tend to respond—and the more likely it is that they will succeed.

egies that individuals can use in interpersonal conflict situations (for that matter, these could also be used in intergroup and organizational conflict resolution). These are the lose-lose, win-lose, and win-win approaches. The win-win strategy is the most effective, but since the other two types are so commonly used, they should also be understood.

Lose-Lose In a lose-lose approach to conflict resolution, both parties lose. It has been pointed out that this approach can take several forms.[7] One of the more common approaches is to compromise or take the middle ground in a dispute. A second approach is to pay off one of the parties in the conflict. These payments often take the form of bribes. A third approach is to use an outside third party or arbitrator. A final type of lose-lose strategy appears when the parties in a conflict resort to bureaucratic rules or existing regulations to resolve the conflict. In all four of these approaches, both parties in the conflict lose. It is sometimes the only way that conflicts can be resolved, but it is generally less desirable than the win-lose or, especially, the win-win strategy.

Win-Lose. A win-lose strategy is a very common way of resolving conflict in American society. In a competitive type of culture, as is generally found in the United States, one party in a conflict situation attempts to marshal its forces to win, and the other party loses. The following list summarizes some of the characteristics of a win-lose situation:

1. There is a clear we-they distinction between the parties.
2. The parties direct their energies toward each other in an atmosphere of victory and defeat.
3. The parties see the issue from their own point of view.
4. The emphasis is on solutions rather than on the attainment of goals, values, or objectives.
5. Conflicts are personalized and judgmental.
6. There is no differentiation of conflict-resolving activities from other group processes, nor is there a planned sequence of those activities.
7. The parties take a short-run view of the issues.[8]

Examples of win-lose strategies can be found in superior-subordinate relationships, line-staff confrontations, union-management relations, and many other conflict situations found in today's organizations. The win-lose strategy can have both functional and dysfunctional consequences for the organization. It is functional in the sense of creating a competitive drive to win, and it can lead to cohesiveness and esprit de corps among the individuals or groups in the conflict situation. On the dysfunctional side, a win-lose strategy ignores other solutions such as a cooperative, mutually agreed-upon outcome; there are pressures to conform, which may stifle a questioning, creative atmosphere for conflict resolution; and highly structured power relationships tend to emerge rapidly. The biggest problem, however, with a win-lose strategy is that someone always loses. Those who suffer the loss may learn something in the process, but losers also tend to be bitter and vindictive. A much healthier strategy is to have both parties in a conflict situation win.

Win-Win. A win-win strategy of conflict resolution is probably the most desirable from a human and organizational standpoint. Energies and creativity are aimed at solving the problems rather than beating the other party. It takes advantage of the functional aspects of win-lose and eliminates many of the dysfunctional aspects. The needs of both parties in the conflict situation are met, and both parties receive rewarding outcomes. A review of the relevant literature revealed that "win-win decision strategies are associated with better judgments, favorable organization experience, and more favorable bargains."[9] Although it is often difficult to accomplish a win-win outcome of an interpersonal conflict, this should be a major goal of the management of conflict.

INTERGROUP BEHAVIOR AND CONFLICT

Conceptually similar to interpersonal behavior is intergroup behavior. The last chapter concentrated on *intra*group behavior and dynamics. There are also some interesting dynamics and resulting conflict that occur between groups. An understanding of the theoretical framework for intergroup behavior is a prerequisite for examining the conflict that often results.

Intergroup Behavior in Organizations

The chapters in Part 5 of the book deal specifically with organization process and design. One way to look at organizations, however, is in terms of interacting groups. Instead of depicting an organization as being made up of interacting individuals, one could think of it as consisting of interacting and overlapping role sets.

Interacting and Overlapping Role Sets. Once again the role concept can be used in the understanding of intergroup behavior. In particular, all organizational participants would have certain expectations of others and of themselves concerning what would be involved in their roles. The organization could be thought of as a set of such roles, and when these roles are in interaction with one another, the organization could more realistically be pictured as a system of overlapping role sets; this often results in conflict.

Robert L. Kahn is most closely associated with the role-set theory of organization. In Kahn's view the organization is made up of overlapping and interlocking role sets. These role sets would normally transcend the boundaries of the classical conception of organizations. Figure 13.8 gives an example of the interacting role-set concept of organization. The figure shows only three possible role sets from a large manufacturing organization. The purchasing agent, executive vice president, and design engineer are called the *focal persons* of the sets shown. The supplier's and consultant's roles are vital in their respective sets but would not be included within traditional organizational boundaries. They are external to the classical organization. The design engineer is a member of the purchasing agent's role set but is also a focal person for another role set. The production manager is shown as a member of two role sets. The overlaps can result in role conflicts and ambiguities. Such dynamics become important in conflict analysis.

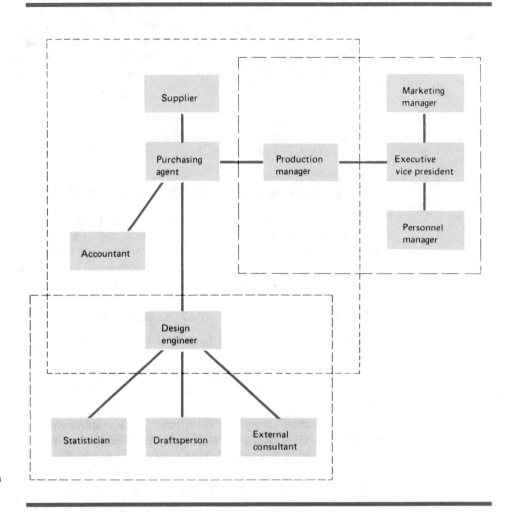

FIGURE 13.8
The organization
as overlapping
role sets.

Antecedents to Intergroup Conflict. Several antecedent conditions have been identified for explaining intergroup conflict. These can be summarized as follows:[10]

1. *Competition for resources.* Most organizations today have very limited resources.
   Groups within the organization vie for budget funds, space, supplies, personnel,
   and support services.
2. *Task interdependence.* If two groups in the organization depend on one another in
   a mutual way or even one-way (as in a sequential technological process), there
   tends to be more conflict than if groups are independent of one another. The more
   diverse the objectives, priorities, and personnel are of the interdependent groups
   (for example, research and production), the more conflict there tends to be.
3. *Jurisdictional ambiguity.* This may involve "turf" problems or overlapping responsibilities. For example, conflict might occur when one group attempts to

assume more control or take credit for desirable activities, or give up its part and any responsibility for undesirable activities.

4. *Status struggles.* This conflict occurs when one group attempts to improve its status and another group views this as a threat to its place in the status hierarchy. One group may also feel it is being inequitably treated in comparison with another group of equal status in terms of rewards, job assignments, working conditions, privileges, or status symbols. Human Resources Departments typically feel they are treated inequitably in relation to sales, finance, or production departments.

The Impact of, and Strategies for, Intergroup Conflict

Presenting interacting groups in terms of the overlapping role set and some antecedents provides a better understanding of the dynamics and resulting conflict that can occur. Groups in conflict have much different behavior from that of smoothly cooperating groups. There is evidence that groups in conflict change both internally and in relation to one another. "Unfortunately, these changes generally result in either a continuance or an escalation of the conflict."[11] In particular, after searching the relevant literature, Daft identified the following characteristics of groups in conflict:

1. There is a clear distinction and comparison between "we" (the in-group) and "they" (the out-group).
2. A group that feels it is in conflict with another group becomes more cohesive and pulls together to present a solid front to defeat the other group.
3. The positive feelings and cohesion within the in-group do not transfer to the members of the out-group. The members of the out-group are viewed as the enemy rather than as neutrals.
4. Threatened group members feel superior—they overestimate their strength and underestimate that of members of other groups.
5. The amount of communication between conflicting groups decreases. When there is communication, it is characterized by negative comments and hostility.
6. If a group is losing in a conflict, the members' cohesion decreases and they experience increased tension among themselves. They look for a scapegoat to blame their failure on.
7. The intergroup conflict and resulting hostility are not the result of neurotic tendencies on the part of individual members. These seem to be a product of group interaction, even when individuals in the group are normal and well adjusted.[12]

The above findings from research help describe and provide an understanding of the behavior of conflicting groups in organizations such as unions and management, production and sales, office personnel and operating personnel, nurses and doctors, and faculty and administrators. There is even some evidence that gender may affect intergroup behavior. Research indicates that although men and women are equally adept at helping groups solve conflict, women tend to seek changes in future behavior while men tend to push for more immediate results.[13]

There is also recent theoretical analysis indicating the importance that the origin of the group (for example, mandated versus voluntary) and the degree of externally imposed task structure (for example, high versus low) may have on the outcomes of intergroup interactions.[14] For example, mandated groups with high external task structure are predicted to have low member satisfaction and minimal quality of output while voluntary groups with low external task structure are predicted to have high member satisfaction and high quality of output. These indications, of course, need to be tested by empirical research, but if the model proves predictive, it could greatly help managers make better decisions in forming and structuring interacting groups.

Flowing out of this profile are a number of strategies that can be employed to reduce the conflict. These can be summarized into four major types:

1. *Avoidance.* This type of strategy attempts to keep the conflict from surfacing at all. Examples would be to simply ignore the conflict or impose a solution. This may be appropriate if the conflict is trivial or if quick action is needed to prevent the conflict from occurring.

2. *Defusion.* Under this strategy, an attempt is made to deactivate the conflict and cool off the emotions and hostilities of the groups involved. Examples would include trying to "smooth things over" by playing down the importance and magnitude of the conflict or of established superordinate goals that need the cooperation of the conflicting groups in order to be accomplished. This strategy is appropriate where a stopgap measure is needed or when the groups have a mutually important goal.

3. *Containment.* Under this strategy, some conflict is allowed to surface, but it is carefully contained by spelling out which issues are to be discussed and how they are to be resolved. To carry out this strategy, the problems and procedures may be structured, and representatives from the conflicting parties may be allowed to negotiate and bargain within the structure established. This is appropriate where open discussions have failed and the conflicting groups are of equal power.

4. *Confrontation.* Under this strategy, which is at the other end of the continuum from avoidance, all the issues are brought into the open, and the conflicting groups directly confront the issues and each other in an attempt to reach a mutually satisfactory solution. This may involve mutual problem solving or even formally redesigning jobs or responsibilities in order to resolve the conflict. This is most appropriate when there is a minimum level of trust, when time is not critical, and when the groups need to cooperate to get the job done effectively.[15]

There are many other strategies that could be used besides those described above. For example, conflict management techniques such as the following can be used: superordinate goal (a common goal that is appealing to conflicting groups); the reduction of interdependence between the conflicting groups; expanding resources so that competition between the groups is minimized; mutual problem solving to get the conflicting groups together in a face-to-face meeting; creation of a formal appeals system; and merging conflicting groups.[16] In addition, the win-win perspective is important, and many of the organization development techniques presented in Chapter 21 are also applicable.

ORGANIZATIONAL CONFLICT

So far, this chapter has focused, in turn, on intraindividual, interpersonal, and intergroup conflict. All these types of conflict take place within the organizational setting. However, now attention is directed at organizational conflict per se, but it must be remembered that intraindividual, interpersonal, and intergroup conflict are all inherent in organizational conflict.

Structural Conflict

Individuals in the organization have many conflicting organizational cross pressures operating on them. For example, in the classical organization there are four predominant types of structural conflict:

1. *Hierarchical conflict.* There may be conflict between the various levels of the organization. The board of directors may be in conflict with top management, middle management may be in conflict with supervisory personnel, or there may be general conflict between management and the workers.
2. *Functional conflict.* There may be conflict between the various functional departments of the organization. Conflict between the production and marketing departments in an industrial organization is a classic example.
3. *Line-staff conflict.* There may be conflict between line and staff. It often results from situations in which staff personnel do not formally possess authority over line personnel.
4. *Formal-informal conflict.* There may be conflict between the formal and informal organizations. For example, the informal organization's norms for performance may be incompatible with the formal organization's norms for performance.

These forms of organizational conflict have been given attention in other chapters. However, the example of line-staff conflict is representative of organizational conflict. In particular, the classic research of Melville Dalton is a good example of an analysis of line-staff conflict.[17] Also covered in Chapter 12, his case study of Milo (a pseudonym), a factory of 8000 employees, has become a classic analysis of line-staff conflict. Through detailed observations, Dalton was able to record actual conflict that occurred between line and staff personnel at this plant. One of his major conclusions was that line managers often view staff advice as a threat. An example was the case of R. Jefferson, a staff engineer who devised a new plan for toolroom operations. At least two line supervisors admitted privately to Dalton that the plan had merit, but they nevertheless rejected it. One of them, H. Clause, explained why:

> Jefferson's idea was pretty good. But his . . . overbearing manner queered him with me. He came out here and tried to ram the scheme down our throats. He made me so . . . mad I couldn't see. The thing about him and the whole white-collar bunch that burns me up is the way they expect you to jump when they come around. . . . I been in this plant twenty-two years. I've worked in tool rooms, too. I've forgot more than most of these college punks'll ever know. I've worked with all kinds of schemes and all kinds of people. You see what I mean—I've been around, and I don't need a punk like Jefferson telling me where to head in. I wouldn't take that kind of stuff from my own kid—and he's an engineer too. No, his [Jefferson's]

scheme may have some good points, but not good enough to have . . . him lording it over you. He acted like we had to use his scheme. . . . that noise! Him and the whole white-collar bunch—I don't mean any offense to you—can go to . . . We've got too . . . many bosses already.[18]

In support of the classic conflict situation, Dalton documented that at Milo the staff personnel were substantially younger and had more formal education than the line supervisors. Combined with social factors, these personal characteristics were given as the major factors explaining the organizational conflicts which existed at Milo. However, in a later study, Dalton found some indication that the traditional line-staff conflict model may be changing, at least in some industries. His study of Transode Corporation, a fictitious name given to an electronics firm that employed a highly technical engineering staff that had no official hierarchy and a group of line officers who were formed into a strict hierarchy, provided insights into how conflict can be reduced. In this situation, friction was decreased by "assigning each individual a specific authority, by obscuring status symbols and by stressing symbols of science, quality, and service that allowed all officers to share the luster of association with a vital product."[19]

A very simple solution to help alleviate line-staff conflict and improve communications would be for all staff personnel to use the approach of "sell before tell" when dealing with line personnel. Taken philosophically and literally, this approach has great merit for improving line-staff relationships and thus resolving organizational conflict.

Besides the classic structural conflicts such as line-staff conflict, more contemporary organization designs (covered in Chapter 18) also contain potential conflict situations. The project and matrix organizations in particular have structurally created conflict. The project manager with responsibility but no authority and the manager in a matrix structure with a functional boss and a project boss present two prominent conflict situations. However, like other types of intraindividual, interpersonal, and intergroup conflict, conflict in modern organization designs can also be healthy. In some cases the modern designs may actually try to promote conflict to benefit the organization.

The Role of Conflict in Today's Organizations

Traditionally, the approach to organizational conflict was very simple and optimistic. It was based on the following assumptions:

1. Conflict is by definition avoidable.
2. Conflict is caused by troublemakers, boat rockers, and prima donnas.
3. Legalistic forms of authority such as "going through channels" or "sticking to the book" are emphasized.
4. Scapegoats are accepted as inevitable.[20]

Management traditionally relied on formal authority and classical organization restructuring to solve their "conflict problem." Individual managers often became hypocritical in order to avoid conflicts from above or below. They tried to either ignore conflict or rationalize it away with the position that there is nothing that can be done about it.

Starting with the wide acceptance of the Argyris thesis that there is a basic incongruence between the needs and characteristics of adult, mature employees and the requirements of the modern formal organization, the behavioral approach to management began to reexamine its assumptions and concerns about conflict. This development has, at least indirectly, been caused by the overall societal concern with conflict on national, organizational, group, and individual bases. The outcome has been a new set of assumptions about organizational conflict, which are almost the exact opposite of the traditional assumptions. Some of the new assumptions about conflict are the following:

1. Conflict is inevitable.
2. Conflict is determined by structural factors such as the physical shape of a building, the design of a career structure, or the nature of a class system.
3. Conflict is integral to the nature of change.
4. A minimal level of conflict is optimal.[21]

Using such assumptions as a starting point, most experts today emphasize the importance of making a cost benefit analysis of the conflict situation at any level and then setting up dispute systems.[22] Also, experts urge an expanded view of conflict in organizations. For example, it is suggested that conflict be viewed as a cognitive bargaining process that should focus on negotiation as a way to manage and resolve conflict.[23]

The next chapter, on stress, will use this chapter's discussion of conflict as a foundation and point of departure.

Summary

The dynamics of interactive behavior at individual, interpersonal, group, and organizational levels, and the resulting conflict, play an increasingly important role in the analysis and study of organizational behavior. Although conflict and stress are conceptually and practically similar, especially at the individual level, they are covered separately (Chapter 14 is devoted to stress). Conflict at the intraindividual level involves frustration, goal conflict, and role conflict and ambiguity. Frustration occurs when goal-directed behavior is blocked. Goal conflict can come about from approach-approach, approach-avoidance, or avoidance-avoidance situations. Role conflict and ambiguity result from a clash in the expectations of the various roles possessed by an individual and can take the forms of person and role conflict, intrarole conflict, or interrole conflict. Interpersonal conflict was examined within the frameworks of transactional analysis and Johari window styles (open self, hidden self, blind self, and undiscovered self) and of the three major strategies of interpersonal conflict resolution (lose-lose, win-lose, and win-win). Next, intergroup conflict was examined from the perspective of overlapping role sets and antecedent causes and the strategies of avoidance, defusion, containment, and confrontation. The broader organizational perspective of conflict can be found in both the classical (hierarchical, functional, line-staff, and formal-informal) and modern (project and matrix) structures. Traditionally, the management of organizational conflict was based on simplistic assumptions. Formal authority and classical restructuring were used in attempts to eliminate it. The more modern approach is to assume the inevitability of conflict, recognize that it is not always bad for the organization, and try to manage it effectively rather than merely try to eliminate it.

Questions for Discussion and Review

1. What is frustration? What are some of its manifestations? How can the frustration model be used to analyze organizational behavior?
2. Explain approach-avoidance conflict. Give a realistic organizational example of where it may occur.
3. What are the three ego states in TA? Give an example of each of the three major transactions. What are strokes in TA? Give examples of some you have received in the last day or two. Can you describe any TA games you have been involved in lately?
4. Briefly summarize the four "selfs" in the Johari window. What implications does each have for interpersonal conflict?
5. How do groups in conflict behave? What are the four strategies that can be used to manage intergroup conflict effectively?
6. How do the traditional assumptions about organizational conflict differ from the modern assumptions? What implications do these new assumptions have for the management of organizational conflict?

References

1. "Survey: Third of Employees Stealing on Job," *Omaha World Herald*, June 11, 1983, p. 2.
2. "Workers' Drug Use Becomes a Drag on U.S. Productivity," *Lincoln Journal*, Mar. 3, 1986, p. 8.
3. Spencer A. Rathus, *Psychology*, 4th ed., Holt, Rinehart and Winston, Fort Worth, 1990, p. 437.
4. Leon Festinger, *A Theory of Cognitive Dissonance*, Stanford University Press, Stanford, Calif., 1957.
5. See David G. Myers, *Social Psychology*, 3d ed., McGraw-Hill, New York, 1990, pp. 178–179.
6. Brian O'Reilly, "Is Your Company Asking Too Much?" *Fortune*, March 12, 1990, p. 39.
7. Alan C. Filley, Robert J. House, and Steven Kerr, *Managerial Process and Organizational Behavior*, 2d ed., Scott, Foresman, Glenview, Ill., 1976, pp. 166–167.
8. Ibid., p. 167.
9. Ibid., p. 177.
10. See Gary Yukl, *Skills for Managers and Leaders*, Prentice Hall, Englewood Cliffs, N.J., 1990, pp. 283–285.
11. James L. Gibson, John M. Ivancevich, and James H. Donnelly, Jr., *Organizations*, 6th ed., Business Publications, Plano, Tex., 1988, p. 314.
12. Richard L. Daft, *Organization Theory and Design*, West, St. Paul, Minn., 1983, pp. 424–425.
13. "Labor Letter," *The Wall Street Journal*, Jan. 10, 1987, p. 1.
14. Janice H. Schopler, "Interorganizational Groups: Origins, Structure, and Outcomes," *Academy of Management Review*, October 1987, pp. 702–713.
15. Daniel C. Feldman and Hugh J. Arnold, *Managing Individual and Group Behavior in Organizations*, McGraw-Hill, New York, 1986, pp. 223–225.
16. See Stephen P. Robbins, *Organization Theory*, 3d ed., Prentice-Hall, Englewood Cliffs, N.J., 1990, pp. 425–431.

17. Melville Dalton, *Men Who Manage*, Wiley, New York, 1959; Melville Dalton, "Conflicts between Staff and Line Managerial Officers," *American Sociological Review*, June 1950, pp. 342–350; and Melville Dalton, "Changing Staff-Line Relationships," *Personnel Administration*, March–April 1966, pp. 3–5, 40–48.

18. Dalton, *Men Who Manage*, p. 75.

19. Dalton, "Changing Staff-Line Relationships," p. 45.

20. Joe Kelly, *Organizational Behavior*, rev. ed., Dorsey-Irwin, Homewood, Ill., 1975, p. 555.

21. Ibid.

22. Jeanne M. Brett, Stephen B. Goldberg, and William L. Ury, "Designing Systems for Resolving Disputes in Organizations," *American Psychologist*, February 1990, pp. 162–170.

23. Robin L. Pinkley, "Dimensions of Conflict Frame: Disputant Interpretations of Conflict," *Journal of Applied Psychology*, vol. 75, no. 2, 1990, p. 117.

REAL CASE: DO JUST THE OPPOSITE

One of the major reasons for organizational conflict is a downturn in the economy. When things start going bad, most companies cut back their expenses and start laying off people. Recent research shows that this may be the worst strategy of all, because it is too defensive in nature. When things get bad, this may be the time for the company to strike out and take advantage of the situation. Simply put, when times get bad successful firms do the opposite of what everyone else is doing. A recent analysis put it this way:

> Old reflexes that used to kick in when recession loomed will have to be re-thought. Don't expect, for instance, to have the luxury of cutting back heavily on marketing and product development. The experts argue that smart companies will find the funds to *increase* advertising and new-product launches. Says Harvard business school professor John Kotter, "It's a different set of responses. You don't just say, 'It's tough times, let's cut.' You take risks and spend more."

Home Depot is a good example. When the economy recently began to falter, the owners of the company appeared on the quarterly satellite broadcast to the salespeople and discussed the psychology of selling during a recession. They offered steps in how to increase sales among customers who were likely to be more resistant than ever to spending money.

Other firms have different approaches. At Geico Insurance, the company used the economic turndown to scan its nationwide markets, see where competitors were hurting most, and beef up advertising and cut prices in these locales. Result: Market share in these areas began rising. At GM, Rolls Royce, and Toyota, new product development times have been shortened so that new offerings can be brought to market more quickly. At Allegheny Ludlum, the Pittsburgh maker of specialty steel, the company pushed ahead with its $85 million finishing mill that will increase capacity by 30 percent. At TJ International, maker of windows and speciality building materials, the company took advantage of the slowdown to tinker with its production facilities and work processes, looking for better ways to manufacture the products. This was not possible when the facilities were being run at full tilt. At Delta Airlines, people were reassigned jobs until there was an upturn in the economy—with some pilots actually unloading baggage from arriving flights.

1. The information in this case illustrates what the best firms do to meet a recession. How do their less effective competitors react to such economic frustration? Use Table 13.1 to formulate your answer and discuss three adjustive reactions.
2. A recession would undoubtedly bring about intergroup conflict in the organization. What are some antecedent conditions that would help explain this conflict? Identify and describe three.
3. How do the managers in this case view conflict? How is this view different from the views of their less effective competitors?

Case: Drinking Up the Paycheck

James Emery is the father of four children. He was raised in a hard-working immigrant family. His needs for achievement and power were developed while he was growing up. Now he finds himself in a low-paying, dead-end assembly line job with a large manufacturing firm. It is all he can do to get through the day, so he has started daydreaming on the job. On payday he often goes to the tavern across the street and generally spends a lot of money. The next day he is not only hung over but also very depressed because he knows that his wife cannot make ends meet and his children often go without the basic essentials.

Now he cannot take it any longer. At first he thought of going to his boss for some help and advice, but he really does not understand himself well enough, and he certainly does not know or trust his boss enough to openly discuss his problems with him. Instead, he went to his union steward and told him about his financial problems and how much he hated his job. The steward told James exactly what he wanted to hear. "This darn company is the source of all your problems. The working conditions are not suited for a slave, let alone us. The pay also stinks. We are all going to have to stick together when our present contract runs out and get what we deserve—better working conditions and more money."

1. Explain James's behavior in terms of the frustration model.
2. Cite a specific example of role conflict in this case.
3. What type of transaction from TA and what style from the Johari window can explain James's relationship with his boss? With his union steward?
4. What type of conflict resolution strategy is the union steward suggesting? Do you think the real problems facing James are working conditions and pay? Why or why not?
5. What, if anything, can be done to help the James Emerys of the world? Keep your answer in terms of human resources management.

Case: Arresting the Neighbor's Kid

Barney Kohl is a police officer assigned to the juvenile department of a large city. Part of the oath that Barney took was to uphold the law consistently for all people. The scope of his job includes investigation of youth drug traffic, alcoholism, and vandalism. Barney is also involved in the community outreach program, which works to build greater understanding and cooperation between the police department and the youth of the community.

Last night, Barney ran into one of the most difficult, if not the most dangerous, problems he has ever faced. While on patrol, he received a radio report to investigate some possible vandalism at a junior high school. Upon reaching the scene he found five youths, aged twelve to fifteen, engaged in malicious acts of vandalism. They were throwing rocks through the windows and had splashed paint against the walls. After calling backup units, he proceeded to run down and arrest the vandals. He was successfully holding the group at bay and was waiting for the backup unit to arrive when he noticed that one of the offenders was his neighbor's son. The city has a parents' responsibility law that makes parents financially liable for the damage caused by their children's actions. The damage looked as if it would be considerable, probably running into the thousands of dollars. Barney knows his neighbor can't afford the costs because he has a physical disability and is out of work. He also knows this incident will lead to great problems in their family and, of course, would place a great strain on his own and his family's relationship with the neighbors.

1. What kind of conflict is this police officer experiencing? What should he do?
2. How do you explain the boys' behavior in terms of the frustration model?
3. If you were asked to conduct a training seminar for police officers on the management of conflict, what topics would you cover? What strategies would you suggest?

14 Job Stress

■ CEOs Work to Manage Their Stress

One of the predictions for the 1990s is that people will begin relocating to small towns in order to put the brakes on their fast-paced lifestyles. However, many managers are very committed to their careers and are unwilling to accept any other lifestyle. How then do these people deal with the stress of their jobs? One recent study by Nelson, Quick, and Quick investigated the methods used by the president of a leading oil field service company, the president of a private sector healthcare company, the chairman and president of a large commercial bank, and a navy admiral. Two female executives were also studied—a president of a commercial real estate firm and the president of a residential real estate firm.

The investigators found that all six executives had their own approach to dealing with stress. These approaches fell into two categories: primary prevention strategies and secondary prevention strategies, and most of the executives used both types of approaches. In the primary prevention area, these strategies included: (1) trying to maintain a perspective on the work by balancing job considerations and family consideration; (2) the effective use of leisure time in the form of relaxing, taking walks, reading, and doing things that were personally enjoyable; (3) the use of time management techniques; keeping a day calendar so that they knew what they had to do and by when it was to be done, and setting aside time for catching up on projects; (4) use of planning and goal setting so that they could monitor their progress and ensure that everything necessary was getting done; and (5) building strong work and nonwork relationships for providing them with information, appraisal, and emotional support. In the secondary prevention area, these strategies included: (1) exercise, (2) relaxation, and (3) prayer and faith. The executives placed greatest focus on such primary prevention strategies as social support and the use of leisure time. Other strategies given a high rating included maintaining perspective and the use of time management. Of the secondary prevention strategies, exercise ranked first. Commenting on the use of these strategies, the researchers noted that "effectively managing stress can allow the CEO to make sound decisions; serve as a source of leadership, support, and inspiration for him [or her]; and win victories on today's economic battlefield."

- **Define** stress by giving attention to what it is not.
- **Identify** the extraorganizational, organizational, and group stressors.
- **Examine** individual dispositions of stress.
- **Discuss** the effects of stress, including physical, psychological, and behavioral problems.
- **Present** both individual and organizational strategies for coping with stress.

The opening example points out that stress is a problem and shows how some managers try to prevent and cope with it. A leading expert on stress, cardiologist Robert Eliot, gives the following prescription for dealing with stress: "Rule No. 1 is, don't sweat the small stuff. Rule No. 2 is it's all small stuff. And if you can't fight and you can't flee, flow."[1] What is happening in today's organizations, however, is that the "small stuff" is getting to employees, and they are not going with the "flow." Job stress or "burnout" is a major buzzword and concern of the times. Estimates of what stress-related illness is costing the American economy range from $75 to $100 billion a year, which is ten times more than all labor strikes combined.[2]

The last chapter, on interactive behavior and conflict, can be used as a foundation and point of departure for this chapter's discussion of stress. Although conflict and stress are conceptually close, especially the intraindividual dimensions of conflict, the perspective, variables, and research are treated differently. Since both conflict and stress are such major contemporary problems affecting organizational behavior, they are given specific attention in this text. This chapter first explores the meaning of stress and why it has emerged as a major topic for the study of organizational behavior and the practice of human resources management. Next the major causes of stress in jobs today (extraorganizational, organizational, and group, and the individual dispositions) are examined. This is followed by an analysis of the effects that job stress has on both the individual and the organization. The last part of the chapter is devoted to the coping strategies that can be used at the individual and organizational levels to manage stress effectively.

THE MEANING OF STRESS

Stress is usually thought of in negative terms. It is thought to be caused by something bad (for example, a college student is placed on scholastic probation, a loved one is seriously ill, or the boss gives a formal reprimand for poor performance). This is a form of distress. But there is also a positive, pleasant side of stress caused by good things (for example, a college student makes the dean's list; an attractive, respected acquaintance asks for a date; an employee is offered a job promotion at another location). This is a form of *eu*stress. This latter term was coined by the pioneers of stress research from the Greek *eu*, which means "good." In other words, stress can be viewed in a number of different ways and has been described as the most imprecise word in the scientific dictionary. The word "stress" has also been compared with the word "sin": "Both are short, emotionally charged words used to refer to something that otherwise would take many words to say."[3]

Although there are numerous definitions and much debate about the meaning of job stress,[4] Ivancevich and Matteson define *stress* simply as "the interaction of the individual with the environment," but then they go on to give a more detailed working definition, as follows: "an adaptive response, mediated by individual differences and/or psychological processes, that is a consequence of any external (environmental) action, situation, or event that places excessive psychological and/or physical demands upon a person."[5] Beehr and Newman define *job stress* as "a condition arising from the interaction of people and their jobs and characterized by changes within people that force them to deviate from their normal functioning."[6] Taking these two definitions and simplifying them for the purposes of this chapter, "stress" is defined as an adaptive response to an external situation that results in physical, psychological, and/or behavioral deviations for organizational participants.

It is also important to point out what stress is *not:*

1. *Stress is not simply anxiety.* Anxiety operates solely in the emotional and psychological sphere, whereas stress operates there and also in the physiological sphere. Thus, stress may be accompanied by anxiety, but the two should not be equated.
2. *Stress is not simply nervous tension.* Like anxiety, nervous tension may result from stress, but the two are not the same. Unconscious people have exhibited stress, and some people may keep it "bottled up" and not reveal it through nervous tension.
3. *Stress is not necessarily something damaging, bad, or to be avoided.* Eustress is not damaging or bad and is something people should seek out rather than avoid. The key, of course, is how the person handles the stress. Stress is inevitable; distress may be prevented or can be effectively controlled.[7]

THE BACKGROUND OF STRESS

Concern about the impact of stress on people has its roots in medicine and specifically in the pioneering work of Hans Selye, the recognized father of stress. In his search for a new sex hormone, he serendipitously (an accidental discovery) discovered that tissue damage is a nonspecific response to virtually all noxious stimuli. He called this phenomenon the *general adaptation syndrome* (GAS), and about a decade later he introduced the term "stress" in his writings.

The GAS has three stages: alarm, resistance, and exhaustion. In the alarm stage an outside stressor mobilizes the internal stress system of the body. There are a number of physiological and chemical reactions such as increased pituitary and adrenaline secretions; noticeable increases in respiration, heart rate, and blood pressure; and a heightening of the senses. If the stressor continues, then the GAS moves into the resistance stage, during which the body calls upon the needed organ or system to deal with the stressor. However, while there may be a great deal of resistance to one stressor during this second stage, there may be little, if any, resistance to other, unrelated stressors. This helps explain why a person going through an emotional strain may be particularly vulnerable to other illness or disease. Finally, if the stressor persists over a long period of time, the reserves of the adaptive mechanisms during the second stage may become drained, and exhaustion sets in.

When this happens, there may be a return to the alarm stage, and the cycle starts again with another organ or system, or the "automatic shutoff valve" of death occurs. This GAS process, of course, can be very hard on the person and takes its toll on the human body.

Besides the physiologically oriented approach to stress represented by the classic GAS model, which remains a vital dimension of modern stress research and stress management, attention is also being given to the psychological (for example, mood changes, negative emotions, and feelings of helplessness) and the behavioral (for example, directly confronting the stressors or attempting to obtain information about the stressors) dimensions of stress. All three dimensions (physiological, psychologial, and behavioral) are important to the understanding of job stress and coping strategies in modern organizations.

THE CAUSES OF STRESS

The antecedents of stress, or the so-called "stressors," affecting today's employees are summarized in Figure 14.1. As shown, these causes come from both outside and inside the organization and from the groups that employees are influenced by and from employees themselves.

Extraorganizational Stressors

Although most analyses of job stress ignore the importance of outside forces and events, it is becoming increasingly clear that these have a tremendous impact. Taking an open-systems perspective of an organization (that is, the organization is greatly affected by the external environment), it is clear that job stress is not just limited to things that happen inside the organization, during working hours. Extraorganizational stressors include things such as societal/technological change, the family, relocation, economic and financial conditions, race and class, and residential or community conditions.[8]

The phenomenal rate of social and technical change, which is given detailed attention in Chapter 21, has had a great effect on people's lifestyles, and this of course is carried over into their jobs. Although medical science has increased the life spans of people and has eradicated or reduced the threat of many diseases, the pace of modern living has increased stress and decreased personal *wellness*. This latter concept of wellness has been defined as "a harmonious and productive balance of physical, mental, and social well being brought about by the acceptance of one's personal responsibility for developing and adhering to a health promotion program."[9] Because people tend to get caught up in the rush-rush, mobile, urbanized, crowded, on-the-go lifestyle of today, their wellness in general has deteriorated, and the potential for stress on the job has increased.

As Chapter 4 indicated, a person's family has a big impact on personality development. A family situation—either a brief crisis, such as a squabble or the illness of a family member, or long-term strained relations with the spouse or children—can act as a significant stressor for employees. So can relocating the family because of a transfer or a promotion. For most people in the 1990s, their financial

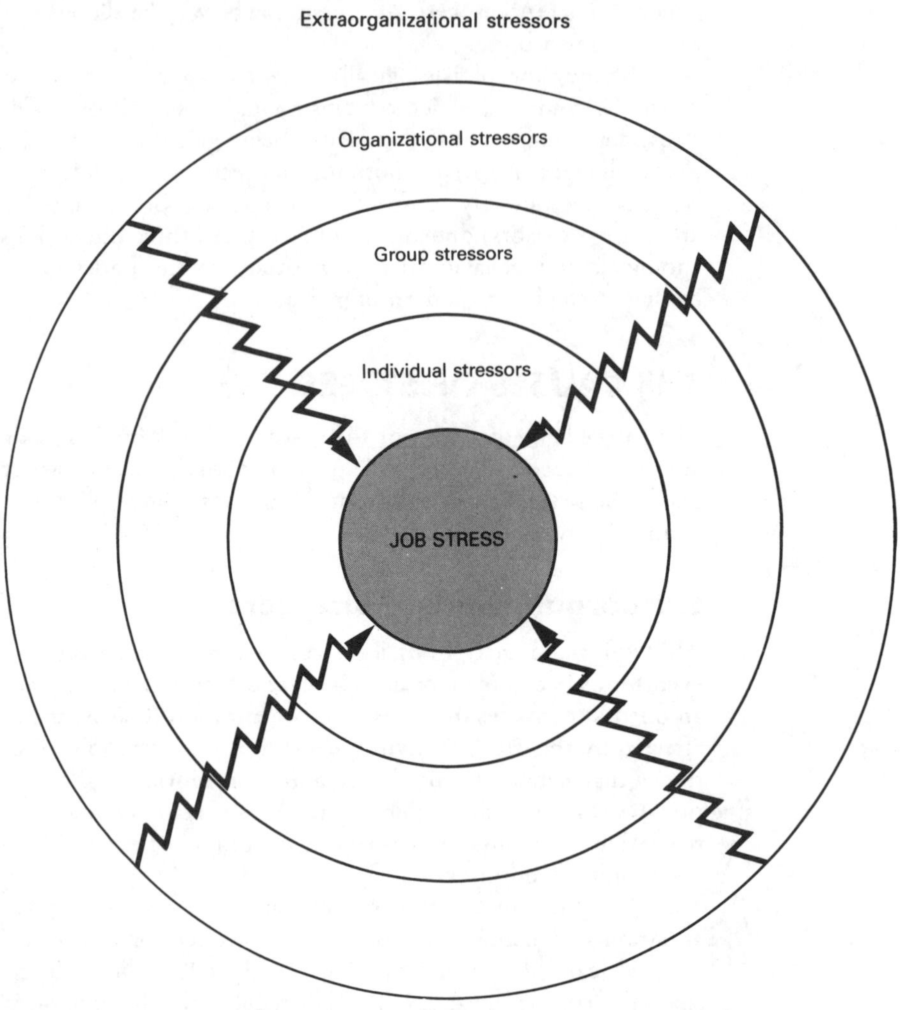

FIGURE 14.1
Categories of stressors affecting job stress.

situation has proved to be a stressor. Many people have been forced to take a second job ("moonlight"), or the spouse has had to enter the work force in order to make ends meet. This reduces time for recreational and family activities. The overall effect on the employees is more stress on their primary jobs. Some stress researchers define these personal life stressors as unresolved environmental demands (e.g., family or financial problems) requiring adaptive behaviors in the form of social readjustments.[10]

Life's changes may be slow (getting older) or sudden (the death of a spouse). These changes have been portrayed in novels and movies as having a dramatic effect on people (for example, the heroine who pines for a dead lover until she herself dies).

TABLE 14.1 Relative Weights of Life Changes

Life Change	Relative Weight
Death of spouse	100
Divorce	73
Jail term	63
Death of close family member	63
Major personal injury or illness	53
Marriage	50
Fired from work	47
Retirement	45
Sex difficulties	39
Business readjustment	39
Change to a different line of work	36
Change in responsibilities at work	29
Trouble with boss	23
Change in work hours or conditions	20
Vacation	13
Christmas	12
Minor violations of the law	11

Source: Adapted from L. O. Ruch and T. H. Holmes, "Scaling of Life Changes: Comparison of Direct and Indirect Methods," *Journal of Psychosomatic Research,* vol. 15, 1971.

Medical researchers have verified that especially sudden life changes do in fact have a very stressful impact on people.[11] They found a definite relationship between the degree of life changes and the subsequent health of the person. Table 14.1 shows the relative standings of certain life changes. The more change, the poorer the subsequent health. These life changes can also directly influence job performance. One psychologist, Faye Crosby, reports that divorce interferes with work more than any other trauma in a person's life. She says, "During the first three months after a spouse walks out, the other spouse—male or female—usually is incapable of focusing on work."[12]

Sociological variables such as race, sex, and class can also become stressors. Sociologists have noted over the years that minorities may have more stressors than whites. More recently, reseach has found that women experience more psychological distress than men, but men are more prone to severe physical illness.[13] For professional women, the particular sources of stress have been identified as discrimination, stereotyping, the marriage/work interface, and social isolation.[14] Also, people in the middle and upper classes may have particular or common stressors. The same is true of the local community or region that one comes from. For example, one researcher identified the condition of housing, convenience of services and shopping, neighborliness, and degree of noise and air pollution as likely stressors.[15]

Organizational Stressors

Besides the potential stressors that occur outside the organization, there are also those associated with the organization itself. Although the organization is made up of groups and individuals, there are also more macro-level dimensions, unique to the organization, that contain potential stressors. Figure 14.2 shows that these macro-

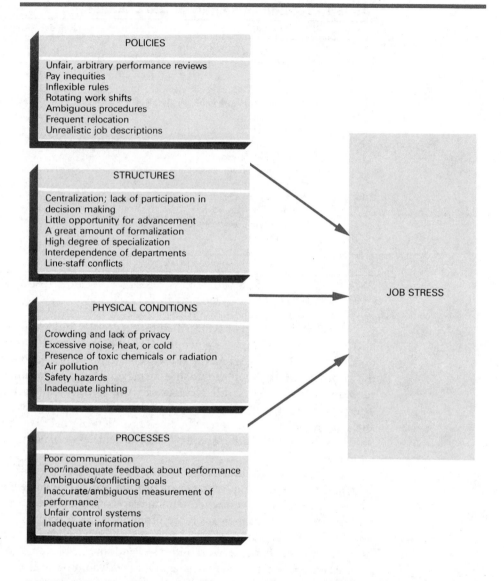

FIGURE 14.2
Macro-level organizational stressors. (*Source:* Adapted from Arthur P. Brief, Randall S. Schuler, and Mary Van Sell, *Managing Job Stress*, Little, Brown, Boston, 1981, p. 66.)

level stressors can be categorized into organizational policies, structures, physical conditions, and processes. Although these areas are given specific attention in Part 5 of this book, it should be noted that as organizations become larger and more complex, there are more and more accompanying stressors for individual employees in their jobs. Most of the stressors shown in Figure 14.2 are the direct result of very large, highly complex organizations. As today and tomorrow's companies attempt to compete in the increasingly competitive world marketplace, these organizational stressors may become more severe. For example, in a recent survey of Fortune 500

CEOs, over three-fourths agreed with the statement that "large U.S. companies will have to push their managers harder if we are to compete successfully with the Japanese and other global competitors."[16]

Group Stressors

Chapters 12 and 13 indicated the tremendous influence that the group has on behavior. The group can also be a potential source of stress. These group stressors can be categorized into three areas:

1. *Lack of group cohesiveness.* Starting with the historically famous Hawthorne studies, discussed in Chapter 2, it has become very clear that cohesiveness, or "togetherness," is very important to employees, especially at the lower levels of organizations. If an employee is denied the opportunity for this cohesiveness because of the task design, because the supervisor does things to prohibit or limit it, or because the other members of the group shut the person out, this can be very stress-producing.

2. *Lack of social support.* Employees are greatly affected by the support of one or more members of a cohesive group. By sharing their problems and joys with others, they are much better off. If this type of social support is lacking for an individual, it can be very stressful.

3. *Intraindividual, interpersonal, and intergroup conflict.* This is the topic of Chapter 13. Conflict is very closely conceptually linked to stress. Conflict is normally associated with incompatible or hostile acts between intraindividual dimensions such as personal goals or motivational needs/values, between individuals within a group, and between groups. Chapter 13 went into the details of these levels of conflict, but for the purposes of this chapter it can be said simply that such conflict can lead to considerable stress for individuals.[17]

Individual Stressors: The Role of Dispositions

In a sense, the other stressors discussed so far (extraorganizational, organizational, and group) all eventually get down to the individual level. There is also more research and agreement on possible situational dimensions and individual dispositions which may affect stress outcomes. For example, role conflict, ambiguity, and individual dispositions such as Type A personality patterns, personal control, learned helplessness, self-efficacy, and psychological hardiness may all affect the level of stress someone experiences.

Role Conflict and Ambiguity. Like the conflict at organizational and group levels, role conflict and the closely related concept of role ambiguity were given specific attention in Chapter 13. Individual employees have multiple roles (family, work, professional, recreational, church, club, community, and so on), and these often make conflicting demands and create conflicting expectations. After a recent extensive search of the empirical research it was concluded that "work schedule, work orientation, marriage, children, and spouse employment patterns may all produce pressures to participate extensively in the work role or the family role."[18] Stress results when the time demands for the work role are incompatible with the time pressures of the family role or vice versa.

Role ambiguity results from inadequate information or knowledge to do a job. This ambiguity may be due to inadequate training, poor communication, or the deliberate withholding or distortion of information by a coworker of supervisor. In any event, the result of role conflict and ambiguity is stress for the individual, and there is a substantial body of research indicating undesirable outcomes for the individual and the organization.[19] Role overload and/or underload (being asked to do too much or too little), which has not received as much attention as role conflict and ambiguity, may be just as stress-provoking.

Type A Characteristics. The discussion of personality in Chapter 4 pointed out the complexity of, and individual differences in, personality dispositions and traits. Personality traits such as authoritarianism, rigidity, masculinity, femininity, extroversion, supportiveness, spontaneity, emotionality, tolerance for ambiguity, anxiety, and the need for achievement have been uncovered by research as being particularly relevant to individual stress.[20] Most recent attention, however, has centered on the so-called "Type A personality."

Although heart researchers have been working on the use of personality types and the resulting behavior patterns in order to predict heart attacks since the 1950s, in the late 1960s Friedman and Rosenman popularized the use of Type A and

TABLE 14.2 Type A–Type B Self-Test

To determine your Type A or Type B profile, circle the number on the continuums (the verbal descriptions represent endpoints) that best represents your behavior for each dimension.

Am casual about appointments	1 2 3 4 5 6 7 8	Am never late
Am not competitive	1 2 3 4 5 6 7 8	Am very competitive
Never feel rushed, even under pressure	1 2 3 4 5 6 7 8	Always feel rushed
Take things one at a time	1 2 3 4 5 6 7 8	Try to do many things at once; think about what I am going to do next
Do things slowly	1 2 3 4 5 6 7 8	Do things fast (eating, walking, etc.)
Express feelings	1 2 3 4 5 6 7 8	"Sit" on feelings
Have many interests	1 2 3 4 5 6 7 8	Have few interests outside work

Total your score: _____ Multiply it by 3: _____. The interpretation of your score is as follows:

Number of points	Type of personality
Less than 90	B
90 to 99	B+
100 to 105	A−
106 to 119	A
120 or more	A+

Source: Adapted from R. W. Bortner, "A Short Rating Scale as a Potential Measure of Pattern A Behavior," *Journal of Chronic Diseases,* vol. 22, 1966, pp. 87–91.

opposing Type B personalities in the study of stress.[21] These were portrayed as relatively stable characteristics and initially Friedman and Rosenman's extensive studies found the Type A profile correlated highly with experienced stress and dangerous physical consequences.

Table 14.2 gives the reader a chance to see whether he or she tends to be a Type A or a Type B personality. A majority of Americans are Type A, and an even higher percentage of managers are Type A; one study found that 60 percent of the managers sampled were clearly Type A and that only 12 percent were Type B.[22]

Friedman and Rosenman define the Type A personality as "an action-emotion complex that can be observed in any person who is aggressively involved in a chronic, incessant struggle to achieve more and more in less and less time, and if required to do so, against the opposing efforts of other things or other persons."[23] Table 14.3 briefly summarizes the Type A and Type B profiles. Obviously, Type A employees (managers, salespersons, staff specialists, secretaries, or rank-and-file operating employees) experience considerable stress. They are the ones who:

1. Work long, hard hours under constant deadline pressures and conditions for overload.
2. Often take work home at night or on weekends and are unable to relax.
3. Constantly compete with themselves, setting high standards of productivity that they seem driven to maintain.
4. Tend to become frustrated by the work situation, to be irritated with the work efforts of others, and to be misunderstood by superiors.[24]

At first, because of Rosenman and Friedman's studies, it was generally thought that Type A's were much more prone to the worst outcome of stress: heart attacks.[25] More recently, however, a number of studies have been unable to confirm their findings.[26] For example, Type A's may release and better cope with their stress than do Type B's. The controversy surrounding the conflicting conclusions are discussed in the accompanying Application Example: Is Being a Type A Dangerous?

The most recent studies seem to indicate that it is not so much the impatience that is closely associated with Type A's, but rather anger and hostility that leads to heart problems. A leading medical researcher recently noted that the term Type A

TABLE 14.3 Profiles of Type A and Type B Personalities

Type A Profile	Type B Profile
Is always moving	Is not concerned about time
Walks rapidly	Is patient
Eats rapidly	Doesn't brag
Talks rapidly	Plays for fun, not to win
Is impatient	Relaxes without guilt
Does two things at once	Has no pressing deadlines
Can't cope with leisure time	Is mild-mannered
Is obsessed with numbers	Is never in a hurry
Measures success by quantity	
Is aggressive	
Is competitive	
Constantly feels under time pressure	

Application Example

Is Being a Type A Dangerous?

The complexities involved in studying behavior are exemplified by the recent controversy surrounding the link between the Type A personality and heart disease. Most people have heard of the Type A personality—competitive, driven, and impatient—and its association with heart disease. Decades of research have supported the link.

Meyer Friedman and Ray Rosenman, California cardiologists, are noted for discovering the link. Their findings were replicated by several larger studies. The most compelling evidence came from the Western Collaborative Group Study (WCGS), an eight-year study ending in 1969. The study showed that Type A men had twice as many heart attacks or other forms of heart disease than anyone else.

However, a seven-year study ending in 1982 found contradictory results. The Multiple Risk Factor Intervention Trial (MRFIT) was sponsored by the National Heart, Lung, and Blood Institute to single out the deadliest risks of heart disease. Their results failed to show that Type A men were more likely to develop heart disease than anyone else.

How do researchers explain such conflicting findings? One test is to compare measurement techniques. Both the WCGS and the MRFIT used structured interviews to identify Type A's. The structured interview is considered to be the most accurate assessment technique for identifying Type A's since it not only evaluates the content of answers but also accounts for tone of voice, facial expressions, and gestures—important indicators of the impatience characteristic of Type A's.

Not only is the technique important but also how it is used. For example, Larry Scherwitz, a psychologist at the University of California, San Francisco, listened to the interview tapes of both the WCGS and the MRFIT. He noticed that the MRFIT interviewers asked the questions faster than the WCGS interviewers. He believes this could have skewed the MRFIT results.

According to Scherwitz, the fast-paced interviewers come across as cold and uninterested. He believes that the hostile Type A's responded by hiding their hostile feelings—making them appear to be Type B's. The more sensitive Type B's, on the other hand, may have reacted more curtly—responding like Type A's. Such responses may have led to mislabeling which could have easily confounded the results.

Rosenman also points out an important flaw with the MRFIT. "Type A's are not going to sign up for studies like this, with once-a-week follow-ups and lots of paperwork. You don't get impatient, hostile people volunteering to do this." Rosenman emphasizes the importance of how subjects are selected. However, he does not indicate how subjects were contacted for the WCGS. Although other areas of the studies' designs need to be considered, these two areas show why rigorous methodology is necessary for conclusive findings.

Whether the Type A personality is dangerous is still a subject for debate. Further research with attention to methodology is needed before any conclusions can be made.

---

probably has outlived its usefulness. He stated, "Being a workaholic, being in a hurry, interrupting people, are not necessarily bad for your heart. What is bad is if you have high levels of hostility and anger, and you don't bother to hide it when dealing with other people."[27] Sometimes, however, this anger and hostility goes along with a Type A person.

Besides the debate surrounding the impact of Type A personality on health is the question of the success of Type A's versus Type B's. It is pretty clear that Type A's are typically on a "fast track" to the top. They are more successful than Type B's. However, at the *very* top they do not tend to be as successful as Type B's, who are more patient and take a broader view of things.[28] The key may be to shift from Type A to Type B behavior, but, of course, most Type A's are unable and *unwilling* to make the shift and/or to cope with their Type A characteristics.

Personal Control and Learned Helplessness. Beside Type A personality patterns, another important disposition is an individual's perception of control. As mentioned in Chapter 5's discussion on job satisfaction, people's feelings about their ability to control the situation will be an important disposition for stress. In particular, if employees feel that they have little control over the work environment and over their own job, they will experience stress.[29] Studies have shown that if employees are given a sense of control over their work environment, such as giving them a chance to be involved in the decision making process that affects them, this will reduce their work stress.[30] Most recently, a large study by Cornell University medical researchers found that those workers who experience a loss of control, especially in relatively low-level jobs, have triple the risk of developing high blood pressure. The researchers concluded that lack of control turns stress into physical problems. They also found that if a high-stress job included latitude to control the situation, there was no increase in blood pressure.[31]

The feeling of loss of control goes back to some of the classic research on learned helplessness conducted by Seligman.[32] In conducting experiments on dogs who could not escape shock, he found that they eventually accepted it and did not even try to escape. Importantly, later when the dogs could learn to easily escape, they did not—they had learned to be helpless. Other studies found that people, too, can learn to be helpless.[33] This helps explain why some employees just seem to have given up and seem to accept stressors in their work environment, even when a change for the better is possible.

Most recently, Seligman and his colleagues have concentrated on people's explanations for their lack of control. Specifically, they suggest that people are most apt to experience helplessness when they perceive the causes of the lack of control:

1. to be related to something about their own personal characteristics (as opposed to outside, environmental forces);
2. as stable and enduring (rather than just temporary); and
3. are global and universal (cutting across many situations, rather than in just one sphere of life).[34]

Further study and research on the sense of control in general and learned helplessness in particular will provide much insight into stress and how to cope with it.

Self-Efficacy. Another important disposition that has recently emerged to help understand stress in the workplace is self-efficacy. (This concept was introduced in Chapter 4 on self theories of personality.) There is increasing evidence that people's self-perception of their capacity to be effective and bring about change may be an important disposition in the ability to withstand stress.[35] For example, Bandura has found that those with high self-efficacy have a relatively low level of physiological arousal (e.g., they have less adrenaline in the bloodstream).[36] Yet, those under stress tend to have high physiological arousal. Thus, those with high self-efficacy tend to remain calmer when faced with a stressful situation. As Rathus points out, "Over-arousal can impair our ability to solve complex stress-related problems by elevating our motivation well beyond optimal levels and by distracting us from tasks at hand. So, people with higher self-efficacy expectations have biological as well as psychological reasons for remaining calmer."[37]

Psychological Hardiness. Everyone has observed individual differences of people faced with stressors. Some people seem to go to pieces at the slightest provocation while others seem unflappable in the face of extremely stressful situations. Those able to successfully cope with extreme stressors seem to have a "hardiness" disposition.

Kobasa and her colleagues studied executives under considerable stress who were both hardy and nonhardy. She found that the hardy executives had a lower rate of stress-related illness and were characterized as having commitment (they become very involved in what they were doing); challenge (they believed that change rather than stability was normal); and control (they felt they could influence the events around them).[38] She suggests that the predisposition of psychological hardiness helps those with it to resist stress by providing buffers between themselves and stressors.

Such buffering from hardiness may be an important quality as organizations now and in the future demand more and more from their employees at all levels. As recently noted:

> Why does the job seem so demanding? It isn't just long hours or clumsy direction from above, though there's plenty of that. All sorts of pressure, from the stress of participatory management techniques to the hyperkinesia of two-career marriages to the dismay of finding your workload increasing as you near 50, just when you thought you could adopt a more dignified pace, are working together to squeeze the oomph from heretofore steely-eyed achievers.[39]

Kobasa's research would say that those with hardiness will be able to survive and even thrive in such an environment, but those who do not possess hardiness may suffer the harmful outcomes of stress that are covered next.

THE EFFECTS OF JOB STRESS

As was pointed out in the introductory comments, stress is not automatically bad for individual employees or their organizational performance. In fact, it is generally recognized that at least low levels of stress can even enhance job performance. For example, one recent study found that mild stress, such as getting a new supervisor or being involuntarily transferred, may result in an increased search for information in the job.[40] This may lead employees to new and better ways of doing their jobs. Also, mild stress may get employees' "juices" flowing and lead to increased activity, change, and overall better performance. People in certain jobs, such as in sales or creative fields (for example, newspaper journalists and television announcers who work under time pressures), would seem to benefit from a mild level of stress. People in other jobs, such as police officers or physicians, may not benefit from constant mild stress.

Research is also emerging that indicates that the level of difficulty and nature of the task being performed and personal dispositions such as Type A, personal control and learned helplessness, self-efficacy and psychological hardiness discussed in previous sections may affect the relationship between stress and performance.[41] However, it is still safe to conclude that:

1. The performance of many tasks is in fact strongly affected by stress.
2. Performance usually drops off sharply when stress rises to high levels.[42]

It is the dysfunctional effects of high levels of stress that should be and are a major concern for contemporary society in general and for effective human resources management in particular. The problems due to high levels of stress can be exhibited physically, psychologically, or behaviorally by the individual.

Physical Problems Due to Stress

Most of the attention and the basic research over the years has been devoted to the impact that stress has on physical health. A high level of stress is accompanied by high blood pressure and high levels of cholesterol and may even result in heart disease,[43] ulcers, and arthritis. There may even be a possible link between stress and cancer.[44]

Obviously, such serious physical ailments have a drastic effect on the individual; not always so obvious, but just as serious, are the effects that physical problems such as heart disease can have on the organization. Ivancevich and Matteson have provided the following worksheet for computing the costs of replacing employees lost to heart disease in a company employing 4000 people.[45]

1. Number of employees	4000
2. Men in age range forty-five to sixty-five (0.25 × line 1)	1000
3. Estimated deaths due to heart disease per year (0.006 × line 2)	6
4. Estimated premature retirement due to heart problems per year (0.003 × line 2)	3
5. Company's annual personnel losses due to heart disorders (sum of lines 3 and 4)	9
6. Annual replacement cost: the average cost of hiring and training replacements for experienced employees (line 5 × $4300)	$38,700
7. Number of employees who will eventually die of heart disease if present rate continues (0.5 × line 1)	2000

These figures are just estimates, but they dramatically illustrate how heart disease alone can affect costs and sheer numbers of employees in a typical organization. Obviously, not all heart disease can be directly linked to stress; environmental conditions and the person's general state of health, heredity, and medical history can also contribute. However, there seems to be enough evidence that stress can and does contribute to this dreaded disease and to other physical problems as well.

Psychological Problems Due to Stress

While considerable attention has been given to the relationship between stress and physical health, especially within the medical community, not as much has been given to the impact of stress on mental health. Yet, at least indirectly if not directly, the psychological problems resulting from stress may be just as important to day-to-day job performance as the physical problems, if not more important.

High levels of stress may be accompanied by anger, anxiety, depression, nervousness, irritability, tension, and boredom. The effects of this on individual employees are changes in mood and other emotional states and, especially relevant to job performance, lowered self-esteem,[46] resentment of supervision, inability to concentrate and make decisions, and job dissatisfaction.[47] These outcomes of stress can have a direct cost effect on the organization. For example, the National Centers for Disease Control reported that psychological stress is the source of numerous job-related insurance claims.[48] Recent court cases have also brought stress-related problems stemming from employment under the employer's workers' compensation insurance. Experts are predicting that if the number of stress-related workers' compensation claims continues to grow at current rates, they will lead all other claims in the 1990s.[49]

Of even greater significance, the outcomes of stress can have a subtle, but very real, effect on the styles and effectiveness of managers in key positions. For example, managers who are under constant stress may become very moody, and their subordinates soon learn not to disturb them, even with important information, because they will just "bite your head off." Such managers may also realize, at times, that they are acting this way; they may feel that they are not living up to the expectations of their important position and suffer a loss of self-esteem. In this state they may also procrastinate and continue to put things off and not make needed decisions. And, finally, they may resent their boss for trying to get them back on the track and begin to hate the job in general. Coworkers, subordinates, and superiors may become very disgusted with such a manager and explain the behavior away as being the result of a "rotten personality," when in fact the problems are the result of stress. If the manager had a heart attack, everyone would feel sorry and say that he or she was under too much stress, but moodiness, low self-esteem, inability to make a decision, and dissatisfaction with the boss and the job cause people to get angry and say that the manager is "no darned good" or "can't get along with anyone." Both a heart attack and a psychological problem may have the same cause (too much stress), and although people may react to them differently, the negative effect on performance is the same in the case of a psychological problem, or perhaps even worse.

Behavioral Problems Due to Stress

As has been the case with other topics covered in this book, the *behavioral* unit of analysis may be most helpful in analyzing the effects of job stress. Direct behaviors that may accompany high levels of stress include undereating or overeating, sleeplessness, increased smoking and drinking, and drug abuse. When it is realized that 6 percent of the population are alcoholics, that another estimated 10 percent are problem drinkers, and that 6 billion doses of amphetamines and barbiturates are consumed annually,[50] the potential problems for employee behavior caused by alcohol and drug abuse become dramatically clear.

Although problems with alcohol have been recognized for a number of years, severe problems stemming from drug abuse have emerged more recently. For example, Kidder, Peabody, the New York–based investment bank, recently spent $100,000 on a drug program and many other firms such as Lockheed and Southern California Rapid Transit have drug-testing programs for their employees.[51]

One company had such a problem with on-the-job drinking that it bought a breath-alcohol meter to test its employees. The president of the union in this firm stated: "there were a couple of people who came to work drunk every day."[52] Although the meter has not been used as yet, one worker was overheard to say, "I guess I'll have to stop going to the bar at lunchtime."[53] Besides being dangerous, as in this company, which used a lot of saws and punches, these problems may be manifested by tardiness, absenteeism, and turnover.

There is some research evidence indicating the relationship between stress and especially absenteeism and turnover.[54] For example, workers may experience stress and react by getting drunk and staying home from work the next day with a hangover. They then feel bad about this drinking. They may feel that they are letting everyone down "the morning after" and eventually quit or be fired from the job. In the meantime the absenteeism rate climbs, and subsequently the turnover rates increase, both of which are very costly to the organization in terms of filling in for absent workers and replacing those who have left. Staying away from a job that is causing stress or quitting the job is a "flight" reaction to the situation. Actually, this may be a healthier reaction than a "fight" reaction, in which the person may stay on the stress-producing job and become angry and/or aggressive.

Like the psychological problems resulting from stress, the behavioral problems are often not attributed to stress by coworkers or supervisors and generate little sympathy. But, also like the psychological and the physical symptoms of stress, the behavioral problems can be controlled, more effectively managed, and even prevented by the individual and the organization. These coping strategies are discussed next.

COPING STRATEGIES FOR STRESS

Much of the discussion so far in this chapter and, at least indirectly, a lot of the material in previous and subsequent chapters (for example, discussions of job design, goal setting, organizational behavior modification, group dynamics, management of conflict, communication skills, political strategies, leadership styles, organization processes and design, decision-making skills, control techniques, management of change, and organization development techniques) suggest ways to manage and more effectively cope with stress. The accompanying Application Example, Taking Time to Manage Time, suggests some simple techniques such as time management that can be used to cope with stress. Generally speaking, however, there are two major approaches to dealing with job stress.

First are the individual strategies, which tend to be more reactive in nature. That is, they tend to be ways of coping with stress that has already occurred. Some

Application Example

Taking Time to Manage Time

One of the major causes of stress for managers comes from time pressures. No matter how fast some managers work and how much time they put in, they are still unable to get all their work done. One of the most effective ways of dealing with this problem is the use of time management techniques. Today many organizations from Chase Manhattan to Exxon to Xerox are training their managers how to get more done in less time. Some of the most helpful guidelines for effective time management are the following:

1. Make out a "to do" list that identifies everything that must be done during the day. This helps keep track of work progress.
2. Delegate as much minor work as possible to subordinates.
3. Determine when you do the best work—morning or afternoon—and schedule the most difficult assignments for this time period.
4. Set time aside, preferably at least one hour, during the day when visitors or other interruptions are not permitted.
5. Have the secretary screen all incoming calls in order to turn away those that are minor or do not require your personal attention.
6. Eat lunch in the office one or two days a week in order to save time and give yourself the opportunity to catch up on paperwork.
7. Discourage drop-in visitors by turning your desk so you do not have eye contact with the door or hallway.
8. Read standing up. The average person reads faster and more accurately when in a slightly uncomfortable position.
9. Make telephone calls between 4:30 and 5:00 P.M. People tend to keep these conversations brief so that they can go home.
10. Do not feel guilty about those things that have not been accomplished today. Put them on the top of the "to do" list for tomorrow.

individual strategies, such as physical exercise, can be both reactive and proactive, but most are geared toward helping the person who is already suffering from stress. The second general approach is to develop a more proactive set of strategies at the organizational level. The idea behind these organizational strategies is to remove existing or potential stressors and thus, like preventive medicine, prevent the onset of stress for individual jobholders.

Individual Coping Strategies

Today, when self-help remedies, do-it-yourself approaches, weight-loss clinics and diets, health foods, and physical exercise are being given so much attention in the mass media and when people are actually taking responsibility, or know they *should* be taking responsibility, for their own wellness, individual coping strategies for dealing with stress make sense. In other words, most people don't have to be convinced of the value of taking charge and actually making a change in their lives.

Some specific techniques that individuals can use to eliminate or more effectively manage inevitable, prolonged stress are the following:

1. *Exercise.* Today, it is not whether you win or lose, but whether you get some good exercise that counts. People of all ages are walking, jogging, swimming, riding bicycles, or playing softball, tennis, or racquetball in order to get some exercise to combat stress. Although this seems to make a great deal of sense and many laypeople and physicians swear by it, there still is no conclusive evidence that exercise will directly reduce the chances of heart disease or stroke. But there seems little doubt that it can help people better cope with stress, even if only as a result of the side effects, such as relaxation, enhanced self-esteem, and simply getting one's mind off work for a while.

2. *Relaxation.* Whether a person simply takes it easy once in a while or uses specific relaxation techniques such as biofeedback or meditation, the intent is to eliminate the immediately stressful situation or manage a prolonged stressful situation more effectively. Taking it easy may mean curling up with a good book in front of a fireplace or watching something "light" (not a violent program or a sports program) on television. Biofeedback was discussed in Chapter 4. Meditation involves muscle and mental relaxation; the person slowly repeats a peaceful phrase or word or concentrates on a mental picture in a quiet location. There is some research evidence that much meditation can have a desirable physical[55] and mental[56] impact on people. Whether it can have a practical impact on job stress is yet to be determined. However, a number of firms are using it. For example, a stockbroker who regularly uses meditation recently stated, "It's widely known that this industry has a lot of stress. So where a lot of people drink alcohol, we meditate. It's not that we don't feel stress. It just doesn't hit us as much."[57]

3. *Behavioral self-control.* Chapter 9 gives specific attention to behavioral self-control. By deliberately managing the antecedents and the consequences of their own behavior, people can achieve self-control. For example, sales managers who have a steady stream of customer complaints all day could change the antecedent by having an assistant screen all complaints and allow only exceptions to reach them. They could also manage the consequences by rewarding themselves with an extra break when they remain calm and collected after interacting with a particularly angry customer. Besides managing their own behavior to reduce stress, people can also become more aware of their limits and of "red flags" that signal trouble ahead. They can avoid people or situations that they know will put them under stress. In other words, this strategy involves individuals' controlling the situation instead of letting the situation control them.

4. *Cognitive therapy.* Besides behavioral self-control techniques, a number of clinical psychologists have entered the stress field in recent years with cognitive therapy techniques. Techniques such as Ellis's rational emotive model[58] and Meichenbaum's cognitive behavior modification have been successfully used to reduce test anxiety[59] and have recently been used as an individual strategy for reducing job stress. One study described the approach as follows:

> Participants were taught that much of their experienced strain (anxiety, tension, etc.) is caused by their cognitions ("self-talks"). This part of the treatment program, then, consisted of off-line lectures and interactive discussions designed to help participants (a) recognize events at work and what cognitions they elicit; (b) become aware of the effects of such cognitions on their physiological and

emotional responses: (c) systematically evaluate the objective consequences of events at work; and (d) replace self-defeating cognitions that unnecessarily arouse strain (e.g., "I'm an incompetent worker who cannot handle the workload") with more adaptive appraisals (e.g., "I handle this workload as well as anyone else," or "the workload is too high and I should approach my supervisor").[60]

When this coping strategy (combined with some simple relaxation techniques) was systematically evaluated by a field experimental design in a social service agency, it was found to have a positive impact on some of both the physiological (epinephrine, a hormone produced by the adrenal glands) and the psychological (depression) variables measured.[61] However, there were no significant effects on some of the other variables measured, and the treatment effects were not replicated in a subsequent intervention on the original control group. Another study evaluated a similar cognitive therapy approach applied to police academy trainees. This study found that in simulated exercises, those who used the cognitive strategy performed more effectively and exhibited greater self-control and less strain than those who did not use the approach.[62] However, there were methodological flaws[63] that probably prevent definitive conclusions at this point on the value of the cognitive approach to managing stress. Yet, as is true of the other strategies discussed so far, there is enough promise to continue its use in trying to cope with stress.

5. *Networking.* One clear finding that has come out of social psychology research over the years is that people need and will benefit from social support. Applied as a strategy to reduce job stress, this would entail forming close associations with trusted empathetic coworkers and colleagues who are good listeners and confidence builders. These friends are there when needed and provide support to get the person through stressful situations. Today, such alliances, especially if deliberately sought out and developed, are called *networks*. Although the relationship between social support and stress reduction appears complicated,[64] there is some research evidence that a networking strategy may be able to help people cope better with job stress[65] and be more effective[66] and successful managers.[67]

Organizational Coping Strategies

Organizational coping strategies are designed by management to eliminate or control organizational-level stressors in order to prevent or reduce job stress for individual employees. Earlier in the chapter, the organizational stressors were categorized in terms of overall policies, structures, physical conditions, and processes/functions (see Figure 14.2). It logically follows that these areas would be the focus of attention in developing organizational coping strategies. In other words, each of the specific stressors would be worked on in order to eliminate or reduce job stress. For example, in the policy area, attention would be given to making performance reviews and pay plans as equitable and as fair as possible. In the structural area, steps would be taken to back away from high degrees of formalization and specialization. The same would be done in the areas of physical conditions (for example, safety hazards would be removed, and lighting, noise, and temperature would be improved) and processes/functions (for example, communication and information would be improved, and ambiguous or conflicting goals would be clarified or resolved). In addition, the Association for Fitness in Business estimates that 12,000 companies today offer stress-coping programs ranging from counseling services, lunchtime stress management seminars, and wellness publications to elaborate company-run fitness centers where employees can sweat out the tension.[68] There is also evidence that the number of stress management programs is increasing and they are being evaluated more rigorously.[69]

In addition to working on each specific organizational stressor identified in Figure 14.2, more generalized strategies might include the following:

1. *Create a supportive organizational climate.* Most large organizations today tend to be highly formalized bureaucratic structures with accompanying inflexible, impersonal climates. This can lead to considerable job stress. A coping strategy would be to make the structure more decentralized and organic, with participative decision making and upward communication flows. In theory, these structural and process changes would create a more supportive climate for employees, give them more control over their jobs, and would prevent or reduce their job stress. The chapters in Part 5 of this book will analyze the details of organization structure and processes and the ramifications that they can have for the effective management of stress; however, as a number of reviews of literature on stress have pointed out, "the evidence bearing on relationships between climate factors and stress is speculative and needs to be empirically tested."[70]

2. *Enrich the design of tasks.* Chapter 7 was specifically devoted to job design. As was brought out there, enriching jobs either by improving job content factors (such as responsibility, recognition, and opportunities for achievement, advancement, and growth[71]) or by improving core job characteristics (such as skill variety, task identity, task significance, autonomy, and feedback[72]) may lead to motivational states or experienced meaningfulness, responsibility, and knowledge of results. Presumably, these enriched tasks will eliminate the stressors found in more routine, structured jobs. However, as Chapter 7 pointed out, not all people respond favorably to enriched job designs; and therefore, at least with some people some of the time, the enriched job may actually lead to increased job stress. For example, an individual with low growth needs, low self-efficacy, lack of hardiness, and/or fear of failure may experience increased stress in an enriched job. Overall, however, careful managing of task design may be an effective way to cope with stress.

3. *Reduce conflict and clarify organizational roles.* Role conflict and ambiguity was identified earlier as a major individual stressor. It is up to management to reduce the conflict and clarify *organizational* roles so that this cause of stress can be eliminated or reduced. Each job should have clear expectations and the necessary information and support so that the jobholder is not left with conflicting demands or an ambiguous understanding of what he or she is to do. A specific role clarification strategy might be to have the person occupying a role obtain a list of expectations from each role sender. This list would then be compared with the focal person's expectations, and any differences would be openly discussed to clarify ambiguities and negotiated to resolve conflict.[73]

4. *Plan and develop career paths and provide counseling.* Traditionally, organizations have shown only passing interest in the career planning and development of their employees. Individuals are left to decide career moves and strategies on their own and, at most, get paternalistic advice once in a while from a supervisor. This situation is analogous to that of students at a large university who are simply names on an adviser's computer printout sheet, which contains the names of hundreds of advisees. This obviously can be a source of considerable uncertainty and stress for both the students and the professor. The same is true for members of any large organization; the stress is created by not knowing what their next move is or how they are going to make it.

Summary

This chapter examined job stress. Although not always bad for the person (for example, the father of stress, Hans Selye, feels that complete freedom from stress is death[74]) or the organization (low levels of stress may lead to performance improvement), stress is still one of the most important and serious problems facing the field of organizational behavior. Defined as an adaptive response to an external situation that results in physical, psychological, and/or behavioral deviations for organizational participants, stress was first studied in terms of Selye's general adaptation syndrome. The three stages of GAS are alarm, resistance, and exhaustion. Since this beginning, which concentrated mainly on the physiological dimensions of stress, attention has also shifted to the psychological and behavioral dimensions.

The causes of stress can be categorized into extraorganizational, organizational, and group stressors and individual stressors and dispositions. In combination or singly, they represent a tremendous amount of potential stress impinging upon today's jobholder—at every level and in every type of organization. The effects of such stress can create physical problems (heart disease, ulcers, arthritis, and maybe even cancer), psychological problems (mood changes, lowered self-esteem, resentment of supervision, inability to make decisions, and job dissatisfaction), and/or behavioral problems (tardiness, absenteeism, turnover, and accidents). A number of individual and organizational strategies have been developed to cope with these stress-induced problems. Exercise, relaxation, behavioral self-control techniques, cognitive therapy techniques, and networking are some potentially useful coping strategies that individuals can apply to help combat existing stress. Taking a more proactive approach, management of organizations could create a more supportive climate, enrich tasks, reduce conflict, and clarify roles. Whether on an individual or an organizational level, steps need to be taken to prevent or reduce job stress.

Questions for Discussion and Review

1. How is stress defined? Is it always bad for the individual? Explain.
2. What is the general adaptation syndrome? What are the stages?
3. What are the general categories of stressors that can affect job stress? Give some examples of each.

4. What are some of the dispositions that may influence an individual's reaction to stress? Give an example of each.

5. Job stress can have physiological, psychological, and behavioral effects. Give an example of each and cite some research findings on the relationship between job stress and these outcomes.

6. Coping strategies for job stress were given for both the individual and the organizational levels. Summarize and evaluate these various strategies for preventing and/or more effectively managing stress.

References

1. "Stress: Can We Cope?" *Time*, June 6, 1983, p. 48.

2. "Unraveling Stress," *The Economist*, Apr. 13, 1985, p. 82; and Nick Nykodym and Katie George, "Stress Busting on the Job," *Personnel*, July 1989, p. 56.

3. John M. Ivancevich and Michael T. Matteson, *Organizational Behavior and Management*, Business Publications Inc., Plano, Tex., 1987, p. 211.

4. See Terry A. Beehr, "The Current Debate about the Meaning of Job Stress," *Journal of Organizational Behavior Management*, Fall/Winter 1986, pp. 5–18.

5. Ivancevich and Matteson, *Organizational Behavior and Management*, pp. 6, 8–9.

6. T. A. Beehr and J. E. Newman, "Job Stress, Employee Health, and Organizational Effectiveness: A Facet Analysis, Model, and Literature Review," *Personnel Psychology*, Winter 1978, pp. 665–699.

7. This is based on Hans Selye, *Stress without Distress*, Lippincott, Philadelphia, 1974; and James C. Quick and Jonathan D. Quick, *Organizational Stress and Preventative Management*, McGraw-Hill, New York, 1984, pp. 8–9.

8. John M. Ivancevich and Michael T. Matteson, *Stress and Work*, Soctt, Foresman, Glenview, Ill., 1980, p. 145.

9. Robert Kreitner, "Personal Wellness: It's Just Good Business," *Business Horizons*, May–June 1982, p. 28.

10. Rabi S. Bhagat and Stephen M. Allie, "Organizational Stress, Personal Life Stress, and Symptoms of Life Strains: An Examination of the Moderating Role of Sense of Competence," *Journal of Vocational Behavior*, vol. 35, 1989, p. 233.

11. T. H. Holmes and R. H. Rahe, "Social Readjustment Rating Scale," *Journal of Psychosomatic Research*, vol. 11, 1967, pp. 213–218.

12. *The Wall Street Journal*, Dec. 23, 1986, p. 1.

13. Todd D. Jick and Linda F. Mitz, "Sex Differences in Work Stress," *Academy of Management Review*, July 1985, pp. 408–420.

14. Debra L. Nelson and James C. Quick, "Professional Women: Are Distress and Disease Inevitable?" *Academy of Management Review*, April 1985, pp. 206–218.

15. R. Marens, "The Residential Environment," in A. Campbell, P. E. Converse, and W. L. Rodgers (eds.), *The Quality of American Life*, Russell Sage, New York, 1976.

16. Sally Solo, "Stop Whining and Get Back to Work," *Fortune*, March 12, 1990, p. 49.

17. Ivancevich and Matteson, *Stress and Work*, pp. 125–129.

18. Jeffrey H. Greenhaus and Nicholas J. Beutell, "Sources of Conflict between Work and Family Roles," *Academy of Management Review*, January 1985, p. 80.

19. For example, see R. L. Kahn, D. M. Wolfe, R. P. Quinn, J. D. Snoeck, and R. A. Rosenthal, *Organizational Stress: Studies in Role Conflict and Ambiguity*, Wiley, New York, 1964; Robert H. Miles, "An Empirical Test of Causal Inference between Role Perceptions of Conflict and Ambiguity and Various Personal Outcomes," *Journal of Applied Psychology*, June 1975, pp. 334–339; Robert H. Miles, "Role Requirements as Sources of Organizational Stress," *Journal of Applied Psychology*, April 1976, pp. 172–179; Andrew D. Szilagyi, Henry P. Sims, and Robert T. Keller, "Role Dynamics, Locus of Control and Employee

Attitudes and Behavior," *Academy of Management Journal,* June 1976, pp. 259–276; and Arthur G. Bedeian and Achilles A. Armenakis, "A Path-Analytic Study of the Consequences of Role Conflict and Ambiguity," *Academy of Management Journal,* June 1981, pp. 417–424.

20. Arthur P. Brief, Randall S. Schuler, and Mary Van Sell, *Managing Job Stress,* Little, Brown, Boston, 1981, p. 94.

21. Meyer Friedman and Ray H. Rosenman, *Type A Behavior and Your Heart,* Knopf, New York, 1974.

22. John H. Howard, David A. Cunningham, and Peter A. Rechnitzer, "Health Patterns Associated with Type A Behavior: A Managerial Population," *Journal of Human Stress,* March 1976, pp. 24–31.

23. Friedman and Rosenman, op. cit.

24. Brief, Schuler, and Van Sell, op. cit., pp. 11–12.

25. R. Rosenman and M. Friedman, "The Central Nervous System and Coronary Heart Disease," *Hospital Practice,* vol. 6, 1971, pp. 87–97.

26. "Unraveling Stress," *The Economist,* April 13, 1985, p. 82, and Jerry E. Bishop, "Prognosis for the 'Type A' Personality Improves in a New Heart Disease Study," *The Wall Street Journal,* Jan. 14, 1988, p. 29.

27. "Heart Disease, Anger Linked Research Shows," *Lincoln Journal,* Jan. 17, 1989, p. 4.

28. Richard M. Steers, *Introduction to Organizational Behavior,* 2d ed., Scott, Foresman, Glenview, Ill., 1984, p. 518.

29. Ronald E. Riggio, *Introduction to Industrial/Organizational Psychology,* Scott, Foresman/Little, Brown, Glenview, Ill., 1990, p. 204.

30. S. E. Jackson, "Participation in Decision Making as a Strategy for Reducing Job Related Strain," *Journal of Applied Psychology,* vol. 68, 1983, pp. 3–19.

31. "Jobs with Little Freedom Boost Heart Risk," *Lincoln Journal,* Apr. 11, 1990, p. 1.

32. M. E. P. Seligman, *Helplessness: On Depression, Development, and Death,* Freeman, San Francisco, 1975.

33. S. Mineka and R. W. Henderson, "Controllability and Predictability in Acquired Motivation," *Annual Review of Psychology,* vol. 36, 1985, pp. 495–529.

34. See L. Y. Abrahamson, J. Garber, and M. E. P. Seligman, "Learned Helplessness in Humans: An Attributional Analysis," in J. Garber and M. E. P. Seligman (eds.), *Human Helplessness: Theory and Applications,* Academic Press, New York, 1980; summarized in Robert S. Feldman, *Understanding Psychology,* 2d ed., McGraw-Hill, New York, 1990, p. 525. Also see: Mark J. Martinko and William L. Gardner, "Learned Helplessness: An Alternative Explanation for Performance Deficits," *Academy of Management Review,* vol. 7, 1982, pp. 413–417.

35. Spencer A. Rathus, *Psychology,* 4th ed., Holt, Rinehart and Winston, Fort Worth, Tex., 1990, pp. 440–441.

36. A. Bandura, C. B. Taylor, S. L. Williams, I. N. Medford, and J. D. Barchas, "Catecholamine Secretion as a Function of Perceived Coping Self-Efficacy," *Journal of Consulting and Clinical Psychology,* vol. 53, 1985, pp. 406–414.

37. Rathus, op. cit., p. 441.

38. S. C. Kobasa, "Stressful Life Events, Personality, and Health: An Inquiry into Hardiness," *Journal of Personality and Social Psychology,* vol. 37, 1979, pp. 1–11; and S. C. Kobasa, S. R. Maddi, and S. Kahn, "Hardiness and Health: A Perspective Study," *Journal of Personality and Social Psychology,* vol. 42, 1982, pp. 168–177.

39. Brian O'Reilly, "Is Your Company Asking Too Much," *Fortune,* March 12, 1990, p. 39.

40. Howard M. Weiss, Daniel R. Ilgen, and Michael E. Sharbaugh, "Effects of Life and Job Stress on Information Search Behaviors of Organizational Members," *Journal of Applied Psychology,* February 1982, pp. 60–62.

41. Beehr and Newman, op. cit.; David C. McClelland and John B. Jemmott, "Power Motivation, Stress and Physical Illness," *Journal of Human Stress,* December 1980, pp. 6–15; John M. Ivancevich, Michael T. Matteson, and Cynthia Preston, "Occupational Stress, Type A Behavior, and Physical Well Being," *Academy of Management Journal,* June 1982, pp. 373–391; and Ahmed A. Abdel-Halim, "Effects of Role Stress–Job Design–Technology Interaction on Employee Work Satisfaction," *Academy of Management Journal,* June 1981, pp. 260–273.

42. Robert A. Baron, *Behavior in Organizations,* 2d ed., Allyn and Bacon, Boston, 1986, p. 223.

43. Thomas G. Cummings and Cary L. Cooper, "A

Cybernetic Framework for Studying Occupational Stress," *Human Relations*, May 1979, pp. 395–418.

44. K. Bammer and B. H. Newberry (eds.), *Stress and Cancer*, Hogrefe, Toronto, 1982.

45. Ivancevich and Matteson, *Stress and Work*, p. 92.

46. J. E. McGrath, "Stress and Behavior in Organizations," in M. D. Dunnette (ed.), *Handbook of Industrial and Organizational Psychology*, Rand McNally, Chicago, 1976.

47. Beehr and Newman, op. cit.; A. A. McLean, *Work Stress*, Addison-Wesley, Reading, Mass., 1980; and Cary L. Cooper and Judi Marshall, "Occupational Sources of Stress," *Journal of Occupational Psychology*, March 1976, pp. 11–28.

48. "Job Stress Said a 'Substantial Health Problem,'" *Lincoln Journal*, Oct. 6, 1986, p. 15.

49. David S. Allen, "Less Stress, Less Litigation," *Personnel*, January 1990, p. 33.

50. Ivancevich and Matteson, *Stress and Work*, p. 96.

51. *The Wall Street Journal*, Oct. 14, 1986, p. 1; and *The Wall Street Journal*, Nov. 11, 1986, p. 35.

52. "Firm Hopes Breath Meter Curbs Workers' Drinking," *Lincoln Journal*, June 11, 1983, p. 13.

53. Ibid.

54. For example, see Lyman W. Porter and Richard M. Steers, "Organizational, Work, and Personal Factors in Employee Turnover and Absenteeism," *Psychological Bulletin*, August 1973, pp. 151–176; Richard M. Steers and Susan R. Rhodes, "Major Influences on Employee Attendance: A Process Model," *Journal of Applied Psychology*, August 1978, pp. 391–407; and W. H. Mobley, R. W. Griffeth, H. H. Hand, and B. M. Meglino, "Review and Conceptual Analysis of the Employee Turnover Process," *Psychological Bulletin*, May 1979, pp. 493–522.

55. Robert K. Wallace and Herbert Benson, "The Physiology of Meditation," *Scientific American*, February 1972, pp. 84–90.

56. Terri Schultz, "What Science Is Discovering about the Potential Benefits of Meditation," *Today's Health*, April 1972, pp. 34–37.

57. "Executives Meditating to Success," *Omaha World-Herald*, Feb. 11, 1986, p. 9.

58. A. Ellis, *Reason and Emotion in Psychotherapy*, Lyle Stuart, New York, 1962.

59. D. H. Meichenbaum, "Cognitive Modification of Test-Anxious College Students," *Journal of Consulting and Clinical Psychology*, vol. 39, 1972, pp. 370–378.

60. Daniel C. Ganster, Bronston T. Mayes, Wesley E. Sime, and Gerald D. Tharp, "Managing Organizational Stress: A Field Experiment," *Journal of Applied Psychology*, October 1982, p. 536.

61. Ibid., pp. 533–542.

62. I. G. Sarson, J. H. Johnson, J. P. Berberich, and J. S. Siegel, "Helping Police Officers to Cope with Stress: A Cognitive Behavioral Approach," *American Journal of Community Psychology*, vol. 7, 1979, pp. 593–603.

63. Ganster, Mayes, Sime, and Tharp, op. cit., p. 534.

64. Anson Seers, Gail W. McGee, Timothy T. Serey, and George B. Graen, "The Interaction of Job Stress and Social Support: A Strong Inference Investigation," *Academy of Management Journal*, June 1983, pp. 273–284.

65. McLean, op. cit.

66. John Kotter, *The General Managers*, Free Press, New York, 1982.

67. Fred Luthans, Stuart A. Rosenkrantz, and Harry W. Hennessey, "What Do Successful Managers Really Do? An Observation Study of Managerial Activities," *Journal of Applied Behavioral Science*, vol. 21, no. 3, 1985, pp. 255–270.

68. Laurie Hays, "But Some Firms Try to Help," *The Wall Street Journal*, Apr. 24, 1987, p. 16D.

69. John M. Ivancevich, Michael T. Matteson, Sara M. Freedman, and James S. Phillips, "Worksite Stress Management Interventions," *American Psychologist*, February 1990, pp. 252–261.

70. Ivancevich and Matteson, *Stress and Work*, p. 212. Also see Newman and Beehr, op. cit.

'71. F. Herzberg, B. Mausner, and B. Snyderman, *The Motivation to Work*, Wiley, New York, 1959.

72. J. Richard Hackman and Greg R. Oldham, "Motivation through the Design of Work: Test of a Theory," *Organizational Behavior and Human Performance*, August 1976, pp. 250–279.

73. J. R. P. French and R. D. Caplan, "Psychosocial Factors in Coronary Heart Disease," *Industrial Medicine*, vol. 39, 1970, pp. 383–397.

74. Selye, *Stress without Distress*.

REAL CASE: GETTING ALONG WITHOUT THE BOSS

When Everett Suters started his own business, he never realized that his personality and disposition had not prepared him for the rigors of the task he was undertaking. Suters is a high achiever and, like most of these people, he believed strongly in the old maxim, "If you want something done right, do it yourself." The problem, however, was that within a short period of time his health began to be affected.

Suters started out working in the sales area of a large corporation. He was very successful at this job because he quickly realized that the most important thing in selling is hard work. If he called on a customer and the individual was not interested in buying his product, he would go on to another location and call on another customer. The more people he called on, the higher his sales volume. His success was determined by how long and how hard he worked.

However, when he started his own business, Suters soon realized that his previous success strategy would not work. As his computer-service business increased its customer base, more and more work fell on Suters' shoulders. He found himself scurrying from one project to the next. There never was any time for planning for the future. The entire day was spent handling rush projects. His appointment calendar was so filled with things to do he even found himself having trouble handling emergency situations. At the same time he began getting angry at his personnel, whom he saw as not working as hard as he nor as concerned with the success of the operation as he was.

Exhausted and burned out after two years, Suters decided to take a month's vacation. It was the only way of ensuring that his health did not totally break down. When he returned, refreshed and ready to start again, Suters found that things were running smoothly. With him out of the way, the staff was able to plan more projects, get things organized, and not have to wait until they got an okay from the boss on everything. Quite obviously, Suters had been burning himself out with overwork and proving to be ineffective in the process.

Now aware that his stress was caused by inefficient management practices and an overcommitment to working harder rather than smarter, Suters began changing his operational methods. He began delegating more authority to his staff and refusing to handle busywork projects that could easily be managed by someone else. He stopped agreeing to help customers with all of their problems and began to face the fact that many of his clients were making unreasonable demands on the company. This freed up a great deal of personal time for more important projects. He also began setting and reviewing organizational priorities so that he knew where the company was going and how it would get there. In summarizing his new approach, Suters pointed to three important steps: (a) plan to do more than you can do; (b) prioritize what you plan to do by importance and urgency; and (c) commit yourself to *less* than you can do and *only* to those projects that are the most important or urgent. In summing up what he has learned as president of his company, Suters says:

> This is not to suggest that it's easy to maintain this management style. As with most addicts, reformed overachievers have to be on the alert constantly to keep from backsliding. Over the course of any year, my company hires new people, and the old syndrome starts to creep back. Even experienced people begin to depend too much on me. So every year I take the cure: three weeks away to prove to myself and to the members of my staff that they can get along without me.

1. What caused Suters' job stress? (Use Figure 14.2 in formulating your answer).
2. What were some of the individual coping strategies Suters employed to help him deal with his stress problem?
3. What lessons can be learned by managers from Suters' personal experience? Identify and describe three of them.

**Case:
Sorry, No
Seats Are
Left; Have a
Nice Flight**

Jim Miller has been a ticket agent for Friendly Airlines for the past three years. This job is really getting to be a hassle. In order to try to reduce the mounting losses that Friendly has suffered in recent months, management have decided to do two things: (1) overbook their flights so that every seat possible will be filled and (2) increase their service to their customers and live up to their name. Jim, of course, is at the point of application of this new policy. When checking in passengers, he is supposed to be very courteous and friendly, and he has been instructed to end every transaction with the statement, "Have a nice flight." The problem, of course, is that sometimes there are more passengers holding confirmed reservations checking in than there are seats on the plane. Rightfully, these people become extremely upset with Jim and sometimes scream at him and even threaten him. During these confrontations Jim becomes "unglued." He breaks into a sweat, and his face turns bright red. The company guidelines on what to do in these situations are very vague. When Jim called his supervisor for advice, he was simply told to try to book passengers on another flight, but be friendly.

1. Is Jim headed for trouble? What would be some physical, psychological, and behavioral outcomes of this type of job stress?
2. What could the company do to help reduce the stress in Jim's job?
3. What individual coping strategies could Jim try in this situation?

**Case:
A Gnawing
Stomach-
ache**

Sandy Celeste was thirty years old when her divorce became final. She was forced to go to work to support her two children. Sandy got married right after graduating from college and had never really held a full-time job outside the home. Nevertheless, because of her enthusiasm, education, and maturity, she impressed the personnel manager at Devon's Department Store and was immediately hired. The position involves supervising three different departments of women's clothing. Sandy's training consisted of approximately two months at another store in the Devon chain. She spent this training period both selling merchandise and learning the supervisor's responsibilities. On the first day of her supervisory job, Sandy learned that, because of size constraints at the store, eight different women's clothing departments are all located in the same area. In addition to Sandy, there are two other supervisors in the other departments. These three supervisors share the service of twenty-eight full- and part-time salespeople. Since the various departments are so jammed together, all the salespeople are expected to know each department's merchandise. Devon's merchandising philosophy is that it will not finish one department or store-wide sale without starting another. Both the clerks and the supervisors, who work on a commission and salary basis, are kept busy marking and remarking the merchandise as one sale stops and another starts. To make matters worse, Devon's expects the employees to remark each item just prior to closing time the night after a big sale. The pressure is intense, and customers are often neglected. However, all the salespeople realize that when the customer suffers, so do their commissions. As a supervisor, Sandy is expected to enforce the company's policy rigidly. Soon after taking the position as supervisor, Sandy began to experience severe headaches and a gnawing stomachache. She would like to quit her job, but realistically she can't because the pay is good and she needs to support her children.

1. To what do you attribute Sandy's health problems? What are some possible extra-organizational, organizational, group, and individual stressors?
2. Is there anything that this company could do to alleviate stress for its supervisors? What individual coping strategies could Sandy try?

15 | Power and Politics

■ The Keating Five

Power and politics are in every organization, but no where are they better reflected than in the halls of Congress where the two often go hand-in-hand. This combination recently resulted in a major problem for five senators, who were accused of using their power to help Charles H. Keating, Jr., president of Lincoln Savings and Loan of Irvine, California. Among other things, Mr. Keating wanted to obtain a reversal of a Federal Home Loan Bank Board regulation that limited high-risk investments by savings and loans. The five senators, in varying degrees, intervened on his behalf.

Lincoln S&L eventually went bankrupt. When the investigators had sifted through the evidence, they concluded that the five senators had gone too far in attempting to help Keating keep his bank afloat. The senators had written letters and contacted regulators in an effort to help Keating's bank, and this largesse had not gone unappreciated. Keating made contributions to the re-election of all five, which proved to be the crux of the problem. Would the senators have done the same for any individual who came and asked for their help or were they influenced by the contributions?

The evidence proved so compelling that the Senate Ethics Committee held hearings, reviewed the materials, and concluded that a full investigation was warranted. All five were called in front of the committee, listened to the charges that were brought against them, and then were given the opportunity to respond to them. Senators found guilty of ethics violations can be expelled.

Many observers believe that with the Keating hearings, the Ethics Committee is sending a message to the rest of the Congress and to the nation at large that power in the political arena must be used judiciously. This message is not being lost on the justice system in general. In the middle of the hearings, another power-ethics case was resolved. Michael Milken, the junk bond king, was found guilty of using illegal power to manipulate the stock market (and according to some, such actions helped create the S&L mess in which people like Keating became ensnared) and was given a ten-year prison sentence. This was the longest sentence ever given to someone found guilty of stock market fraud. These developments are obviously going to have a great deal of influence on the way power and politics are used by organizations in the 1990s.

Learning Objectives

- **Define** power and its relationship to authority and influence.
- **Identify** the various classifications of power.
- **Discuss** the contingency approach to power.
- **Explain** a macro view of power.
- **Relate** the political implications of power.
- **Present** some political strategies for power acquisition in modern organizations.

Over the years, groups, informal organization, interactive behavior, conflict, and stress have received considerable attention as important dynamics of organizational behavior; power and politics, however, have not. Yet it is becoming clear, and anyone who has spent any time in a formal organization can readily verify, that organizations are highly political and power is the name of the game. Power and politics must be brought "out of the closet" and recognized as an important dynamic in organizational behavior. For example, the dynamics of power—how to use it and how to abuse it—was recently discovered by Joseph O'Donnell, who was abruptly fired from his high-level executive position with JWT Group Inc. when he proposed stripping the CEO and chairman Don Johnston of his day-to-day operating duties. In other cases, however, such a grab for power has worked. Lewis Glucksman, for instance, pushed Peter Peterson from the head of Lehman Brothers a few years ago,[1] and every day, in organizations at all levels, power plays and political moves take place.

The first part of the chapter defines what is meant by power and describes how it is related to authority and influence. The next part concentrates on the various classifications of power. Particular attention is given to the French and Raven classification of the sources of power. After an examination of some of the research results on power types, attention is given to some contingency approaches (for example, the influenceability of the target and an overall contingency model of power). Next, a more macro perspective of power is presented. Structured determinants of power are emphasized. The last part is concerned with organizational politics. Particular attention is given to a political perspective of power in today's organizations and to some specific political strategies for its acquisition.

THE MEANING OF POWER

Although the concepts in the field of organizational behavior seldom have universally agreed upon definitions, *power* may have even more diverse definitions than most. Almost every author who writes about power defines it differently. Going way back, for example, the famous pioneering sociologist Max Weber defined power as "the probability that one actor within a social relationship will be in a position to carry out his own will despite resistance."[2] More recently, a search of the literature on power found it referred to as the ability to get things done despite the will and resistance of others or the ability to "win" political fights and outmaneuver the opposition. The power theorists stress the positive sum of power, suggesting it is the raw ability to mobilize resources to accomplish some end without reference to any organized opposition.[3] Robbins has supplied one of the most detailed, and perhaps most understandable, definitions: "Power refers to a capacity that A has to influence the behavior of B, so that B does something he or she would not otherwise do. This definition implies (1) a *potential* that need not be actualized to be effective, (2) a *dependence* relationship, and (3) the assumption that B has some *discretion* over his or her own behavior."[4]

Usually, definitions of power are intertwined with the concepts of authority and influence. For example, the definition above uses the word *influence* in describing power, the pioneering theorist Chester Barnard defined power in terms of "informal authority," and many modern organizational sociologists define authority as "legitimate power."[5] These distinctions between concepts need to be cleared up in order to understand power.

The Distinctions Between Power, Authority, and Influence

In Chapter 6 the power motive was defined as the need to manipulate others and have superiority over them. Extrapolating from this definition of the need for power, "power" itself can be defined as *the ability to get an individual or group to do something—to get the person or group to change in some way.* The person who possesses power has the ability to manipulate or change others. Such a definition of power distinguishes it from authority and influence.

Authority legitimatizes and is a source of power. Authority is the right to manipulate or change others. Power need not be legitimate. In addition, the distinction must be made between top-down classical, bureaucratic authority and Barnard's concept of bottom-up authority based upon acceptance. In particular, Barnard defined *authority* as "the character of a communication (order) in a formal organization by virtue of which it is accepted by a contributor to or 'member' of the organization as governing the action he contributes."[6]

Such an acceptance theory of authority is easily differentiated from power. Grimes notes: "What legitimizes authority is the promotion or pursuit of collective goals that are associated with group consensus. The polar opposite, power, is the pursuit of individual or particularistic goals associated with group compliance."[7]

Influence is usually conceived of as being broader in scope than power. It involves the ability to alter other people in general ways, such as by changing their satisfaction and performance. Influence is more closely associated with leadership than power is, but both obviously are involved in the leadership process. Thus, authority is different from power because of its legitimacy and acceptance, and influence is broader than power, but it is so conceptually close that the two terms can be used interchangeably.

The above discussion points out that an operational definition of power is lacking, and this vagueness is a major reason why power has been largely ignored in the study of organizational behavior. Yet, especially when it is linked to the emerging concern for organizational politics, the study of power can greatly enhance the understanding of organizational behavior.

The Classifications of Power

Any discussion of power usually begins and sometimes ends with the five categories of the sources of power identified by social psychologists John French and Bertram Raven.[8] Describing and analyzing these five classic types of power (reward, coercive, legitimate, referent, and expert) serves as a necessary foundation and point of departure for the entire chapter. Most of the examples and applications to organizational behavior come from these five types of power.

Reward Power. This source of power depends on the person's having the ability and resources to reward others. In addition, the target of this power must value these rewards. In an organizational context, managers have many potential rewards such as pay increases, promotions, favorable work assignments, more responsibility, new equipment, praise, feedback, and recognition available to them. In operant learning terms, this means that the manager has the power to administer positive reinforcers. In expectancy motivation terms, this means that the person has the power to provide positive valences and that the other person perceives this ability.

To understand this source of power more completely, it must be remembered that the recipient holds the key. If managers offer subordinates what they think is a reward (for example, a promotion with increased responsibility), but subordinates do not value it (for example, they are insecure or have family obligations that are more important to them than a promotion), then managers do not really have reward power. By the same token, managers may not think they are giving a reward to subordinates (they calmly listen to chronic complainers), but if subordinates perceive this as rewarding (the managers are giving them attention by intently listening to their complaining), the managers nevertheless have reward power. Also, managers may not really have the rewards to dispense (they may say that they have considerable influence with top management to get their people promoted, but actually they don't), but as long as their people think they have it, they do indeed have reward power.

Coercive Power. This source of power depends on fear. The person with coercive power has the ability to inflict punishment or aversive consequences on the other person or, at least, to make threats that the other person believes will result in punishment or undesirable outcomes. This form of power has contributed greatly to the negative connotation that power has for most people. In an organizational context, managers frequently have coercive power in that they can fire or demote subordinates or dock their pay, although unions have certainly stripped some of this power away over the years. Management can also directly or indirectly threaten an employee with these punishing consequences. In operant learning terms, this means that the person has the power to administer punishers or negatively reinforce (terminate punishing consequences, which is a form of negative control). In expectancy motivation terms, this means that power comes from the expectation on the part of the other persons that they will be punished if they do not conform to the powerful person's desires. For example, there is fear of punishment if they do not follow the rules, directives, or policies of the organization. It is probably this fear that gets most people to come to work on time and look busy when the boss walks through the area. In other words, much of organizational behavior may be explained in terms of coercive power rather than reward power.

Legitimate Power. This power source, identified by French and Raven, stems from the internalized values of the other persons which give the legitimate right to the agent to influence them. The others feel they have the obligation to accept this power. It is almost identical to what is usually called *authority* and is closely aligned with both reward and coercive power because the person with legitimacy is also in a position to reward and punish. However, legitimate power is unlike reward and coercive power in that it does not depend on the relationships with others but rather on the position or role that the person holds. For example, people obtain legitimacy because of their title (captain or executive vice president) or position (oldest in the family or officer of a corporation) rather than their personalities or how they affect others.

Legitimate power can come from three major sources. First, the prevailing cultural values of a society, organization, or group determine what is legitimate. For example, in some societies, the older people become, the more legitimate power they possess. The same may be true for certain physical attributes, sex, or vocation. In an organizational context, managers generally have legitimate power because employees believe in the value of private property laws and in the hierarchy where higher positions have been designated to have power over lower positions. The same holds true for certain functional positions in an organization. An example of the latter would be engineers who have legitimacy in the operations area of a company, while accountants have legitimacy in financial matters. The prevailing values within a group also determine legitimacy. For example, in a street gang the toughest member may have legitimacy, while in a work group the union steward may have legitimacy.

Second, people can obtain legitimate power from the accepted social structure. In some societies there is an accepted ruling class. But an organization or a family may also have an accepted social structure that gives legitmate power. For example, when blue-collar workers accept employment from a company, they are in effect accepting the hierarchical structure and granting legitimate power to their supervisors.

A third source of legitimate power can come from being designated as the agent or representative of a powerful person or group. Elected officials, a chairperson of a committee, and a member of the board of directors of a corporation or a union or management committee would be examples of this form of legitimate power.

Each of these forms of legitimate power creates an obligation to accept and be influenced. But, in actual practice, there are often problems, confusion, or disagreement about the range or scope of this power. Consider the following:

> An executive can rightfully expect a supervisor to work hard and diligently; may he also influence the supervisor to spy on rivals, spend weekends away from home, join an encounter group? A coach can rightfully expect [her] players to execute specific plays; may [she] also direct their life styles outside the sport? A combat officer can rightfully expect his men to attack on order; may he also direct them to execute civilians whom he claims are spies? A doctor can rightfully order a nurse to attend a

patient or observe an autopsy; may [she] order [him or] her to assist in an abortion against [his or] her own will?[9]

These gray areas point to the real concern that many people in contemporary society have regarding the erosion of traditional legitimacy. These uncertainties also point to the complex nature of power.

Referent Power. This type of power comes from the desire on the part of the other persons to identify with the agent wielding power. They want to identify with the powerful person, regardless of the outcomes. The others grant the person power because he or she is attractive and has desirable resources or personal characteristics.

Advertisers take advantage of this type of power when they use celebrities, such as movie stars or sports figures, to do testimonial advertising. The buying public identifies with (finds attractive) certain famous people and grants them power to tell them what product to buy. For example, a review of research has found that arguments, especially emotional ones, are more influential when they come from beautiful people.[10]

Timing is an interesting aspect of the testimonial advertising type of referent power. Only professional athletes who are in season (for example, baseball players in the summer and early fall, football players in the fall and early winter, and basketball players in the winter and early spring) are used in the advertisements, because then they are very visible, they are in the forefront of the public's awareness, and consequently they have referent power. Out of season the athlete is forgotten and has little referent power. Exceptions, of course, are the handful of superstars (for example, George Brett, Sugar Ray Leonard, Joe Montana, and Magic Johnson) who transcend seasons and have referent power all year long, and even after they have retired.

In an organizational setting, referent power is much different from the other types of power discussed so far. For example, managers with referent power must be attractive to subordinates so that subordinates will want to identify with them, regardless of whether the managers later have the ability to reward or punish or whether they have legitimacy. In other words, the manager who depends on referent power must be personally attractive to subordinates.

Expert Power. The last source of power identified by French and Raven is based on the extent to which others attribute knowledge and expertise to the power seeker. Experts are perceived to have knowledge or understanding only in certain well-defined areas. All the sources of power depend on the target's perceptions, but expert power may be even more dependent on this than the others. In particular, the target must perceive the agent to be credible, trustworthy, and relevant before expert power is granted.

Credibility comes from having the right credentials; that is, the person must really know what he or she is talking about and be able to show tangible evidence of this knowledge. For example, if a highly successful football coach gives an aspiring young player some advice on how to do a new block, he will be closely listened to—he will be granted expert power. The coach has expert power in this case because he is so knowledgeable about football. His evidence for this credibility is the fact that he is a former star player and has coached championship teams. If this coach tried to give advice on how to play basketball or how to manage a corporation, he would have no credibility and thus would have no expert power. For avid football fans or players, however, this coach might have general referent power (that is, he is very attractive to them), and they would be influenced by what he has to say on any subject—basketball or corporate management.

In organizations, staff specialists have expert power in their functional areas, but not outside. For example, engineers are granted expert power in production matters but not in personnel or public relations problems. The same holds true for other staff experts such as computer experts or accountants. For example, the computer person in a small office may be the only one who really understands it and how to use it, and this knowledge gives him or her considerable power.

As already implied, however, expert power is highly selective, and, besides credibility, the agent must also have trustworthiness and relevance. By trustworthiness, it is meant that the person seeking expert power must have a reputation for being honest and straightforward. In the case of political figures, scandals such as the Iran-*contra* affair could undermine their expert power in the eyes of the American public. In addition to credibility and trustworthiness, a person must have relevance and usefulness to have expert power. Going back to the earlier example, if the football coach gave advice on world affairs, it would be neither relevant nor useful, and therefore the coach would not have expert power.

It is evident that expertise is the most tenuous type of power, but managers, and especially staff specialists, who seldom have the other sources of power available to them, often have to depend upon their expertise as their only source of power. As organizations become increasingly technologically complex and specialized, the expert power of organization members at all levels may become more and more important. This is formally recognized by some companies that deliberately include lower-level staff with expert power in top-level decision making. For example, the president of a high-tech firm stated: "In general, the faster the change in the know-how on which a business depends, the greater the divergence between knowledge and position power is likely to be. Since our business depends on what it knows to survive, we mix 'knowledge-power people' with 'position-power people' daily, so that together they make the decisions that will affect us for years to come."[11] Some organizations are using their expertise to fend off the competition. The International Application Example, Keeping the Inside Track, illustrates how Intourist, the giant Soviet tourism agency, is doing this to hold off competition.

It must also be remembered that French and Raven did recognize that there may be other sources of power. For instance, some organizational sociologists such as Crozier[12] recognize the source of power of task interdependence (where two or more organizational participants must depend on one another). An example would be an executive who has legitimate power over a subordinate, but because the executive must depend on the subordinate to get the job done correctly and on time, the subordinate also has power over the executive.[13] There is research evidence that subordinates in such an interdependent relationship with their boss receive better pay raises.[14] French and Raven also point out that the sources are interrelated (for

Keeping the Inside Track

Competition is coming to the Soviet Union, but Intourist, which has monopolized foreign tourism for decades, is finding that the use of expert power can help it fend off many of these threats. The two biggest internal competitors are Intourbureau and Sputnik. Intourbureau was set up in 1967 to handle trade-union exchange programs, and in recent years it has ventured into commercial travel. Today, it has hotels in twenty-five cities and hosts about 200,000 foreign visitors annually. Sputnik handles tours for young Soviets (thirty-five years of age or under) who want to visit other locales around the country.

The biggest problem that Intourist faces is that many people dislike doing business with it. The agency is famous for lost reservations, lackadaisical tour guides, dingy rooms, and rude employees. On the other hand, Intourist has the necessary infrastructure to compete. For years, tourists to the Soviet Union have learned to call Intourist and have it take care of all of their reservations. This helps explain why the agency handles about 2 million of the nation's 2.5 million foreign tourists each year and arranges Soviet travel abroad. Moreover, Intourist owns 110 hotels and is affiliated with more than 800 travel agents in other countries. And it is now expanding operations so that by the end of the 1990s it is estimated that the agency will have five times as many rooms as it did at the beginning.

Will past experience and reputation help Intourist crush the competition? This outcome is unlikely, given the influx of foreign competitors who are attempting to lure tourists to their own facilities. Examples are Radisson Hotels, the Sheraton, and Pan American, all of which, either individually or in a joint-venture arrangement, are getting into the tourism business in the Soviet Union. In some cases, they are teaming up with competitors of Intourist; in other cases, they are dealing directly with Soviet cities—as in the case of the Sheraton Moscow Hotel, a partnership between Pan Am and the city of Moscow. Thus, while Intourist will continue to be a major player in the tourism business, its power is beginning to erode in the face of competition.

example, the use of coercive power by managers may reduce their referent power), and the same person may exercise different types of power under different circumstances and at different times. The latter point has recently led to some contingency models of power in organizations.

Contingency Approaches to Power

As in other areas of organizational behavior and management, contingency approaches to power are beginning to emerge. Some authors have summarized the research literature into contingency statements such as the following:

1. The greater the professional orientation of group members, the greater relative strength referent power has in influencing them.
2. The less effort and interest high-ranking participants are willing to allocate to a task, the more likely lower-ranking participants are to obtain power relevant to this task.[15]

Besides these overall contingency observations, there is increasing recognition of the moderating impact of the control of strategic contingencies such as organizational interdependence and the extent to which a department controls critical operations of other departments[16] or the role of the influence target in the power relationship. The characteristics of influence targets (that is, their influenceability) have an important moderating impact on the types of power that can be successfully used. An examination of these characteristics of the target and an overall contingency model is presented next.

Influenceability of the Targets of Power. Most discussions of power imply a unilateral process of influence from the agent to the target. It is becoming increasingly clear, however, that power involves a reciprocal relationship between the agent and the target, which is in accordance with the overall social learning perspective taken in other chapters of the book. The power relationship can be better understood by examining some of the characteristics of the target. The following characteristics have been identified as being especially important to the influenceability of targets.[17]

1. *Dependency.* The greater the targets' dependency on their relationship to agents (for example, when a target cannot escape a relationship, perceives no alternatives, or values the agent's rewards as unique), the more targets are influenced.
2. *Uncertainty.* Experiments have shown that the more uncertain people are about the appropriateness or correctness of a behavior, the more likely they are to be influenced to change that behavior.
3. *Personality.* There have been a number of research studies showing the relationship between personality characteristics and influenceability. Some of these findings are obvious (for example, people who cannot tolerate ambiguity or who are highly anxious are more susceptible to influence, and those with high needs for affiliation are more susceptible to group influence), but some are not (for example, both positive and negative relationships have been found between self-esteem and influenceability).
4. *Intelligence.* There is no simple relationship between intelligence and influenceability. For example, highly intelligent people may be more willing to listen, but, because they also tend to be held in high esteem, they also may be more resistant to influence.
5. *Sex.* Although traditionally it was generally acknowledged that women were more likely to conform to influence attempts than men because of the way they were raised, there is now evidence that this is changing.[18] As women's and society's views of the role of women are changing, there is less of a distinction by sex of influenceability.
6. *Age.* Social psychologists have generally concluded that susceptibility to influence increases in young children up to about age eight or nine and then decreases with age until adolescence, when it levels off.
7. *Culture.* Obviously, the cultural values of a society have a tremendous impact on the influenceability of its people. For example, some cultures, such as Western

cultures, emphasize individuality, dissent, and diversity, which would tend to decrease influenceability, while others, such as many in the Far East, emphasize cohesiveness, agreement, and uniformity, which would tend to promote influenceability. As the accompanying International Application Example, Taking as Long as It Takes, indicates, controlling the agenda and time in foreign cultures may be used to gain power and influenceability. These individual differences in targets greatly complicate the effective use of power and point up the need for contingency models.

An Overall Contingency Model for Power. Many other contingency variables in the power relationship besides the target could be inferred from the discussion of the

Taking as Long as It Takes

In recent years many American firms doing business internationally have found, to their chagrin, that their overseas hosts have been using the agenda to gain power over visiting dignitaries. Here is a story related by a business lawyer who recently returned from Japan.

"I went to Japan to negotiate a licensing agreement with a large company there. We had been in contact with these people for three months and during that time had hammered out a rough agreement regarding the specific terms of the contract. The president of the firm thought that it would be a good idea if I, the corporate attorney, went to Tokyo and negotiated some of the final points of the agreement before we signed. I arrived in Japan on a Sunday with the intention of leaving late Friday evening. When I got off the plane, my hosts were waiting for me. I was whisked through customs and comfortably ensconced in a plush limousine within 30 minutes.

The next day began with my host asking me for my return air ticket so his secretary could take care of confirming the flight. I was delighted to comply. We then spent the next four days doing all sorts of things—sightseeing, playing golf, fishing, dining at some of the finest restaurants in the city. You name it, we did it. By Thursday I was getting worried. We had not yet gotten around to talking about the licensing agreement. Then on Friday morning we had a big meeting. Most of the time was spent discussing the changes my hosts would like to see made in the agreement. Before I had a chance to talk, it was time for lunch. We finished eating around 4 P.M. This left me only four hours before I had to leave for the airport. During this time I worked to get them to understand the changes we wanted made in the agreement. Before I knew it, it was time to head for the airport. Halfway there my host pulled out a new contract. 'Here are the changes we talked about,' he said. 'I have already signed for my company. All you have to do is sign for yours.' Not wanting to come home empty-handed, I signed. It turned out that the contract was much more favorable to them than to us. In the process, I learned a lesson. Time is an important source of power. When you know the other person's agenda, you have an idea of what the individual's game plan must be and can work it to your advantage. Since this time, I have all my reservations and confirmations handled stateside. When my guest asks me how long I will be staying, I have a stock answer, 'As long as it takes.'"

various types of power, for example, credibility and surveillance. All these variables can be tied together and related to one another in an overall contingency model.

The classic work on influence processes, by social psychologist Herbert Kelman, can be used to structure an overall contingency model of power. Figure 15.1 shows such a model. It recognizes that there are several sources of power combine into three major processes of power.

According to the model, the target will *comply* in order to gain a favorable reaction or avoid a punishing one from the agent. This is the process that most supervisors in work organizations must rely upon. But in order for compliance to work, supervisors must be able to reward and punish (that is, have control over the means to their subordinates' ends) and keep an eye on their subordinates (that is, have surveillance over them).

People will *identify*, not in order to obtain a favorable reaction from the agent, as in compliance, but because it is self-satisfying to do so. But in order for the identification process to work, the agent must have referent power—be very attractive to the target—and be salient. For example, a research study by Kelman found that students were initially greatly influenced by a speech given by a very handsome star athlete; that is, they identified with him. However, when the students were checked six months after the speech, they were not influenced. The handsome athlete was no longer salient; that is, he was no longer in the forefront of their awareness, and his words carried no influence. As discussed earlier, except for the handful of

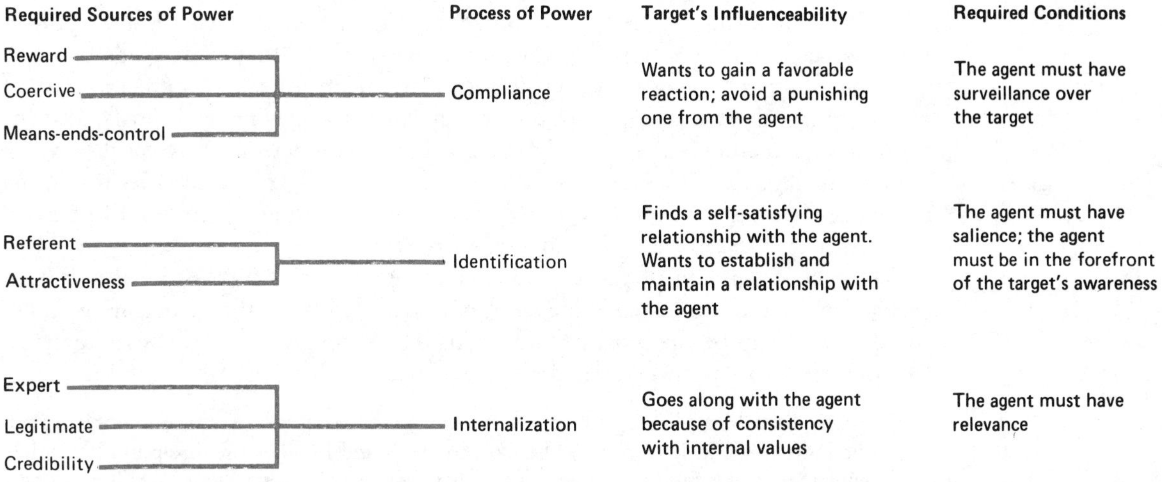

Required Sources of Power	Process of Power	Target's Influenceability	Required Conditions
Reward Coercive Means-ends-control	Compliance	Wants to gain a favorable reaction; avoid a punishing one from the agent	The agent must have surveillance over the target
Referent Attractiveness	Identification	Finds a self-satisfying relationship with the agent. Wants to establish and maintain a relationship with the agent	The agent must have salience; the agent must be in the forefront of the target's awareness
Expert Legitimate Credibility	Internalization	Goes along with the agent because of consistency with internal values	The agent must have relevance

FIGURE 15.1

An overall contingency model of power.

(*Source:* Adapted from Herbert C. Kelman, "Compliance, Identification, and Internalization: Three Processes of Attitude Change," *Journal of Conflict Resolution,* March 1958, pp. 51–60.)

superstars, athletes are soon forgotten and have no power over even their most avid fans. Once they have graduated or are out of season, they lose their salience and, thus, their power.

Finally, people will *internalize* because of compatibility with their own value structure. But, as Figure 15.1 shows, in order for people to internalize the agent must have expert or legitimate power (credibility) and, in addition, be relevant. Obviously, this process of power is most effective. Kelman, for example, found that internalized power had a lasting impact on his subjects.

McClelland's Two Faces of Power. Whereas French and Raven's work has much relevance for the dynamics of organizational behavior, David McClelland has, as Chapter 6 pointed out, done considerable work on the impact of the motivational need for power (what he calls *n Pow*) on organizational power. He also is convinced that there are two major types of power, one negative and one positive.

Over the years, power has often had a negative connotation. The commonly used term *power-hungry* reflects this negative feeling about power. According to McClelland, power

> . . . is associated with heavy drinking, gambling, having more aggressive impulses, and collecting "prestige supplies" like a convertible or a Playboy Club Key. People with this personalized power concern are more apt to speed, have accidents, and get into physical fights. If . . . possessed by political officeholders, especially in the sphere of international relations, the consequences would be ominous.[19]

McClelland feels that this negative use of power is associated with *personal power.* He feels that it is primitive and does indeed have negative consequences.

The contrasting "other face" of power identified by McClelland is *social power.* It is characterized by a "concern for group goals, for finding those goals that will move people, for helping the group to formulate them, for taking some initiative in providing members of the group with the means of achieving such goals, and for giving group members the feeling of strength and competence they need to work hard for such goals."[20] Under this definition of social power, the manager may often be in a precarious position of walking a fine line between an exhibition of personal dominance and the more socializing use of power.

As the discussion of power and achievement motives in Chapter 6 indicates, McClelland has accumulated evidence that seems to indicate that managers who use social power may be the most effective. His data show that the successful manager has four discernible power-related characteristics:

> Firstly he believes in an authority system, that the institution is more important than the individuals in it. Secondly, he likes to work and he likes the discipline of work, which leads to orderly management. Thirdly, he is altruistic in that he will sacrifice his own self-interest for the welfare of the company and does this in some obvious way that everybody can see. And fourthly, he believes in justice above everything else, that people must have even-handed treatment.[21]

McClelland's position on the importance of power to successful management is in direct opposition to the more humanistic positions, which emphasize the importance of democratic values and participative decison making. There is also recent empirical evidence that would counter McClelland's view. One study found that those with a high need for power may suppress the flow of information, especially information that contradicts their preferred course of action, and thus have a negative impact on effective managerial decision making.[22] But regardless of the controversy surrounding the definition and classification of power—be it by French and Raven or McClelland—it is clear that power is inevitable in today's organizations.

How power is used and what type of power is used will vitally affect human performance and organizational goals. In French and Raven's terms, the use of expert and referent power in organizations may be more effective than traditionally used legitimate and coercive power. In McClelland's terms, social power may be of greater value to the organization than traditionally used personal power. It is becoming increasingly clear that today, and in the years ahead, effective human performance, the management of change, and the reduction of stress in the workplace may result from empowerment of employees at all levels of the organization.

Empowerment of Employees. As was discussed in Chapter 4 on personality and Chapter 14 on job stress, the extent to which organizational participants have a sense of personal power and control has become recognized as critical to their performance and well being. This has become known as empowerment. For example, successful hotel chains such as Marriott and retailers such as Wal-Mart are known for empowering their employees to make things right for the customer, at any cost. If a guest at a Marriott hotel questions a minor charge on the bill when checking out, the clerk, not just the manager, is empowered to make the decision to eliminate the charge. When a customer returns an item at Wal-Mart, the customer service counter clerk is empowered to make the decision to refund the money for the item, even without a sales slip. This not only provides quality service to customers, but also gives the employees a sense of personal power and control over their work.

Here are some specific suggestions of ways management can empower their employees:[23]

1. Express confidence in employees' abilities and hold high expectations concerning their performance.
2. Allow employees to participate in the decision-making process.
3. Allow employees freedom and autonomy in how they perform their jobs.
4. Set inspirational and/or managerial goals for employees.
5. Use legitimate power in a prudent and positive way and limit the use of coercive power.

Unfortunately, there are many barriers to empowerment of employees. There is still widespread belief among managers that to empower subordinates is to lose one's own power. One way to overcome such a perception is to make sure that managers who empower their employees are not blamed for their people's failures nor ignored when their people succeed.[24]

A More Macro View of Power

Although the discussion of power so far at least has organizational implications (especially the contingency models), there is a view from organization theory that structure actually determines power. For example, Pfeffer states:

The design of an organization, its structure, is first and foremost the system of control and authority by which the organization is governed. . . . Thus, organizational structures create formal power and authority by designating certain persons to do certain tasks and make certain decisions and create informal power through the effect on information and communication structures within the organization.[25]

The position one occupies in the structure also is a determinant of power. For example, those at the top of the hierarchical structure (that is, upper-level management) have power sources such as formal position, resources, and control of decision premises, while lower-level managers may get their power from physical location or information flow.[26]

Besides the power implications of vertical structuring, there are also power differentials on each horizontal level of the structure. For example, even though the heads of the various functions of a business firm are on the same level, they do not possess the same power.

For example, which functional department head—production, marketing, or finance—has the most power will depend on the type of firm. In a manufacturing concern, production and engineering have the most power, but in a big oil company, marketing may have the most power. These horizontal power differentials, of course, will be contingent on a number of environmental factors such as the technology and the economy. In recent years, because of the economic and political climate, the financial and legal departments of many American organizations have become very powerful, but in Japan the operations, quality-control and personnel functions are more powerful. In other words, like the more micro analysis of power, the macro analysis of power must also recognize the contingency approach. Some recently suggested contingency variables—to summarize what has just been discussed—are areas such as organizational environment, culture, structure, and process.[27]

POLITICAL IMPLICATIONS OF POWER

Power and politics are very closely related concepts. A popular view of organizational politics is how one can pragmatically get ahead in an organization. Alvin Toffler, the noted author of *Future Shock*, *The Third Wave* and, *Powershift*, observed that "companies are always engaged in internal political struggles, power struggles, infighting, and so on. That's normal life."[28] Another view, however, deals with the acquisition of power. In this latter view, power and politics become especially closely intertwined. A recognition of the political realities of power acquisition in today's organizations and an examination of some specific political strategies for acquiring power are of particular interest for understanding the dynamics of organizational behavior.

A Political Perspective of Power in Organizations

As Chapter 18 will discuss in detail, the classical organization theorists portrayed organizations as highly rational structures in which authority meticulously followed the chain of command and in which managers had legitimatized power. The discussion in Chapter 12 of informal managerial roles and organization portrayed another, more realistic view of organizations. It is in this more realistic view of organizations that the importance of the political aspects of power comes to the forefront.

Walter Nord has tried to dispel some of the dreams of ideal, rationally structured and humanistic organizations by pointing out some of the stark realities of political power. He suggests four postulates of power in organizations that help focus on the political realities:

1. Organizations are composed of coalitions which compete with one another for resources, energy, and influence.
2. Various coalitions will seek to protect their interests and positions of influence.
3. The unequal distribution of power itself has dehumanizing effects.
4. The exercise of power within organizations is one very crucial aspect of the exercise of power within the larger social system.[29]

In other words, the political power game is very real in today's organizations.

Some of today's large corporations have even formalized their political nature by creating political action committees (PACs) to support certain government positions. For example, the president of NBC, Robert Wright, created a stir when he proposed the network create a PAC and purportedly suggested that employees who don't contribute "should question their own dedication to the company and their expectations."[30] But like other aspects of organizational dynamics, politics is not a simple process; it can vary from organization to organization and even from one subunit of an organization to another. A comprehensive definition drawing from the literature is that "organizational politics consists of intentional acts of influence undertaken by individuals or groups to enhance or protect their self-interest when conflicting courses of action are possible."[31] The political behavior of organizational participants tends to be opportunistic for the purpose of maximizing self-interest.[32]

Research on organizational politics has identified several areas that are particularly relevant to the degree to which organizations are political rather than rational. These areas can be summarized as follows:

1. *Resources.* There is a direct relationship between the amount of politics and how critical and scarce the resources are. Also, politics will be encouraged when there is an infusion of new, "unclaimed" resources.
2. *Decisions.* Ambiguous decisions, decisions on which there is lack of agreement, and uncertain, long-range strategic decisions lead to more politics than routine decisions.
3. *Goals.* The more ambiguous and complex the goals become, the more politics there will be.
4. *Technology and external environment.* In general, the more complex the internal technology of the organization, the more politics there will be. The same is true of organizations operating in turbulent external environments.
5. *Change.* A reorganization or a planned organization development (OD) effort (see Chapter 21, on various OD techniques) or even an unplanned change brought about by external forces will encourage political maneuvering.[33]

The above implies that some organizations and subunits within the organization will be more political than others. By the same token, however, it is clear that most of today's organizations meet the above requirements for being highly political.

That is, they have very limited resources; make ambiguous, uncertain decisions; have very unclear yet complex goals; have increasingly complex technology; and are undergoing drastic change. This existing situation facing organizations makes them more political, and the power game becomes increasingly important. Miles states: "In short, conditions that *threaten* the status of the powerful or *encourage* the efforts of those wishing to increase their power base will stimulate the intensity of organizational politics and increase the proportion of decision-making behaviors that can be classified as political as opposed to rational."[34] For example, with the political situation of today's high-tech, radically innovative firms, it has been suggested that medieval structures of palace favorites, liege lordship, and fiefdoms may be more relevant than the more familiar rational structures.[35] The next section presents some political strategies for power acquisition in today's organizations.

Specific Political Strategies for Power Acquisition

Once it is understood and accepted that contemporary organizations are in reality largely political systems, some very specific strategies can be identified to help organization members more effectively acquire power.

For over twenty years, various political strategies for gaining power in organizations have been suggested. Table 15.1 gives a representative summary of these strategies. Research is also being done on political tactics. For example, Yukl and Falbe recently derived eight political or influence tactics that are commonly found in today's organizations. These tactics are identified in Table 15.2. Yukl and Falbe found that the consultation and rational persuasion tactics were used most frequently.[36] Some modern organization theorists take more analytical approaches than most of the strategies suggested in Table 15.1 and Table 15.2, and they depend more on concepts such as uncertainty in their political strategies for power. For example,

TABLE 15.1 Political Strategies for Attaining Power in Organizations

Taking counsel
Maintaining maneuverability
Promoting limited communication
Exhibiting confidence
Controlling access to information and persons
Making activities central and nonsubstitutable
Creating a sponsor-protegé relationship
Stimulating competition among ambitious subordinates
Neutralizing potential opposition
Making strategic replacements
Committing the uncommitted
Forming a winning coalition
Developing expertise
Building personal stature
Employing trade-offs
Using research data to support one's own point of view
Restricting communication about real intentions
Withdrawing from petty disputes

Source: Adapted from Robert H. Miles, *Macro Organizational Behavior.* Goodyear, Santa Monica, Calif., 1980, pp. 174–175.

TABLE 15.2 Political Tactics Derived from Research

Tactics	Description
Pressure tactics	The use of demands, threats, or intimidation to convince you to comply with a request or to support a proposal.
Upward appeals	Persuading you that the request is approved by higher management, or appeals to higher management for assistance in gaining your compliance with the request.
Exchange tactics	Making explicit or implicit promises that you will receive rewards or tangible benefits if you comply with a request or support a proposal, or remind you of a prior favor to be reciprocated.
Coalition tactics	Seeking the aid of others to persuade you to do something or using the support of others as an argument for you to agree also.
Ingratiating tactics	Seeking to get you in a good mood or to think favorably of the influence agent before asking you to do something.
Rational persuasion	Using logical arguments and factual evidence to persuade you that a proposal or request is viable and likely to result in the attainment of task objectives.
Inspirational appeals	Making an emotional request or proposal that arouses enthusiasm by appealing to your values and ideals, or by increasing your confidence that you can do it.
Consultation tactics	Seeking your participation in making a decision or planning how to implement a proposed policy, strategy, or change.

Source: Adapted from Gary Yukl and Cecilia M. Falbe, "Influence Tactics and Objectives in Upward, Downward, and Lateral Influence Attempts," *Journal of Applied Psychology*, vol. 75, 1990, p. 133.

Pfeffer's strategies include managing uncertainty, controlling resources, and building alliances.[37] Others take a more pragmatic approach such as the recent analysis that suggests that successful political behavior involves keeping people happy, cultivating contacts, and wheeling and dealing.[38]

One of the more comprehensive and relevant lists of strategies for modern managers comes from DuBrin.[39] A closer look at his suggested strategies provides important insights into power and politics in modern organizations.

Maintain Alliances with Powerful People. As has already been pointed out, the formation of coalitions (alliances) is critical to the acquisition of power in an organization. An obvious coalition would be with members of other important departments or with members of upper-level management. Not so obvious but equally important would be the formation of an alliance with the boss's secretary or staff assistant, that is, someone who is close to the powerful person. A recent ethnographic study of a city bus company found that a series of dyadic alliances went beyond the formal system and played an important role in getting the work done both within and between departments.[40] For example, alliances between supervisors and certain drivers got the buses out on the worst winter snow days, and kept them running during sparse summer vacation periods.

Embrace or Demolish. Machiavellian principles can be applied as strategies in the power game in modern organizations. One management writer has applied these principles to modern corporate life. For example, for corporate takeovers, he draws on Machiavelli to give the following advice:

> The guiding principle is that senior men in taken-over firms should either be warmly welcomed and encouraged or sacked; because if they are sacked they are powerless, whereas if they are simply downgraded they will remain united and resentful and determined to get their own back.[41]

Divide and Rule. This widely known political and military strategy can also apply to the acquisition of power in a modern organization. The assumption, sometimes unwarranted, is that those who are divided will not form coalitions themselves. For example, in a business firm the head of finance may generate conflict between marketing and production in hopes of getting a bigger share of the limited budget from the president of the company.

Manipulate Classified Information. The observational studies of managerial work have clearly demonstrated the importance of obtaining and disseminating information.[42] The politically astute organization member carefully controls this information in order to gain power. For example, the purchasing agent may reveal some new pricing information to the design engineer before an important meeting. Now the purchasing agent has gained some power because the engineer owes the purchasing agent a favor.

Make a Quick Showing. This strategy involves looking good on some project or task right away in order to get the right people's attention. Once this positive attention is gained, power is acquired to do other, usually more difficult and long-range projects.

Collect and Use IOUs. This strategy says that the power seeker should do other people favors but should make it clear that they owe something in return and will be expected to pay up when asked. The "Godfather" in the famous book and movie of that name very effectively used this strategy to gain power.

Avoid Decisive Engagement (Fabianism). This is a strategy of going slow and easy—an evolutionary rather than a revolutionary approach to change. By not "ruffling feathers," the power seeker can slowly but surely become entrenched and gain the cooperation and trust of others.

Progress One Step at a Time (Camel's Head in the Tent). This strategy involves taking one step at a time instead of trying to push a whole major project or reorganization attempt. One small change can be a foothold that the power seeker can use as a basis to get other, more major things accomplished.

Wait for a Crisis (Things Must Get Worse before They Get Better). This strategy uses the reverse of "no news is good news"; that is, bad news gets attention. For example, many deans in large universities can get the attention of central administration and the board of regents or trustees only when their college is in trouble, for instance, if their accreditation is threatened. Only under these crisis conditions can they get the necessary funding to move their college ahead.

Take Counsel with Caution. Finally, this suggested political strategy is concerned more with how to keep power than with how to acquire it. Contrary to the traditional prescriptions concerning participative management and empowerment of employees, this suggests that at least some managers should avoid "opening up the gates" to their subordinates in terms of shared decision making. The idea here is that allowing subordinates to participate and to have this expectation may erode the power of the manager.

A Final Word on Power and Politics

Obviously, the strategies discussed above are only representative, not exhaustive, of the possible politically based strategies for acquiring power in organizations. Perhaps even more than in the case of many of the other topics covered in the book, there is little research backup for these ideas on power and, especially, politics. There is also a call for a framework and guidelines to evaluate the ethics of power and politics in today's organizations. This ethical concern goes beyond the notions of success or effectiveness. As one analysis pointed out, "when it comes to the ethics of organizational politics, respect for justice and human rights should prevail for its own sake."[43] Besides the possible ethical implications of power and politics carried to the extreme, there may be dysfunctional effects such as morale being weakened, victors and victims being created, and energy and time being spent on planning attacks and counterattacks instead of concentrating on getting the job done.[44] There is some empirical evidence that those managers who are observed to engage in more political activity are relatively more successful in terms of promotions, but are relatively less effective in terms of subordinate satisfaction and commitment and the performance of their unit.[45]

One thing about power and politics, however, is certain: Modern, complex organizations tend to create a climate that promotes power seeking and political maneuvering. It is a fact of modern organizational life, and it is hoped that future research will be forthcoming that will help managers better understand the dynamics, meaning, and successful application of power and politics.

Summary

This chapter has examined one of the most important and realistic dynamics of organizational behavior—power and politics. *Power* and *politics* have a number of different meanings. Power can be distinguished from authority and influence, but most definitions subsume all three concepts. Most of the attention given to power over the years has centered on the French and Raven classification of power types: reward, coercive, legitimate, referent, and expert. More recently, some contingency models for power have been developed which take into consideration the influence-ability of the targets of power (that is, their dependency, uncertainty, personality, intelligence, sex, age, and culture). Overall contingency models are also beginning to emerge. Closely related to the contingency models of the French and Raven power types is the view of power by McClelland. McClelland suggests that there are two faces of power: negative personal power and positive social power. Finally, a more macro view of power in organizations is needed for comprehensive understanding. Both vertical and horizontal structural arrangements have implications for power in organizations.

Politics is very closely related to power. This chapter gave particular attention to a political perspective of power in modern organizations, in terms of resources, decisions, goals, technology, external environment, and change, and to strategies for the acquisition of power. Some specific political strategies are to maintain alliances with powerful people, embrace or demolish, divide and rule, manipulate classified information, make a quick showing, collect and use IOUs, avoid decisive engagement, progress one step at a time, wait for a crisis, and take counsel with caution. Above all, it should be remembered that both power and politics represent the realities of modern organizational life. The study of these important dynamics can significantly improve the understanding of organizational behavior.

Questions for Discussion and Review

1. How would you define "power" in your own words? How does power differ from authority? From influence?
2. Identify, briefly summarize, and give some realistic examples of each of the French and Raven power types.
3. Using the contingency model of power, who would you use to advertise products in the fall, winter, spring and summer? Explain your choices.
4. In the chaper it is stated: "The political power game is very real in today's organizations." Explain this statement in terms of the discussion in the chapter and any firsthand experience you have had to verify it.
5. Identify three or four of the political strategies that are discussed in the chapter. Explain how these might actually help someone acquire power in a modern organization.

References

1. "Trying a Palace Coup Can Be Hazardous to an Executive's Career," *The Wall Street Journal*, Feb. 17, 1987, p. 1.
2. A. M. Henderson and Talcott Parsons (trans. and ed.), *Max Weber: The Theory of Social and Economic Organization*, Free Press, New York, 1947, p. 152.
3. David Krackhardt, "Assessing the Political Landscape: Structure, Cognition, and Power in Organizations," *Administrative Science Quarterly*, vol. 35, 1990, p. 343.
4. Stephen P. Robbins, *Organizational Behavior*, 4th ed., Prentice-Hall, Englewood Cliffs, N.J., 1990, p. 339.

5. A. J. Grimes, "Authority, Power, Influence and Social Control: A Theoretical Synthesis," *Academy of Management Review*, October 1978, p. 725.

6. Chester I. Barnard, *The Functions of the Executive*, Harvard University Press, Cambridge, Mass., 1938, p. 163.

7. Grimes, op. cit., p. 726.

8. John R. P. French, Jr., and Bertram Raven, "The Bases of Social Power," in D. Cartwright (ed.), *Studies in Social Power*, University of Michigan, Institute for Social Research, Ann Arbor, 1959.

9. H. Joseph Reitz, *Behavior in Organizations*, 3d ed., Irwin, Homewood, Ill., 1987, p. 435.

10. David G. Myers, *Social Psychology*, 3d ed., McGraw-Hill, New York, 1990, p. 240.

11. Andrew S. Grove, "Breaking the Chains of Command," *Newsweek*, Oct 3, 1983, p. 23.

12. M. Crozier, *The Bureaucratic Phenomenon*, University of Chicago Press, Chicago, 1964.

13. Gregory B. Northcraft and Margaret A. Neale, *Organizational Behavior*, Dryden, Chicago, 1990, pp. 342–343.

14. Kathryn M. Bartol and David C. Martin, "When Politics Pays: Factors Influencing Managerial Compensation Decisions," *Personnel Psychology*, vol. 43, 1990, p. 599.

15. Robbins, op. cit. (1st ed., 1979), p. 276.

16. Carol Stoak Saunders, "The Strategic Contingencies Theory of Power: Multiple Perspectives," *Journal of Management Studies*, January 1990, p. 4.

17. Adapted from Reitz, op. cit., pp. 441–443.

18. Ibid., pp. 442–443.

19. David C. McClelland, "The Two Faces of Power," *Journal of International Affairs*, vol. 24, no. 1, 1970, p. 36.

20. Ibid., p. 41.

21. "McClelland: An Advocate of Power," *International Management*, July 1975, pp. 27–28.

22. Eugene M. Fodor and Terry Smith, "The Power Motive as an Influence on Group Decision Making," *Journal of Personality and Social Psychology*, January 1982, pp. 178–185.

23. See Ronald E. Riggio, *Introduction to Industrial/Organizational Psychology*, Scott, Foresman/Little, Brown, Glenview, Ill., 1990, p. 322.

24. Edwin P. Hollander and Lynn R. Offermann, "Power and Leadership in Organizations," *American Psychologist*, February 1990, p. 184.

25. Jeffrey Pfeffer, "The Micropolitics of Organizations," in Marshall W. Meyer et al. (eds.), *Environments and Organizations*, Jossey-Bass, San Francisco, 1978, pp. 29–50. Also see Jeffrey Pfeffer, *Power in Organizations*, Pitman, Marshfield, Mass., 1981.

26. Richard L. Daft, *Organization Theory and Design*, West, St. Paul, Minn., 1983, pp. 384–385, 389. Also see Stephen P. Robbins, *Organization Theory*, 3d ed., Prentice-Hall, Englewood Cliffs, N.J., 1990, pp. 265–270.

27. Anthony T. Cobb, "Political Diagnosis: Applications in Organizational Development," *Academy of Management Review*, July 1986, p. 490.

28. Alvin Toffler, "Powershift—In the Workplace," *Personnel*, June 1990, p. 21.

29. Walter Nord, "Dreams of Humanization and the Realities of Power," *Academy of Management Review*, July 1978, pp. 675–677.

30. "Labor Letter," *The Wall Street Journal*, Dec. 23, 1986, p. 1.

31. Barbara Gray and Sonny S. Ariss, "Politics and Strategic Change across Organizational Life Cycles," *Academy of Management Review*, October 1985, p. 707.

32. Patricia M. Fandt and Gerald R. Ferris, "The Management of Information and Impressions: When Employees Behave Opportunistically," *Organizational Behavior and Human Decision Processes*, vol. 45, 1990, p. 140.

33. Robert H. Miles, *Macro Organizational Behavior*, Goodyear, Santa Monica, Calif., 1980, pp. 182–184.

34. Ibid., p. 182.

35. Jone L. Pearce and Robert A. Page, Jr., "Palace Politics: Resource Allocation in Radically Innovative Firms," *The Journal of High Technology Management Research*, vol. 1, 1990, pp. 193–205.

36. Gary Yukl and Cecilia M. Falbe, "Influence Tactics and Objectives in Upward, Downward, and Lateral Influence Attempts," *Journal of Applied Psychology*, vol. 75, 1990, pp. 132–140.

37. Jeffrey Pfeffer, "Power and Resource Allocation in Organizations," in Barry M. Staw and Gerald R. Salancik (eds.), *New Directions in Organizational Behavior*, St. Clair, Chicago, 1977, pp. 255–260.

38. Andrew Kakabadse, "Organizational Politics," *Management Decision*, vol. 25, no. 1, 1987, pp. 35–36.

39. These strategies are discussed fully in Andrew J. DuBrin, *Human Relations*, Reston, Reston, Va.,

1978, pp. 113–122; DuBrin, in turn, abstracted them from the existing literature on power and politics. Also see Andrew J. DuBrin, *Winning Office Politics,* Prentice-Hall, Englewood Cliffs, N.J., 1990, Ch. 8 and 9.

40. Nancy C. Morey and Fred Luthans, "The Use of Dyadic Alliances in Informal Organization: An Ethnographic Study," *Human Relations* (in press).

41. Anthony Jay, *Management and Machiavelli,* Holt, New York, 1967, p. 6.

42. Fred Luthans, Richard M. Hodgetts, and Stuart A. Rosenkrantz, *Real Managers,* Ballinger, Cambridge, Mass., 1988.

43. Gerald F. Cavanagh, Dennis J. Moberg, and Manuel Velasquez, "The Ethics of Organizational Politics," *Academy of Management Review,* July 1981, p. 372.

44. Robert P. Vecchio, *Organizational Behavior,* Dryden, Chicago, 1988, p. 270.

45. Luthans, Hodgetts, and Rosenkrantz, op. cit.

REAL CASE: FIGHTING BACK

One of the areas in which organizations are finding power to be an extremely important consideration is that of patent protection. When a firm secures a patent, it gains power over the marketplace. However, if this patent cannot be defended against violators, it has little value. A good example of a patent protection battle is that of Fusion Systems, a small, high-tech American firm, and Mitsubishi, the giant Japanese conglomerate.

A few years ago, Fusion developed a core technology that allowed it to manufacture high-intensity ultraviolet lamps powered by 500 to 6,000 watts of microwave energy. The company obtained patents in the United States, Europe, and Japan. One of its first big orders came from the Adolph Coors Company for lamp systems to dry the printed decoration on beer cans. Other customers included Hitachi, IBM, 3M, Motorola, Sumitomo, Toshiba, NEC, and Mitsubishi. The last purchased Fusion's lamp system and immediately sent it to the research and development lab to be reverse engineered. Once Mitsubishi had stripped down the product, it began filing patent applications that copied and surrounded Fusion's high-intensity microwave lamp technology. Fusion was unaware of what was going on until it began investigating and found that Mitsubishi had filed nearly 300 patent applications directly related to its own lamp technology. When Fusion tried to settle the matter through direct negotiations, the firm was unsuccessful. In addition, Mitsubishi hired the Stanford Research Institute to study the matter and the Institute concluded that the Japanese company's position was solid. However, the chairman of the applied physics department at Columbia University, who was hired by Fusion, disagreed and—after reviewing the patent materials from both companies—concluded that Mitsubishi had relied heavily on technology developed at Fusion and that Mitsubishi's lamp represented no significant additional breakthrough.

Mitsubishi then offered Fusion a deal: Mitsubishi would not sue Fusion for patent infringement if Fusion would pay Mitsubishi a royalty for the privilege of using "its" patents in Japan. Mitsubishi would then get a royalty-free, worldwide cross license of all of Fusion's technology. Fusion responded by going to the Office of the U.S. Trade Representative and getting help. The company also found a sympathetic ear from the Senate Finance Committee and the House Republican Task Force on Technology Transfer, as well as from the Secretary of Commerce and the American ambassador to Japan. At present the dispute continues, but Mitsubishi is beginning to give ground in the face of political pressure. At the same time, Fusion is continuing to develop new innovations in its core field of expertise and remains the leader in both Japanese and worldwide markets. The company believes that as long as it maintains the exclusive rights to this technology, competitors will not be able to erode its market power.

1. What type of power does a patent provide to a company? Is this the same kind of power that people within a firm attempt to gain?
2. What types of political strategies has Mitsubishi used to try to gain power over Fusion? Using the material in Table 15.1, identify and describe three.
3. How has Fusion managed to retaliate successfully? Using the material in Table 15.2, identify and describe three tactics they have employed.

Case: Throwing Away a Golden Opportunity

Roger Allen was a man on the move. Everyone in the firm felt that someday he would be company president. To listen to his boss, Harry Walden, it was only a matter of time before Roger would be at the helm.

The current president of the firm was a marketing person. She had worked her way up from field salesperson to president by selling both the product and herself to customers and the company alike. In a manner of speaking, the marketing department was the "well-oiled" road to the top. Roger was the number 1 salesperson and, according to the grapevine, was due to get Harry Walden's job when the latter retired in two years. However, Roger was not sure that he wanted to be vice president of marketing. Another slot was opening up in foreign sales. Roger knew nothing about selling to Europe, but this was the firm's first venture outside the United States, and he thought he might like to give it a try. He talked to Harry about it, but the vice president tried to discourage him. In fact, Harry seemed to think that Roger was crazy to consider the job at all. "Kid," he said, "that's no place for you. Things are soft and cozy back here. You don't have to prove yourself to anyone. You're the number 1 boy around here. Just sit tight and you'll be president. Don't go out and make some end runs. Just keep barreling up the middle for 4 yards on each carry, and you'll score the big touchdown." Roger was not convinced. He thought perhaps it would be wise to discuss the matter with the president herself. This he did. The president was very interested in Roger's ideas about international marketing. "If you really think you'd like to head up this office for us, I'll recommend you for the job."

After thinking the matter over carefully, Roger decided that he would much rather go to Europe and try to help establish a foothold over there than sit back and wait for the stateside opening. He told his decision to Harry. "Harry, I've talked to the president, and she tells me that this new opening in foreign sales is really going to get a big push from the company. It's where the action is. I realize that I could sit back and take it easy for the next couple of years, but I think I'd rather have the international job." Harry again told Roger that he was making a mistake. "You're throwing away a golden opportunity. However, if you want it, I'll support you."

A week later, when the company selected someone else from sales to head the international division, Roger was crushed. The president explained the situation to him in this way: "I thought you wanted the job and I pushed for you. However, the other members of the selection committee voted against me. I can tell you that you certainly didn't sell Harry very strongly on your idea. He led the committee to believe that you were really undecided about the entire matter. In fact, I felt rather foolish telling them how excited you were about the whole thing, only to have Harry say he'd talked to you since that time and you weren't that sure at all. When Harry got done, the committee figured you had changed your mind after talking to me, and they went on to discuss other likely candidates."

1. Who had power in this organization? What type of power did Harry Walden have?
2. Do you think Roger played company politics well? If so, why didn't he get the international sales job?
3. At this point, what would you do if you were Roger? What political strategies could he use?

INTEGRATIVE CONTEMPORARY CASE FOR PART 4

Superteams
at Work*

Many American companies are discovering what may be *the* productivity breakthrough of the 1990s. Call the still-controversial innovation a self-managed team, a cross-functional team, a high-performance team, or, to coin a phrase, a superteam. Says Texas Instruments CEO Jerry Junkins: "No matter what your business, these teams are the wave of the future." Corning CEO Jamie Houghton, whose company has 3,000 teams, echoes the sentiment: "If you really believe in quality, when you cut through everything, it's empowering your people, and it's empowering your people that leads to teams."

We're not talking here about the teamwork that's been praised at Rotary Club luncheons since time immemorial, or the quality circles so popular in the 1980s, where workers gathered once a week to save paper clips or bitch about the fluorescent lights. What makes superteams so controversial is that they ultimately force managers to do what they had only imagined in their most Boschian nightmares: give up control. Because if superteams are working right, *mirabile dictu*, they manage themselves. No boss required. A superteam arranges schedules, sets profit targets, and—gulp—may even know everyone's salary. It has a say in hiring and firing team members as well as managers. It orders material and equipment. It strokes customers, improves quality, and, in some cases, devises strategy.

Superteams typically consist of between three and 30 workers—sometimes blue collar, sometimes white collar, sometimes both. In a few cases, they have become a permanent part of the work force. In others, management assembles the team for a few months or years to develop a new product or solve a particular problem. Companies that use them—and they work as well in service or finance businesses as they do in manufacturing—usually see productivity rise dramatically. That's because teams composed of people with different skills, from different parts of the company, can swoop around bureaucratic obstacles and break through walls separating different functions to get a job done.

Ten years ago there were practically no superteams. Only a handful of companies—Procter & Gamble, Digital Equipment, TRW—were experimenting with them. But a recent survey of 476 FORTUNE 1,000 companies, published by the American Productivity & Quality Center in Houston, shows that while only 7 percent of the work force is organized in self-managed teams, half the companies questioned say they will be relying significantly more on them in the years ahead. Those who have already taken the plunge have seen impressive results:

- At a General Mills cereal plant in Lodi, California, teams schedule, operate, and maintain machinery so effectively that the factory runs with no managers present during the night shift.

* *Source:* Brian Dumaine, "Who Needs a Boss?" *Fortune*, May 7, 1990, pp. 52–55, 58, 60. Copyright 1990, Time Inc. All rights reserved. Reprinted by permission from TIME.

- At a weekly meeting, a team of Federal Express clerks spotted—and eventually solved—a billing problem that was costing the company $2.1 million a year.
- A team of Chaparral Steel millworkers traveled the world to evaluate new production machinery. The machines they selected and installed have helped make their mill one of the world's most efficient.
- 3M turned around one division by creating cross-functional teams that tripled the number of new products.
- After organizing its home office operations into superteams, Aetna Life & Casualty reduced the ratio of middle managers to workers—from 1 to 7 down to 1 to 30—all the while improving customer service.
- Teams of blue-collar workers at Johnsonville Foods of Sheboygan, Wisconsin, helped CEO Ralph Stayer make the decision to proceed with a major plant expansion. The workers told Stayer they could produce more sausage, faster than he would have ever dared to ask. Since 1986, productivity has risen at least 50 percent.

Like latter-day Laocoöns, the companies using superteams must struggle with serpentine problems. How do you keep a team from veering off track? How should it be rewarded for inventing new products or for saving money? How much spending authority should a team have? What happens to the opportunity for team members to advance as the corporate hierarchy flattens? How should disputes among its members be resolved? Answers vary from company to company. Read on to see how some organizations are coping.

Superteams aren't for everyone. They make sense only if a job entails a high level of dependency among three or more people. Complex manufacturing processes common in the auto, chemical, paper, and high-tech industries can benefit from teams. So can complicated service jobs in insurance, banking, and telecommunications. But if the work consists of simple assembly line activity like stuffing pimentos into olives, teams probably don't make sense. Says Edward Lawler, a management professor at the University of Southern California: "You have to ask, 'How complex is the work?' The more complex, the more suited it is for teams."

Lawler is getting at the heart of what makes superteams tick: cross-functionalism, as the experts inelegantly put it. The superteam draws together people with different jobs or functions—marketing, manufacturing, finance, and so on. The theory is that by putting their heads together, people with different perspectives on the business can solve a problem quickly and effectively.

Contrast that to the Rube Goldberg approach a hierarchical organization would usually take. A person with a problem in one function might have to shoot it up two or three layers by memo to a vice president who tosses it laterally to a vice president of another function who then kicks it down to the person in his area who knows the answer. Then it's back up and down the ladder again. Whew.

Federal Express has been particularly successful using superteams in its back-office operations in Memphis. Two years ago, as part of a companywide push to convert to teams, Fedex organized its 1,000 clerical workers into superteams of five to ten people, and gave them the training and authority to manage themselves. With the help of its teams, the company cut service glitches, such as incorrect bills and lost packages, by 13 percent in 1989.

At lunch with one team, this reporter sat impressed as entry-level workers, most with only high school educations, ate their chicken and dropped sophisticated management terms like *kaizen*, the Japanese art of continuous improvement, and *pareto*, a form of problem solving that requires workers to take a logical step-by-step approach. The team described how one day during a weekly meeting, a clerk from quality control pointed out a billing problem. The bigger a package, he explained, the more Fedex charges to deliver it. But the company's wildly busy delivery people sometimes forgot to check whether customers had properly marked the weight of packages on the air bill. That meant that Fedex, whose policy in such cases is to charge customers the lowest rate, was losing money.

The team switched on its turbochargers. An employee in billing services found out which field offices in Fedex's labyrinthine 30,000-person courier network were forgetting to check the packages, and then explained the problem to the delivery people. Another worker in billing set up a system to examine the invoices and make sure the solution was working. Last year alone the team's ideas saved the company $2.1 million.

In 1987, Rubbermaid began to develop a so-called auto office, a plastic, portable device that straps onto a car seat; it holds files, pens, and other articles and provides a writing surface. The company assembled a cross-functional team composed of, among others, engineers, designers, and marketers, who together went into the field to ask customers what features they wanted. Says Rubbermaid vice president Lud Huck: "A designer, an engineer, and a marketer all approach research from a different point of view."

Huck explains that while a marketer might ask potential customers about price, he'd never think to ask important design questions. With contributions from several different functions, Rubbermaid brought the new product to market last year. Sales are running 50 percent above projections.

Companies making the move to superteams often discover middle managers who feel threatened, and refuse—even for a millisecond—to think outside their narrow functional specialties, or chimneys, as they're labeled at some companies. Understandable, since the managers probably made it to where they are by being marketing whizzes or masters of the bean-counting universe. Why help some poor slob in engineering? For superteams to work, functional chimneys must be broken down and middle managers persuaded to lend their time, people, and resources to other functions for the good of the entire corporation.

Robert Hershock, a group vice president at 3M, is an expert chimney breaker. In 1985 he introduced teams to his division, which makes respirators and industrial safety equipment, because it was desperately in need of new products. The old boss had simply told his underlings what to develop. R&D would sketch it up and deliver the concept to sales for comment, leaving manufacturing and marketing scrambling to figure out how to make or position the new offering. Says Hershock: "Every function acted as if it didn't need anyone else."

He formed an operating team made up of himself and six top managers, each from a different function. With suggestions from all interested parties, he hoped to chart new-product strategies that everyone could get behind. Under the operating team he established ten self-managed "action teams," each with eight to ten people, again from different functions. They were responsible for the day-to-day development of new products.

It wasn't all sweetness and light. Hershock says one manager on the operating team dragged his feet all the way. "He'd say he wasn't in favor of this or that," recalls Hershock. "He'd say to his people, 'Meet with the action teams because Hershock said so, but don't commit to anything. Just report back to me what was said.'" Hershock worked to convince the man of the benefits of the team approach, but to no avail. Eventually the manager went to Hershock and said, "I didn't sleep all weekend, I'm upset." The manager found a good job in another division. "You need to have a sense of who's not buying in and let the teams kick people off who aren't carrying their weight," Hershock concludes. Today his division is one of 3M's most innovative and fastest growing.

It's easier to build superteams into a new office or factory than to convert an old one to them. When an operation is just starting up, a company can screen people carefully for educational skills and the capacity to work on a team, and can train them without worrying about bad old work habits like the "it's not my problem" syndrome. Nonetheless, General Mills is organizing superteams in all its existing factories. Randy Darcy, director of manufacturing, says transforming an old plant can take several years, vs. only a year to 18 months for a new plant. Says Darcy: "It costs you up front, but you have to look at it as a capital project. If you consider the productivity gains, you can justify it on ROE."

Can you ever. General Mills says productivity in its plants that use self-managed teams is as much as 40 percent higher than at its traditional factories. One reason is that the plants need fewer middle managers. At one of General Mills' cereal plants in Lodi, workers on the night shift take care of everything from scheduling to maintenance. The company has also found that superteams sometimes set higher productivity goals than management does. At its Carlisle, Pennsylvania, plant, which makes Squeezit juice, superteams changed some equipment and squeezed out a 5 percent production increase in a plant management thought was already running at full capacity.

But you will never get large productivity gains unless you give your teams real authority to act. This is a theme that Johnsonville's Stayer, who teaches a case on teams at the Harvard business school, preaches with messianic zeal.

"The strategic decision," he explains, "is who makes the decision. There's a lot of talk about teamwork in this country, but we're not set up to generate it. Most quality circles don't give workers responsibility. They even make things worse. People in circles point out problems, and it's someone else's problem to fix."

In 1986 a major food company asked Johnsonville to manufacture sausage under a private label. Stayer's initial reaction was to say no, because he thought the additional volume would overload his plant and force his people to work grueling hours. But before declining, he assembled his 200 production workers, who are organized in teams of five to 20, and asked them to decide whether *they* wanted to take on the heavier workload. Stayer discussed the pros: Through economies of scale, the extra business would lower costs and thus boost profits; since everyone's bonus was based on profitability, everyone would make more money. And the cons: long hours, strained machinery, and the possibility of declining quality.

After the teams deliberated for ten days, they came back with an answer: "We can do it. We'll have to work seven days a week at first, but then the work will level off." The teams decided how much new machinery they would need and how many new people; they also made a schedule of how much to produce per day. Since Johnsonville took on the new project, productivity has risen over 50 percent in the factory. Says Stayer: "If I had tried to implement it from above, we would have lost the whole business."

Some large organizations still feel a need to exercise oversight of superteams' activities. What to do with a team that louses up quality or orders the wrong machinery? James Watson, a vice president of Texas Instruments' semiconductor group, may have the answer. At one of TI's chip factories in Texas, Watson helped create a hierarchy of teams that, like a shadow government, works within the existing hierarchy.

On top is a steering team consisting of the plant manager and his heads of manufacturing, finance, engineering, and human resources. They set strategy and approve large projects. Beneath the steering team, TI has three other teams: corrective-action teams, quality-improvement teams, and effectiveness teams. The first two are cross-functional and consist mainly of middle managers and professionals like engineers and accountants. Corrective-action teams form to tackle short-lived problems and then disband. They're great for those times when, as the technophantasmic novelist Thomas Pynchon writes, there's fecoventilatory collision: the s— hits the fan.

By contrast, TI's quality-improvement teams work on long-term projects, such as streamlining the manufacturing process. The corrective-action and quality-improvement teams guide and check effectiveness teams, which consist of blue-collar employees who do day-to-day production work, and professional workers.

What's to keep this arrangement from becoming just another hierarchy? "You have to keep changing and be flexible as business conditions dictate," says Watson. He contends that one of the steering team's most important responsibilities is to show a keen interest in the teams beneath it. "The worst thing you can do to a team is to leave it alone in the dark. I guarantee that if you come across someone who says teams didn't work at his company, it's because management didn't take interest in them." Watson suggests that the steering team periodically review everyone's work, and adds, "It does not have to be a big dog-and-pony show. Just walk around and ask, 'How are you doing?'"

Last spring a group of executives from a Fortune 500 manufacturer traveled to Midlothian, Texas, to learn how Chaparral Steel managed its teams. Efficient superteams have helped make Chaparral one of the world's most productive steel companies. During the tour, one executive asked a Chaparral manager, "How do you schedule coffee breaks in the plant?"

"The workers decide when they want a cup of coffee," came the reply.

"Yes, but who tells them when it's okay to leave the machines?" the executive persisted.

Looking back on the exchange, the Chaparral manager reflects, "The guy left and still didn't get it."

Why do Chaparral workers know when to take a coffee break? Because they're trained to understand how the whole business operates. Earl Engelhardt, who runs the company's educational program, teaches mill hands "The Chaparral Process," a course that not only describes what happens to a piece of steel as it moves through the company, but also covers the roles of finance, accounting, and sales. Once trained, a worker understands how his job relates to the welfare of the entire organization. At team meetings, many of which are held in the company's modest boardroom, talk is of backlogs and man-hours per ton. Financial statements are posted monthly in the mill, including a chart tracking operating profits before taxes—the key measure for profit sharing.

In the early 1980s the company sent a team leader and three millworkers, all of whom had been through "The Chaparral Process," to Europe, Asia and South America to evaluate new mill stands. These large, expensive pieces of equipment flatten and shape hot steel as it passes through the mill, much as the rollers on old washing machines used to wring clothes. After team members returned from their first trip, they discussed the advantages and disadvantages of various mill stands with other workers and with top management. Then they narrowed the field and flew off again. Eventually the team agreed on the best mill stand—in this case a West German model—and top management gave its blessing.

The team then ordered the mill stands and oversaw their installation, even down to negotiating the contracts for the work involved. At other companies it can take as long as several years to buy and install such a complicated piece of equipment. The Chaparral team got the job done in a year. Perhaps even more amazing, the mill stands—notoriously finicky pieces of machinery—worked as soon as they were turned on.

There remains considerable debate among employees, managers, and consultants over the best way to compensate team members. Most companies pay a flat salary. And instead of handing out automatic annual raises, they often use a pay-for-skills system that bases any increase not on seniority but on what an employee has learned. If, say, a steelworker learns how to run a new piece of equipment, he might get a 5 percent raise.

While the young and eager tend to do well with pay-for-skills, some old-school blue-collar workers like Chaparral Steel's Neil Parker criticize aspects of the system. Says he: "New guys come in who are aggressive, take all the courses, and get promoted ahead of guys who have been here years longer and who showed up for overtime when the company really needed us. It's not fair." As Parker suggests, pay-for-skills does set up a somewhat Darwinian environment at the mill, but that's just the way Chaparral's management likes it.

When teams develop a hot new product, like Rubbermaid's auto office, or save money, like the Federal Express team that caught $2.1 million in billing errors, you would think they would clamor for rewards. Not necessarily. In many cases, surprisingly, a little recognition is reward enough. The Fedex team members seem perfectly content with a gold quality award pin and their picture in the company newsletter. Says one: "We learn more in teams, and it's more fun to work in teams. It's a good feeling to know someone is using your ideas."

In his book *Managing New Products*, Thomas Kuczmarski, a consultant to many of the Fortune 500 industrials, argues that recognition isn't enough. "In most companies multidisciplinary teams are just lip service because companies don't provide the right motivation and incentive. Most top managers think people should just find 20 percent more time to work on a new team project. It's a very naive and narrow-minded approach." His modest proposals: If a new product generates $1 million in profits, give each of the five team members $100,000 the first year. Or have each member write a check for $10,000 in return for 2 percent of the equity in the new product. If it flies they're rich; if it flops they lose their money.

Kuczmarski admits that no major corporation has adopted his provocative system, although he says a few are on the verge of doing so. One objection: Jack Okey, a Honeywell team manager, flatly states that it would be bad for morale to have, say, a junior engineer making more than a division vice president. "If you want to be an entrepreneur, there are plenty of entrepreneurial opportunities outside the company. You can have entrepreneurial spirit without entrepreneurial pay."

Perhaps. Awards dinners and plaques for jobs well done are common in the world of teams, but Texas Instruments vice president James Watson thinks more can be done. He cites the example from Japan, where there is a nationwide competition among manufacturers' teams. Sponsored by the Union of Japanese Scientists and Engineers, the competition pits teams selected by their companies against one another. Once a year the teams travel to Tokyo to make presentations before judges, who decide which performs best at everything from solving quality problems to continuously improving a manufacturing process. The winners get showered with prizes and media coverage.

Sometimes, despite everyone's best efforts, teams get hung up. Leonard Greenhalgh, a professor of management at Dartmouth's Tuck School, says the most common problem is the failure by team members to understand the feelings and needs of their co-workers. At GTE's training center in Connecticut, Greenhalgh had middle managers do role-playing to bring out how such problems can creep up. In a fictionalized case, a team of six pretended they were Porsche managers who had to set next year's production schedule. Each was given a different function and agenda. The Porsche sales manager, for instance, wanted to manufacture more of the popular Carrera convertibles, but the general counsel thought it a bad idea because of the liability problems generally associated with convertibles.

The GTE managers spent several hours arriving at a consensus. Says Greenhalgh: "Typically, a team lacks skills to build a strong consensus. One coalition tries to outvote the other or browbeat the dissenters." To make sure everyone is on board, says Greenhalgh, it's important that each team member feel comfortable airing his opinions. But that can take some training for all group members in how to respond. For instance, the GTE managers learned it's better not to blurt out an intimidating, "I disagree," but rather, "That's an interesting way to look at it; what about this?"

Companies using teams sometimes run into another problem: With fewer middle-manager positions around, there's less opportunity for advancement. The experts say they need to emphasize that because team members have more responsibility, their work is more rewarding and challenging. Harvard business school professor Anne Donnellon, who is doing a major new study of teams, sees this approach already working at some Fortune 500 companies: "People are adjusting to career-ladder shortening. If a team is operating well, I hear less talk about no opportunity for promotion and more about the product and the competition. They're focusing on getting the work done. After all, people want rewarding work."

If you've done everything you can think of, and your team is still running on only three cylinders, you might consider something as prosaic as changing the office furniture. Aetna Life recently reorganized its home office operations into self-managed teams—combining clerks, technical writers, underwriters, and financial analysts—to handle customer requests and complaints. To facilitate teamwork, Aetna is using a new line of "team" furniture, designed by Steelcase.

The furniture establishes small areas that the folks at Steelcase call neighborhoods. A central work area with a table lets teams meet when they need to, while nearby desks provide privacy. Says William Watson, an Aetna senior vice president: "I can't tell you how great it is. Everyone sits together, and the person responsible for accounting knows who prepares the bills and who puts the policy information in the computers to pay the claims. You don't need to run around the building to get something done."

The most important thing to remember about teams is that organizing them is a long, hard process, not a quick fix that can change your company in a few weeks. Says Johnsonville's Stayer: "When I started this business of teams, I was anxious to get it done and get back to my real job. Then I realized that, hey, this *is* my real job!"—letting the teams loose. For those up to the challenge, there will be real results as well.

1. One statement in the case is that superteams aren't for everyone. What are some situations or contingencies that are particularly suitable for making superteams an effective approach? Give some specific examples of where and how teams have been effective.
2. How does conflict occur in teams? What can be done to manage such conflict?
3. Obviously, group dynamics, interactive behavior, and conflict play a role in superteams at work. What about stress, power, and politics? Can superteams lead to increased stress? What about their use as a way to cope with stress? What implications do superteams have for power and politics?

EXPERIENTIAL EXERCISES FOR PART 4

EXERCISE: GROUPS AND CONFLICT RESOLUTION

Goals:
1. To compare individual versus group problem solving and decision making
2. To analyze the dynamics of groups
3. To demonstrate conflict and ways of resolving it

Implementation:
1. Divide any number of people into small groups of four or five.
2. Take about fifteen minutes for individual responses and thirty minutes for group consensus.
3. Each individual and group should have a worksheet. Pencils, a flip chart (newsprint or blackboard), marker pens, or chalk may also be helpful to the groups.

Process:
1. Each individual has fifteen minutes to read the story and answer the eleven questions about the story. Each person may refer to the story as often as needed but may not confer with anyone else. Each person should circle "T" if the answer is clearly true, "F" if the answer is clearly false, and "?" if it isn't clear from the story whether the answer is true or false.
2. After fifteen minutes each small group makes the same decisions using group consensus. No one should change his or her answers on the individual questions. The ground rules for group decisions are:
   a. Group decisions should be made by consensus. It is illegal to vote, trade, average, flip a coin, etc.
   b. No individual group member should give in only to reach agreement.
   c. No individual should argue for his or her own decision. Instead, each person should approach the task using logic and reason.
   d. Every group member should be aware that disagreements may be resolved by facts. Conflict can lead to understanding and creativity if it does not make group members feel threatened or defensive.
3. After thirty minutes of group work, the exercise leader should announce the correct answers. Scoring is based on the number of correct answers out of a possible total of eleven. Individuals are to score their own individual answers, and someone should score the group decision answers. The exercise leader should then call for:
   a. The group-decision score in each group
   b. The average individual score in each group
   c. The highest individual score in each group
4. Responses should be posted on the tally sheet. Note should be taken of those groups in which the group score was (1) higher than the average individual score or (2) higher than the best individual score. Groups should discuss the way in which individual members resolved disagreements and the effect of the ground rules on such behavior. They may

consider the obstacles experienced in arriving at consensus agreements and the possible reasons for the difference between individual and group decisions.

The story: A businessman had just turned off the lights in the store when a man appeared and demanded money. The owner opened a cash register. The contents of the cash register were scooped up, and the man sped away. A member of the police force was notified promptly.

Statements about the story:

1. A man appeared after the owner had turned off his store lights.	T	F	?
2. The robber was a man.	T	F	?
3. A man did not demand money.	T	F	?
4. The man who opened the cash register was the owner.	T	F	?
5. The store owner scooped up the contents of the cash register and ran away.	T	F	?
6. Someone opened a cash register.	T	F	?
7. After the man who demanded the money scooped up the contents of the cash register, he ran away.	T	F	?
8. While the cash register contained money, the story does *not* state *how much*.	T	F	?
9. The robber demanded money of the owner.	T	F	?
10. The story concerns a series of events in which only three persons are referred to: the owner of the store, a man who demanded money, and a member of the police force.	T	F	?
11. The following events in the story are true: someone demanded money, a cash register was opened, its contents were scooped up, and a man dashed out of the store.	T	F	?

Tally Sheet

GROUP NUMBER	GROUP SCORE	AVG. INDIVIDUAL SCORE	BEST INDIVIDUAL SCORE	GROUP SCORE BETTER THAN AVG. INDIV.?	GROUP SCORE BETTER THAN BEST INDIV.?

EXERCISE: POWER AND POLITICS

Goals:

1. To gain some insights into your own power needs and political orientation
2. To examine some of the reasons people strive for power and what political strategies can be used to attain it

Implementation:

Directions: Answer each question below with "mostly agree" or "mostly disagree," even if it is difficult for you to decide which alternative best describes your opinion.

	Mostly Agree	Mostly Disagree
1. Only a fool would correct a boss's mistakes.	_____	_____
2. If you have certain confidential information, release it to your advantage.	_____	_____
3. I would be careful not to hire a subordinate with more formal education than myself.	_____	_____
4. If you do a favor, remember to cash in on it.	_____	_____
5. Given the opportunity, I would cultivate friendships with powerful people.	_____	_____
6. I like the idea of saying nice things about a rival in order to get that person transferred from my department.	_____	_____
7. Why not take credit for someone else's work? They would do the same to you.	_____	_____
8. Given the chance, I would offer to help my boss build some shelves for his or her den.	_____	_____
9. I laugh heartily at my boss's jokes, even when they are not funny.	_____	_____
10. I would be sure to attend a company picnic even if I had the chance to do something I enjoyed more that day.	_____	_____
11. If I knew an executive in my company was stealing money, I would use that against him or her in asking for favors.	_____	_____
12. I would first find out my boss's political preferences before discussing politics with him or her.	_____	_____
13. I think using memos to zap somebody for his or her mistakes is a good idea (especially when you want to show that person up).	_____	_____
14. If I wanted something done by a coworker, I would be willing to say "If you don't get this done, our boss might be very unhappy."	_____	_____
15. I would invite my boss to a party at my house, even if I didn't like him or her.	_____	_____
16. When I'm in a position to, I would have lunch with the "right people" at least twice a week.	_____	_____
17. Richard M. Nixon's alleged bugging of the Democratic headquarters would have been a clever idea if he hadn't been caught.	_____	_____
18. Power for its own sake is one of life's most precious commodities.	_____	_____
19. Having a high school named after you would be an incredible thrill.	_____	_____
20. Reading about job politics is as much fun as reading an adventure story.	_____	_____

Interpretation scores:

Each statement you check "mostly agree" is worth one point toward your power and political orientation score. If you score 16 or over, it suggests that you have a strong inclination toward playing politics. A high score of this nature would also suggest that you have strong needs for power. Scores of 5 or less would suggest that you are not inclined toward political maneuvering and that you are not strongly power driven.

The customary caution is again in order. This questionnaire is designed primarily to encourage you to think carefully about the topic of power and politics. It lacks the scientific validity of a legitimate, controlled test.

PART **5**

THE PROCESSES AND STRUCTURE OF ORGANIZATIONAL BEHAVIOR

16 Communication

■ A Tragic Breakdown in Communication

The space shuttle *Challenger* tragedy (in which a schoolteacher and six astronauts were killed) was an unfortunate example of a breakdown in organizational communication. Head NASA administrators, who made the final decision to launch the shuttle, were not fully informed of the engineers' serious reservations regarding the safety of the shuttle. This lack of upward communication resulted in a national tragedy and raised the question of whether our ability to create highly technological systems exceeds our ability to control them in practice.

The major obstacle in the communication flow seemed to be at the Marshall Center, one of NASA's organizational units. The communication system itself provided for upward communication. Top administrators were plugged into a communication network that allowed everyone at a console to listen to discussions during the 48-hour countdown. However, the Marshall Center did not pass on the discussion regarding the shuttle's safety because managers felt the decision could be handled appropriately at their level. This is an example of how intermediate organization levels often determine what is actually heard at the top. NASA insiders agree that the safety debate was unprecedented in its intensity and should have been conveyed upward.

The communication breakdown that led to the fatal launch decision was indicative of the problems that besieged the entire space shuttle program. For instance, the shuttle schedule did not include reporting arrangements that would have allowed top administrators to review lower-level decisions. In addition, there was a lack of horizontal communication between the organizational units. Although the Marshall, Kennedy, and Johnson space centers are supposed to work closely together, they operate as virtually independent units.

Several suggestions have been made for improving organizational communication at NASA. Jerome F. Lederer, a former NASA executive, suggests that NASA's safety oversight team should report directly to James C. Fletcher, the new NASA administrator. At present the safety team reports to the headquarters engineering office. Since the safety team oversees decisions made by the engineering office, there is a conflict of interest within this reporting relationship. Former NASA general counsel S. Neil Hosenball suggests that engineers from contractors be present at headquarters so their ideas do not become lost in the bureaucratic channels. NASA budget analyst Richard Cook promotes the development of a computer system that tracks the flow of engineering and production problems.

The communication problems facing NASA are typical of those found in many large organizations, both government and business. The people at the top are often isolated from what is actually going on in the organization. Upward communication channels need to be improved so that top managers receive all the available information for making decisions. It is unfortunate that at NASA the breakdown cost lives instead of profits.

Learning Objectives

- **Define** the perspective, historical background, and meaning of communication in organizations.
- **Explain** the nature of management information systems.
- **Identify** the dimensions of nonverbal communication.
- **Analyze** interpersonal communication.
- **Discuss** the downward (supervisor-subordinate), upward (subordinate-initiated), and horizontal (interactive) organizational communication systems.

Communication is one of the most frequently discussed dynamics in the entire field of organizational behavior, but it is seldom clearly understood. In practice, effective communication is a basic prerequisite for the attainment of organizational goals, but it has remained one of the biggest problems facing modern management. Communication is an extremely broad topic and of course is not restricted to the organizational behavior field. Some estimates of the extent of its use go up to about three-fourths of an active human being's life, and even higher proportions of a typical manager's time. The comprehensive study reported in Chapter 11 that directly observed a wide cross-section of what were called "real managers" in their day-to-day behaviors found that they devote about a third of their activity to routine communication—exchanging routine information and processing paperwork.[1] Importantly, however, the communication activity made the biggest relative contribution to effective managers. Figure 16.1 summarizes these findings.

There seems little doubt that communication plays an important role in managerial and organizational effectiveness. Yet, on the other side of the same coin, communication is commonly cited as being at the root of practically all the problems of the world. It is given as the explanation for lovers' quarrels, ethnic prejudice, war between nations, the generation gap, industrial disputes, and organizational conflict. These are only representative of the numerous problems attributed to ineffective communication. Obviously, this thinking can go too far: communication can become a convenient scapegoat or crutch. Not all organization and interpersonal difficulties are the result of communication breakdown. Other matters discussed in this book—motivation, decision making and control, stress, organization structure, to name but a few—can also contribute to problems. Yet it is also true that the communication process is a central problem in most human and organizational activities.

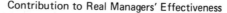

Contribution to Real Managers' Effectiveness

(N = 178, drawn from participant observation data related to combined effectiveness measure of unit performance and subordinate satisfaction and commitment)

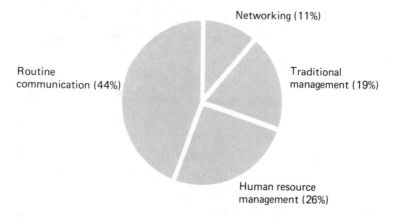

Networking (11%)

Routine communication (44%)

Traditional management (19%)

Human resource management (26%)

FIGURE 16.1
The Contribution of Communication Activities to Real Managers' Effectiveness. (*Source:* Fred Luthans, Richard M. Hodgetts, and Stuart A. Rosen-krantz, *Real Managers,* Ballinger, Cambridge, Mass., 1988, p. 68. Reprinted with permission, copyright 1988, Ballinger Publishing Company.)

First, the historical background of the role of communication in organizational behavior and management will be briefly discussed, and a precise definition of communication given. Then will come a brief discussion of management information systems, telecommunication technology, and nonverbal communication. The heart of the chapter examines the downward, upward, and interactive communication systems. A personal as opposed to a *linear* information-flow perspective of communication is used throughout the chapter.

HISTORICAL BACKGROUND OF THE ROLE OF COMMUNICATION

Early discussions of management gave very little emphasis to communication. Although communication was implicit in the management function of command and the structural principle of hierarchy, the early theorists never fully developed or integrated it into management theory. At the same time, they did generally recognize the role of informal communication in relation to the problem of supplementing the formal, hierarchical channels. But the pioneering management theorist Henri Fayol was about the only one who gave a detailed analysis of, and supplied a meaningful solution to, the problem of communication.

Fayol's Contribution

Figure 16.2 shows how Fayol presented a simplified version of the formal organization. If the formal channels in this organization were strictly followed and F wanted to communicate with P, the communication would have to go through E—D—C—B—A—L— M—N—O—P and back again. In other words, F would have to go

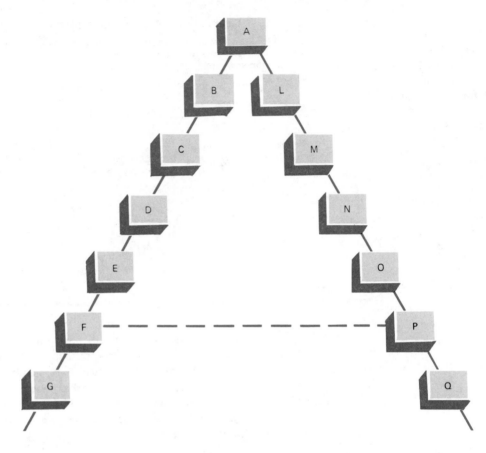

FIGURE 16.2
Fayol's gangplank
concept.
(*Source:* Henri
Fayol, *General and
Industrial Manage-
ment,* trans. by
Constance Storrs,
Pittman, London,
1949, p. 34.)

through a total of twenty positions. On the other hand, if F could lay a "gangplank" to P, it would, in the words of Fayol,

> . . . allow the two employees F and P to deal at one sitting, and in a few hours, with some question or other which via the scalar chain would pass through twenty transmissions, inconvenience many people, involve masses of paper, lose weeks or months to get to a conclusion less satisfactory generally than the one which could have been obtained via direct contact as between F and P.[2]

This gangplank concept has direct implications for horizontal communication systems in modern formal organizations. Unfortunately, such classical insights were few and far between.

Barnard's Contribution

It largely was Chester Barnard in the late 1930s who meaningfully developed communication as a vital dynamic of organizational behavior. He was convinced that communication is the major shaping force in the organization. He ranked it with common purpose and willingness to serve as one of the three primary elements of the organization. To him, communication both makes the organization cooperative system dynamic and links the organization purpose to the human participants. Communication techniques, which he considered to be written and oral language, were deemed not only to be necessary to attain organization purpose but also to be a potential problem area for the organization. In Barnard's words, "The absence of a suitable technique of communication would eliminate the possibility of adopting some purposes as a basis of organization. Communication technique shapes the form and the internal economy of organization."[3]

Barnard also interwove communication into his concept of authority. He emphasized that meaning and understanding must occur before authority can be communicated from superior to subordinate. He listed seven specific communication factors which are especially important in establishing and maintaining objective authority in an organization. He believed them to be, in brief, the following:

1. The channels of communication should be definitely known.
2. There should be a definite formal channel of communication to every member of an organization.
3. The line of communication should be as direct and short as possible.
4. The complete formal line of communication should normally be used.
5. The persons serving as communication centers should be competent.
6. The line of communication should not be interrupted while the organization is functioning.
7. Every communication should be authenticated.[4]

Modern Perspective

Since the original contributions by Fayol and Barnard, the dynamics of communication have been one of the central concerns, if not *the* central concern, of organizational behavior and management theorists. Except in the principles of those management textbooks which still rely heavily on a classical process framework, communication is given major attention. In addition, there has been a deluge of books and articles which deal specifically with interpersonal and organizational communication. Unfortunately, practically all this vast literature gives only a surface treatment of the subject and is seldom based upon systematic research findings. For example, there have been complaints about an uncritical acceptance of the effectiveness of open communication, when a contingency perspective would be more in line with the evidence.[5]

One exception was the Real Managers study reported in Chapter 11 and mentioned in the introductory comments of this chapter. One part of this study combined direct observation of managers in their natural setting with self-report measures to try to determine how they communicated.[6] The model shown in Figure 16.3 gives the results. The first dimension of the managerial communication model represents a continuum ranging from the Humanistic Interactor (who frequently interacts both up and down the organization hierarchy and exhibits human-oriented activities) to the Mechanistic Isolate (who communicates very little, except on a formal basis). The other dimension describes a continuum from the Informal Developer (who communicates spontaneously in all directions and exhibits activities

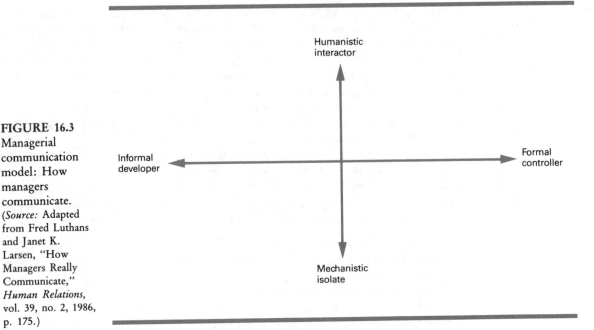

FIGURE 16.3
Managerial communication model: How managers communicate. (*Source:* Adapted from Fred Luthans and Janet K. Larsen, "How Managers Really Communicate," *Human Relations,* vol. 39, no. 2, 1986, p. 175.)

related to developing his or her people) to Formal Controller (who uses formally scheduled communication interaction and exhibits monitoring/controlling activities.)[7] This empirically derived model describes two major dimensions of managerial communication. It provides a framework for *how* managers communicate on a day-to-day basis and can be used as a point of departure for formally defining communication and the processes and systems of communication in today's organizations.

THE DEFINITION OF COMMUNICATION

The term *communication* is freely used by everyone in modern society, including members of the general public, organizational behavior scholars, and management practitioners. In addition, as noted earlier, the term is employed to explain a multitude of sins both in the society as a whole and in work organizations. Despite this widespread usage, very few members of the general public—and not a great many more management people—can precisely define the term. Part of the problem is that communication experts have not agreed upon a definition themselves.

Most definitions of "communication" used in organizational behavior literature stress the use of symbols to transfer the meaning of information. For example, a recent analysis stresses that communication is the understanding, not of the visible, but of the invisible and hidden. These hidden and symbolic elements embedded in the culture give meaning to the visible communication process.[8] Equally, if not of more importance, however, is the fact that communication is a personal process that involves the exchange of behaviors. The personal aspects have been noted in no uncertain terms by most organizational behavior scholars. For example, Ivancevich and Matteson recently noted that "communication among people does not depend on technology, but rather on forces in people and their surroundings. It is a 'process' that occurs 'within' people."[9]

In addition to its being a personal process, a communication expert emphasizes the *behavioral* implications of communication by pointing out that "the only means by which one person can influence another is by the behaviors he performs—that is, the communicative exchanges between people provide the sole method by which influence or effects can be achieved."[10] In other words, the behaviors that occur in an organization are vital to the communication process. This personal and behavioral exchange view of communication takes many forms.

The continuum in Figure 16.4 can be used to identify the major categories of communication that are especially relevant to the study of organizational behavior. On the one extreme is the computer-based management information systems (MIS) and telecommunication technology approach, and on the other extreme is nonverbal communication. The middle ground is occupied by organizational and interpersonal approaches, which represent the perspective taken in this chapter. A very brief overview of the MIS, telecommunication and nonverbal approaches is necessary to put the discussion of the organizational and interpersonal communication approaches into proper perspective.

Management Information Systems

At first, in the management literature, information systems were only associated with computer systems. Now, in the organizational behavior field, information processing is seen as a way to explain the cognitive aspects of humans. Similar to a computer system, people's cognitive processes attain information (input) from the environment, store it, retrieve and manipulate it, then respond to it overtly (output).[11] Today, it is recognized that there are different information processing models[12] that can be used to explain human cognitions as well as organizational communication.

Applied to organizational communication, the terminology of management information systems, or MIS, is commonly used. Although management information systems do not have to be computerized, normally they are. With the common use of personal computers today, almost all information processing is done by

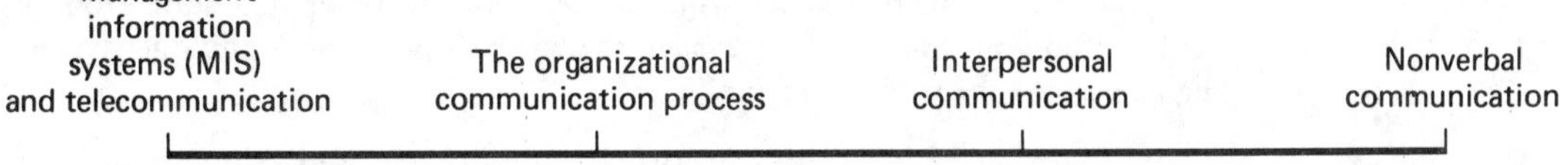

| Management information systems (MIS) and telecommunication | The organizational communication process | Interpersonal communication | Nonverbal communication |

FIGURE 16.4
The continuum of communication in organizational behavior.

computers. MIS involves generating, processing, and transmitting information. The system itself involves not only computer hardware and software but also data and people—both MIS personnel and users.

Although MIS is usually associated with integrated networks of information that support management decision making,[13] MIS can also be used for strategic planning[14] (for example, American Hospital Supply used MIS to change the perspective and direction of the company), improved customer service (for example, some airlines are providing gate agents with relevant information to personalize service at the gate),[15] and for communication per se. The next chapter, on decision making, will devote attention to how computerized systems, especially artificial intelligence and expert systems, can support decision making, but for now it can be said that MIS can be used as part of the interpersonal and organizational communication systems. For example, managers can get on the system to ask others for information about solving problems or can use the system to monitor the literature on particular technological developments.

Because of the information explosion now occurring in all organizations, the systematic management of this information is becoming increasingly difficult. For example, the legal department of Xerox has over 300,000 documents on computer disks and the number is growing by 120,000 per year. Whereas information systems have no trouble processing data that fit into lists of structured records (for example, inventory updates), retrieving specifically required text from documents is another matter. As one MIS expert recently noted, "Finding precisely what you're looking for in a mass of unorganized text—nothing more, nothing less—is a problem of nearly intractable complexity."[16] In other words, there are still plenty of challenges left in the contribution that MIS can make to more effective communication in organizations.

Telecommunication Technology

Closely related to computerized MIS is the telecommunications explosion. In fact, the boundaries between computing and communicating are becoming very blurred. Today, computers communicate and telecommunication networks compute.[17] In addition to computers, telecommunications utilize telephone and television technologies and both a wireless system of portable phones and a wired system built around fiber-optic links.

Over the wireless system:

> . . . you will eventually be able to have your car engine diagnosed from your house or the road, via a digital phone link between the garage's and your car's computer. Or you will be able to take out your pocket phone while driving home from work and dial up your home control system to switch on your air conditioner, turn on the lights or start the coffee machine.[18]

In the wired world of fiber optics, information is transmitted as pulses of laser light through ultrapure glass fibers. Here is a description of what this fiber optics system can do:

> The most advanced system today can transmit information at the rate of 3.4 billion bits per second, or the equivalent of 48,000 telephone conversations on a single pair

of fibers. Of course, fiber optics will be important not so much for its role in accommodating voice traffic as for its role in accommodating the exposively growing traffic generated by facsimile, computer networking, and video.[19]

In other words, whether wireless or over fiber optics, the telephone, television, and computer will combine to form a very powerful, but user-friendly, communication system.

Some of the telecommunication techniques already widely used to communicate in today's organizations are telephone caller ID, electronic mail, voice messaging, and electronic bulletin boards. Caller ID displays the number of the person calling. This number can be connected to a computer for many uses. American Express, for example, uses such a system at its customer-relations center. When customers call, the computer uses the number to retrieve their name and bring up the AMEX file to the screen *before* the customer representative even picks up the phone.[20]

Electronic mail (E-mail) uses electronic circuitry to transmit written messages via computer terminals instantaneously to other people within the organization or to other organizations around the world. In addition to sending messages, E-mail can be used to transfer computer files (spreadsheets, database files, and address lists) as well as for electronic data interchange (EDI), an automated form of ordering and inventory control. E-mail providers may also be hooked into various computer databases that give users access to up-to-the-minute news and financial information, credit reports, airline schedules, electronic banking, and even home shopping.[21]

In voice messaging, the computer acts as a sophisticated answering machine. The computer answers the phone, relays memos, gives out information, and takes messages. For example, Plunkett, Gibson, & Allen, a large law firm in Texas, receives an average of a thousand incoming calls per day. The firm was having trouble with the volume of calls and client service suffered. They installed a voice-message system and clients are now promptly greeted with personal messages from their attorney and have the option of leaving a detailed, confidential message. Attorneys can get their messages from inside or outside the office, twenty-four hours a day. When they return calls, they already have all the information necessary to assist the client. Research indicates that the average business phone call lasts four to five minutes, but the average voice message is less than a minute. Plunkett, Gibson, & Allen's voice-message system resulted in a 60 percent reduction in the number of internal calls and the amount of paperwork. The system also resulted in greatly improved client service.[22]

Whereas E-mail and voice messaging tend to be for individual users, electronic bulletin boards are like the traditional corkboard in public access areas except for using a computer and a modem instead of paper and thumbtacks. Electronic boards use computers to communicate routine information or to reduce paperwork and filing by storing policy manuals, job descriptions, telephone directory listings, and other documents to which managers and employees can gain access. Besides internal use in an organization, there are an increasing number of general public access bulletin boards that are run by commercial database companies organized around a particular interest, such as software or a professional group. Besides making contacts, electronic bulletin boards can also become important to a firm's daily operations. For example, at Language Exchange Inc., a language teaching and translation service based in Washington, D.C., translators dial into the Language Exchange Bulletin Board to pick up documents that have been scanned into the system. They make their translations and send them back to the bulletin board, where the documents are then edited, proofread, typeset, or sent directly to the client. The company estimates they can handle ten times the former business with this bulletin-board system.[23]

There seems to be no limit to the role that telecommunication technology will play in organizational communication. There is tremendous growth in the use of all areas of the technology. As one business executive noted, "Sooner or later, everybody will be using telecommunication technology and the world will be a better place, or at least a simpler place."[24]

Nonverbal Communication

The opposite of the computer-based MIS, telecommunication approach to communication is nonverbal communication. Although verbal communication has long been recognized as being important, nonverbal communication has only recently been given attention in the study of communication. Sometimes called the "silent language," *nonverbal communication* can be defined as "nonword human responses (such as gestures, facial expressions) *and* the perceived characteristics of the environment through which the human verbal and nonverbal messages are transmitted."[25] Thus, whether a person says something or, equally important, does *not* say anything, communication still can take place.

There are many forms of nonverbal communication. Probably the most widely recognized is body language. Body movements convey meanings and messages. This includes facial expressions and what people do with their eyes, feet, hands, and posture. For example, good salespeople, advertisers, and even poker players capitalize on their knowledge of people's eyes. As explained by Preston:

> . . . when an individual is excited or aroused, the pupils of the eyes will dilate. When haggling over a price, a buyer will unconsciously signal an alert seller that a particular price is acceptable. . . . Some colors or shapes cause more excitement than others, and the reaction registers in the shopper's eyes. With this research information, marketing people redesign their products to better appeal to buyers in a competitive environment. Good poker players watch the eyes of their fellow players as new cards are dealt. The pupil dilation very often will show if the card being dealt improves the player's hand.[26]

Besides the obvious meanings attached to things such as a firm handshake or touching the other person when making an important point, at least one communication expert believes that what the person does with the lower limbs is the key to body language. He explains:

> That is where the tension and anxiety show. The person may claim to be relaxed, yet the legs are crossed tightly, and one foot thrusts so rigidly in the air that it appears to be on the verge of breaking off. *Insight:* People concentrate on hiding their tension from the waist up. Their real state is revealed in their legs and feet.[27]

Even a person's clothing can become important in body language. For example, in his best-selling book *Dress for Success,* John Molloy points out: "The most authoritative pattern is the pinstripe, followed in descending order by the solid, the chalk stripe and the plaid. If you need to be more authoritative, stick with dark pinstripes."[28] In addition to dress, physical appearance in general seems important. From her research with clients, one consultant concluded that physical attractiveness is "the single most important quality in determining your success at every stage in your life. People who are attractive are judged to be nicer people, more intelligent, more capable, more desirable mates and better employees."[29]

Besides the truly silent dimensions of nonverbal communication such as body language, time (for example, being late or early), or space (for example, how close one gets during a conversation or seating arrangements in a committee meeting), there are also *ways* in which people verbalize that are an important dimension of nonverbal communication. Sometimes called *paralanguage,* these include things such as voice quality, volume, speech rate, pitch, nonfluencies (saying "ah," "um," or "uh"), laughing, and yawning.[30] Also, *who* says a word (for example, whether the boss or a coworker asks for "volunteers") and in what *environmental context* it is said (for example, in the boss's office or out on the golf course) makes a difference.

As with other forms of communication, there are specific guidelines that can be used to increase the accuracy of interpreting other's nonverbal behavior. Here are some suggestions to improve nonverbal communication:

1. *Look at what is happening in the situation.* When nonverbal behavior is an emotional response, it reflects what is going on at the moment and can be used to better understand the person's nonverbal behavior.
2. *Consider the discrepancies between the nonverbal behavior and the verbal statements.* If there is a mismatch, then this should be a signal for closer examination of what is going on. Sometimes the nonverbal signals are more accurate than the verbals.
3. *Watch for subtleties in the nonverbal behavior.* For example, the difference between a real smile and fake one can usually be detected.[31]

Cultural differences can also play an important role in effective nonverbal communication. The following are a few guidelines affecting communication in foreign cultures: expect more physical closeness in Latin America; the use of "thumbs up" is fine almost anywhere except Australia; and take your hands out of your pockets when meeting a Japanese person. The accompanying International Application Example gives some further guidelines for both nonverbal and verbal communication in foreign cultures. Overall, nonverbal dimensions are extremely important to interpersonal and organizational communication and must be given as much recognition as the more technical transmissions from information systems and telecommunications.

Organizational and Interpersonal Communication

The organizational and interpersonal approaches to communication represent the middle ground between management information systems/telecommunications on

Nonverbal and Verbal Communication

One of the best ways of coping with foreign cultures and customs is to be careful in the use of both verbal and nonverbal communication. This means saying and doing the right things and, perhaps even more important, not saying or doing wrong things. Here are some guidelines that American managers are finding useful in treading their way through the intercultural maze of foreign countries.

1. In Europe, act as if you are calling on a rich old aunt. Dress well, do not chew gum, do not smoke without first seeking permission, do not use first names unless invited to do so by the other party, be punctual to meetings, and, if you are unsure of the proper dress, err on the side of conservatism.
2. When in France, speak English to your hosts. They know how to speak English and typically are appalled at the performance of foreigners trying to communicate in their tongue. Stick to the language you know best. Also, be on time for all engagements. The French are sticklers for promptness.
3. Remember that the Germans differ from the French in a number of ways. One of these is that they are even bigger sticklers for promptness. Also, remember that gentlemen walk and sit to the left of all ladies and men of senior business rank. Do not get on the wrong side.
4. In Britain, social events are not used for discussing business. This is left at the office. Also, remember that the British religiously keep engagement calendars, so if you are inviting some people to lunch or dinner, send your invitation well in advance or you are likely to find that date already filled in your prospective guest's calendar, if you are attending a formal dinner, it is common to toast Her Majesty's health after the main course. This is the signal that you may now smoke. Do not light up prior to this time. Also, remember that while promptness is valued, if you are invited to dinner at 8 P.M., you may show up five or ten minutes late, but it is not good manners to show up early.
5. In Italy, it is common to shake hands with everyone. However, do not expect them to remember your name. No one does on the first introduction. Also, get in the habit of calling people by their title. For example, university graduates often prefer to be addressed as such, and there are different titles depending on the individual's field of study.
6. In Spain, punctuality is taken seriously only when attending a bullfight. Most offices and shops close for siesta from 1:30 P.M. to 4:30 P.M., and restaurants do not usually reopen until after 9 P.M. or get into full swing before 11 P.M. An early dinner in Spain often ends around midnight; a late dinner goes into the wee hours of the morning. If you are invited to dinner and are unaccustomed to late hours, take an afternoon nap. You are going to need it if you hope to last through dessert.

the one extreme and nonverbal communication on the other. Traditionally, the organization structure was viewed as a network over which there were linear information flows. Especially in classical organization structures, communication consisted simply of the following:

1. Instructions and commands to do or not to do something are always communicated down the chain of command, and only from one person to others directly below that person in the hierarchy.

2. Reports, inquiries, and requests are always communicated up the chain of command, and only to the one person directly above the communicator in the hierarchy.
3. Subgroups do not communicate directly with other subgroups at their level on the chart, but instead communicate up the chain of command until the message arrives at an office where both subgroups share a supervisor, and then down the chain of command to the recipient subgroup.
4. The staff plays the role of communication gadfly; that is, it is given free rein to collect and disseminate nonauthoritative information in its role as an extension of the boss.[32]

In more recent times, organizational communication incorporates the whole spectrum of organization design, information systems/telecommunications, and interpersonal processes. Analysis is made of the types of communication by level of the organization. For example, a recent study found that, contrary to common belief, upper-level managers did not necessarily use electronic mail less than did lower-level clerical workers.[33] For the study of organizational behavior, however, the focus on interpersonal rather than organizational communication is most relevant.

INTERPERSONAL COMMUNICATION

In interpersonal communication, the major emphasis is on transferring information from one person to another. Communication is looked upon as a basic method of effecting behavioral change, and it incorporates the psychological processes (perception, learning, and motivation), on the one hand, and language, on the other. Listening sensitivity and nonverbal communications are also closely associated with this approach. For example, Bill Marriott, Jr., the CEO of the hotel chain, spends nearly half his time listening and talking to front-line employees. Importantly, he listens and then talks to his people.[34]

The Importance of Feedback

The often posed philosophical question that asks, "Is there a noise in the forest if a tree crashes to the ground but no one is there to hear it?" demonstrates some of the important aspects of interpersonal communication.[35] From a communications perspective, the answer is "no." There are sound waves but no noise because no one perceives it. There must be both a sender and a receiver in order for interpersonal communication to take place. The sender is obviously important to communication, but so is the neglected receiver who gives feedback to the sender.

The importance of feedback cannot be overemphasized because effective interpersonal communication is highly dependent on it. Proper follow-up and feedback requires establishing an informal and formal mechanism by which the sender can check on how the message was actually interpreted. Feedback makes communication a two-way process.[36]

Table 16.1 summarizes some characteristics of effective and ineffective feed-

TABLE 16.1 Characteristics of Feedback for Effective and Ineffective Interpersonal Communication in Human Resources Management

Effective Feedback	Ineffective Feedback
1. Intended to help the employee	1. Intended to belittle the employee
2. Specific	2. General
3. Descriptive	3. Evaluative
4. Useful	4. Inappropriate
5. Timely	5. Untimely
6. Employee readiness for feedback	6. Makes the employee defensive
7. Clear	7. Not understandable
8. Valid	8. Inaccurate

Source: Fred Luthans and Mark J. Martinko, *The Practice of Supervision and Management*, McGraw-Hill, New York, 1979, p. 183.

back for employee performance. The following list explains these characteristics in more detail:

1. *Intention.* Effective feedback is directed toward improving job performance and making the employee a more valuable asset. It is not a personal attack and should not compromise the individual's feeling of self-worth or image. Rather, effective feedback is directed toward aspects of the job.
2. *Specificity.* Effective feedback is designed to provide recipients with specific information so that they know what must be done to correct the situation. Ineffective feedback is general and leaves questions in the recipients' minds. For example, telling an employee that he or she is doing a poor job is too general and will leave the recipient frustrated in seeking ways to correct the problem.
3. *Description.* Effective feedback can also be characterized as descriptive rather than evaluative. It tells the employee what he or she has done in objective terms, rather than presenting a value judgment.
4. *Usefulness.* Effective feedback is information that an employee can use to improve performance. It serves no purpose to berate employees for their lack of skill if they do not have the ability or training to perform properly. Thus, the guideline is that if it is not something the employee can correct, it is not worth mentioning.
5. *Timeliness.* There are also considerations in timing feedback properly. As a rule, the more immediate the feedback, the better. This way the employee has a better chance of knowing what the supervisor is talking about and can take corrective action.
6. *Readiness.* In order for feedback to be effective, employees must be ready to receive it. When feedback is imposed or forced upon employees, it is much less effective.
7. *Clarity.* Effective feedback must be clearly understood by the recipient. A good way of checking this is to ask the recipient to restate the major points of the discussion. Also, supervisors can observe facial expressions as indicators of understanding and acceptance.
8. *Validity.* In order for feedback to be effective, it must be reliable and valid. Of course, when the information is incorrect, the employee will feel that the super-

visor is unnecessarily biased, or the employee may take corrective action which is inappropriate and only compounds the problem.[37]

Other Important Variables in Interpersonal Communication

Besides feedback, other variables, such as trust, expectations, values, status, and compatibility, greatly influence the interpersonal aspects of communication. If the subordinate does not trust the boss, there will be ineffective communication. The same is true of the other variables mentioned. People perceive only what they expect to perceive; the unexpected may not be perceived at all. The growing generation gap can play havoc with interpersonal communication; so can status differentials and incompatibilities of any sort. Giving attention to, and doing something about, these interpersonal variables can spell the difference between effective and ineffective communication.

Interpersonal communication plays a central role in the organizational communication process and is directly relevant to the study of organizational behavior. It is given further attention in this chapter in terms of upward and downward communication and interactive communication.

SUPERIOR-SUBORDINATE COMMUNICATION

Traditionally, one of the dominant themes of organizational communication has been the so-called "downward" system. However, when a personal perspective replaces a linear information flow perspective, the downward system is more accurately portrayed as superior-subordinate communication. There are interpersonal linkages, not just information flows, in the downward system.

The Purposes and Methods of Downward Communication

Katz and Kahn have identified five general purposes of superior-subordinate communication in an organization:

1. To give specific task directives about job instructions
2. To give information about organizational procedures and practices
3. To provide information about the rationale of the job
4. To tell subordinates about their performance
5. To provide ideological information to facilitate the indoctrination of goals[38]

In the past, most organizations have concentrated on and accomplished only the first two of these purposes; to a large extent, this is still the case today. In general, superior-subordinate communication on job performance and the rationale-ideological aspects of jobs have been neglected.

A communication system that gives only specific directives about job instructions and procedures and fails to provide information about job performance or rationale-ideological information about the job has a negative organizational impact. This type of downward orientation promotes an authoritative atmosphere which tends to inhibit the effectiveness of the upward and horizontal systems of communication. Communicating the rationale for the job, the ideological relation of the job to the goals of the organization, and information about job performance to employees can, if properly handled, greatly benefit the organization. As Katz and Kahn point out: "If people know the reasons for their assignment, this will often insure their carrying out the job more effectively; and if they have an understanding of what their job is about in relation to their subsystem, they are more likely to identify with organizational goals."[39] This does not imply that management should tell assembly line workers that their jobs are extremely important to the success of the company—that the company would fold unless they put on a bolt right or welded a fender properly. Obviously, this type of communication can backfire. The workers would justifiably reason: "Who are they trying to kid? My job isn't *that* important. It is just another hypocritical con job by management." What is meant is that providing *full* information about the job, its ramifications for the rest of the organization, and the quality of the employee's performance in it should be an important function of superior-subordinate communication. This can be especially true in dealing with employees who are not native born, as seen in the International Application Example: Different Cultures, Different Meanings.

International Application Example

Different Cultures, Different Meanings

As more and more organizations do business in the international arena, communication is going to become a growing problem. This is true not only for verbal and written communication but nonverbal as well. For example, many Americans are accustomed to conveying information by shrugging their shoulders, raising their eyebrows, clenching their fist with the thumb out and extended or placing the thumb and index finger together to form an "O". Do international business people understand these nonverbal gestures? If so, do they give the gestures the same interpretation as do Americans?

One recent research study showed pictures of twenty gestures such as those described in the above paragraph and asked people from various countries to identify them. The respondents were asked to write out their answers so that the responses could be compared both within and between international groups. If the response had no meaning, they were to indicate this also. In all, there were seven different groups of respondents: Colombian, Venezuelan, Peruvian, Jamaican, Indian, Thai, and Japanese. The researchers found that of the twenty pictures, only one had the same meaning for all groups. Overall, the respondents identified 40 percent of the gestures the same way as in the United States, 40 percent differently, and there were mixed responses on the remaining 20 percent. The results showed that the Thai and Japanese respondents agreed with the American meanings on fewer than half of the gestures, while the Venezuelan and Jamaican respondents agreed on about two-thirds of them.

This research points to the importance of communication in the international arena. There are people from many parts of the world who have very different meanings for the same nonverbal communications. For example, the A-okay sign that is conveyed by placing the thumb and forefinger in an "O" shape is an obscene gesture in Latin America and the Middle East, but a very common and positive gesture in the United States. Unless business people are aware of the fact that nonverbal communications can differ radically from one part of the world to the next, there will continue to be communication breakdowns and, in some cases, considerable embarrassment.

Media Used for Downward Communication

Besides the increasing use of the telecommunication techniques discussed earlier, traditionally downward communication systems relied on many types of print and oral media to disseminate information. Some examples of written media are organizational handbooks, manuals, magazines, newspapers, and letters sent to the home or distributed on the job; bulletin-board items, posters, and information displays; and standard reports, descriptions of procedures, and memos. For example, United Airlines has a daily *Employee Newsline* and a monthly employee newspaper. Of particular interest, however, is its biweekly *Supervisors' Hotlines,* which both informs supervisors and encourages them to communicate accurate information in the *Hotline* to those who report to them.[40]

Examples of oral media utilized in the system are direct verbal orders or instructions from superiors, speeches, meetings, closed-circuit television sets, public address systems, and telephones. Arthur Morrissette, president and founder of Interstate Van Lines in Springfield, Virginia, has key managers address their employees every morning and every couple of weeks; he even has a sing-along where employees belt out the lyrics to the company anthem.[41]

The numerous types of media give an indication of the avalanche of information that is descending on personnel from the downward system. An example would be the manager of a metal-fabricating division of a large firm:

> He received six hundred pages of computer printout each day detailing the output of each production line, the location of various materials, and other indexes of the operation. He said that it would take him approximately three full days to simplify the information into usable form. Instead, he found an empty storage room, stacked the printouts there, and subcontracted with a trash removal firm to remove the printouts, untouched, once a month.[42]

Unfortunately, this is not an extreme example. The author observed that in the basement of one large organization, the trash bin used for miscellaneous throwaway items was always neatly stacked and never full. However, next to it was a bin marked for discarded computer printout paper that was always overflowing into the aisle and was stacked dangerously high, literally threatening to become a dangerous avalanche at any time.

Ways to Improve Downward Communication

Quality of information has often been sacrificed for quantity. Also, social psychology experiments over the years have clearly demonstrated people's willingness to ignore useful information and use useless information.[43] Some organizations have tried to solve their downward communication problems by the telecommunication and management information systems discussed earlier. For example, the New York Transit Authority has an information system whereby if one of its buses breaks down, six months of service records are immediately available on a computer monitor at the service depot.[44] These emerging technologies help solve some of the information overload problem of the downward system. In addition, a research study found that although decision makers who perceive information overload may be more satisfied than those who perceive information underload, they may not perform as well.[45]

The biggest problem, however, is ignoring the importance of the receiver. This problem, of course, is symptomatic of taking a linear (in this case, downward) information flow perspective, as opposed to a personal perspective. After an extensive review of the literature, one communications researcher concluded that the downward flow of information can affect receivers in the following ways:

1. People's interpretations of communications follow the path of least resistance.
2. People are more open to messages which are consonant with their existing image, their beliefs, and their values.
3. Messages which are incongruent with values tend to engender more resistance than messages which are incongruent with rational logic.
4. To the extent that people positively value need fulfillment, messages which facilitate need fulfillment are more easily accepted than messages which do not.
5. As people see the environment changing, they are more open to incoming messages.
6. The total situation affects communication; a message interpreted as congruent in one situation may be interpreted as incongruent in another.[46]

If managers understand these impacts of communication on subordinates and do something about them, communication can become more effective. There is a series of studies indicating that if subordinates do get needed information (that is, if superior-subordinate communication is effective), they perform better as individuals and in groups.[47]

SUBORDINATE-INITIATED COMMUNICATION

Just as the downward system becomes superior-subordinate communication from a dynamic, interpersonal perspective, the upward system becomes subordinate-initiated communication in the personal view. In the traditional view, the classical organization structure formally provided for vertical information flows, downward and upward. However, in practice, except for feedback controls, the downward system completely dominated the upward system. Whereas the downward system is highly directive—giving orders, instructions, information, and procedures—the upward system is characteristically nondirective in nature. While bureaucratic authority facilitates a directive atmosphere, a free, participative supervisory approach is necessary for subordinate-initiated communication.

Traditionally, bureaucratic authority has prevailed over the more participative styles, with the result that subordinate-initiated communication has often been outwardly stifled, badly misused, or conveniently ignored by management. Too often, subordinates simply fear to give upward communication, especially if it is bad news. An example would be the "computer company president who had to tell his chairman—a substantial shareholder—and the assembled directors that results wouldn't be up to plan. The exec went about it the right way, providing a full explanation and detailed plans for getting back on track. The chairman fired him on the spot anyway."[48]

Methods of Improving the Effectiveness of Upward Communication

The hierarchical structure is about the only formal method that the classical approach used to communicate upward, and, as has been pointed out, in practice this has not worked out well. Other techniques and channels for subordinate-initiated communication are necessary. The following are some possible ways to promote more effective subordinate-superior communications:

1. *The grievance procedure.* Provided for in most collective bargaining agreements, the grievance procedure allows employees to make an appeal upward beyond their immediate superior. It protects individuals from arbitrary action by their direct superior and encourages communication about complaints. A growing number of companies, such as Federal Express, General Electric, and Borg-Warner, have been instituting peer-review boards to resolve grievances.[49] These boards mostly consist of three peers (those on the same level or below) and two management representatives, and their decisions are binding on both parties.

2. *The open-door policy.* Taken literally, this means that the superior's door is always open to subordinates. It is a continuous invitation for subordinaes to come in and talk about anything that is troubling them. Unfortunately, in practice the open-door policy is more fiction than fact. The boss may slap the subordinate on the back and say, "My door is always open to you," but in many cases both the subordinate and the boss know the door is really closed. It is a case where the adage "actions speak louder than words" applies.

3. *Counseling, attitude questionnaires, and exit interviews.* The personnel department can greatly facilitate subordinate-initiated communication by conducting nondirective, confidential counseling sessions; periodically administering attitude questionnaires; and holding meaningful exit interviews for those who leave the organization. Much valuable information can be gained from these forms of communication.

4. *Participative techniques.* Participative decision techniques can generate a great deal of communication. This may be accomplished by either informal involvement of subordinates or formal participation programs such as the use of junior boards, union-management committees, suggestion boxes, and quality circles. There is also empirical research evidence indicating that participants in communication networks are generally more satisfied with their jobs, are more committed to their organizations, and are better performers than those who are not involved in the communication process.[50]

5. *The ombudsperson.* A largely untried but potentially significant technique to enable management to obtain more subordinate-initiated communication is the use of an ombudsperson. The concept has been used primarily in Scandinavia to provide an outlet for persons who have been treated unfairly or in a depersonalized manner by large, bureaucratic government. It has more recently gained popularity in American state governments, military posts, and universities. Although it is just being introduced in a few business organizations, if set up and handled properly, it may work where the open-door policy has failed. As business organizations become larger and more depersonalized, the ombudsperson may fill an important void that exists under these conditions.

Perhaps the best and simplest way to improve upward communication is for managers to develop good listening habits and systems for listening. For example, the top managers of a Canadian forest products company felt they were great communicators until an employee survey revealed differently. Here is what they did to solve the problem:

> The two owners undertook a series of thirty dinners in the course of the next year. Ten employees and their spouses, eventually including everyone at the mill, went to dinner with their bosses. After the meal, there was a sociable and often long and intense question-and-answer session, "We all wanted to be listened to," says the president. "By the end of the evening, I'd often see a remarkable change in attitude on the part of even the crustiest of the union guys."[51]

Some practical guidelines to facilitate active listening are: (1) maintaining attention; (2) using restatement; (3) showing empathy; (4) using probes to draw the person out; (5) encouraging suggestions; and (6) synchronizing the interaction by knowing when to enter a conversation and when to allow the other person to speak.[52]

Types of Information for Upward Communication

Overall, subordinates can supply basically two types of information: (1) personal information about ideas, attitudes, and performance and (2) more technical feedback information about performance, a vital factor for the control of any organization. The personal information is generally derived from what subordinates tell their superiors. Some examples of such information are:

1. What the persons have done
2. What those under them have done
3. What their peers have done
4. What they think needs to be done
5. What their problems are
6. What the problems of the unit are
7. What matters of organizational practice and policy need to be reviewed[53]

The other type of upward information, feedback for control purposes, is necessary if the organization is to survive. As has been pointed out, "Decision centers utilize information feedback to appraise the results of the organization's performance and to make any adjustments to insure the accomplishment of the purposes of the organization."[54] The role that feedback communication plays has already been stressed earlier in the chapter. Its role in the decision process is covered in Chapter 17.

INTERACTIVE COMMUNICATION IN ORGANIZATIONS

The classical hierarchical organization structure gives formal recognition only to vertical communication. Nevertheless, most of the classical theorists saw the need to supplement the vertical with some form of horizontal system, as Fayol did with his gangplank concept. Horizontal communication is required to make a coordinated effort in achieving organizational goals. The horizontal requirement becomes more apparent as the organization becomes larger, more complex, and more subject to dramatic change. The modern organization designs that will be discussed in Chapter 18, the project and matrix, recognize this need by formally incorporating horizontal flows into the structure. However, as with vertical (downward and upward) flows in the organization structure, the real key to horizontal communication is found in people and behaviors. Because of the dynamic, interpersonal aspects of communication, the *interactive* form seems more appropriate than the *horizontal* form. The horizontal flows of information (even in a matrix structure) are only part of the communication process that takes place across an organization.

The Extent and Implications of Interactive Communication

Most management writers today stress the important but overlooked role that interactive communication plays in organizations. In most cases the vertical communication process overshadows the horizontal. For example, the recent study of "real managers" reported at the beginning of the chapter found that approximately 100 interactions per week reportedly occurred between managers and their subordinates (both to them and from them). "While there was far more communication downward (between managers and their subordinates) than upward (between managers and their superiors), there were no specific differences determined by initiation of interaction."[55] The horizontal communication in this study was mainly represented by the networking activity (socializing/politicking and interacting with outsiders) that was shown to be related to successful managers (those promoted relatively fast) more than any other activity.[56] Other studies have also found a relationship, although complex, between communication activities and leadership.[57]

Just as in other aspects of organizational communication, there are many behavioral implications contained in the interactive process. Communication with peers, that is, with persons of relatively equal status on the same level of an organization, provides needed social support for an individual. People can more comfortably turn to a peer for social support than they can to those above or below them. The result can be good or bad for the organization. If the support is couched in terms of task coordination to achieve overall goals, interactive communication can be good for the organization. On the other hand, "if there are no problems of task coordination left to a group of peers, the content of their communication can take forms which are irrelevant to or destructive of organizational functioning."[58] In addition, interactive communication among peers may be at the sacrifice of vertical communication. Persons at each level, giving social support to one another, may freely communicate among themselves but fail to communicate upward or downward. In fact, in the study of "real managers," Figure 16.1 showed that networking had the least relative relationship with effective managers (those with satisfied and committed subordinates and high-performing units), but routine communication activities (exchanging information and processing paperwork) had the highest.[59]

The Purposes and Methods of Interactive Communication

Just as there are several purposes of vertical communication in an organization, there are also various reasons for the need for interactive communication. Basing his inquiry on several research studies, a communications scholar has summarized four of the most important purposes of interactive communication:

1. *Task coordination.* The department heads may meet monthly to discuss how each department is contributing to the system's goals.
2. *Problem solving.* The members of a department may assemble to discuss how they will handle a threatened budget cut; they may employ brainstorming techniques.
3. *Information sharing.* The members of one department may meet with the members of another department to give them some new data.
4. *Conflict resolution.* The members of one department may meet to discuss a conflict inherent in the department or between departments.[60]

The examples for each of the major purposes of interactive communication are mainly departmental or interdepartmental meetings. Such meetings and the system of committees that exist in most organizations have been the major methods of interactive communication. In addition, most organizations' procedures require written reports to be distributed across departments. The quantity, quality, and human implications discussed in relation to the vertical communication process are also inherent in the traditional methods of interactive communication.

Also like downward communication, telecommunication technology via computers and television has had a recent impact on interactive communication in organizations. Via their computer terminals, members of an organization at the same location or dispersed throughout the world can communicate with one another. For example, to stimualte sharing ideas and technological developments among its engineers, Hewlett-Packard has about sixty computer conferences running simultaneously.[61] Live television hookups can also be used to hold meetings with participants at various geographical locations. This is less costly and time-consuming than bringing everyone into one location and, because it is face-to-face, improves communication over traditional telephone conferencing.

Because of the failure of the classical structures to meet the needs of interactive communication, the informal organization and groups have filled the void. Informal contacts with others on the same level are a primary means of interactive communication. The informal system of communication can be used to spread false rumors and destructive information, or it can effectively supplement the formal channels of communication. It can quickly disseminate pertinent information that assists the formal systems to attain goals. However, whether the informal system has negative or positive functions for the organization depends largely on the goals of the person doing the communicating. Like any communication system, the entire informal system has a highly personal orientation, and, as has been pointed out earlier, personal goals may or may not be compatible with organizational goals. The degree of compatibility that does exist will have a major impact on the effect that the grapevine has on organizational goal attainment.

Some organization theorists are critical of the grapevine because its speed makes control of false rumors and information difficult to manage. By the same token, however, this speed factor may work to the advantage of the organization. Since the informal system is so personally based and directed, it tends to be much faster than the formal downward system of information flow. Important relevant information that requires quick responsive action by lower-level personnel may be more effectively handled by the informal system than by the formal system. Thus, the informal system is a major way that interactive communication is accomplished. The formal horizontal and upward systems are often either inadequate or completely ineffective. The informal system is generally relied upon to coordinate the units horizontally on a given level.

Summary

At every level of modern society, communication is a problem. One of the problems when applied to organizations has been the failure to recognize that communications involves more than just linear information flows; it is a dynamic, interpersonal process that involves behavior exchanges. Knowledge of management information systems, telecommunication technology and nonverbal approaches are necessary background for understanding interpersonal and organizational communication.

The contemporary view is that communication is a dynamic, personal process. The three major dimensions of communication from this perspective are superior-subordinate, subordinate-initiated, and interactive processes. Each has varied purposes and methods. The downward system is generally adequate in the superior-subordinate process, but better techniques are needed to improve the upward and horizontal systems. All three processes in organizations can greatly benefit from increased attention given to the dynamic, interpersonal aspects of communication.

Questions for Discussion and Review

1. Explain Fayol's "gangplank" concept. What are some of its advantages and disadvantages?
2. Compare and contrast the various telecommunication techniques for effective communication.
3. Why is feedback so important to communication? What are some guidelines for the effective use of feedback?
4. What are some of the major purposes and methods of supervisor-subordinate communication?
5. What are some techniques for improving subordinate-initiated communication?
6. What are the major purposes and methods of interactive communication?

References

1. Fred Luthans, Richard M. Hodgetts, and Stuart A. Rosenkrantz, *Real Managers,* Ballinger, Cambridge, Mass., 1988, p. 27 and chap. 6.
2. Henri Fayol, *General and Industrial Management* (trans. by Constance Storrs), Pitman, London, 1949, p. 35.
3. Chester I. Barnard, *The Functions of the Execu-tive,* Harvard University Press, Cambridge, Mass., 1938, p. 90.
4. Ibid., pp. 175–181.
5. Eric M. Eisenberg and Marsha G. Witten, "Reconsidering Openness in Organizational Communication," *Academy of Management Review,* July 1987, pp. 418–426.

6. Fred Luthans and Janet K. Larsen, "How Managers Really Communicate," *Human Relations*, vol. 39, no. 2, 1986, pp. 161–178.

7. Ibid.

8. Bernard J. Reilly and Joseph A. Di Angelo, Jr., "Communication: A Cultural System of Meaning and Value," *Human Relations*, February 1990, p. 129.

9. John M. Ivancevich and Michael T. Matteson, *Organizational Behavior and Management*, Business Publications, Plano, Tex., 1987, p. 631.

10. Aubrey Fisher, *Small Group Decision Making*, McGraw-Hill, New York, 1974, p. 23.

11. Spencer A. Rathus, *Psychology*, 4th ed., Holt, Rinehart and Winston, Fort Worth, 1990, p. 367.

12. See Robert G. Lord and Karen J. Maher, "Alternative Information Processing Models and Their Implications for Theory, Research, and Practice," *Academy of Management Review*, January 1990, pp. 9–28.

13. David H. Holt, *Management*, Prentice-Hall, Englewood Cliffs, N.J., 1987, p. 55.

14. See Albert L. Lederer and Raghu Nath, "Making Strategic Information Systems Happen," *Academy of Management Executive*, August 1990, pp. 76–83.

15. See Blake Ives and Richard O. Mason, "Can Information Technology Revitalize Your Customer Service?" *Academy of Management Executive*, November 1990, pp. 52–69.

16. Christopher Locke of Carnegie Mellon quoted in "The Next Frontier Is the Text Frontier," *Business Week*, June 18, 1990, p. 178.

17. Randall L. Tobias, "Telecommunications in the 1990s," *Business Horizons*, January–February 1990, p. 81.

18. Jeffery Ferry, "The Wired World," *Vis a Vis*, May 1990, p. 25.

19. Tobias, op. cit., p. 82.

20. Ferry, op. cit., p. 26.

21. Jill MacNeice, "Calls by Computer," *Nation's Business*, July 1990, p. 29.

22. Mike Bransby, "Voice Mail Makes a Difference," *The Journal of Business Strategy*, January/February, 1990, p. 8.

23. MacNeice, op. cit., p. 29.

24. Ferry, op. cit., p. 25.

25. Don Hellriegel, John W. Slocum, Jr., and Richard W. Woodman, *Organizational Behavior*, 4th ed., West, St. Paul, Minn., 1986, p. 221.

26. Paul Preston, *Communication for Managers*, Prentice-Hall, Englewood Cliffs, N.J., 1979, p. 161.

27. Martin G. Groder, "Incongruous Behavior: How to Read the Signals," *Bottom Line*, Mar. 30, 1983, p. 13.

28. John T. Molloy, *Dress for Success*, Warner Books, New York, 1975, p. 46.

29. V. Hale Starr, quoted in "Expert: Non-Verbal Body Language Counts," *Omaha World Herald*, Dec. 20, 1982, p. 2.

30. Dalmor Fisher, *Communication in Organizations*, West, St. Paul, Minn., 1981.

31. See Robert S. Feldman, *Understanding Psychology*, 2d ed., McGraw-Hill, New York, 1990, pp. 329–330.

32. Eugene Walton, *A Magnetic Theory of Organizational Communication*, U.S. Naval Ordnance Test Station, China Lake, Calif., 1962.

33. Ronald E. Rice and Douglas E. Shook, "Relationships of Job Categories and Organizational Levels to Use of Communication Channels, Including Electronic Mail: A Meta-Analysis and Extension," *Journal of Management Studies*, March 1990, p. 195.

34. James L. Heskett, *Managing in the Service Economy*, Harvard Business School Press, Boston, 1986, p. 127.

35. Peter F. Drucker, *Management*, Harper & Row, New York, 1974, p. 483.

36. Andrew D. Szilagyi, Jr., and Marc J. Wallace, Jr., *Organizational Behavior and Performance*, Scott, Foresman, Glenview, Ill., 1987, p. 410.

37. Fred Luthans and Mark J. Martinko, *The Practice of Supervision and Management*, McGraw-Hill, New York, 1979, pp. 180–182.

38. Daniel Katz and Robert Kahn, *The Social Psychology of Organizations*, 2d ed., Wiley, New York, 1978, p. 440.

39. Ibid., p. 443.

40. Heskett, op. cit., p. 127.

41. Nelson W. Aldrich, Jr., "Lines of Communication," *Inc.*, June 1986, p. 142.

42. Szilagyi and Wallace, op. cit, p. 408.

43. See David G. Myers, *Social Psychology*, 3d ed., McGraw-Hill, New York, 1990, p. 117.

44. "Manager's On-Line Design Keeps New Yorkers Rolling," *Computerworld*, Dec. 10, 1984, p. 8.

45. Charles A. O'Reilly, "Individuals and Information Overload in Organizations." *Academy of*

Management Journal, December 1980, pp. 684–696.

46. Donald F. Roberts, "The Nature of Communication Effects," in Wilbur Schramm and Donald F. Roberts (eds.), *The Process and Effects of Mass Communication,* rev. ed., University of Illinois Press, Chicago, 1971, pp. 368–371.

47. Charles A. O'Reilly, "Supervisors and Peers as Information Sources, Group Supportiveness, and Individual Performance," *Journal of Applied Psychology,* October 1977, pp. 632–635; and Charles A. O'Reilly and Karlene H. Roberts, "Task Group Structure, Communication, and Effectiveness in Three Organizations," *Journal of Applied Psychology,* December 1977, pp. 674–681.

48. Walter Kiechel III, "Breaking Bad News to the Boss," *Fortune,* Apr. 9, 1990, p. 111.

49. Larry Reibstein, "More Firms Use Peer Review Panel to Resolve Employees' Grievances," *The Wall Street Journal,* Dec. 3, 1986, p. 25.

50. Karlene H. Roberts and Charles A. O'Reilly, "Some Correlations of Communication Roles in Organizations," *Academy of Management Journal,* March 1979, pp. 42–57.

51. Tom Peters, *Thriving on Chaos: Handbook for a Management Revolution,* Knopf, New York, 1987, p. 305.

52. Gary Yukl, *Skills for Managers and Leaders,* Prentice-Hall, Englewood Cliffs, N.J., 1990, pp. 111–115.

53. Katz and Kahn, op. cit., p. 446.

54. William G. Scott and Terence R. Mitchell, *Organization Theory,* rev. ed., Irwin, Homewood, Ill., 1972, p. 147.

55. Luthans and Larsen, op. cit., p. 168.

56. Fred Luthans, Stuart A. Rosenkrantz, and Harry W. Hennessey, "What Do Successful Managers Really Do? An Observational Study of Managerial Activities," *Journal of Applied Behavioral Science,* vol. 21, no. 3, 1985, pp. 255–270.

57. J. Fulk and E. R. Wendler, "Dimensionality of Leader-Subordinate Interactions: A Path-Goal Investigation," *Organizational Behavior and Human Performance,* vol. 30, 1982, pp. 241–264; and Larry E. Penley and Brian Hawkins, "Studying Interpersonal Communication in Organizations: A Leadership Application," *Academy of Management Journal,* June 1985, pp. 309–326.

58. Katz and Kahn, op. cit., p. 445.

59. Luthans, Hodgetts, and Rosenkrantz, op. cit., chap. 4.

60. Gerald M. Goldhaber, *Organizational Communication,* Wm. C. Brown, Dubuque, Ia., 1974, p. 121.

61. Henry C. Mishkoff, "The Network Nation Emerges," *Management Review,* August 1986, pp. 29–31.

REAL CASE: 800 TO THE RESCUE

One of the major trends that has changed American industry over the last five years has been the rise of consumer demands for higher quality goods and services. It is becoming tougher and tougher to please customers, and yet those firms that fail to do so are finding themselves losing market share. How can companies keep up with these demands? One way is by developing strategies that help them communicate with their customers and quickly respond to problem areas.

One of the best examples is provided by the rise in toll-free telephone numbers that give the customer 24-hour service. This approach has proven so popular that over the last ten years AT&T's 800-line network has grown from 1.5 billion to 8 billion customers. These lines are extremely important in providing companies with feedback regarding how well they are serving their customers and how they can improve. Take the case of Cadillac, which has added 22 toll-free numbers since 1984. As a result of this feedback, the company has eliminated the deductibles on warranties and has become the first American carmaker to institute 24-hour roadside service. In fact, the company's emphasis on service plus improvements in the quality of its cars helped it win the Malcolm Baldrige Award in 1990.

General Electric is another good example. Its 800-number network, first installed in 1982 and receiving 1,000 calls weekly, now handles 65,000 calls a week. The firm has found this channel of communication to be so important that it recently raised its requirements for the 150 phone reps that staff these phones. Now they must have a college degree and sales experience. They also have to be able to spot trends in consumer complaints and then alert the appropriate division to take swift action. For example, when the reps started receiving calls from mothers complaining that the end-of-the-cycle signal on clothes dryers disturbed their napping babies, the company responded by changing the signal so that it now can be turned off by the user.

Colgate-Palmolive uses its 800 line to poll consumers and learn how they feel about the company's products. This helps the firm identify problems and make changes necessary to meet customer needs. As the company president puts it, "Our customers want a specific product that does a specific job, and they are less willing to settle for the happy medium. We must interact with them to fill their needs."

1. How important is communication feedback to these firms?
2. In addition to the use of 800-lines, how else can firms improve their communication with customers?
3. What can organizations do to ensure that internal barriers are overcome so that proper action is taken with regard to customer concerns?

**Case:
Doing My
Own Thing**

Rita Lowe has worked for the same boss for eleven years. Over coffee one day, her friend Sara asked her, "What is it like to work for old Charlie?" Rita replied, "Oh, I guess it's okay. He pretty much leaves me alone. I more or less do my own thing." Then Sara said, "Well, you've been at that same job for eleven years. How are you doing in it? Does it look like you will ever be promoted? If you don't mind me saying so, I can't for the life of me see that what you do has anything to do with the operation." Rita replied, "Well, first of all, I really don't have any idea of how I am doing. Charlie never tells me, but I've always taken the attitude that no news is good news. As for what I do and how it contributes to the operation around here, Charlie mumbled something when I started the job about being important to the operation, but that was it. We really don't communicate very well."

1. Analyze Rita's last statement: "We really don't communicate very well." What is the status of superior-subordinate communication in this work relationship? Katz and Kahn identified five purposes of the superior-subordinate communication process. Which ones are being badly neglected in this case?
2. It was said in this chapter that communication is a dynamic, personal process. Does the situation described verify this contention? Be specific in your answer.
3. Are there any implications in this situation for subordinate-initiated communication and for interactive communication? How could feedback be used more effectively?

**Case:
Bad Brakes**

Michelle Adams is the maintenance supervisor of a large taxicab company. She had been very concerned because the cabdrivers were not reporting potential mechanical problems. Several months ago she implemented a preventive maintenance program. This program depended upon the drivers' filling out a detailed report when they suspected any problem. But this was not happening. On a number of occasions a cab left the garage with major problems that the previous driver was aware of but had not reported. Calling out the field repair teams to fix the breakdown was not only costing the company much time and trouble but also was very unsafe in some cases and created a high degree of customer ill will. The drivers themselves suffered from a loss of fares and tips, and in some cases their lives were endangered by these mechanical failures. After many verbal and written threats and admonishments, Michelle decided to try a new approach. She would respond directly to each report of a potential mechanical problem sent in by a driver with a return memo indicating what the maintenance crew had found wrong with the cab and what had been done to take care of the problem. In addition, the personal memo thanked the driver for reporting the problem and encouraged reporting any further problems with the cabs. In less than a month the number of field repair calls had decreased by half, and the number of turned-in potential problem reports had tripled.

1. In communications terms, how do you explain the success of Michelle's follow-up memos to the drivers?
2. Explain and give examples of the three communications systems in this company (that is, superior-subordinate, subordinate-initiated, and interactive).

17 Decision Making

■ Zero Defections

Decision making is an important process for organizational effectiveness. In the manufacturing area, effective decisions are aimed at achieving "zero defects." In recent years, this focus has also been applied to the service sector in order to create "zero defections."

Marketing indicates when it comes to delivering services, successful companies keep their customers coming back again and again. Those who cannot, will have serious problems because the initial cost of getting a customer is usually so high that the company can profit only if it gets repeat business. In accomplishing this objective, many firms have made the decision to do whatever it takes to get the customer's business and keep it. This effort often means delegating to the lowest operating level. The goal is to make the right decision for the customer, at any cost.

A good example is Silvio de Bortoli, general manager of a Cancun resort in Mexico who is renowned for his ability to satisfy his customers. When he recently received word that some tourists flying in from the United States were having flight trouble, he gathered his people and hurried to the airport. The plane had been six hours late taking off, made two unscheduled stops, and circled for thirty minutes before landing. By that time, the aircraft had run out of food and—to make matters worse—the landing was so rough that oxygen masks and luggage dropped from the overhead compartments. As the passengers disembarked, de Bortoli had set up a stereo to play lively music, had snacks and drinks for all the people, had his staff help them with their bags, and provided a chauffeured ride to the resort for everyone. De Bortoli couldn't improve the flight, but his quick decision on how to recover made a lasting impression on customers and, of course, led to repeat business and having grateful customers telling many others.

A different way to accomplish customer service is the method of British Airways. It installed Video Point booths at Heathrow Airport in London. Immediately upon arrival, travelers can tape their reaction to the service they have just received. If there has been a problem, the airline will learn about it in short order, and customer service reps who view the tapes can begin taking steps to prevent a recurrence.

Another example is the Maine Savings Bank in Portland. The bank offers its patrons $1 for every letter they write suggesting ways to improve service. The bank is now receiving 500 letters a month giving it 500 ideas for improving service—ideas which, before the program, would not have surfaced. Still another example is the Minneapolis Marriott Hotel, which sends a "Sweet Dreams" package consisting of a cordial, a small bud vase with a carnation, and homemade cookies to customers having difficulties the hotel cannot immediately fix. By giving their personnel decision-making authority to "make it right" for the customer, companies are finding that they are able to attract more customers and keep defections to a minimum.

Learning Objectives

- **Define** the phases in the decision-making process.
- **Identify** the models of behavioral decision making.
- **Present** the behaviorally oriented participative decision-making techniques.
- **Discuss** the creative process and group decision making.

In this chapter, the important processes of decision making are given attention. A *process* is any action which is performed by management to achieve organizational objectives. Thus, decision making is an organizational process because it transcends the individual and has an effect on organizational goals. First, the overall nature of the decision-making process is explored. Then, the models of behavioral decision making are described. Next, the traditional and modern participative techniques are presented as behaviorally oriented decision techniques. Finally, the creative process and group decision making are given attention.

THE NATURE OF DECISION MAKING

Decision making is almost universally defined as *choosing between alternatives*. It is closely related to all the traditional management functions. For example, when a manager plans, organizes, and controls, he or she is making decisions. The classical theorists, however, did not generally present decision making this way. Classical theorists such as Fayol and Urwick were concerned with the decision-making process only to the extent that it affects delegation and authority, while Frederick W. Taylor alluded to the scientific method only as an ideal approach to making decisions. Like most other aspects of modern organization theory, the beginning of a meaningful analysis of the decision-making process can be traced to Chester Barnard. In *The Functions of the Executive*, Barnard gave a comprehensive analytical treatment of decision making and noted: "The processes of decision . . . are largely techniques for narrowing choice."[1]

Most discussions of the decision-making process break it down into a series of steps. For the most part, the logic can be traced to the ideas developed by Herbert A. Simon, the well-known Nobel Prize–winning organization and decision theorist, who conceptualizes three major phases in the decision-making process:

1. *Intelligence activity.* Borrowing from the military meaning of *intelligence,* Simon describes this initial phase as consisting of searching the environment for conditions calling for decision making.
2. *Design activity.* During the second phase, inventing, developing, and analyzing possible courses of action take place.
3. *Choice activity.* The third and final phase is the actual choice—selecting a particular course of action from among those available.[2]

Closely related to these phases, but with a more empirical basis (that is, tracing actual decisions in organizations), are the stages of decision making of Mintzberg and his colleagues:

1. *The identification phase,* during which *recognition* of a problem or opportunity arises and a *diagnosis* is made. It was found that severe, immediate problems did not have a very systematic, extensive diagnosis but that mild problems did.
2. *The development phase,* during which there may be a *search* for existing standard procedures or solutions already in place or the *design* of a new, tailormade solution. It was found that the design process was a groping, trial-and-error process in which the decision makers had only a vague idea of the ideal solution.
3. *The selection phase,* during which the choice of a solution is made. There are three ways of making this selection: by the *judgment* of the decision maker, on the basis of experience or intuition rather than logical analysis; by *analysis* of the alternatives on a logical, systematic basis; and by *bargaining* when the selection involves a group of decision makers and all the political maneuvering that this entails. Once the decision is formally accepted, an *authorization* is made.[3]

Figure 17.1 summarizes these phases of decision making based on Mintzberg's research.

Whether expressed in Simon's or Mintzberg's phases, there seem to be identifiable, preliminary steps leading to the choice activity in decision making. Also, it should be noted that decision making is a dynamic process, and there are many feedback loops in each of the phases. "Feedback loops can be caused by problems of timing, politics, disagreement among managers, inability to identify an appropriate alternative or to implement the solution, turnover of managers, or the sudden appearance of a new alternative."[4] The essential point is that decision making is a dynamic process.

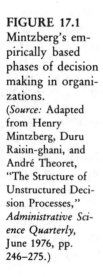

FIGURE 17.1 Mintzberg's empirically based phases of decision making in organizations. (*Source:* Adapted from Henry Mintzberg, Duru Raisin-ghani, and André Theoret, "The Structure of Unstructured Decision Processes," *Administrative Science Quarterly,* June 1976, pp. 246–275.)

BEHAVIORAL DECISION MAKING

Why does a decision maker choose one alternative over another? The answer to this question has been a concern of organizational behavior theorists as far back as March and Simon's classic book *Organizations* in 1958. Subsequently, however, the field became more interested in such topics as motivation and goal setting, and emphasis on decision making waned. The field of behavioral decision making was mainly developed outside the mainstream of organizational behavior theory and research by cognitive psychologists and decision theorists in economics and information science. Very recently, however, there has been a resurgence of interest in behavioral decision making and it has moved back into the mainstream of the field of organizational behavior.[5]

Whereas classical decision theory operated under the assumption of rationality and certainty, the new behavioral decision theory does not. Behavioral decision-making theorists argue that individuals have cognitive limitations and, because of the complexity of organizations and the world in general, they must act under uncertainty and often ambiguous and incomplete information.[6] The Application Example, Avon's Calling: But No One Answered, shows how this happens in the real world.

Application Example

Avon's Calling: But No One Answered

Decision making is recognized as an important process for organizational effectiveness. Managers who make good decisions can contribute to goals and performance; those who do not can create dire consequences for the organization. Take the case of Avon Products Inc. When Hicks Waldron took over the beauty products firm in 1983, he had his work cut out for him. Earnings had been falling since 1979, and the stock had tumbled from a high of $140 in 1973 to a meager $25 a share. Eager to turn the company around, Waldron made some decisions without first gathering the necessary information or considering other possible alternatives. For example, Waldron decided to reward sales representatives who generated the bigger orders. Unfortunately, Waldron ignored the fact that a significant amount of Avon's sales were from small-order customers and a lot of this business was lost.

With troubles brewing at Avon's core business of beauty products, Waldron decided to diversify. In 1984 he bought Foster Medical Care, a medical equipment rental company. This decision proved fruitful. Foster showed 100 percent annual growth for the next two years. But then this subsidiary ran into trouble. In particular, in his struggle to reverse the decline of the beauty products line, he delegated all authority to Foster Medical Care to run their end of the company. Foster, however, did not use this authority well. Since oxygen therapy accounts for 22 percent of Foster's total revenues, Foster's management should have been aware of their environment, especially government guidelines for Medicare reimbursements. In short order, the government announced it would not reimburse oxygen treatments unless patients were certified by their physicians. The government gave oxygen therapy concerns such as Foster one year to get their patients recertified. However, at the year's end, Foster had not completed the necessary paperwork. As a result, they lost $10 to $11 million in Medicare revenues.

The foundation and point of departure for developing and analyzing various models of behavioral decision making is mainly the degree and meaning of rationality.

Decision Rationality

The most often used definition of *rationality* in decision making is that it is a means to an end. If appropriate means are chosen to reach desired ends, the decision is said to be rational. However, there are many complications to this simple test of rationality. To begin with, it is very difficult to separate means from ends because an apparent end may be only a means for some future end. This idea is commonly referred to as the *means-ends chain* or *hierarchy*. Simon points out that "the means-end hierarchy is seldom an integrated, completely connected chain. Often the connection between organization activities and ultimate objectives is obscure, or these ultimate objectives are incompletely formulated, or there are internal conflicts and contradictions among the ultimate objectives, or among the means selected to attain them."[7]

Besides the complications associated with the means-ends chain, it may even be that the concept is obsolete. Decision making relevant to the national economy supports this position. Decision makers who seek to make seemingly rational adjustments in the economic system may in fact produce undesirable, or at least unanticipated, end results. Simon also warns that a simple means-ends analysis may have inaccurate conclusions.

One way to clarify means-ends rationality is to attach appropriate qualifying adverbs to the various types of rationality. Thus, *objective* rationality can be applied to decisions that maximize given values in a given situation. *Subjective* rationality might be used if the decision maximizes attainment relative to knowledge of the given subject. *Conscious* rationality might be applied to decisions in which adjustment of means to ends is a conscious process. A decision is *deliberately* rational to the degree that the adjustment of means to ends has been deliberately sought by the individual or the organization; a decision is *organizationally* rational to the extent that it is aimed at the organization's goals; and a decision is *personally* rational if it is directed toward the individual's goals.[8]

Models of Behavioral Decision Making

There are many descriptive models of behavioral decision making. In effect, these have become models for much of management decision-making behavior. The models attempt to describe theoretically and realistically how practicing managers make decisions. In particular, the models strive to determine to what degree management decision makers are rational. The models range from complete rationality, as in the case of the *economic* or *econologic* model, to complete irrationality, as in the case of the *social* model. Figure 17.2 summarizes on a continuum the two major extremes and the in-between models of Simon's bounded rationality and the judgmental heuristics model coming out of cognitive psychology. These models deal specifically with management decision-making behavior.

| Econologic model | Simon's bounded rationality model | Judgmental heuristics and biases model | Social model |

FIGURE 17.2
The continuum of decision-making behavior.

The Econologic Model. This model comes from the classical economic model, in which the decision maker is perfectly and completely rational in every way. Regarding decision-making activities, the following conditions are assumed:

1. The decision will be completely rational in the means-ends sense.
2. There is a complete and consistent system of preferences which allow a choice among the alternatives.
3. There is complete awareness of all the possible alternatives.
4. There are no limits to the complexity of computations that can be performed to determine the best alternatives.
5. Probability calculations are neither frightening nor mysterious.[9]

With this almost infallible ability, the decision maker always strives to maximize outcomes in the business firm, and decisions will be directed to the point of maximum profit where marginal cost equals marginal revenue (MC = MR).

Most economists and quantitative decision theorists do not claim that this depiction is a realistic descriptive model of modern decision-making behavior. But because this rational model and its accompanying quantitative methods have traditionally been embraced by the business schools, many of today's managers still equate "good" management decision making with this approach. This may be dangerous and may be a leading cause of many of today's problems. As Peters and Waterman observed: "The numerative, rationalist approach to management dominates the business schools. It seeks detached, analytical justification for all decisions. It is right enough to be dangerously wrong, and it has arguably led us seriously astray."[10]

Obviously, Peters and Waterman are not saying "throw the rascal out," nor are other critics of the rational model. It has made and will continue to make a significant contribution to effective decision making. For example, the most successful consumer marketers, such as Procter & Gamble, Chesebrough-Pond's, and Ore-Ida, are known for their rational approach and accompanying quantitative backup. The point that Peters and Waterman are making is that the rational model is not the be-all and end-all of effective decision making and that, if carried to the extreme, it can actually be harmful to the decision-making process.

The Social Model. At the opposite extreme from the econologic model is the social model of psychology. Sigmund Freud presented humans as bundles of feelings, emotions, and instincts, with their behavior guided largely by their unconscious desires. Obviously, if this were an accurate description, people would not be capable of making effective decisions.

Although most contemporary psychologists would take issue with the Freudian description of humans, almost all would agree that social influences have a significant impact on decision-making behavior. Furthermore, social pressures and influences may cause managers to make irrational decisions. The well-known conformity experiment by Solomon Asch demonstrates human irrationality.[11] His study utilized several groups of seven to nine subjects each. They were told that their task was to compare the lengths of lines. All except one of the "subjects" in each group had prearranged with the experimenter to give clearly wrong answers on twelve of the eighteen line-judgment trials. About 37 percent of the 123 naive subjects yielded to the group pressures and gave incorrect answers to the twelve test situations. In other words, more than one-third of the experimental subjects conformed to a decision they knew was wrong.

If over one-third of Asch's subjects conformed under "right and wrong," "black and white" conditions of comparing the lengths of lines, a logical conclusion would be that the real, "gray" world is full of irrational conformists. It takes little imagination to equate Asch's lines with the alternatives of a management decision. There seems to be little doubt of the importance of social influences in decision-making behavior.

There is still much to be learned about the impact of social pressures on decision-making behavior. This even applies to how one makes decisions in the international arena. Knowing the correct social protocol can be very important to U.S. managers in an international assignment. The accompanying International Application Example gives some of these basic rules.

Certainly, the completely irrational person depicted by Freud is too extreme a case to be useful. On the other hand, as the chapters in this book have pointed out, there is little question of the important role that human behavior can and does play in management decision making. Some management behavior is irrational but still very realistic. For example, the author and a colleague conducted two studies that showed that subjects in both laboratory and field settings who did not have computer experience were more influenced in their decision activities by information presented on computer printout paper than they were by information presented on regular paper.[12] On the other hand, for those subjects with computer experience, the reverse was true. In other words, decision makers are influenced in their choice activities even by the type of format in which information is presented to them. Managers without computer experience may be in awe of the computer and place more value on computer-generated information than is justified, while those with computer experience may be highly skeptical and may underrate the importance of computer-generated information.

Simon's Bounded Rationality Model. To present a more realistic alternative to the econologic model, Herbert Simon proposed what he called "administrative man." He felt that management decision-making behavior could best be described as follows:

**International
Application
Example**

Some Basic Rules of Protocol

There are many rules of protocol that Americans serving in foreign assignments should recognize. Some are confusing; most are not. In any event, it is important to know these guidelines in order to be as effective as possible. Here are the most useful rules:

1. In many countries of the world, a person's name denotes social rank or family status. A mistake can be an outright insult. So American managers who are going to be meeting some important nationals should find out who they are beforehand and write their names out and memorize them for correct pronunciation.
2. Keep in mind that there are different rules of protocol in different cultures. For example, in Latin America people's names are a combination of the father's and the mother's, but only the father's name is used in conversation. In Spanish-speaking countries, the father's name comes first. For example, Carolos Migoya-Gutierrez is called Mr. Migoya. However, in Portuguese-speaking countries, it is the other way around, i.e., Mr. Gutierrez. To make it even more confusing, in Asia the rules often vary by country. For example, in Korea which of a man's names to use is determined by whether he is the first son or the second son. In Japan, people should be addressed by their surname, while in Thailand you should call people by their given name, i.e., Mr. Ho Chin would be called Mr. Ho. How can an American manager be sure of not making a mistake? The one best way is: ask your host.
3. In the United States it is acceptable to bypass food you do not like. When overseas, however, you should take whatever is put on your plate and make a valiant effort to eat it regardless of taste. If it's something you have never had before, do not ask what it is. You may be unpleasantly surprised.
4. Before getting to the destination, find out the types of clothes that people wear. Remember that color is as important as fashion. If the American male manager is in doubt, a conservative business suit will usually be acceptable, although in the Philippines a barong (a loose, frilly, usually white or cream-colored shirt with tails out) is proper dress, and in Latin countries a guayabera (similar to a barong) will get him through. For women there would be different rules.
5. Despite what is commonly heard about locals in other countries wanting Americans to speak their language, English is still the primary tongue in the international arena. Most educated people understand this language, and many speak it fluently. Unless American managers are absolutely sure of what they are going to say in a foreign tongue, they should stick with English.

1. In choosing between alternatives, managers attempt to *satisfice,* or look for the one which is satisfactory or "good enough." Examples of satisficing criteria would be adequate profit or share of the market and fair price.
2. They recognize that the world they perceive is a drastically simplified model of the real world. They are content with this simplification because they believe the real world is mostly empty anyway.
3. Because they satisfice rather than maximize, they can make their choices without first determining all possible behavior alternatives and without ascertaining that these are in fact all the alternatives.

4. Because they treat the world as rather empty, they are able to make decisions with relatively simple rules of thumb or tricks of the trade or from force of habit. These techniques do not make impossible demands upon their capacity for thought.[13]

In contrast to the econologic model, Simon's model is rational and maximizing, but it is bounded. Decision makers end up satisficing because they do not have the ability to maximize. The case against maximizing behavior has been summed up by noting that objectives are dynamic rather than static; information is seldom perfect; there are obvious time and cost constraints; alternatives seldom lend themselves to quantified preference ordering; and the effect of environmental forces cannot be disregarded.[14] Simon's model recognizes these limitations. The econologic model's assumptions are viewed as unrealistic. But in the final analysis, the difference between the econologic model and Simon's model is one of degree because, under some conditions, satisficing approaches maximizing, whereas in other conditions satisficing and maximizing are very far apart.

There are many economic, social, and organizational variables which influence the degree to which satisficing becomes maximizing. An example of an economic variable is market structure. The more competitive the market, the more satisficing may approach maximizing. In an agricultural products market situation, satisficing will by necessity become maximizing. Economists generally recognize that in a purely competitive environment, profit maximization lends itself to the very survival of the firm. Thus, the decision maker must make maximizing decisions. In an oligopolistic market situation (for example, the automobile and steel industries), satisficing is quite different from maximizing. Oligopolistic firms can still survive on the basis of adequate profit or share of the market. They do not have to operate at the point where marginal cost equals marginal revenue, and, in fact, they may be unavoidably prevented from maximizing.

Besides the economic market constraints, there are many socially based obstacles which prevent maximization in practice. Some of these social barriers are not consciously recognized by the management decision maker. Examples are resistance to change, desire for status, concern for image, organizational politics, and just plain stupidity. On the other hand, the decision maker may in some cases consciously avoid maximizing. Examples of the latter behavior include decisions which discourage competitive entry or antitrust investigation, restrain union demands, or maintain consumer goodwill.

Judgmental Heuristics and Biases Model. Although Simon's bounded rationality model and the concept of satisficing are an important extension of the wholly rational econologic model, as Bazerman points out, it does not describe *how* judgment will be biased.[15] Thus, to take the bounded rationality model one step further, a model which identifies specific systematic biases that influence judgment has recently emerged.

The judgmental heuristics and biases model is mostly drawn from Kahneman and Tversky, cognitive decision theorists, who suggested that decision makers rely on heuristics (simplifying strategies or rules of thumb).[16] Such judgmental heuristics reduce the information demands on the decision maker and realistically help in the following ways:

1. Summarize past experiences and provide an easy method to evaluate the present.
2. Substitute simple rules of thumb or "standard operating procedures" for complex information collection and calculation.
3. Save considerable mental activity and cognitive processing.[17]

Importantly, however, even though these cognitive heuristics simplify and help the decision maker, under certain conditions, their use can lead to errors and systematically biased outcomes. Three major biases are identified that help explain how people's judgment deviates from a fully rational process. (Before reading about these biases, answer the questions in Figure 17.3)

1. *The Availability Heuristic.* This cognitive input into judgment refers to decision makers' tendencies to assess the frequency, probability, or likelihood of an event occurring by how readily they can remember it.[18] "An event that evokes emotions and is vivid, easily imagined, and specific will be more 'available' from memory than will an event that is unemotional in nature, bland, difficult to imagine, or vague."[19] An example would be a human resource manager's assessment of the probability of the effectiveness of a newly hired skilled worker from the local technical school, based on her recollection of the successes and failures of those graduates she has hired in recent years. This heuristic can be very valuable to decision makers because events that happen most frequently or are most vivid tend to lead to accurate judgments. By the same token, however, errors or bias results from this heuristic when the ease of recall is influenced by factors unrelated to the frequency of an event's occurrence.[20] For example, the most common response to question one in Figure 17.3 is (a), that there are more words that start

FIGURE 17.3
A Judgment Quiz.
(*Source:* Adapted from Max H. Bazerman, *Judgment in Managerial Decision Making,* Wiley, New York, 1986 and 1990.)

1. Are there more words in the English language that (*a*) begin with the letter "r" or (*b*) have "r" as the third letter?

2. On one day in a large metropolitan hospital, eight births were recorded by gender in the order of their arrival. Which of the following orders of births (B = boy, G = girl) was most likely to be reported?

   a. BBBBBBBB

   b. BBBBGGGG

   c. BGBBGGGB

3. A newly hired engineer for a computer firm in the Boston metropolitan area has four years of experience and good all-around qualifications. When asked to estimate the starting salary for this employee, my secretary (knowing very little about the profession or the industry) guessed an annual salary of $23,000. What is your estimate?
   $ _____ per year.

with the letter "r." However the correct answer, by far, is (b); there are many more words with "r" as the third letter.[21] This is explained by the availability bias. More people can recall words that start with "r" and it is difficult to think of those that have "r" as the third letter, so they falsely conclude that there must be more words that start with "r." In other words, those words that start with "r" are more readily available in the typical person's memory, but this is a case where the remembered information is wrong and an error in judgment results.

2. *The Representativeness Heuristic.* This second major heuristic uses decision rules of thumb based on the likelihood of an event's occurrence as judged by the similarity of that occurrence to stereotypes of similar occurrences. Managers would be using a representativeness heuristic when they predict the success of a new product based on the similarity of that product to past successful and unsuccessful product types.[22] However, as with the availability heuristic, this representativeness thinking can be biased and lead to errors. For example, most people choose response (c) for question 2 in Figure 17.3 because it appears to be most random. The reasoning is that both (a) and (b) are too ordered and are unlikely to occur. However, this is faulty logic. The correct response is that all three of the options are equally likely to occur. As explained by Northcraft and Neale, "the problem here is that we believe that a sequence of independent events (such as eight births) generated from a random process should resemble the essential characteristics of a random process, even when the sequence is too short for that process to express itself statistically. Decision makers expect a few examples of a random event to behave in the same way as large numbers of the event."[23]

3. *The Anchoring and Adjustment Heuristic.* In this heuristic, the decision maker makes a judgment by starting from an initial value or anchor and then adjusts to make the final decision. Bazerman goes on to explain that "The initial value, or starting point, may be suggested from historical precedent, from the way in which a problem is presented, or from random information. For example, managers make salary decisions by adjusting from an employee's past year's salary."[24] However, as with the others, bias and resulting error in judgment can creep into this decision rule. For example, in question 3 of Figure 17.3 most people do not think they are affected by the secretary's estimate. Yet, Bazerman clearly found that they are. When he raised the secretary's estimate to $80,000, individuals give much higher estimates, on average, than when the secretary's estimate was at $23,000.[25] In other words, people use the secretary's estimate as an anchor (even though it is irrelevant information) and adjust from there.

Overall, even though the judgmental heuristics and biases model is based on relatively complex cognitive processing, it is quite descriptive of how managers actually make decisions. Despite the fact that this cognitive approach has only recently emerged in the mainstream of organizational behavior, there is a sound theoretical base and a growing stream of research.[26]

In the final analysis, all the decision models presented are appropriate under certain conditions and are used in combination with one another. This last one, however, has been largely ignored up to very recent times. Obviously, it has to be taken into consideration for effective decision making in today's organizations. Besides the heuristics and biases model, the behavioral techniques discussed next can also be helpful for effective decision making.

BEHAVIORALLY ORIENTED DECISION-MAKING TECHNIQUES

Most of the behavioral techniques, at least traditionally, have revolved around participation. Used as a technique, participation involves individuals or groups in the decision-making process. It can be formal or informal, and it entails intellectual and emotional as well as physical involvement. The actual amount of participation in making decisions ranges from one extreme of no participation, wherein the superior makes the decision and asks for no help or ideas from anyone, to the other extreme of full participation, where everyone connected with, or affected by, the decision is completely involved. In practice, the degree of participation will be determined by factors such as the experience of the person or group and the nature of the task. The more experience and the more open and unstructured the task, the more participation there will tend to be.

In today's organizations there is an awakened interest in participation. As was recently noted, "Interest in participation among American managers, unions, and workers has been spurred by the competitive assault on U.S. companies by companies with more participatory industrial relations systems, by the challenges of new production technologies, and by the disappointing productivity performance of American companies."[27] Participative techniques have been talked about ever since the early human relations movement, and now some organizations and individual managers are actually trying them.

Participation techniques can be applied informally on an individual or a group basis or formally on a program basis. Individual participation techniques are those in which a subordinate somehow affects the decision making of a superior. Group participation utilizes consultative and democratic techniques. Under consultative participation, the superiors ask for and receive involvement from subordinates, but they maintain the right to make the decision. In the democratic form, there is total participation, and the group, not the individual head, makes the final decision by consensus or majority vote.

Although participation has long been discussed and advocated, only recently has there been research support that it enhances employee performance. A recent comprehensive review of the research literature concluded that "Participation generally fosters a sense of identification with the firm, a positive quality of working life, and enhanced mental health as needs for autonomy, responsibility, and material well-being are fulfilled. Participation has been shown to result in higher productivity, decreased turnover, and increased job satisfaction."[28]

Examples of formal programs of participation range all the way from the classic Scanlon Plan and widely-used suggestion plans or boxes to the more recent quality circles popularized by the Japanese and teams or self-managed work groups.

Traditional Participative Techniques

The Scanlon Plan is a pioneering form of labor-management cooperation. The plan, originated by Joseph Scanlon (who was at first with the steelworkers' union and later MIT) about fifty years ago, consists of a system of committees which encourage labor to participate in management decisions. The unique feature of the Scanlon Plan is that the rewards for an individual's successful suggestion are equally divided among all members of the group. A comprehensive analysis of the Scanlon Plan tested several hypotheses that were derived from the extensive literature on the plan during the preceding thirty years. After examining twenty-three firms that had the Scanlon Plan in operation, researchers concluded that success was positively related to (1) the average level of participation in decision making reported by employees, (2) the number of years the company had been using the plan, and (3) management's—especially the chief executive officer's—attitudes toward, and expectations of, the plan.[29]

Commonly used suggestion plans or boxes are also a traditional participation program. At A&P grocery stores, the company cut back wages but gives bonuses for suggestions and inputs to its participation program. In the Philadelphia area alone, A&P has paid out $10 million in bonuses in a five-year period.[30] Suggestion systems in general are commonly thought to be seldom used and of little value to the companies using them and the employees who participate. Yet an estimate of a recent year was that suggestion box ideas saved companies $2.2 billion and paid out $160 million to those making the suggestions.[31] If employee responses are properly handled and adequately rewarded, the suggestion box can be a very effective method of obtaining participation in the decision-making process from anyone in the organization.

Modern Participative Techniques

Modern participative techniques revolve around participative decision making pushed down to the worker level, and the use of work teams or self-managed groups discussed in Chapter 7. These techniques have been used extensively overseas for a number of years, but are also becoming popular in more enlightened U.S. firms. Table 17.1 summarizes the applications abroad and what Hewlett-Packard does with these techniques in the United States.

These modern participative techniques are recognized as successful by both practicing organizations (for example, General Mills claims that since it implemented participative teams, productivity has increased 40 percent[32]) and the recent research literature.[33] Some specific examples of money-saving ideas and innovations that came out of Chevron's participative program are the following:

- A transportation foreman proposed that Chevron quit providing lube oil, lubricants, and hydraulic oil to chartered boats. Eliminating these provisions resulted in significant yearly savings, and no increase in vessel rates. Research with other companies taking similar actions verified that boat rates did not increase.
- An electrical foreman discovered that the lights on four offshore platforms were

TABLE 17.1 Applications and Use of Modern Participative Techniques Across Cultures

Type of Participative Technique	Japanese Firms	Spanish Co-ops	Swedish Auto Firms	Hewlett-Packard
Decision making at the worker level	Widespread quality circles with the power to change the deployment of workers within workshops and the way jobs are concluded.	Experiments with shop-floor re-designs, small work teams, and quality circles along Japanese and Swedish lines are being diffused among the co-ops.	Workers design and organize their own jobs within a team framework to accomplish their common assignment. The design of the factory supports their self-paced team work.	700 quality circles at peak. Implementing self-directed work teams. Cooperative product design. Quality program.
Team of self-managed groups	Organization structures, such as broad job specification, group responsibility, and job rotation, require and promote teamwork.	Experiments with small work teams and quality circles along Japanese and Swedish lines are being diffused among the co-ops.	Self-directed assembly groups with frequent job rotation and enrichment.	Units are kept small. Communication emphasized. Participative decision-making practiced. Implementing self-directed work teams in new factories.

Source: Adapted from David I. Levine, "Participation, Productivity, and the Firm's Environment," *California Management Review,* Summer 1990, p. 88.

cally shut the lights off during the day, electricity consumption was reduced dramatically.

- A mechanical foreman recognized that sending excess valves to an outside vendor for machining and lapping was a "resource loss." He designed and built a valve-lapping machine that eliminated the need for sending valves to vendors.
- A production foreman noticed that the workboat assigned to his offshore field and the workboat assigned to an adjacent field together averaged more than twenty-four hours per day of standby time. He developed a plan to release one boat and share the other between fields.[34]

The best-known group participative technique is the quality circle. Introduced in Chapter 12, quality circles really started in this country but were developed and as indicated in Table 17.1 are widely used in Japan. Recently they have been imported back to this country. Quality circles "typically are small groups of volunteers from the same work areas who meet regularly to identify, analyze, and solve quality and related problems in their area of responsibility. Members of a group choose a particular problem to study, gather data, and use such methods as brainstorming, Pareto analysis, histograms, and control charts to form a recommendation that can be presented to management."[35] Now groups are trained in communication and problem-solving skills and in quality/measurement strategies and techniques.

Participation Techniques in Perspective

There are many positive and negative attributes of the participation techniques of decision making. Balancing these off in evaluating the effectiveness of participative decision making is difficult because of moderating factors such as leadership style or personality of the parties involved and situational, environmental, contextual factors,[36] and ideology.[37] Also, even though there is general research support, as was pointed out in the introductory comments, an extensive review of research found that the different forms of participative techniques had markedly different outcomes. For example, informal participation was found to have a positive effect on employee productivity and satisfaction; representative participation had a positive impact on satisfaction, but not productivity; and short-term participation was ineffective by both criteria.[38]

One problem is the tendency toward pseudoparticipation. Many managers ask for participation, but whenever subordinates take them up on it by making a suggestion or trying to give some input into a decision, they are put down or never receive any feedback. In some cases managers try to get their subordinates involved in the task but not in the decision-making process. This can lead to a boomerang effect regarding employee satisfaction. If the superior claims to want participation from subordinates but never lets them become intellectually and emotionally involved and never utilizes their suggestions, the results may be disastrous. Also, participation can be very time-consuming, and it has the same general disadvantages of committees. From a behavioral standpoint, however, the advantages far outweigh the disadvantages. Most of the benefits are touched upon throughout this book. Perhaps the biggest advantage is that the participation techniques recognize that each person can make a meaningful contribution to the attainment of organizational objectives.

CREATIVITY AND GROUP DECISION MAKING

By far, the most advances that have been made in decision making over the past several years have been quantitative in nature. Only the participative behavioral techniques discussed so far have been available to managers, and there have been few scattered attempts to develop new techniques for helping make more creative and problem-solving types of decisions. Yet it is the latter decisions which are the major challenge facing modern management.

The Process of Creativity

A key challenge for organizations in the 1990s is to have more creativity and innovation. An example of a highly successful creative firm is Raychem Corporation, which on its twenty-fifth anniversary had developed over 200,000 products, more than 900 U.S. patents with some 300 pending, and 3,000 foreign patents with another 9,000 pending.[39] Unfortunately, such creative companies are still the exception rather than the rule.

Creative ideas from both individuals and groups are scarce. One of the problems may be that students educated in business schools know how to crunch numbers and develop models, but they have no knowledge of the creative process or how to develop creative solutions to problems. For example, General Foods held a competition in which student teams from prestigious business schools were given the charge to develop a new marketing plan that would stem the plunging sales of Sugar-Free Kool-Aid. Although they used models and the right terminology, they offered very few original ideas that the company could or would be able to use. The marketing manager concluded, "There were a couple of ideas that were of interest, but nothing we haven't looked at before."[40] A starting point for getting around this problem would be to understand the meaning and dimensions of creativity.

A simple, but generally recognized definition of *creativity* is that it involves combining responses or ideas of individuals or groups in novel ways.[41] The creative process is very complex. Creative solutions to even the simplest problems have wide variation. For instance, how would you respond to the problem of coming up with as many uses for a newspaper as possible? Compare your solution to the following proposed by a ten-year-old boy:

> You can read it, write on it, lay it down and paint a picture on it. . . . You could put it in your door for decoration, put it in the garbage can, put it on a chair if the chair is messy. If you have a puppy, you put newspaper in its box or put it in your backyard for the dog to play with. When you build something and you don't want anyone to see it, put newspaper around it. Put newspaper on the floor if you have no mattress, use it to pick up something hot, use it to stop bleeding, or to catch the drips from drying clothes. You can use a newspaper for curtains, put it in your shoe to cover what is hurting your foot, make a kite out of it, shade a light that is too bright. You can wrap fish in it, wipe windows, or wrap money in it. . . . You put washed shoes in newspaper, wipe eyeglasses with it, put it under a dripping sink, put a plant on it, make a paper bowl out of it, use it for a hat if it is raining, tie it on your feet for slippers. You can put it on the sand if you have no towel, use it for bases in baseball, make paper airplanes with it, use it as a dustpan when you sweep, ball it up for the cat to play with, wrap your hands in it if it is cold.[42]

Obviously, this boy describing the uses of a newspaper was very creative, but what caused his creativity?

Feldman points out that it is much easier to provide examples of creativity than it is to identify causes. However, he identifies two major dimensions that can help explain the creative process:

1. *Divergent thinking.* This refers to a person's ability to generate novel, but still appropriate, responses to questions or problems. This is in contrast to convergent thinking which leads to responses that are based mainly on knowledge and rational logic. In the newspaper problem, convergent thinking would answer, "You read it," but divergent thinking would say, "make a kite out of it." The latter—divergent thinking—is considered more creative.
2. *Cognitive Complexity.* This refers to a person's use of and preference for elaborate, intricate, and complex stimuli and thinking patterns. Creative people tend to have such cognitive complexity and display a wide range of interests, are independent, and are interested in philosophical or abstract problems. Importantly, however, creative people are not necessarily more intelligent (if intelligence is

defined by standard tests of intelligence or grades in school, which tend to focus more on convergent thinking skills).[43]

Group Decision Making

Creativity in decision making can apply to individuals or groups. Since individual decision making has largely given way to group decision making in today's organizations, an understanding of group dynamics as discussed in Chapter 12 becomes relevant to decision making. For example, that chapter's discussion of groupthink problems and phenomena such as the risky shift (that a group may make more risky decisions than the individual members would on their own) help one to better understand the complexity of group decision making. In fact, a number of social decision schemes have emerged from social psychology research in recent years.

These schemes or rules can predict the final outcome of group decision making based on the individual members' initial positions. Rathus has summarized these as follows:

1. *The majority-wins scheme.* In this commonly used scheme, the group arrives at the decision that was initially supported by the majority. This scheme appears to guide decision making most often when there is no objectively correct decision. An example would be a decision about what car model to build when the popularity of various models has not been tested in the "court" of public opinion.
2. *The truth-wins scheme.* In this scheme, as more information is provided and opinions are discussed, the group comes to recognize that one approach is objectively correct. For example, a group deciding whether to use SAT scores in admitting students to college would profit from information about whether these scores actually predict college success.
3. *The two-thirds majority scheme.* This scheme is frequently adopted by juries, who tend to convict defendants when two-thirds of the jury initially favors conviction.
4. *The first-shift rule.* In this scheme, the group tends to adopt the decision that reflects the first shift in opinion expressed by any group member. If a car-manufacturing group is equally divided on whether or not to produce a convertible, it may opt to do so after one group member initially opposed to the idea changes her mind. If a jury is deadlocked, the members may eventually follow the lead of the first juror to change his position.[44]

Besides the above schemes, there are also other phenomena such as the status quo tendency (when individuals or groups are faced with decisions, they resist change and will tend to stick with existing goals or plans) which affect group decision making. Suggestions such as the following can be used to help reduce and combat the status quo tendency and thus make more effective group decisions:

- When things are going well, decision makers should still be vigilant in examining alternatives.
- It can help to have separate groups monitor the environment, develop new technologies, and generate new ideas.
- To reduce the tendency to neglect gathering negative long-term information, managers should solicit worst-case scenarios as well as forecasts that include long-term costs.

- Build checkpoints and limits into any plan.
- When limits are reached, it may be necessary to have an outside, independent, or separate review of the current plan.
- Judge people on the way they make decisions and not only on outcomes, especially when the outcomes may not be under their control.
- Shifting emphasis to the quality of the decision process should reduce the need of the decision maker to appear consistent or successful when things are not going well.
- Organizations can establish goals, incentives, and support systems that encourage experimenting and taking risks.[45]

In addition to simple guidelines such as the above, group decision techniques such as Delphi and nominal grouping can also be used to help eliminate the dysfunctions of groups and help them make more effective decisions.

The Delphi Technique

Although Delphi was first developed by N. C. Dalkey and his associates in 1950 at the Rand Corporation's Think Tank, it has only recently become popularized as a group decision-making technique, for example, for long-range forecasting. Today, numerous organizations in business, education, government, health, and the military are using Delphi. No decision technique will ever by able to predict the future completely, but the Delphi technique seems to be as good a crystal ball as is currently available.

The technique, named after the oracle at Delphi in ancient Greece, has many variations, but generally it works as follows:

1. A group (usually of experts, but in some cases nonexperts may be deliberately used) is formed, but, importantly, the members are not in face-to-face interaction with one another. Thus, the expenses of bringing a group together are eliminated.
2. Each member is asked to make anonymous predictions or input into the problem decision the panel is charged with.
3. Each panel member then receives composite feedback from what the others have inputted. In some variations the reasons are listed (anonymously), but mostly just a composite figure is used.
4. On the basis of the feedback, another round of anonymous inputs is made. These iterations take place for a predetermined number of times or until the composite feedback remains the same, which means everyone is sticking with his or her position.

A major key to the success of the technique lies in its anonymity. Keeping the responses of panel members anonymous eliminates the problem of "saving face" and encourages the panel experts to be more flexible and thus to benefit from the estimates of others. In the traditional interacting group decision-making technique, the experts may be more concerned with defending their vested positions than they are with making a good decision.

Many organizations testify to the success they have had so far with the Delphi technique. McDonnell Douglas Aircraft uses the technique to forecast the future uncertainties of commercial air transportation. Weyerhaeuser, a building supply company, uses it to predict what will happen in the construction business, and Smith, Kline, and French, a drug manufacturer, uses it to study the uncertainties of medicine. TRW, a highly diversified, technically oriented company, has fourteen Delphi panels averaging seventeen members each. The panels suggest products and services which have marketing potential and predict technological developments and significant political, economic, social, and cultural events. Besides business applications, the technique has been used successfully on various problems in government, education, health, and the military. In other words, Delphi can be applied to a wide variety of program planning and decision problems in any type of organization.

The major criticisms of the Delphi technique center on its time consumption, cost, and Ouija-board effect. The third criticism implies that, much like the parlor game of that name, Delphi can claim no scientific basis or support. To counter this criticism, Rand has attempted to validate Delphi through controlled experimentation. The corporation set up panels of nonexperts who use the Delphi technique to answer questions such as, "How many popular votes were cast for Lincoln when he first ran for President?" and "What was the average price a farmer received for a bushel of apples in 1940?" These particular questions were used because the average person does not know the exact answers but knows something about the subjects. The result of these studies showed that the original estimates by the panel of nonexperts were reasonably close to being correct, but with the Delphi technique of anonymous feedback, the estimates greatly improved.

The Nominal Group Technique

Closely related to Delphi is the nominal group approach to group decision making. The nominal group has been used by social psychologists in their research for almost three decades. A nominal group is simply a "paper group." It is a group in name only because no verbal exchange is allowed between members. In group dynamics research, social psychologists would pit a fully interacting group against a nominal group (a group of individuals added together on paper but not verbally interacting). In terms of number of ideas, uniqueness of ideas, and quality of ideas, research has found nominal groups to be superior to real groups. The general conclusion is that interacting groups inhibit creativity. This, of course, applies only to idea generation because the interactive effect of group members is known to have a significant effect on other variables. The latter type of effect was given attention in Chapter 12, on group dynamics.

When the nominal group approach is used as a specific technique for decision making in organizations, it is labeled the *nominal group technique* (NGT) and consists of the following steps:

1. Silent generation of ideas in writing
2. Round-robin feedback from group members, who record each idea in a terse phrase on a flip chart or blackboard
3. Discussion of each recorded idea for clarification and evaluation
4. Individual voting on priority ideas, with the group decision being mathematically derived through rank ordering or rating[46]

The difference between this approach and Delphi is that the NGT members are usually acquainted with one another, have face-to-face contact, and communicate with one another directly in the third step. Although more research is needed, there is some evidence that NGT-led groups come up with many more ideas than traditional interacting groups and may do as well as, or slightly better than, groups using Delphi.[47] A study also found that NGT-led groups performed at a level of accuracy that was equivalent to that of the most proficient member.[48] However, another study found that NGT-led groups did not perform as well as interacting groups whose participants were pervasively aware of the problem given the group and when there were no dominant persons who inhibited others from communicating ideas.[49] Thus, as is true of most of the techniques discussed in this book, there are moderating effects. A review of the existing research literature on Delphi and NGT concluded:

> In general, the research on both Delphi and nominal group techniques suggests that they can help improve the quality of group decisions because they mitigate the problems of interacting groups—individual dominance and groupthink. A skillful chairperson, therefore, may adapt these techniques to particular decision-making situations.[50]

Summary

This chapter has been devoted to the process of decision making. *Decision making* is defined as choosing between two or more alternatives. However, viewed as a process, the actual choice activity is preceded by gathering information and developing alternatives. The models of behavioral decision making include the completely rational econologic model on one extreme, Herbert Simon's bounded rationality model and the judgmental heuristics and biases model in the middle range, and the irrationally based social model on the other extreme. Each of these models give insights into decision-making rationality, but the judgmental model from cognitive psychology has recently emerged as having the biggest impact on decision-making theory and practice.

The techniques for decision making have been dominated mainly by quantitative models. The behavioral techniques do not begin to approach the sophistication of the quantitative techniques. Yet it is the creative, problem-solving management decisions which are crucial for organizational success. Understanding of the traditional (Scanlon Plan and suggestion plans or boxes) and modern (decision making at the worker level, team/self-managed groups, and quality circles) participative techniques and the creative and group decision-making process and techniques (Delphi and nominal grouping) can lead to more effective decision making for the future.

Questions for Discussion and Review

1. What are the three steps in Simon's decision-making process? Relate these steps to an actual decision.

2. Compare and contrast the econologic model and the social model.
3. Describe the major characteristics of Simon's bounded rationality model. Do you think this model is descriptive of practicing executives?
4. Identify the three major judgmental biases. How do they differ from one another? Give an example of each in management decision making.
5. What are the traditional and modern participation techniques? If you were in charge of the production department at a manufacturing plant, which technique or techniques would you implement and why?
6. What is the difference between divergent and convergent thinking and what is their relationship to the process of creativity?
7. Explain a hypothetical situation in which Delphi and/or NGT could be used.

References

1. Chester I. Barnard, *The Functions of the Executive*, Harvard University Press, Cambridge, Mass., 1938, p. 14.
2. Herbert A. Simon, *The New Science of Management Decision*, Harper, New York, 1960, p. 2.
3. Henry Mintzberg, Duru Raisin-ghani, and André Theoret, "The Structure of 'Unstructured' Decision Processes," *Administrative Science Quarterly*, June 1976, pp. 246–275.
4. Richard L. Daft, *Organization Theory and Design*, West, St. Paul, Minn., 1983, pp. 357–358.
5. See Max H. Bazerman, *Managerial Decision Making*, 2d ed., Wiley, New York, 1990.
6. See James L. Bowditch and Anthony F. Buono, *A Primer on Organizational Behavior*, 2d ed., Wiley, New York, 1990, p. 99.
7. Herbert A. Simon, *Administrative Behavior*, 2d ed., Macmillan, New York, 1957, p. 64.
8. Ibid., pp. 76–77.
9. Ibid., p. xxiii.
10. Thomas J. Peters and Robert H. Waterman, Jr., *In Search of Excellence: Lessons from America's Best-Run Companies*, Harper & Row, New York, 1982, p. 29.
11. Solomon E. Asch, "Opinions and Social Pressure," *Scientific American*, November 1955, pp. 31–35.
12. Fred Luthans and Robert Koester, "The Impact of Computer-Generated Information on the Choice Activity of Decision Makers," *Academy of Management Journal*, June 1976, pp. 328–332; and Robert Koester and Fred Luthans, "The Impact of

the Computer on the Choice Activity of Decision Makers: A Replication with Actual Users of Computerized MIS," *Academy of Management Journal*, June 1979, pp. 416–422.
13. Simon, *Administrative Behavior*, pp. xxv–xxvi.
14. E. Frank Harrison, *The Managerial Decision-Making Process*, Houghton Mifflin, Boston, 1975, p. 69.
15. The analysis of the judgmental heuristics model largely comes from Bazerman, op. cit.
16. For example, see: D. Kahneman and A. Tversky, "Subjective Probability: A Judgment of Representativeness," *Cognitive Psychology*, vol. 3, 1972, pp. 430–454; D. Kahneman and A. Tversky, "On the Psychology of Prediction," *Psychological Review*, vol. 80, 1973, pp. 237–251; D. Kahneman and A. Tversky, "Prospect Theory: An Analysis of Decision Under Risk," *Econometrica*, vol. 47, 1979, pp. 263–291; A. Tversky and K. Kahneman, "Availability: A Heuristic for Judging Frequency and Probability," *Cognitive Psychology*, vol. 5, 1973, pp. 207–232; and A. Tversky and D. Kahneman, "Judgment Under Uncertainty: Heuristics and Biases," *Science*, vol. 185, 1974, pp. 1124–1131.
17. See: Gregory B. Northcraft and Margaret A. Neale, *Organizational Behavior*, Dryden, Chicago, 1990, p. 184.
18. Tversky and Kahneman, "Availability: A Heuristic," op. cit.; and Tversky and Kahneman, "Judgment Under Uncertainty," op. cit.
19. Bazerman, op. cit., p. 7.

20. Northcraft and Neale, op. cit., p. 185.
21. Kahneman and Tversky, "On the Psychology of Prediction," op. cit.
22. Bazerman, op. cit., p. 7.
23. Northcraft and Neale, op. cit., p. 187.
24. Bazerman, op. cit., p. 7.
25. Ibid., p. 28.
26. For example, see issues of the *Journal of Behavioral Decision Making* and the *Journal of Risk and Uncertainty,* as well as the standard journals such as *Organizational Behavior and Human Decision Processes.*
27. David L. Levine, "Participation, Productivity, and the Firm's Environment," *California Management Review,* Summer 1990, p. 86.
28. Barry A. Macy, Mark F. Peterson, and Larry W. Norton, "A Test of Participation Theory in a Work Re-design Field Setting: Degree of Participation and Comparison Site Contrasts," *Human Relations,* vol. 42, 1989, p. 1110.
29. J. Kenneth White, "The Scanlon Plan: Causes and Correlates of Success," *Academy of Management Journal,* June 1979, pp. 292–312.
30. "Worker Participation at A&P Stores Gives the Chain a Boost," *The Wall Street Journal,* Jan. 6, 1987, p. 1.
31. Labor Letter, *The Wall Street Journal,* Sept. 12, 1989, p. A1.
32. Brian Dumaine, "Who Needs a Boss?" *Fortune,* May 7, 1990, p. 52.
33. Eric Sundstrom, Kenneth P. DeMeuse, and David Futrell, "Work Teams," *American Psychologist,* February 1990, pp. 120–133.
34. Kevin J. Lewis, "HR Keeps Chevron Well Oiled," *Personnel,* January 1990, p. 18.
35. George Munchus, "Employer-Employee Based Quality Circles in Japan: Human Resource Policy Implications for American Firms," *Academy of Management Review,* April 1983, p. 255.
36. David M. Schweiger and Carrie R. Lena, "Participation in Decision Making," in Edwin A. Locke (ed.), *Generalizing from Laboratory to Field Settings,* Lexington Books, Lexington, Mass., 1986, p. 148.
37. Stewart Black and Newton Margulies, "An Ideological Perspective on Participation: A Case for Integration," *Journal of Organizational Change Management,* vol. 2, no. 1, 1989, pp. 13–34.
38. John L. Cotton, David A. Vollrath, Kirk L. Froggatt, Mark L. Lengnick-Hall, and Kenneth R. Jennings, "Employee Participation: Diverse Forms and Different Outcomes," *Academy of Management Review,* January 1988, pp. 8–22.
39. William Taylor, "The Business of Innovation," *Harvard Business Review,* March–April 1990, p. 97.
40. Trish Hall, "When Budding MBAs Try to Save Kool-Aid, Original Ideas Are Scarce," *The Wall Street Journal,* Nov. 25, 1986, p. 31.
41. M. D. Mumford and S. B. Gustafson, "Creativity Syndrome: Integration, Application, and Innovation," *Psychological Bulletin,* vol. 103, 1988, pp. 27–43.
42. This description is part of a study reported in W. C. Ward, N. Kogan, and E. Pankove, "Incentive Effects in Children's Creativity," *Child Development,* vol. 43, 1972, pp. 669–676 and is found in Robert S. Feldman, *Understanding Psychology,* 2d ed., McGraw-Hill, New York, 1990, p. 243.
43. Ibid., pp. 242–243.
44. Spencer A. Rathus, *Psychology,* 4th ed., Holt, Rinehart and Winston, Fort Worth, 1990, pp. 634–635.
45. William S. Silver and Terence R. Mitchell, "The Status Quo Tendency in Decision Making," *Organizational Dynamics,* Spring 1990, pp. 45–46.
46. Andre L. Delbecq, Andrew H. Van deVen, and David H. Gustafson, *Group Techniques for Program Planning,* Scott, Foresman, Glenview, Ill., 1975, p. 8.
47. A. H. Van deVen, *Group Decision-Making Effectiveness,* Kent State University Center for Business and Economic Research Press, Kent, Ohio, 1974.
48. John Rohrbaugh, "Improving the Quality of Group Judgment: Social Judgment Analysis and the Nominal Group Technique," *Organizational Behavior and Human Performance,* October 1981, pp. 272–288.
49. Thad B. Green, "An Empirical Analysis of Nominal and Interacting Groups," *Academy of Management Journal,* March 1975, pp. 63–73.
50. David R. Hampton, Charles E. Summer, and Ross A. Webber, *Organizational Behavior and the Practice of Management,* 5th ed., Scott, Foresman, Glenview, Ill., 1987, p. 274.

REAL CASE: GETTING ADDITIONAL INFORMA- TION

In recent years managers have begun to realize one important fact about decision making: the more information they can gather on a particular area or problem, the more likely it is that they can make a good decision. The result has been the mushrooming of the information processing business.

As early as the 1970s, many entrepreneurs with a close eye on what was needed in management decision making and control were forecasting an "information market" boom. They believed that both business firms and consumers would be willing to pay to have information provided to them. For example, General Motors might want to know the most recent articles or news releases on cars with front-wheel drive. One way to get this information would be to have someone in the public relations department cut and clip every piece of information found in all the newspapers and journals that the company purchased. An easier way, however, would be to subscribe to a news retrieval service that would provide all this same information for the asking. All subscribers have to do is use the computer to tell the retrieval service the types of information they want. The computer will then search its files and print out everything related to the topic areas requested by the customer.

Today, a number of firms are providing information services to clients. Examples are the following:

- Dow Jones News/Retrieval accumulates information collected by the company's news organization, divides it into categories such as financial data, stock prices, and international news, and sells each separately to subscribers.
- Reuters, the news agency, sells software that allows currency and commodities traders to spot opportunities based on their own strategies. The data used by the software are obtained from Reuters's database.
- The Institute for Scientific Information scans approximately 7000 scientific and medical journals and indexes them for 300,000 customers.
- Telerate sells financial information on such things as money market and foreign currency rates.

In addition to the examples above, a number of other new information services are springing up. One is that of Strategic Intelligence Systems (SIS) Inc., which has built databases on eighteen separate industries. These data include economic trends, product development, and other information useful for strategy formulation and implementation. By interviewing its clients and finding out the kinds of information they need, SIS helps client managers make better decisions. Another service is CompuServe Inc., which provides its subscribers everything from airline schedules to stock reports to electronic shopping services to games. As management finds itself needing more and more timely information for decision making, computerized information services are likely to become increasingly important.

1. When managers use the services to provide themselves with information, what phase of the decision-making process are they focusing on?
2. Of what value are information services to today's decision makers? Do these services allow the manager to make decisions along the line of the econological model?
3. Are we likely to see greater use of these information services in the future? Why or why not?

**Case:
Harry Smart
or Is He?**

Harry Smart, a very bright and ambitious young executive, was born and raised in Boston and graduated from a small New England college. He met his future wife, who was also from Boston, in college. They were married the day after they both graduated cum laude. Harry then went on to Harvard, where he received an MBA. He is now in his seventh year with Brand Corporation, which is located in Boston.

As part of an expansion program, the board of directors of Brand has decided to build a new branch plant. The president personally selected Harry to be the manager of the new plant and informed him that a job well done would guarantee him a vice presidency in the corporation. Harry was appointed chairperson, with final decision-making privileges, of an ad hoc committee to determine the location of the new plant. At the initial meeting, Harry explained the ideal requirements for the new plant. The members of the committee were experts in transportation, marketing, distribution, labor economics, and public relations. He gave them one month to come up with three choice locations for the new plant.

A month passed and the committee reconvened. After weighing all the variables, the experts recommended the following cities in order of preference: Kansas City, Los Angeles, and New York. Harry could easily see that the committee members had put a great deal of time and effort into their report and recommendations. A spokesperson for the group emphasized that there was a definite consensus Kansas City was the best location for the new plant. Harry thanked them for their fine job and told them he would like to study the report in more depth before he made his final decision.

After dinner that evening he asked his wife, "Honey, how would you like to move to Kansas City?" Her answer was quick and sharp, "Heavens, no!" she said. "I've lived in the East all my life, and I'm not about to move out into the hinterlands. I've heard the biggest attraction in Kansas City is the stockyards. That kind of life is not for me." Harry weakly protested, "But, honey, my committee strongly recommends Kansas City as the best location for my plant. Their second choice was Los Angeles and the third was New York. What am I going to do?" His wife thought a moment and then replied, "Well, I would consider moving to New York, but if you insist on Kansas City, you'll have to go by yourself!"

The next day Harry called his committee together and said, "You should all be commended for doing an excellent job on this report. However, after detailed study, I am convinced that New York will meet the needs of our new plant better than Kansas City or Los Angeles. Therefore, the decision will be to locate the new plant in New York. Thank you all once again for a job well done."

1. Did Harry make a rational decision?
2. What model of behavioral decision making does this incident support?
3. What decision techniques that were discussed in the chapter could be used by the committee to select the new plant site?

■ Keeping It Simple

Some organizations have found that as they get larger and more complex, there is a need for a new, innovative structure to hold things together. However, others have found that a classic design with a few modifications is all that is required for them to continue their successful operation. Roger Vergé, the world-famous French chef, is a good example of the latter. Vergé's restaurant, le Moulin de Mougins, is one of only nineteen in France and thirty in all of Europe that have been given the highest rating by the Michelin Guide. The price of a meal can be steep: $160 per person for dinner—assuming that the diners do not splurge on the wines—including an 18 percent government tax and a 15 percent service charge. Nevertheless, the restaurant is filled to capacity for both lunch and dinner sittings.

How does Vergé manage to keep the quality so high and the customers coming back? By organizing the operation so that everything is built around service. Vergé stays at the front entrance and greets his guests personally, while his main chef attends to the preparation of the food. Although Vergé, himself, is a world-renowned chef, he has found that in a well-organized restaurant there must be a chef overseeing the kitchen. Therefore, Vergé assumes the role of preparing the menu and creating new recipes, while the main chef sees that the food is cooked properly. Assisting this chef are twenty-five cooks, while outside in the dining room there are seventy-five waiters and other staff personnel to attend to the needs of the hundred and fifty guests. Since Vergé has only one sitting at lunch and one at dinner, the ratio of personnel to customers is around 2:3.

The chain of command is direct and personal. When Vergé wants something done, he communicates it face-to-face. Moreover, some of his people have been with him for so long that they can anticipate how he wants things handled. Result: The restaurant is able to maintain the most consistent and highest standards in the industry.

Vergé is now expanding his operations and opening two less expensive restaurants to cater to a broader market. He has also teamed up with two other world-famous chefs to manage the French restaurant at the Epcot Center in Florida's Walt Disney World, and has loaned his name to a new restaurant being developed in Tokyo. Throughout it all, however, Vergé realizes that effectively run restaurants can serve only a limited number of guests, and require a well-functioning organization structure simple in design and rapid in response. As a result, while many organizations are finding that matrix and free-form designs are important to their success, Vergé is sticking to the basics, content to run a small successful chain of high-quality restaurants and take home an annual salary of $500,000.

Learning Objectives

- **Define** the bureaucratic model.
- **Analyze** the dysfunctions of bureaucracy.
- **Discuss** the modifications of bureaucracy, including centralization/decentralization, flat/tall, departmentation, and staff dimensions.
- **Explain** the modern organization theories of open systems, information processing, contingency, and ecology.
- **Present** the modern project and matrix designs of organization.

In this chapter, the inductive conceptual framework moves to the extreme macro level of analysis for organizational behavior. This chapter is concerned with organization theory and design. Organization structure represents the skeletal framework for organizational behavior. As the discussion of the conceptual framework in Chapter 1 pointed out, the organization structure is the dominant environmental factor that interacts with the person and the behavior. This chapter presents the organization from the viewpoint of classical and modern theory and design. The bureaucratic model of organization dominates the classical approach. After presenting and discussing this model, the chapter gives an overview and analysis of some of the extensions and modifications represented by the concepts of centralization and decentralization, flat and tall structures, departmentation, and line and staff.

Although the classical approach is still much in evidence today, organizations are in the process of dramatic change. Traditional ways of structuring are no longer always relevant to the modern situation. New theories and structural designs are emerging to meet new demands of growth, complexity, and change. In general, the modern approach to organization assumes more complexity and is more comprehensive in nature. For example, one modern organization theorist has noted: "Organization structure is more than boxes on a chart; it is a pattern of interactions and coordination that links the technology, tasks, and human components of the organization to ensure that the organization accomplishes its purposes."[1] The chapter reflects this more comprehensive theoretical understanding of organizations and presents some specific, newer structural designs. After a brief look at the roots of modern organizational theory, the chapter discusses the systems, information processing, contingency and ecological theories of organization. This is followed by a description and an analysis of project and matrix designs.

THE BUREAUCRATIC MODEL

A logical starting point in the analysis of any theory is the ideal. Max Weber, one of the pioneers of modern sociology, presented what he thought was an ideal organization structure called a *bureaucracy*. His concern for the ideal was a natural extension of his interest in the development and change of Western society. He believed that rationalization is the most persistant cultural value of Western society. On an organizational level, the bureaucracy represented a completely rational form.

The Characteristics of Bureaucracy

Weber specified several characteristics of an ideal organization structure. The four major ones are the following:

1. *Specifications and division of labor.* Weber's bureaucracy contained "A specified sphere of competence. This involves (a) a sphere of obligations to perform functions which has been marked off as part of a systematic division of labor (b) The provision of the incumbent with the necessary authority . . . (c) That the necessary means of compulsion are clearly defined and their use is subject to definite conditions."[2] This statement implies that Weber recognized the importance of having the authority and power to carry out assigned duties. In addition, the bureaucrats must know the precise limits of their sphere of competence so as not to infringe upon that of others.

2. *Positions arranged in a hierarchy.* Weber stated: "The organization of offices follows the principle of hierarchy: that is, each lower office is under the control and supervision of a higher one."[3] This bureaucratic characteristic forces control over every member in the structure. Some organization theorists, such as Herbert Simon, have pointed out that hierarchy is the natural order of things. An example lies in the biological subsystems, such as the digestive and circulatory systems; these are composed of organs, the organs are composed of tissues, and the tissues are composed of cells. Each cell is in turn hierarchically organized into a nucleus, cell wall, and cytoplasm. The same is true of physical phenomena such as molecules, which are composed of electrons, neutrons, and protons.[4] In a manner analogous to the biological and physical structures, hierarchy is a basic characteristic of complex organization structures.

3. *A system of abstract rules.* Weber felt a need for "a continuous organization of official functions bound by rules."[5] A rational approach to organization requires a set of formal rules to ensure uniformity and coordination of effort. A well-understood system of regulations also provides the continuity and stability that Weber thought were so important. Rules persist, whereas personnel may frequently change. They may range from no smoking in certain areas to the need for board approval for multithousand-dollar capital expenditures.

4. *Impersonal relationship.* It was Weber's belief that the ideal official should be dominated by "a spirit of formalistic impersonality, without hatred or passion, and hence without affection or enthusiasm."[6] Once again, Weber was speaking from the viewpoint of ideal rationality and not of realistic implementation. He felt that in order for bureaucrats to make completely rational decisions, they must avoid emotional attachment to subordinates and clients/customers.

The four characteristics just described are not the only ones recognized and discussed by Weber. Another important aspect of the ideal bureaucracy is that employment is based on technical qualifications. The bureaucrat is protected against arbitrary dismissal, and promotions are made according to seniority and/or achievement. In total, it must be remembered that Weber's bureaucracy was intended to be an ideal construct: no real-world organization exactly follows the Weber model. The widely recognized modern organization theorist Peter M. Blau summarizes Weber's thinking as follows:

> Weber dealt with bureaucracy as what he termed an ideal type. This methodological concept does not represent an average of the attributes of all existing bureaucracies (or other social structures), but a pure type, derived by abstracting the most characteristic aspects of all known organizations. [7]

It has been pointed out that the classical, rational approach to structure is of value to managers of formal work organizations that have no conflict or whose subordinates have no power, [8] but, of course, this is the ideal, not reality. The ideal is only the starting point, not the end, of organizational analysis.

Bureaucratic Dysfunctions

With the exception of Weber, sociologists and philosophers have been very critical of bureaucracies. For example, Karl Marx believed that bureaucracies are used by the dominant capitalist class to control the other, lower social classes. According to Marx, bureaucracies are characterized by strict hierarchy and discipline, veneration of authority, incompetent officials, lack of initiative and imagination, fear of responsibility and a process of self- aggrandizement. [9] This interpretation of bureaucracy is basically a list of functions opposite to what Weber proposed. The Weber model can serve equally well in analyzing either the functional or the dysfunctional ramifications of classical organization structure.

The Dysfunctions of Specialization. The Weber bureaucratic model emphasizes that specialization serves efficiency. The model ignores, but can be used to point out, the dysfunctional qualities of specialization. Empirical investigation has uncovered both functional and dysfunctional consequences. In other words, specialization has been shown to lead to increased productivity and efficiency but also to create conflict between specialized units, to the detriment of the overall goals of the organization. For example, specialization may impede communication between units. The management team of a highly specialized unit has its own terminology and similar interests, attitudes, and personal goals. Because "outsiders are different," the specialized unit tends to withdraw into itself and not fully communicate with units above, below, or horizontal to it.

The Dysfunctions of Hierarchy. What was said of specialization also holds true for the other characteristics of a bureaucracy. The functional attributes of a hierarchy are that it maintains unity of command, coordinates activities and personnel, reinforces authority, and serves as a formal system of communication. In theory, the hierarchy has both a downward and an upward orientation, but in practice, it has often turned out to have only a downward emphasis. Thus, individual initiative and participation are often blocked, upward communication is impeded, and there is no formal recognition of horizontal communication. Personnel who follow only the formal hierarchy may waste a great deal of time and energy.

The Dysfunctions of Rules. Bureaucratic rules probably have the most obvious dysfunctional qualities. Contributing to the bureaucratic image of red tape, rules often become the ends for more effective goal attainment. The famous management consultant Peter Drucker cites the following common misuses of rules that require reports and procedures:

First is the mistaken belief that procedural rules are instruments of morality. They should not determine what is right or wrong conduct.

Second, procedural rules are sometimes mistakenly substituted for judgment. Bureaucrats should not be mesmerized by printed forms; forms should be used only in cases where judgment is not required.

The third and most common misuse of procedural rules is as a punitive control device from above. Bureaucrats are often required to comply with rules that have nothing to do with their jobs—for example, plant managers who have to accurately fill out numerous forms for staff personnel and corporate management which they cannot use in obtaining their own objectives.[10]

Drucker would like to see every procedural rule put on trial for its life at least every five years. He cites the case of an organization in which all reports and forms were totally done away with for two months. At the end of the suspension, three-fourths of the reports and forms were deemed unnecessary and were eliminated.[11]

Dysfunctions of the Impersonal Characteristics. The impersonal quality of the bureaucracy has even more dysfunctional consequences than specialization, hierarchy, and rules. Behaviorally oriented organization theorists and researchers have given a great deal of attention to the behavioral dysfunctions of bureaucratic structures. Much discussion in this book is critical of the impersonal characteristic of bureaucracies. The same is true of today's consumers and employees. Everyone has horror stories and everyday irritations dealing with impersonal bureaucracies.

The Modern View of Bureaucracies

The acknowledged bureaucratic dysfunctions have led most people to readily accept Parkinson's popular "laws" (for example, bureaucratic staffs increase in inverse proportion to the amount of work done[12]) and the popular "Peter principle" (managers rise to their level of incompetence in bureaucracies[13]). These "laws" and "principles" have received wide public acceptance because everyone has observed and experienced what Parkinson and Peter wrote about. But as one organizational scholar has noted:

These two writers have primarily capitalized on the frustrations toward government and business administration felt by the general public, which is not familiar with the processes necessitated by large-scale organization. Parkinson and Peter made a profit on their best sellers; they added little to the scientific study of organizations.[14]

In addition to the popularized criticisms of bureaucracy, a more academic analysis also uncovers many deficiencies. Bennis summarized some of them as follows:

1. Bureaucracy does not adequately allow for personal growth and the development of mature personalities.

2. It develops conformity and "groupthink."
3. It does not take into account the "informal organization" and the emergent and unanticipated problems.
4. Its systems of control and authority are hopelessly outdated.
5. It has no juridical process.
6. It does not possess adequate means for resolving differences and conflicts between ranks and, most particularly, between functional groups.
7. Communication and innovative ideas are thwarted or distorted as a result of hierarchical divisions.
8. The full human resources of bureaucracy are not being utilized because of mistrust, fear of reprisals, etc.
9. It cannot assimilate the influx of new technology or scientists entering the organization.
10. It modifies personality structure in such a way that the person in a bureaucracy becomes the dull, gray, conditioned "organization man."[15]

Parkinson, Peter, and Bennis represent the extreme critics of bureaucratic organization. Nevertheless, during the past few years popular writers, scholars, practitioners, and the general public have felt increasing dissatisfaction and frustration with classical bureaucratic structures. This is reflected in the consumerism movement, which is largely a grass-roots reaction to the impersonality of large bureaucracies, and the tremendous appeal of best-selling books such as *In Search of Excellence: Lessons from America's Best-Run Companies*[16] and *The One Minute Manager*,[17] whose basic theme is that organizations should be made more fluid and less bureaucratic and that it should be realized that there are effective alternatives to the rational model of organizations.

In Tom Peters's latest book, he colorfully describes how he would like managers to engage in bureaucracy bashing:

> Rant and rave. Tear up papers. Refuse to read them. Don't attend meetings. . . . Be outrageous. Get rid of all your file cabinets. . . . Put big cardboard boxes around your desk, and throw all the junk you receive into them—unread. Put a big red label on the boxes: "This week's unread paperwork."[18]

He recognizes that such drastic actions may jeopardize one's career, but feels that unless it is done, organizations depending on bureaucratic structuring—especially those which use vertical processing of information—will not be competitive or even, in the long run, survive.

Taken in perspective, the argument is not necessarily that the classical bureaucratic model is completely wrong but, rather, that the times have rendered many of those concepts and principles irrelevant. Bureaucratic organization is thought to be too inflexible to adapt readily to the dynamic nature and purpose of many of today's organizations and public needs. Flexibility and adaptability are necessary requirements for modern organization structures. The increasing size of organizations (as a result of both mergers and internal growth), computerization and the tremendous strides made in all types of technology, and the huge social and economic upheavals in recent years are but a few of the things which have contributed to a new organizational environment. There has even been a call for Mikhail Gorbachev's concept of perestroika (openness) be applied to restructuring American corporations.[19]

In the past decade, over half of the Fortune 500 firms went through major restructuring.[20] Much of this restructuring is the result of external forces—a slumping economy, foreign competition,[21] and merger and acquisition activity. The traditional bureaucratic organization structure has not been able to deal with these dramatic changes. Something else is needed. The rest of this chapter discusses this "something else" besides bureaucratic principles that can be and is being used to structure today's organizations.

MODIFICATIONS OF BUREAUCRATIC STRUCTURING

The classical bureaucratic model has served as a point of departure for modified vertical and horizontal structural arrangements in recent years. Vertical analysis concentrates on centralization versus decentralization and on flat versus tall structuring. These represent modifications of the classical principles of delegation of authority and limited span of control. Decentralization expands the principle of delegation to the point of an overall philosophy of organization and management. A *tall* organization structure means a series of narrow spans of control, and a *flat* structure incorporates wide spans. The bureaucratic principle of hierarchy is also closely related to the vertical concept.

Horizontal structural analysis is concerned with organizing one level of the hierarchy. The concepts of departmentation and of line and staff represent this approach. They are derived chiefly from the bureaucratic doctrine of specialization. Departmentation concentrates on organizing each level to attain optimum benefit from high degrees of specialization. The staff concept attempts to resolve the vertical and horizontal conflicts that appeared in the classical scheme. In general, the concepts discussed in the rest of this chapter carry the classical concepts one step further. They give greater weight to the human element and recognize that simple, mechanistic structural arrangements are not satisfactory for complex organizations.

Centralization and Decentralization

The terms *centralization* and *decentralization* are freely tossed about in the management and organization theory literature and in actual management and organization design. Most often, both the scholar and the practitioner neglect to define what they mean by the concept. There are three basic types of centralization and decentralization.

Types and Meaning. The first type is *geographic*, or *territorial*, concentration (centralization) or dispersion (decentralization) of operations. For example, the term *centralized* can be used to refer to an organization that has all its operations under one roof or in one geographic region. On the other hand, the dispersion of an organization's operations throughout the country or the world is a form of decentralization. This type of centralization-decentralization has become particularly relevant as organizations today begin to create international structures.[22] The word "geographic" is often not stated, which adds to the confusion.

The second type is *functional* centralization and decentralization. A good example is the personnel function of an organization. A separate personnel department that performs personnel functions for the other departments is said to be centralized. However, if the various functional departments (for example, marketing, production, and finance) handle their own personnel functions, then personnel is considered to be decentralized. Both *geographic* and *functional centralization* and *decentralization* are descriptive terms rather than analytical terms.

The third type is the only analytical use of the concept. This is where the terms *centralization* and *decentralization* refer to the retention or delegation of decision-making prerogatives or command. From an organization theory and analysis standpoint, this third type is the most relevant use of the concepts of centralization and decentralization. They are relative concepts because every organization structure contains both features, and the concepts differ only in degree.

Contrary to common belief, it is not possible to determine whether an organization is centralized or decentralized merely by looking at the organization chart. The determining factor is how much of the decision making is retained at the top and how much is delegated to the lower levels. This amount of retention or delegation is not reflected on the organization chart.

Optimum Degree of Decentralization. Traditionally, the implication has been that decentralization is somehow better than centralization. In truth, neither concept is an ideal or intrinsically good or bad. Generally speaking, decentralization is much more compatible with the behavioral aspects of management. This relevancy is due in part to the lower-level participation in decision making and empowerment of employees that results from decentralization. Increased motivation is an extremely important by-product. Besides the behavioral benefits, more effective decisions are possible because of the speed and firsthand knowledge that decentralization provides. Decentralization also affords invaluable experience in decision making for lower-level executives. Finally, it allows more time for top management to concentrate on policymaking and creative innovation.

Many organizations are still experiencing success in moving from centralization to decentralization. For example, under the leadership of General W. L. (Bill) Creech, the Tactical Air Command (TAC) moved from a highly centralized to a highly decentralized structure. By making subunits more autonomous and creating pride of ownership, he was able to turn the Air Force's worst command into its best.[23] As a result of his success the Pentagon now gives commanders new authority to abolish regulations, streamline procedures, and do whatever is necessary to get the job done.

In business, Johnson & Johnson, the highly successful and largest U.S. pharmaceutical firm, has 165 units worldwide. Each has considerable autonomy. Although corporate headquarters in New Jersey sets overall corporate policies on financial and certain administrative matters, the unit presidents, many in their late thirties and early forties, have full responsibility for their unit's research and development, manufacturing, marketing, and sales. For example, Johnson & Johnson sent thirty-eight-year-old Carl Spalding to head up its consumer products unit in South Africa. He not only independently ran the business but also had to hire, train, and promote black employees, even build housing for them, often in violation of local apartheid laws.[24] This is decentralization in action.

It is fair to say that, overall, decentralization has supported, and in some cases has stimulated, the behavioral approach to management. At the same time, there is little doubt that a wide discrepancy exists between the theory of decentralization and its practice. Yet, because of its wide acceptance, decentralization has had a definite impact on developing a managerial attitude favoring the implementation of behavioral concepts in organizations. However, it is now recognized that a third dimension such as cooperation may also be structurally needed, in addition to centralization and decentralization. Teamwork or cooperation may even be added to create a triangular design so that the organization becomes a function of three variables—autonomy (decentralization), control (centralization), and cooperation (teamwork).[25]

Flat and Tall Structures

In organizational analysis, the terms *flat* and *tall* are used to describe the total pattern of spans of control and levels of management. Whereas the classical principle of span of control is concerned with the number of subordinates one superior can effectively manage, the concept of flat and tall is more concerned with the vertical structural arrangements for the entire organization. The nature and scope are analogous to the relationship between delegation and decentralization. In other words, span of control is to flat and tall structures as delegation is to decentralization.

The tall structure has very small or narrow spans of control whereas the flat structure has large or wide spans. In tall structures, the small number of subordinates assigned to each superior allows for tight controls and strict discipline. Classical bureaucratic structures are typically very tall.

Advantages and Disadvantages.   Tall structures assume a role in assessing the value of flat structures similar to that of centralization in assessing the relative merits of decentralization. Tall structures are often negatively viewed in modern organizational analysis. More accurately, there are advantages and disadvantages to both flat and tall structures. Furthermore, flat and tall are only relative concepts; there are no ideal absolutes.

Both flat and tall structures could have the same number of personnel. However, the tall structure could have four levels of management, and the flat one only two levels. The tall structure has the definite advantage of facilitating closer control over subordinates. Notice that the term *closer* and not *better* control was used. The classicists, of course, equated *closer* with *better;* the more behaviorally oriented theorists do not. The very nature of flat structures implies that superiors cannot possibly keep close control over many subordinates. Therefore, they are almost forced to delegate a certain amount of the work. Thus, wide spans structurally encourage decentralization. The behavioral theorists would say that this opens up the opportunities for individual initiative and self-control.

Behavioral Implications of Flat versus Tall Structures. One behavioral implication that is often overlooked in analyzing flat versus tall structures is the opportunity that tall structures offer for more personal contact between superiors and subordinates. This contact is generally assumed to be negative and conflicting, but it need not be. In a tall structure, the superior may create a positive rapport with his or her subordinates that may not be possible in a flat structure.

Another consideration besides personal contact is the levels of communication in the two structures. In the flat structure there are few levels, which means that both downward and upward communication are simplified. There should be less distortion and inaccuracy. The red tape and endless communication channels associated with a bureaucratic tall structure are not present in a flat structure. On the other hand, the increased equality that exists between subordinates in a flat structure may lead to communication problems. If no status or authority differentials are structurally created, a heavy burden is placed upon horizontal communications. As Chapter 16 brought out, the horizontal communication system is notably deficient in most organizations. The problem may be compounded in flat organizations, where more dependence is placed on this type of communication, but it is not structurally facilitated. Also, coordination may be seriously impaired by a flat structure for the same reason.

Overall, the flat structure, at least from a behavioral standpoint, is generally preferable to the tall structure. It can take advantage of the positive attributes of decentralization and personal satisfaction and growth. Although managers who have wide spans will have to give a great deal of attention to selecting and training subordinates, a flat structure has the advantage of providing a wealth of experience in decision making.

Together with these advantages, however, it must be remembered that flat structures only encourage decentralization and individual responsibility and initiative. The supervisor of a small span does not always keep close control and may occasionally decentralize, and the supervisor of a large span does not always create an atmosphere of self-control and decentralization. The degree of centralization or its reverse depends on the overall management and organization philosophy and policies and on individual leadership style and personality. All a flat or a tall arrangement does is structurally promote, not determine, centralization or decentralization and the approach taken toward the behavioral aspects of managing.

Departmentation

Departmentation is concerned with horizontal organization on any one level of the hierarchy, and it is closely related to the classical bureaucratic principle of specialization. There are several types of departmentation. Traditionally, purpose, process, persons or things, and place were the recognized bases for departmentation.[26] In more recent terminology, *product* is substituted for *purpose*, *functional* has replaced *process*, and *territorial* or *geographic* is used instead of *place*. In addition, time, service, customer, equipment, and alphanumeric have also become recognized types of departmentation. Each of these latter types of departmentation is fairly self-explanatory. Examples of each are as follows:

1. *Time* may be divided into first shift, second shift, and third shift.
2. *Service* may reflect first class, second class, and tourist class on a passenger ship.
3. *Customer organization* may exist in a large commercial loan department that lends to farmers, small businesses, and large industries.
4. *Equipment* may be broken down in a production unit into drill-press, punch-press, and polishing departments.
5. *Alphanumeric* departmentation may be utilized in telephone servicing where numbers 0000 to 5000 are placed in one department and numbers 5001 to 9999 are placed in another.

Because organizations of any size will contain more than one hierarchical level, there will always be different types of departmentation represented. A typical large industrial corporation may be territorially organized on the first major horizontal level, and each succeeding level may be organized by product, function, time, and equipment. Confusion is often created when a given organization is identified as having one type of departmentation; for example, General Motors has traditionally been known as a product-departmentalized structure. The confusion can be cleared up it if is remembered that an organization is identified as having one particular type of departmentation because at the primary level (that is, the first major organization breakdown) it is organized and identified in this way. General Motors has been known as a product-departmentalized company because the primary level was organized into automotive and nonautomotive product divisions. However, it must be noted that many other types of departmentation are found in the lower levels of GM or any other organization that is designated by only one particular type of departmentation.

Functional Departmentation. By far the most widely used and recognized type of departmentation is functional in nature and may be found in all types of organization. For example, in a manufacturing organization the major functions usually are production, marketing, and finance—the vital functions that enable a manufacturing concern to operate and survive. On the other hand, in a railroad organization the major functions may be operations, traffic, and finance, and in a general hospital they may be medical service, housekeeping, dietetics, and business. Although the titles are different, the railroad and hospital functions are nevertheless analogous to the manufacturing functions in terms of importance and purpose. The titles of various functional departments may differ among industries and even in organizations within the same industry. All businesses, hospitals, universities, government agencies, and religious organizations, as well as the military, contain vital functions and can be functionally departmentalized.

The greatest single advantage of functional departmentation is that it incorporates the positive aspects of specialization. Theoretically, functionalism should lead to the greatest efficiency and the most economical utilization of employees. In practice, however, certain dysfunctions that were discussed with regard to specialization may also negate the advantages of functional departmentation. For example, functional empires may be created that conflict to the point of detracting from overall goal attainment.

A typical case is that of the salesperson who is guided by the sales department goal of maximizing the number of units sold. In order to sell 2000 units to a customer, this salesperson may have to promise delivery by the end of the week and require no money down. The production department, on the other hand, has a goal of keeping costs as low as possible and therefore does not carry a very large inventory. It cannot possibly supply the customer with 2000 units by the end of the week. Finance has still another goal. It must keep bad-debt expense at a minimum and therefore must require substantial down payments and thorough credit checks on every customer. In this situation, the sales department is in conflict with production and finance. If the salesperson goes ahead and makes the sale under the conditions in the example, the customer may not receive the order on time, and if and when it is received, the customer may not be able to pay the bill. In either outcome, the company goals of customer goodwill and minimization of bad-debt expense will suffer because of the salesperson's action.

It is easy to place the blame in the above example on the individual salesperson or on the lack of management coordination and communication. They are both definitely contributing factors. However, an equal, if not overriding, difficulty is the subgoal loyalties that are fostered by functionalization. A true story told by Peter Drucker provides an example of this mentality:

> A railroad company reported a $20,000 per year cost item for broken glass doors in their passenger stations. Upon investigation it was found that a young accountant had "saved" the company $200 by limiting each station to one key for the rest room. Naturally, the key was always lost and the replacement cost only 20 cents. The catch, however, was that the key cost was set up by financial control to be a capital expenditure which required approval from the home office. This home office approval accompanied by the appropriate paperwork took months to accomplish. On the other hand, emergency repairs could be paid immediately out of the station's cash account. What bigger emergency than not being able to get into the bathroom? Each station had an axe and the result was $20,000 for broken bathroom glass doors.[27]

The presentation of such examples does not imply that conflict is always bad for the organization. In fact, as Chapter 13 pointed out, many modern organization theorists think that conflict has a good effect on the organization that, in fact, outweighs the bad. Yet, as in the cases cited above, where functionalization creates conflict that hinders overall goal attainment, conflict is detrimental.

Product Departmentation. At the primary level, many organizations have chosen to organize along product or unit rather than along functional lines. The product form of departmentation is particularly adaptable to the tremendously large and complex modern organizations. It goes hand in hand with profit-centered decentralization. It allows the giant corporations, such as General Motors, General Electric, and Du Pont, to be broken down into groups of self-contained, smaller product organizations. Thus, the advantages of both large and small size can occur in one large organization. As companies such as Kodak, described in the accompanying Application Example, begin to diversify their product lines, product departmentation will take on even more importance.

Product Diversification Forces Restructuring at Kodak

Executives at Kodak used to point out that few firms could achieve the high profit margins that their company received from its photography business. In fact, photography was just about the only business that Kodak was in. Today, all of this has changed. The photo industry has become very competitive, costs have risen, and profits have plummeted for many firms. In responding to these developments, Kodak has now become a multiproduct firm with a host of autonomous units in its organization structure.

In an effort to expand quickly, Kodak has begun acquiring firms. For example, it recently purchased Texas-based Fox Photo for $96 million, now making it the nation's largest wholesale photofinisher. At the same time, Kodak is introducing a host of new products into the marketplace, including printers, optical memory systems, a medical imaging device, and a 35-millimeter "point-and-shoot" camera. The company is also slashing its work force by 13,000 people, thereby reducing its overhead. The old days of being a single-product company are gone. Kodak is now positioned to be a multi-product line firm that is better able to respond to its external environment. These developments at Kodak have required considerable restructuring of its organization. Only time will tell if this will pay off.

The classical principle of specialization was earlier said to be the greatest benefit derived from functional departmentation. Although often ignored, specialization can also be applied to product departmentation. This was brought out as follows: "The executive who heads a battery manufacturing department generally knows more about production than other functional executives, but he also knows more about batteries than other production executives."[28] However, a greater advantage of organization on a product basis is the matter of control. Because of their self-contained nature, product departments are very adaptable to accounting-control techniques and management appraisal. Product department performance, measured according to several different criteria, can usually be objectively determined. Another advantage is that product departments can be readily added or dropped with a minimum of disruption to the rest of the organization.

As a structural form, product departmentation is very compatible with the behavioral approach. Many of the conflicts that exist in the upper level under functional departmentation are generally resolved by product departmentation. Under product organization, however, the functional conflicts may disappear at the upper levels but reappear in the lower levels that are functionalized. Yet, from the standpoint of overall organizational goals, functional conflict at lower levels may be preferable. Besides reducing the potential for conflict, product division can provide many of the same behavioral advantages offered by decentralization and flat structures. These include more opportunity for personal development, growth, and self-control. Once again, this is not a universal truth, because the advantages still depend on many other personal and organizational variables. All in all, however, product or unit organization, because of its self-contained characteristics, is potentially more structurally adaptable to the behavioral aspects of organization than functional departmentation is.

The Staff Concept of Organization

Staff organization goes way back in history. The military is given credit for its development. As early as the seventeenth century, Gustavus Adolphus of Sweden used a military general staff. The Prussians, with some influence from the French, refined the theory and practice of this concept. At the beginning of the twentieth century, the European version of military staff was installed in the U.S. armed forces. However, it was not until after the Great Depression that the staff concept was widely adapted to American business and industry.

Staff is not a clear-cut organizational concept. It often creates confusion and problems for the organization. Many of the problems stem from conflicting definitions regarding line and staff and the hybrid forms of staff used by many organizations. The military has escaped some of these problems because it has precisely defined and successfully implemented a pure staff system. Under the "pure" military approach, line carries command or decision-making responsibilities, whereas staff gives advice.

Almost every type of modern American organization has attempted to adopt to some degree the military staff concept. In contrast to the military, however, business, hospital, educational, and government organizations have not given proper attention to defining operationally the difference between line and staff. In the military, there definitely exists an informal, implied staff authority, but everyone understands the system and realizes that conflicts can be resolved by reverting to pure line-staff relationships. Unfortunately, this is generally not the case in other types of organizations. What usually develops is a lack of understanding of the line-staff roles and relationships, which often results in a breakdown of communication and open conflict. A typical example is the business corporation which has a myriad of line-staff roles and relationships. It is not unusual to find many lower and middle managers who do not really know whether and when they are line or staff. One reason is that they generally wear more than one hat. Normally, managers are line within their own departments and become line or staff when dealing with outside departments. The manager's functional authority is often not spelled out in the policies of the organization. As a result, personal conflicts and dual-authority situations are rampant. Chapter 13 gave specific attention to the problems of role ambiguity and conflict that can result from such line-staff relationships.

Although these weaknesses exist in a hybrid staff concept, benefits have also been derived. The larger, more technologically complex organizations depended a great deal on staff specialization during the 1960s and 1970s. However, there is evidence that in recent years many of these companies have gone "overboard" by adding too many staff personnel. This "staff proliferation" exists especially at corporate levels, and some management analysts feel that it has been a major reason for the problems many companies have had in recent years. For example, there is recent research evidence that indicates that staff personnel may have less job commitment than do their line counterparts.[29]

Peters and Waterman noted that their "excellently managed" companies had comparatively few corporate staff personnel. For example, Emerson Electric has 54,000 employees, but fewer than 100 in its corporate headquarters; Dana has 35,000 employees, but decreased its corporate staff from about 500 in 1970 to around 100 today; and Schlumberger, a $6 billion diversified oil service company, runs its worldwide empire with a corporate staff of 90.[30] Because of the success of these companies with small staffs and the need to cut back on personnel costs as a result of the poor economy, all companies today are taking a hard look at their need for corporate staff personnel, and many are drastically reducing them.[31] They are beginning to look at more radical alternatives, rather than just modifications of classical structures. The next section presents these alternative ways of theorizing and of structuring organizations.

THE ROOTS OF MODERN ORGANIZATION THEORY

There are some recent arguments that Weber's view of the classical bureaucratic model was mistranslated and that he really did not intend for it to be an ideal type of structure. Instead, he was merely using bureaucracy was an example of the structural form taken by the political strategy of rational-legal domination.[32] In other words, some of the original theories of classical structure may contain underpinnings for modern organization theory.

The real break with classical thinking on organizational structure is generally recognized to be the work of Chester Barnard. In his significant book, *The Functions of the Executive*, he defined a *formal organization* as a system of consciously coordinated activities of two or more persons.[33] It is interesting to note that in this often cited definition, the words "system" and "persons" are given major emphasis. People, not boxes on an organization chart, make up a formal organization. Barnard was critical of the existing classical organization theory because it was too descriptive and superficial.[34] He was especially dissatisfied with the classical bureaucratic view that authority should come from the top down. Barnard, utilizing a more analytical approach, took an opposite viewpoint. As Chapter 15 pointed out, he maintained that authority really came from the bottom up.

Besides authority, Barnard stressed the cooperative aspects of organizations. This concern reflects the importance that he attached to the human element in organization structure and analysis. It was Barnard's contention that the existence of a cooperative system is contingent upon the human participants' ability to communicate and their willingness to serve and strive toward a common purpose.[35] Under such a premise, the human being plays the most important role in the creation and perpetuation of formal organizations.

From this auspicious beginning, modern organization theory has evolved in four major directions. The first major development in organization theory was to view the organization as a system made up of interacting parts. Especially the open-systems concept, which stresses the input of the external environment, has had a tremendous impact on modern organization theory. This was followed by an analysis of organizations in terms of their ability to process information in order to reduce the uncertainty in managerial decision making. The next development in organization theory has been the contingency approach. The premise of the contingency approach is that there is no single best way to organize. The organizational design must be fitted to the existing environmental conditions. The cultural environment even plays a role in organization structure. The accompanying International Application Example humorously depicts this cultural impact in its hypothetical structures

International Application Example

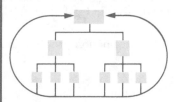

Executive Epigrams by Country

An epigram typically is a poem or line of verse that is witty and/or satirical. Some international business managers have taken this idea one step further and created what today are called executive epigrams. These are charts that humorously depict the organization structure by country in which they operate. The following figure shows some of them along with the logic behind the specific structure.

In the United States everyone in the organization is convinced that he or she has a direct pipeline to the top person.

American

Italian organization have terrible lateral communication.

Italian

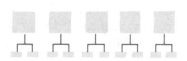

In Albania the second in command is typically bypassed by the boss who goes further down the line in his direct communications.

Albanian

Arab countries have no communication between the personnel.

Arabian

British organizations have excellent lateral communication but very little upward communication

British

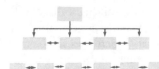

In Ireland, the bosses report to the workers — or so it seems.

Irish

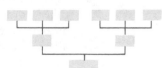

Norwegian

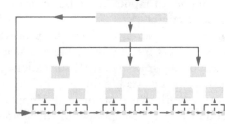

In Norway, no one in the hierarchy tells the lower-line workers anything. Their information is provided by subordinates who represent them on the board of directors.

by country. The newest theoretical approach is a natural selection—or ecological—view of organizations. This organizational ecology theory challenges the contingency approach. While the contingency approach suggests that organizations change through internal transformation and adaptation, the ecological approach says that it is more a process of the "fittest survive"; there is a process of organizational selection and replacement.[36] All of these modern theories serve as the foundation for the actual design of practicing organizations, which is covered at the end of this chapter.

The Organization as an Open System

Both the closed- and open-systems approaches are utilized in modern organization theory and practice. However, in today's dramatically changing environment an open-systems approach is becoming much more relevant and meaningful. The key for viewing organizations as open systems is the recognition of the external environment as a source of significant input. In systems terminology, the boundaries of the organization are permeable to the external environment (social, legal, technical, economic, and political).

The simplest open system consists of an input, a transformation process, and an output. This is depicted thus:

$$\text{Input} \rightarrow \text{Transformation process} \rightarrow \text{Output}$$

A system cannot survive without continuous input, the transformation process, and output.

There are many types of inputs, transformation processes, and outputs. For example, one kind of input actually enters the open system in the "closed" sense. In other words, this type of input has a direct effect on the internal system rather than an outside effect—in systems jargon, it loads the system. Another type of input affects the system in an "open" sense. Generally, this input would consist of the entire environmental influence on the system. Still another kind of input takes the form of replacement or recycling. When a component of the system is ejected or leaves, the replacement becomes an input. This recycling process perpetuates the system. Specific examples of inputs into a business organization include monetary, material, and human resources.

At the heart of the open system are the processes, operations, or channels which transform the inputs into outputs. Here is where the internal organization design plays an important role. The transformation process consists of a logical network of subsystems, which lead to the output. The subsystems are translated into a complex systems network that transforms the inputs into the desired outputs.

The third and final major component of any simple open system is the output. This is represented by the product, result, outcome, or accomplishment of the system. Specific examples of the outputs of a business organization system that correspond to the inputs of monetary, material, and human resources are profit or loss, product sales, and role behaviors.

The simple open-systems concept has universal applicability. Any biological, human, social, economic, or technical phenomenon can be conceptualized in open-systems terms. As has been shown, an economic institution receives inputs of people, raw materials, money, laws, and values. The system then transforms these inputs via complex organizational subsystems into outputs, such as products, services, taxes, dividends, and pollution. From an organization structure standpoint, the critical factor is the design of the transformation process. Oddly, this transformation design involves a closed-systems analysis. In other words, the closed system is a subsystem of the open system. The closed-systems aspects of the transformation process are concerned with the interrelated and interdependent organizational subsystems of structure, processes, and technology. These subsystems must be organized in such a way that they will lead to maximum goal attainment or output.

Although the approach has decreased in popularity in recent years, it has been pointed out that, to date, very little research on organizations has been guided by open-systems thinking.[37] It is not that the open-systems approach has proved to be wrong or lacking in some way but rather that "in order to most fruitfully utilize the systems paradigm of organizations, scholars in the field must re-examine their beliefs about the paradigm and, perhaps, re-educate themselves about how they should think about and study organizations as systems."[38]

Information Processing View of Organizations

The view of organizations as information processing systems facing uncertainty serves as a transition between systems theory, which has just been discussed, and contingency theory, which is discussed next. The information processing view makes three major assumptions about organizations.[39] First, organizations are open systems that face external, environmental uncertainty (for example, technology or the economy) and internal, work-related task uncertainty. Jay Galbraith defines task uncertainty as "the difference between the amount of information required to perform the task and the amount of information already possessed by the organization."[40] The organization must have mechanisms and be structured in order to diagnose and cope with this environmental and task uncertainty. In particular, the organization must be able to gather, interpret, and use the appropriate information to reduce the uncertainty. Thus, the second assumption is as follows: "Given the various sources of uncertainty, a basic function of the organization's structure is to create the most appropriate configuration of work units (as well as the linkages between these units) to facilitate the effective collection, processing, and distribution of information."[41] In other words, organizations are information processing systems.

The final major assumption of this view deals with the importance of the subunits or various departments of an organization. Because the subunits have different degrees of differentiation (that is, they have different time perspectives, goals, technology, and so on) the important question is not what the overall organization design should be but, rather, "(a) What are the optimal structures for the different subunits within the organization (e.g., R&D, sales, manufacturing); (b) What structural mechanisms will facilitate effective coordination among differentiated yet interdependent subunits?"[42]

Taking the answers to these questions as a point of departure, Tushman and

Nadler draw on the extensive relevant research to formulate the following propositions about an information processing theory of organizations:

1. The tasks of organization subunits vary in their degree of uncertainty.
2. As work-related uncertainty increases, so does the need for increased amount of information, and thus the need for increased information processing capacity.
3. Different organizational structures have different capacities for effective information processing.
4. An organization will be more effective when there is a match between the information processing requirements facing the organization and the information processing capacity of the organization's structure.
5. If organizations (or subunits) face different conditions over time, more effective units will adapt their structures to meet the changed information processing requirements.[43]

The above propositions summarize the current state of knowledge concerning the information processing view of organizations. "The key concept is information, and the key idea is that organizations must effectively receive, process, and act on information to achieve performance."[44] Although the focal point of this approach is the interface between environmental uncertainty—both external and internal—and information processing, it is very closely related to systems and contingency theories, and some organization theorists would argue that it could even be subsumed under either one.

Contingency and Ecological Organization Theories

The most recent organization theories focus even more on the environment than do the open systems and information processing views. However, the modern contingency and ecological organization theories treat the environment in almost opposite ways. Contingency theories are proactive and are analogous to the development of contingency management as a whole; they relate the environment to specific organization strucures. More specifically, the contingency models relate to how the organization structure adjusts to fit with both the internal environment such as work technology[45] and the external environment such as the economy or legal regulations.[46]

Recently, some organization theorists feel that contingency theory should be replaced by an ecological view.[47] This new approach is best represented by what is called "population-ecology."[48] Very simply, this population-ecology approach can be summarized as follows:

1. It focuses on groups or populations of organizations rather than individual ones. For example, for the population of grocery organizations after World War II, there was an even split between "mom and pop" stores and supermarkets. The environment selected out the small "mom and pop" operations because they were not efficient and only the supermarkets survived.
2. Organizational effectiveness is simply defined as survival.
3. The environment is assumed to be totally determining. At least in the short or intermediate term, management is seen to have little impact on an organization's survival.

4. The carrying capacity of the environment is limited. Therefore, there is a competitive arena where some organizations will succeed and others will fail.[49]

Obviously, this ecology theory is a much different view of organizations than the classical or even modern approaches. A more rational, proactive approach to management that is able to change the organization structure to fit the changing demands of the environment is more accepted and practical than environmental determination. Yet the ecological theory helps explain why organizations in the same industry (common populations) tend to have similar structural characteristics and why certain types of organizations survive while others die.[50]

MODERN ORGANIZATION DESIGNS

Along with organization theorists, many practicing managers are becoming disenchanted with traditional ways of designing their organizations. Up until a few years ago, most managers attempted only timid modifications of classical structures and balked at daring experimentation and innovation. However, many of today's managers have finally overcome this resistance to making drastic organizational changes. They realize that the simple solutions offered by the classical theories are no longer adequate for many of their complex problems. In particular, the needs for flexibility, adaptability to change, and overcoming environmental uncertainty are among the biggest challenges facing a growing number of modern organizations.

Recently, some new organization forms designed to accommodate radical change have been suggested. One such form is the so-called "learning organization." Unlike the traditional designs, the learning organization cannot be shown in a figure, but instead is "a very big conceptual catchall to help us make sense of a set of values and ideas we've been wrestling with, everything from customer service to corporate responsiveness and speed."[51] Although no practicing organization completely fits the learning organization, going into the 1990s most experts agree that Honda comes the closest. As one manager from the company's Marysville, Ohio, factory describes it: "The Honda philosophy is a way of life. It's characterized by closeness, communication, and frankness at all levels. Honda employs thinking people, creative people. We want people to sound off."[52] Importantly, successful firms are striving to become learning organizations, firms ranging from giants such as Ford to smaller, but excellent, organizations such as Analog Devices and Quad/Graphics.

Other new, more academic organizational designs are being suggested. For example, Miles and Snow identified what they call the *dynamic network*. This involves a unique combination of strategy, structure, and management processes. They also suggest that in the future, new insights and terminology, such as vertical desegregation, internal and external brokering, and full-disclosure information systems, will become commonplace.[53] For now, however, the more widely recognized project and matrix structures will be discussed.

Project Designs

From a rather restricted beginning in the aerospace industry and in those firms having contracts with the Department of Defense, the use of project designs has increased in all organizations that require a great deal of planning, research, and coordination. In addition to the aerospace industry, project designs are becoming widely used in other industrial corporations and also in financial institutions, health care facilities, government agencies, and educational institutions. Projects of various degrees of importance and magnitude are always under way in modern organizations. The project structure is created when management decides to focus a great amount of talent and resources for a given period on a specific project goal.

There are different ways in which the project approach can be designed. Figure 18.1*a* shows that the project managers under this design have no activities or personnel reporting directly to them. The project manager, along with the heads of quality control, research and development, contract administration, and scheduling, acts in a staff capacity to the general manager. The project manager must rely on influence and persuasion in performing a monitoring role, with direct line authority exercised only by the general manager.

Another type is shown in Figure 18.1*b*. Here, project managers have all the personnel necessary for the project. They have staff and functional line personnel

FIGURE 18.1(*a*)
Types of project designs.

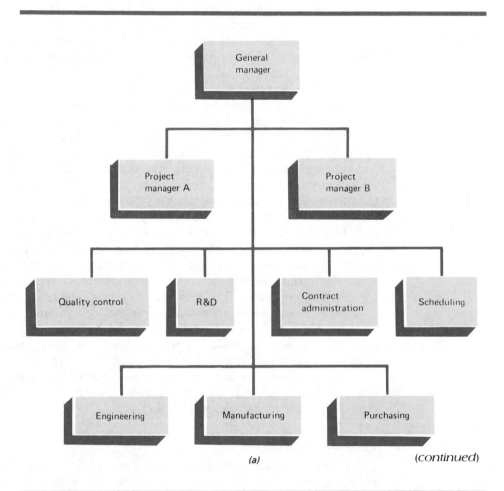

(a)

(continued)

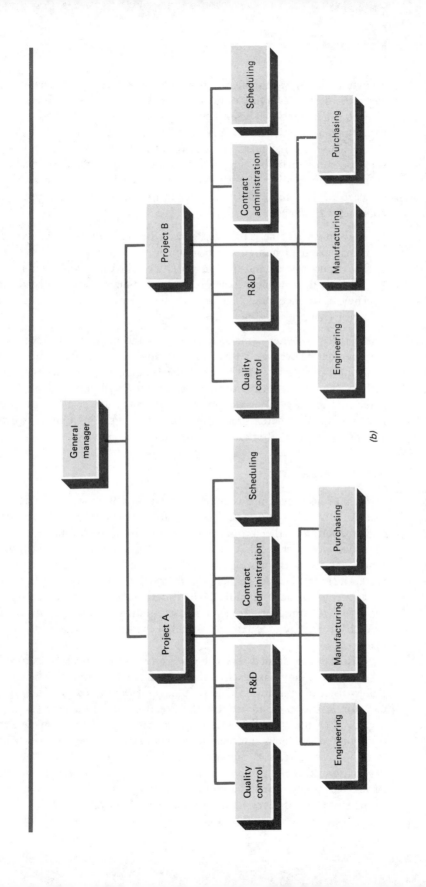

FIGURE 18.1(b)
Types of project designs.

reporting directly to them. Figure 18.1*b* shows that the project managers under the aggregate design have full authority over the entire project. In reality, the aggregate project organization is very similar to the traditional product or unit form of departmentation, which was presented earlier in the chapter.

There are other possible variations besides the two shown in Figure 18.1, and the project organization almost always coexists with the more traditional functional structure. But project experts stress that even though there are many similarities between project and functional organizations, project managers must take a new approach to their jobs:

1. They must become reoriented away from the purely functional approach to the management of human and nonhuman resources.
2. They must understand that purposeful conflict may very well be a necessary way of life as they manage their project across many vertical organizational lines.
3. They must recognize that project management is a dynamic activity in which major changes are almost the order of the day.[54]

These three statements make it clear that the project concept is a philosophy of management as well as a form of structural organization. The same is true of its behavioral perspective. Here are some suggestions for putting a project team together: "Don't put on the team an expert who will dominate its deliberations. And make sure that service on the project represents a career plus, that people detailed to it go on to jobs better than the ones they left."[55] In other words, the project viewpoint is quite different from the functional one.

Matrix Designs

When a project structure is superimposed on a functional structure, the result is a matrix. Sometimes the matrix organization is considered to be a form of project organization, and the terms are used interchangeably. However, a more accurate portrayal would show that the matrix organization is a project organization *plus* a functional organization. Figure 18.2 shows a very simplified matrix organization. Here, the functional department heads have line authority over the specialists in their departments (vertical structure). The functional specialists are then assigned to given projects (horizontal structure). These assignments are usually made at the beginning of each project by a collaboration between the appropriate functional and project managers.

It has been argued that the matrix structure evolves as shown in Table 18.1. Once the company has reached the matrix stage, there are also stages or degrees of this form of organization. This first stage of the matrix is usually just a temporary task force; this is followed by the creation of permanent teams or committees organized around specific needs or problems. The last stage occurs when a manager is appointed and held responsible for coordinating the activities and inputs of the teams or committees.[56] Similar to a project manager, the matrix manager needs negotiation skills and a high tolerance for ambiguous power relationships.[57] There is also recent support for the use of matrix designs as being appropriate and responsive to the strategies of diversified multinational corporations.[58]

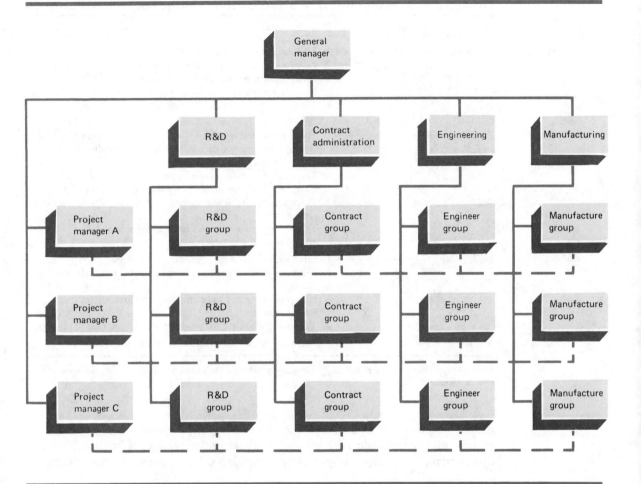

FIGURE 18.2
An example of a matrix design.

Direct Violation of Classical Principles. Matrix designs violate the classical organizational principles. The hierarchy principle and the principle of unity of command are flagrantly violated. Furthermore, the matrix concept does not coincide with the usual line-staff arrangements discussed earlier in the chapter. Obviously, a great deal of conflict is generated in matrix organizations. An organizational specialist with IBM has observed that besides fostering conflict, the matrix structure discourages informal groups and the nurturing of supervisor-subordinate relations. After ten years of experience with the transition from traditional hierarchical to matrix organizations, he concluded that the matrix structure "has seemingly reduced participant motivation for all but the most aggressive personalities and has reduced corporate loyalty and identification with the organization."[59] An extensive empirical investigation of the engineering division of an aircraft manufacturing firm found that the

TABLE 18.1 Determinants of the Evolutionary Stages of Matrix Designs

Organization Design	Determinants
Functional ⟶	1. Efficiency is the major objective. 2. Competitive advantage is along a single parameter such as technology, price, performance, or delivery. 3. Markets are relatively stable and predictable. 4. There is a narrow range of products with long-term perspectives.
Project ⟶	1. There are several simultaneous objectives (for example, performance, cost, price, schedule, technology, and efficiency). 2. There is moderate market change. 3. There are differentiated clients/customers and markets. 4. There is a moderate number of products or projects. 5. There are specific time horizons for each client/customer or project. 6. There is interconnectedness between outside and local organizations.
Product/matrix ⟶	1. Innovation is the major objective. 2. There are differentiated products, markets, and customers/clients. 3. High variability and uncertainty characterize the product-market mix. 4. The time perspective for products varies from medium to long.
Matrix ⟶	1. There are the same determinants as for product/matrix.

Source: Adapted from Harvey F. Kolodny, "Evolution to a Matrix Organization," *Academy of Management Review,* October 1979, p. 551.

matrix structure led to a decrease in the quality of communication and negative effects on relevant role perceptions, work attitudes, and coordination.[60] These disadvantages are balanced by many positive aspects of the matrix organization.

Advantages of Matrix Designs. The matrix organization attempts to combine the best of both worlds. In an eclectic manner, it includes the positive aspects of both the functional and the project designs. These advantages can be summarized as follows:

1. The project is emphasized by designating one individual as the focal point for all matters pertaining to it.
2. Utilization of personnel can be flexible because a reservoir of specialists is maintained in functional organizations.
3. Specialized knowledge is available to all programs on an equal basis; knowledge and experience can be transferred from one project to another.
4. Project people have a functional home when they are no longer needed on a given project.
5. Responsiveness to project needs and customer desires is generally faster because lines of communication are established and decision points are centralized.
6. Management consistency between projects can be maintained through the deliberate conflict operating in the project-functional environment.

7. A better balance between time, cost, and performance can be obtained through the built-in checks and balances (the deliberate conflict) and the continuous negotiations carried on between the project and the functional organizations.[61]

Theorists who advocate a matrix structure maintain that these advantages outweigh the inherent disadvantages. In particular, "Matrix organizations tend to have high levels of performance in dealing with complex, creative work products. Also, because of the amount of interaction among members in matrix structures, and the high levels of responsibility they possess, matrix organizations usually have greater worker job satisfaction."[62]

Many contemporary organizations which are facing tremendous structural and technical complexity have no choice but to move to a matrix arrangement. The critical need for coordination and functional interrelationships can be met by adding a horizontal dimension to the functional structure.

Summary

Bureaucracy dominates classical organization theory and structure. Weber's bureaucratic model consists of specialization, hierarchy, rules, and impersonal relationships. Weber believed that this model was an ideal organization structure that would lead to maximum efficiency. Unfortunately, it does not always turn out this way in practice. In fact, there are probably as many dysfunctions as there are functions of bureaucracy. Specialization or hierarchy can lead to organizational efficiencies, but either can provoke detrimental conflict and impede the communication process. Rules often become ends in themselves rather than means toward goal attainment, and everyone can attest to the dysfunctional consequences of the impersonal characteristic of bureaucracies. Because of these and a number of other dysfunctions, many of today's theorists are predicting the decline and fall of the classical bureaucratic form of organization.

Decentralization, flat structures, departmentation, and staff organization have developed to extend and modify the pure bureaucratic classical principles of organization. In general, the behavioral approach is more compatible with the modified structural concepts, but the dramatic changes that have occurred in recent years have led to the search for new, alternative ways to organize.

Modern organization theory was presented from the perspective of systems, information process, contingency, and ecological approaches. Systems theory emphasizes the impact of the external environment. The information processing approach views the importance of information flows in an organization to cope with internal differentiation and external environmental uncertainty. Contingency theory gives specific attention to adapting to the environment by relating it to organization structure and design. The ecological theory assumes environmental determinism; there is a natural selection and replacement of organizations.

The new organizational models that have recently come on the scene have been developed primarily to meet the dramatically changing needs of today's organizations. Examples of recently emerging designs are learning organizations and dynamic networks. Even the more established project and matrix structures represent a significant departure from the classical, bureaucratic model. The new structures flagrantly violate classical principles such as unity of command and equal authority and responsibility. Nevertheless, organizations with technologies that require flexibility and adaptability to change are willing to sacrifice the classical concepts. Only time will tell whether the new structural forms are suitable replacements for the classical structure. On the other hand, there seems little doubt that the new approaches have already proved themselves valuable enough to become a significant part of organization theory and practice.

Questions for Discussion and Review

1. What are the major characteristics of Weber's bureaucratic model? Discuss the functions and dysfunctions of each.
2. Do you agree or disagree with those who are predicting the fall of bureaucracy? Defend your answer.
3. What are the various kinds of centralization and decentralization? Which one is most relevant to organizational analysis? Why?
4. Defend centralization as an important organizational concept. Do the same for decentralization.
5. Critically analyze functional versus product (unit) departmentation.
6. Why are many companies today cutting back on their corporate staff? What will happen to the specialized functions they performed for line managers?
7. What was Chester Barnard's contribution to organization theory?
8. How does the open-systems theory differ from the information processing, contingency, and ecological approaches? How does the open-systems concept apply to organizations? How does the information processing concept apply to organizations? How does the contingency concept apply to organizations? How does the ecological concept apply to organizations?
9. What are two different types of project structures? How does the project manager differ from the traditional functional manager?
10. The matrix design of organization is variously said to rest on classical, behavioral, systems, information processing, and contingency bases. Explain how each of these approaches could serve as the basis for the matrix design.

References

1. Robert Duncan, "What's the Right Organization Structure?" *Organizational Dynamics*, Winter 1979, p. 59.
2. A. M. Henderson and Talcott Parsons (trans. and ed.), *Max Weber: The Theory of Social and Economic Organization*, Free Press, New York, 1947, p. 330.
3. Ibid., p. 331.
4. Herbert A. Simon, *The New Science of Management Decision*, Harper, New York, 1960, pp. 40–41.
5. Henderson and Parsons, op. cit.
6. Ibid., p. 340.
7. Peter M. Blau, *Bureaucracy in Modern Society*, Random House, New York, 1956, p. 34.
8. Gregory K. Dow, "Configuration and Coactiva-

tional View of Organization Structure," *Academy of Management Review,* January 1988, p. 61.

9. Rolf E. Rogers, *Organizational Theory,* Allyn and Bacon, Boston, 1975, p. 4.

10. Peter Drucker, *The Practice of Management,* Harper, New York, 1954, pp. 133–134.

11. Ibid., p. 135.

12. C. Northcote Parkinson, *Parkinson's Law and Other Studies in Administration,* Houghton Mifflin, Boston, 1957.

13. Laurence J. Peter, *The Peter Principle,* Morrow, New York, 1969.

14. Rogers, op. cit., p. 4.

15. Warren Bennis, "Beyond Bureaucracy," *Trans-Action,* July–August 1965, p. 33.

16. Thomas J. Peters and Robert H. Waterman, Jr., *In Search of Excellence: Lessons from America's Best-Run Companies,* Harper & Row, New York, 1982.

17. Kenneth Blanchard and Spencer Johnson, *The One Minute Manager,* Morrow, New York, 1982.

18. Tom Peters, *Thriving on Chaos: Handbook for a Management Revolution,* Knopf, New York, 1987, p. 459.

19. Hal O. Carroll, "Perestroika in the American Corporation," *Organizational Dynamics,* Spring 1990, pp. 5–21.

20. Walter Kiechel, "The Organization That Learns," *Fortune,* March 12, 1990, p. 133.

21. Peter Enderwick, "Multinational Corporate Restructuring and International Competitiveness," *California Management Review,* Fall 1989, pp. 44–58.

22. Saul W. Gellerman, "In Organizations, as in Architecture, Form Follows Function," *Organizational Dynamics,* Winter 1990, p. 64.

23. Jay Finegan, "Four-Star Management," *Inc.,* January 1987, pp. 48, 51.

24. Jeremy Main, "Wanted: Leaders Who Can Make a Difference," *Fortune,* Sept. 28, 1987, p. 94.

25. Robert W. Keidel, "Triangular Design: A New Organization Geometry," *Academy of Management Executive,* November 1990, pp. 21–37.

26. Luther Gulick, "Notes on the Theory of Organization," in Luther Gulick and Lyndall Urwick (eds.), *Papers on the Science of Administration,* Institute of Public Administration, New York, 1937, p. 15.

27. Drucker, op. cit., p. 125.

28. Henry H. Albers, *Principles of Management,* 4th ed., Wiley, New York, 1974, p. 95.

29. Meni Koslowsky, "Staff/Line Distinctions in Job and Organizational Commitment," *Journal of Occupational Psychology,* vol. 63, 1990, pp. 167–173.

30. Peters and Waterman, op. cit., p. 311.

31. Thomas Moore, "Goodbye, Corporate Staff," *Fortune,* Dec. 21, 1987, p. 65.

32. Richard M. Weiss, "Weber on Bureaucracy: Management Consultant or Political Theorist?" *Academy of Management Review,* April 1983, pp. 242–248.

33. Chester I. Barnard, *The Functions of the Executive,* Harvard, Cambridge, Mass., 1938, p. 73.

34. Ibid., p. vii.

35. Ibid., p. 82.

36. Glen R. Carroll, "Organizational Ecology in Theoretical Perspective," in Glen R. Carroll (ed.), *Ecological Models of Organizations,* Ballinger, Cambridge, Mass., 1988, pp. 1–2.

37. Donde P. Ashmos and George P. Huber, "The Systems Paradigm in Organization Theory: Correcting the Record and Suggesting the Future," *Academy of Management Review,* October 1987, pp. 607–621.

38. Ibid., p. 618.

39. These assumptions are identified in Michael L. Tushman and David A. Nadler, "Information Processing as an Integrating Concept in Organization Design," *Academy of Management Review,* July 1978, pp. 614–615.

40. Jay Galbraith, *Designing Complex Organizations,* Addison-Wesley, Reading, Mass., 1973, p. 5.

41. Tushman and Nadler, op. cit., p. 614.

42. Ibid., p. 615.

43. Ibid.

44. James L. Gibson, John M. Ivancevich, and James H. Donelly, Jr., *Organizations,* 6th ed., Business Publications, Plano, Tex., 1988, p. 513.

45. For a recent summary of this research see Minoo Tehrani, John R. Montanari, and Kenneth P. Carson, "Technology as a Determinant of Organization Structure: A Meta-Analytic Review," *Academy of Management Best Papers Proceedings,* 1990, pp. 180–184.

46. See Derek S. Pugh and David J. Hickson, *Writers on Organizations,* Sage, Newbury Park, Calif., 1989. Chapter 2 provides all the major environmental models of organization.

47. Carroll, op. cit., pp. 1–2.

48. For the original presentation of this model see Michael T. Hannon and John J. Freeman, "The Population Ecology of Organizations," *Amer-*

ican Journal of Sociology, March 1977, pp. 929–964.

49. Stephen P. Robbins, *Organization Theory,* 3d ed., Prentice-Hall, Englewood Cliffs, N.J., 1990, p. 226.

50. Ibid., p. 229.

51. Robert Quinn, quoted in Kiechel, op. cit., p. 133.

52. Pat Sparks, quoted in Kiechel, op. cit., p. 136.

53. Raymond E. Miles and Charles C. Snow, "Organizations: New Concepts for New Forms," *California Management Review,* Spring 1986, p. 62.

54. David I. Cleland and William R. King, *Systems Analysis and Project Management,* McGraw-Hill, New York, 1968, p. 152.

55. Robert H. Waterman, Jr., quoted in Kiechel, op. cit., pp. 134–136.

56. Don Hellriegel, John W. Slocum, Jr., and Richard W. Woodman, *Organizational Behavior,* West, St. Paul, Minn., 1986, p. 417.

57. H. F. Kolodny, "Managing in a Matrix," *Business Horizons,* March–April 1981, pp. 17–35.

58. Jay R. Galbraith and Robert K. Kazanjian, "Organizing to Implement Strategies of Diversity and Globalization: The Role of Matrix Designs," *Human Resource Management,* Spring 1986, pp. 37–54.

59. Michael V. Fiore, "Out of the Frying Pan into the Matrix," *Personnel Administration,* July–August 1979, p. 6.

60. William F. Joyce, "Matrix Organization: A Social Experiment," *Academy of Management Journal,* September 1986, pp. 536–561.

61. Cleland and King, op. cit., p. 172.

62. Ronald E. Riggio, *Introduction to Industrial/Organizational Psychology,* Scott, Foresman/Little, Brown, Glenview, Illinois, 1990, p. 344.

REAL CASE: PEOPLE ARE THE REAL KEY

One of the most interesting ideas about matrix organizations that is getting a lot of attention these days is the need for a people focus. Many organizations have found that as their enterprises grew and international operations became more important, they needed to change from a basic line-staff structure to a matrix or free-form design. The problem with this transition was that the new structure often created more problems than it solved. This was brought out in the following analysis of matrix structures:

> In practice . . . the matrix proved all but unmanageable—especially in an international context. Dual reporting led to conflict and confusion; the proliferation of channels created informational logjams as a proliferation of committees and reports bogged down the organization; and the overlapping responsibilities produced turf battles and a loss of accountability. Separated by barriers of distance, language, time, and culture, managers found it virtually impossible to clarify the confusion and resolve the conflicts.

As a result, companies that are interested in matrix designs are now placing strong emphasis on three steps. First, they are building a shared vision regarding what the organization is all about and how all parts of it integrate. For example, the NEC Corporation has provided its people with a clear statement of its focus, distinctive competencies, and strategic imperatives. Everyone knows what the company intends to do. Second, there is careful recruitment and selection of personnel for matrix structures. In the case of Procter & Gamble, for example, project managers are chosen based on past performance, ability to deal with ambiguity, and ability to manage complexity. Third, organizations are giving project managers more authority and freedom from top management directives so that they can respond to local needs. Philips, the giant consumer electronics firm that is headquartered in the

Netherlands, has set up a World Policy Council that helps coordinate international operations and ensure that the linkage between them and the home office is both smooth and profitable. The reason that these types of developments are so important has been well stated by a senior executive who noted, "The challenge is not so much to build a matrix structure as it is to create a matrix in the minds of our managers." As a result, instead of having built-in conflict within the organization that leads to problems, this approach lets individuals make judgements and negotiate the trade-offs that drive the organization toward a shared strategic objective.

1. How does the approach described in this case illustrate the use of centralization and decentralization in international matrix structures?
2. In what way is the matrix structure an open system?
3. Why is the approach described in this case superior to that used by many organizations that employ matrix structures?

**Case:
The Grass
Is Greener—
or Is It?**

Alice Jenkins had been a supervisor of caseworkers in the county welfare department for nine years. The bureaucratic procedures and regulations became so frustrating that she finally decided to look for a job in private industry. She had an excellent education and employment record and soon landed a supervisory position in the production end of a large insurance firm. After a few weeks on her new job she was having coffee with one of the supervisors of another department. She said, "I just can't win for losing. I quit my job at county welfare because I was being strangled by red tape. I thought I could escape that by coming to work in private industry. Now I find out that it is even worse. I was under the illusion that private industry did not have the bureaucratic problems that we had in welfare. Where can I go to escape these insane rules and impersonal treatment?"

1. Is Alice just a chronic complainer, or do you think her former job was as intolerable as her present job, as she indicates? Do you think Alice is typical of most employees in similar types of positions?
2. How would you answer Alice's last question? Can you give an example of a large organization that you are familiar with that is not highly bureaucratized? Does the county welfare department or the insurance company have to be bureaucratized?
3. Can the concepts of decentralization, flat structures, departmentation, and staff be used in a welfare department or in the clerical area of a large insurance company? Give some examples if possible.

**Case:
The
Outdated
Structure**

Jake Harvey has a position on the corporate planning staff of a large company in a high-technology industry. Although he has spent most of his time on long-range, strategic planning for the company, he has been appointed to a task force to reorganize the company. The president and board of directors are concerned that they are losing their competitive position in the industry because of an outdated organization structure. Being a planning expert, Jake convinced the task force that they should proceed by first determining exactly what type of structure they have now, then determining what type of environment the company faces now and in the future, and then designing the organization structure accordingly. In the first phase they discovered that the organization is currently structured along classical bureaucratic lines. In the second phase they found that they are competing in a highly dynamic, rapidly growing, and uncertain environment that requires a great deal of flexibility and response to change.

1. What type or types of organization design do you feel this task force should recommend in the third and final phase of the approach to their assignment?
2. Explain how the systems, information processing, contingency and ecological theories of organization can each contribute to the analysis of this case.
3. Do you think Jake was correct in his suggestion of how the task force should proceed? What types of problems might develop as by-products of the recommendation you make in question 1?

INTEGRATIVE CONTEMPORARY CASE FOR PART 5

Managing in
Times of
Uncertainty*

The Nineties are shaping up as the decade in which we came, we saw, and we ran for cover. The economy is wobbling, the Germanys are merging, and foreign competitors are becoming tougher. Workers, many aging and underskilled, are clamoring to be empowered. And customers are demanding the highest quality, latest technology, and speediest delivery—all at the lowest cost. Says Walker Lewis, head of Strategic Planning Associates, a Washington, D.C., consulting firm: "This may be a time of immense uncertainty, but it is a *certainty* that Western companies are in for ten years of competitive hell."

Facing this inferno, how can companies possibly prepare for the future? How can they plot strategies when the shape of the battlefield keeps changing? The old methods won't do. At too many companies strategic planning has become overly bureaucratic, absurdly quantitative, and largely irrelevant. In executive suites across America, countless five-year plans, updated annually and solemnly clad in three-ring binders, are gathering dust—their impossibly specific prognostications about costs, prices, and market share long forgotten. Asks John Walter, CEO of R.R. Donnelley & Sons, America's largest printer: "Do I have the books in my closet with all the numbers in them? Yes. Do I look at them? No."

That doesn't mean Walter and other CEOs have abandoned themselves to the Fates and the Furies. They have, instead, begun to forge companies that think and act strategically—not just once a year but every day. The term "strategic planning," popularized in the Sixties, no longer accurately describes what they do. The phrase gaining currency is "strategic thinking." Executives use it to describe what a company does in becoming smart, targeted, and nimble enough to prosper in an era of constant change. William Lawrence, executive vice president for planning, technology, and government affairs at TRW, speaks for many when he says, "The key words for the Nineties are 'focus' and 'flexibility.'"

Focus means figuring out, and building on, what the company does best. It means identifying the evolving needs of your customers, then developing the key skills—often called the core competencies—critical to serving them. It means setting a clear, realistic mission and then working tirelessly to make sure everyone—from the chairman to the middle manager to the hourly employee—understands it.

Such self-assessment led Cleveland-based TRW, once a loosely knit agglomeration of 80 businesses, to shed nearly half its units and grab early leadership in the burgeoning market for automotive air bags. It led Chicago-based Donnelley to become a high-tech global communications company that adds value not just by putting ink on paper (that's only 5 percent of the equation) but also by transmitting, customizing, and packaging information.

* *Source:* Ronald Henkoff, "How to Plan for 1995," *Fortune*, December 31, 1990, pp. 70, 72, 74, 76, 79. Copyright 1990, Time Inc. All rights reserved. Reprinted by permission from TIME.

Flexibility means sketching rough scenarios of the future—what General Electric Chairman Jack Welch calls bands of possibilities—then being ready to pounce on opportunities as they arise. Says Welch, "I'm no guru. I'm not here to predict the world. I'm here to be sure I've got a company that is strong enough to respond to whatever happens." GE was once the corporate citadel of quantitative forecasting. The 350-member planning staff churned out voluminous reports, meticulously detailed and exquisitely packaged. Now GE has but a score of full-time planners. Called business development specialists, they are there only to advise line managers, who have the prime responsibility for formulating strategy.

The heads of GE's 13 businesses each year develop five *one-page* "charts," memos that alert them to possible opportunities and obstacles in their industries over the next 24 months. When Hungary opened its doors to foreign ownership in state-run companies, GE needed just 60 days to cut a deal for 50 percent of Tungsram, the country's leading lighting company. Tungsram had been on GE's charts for years.

There is no neat, patentable formula for managing in times of uncertainty. Says Michael Porter, Harvard business school professor and acclaimed authority on strategy: "The state of practice in this area is very primitive." For the typical large American corporation, diversified into a hodgepodge of enterprises and involved in manufacturing, marketing, distribution, and myriad other activities, just determining what it does for a living—how it adds value— is no easy task. Says Benjamin Tregoe, chairman of Kepner-Tregoe, a Princeton, New Jersey, consulting firm: "Everyone talks about sticking to the knitting, but a lot of companies don't know what their knitting is."

An outfit that lost sight of its knitting—and then rediscovered it—is Northern Trust Corp., an asset management and bank holding company based in Chicago. Long expert at ministering to the private banking needs of affluent Illinoisans, Northern aggressively expanded into such areas as energy and real estate lending in the late Seventies and early Eighties. But the bank was outgunned by bigger, richer, more seasoned competitors. A string of bad loans to Third World countries forced it to take a $179 million write-off in 1987 and post the only loss in its history. Says senior vice president Frederick Waddell: "We found out that we were only marginal players in these areas."

So last spring the 13 members of Northern's policy committee, accompanied by a senior vice president of Boston Consulting Group, ensconced themselves in a hotel in Lake Bluff, north of Chicago. During three days of suburban soul-searching, the managers assessed the company's strengths and weaknesses and hammered out a ten-page vision for the next decade. Northern decided to refocus on its core skills—asset management, private banking, and targeted commercial lending mainly for local mid-size companies.

Capitalizing on its expertise in serving wealthy customers, Northern has been expanding into Florida, Texas, Arizona, and California, and has its eye on the Northeast. The bank has also exported its operational excellence to

London, becoming a leader in cash management and custodial services for international pension funds. Recognizing that its key asset is people, Northern has beefed up management training programs and—thinking even further ahead—has donated $1 million to a Chicago community group to help improve preschool, elementary, and secondary education. While other banks founder, Northern—one of only four U.S. financial institutions that derive more income from fees than from interest—looks to be on course for another year of record earnings.

It often takes a crisis to jar companies into thinking realistically about the future. At Trinova, a Maumee, Ohio, manufacturer of engineered components and systems, the catalyst was would-be corporate raiders who wanted to break up the company and sell off pieces. Trinova—you may remember it as Libbey-Owens-Ford—was until recently a loose confederation of three businesses with no clear mandate. Admits CEO Darryl Allen: "We didn't really have a good understanding of what we were, let alone what we wanted to be.

Figuring those things out took Allen and his senior managers six years. They decided that Trinova's glass business was too capital-intensive and too dependent on the notoriously cyclical automotive industry, so they sold it to Pilkington Bros., a leading British glassmaker.

In a world awash with forecasts, opinions, theories, seminars, consultants, and concepts, many companies have come to the conclusion that the only oracles worth listening to are their customers. Trinova asked itself what kinds of products and services its customers would likely need 15 years down the road and what kind of core competencies the company would have to develop to serve them. Its Vickers division, for example, was already a global leader in hydraulic components (such as pumps and valves) for airplanes. But Vickers's customers were thinking about enhancing or replacing some of their hydraulic components with electric, electromechanical, and electronic parts and systems.

So Vickers resolved to master those new technologies through acquisitions, joint ventures, licensing agreements, and its own R&D. Says Allen, an accountant and *Star Trek* freak: "I've got to have these capabilities. We never want to lose a customer because we don't have the technology." Trinova doesn't know exactly what Boeing and McDonnell Douglas will be ordering in 2005, but it is confident that it has the skills and flexibility to meet their evolving needs.

Many companies have trouble mustering such farsightedness. That's because, in most organizations, the future doesn't have a lobbying group. Managers are preoccupied with—and rewarded for—the critical present-day tasks of boosting sales, increasing market share, and enhancing profit margins. Says C. K. Prahalad, professor of corporate strategy and international business at the University of Michigan and an adviser to Trinova and other large multinationals: "In most American companies the urgent has driven out the important."

The traditional building block of American corporations, the semi-autonomous strategic business unit, can actually impede a company's ability to focus on the future. Most companies, Prahalad argues, still use rigid financial formulas for deciding whether they should invest in, milk, or dump individual units—an approach that not only focuses on current market conditions but also makes it easy for competitors to guess what a company will do with a particular business. Why did American companies pull out of the color TV business? Because traditional strategic analysis said it was a "mature" industry. The remaining players, who now compete in the robust markets for VCRs and video cameras, and will likely get into such new products as high-definition TV, thought otherwise.

The division into strategic business units can also interfere with a company's ability to identify its core competencies—and key people. Says Walker Lewis of Strategic Planning Associates: "Core skills often have nothing to do with the way the company is organized." At GE, Jack Welch is trying to create what he calls a boundaryless organization in which technology, information, managers, and management practices flow freely from one division to another. When inspectors at the aircraft engine division check the integrity of metal parts, for example, they use X-ray technology developed by the medical systems unit.

Focusing on the future needs of customers has prompted R.R. Donnelley to reinvent not just itself but its competition as well. CEO John Walter, who is 43 and has the mediagenic countenance of a political candidate, believes his company's prime rivals aren't other printing companies but televisions, radios, telephones, computers—any medium of communication that can lure his customers away from print.

To keep current customers and win new ones, Donnelley has invested heavily in advanced technology and has stepped up expansion overseas. Using satellites, the company can print a securities prospectus simultaneously in the U.S., Europe, and Japan. When a computer manufacturer wants a new user manual, Donnelley can use digital technology to do the job on glossy paper, magnetic disk, compact disc, or all three. What's next? Perhaps customized yellow pages (each would encompass a circular geographic area with the consumer's house at the center) or college textbooks tailor-made for a professor's class. Says Walter: "Probably 50 percent of our revenues by 1995 or 2000 will come from business that we weren't in ten years ago."

As chief executives strive to get their companies to think strategically, they are rediscovering the importance of their line managers, especially their middle managers. That's right, middle managers—the Rodney Dangerfields of corporate America. Reshuffled, depowered, and pensioned off during the past decade, they are reemerging as the missing link in the drive to turn visions into realities. Says Jeanie Duck, a vice president at Boston Consulting Group in Chicago: "I am frankly amazed at the number of companies I see where people don't know what the strategies are. The CEOs have ennobled the worker. Now they're asking, 'What about the middle manager?'"

Andrew Grove, the plucky Ph.D. who is CEO of Intel, the Santa Clara, California, semiconductor giant, has recently come to a somewhat humbling conclusion about his own role in plotting strategy. He believes that the most important strategic decisions get made in the trenches, not in the cloistered precincts of the executive suite or the VDT-lit aeries of the professional planners. Says he: "People formulate strategy with their fingertips. Day in and day out they respond to things, by virtue of the products they promote, the price concessions they make, the distribution channels they choose."

The Hungarian-born Grove worries that the vision and mission statements that issue from on high often bear only scant relation to reality: "You look at corporate strategy statements, and a lot of them are such pap. You know how they go: 'We're going to be worldclass this and a leader in that, and we're going to keep all our customers smiling.'" Grove believes that such a statement can be valuable (Intel has one of its own), but only if used as a constant guide for the actions of managers and workers. The acid test of a statement's effectiveness, Grove says, is how well it "helps a manager who is earning $60,000 or $80,000 a year actually do what he does."

A prime example of strategic delusion, says Grove, was Intel's stated plan in the early Eighties to be a major player in both memory chips and microprocessors. Intel pulled out of the dynamic random access memory (DRAM) business in 1985—and focused its energies almost exclusively on microprocessors—after the company suffered heavy losses at the hands of Japanese competitors. Grove, who teaches case studies about the DRAM decision at Harvard and Stanford, says it is now clear to him that the company had already "decided" to retreat from memory chips, perhaps as early as 1983, by dint of its marketing, pricing, and investment choices. Says he: "We were fooled by our own strategic rhetoric."

Grove believes Intel's current mission, "to become the premier building block supplier to the new computer industry," is more realistic. The company intends to keep concentrating on microprocessors, such as its hugely successful 386 chip, the brains of the IBM personal computer and many others. But Intel has also begun, on a small scale, to make personal computers that are sold by customers (including AT&T and Unisys) under their own names. Says Grove: "I have to invest in capabilities. Should there be a shift in the marketplace by our customers to increasingly buy finished or semifinished systems, I want to be able to respond to it."

Grove now recognizes that keeping his generals and his troops marching in the same direction requires constant cajoling and quarreling up and down the ranks, over everything from capital allocations to marketing campaigns to geographic priorities. Says the plainspeaking CEO: "It is not a pretty sight." But without such disputation, top management might end up with all the strategic sway of Napoleon during the retreat from Moscow. The French leader, to quote Tolstoy, "was like a child holding on to the straps inside a carriage and imagining that he is driving it."

At the Micro Switch division of Honeywell, general manager Ramon

Alvarez uses his office as a bully pulpit for declaiming the virtues of strategic thinking. Alvarez, who became head of the Freeport, Illinois, operation four years ago, says the company's prior approach to strategy was elitist and academic: "We got so enamored of the process and the final book that we forgot about execution." Now he holds open forums, publishes newsletters, and makes videotapes. Every Friday afternoon, Alvarez or one of his senior managers sets aside 3½ hours of telephone time to field questions and complaints from any of the company's 5,000 employees.

Alvarez's message to his workers is unvarying: If Micro Switch wants to maintain its position as one of the world's top three switch and sensor suppliers, high product quality alone won't do it. The company must continuously improve productivity, technology, and customer service.

Still, even the most focused, customer-oriented, boundaryless company can be tripped up by external surprises. The managers of Southern California Edison, an electric utility serving 3.9 million customers in central and southern California, came to the mind-numbing realization four years ago that their strategic planning system was a bad joke. Every long-range plan they had painstakingly constructed over the past two decades had been rendered virtually useless by unexpected events—from OPEC price-fixing to new restrictions on sulfur emissions to accidents at Three Mile Island and Chernobyl. Says Vikram Budhraja, manager of electrical systems planning: "These were events that no one could have foreseen, but they had a dramatic impact on our business."

So Edison adopted a technique known as scenario planning. Looking ahead ten years, the utility came up with 12 possible versions of the future—incorporating an economic boom, a Middle East oil crisis, expanded environmentalism, and other developments. Each scenario carries implications for how much power Edison would need to generate, from 5,000 megawatts more to 5,000 megawatts less than the 15,000 megawatts it was producing in 1987.

To cope with such radical variations in demand, Edison has built flexibility into its system. It can repower or depower oil-and-gas generating plants, buy juice from other utilities, and intensify or diminish its campaign to help customers use less electricity. Edison is stepping up conservation in response to new state regulations that reward utilities for encouraging reduced consumption. Says Vikram Budhraja: "We couldn't have done this as well if we hadn't planned for this possibility."

Royal Dutch/Shell, which has been doing scenario planning for 19 years and is widely regarded as the master of the craft, currently has two 20-year scenarios in place. The first, called "Sustainable World," predicts increased concern about global warming trends and an expanded emphasis on conservation, recycling, and emissions controls. The second scenario, ominously entitled "Mercantilist World," postulates an increase in protectionism, a slump in world growth, and a de-emphasis of environmentalism.

Group planning coordinator Peter Hadfield believes that scenario planning has helped Shell be better prepared than its competitors for external shocks. In the early Eighties, for example, while most forecasters were predicting a steadily increasing price for crude oil, Shell, in one of its scenarios, had entertained the possibility that the price would slide to $15 a barrel. As a hedge against such an eventuality, the company began looking into cost-saving exploration technologies. When the slump hit, Shell was able to sustain a higher level of drilling activity than many of its competitors. Shell realizes that its two scenarios don't encompass everything that might happen in the future, and that neither will be a perfect predictor. Says Hadfield: "They're there to condition the organization to think."

While constructing alternative visions of the future can be helpful, it can also carry a price. Says Harvard business school's Michael Porter, "If you try to be flexible and be ready for everything, you could end up raising your costs and not being good at anything." Managers ultimately have to make choices, as Grove and his colleagues learned the hard way at Intel. Says he: "I'd rather have all my eggs in one basket and spend my time worrying about whether that's the right basket, than try to put one egg in every basket. Because then you have no upside." When it comes to thinking and acting strategically, managers still have to depend, to some degree, on a few devilishly unquantifiable factors, like experience, instinct, guesswork, and luck. Has the future got you down? Don't fret about it. Focus your company, listen to your customers, empower your managers, and follow your gut.

1. The opening sentence of the case says that the decade of the nineties is becoming the one in which we came, we saw, and we ran for cover. Explain this statement and why you agree or disagree.
2. What communication theories and techniques can be effectively applied in this Age of Uncertainty?
3. What decision making theoretical models are most relevant to the situation facing today's managers?
4. What implications does the Age of Uncertainty have for organization design?

EXPERIENTIAL EXERCISES FOR PART 5

Goals:

1. To identify some of the important organizations in your life
2. To determine relevant, specific characteristics of organizations
3. To describe some of the important functions of management in organizations

Implementation:

Read the "Overview" and "Procedure" sections. Complete the "Profile of Organizations" form, which follows these sections.

Overview:

Undoubtedly, you have had recent experiences with numerous organizations. Ten to fifteen minutes of reflective thinking should result in a fairly large list of organizations. Don't be misled by thinking that only large organizations, such as your college or General Motors, are relevant for consideration. How about the clinic, with the doctors, nurses, and secretary/bookkeeper? Or the corner garage or service station? The local tavern, McDonald's, and the neighborhood theater are all organizations. You should have no difficulty listing several organizations with which you have had recent contact.

The second part of the exercise, however, is tougher. Describe several of the key characteristics of the organizations that you have listed. One of the major issues in studying and describing organizations is deciding *what* characteristics or factors are important. Some of the more common characteristics considered in the analysis of organizations are:

1. Size (small to very large)
2. Degree of formality (informal to highly structured)
3. Degree of complexity (simple to complex)
4. Nature of goals (what the organization is trying to accomplish)
5. Major activities (what tasks are performed)
6. Types of people involved (age, skills, educational background, etc.)
7. Location of activities (number of units and their geographic location)

You should be able to develop a list of characteristics that you think are relevant for each of your organizations.

Now to the third, final, and most difficult task. Think about what is involved in the management of these organizations. For example, what kinds of functions do their managers perform? How does one learn the skills necessary to be an effective manager? Would you want to be a manager in any of these organizations?

In effect, in this exercise you are being asked to think specifically about organizations you have been associated with recently, develop your own conceptual model for looking at their characteristics, and think more specifically about the managerial functions in each of these organizations. You probably already know a great deal more about organizations and their management than you think. This exercise should be useful in getting your thoughts together.

Procedure:

Step 1. Prior to class, list up to ten organizations (for example, work, living group, club) in which you have been involved or with which you have had recent contact.

Step 2. Enter five organizations from your list on the following form.

1. List the organization.
2. Briefly outline the characteristics that you consider most significant.
3. Describe the managerial functions in each of these organizations.

Step 3. During the class period, meet in groups of five or six to discuss your list of organizations, the characteristics you consider important, and your descriptions of their management. Look for significant similarities and differences across organizations.

Step 4. Basing your selections on this group discussion, develop a list entitled "What we would like to know about organizations and their management." Be prepared to write this list on the blackboard or on newsprint and to share your list with other groups in the class.

Profile of Organizations

Organization	Key characteristics	Managerial functions
1.		
2.		
3.		
4.		
5.		

EXERCISE: PAPER PLANE CORPORATION

Goals:

1. To work on an actual organizational task
2. To experience the managerial functions of organizing, decision making, and control

Implementation:

Unlimited groups of six participants each are used in this exercise. These groups may be directed simultaneously in the same room. Approximately a full class period is needed to complete the exercise. Each person should have assembly instructions and a summary sheet, which are shown on the following pages, and ample stacks of paper (8½ by 11 inches). The physical setting should be a room large enough so that the individual groups of six can work without interference from the other groups. A working space should be provided for each group.

1. The participants are doing an exercise in production methodology.
2. Each group must work independently of the other groups.
3. Each group will choose a manager and an inspector, and the remaining participants will be employees.
4. The objective is to make paper airplanes in the most profitable manner possible.
5. The facilitator will give the signal to start. This is a ten-minute, timed event utilizing competition among the groups.
6. After the first round, everyone should report his or her production and profits to the entire group. Each person also should note the effect, if any, of the manager in terms of the performance of the group.
7. This same procedure is followed for as many rounds as there is time.

Paper Plane Corporation: Data Sheet

Your group is the complete work force for Paper Plane Corporation. Established in 1943, Paper Plane has led the market in paper plane production. Presently under new management, the company is contracting to make aircraft for the U.S. Air Force. You must establish an efficient production plant to produce these aircraft. You must make your contract with the Air Force under the following conditions:

1. The Air Force will pay $20,000 per airplane.
2. The aircraft must pass a strict inspection made by the facilitator.
3. A penalty of $25,000 per airplane will be subtracted for failure to meet the production requirements.
4. Labor and other overhead will be computed at $300,000.
5. Cost of materials will be $3000 per bid plane. If you bid for ten but make only eight, you must pay the cost of materials for those which you failed to make or which did not pass inspection.

INSTRUCTIONS FOR AIRCRAFT ASSEMBLY

STEP 1: Take a sheet of paper and fold it in half, then open it back up.

STEP 2: Fold upper corners to the middle.

STEP 3: Fold the corners to the middle again.

STEP 4: Fold in half.

STEP 5: Fold both wings down.

STEP 6: Fold tail fins up.

 COMPLETED AIRCRAFT

Summary Sheet

Round 1:

Bid: _____ Aircraft @ $20,000 per aircraft = _____
Results: _____ Aircraft @ $20,000 per aircraft = _____
Less: $300,000 overhead
_____ × $3000 cost of raw materials
_____ × $25,000 penalty
Profit: _____

Round 2:

Bid: _____ Aircraft @ $20,000 per aircraft = _____
Results: _____ Aircraft @ $20,000 per aircraft = _____
Less: $300,000 overhead
_____ × $3000 cost of raw materials
_____ × $25,000 penalty
Profit: _____

Round 3:

Bid: _____ Aircraft @ $20,000 per aircraft = _____
Results: _____ Aircraft @ $20,000 per aircraft = _____
Less: $300,000 overhead
_____ × $3000 cost of raw materials
_____ × $25,000 penalty
Profit: _____

PART 6

THE ENVIRONMENTAL CONTEXT OF ORGANIZATIONAL BEHAVIOR: ORGANIZATION CULTURE, INTERNATIONAL, ORGANIZATIONAL BEHAVIOR, AND CHANGE

19 Organizational Culture

■ Apple Seeks a New Culture

In the mid-1980s, Apple Computer began shaping a new culture for itself. The company was determined to shed its image of a firm that built computers for hobbyists. It wanted to successfully invade the grammar school and high school market and make serious inroads into the business market. For a while, the firm was successful. However, by the early 1990s, it was becoming obvious that the competition was beginning to outflank Apple. Competitive clone manufacturers were introducing machines that were a good deal less expensive than Apple offerings. A major player—Microsoft Corp.—introduced *Windows* 3.0, giving IBM compatibles a snazzier screen that rivaled Apple's famous friendly Mac. Result: Apple president John Sculley has decided to change the corporate culture again.

The latest plan is to give Apple a pragmatic corporate culture that will make it appealing to customers looking for low price as well as those who want machines that can perform a wide number of operating functions. In short, the new culture will appeal to both business and nonbusiness markets by showing each that Apple can meet their needs.

In an effort to create this culture as quickly as possible, Sculley has shaken up the top management ranks, replaced personnel, and taken personal control of new product development. Other changes that are being made include: (1) emphasis on producing low-cost computers that can meet the clones head-to-head; (2) research and development efforts toward developing laptop and notebook computers, since this is going to be one of the major market niches of the 1990s; (3) development of strong software prowess to beat back challenges from Microsoft's *Windows* and IBM's OS/2 computer; and (4) development of closer relationships with other computer makers for the purpose of licensing its technology.

Will these efforts work? Only time will tell. However, one thing is certain. Apple Computer cannot remain complacent. By redirecting its strategy, the company has created some internal dissension. There is talk that Sculley really does not know where he is taking the company. This was the same argument that was made seven years ago when he changed direction; and if the past is any indication of the future, Sculley will be right again. About the only thing everyone does agree on is that this is certainly not going to be the last time that Apple changes its culture!

561

- **Define** organizational culture and its characteristics.
- **Relate** how an organizational culture is created.
- **Describe** how an organizational culture is maintained.
- **Explain** some ways of changing organizational culture.

This chapter is concerned with organizational culture. The cultural concept has been a mainstay in the field of anthropology from its beginnings and even was given attention in the early development of organizational behavior.[1] However, only recently has it surfaced as a major dimension for understanding organizational behavior. Today, however, as the introductory comments of a special issue of a management journal noted, organizational culture "has acquired the status of the dominant buzz-word in the U.S. popular and academic management literature."[2] Edgar Schein, who has done considerable research and writing on organizational culture, has also noted, "What has really thrust the concept into the forefront is the recent emphasis on trying to explain why U.S. companies do not perform as well as some of their counterpart companies in other societies, notably, Japan."[3]

The first half of the chapter presents the overall nature of organizational culture, including its definition and characteristics and the dimensions of uniformity, strong and weak, and types of cultures. The last half is devoted to creating and maintaining a culture. Real-world examples are provided throughout.

THE NATURE OF ORGANIZATIONAL CULTURE

People are affected by the culture in which they live. For example, a person growing up in a middle-class family will be taught the values, beliefs, and expected behaviors common to that family. The same is true for organizational participants. An individual working for 3M, PepsiCo, Wal-Mart, or any other organization with a firmly established culture will be taught the values, beliefs, and expected behaviors of that organization. Society has a *social* culture; where people work has an *organizational* culture.

Definition and Characteristics

When people join an organization they bring with them the values and beliefs they have been taught. Quite often, however, these values and beliefs are insufficient for helping the individual succeed in the organization. The person needs to learn how the particular enterprise does things. A good example is the U.S. Marine Corps. During boot camp drill instructors teach recruits the "Marine way." The training attempts to psychologically strip down the new recruits and then restructure their way of thinking. They are taught to think and act like Marines. Anyone who has been in the Marines or knows someone who has will verify that the Corps generally accomplishes its objective. In a less dramatic way, organizations do the same thing.

Schein has comprehensively defined *organizational culture* as:

> a pattern of basic assumptions—invented, discovered, or developed by a given group as it learns to cope with its problems of external adaptation and internal integration

—that has worked well enough to be considered valuable and, therefore, to be taught to new members as the correct way to perceive, think, and feel in relation to those problems.[4]

A recent review of organizational culture notes the differing perspectives and the problems associated with the conceptualization of organizational culture in the literature.[5] Most of the definitions, however, stress the importance of shared norms and values.

Organizational culture has a number of important characteristics. Some of the most readily agreed upon are the following:

1. *Observed behavioral regularities.* When organizational participants interact with one another, they use common language, terminology, and rituals related to deference and demeanor.
2. *Norms.* Standards of behavior exist including guidelines on how much work to do, which in many organizations come down to "Do not do too much; do not do too little."
3. *Dominant values.* There are major values that the organization advocates and expects the participants to share. Typical examples are high product quality, low absenteeism, and high efficiency.
4. *Philosophy.* There are policies that set forth the organization's beliefs about how employees and/or customers are to be treated.
5. *Rules.* There are strict guidelines related to getting along in the organization. Newcomers must learn these "ropes" in order to be accepted as full-fledged members of the group.
6. *Organizational climate.* This is an overall "feeling" that is conveyed by the physical layout, the way in which participants interact, and the way in which members of the organization conduct themselves with customers or other outsiders.

None of the above characteristics by themselves represent the culture of an organization. However, collectively, they can reflect the organizational culture.

Uniformity of Culture

A common misconception is that an organization has a uniform culture. However, at least as anthropology uses the concept, it is probably more accurate to treat organizations "as if" they had a uniform culture. "All organizations 'have' culture in the sense that they are embedded in specific societal cultures and are part of them."[6] According to this view, an organizational culture is a common perception held by the organization's members. Everyone in the organization would have to share this perception. However, realistically, all may not do so to the same degree. As a result, there can be a dominant culture as well as subcultures throughout a typical organization.

A *dominant culture* is a set of core values shared by a majority of the organization's members. For example, most employees at Delta Airlines seem to subscribe to such values as hard work, company loyalty, and the need for customer service. At Hewlett-Packard, most of the employees seem to share a concern for product innovativeness, product quality, and responsiveness to customer needs. At Wal-Mart stores, the associates—a term Wal-Mart uses for its employees that is very symptomatic of its culture—share a concern for customer service, hard work, and company loyalty. These values create a dominant culture in these organizations that helps guide the day-to-day behavior of employees.

Important, but often overlooked, are the subcultures in an organization. A *subculture* is a set of values shared by a minority, usually a small minority, of the organization's members. Subcultures typically are a result of problems or experiences that are shared by members of a department or unit. For example, after the AT&T breakup several years ago, the Consumer Products division, which has its own subculture in the huge corporation, was in deep trouble. It was rapidly losing market share of residential phones to quick-thinking, innovative competitors. Division losses were in the eight digits. Top-level corporate management gave the mandate to either turn it around quickly or they would drop the whole division. This obviously spurred the division into action. The division managers felt that it was unthinkable for their company—that grew out of Alexander Graham Bell's invention over a hundred years ago—to cease making phones. They slashed the division's bureaucracy, reducing seven layers to four, moved manufacturing offshore; and in less than two years, AT&T's Consumer Products Division became the industry's most ferocious competitor.[7]

Subcultures can weaken and undermine an organization if they are in conflict with the dominant culture and/or the overall objectives. Successful firms, however, find that this is not always the case. Most subcultures are formed to help the members of a particular group deal with the specific, day-to-day problems with which they are confronted. The members may also support many, if not all, of the core values of the dominant culture. In the case of AT&T's Consumer Products Division, they became a model for the cultural changes that top level management was trying to accomplish for the whole corporation.[8]

Strong and Weak Cultures

Some organizational cultures could be labeled "strong," others "weak." As shown in the Application Example, strong organization cultures are often shaped by strong leaders. However, besides this leadership factor, there seem to be two major factors that determine the strength of an organizational culture: sharedness and intensity. *Sharedness* refers to the degree to which the organizational members have the same core values. *Intensity* is the degree of commitment of the organizational members to the core values.

The degree of sharedness is affected by two major factors: orientation and rewards. In order for people to share the same cultural values, they must know what these values are. Many organizations begin this process with an orientation program. New employees are told about the organization's philosophy and method of operating. This orientation continues on the job where their boss and coworkers share these values through both word of mouth and day-to-day work habits and example. Sharedness is also affected by rewards. When organizations give promotions, raises, recognition, and other forms of reward to those who adhere to the core values, these actions help others better understand these values. Some organizations have been

Application
Example
IIII➡

Strong Managers, Strong Cultures

Successful companies have strong cultures. However, they also have strong managers who introduce, reinforce, and/or nurture those cultures. During the 1980s, many CEOs were successful in taking over a firm that had problems, cutting the work force, and whipping it into shape. The successful managers of the 1990s are using a much different approach. Rather than relying on firings, fear, and guilt to rebuild the organization, these managers are working to create pride and enthusiasm in the firm. These individuals set themselves up as role models who establish overall direction and then work long hours to help the company reach agreed-upon goals. The personnel, influenced by this example, join in and help turn the firm around. There are many examples of managers who are using this approach: Barry Gibbons of Burger King, Richard Miller of Wang Laboratories, Richard Mayer of General Foods USA, Stephen Berkley, head of Quantum, a disk-drive maker, and Leo McKernan of Clark Equipment.

What are some of the specific techniques they employ? One is the use of positive ideas. They continually talk about how things can be done more efficiently or differently, and they encourage the personnel to think in positive terms as well. Second, they meet with managers throughout the company to get this message across to them, so that everyone understands that the organization is going to spare no effort to turn out the best possible product or service. Third, they look for the best people, many of whom have been bypassed for promotions, and give these individuals the jobs for which they are best suited. This serves as a strong incentive for others who want to help, but who have been limited in their efforts by previous managers who have discouraged teamwork and creative ideas. Fourth, they work to develop pride in their people. Do these ideas really work? Experience has shown that when headhunters are asked to find managers who can turn losing companies into winners, individuals who exhibit these four behaviors are at the top of the list of candidates.

labeled "the best to work for" because the rewards that they give to their people are exemplary and help reinforce commitment to core values. For example, a majority of companies recently surveyed offered "perks" such as a company car, country club membership, first-class air travel, and personal financial counseling to their upper-level management.[9]

The degree of intensity is a result of the reward structure. When employees realize that they will be rewarded for doing things "the organization's way," their desire to do so increases. Conversely, when they are not rewarded or they feel there is more to be gained by not doing things the organization's way, commitment to core values diminishes. Although recognition and other nonfinancial rewards are important, money still plays an important role. For example, Westinghouse and Red Lobster allocate merit budgets in order to reward those who carry out the cultural values of cooperation and serving internal and external customers.[10]

Table 19.1 provides an example of how an organization can determine whether it has a strong or weak culture. Notice from the answer key that such highly successful companies as Procter & Gamble, PepsiCo, and Coca Cola all have strong cultures.

TABLE 19.1 Computing an Organizational Culture Socialization Score

Respond to the items below as they apply to the handling of professional employees. Upon completion, compute the total score. For comparison, scores for a number of strong, intermediate, and weak culture firms are to be found at the bottom of the page.

	Not True of This Company				Very True of This Company
1. Recruiters receive at least one week of intensive training.	1	2	3	4	5
2. Recruitment forms identify several key traits deemed crucial to the firm's success, traits are defined in concrete terms and interviewer records specific evidence of each trait.	1	2	3	4	5
3. Recruits are subjected to at least four in-depth interviews.	1	2	3	4	5
4. Company actively facilitates de-selection during the recruiting process by revealing minuses as well as pluses.	1	2	3	4	5
5. New hires work long hours, are exposed to intensive training of considerable difficulty and/or perform relatively menial tasks in the first months.	1	2	3	4	5
6. The intensity of entry level experience builds cohesiveness among peers in each entering class.	1	2	3	4	5
7. All professional employees in a particular discipline begin in entry level positions regardless of prior experience or advanced degrees.	1	2	3	4	5
8. Reward systems and promotion criteria require mastery of a core discipline as a precondition of advancement.	1	2	3	4	5
9. The career path for professional employees is relatively consistent over the first six to ten years with the company.	1	2	3	4	5
10. Reward systems, performance incentives, promotion criteria and other primary measures of success reflect a high degree of congruence.	1	2	3	4	5
11. Virtually all professional employees can identify and articulate the firm's shared values (i.e., the purpose or mission that ties the firm to society, the customer or its employees).	1	2	3	4	5
12. There are very few instances when actions of management appear to violate the firm's espoused values.	1	2	3	4	5
13. Employees frequently make personal sacrifices for the firm out of commitment to the firm's shared values.	1	2	3	4	5
14. When confronted with trade-offs between systems measuring short-term results and doing what's best for the company in the long term, the firm usually decides in favor of the long-term.	1	2	3	4	5
15. This organization fosters mentor-protégé relationships.	1	2	3	4	5
16. There is considerable similarity among high potential candidates in each particular discipline.	1	2	3	4	5

Compute your score: _____

For comparative purposes:	Scores	
Strongly socialized firms	65–80	IBM, P&G, Morgan Guaranty
	55–64	ATT, Morgan Stanley, Delta Airlines
	45–54	United Airlines, Coca Cola
	35–44	General Foods, PepsiCo.
	25–34	United Technologies, ITT
Weakly socialized firms	Below 25	Atari

Source: Richard Pascale, "The Paradox of Corporate Culture: Reconciling Ourselves to Socialization." Copyright © by the Regents of the University of California. Reprinted from the *California Management Review*, vol. 27, no. 2, Winter 1985, pp. 39, 40. By permission of the Regents.

Types of Cultures

Many paradigms or models have recently been constructed to describe organizational culture. One of the most comprehensive and widely known is that by Deal and Kennedy.[11] Table 19.2 describes the four basic types of cultural profiles they uncovered. Each is characterized by a combination of two factors: the type of risks managers assume and the type of feedback that results from their decisions.

Most organizations are some hybrid of these cultural profiles; they do not neatly fit into any one of them. However, within the organization there are sub-cultures that do tend to fit into one of these four profiles. For example, according to Table 19.2, IBM's cultural profile would be that of a "work hard/play hard" company. However, because the corporation is so large and has so many different departments, this overall profile describes the enterprise in general terms only. On the other hand, people in the sales area would most certainly fit into this profile. This is in contrast to personnel in the research and development area who would be operating in a subculture best described in Table 19.2 as "bet your company."[12]

CREATING AND MAINTAINING A CULTURE

Some organizational cultures may be the direct, or at least indirect, result of actions taken by the founders. However, this is not always the case. Sometimes founders create weak cultures, and if the organization is to survive, a new top manager must be installed who will sow the seeds for the necessary strong culture. Thomas Watson, Sr., of IBM is a good example. When he took over the CTR Corporation, it was a small firm manufacturing computing, tabulating, and recording equipment. Through his dominant personality and the changes he made at the firm, Watson created a culture that led to the modern-day IBM corporation. He molded it to become the largest computer firm and one of the most recognized companies in any industry in the world.

At other times, a culture must be changed because the environment changes and the previous core cultural values are not in step with those needed for survival. The opening vignette on Apple Computer is a good example. When Steve Jobs and his partner started Apple, they wanted to create a culture where people could be creative, work on projects that interested them, and turn out a product that would be innovative. However, as they began broadening their horizons and trying to appeal to both the educational and the business market, the firm began to run into trouble. Its culture was not designed to compete head to head with IBM and the other computer giants. Steve Jobs was a thinker and creator, not an organizer and a manager. Apple began to lose money. A change in leadership and culture was needed. Jobs left Apple and directed his talents in starting a new venture, Next, Inc.[13] The following sections take a close look at how organizational cultures get started, maintained, and changed.

How Organizational Cultures Start

While organizational cultures can develop in a number of different ways, the process usually involves some version of the following steps:

1. A single person (founder) has an idea for a new enterprise.

TABLE 19.2 Organizational Culture Profiles

Name of the culture	TOUGH-GUY, MACHO	WORK HARD/ PLAY HARD	BET YOUR COMPANY	PROCESS
Type of risks that are assumed	High	Low	High	Low
Type of feedback from decisions	Fast	Fast	Slow	Slow
Typical kinds of organizations that use this culture	Construction, cosmetics, television, radio, venture capitalism, management consulting	Real estate, computer firms, auto distributors, door-to-door sales operations, retail stores, mass consumer sales	Oil, aerospace, capital goods manufacturers, architectural firms, investment banks, mining and smelting firms, military	Banks, insurance companies, utilities, pharmaceuticals, financial-service organizations, many agencies of the government
The ways survivors and/or heroes in this culture behave	They have a tough attitude. They are individualistic. They can tolerate all-or-nothing risks. They are superstitious.	They are super salespeople. They often are friendly, hail-fellow-well-met types. They use a team approach to problem solving. They are non-superstitious.	They can endure long-term ambiguity. They always double-check their decisions. They are technically competent. They have a strong respect for authority.	They are very cautious and protective of their own flank. They are orderly and punctual. They are good at attending to detail. They always follow established procedures.
Strengths of the personnel/culture	They can get things done in short order.	They are able to quickly produce a high volume of work.	They can generate high-quality inventions and major scientific breakthroughs.	They bring order and system to the workplace.
Weaknesses of the personnel/culture	They do not learn from past mistakes. Everything tends to be short-term in orientation. The virtues of cooperation are ignored.	They look for quick-fix solutions. They have a short-term time perspective. They are more committed to action than to problem solving.	They are extremely slow in getting things done. Their organizations are vulnerable to short-term economic fluctuations. Their organizations often face cash-flow problems.	There is lots of red tape. Initiative is down-played. They face long hours and boring work.
Habits of the survivors and/or heroes	They dress in fashion. They live in "in" places. They like one-on-one sports such as tennis. They enjoy scoring points off one another in verbal interaction.	They avoid extremes in dress. They live in tract houses. They prefer team sports such as touch football. They like to drink together.	They dress according to their organizational rank. Their housing matches their hierarchical position. They like sports such as golf, in which the outcome is unclear until the end of the game. The older members serve as mentors for the younger ones.	They dress according to hierarchical rank. They live in apartments or no-frills homes. They enjoy process sports like jogging and swimming. They like discussing memos.

Source: Adapted from Terence E. Deal and Allan A. Kennedy, *Corporate Cultures: The Rites and Rituals of Corporate Life,* © 1982, Addison-Wesley, Reading, Mass. Excerpts from Chap. 6. Used with permission.

2. The founder brings in one or more other key people and creates a core group that shares a common vision with the founder. That is, all in this core group believe that the idea is a good one, is workable, is worth running some risks for, and is worth the investment of time, money, and energy that will be required.

3. The founding core group begins to act in concert to create an organization by raising funds, obtaining patents, incorporating, locating space, building, and so on.

4. At this point, others are brought into the organization, and a common history begins to be built.[14]

Most of today's successful corporate giants in all industries basically followed these steps. Three well-known representative examples are IBM, McDonald's, and Wal-Mart.

- *International Business Machines.* Thomas Watson, Sr., the founder, began his business career selling office machines for the National Cash Register Company. This experience taught him both the benefits and techniques of effective salesmanship and the value of a good product. Years later when he left the company to join CTR, Watson took these concepts with him. In particular, he stressed the need for product research and development and the importance of marketing. These two ideas helped form the core cultural values of IBM's approach to business. During the 1930s and 1940s the company introduced electronic office machines, and beginning in the 1950s it complemented this line with computers. Today, Watson's core values continue to guide IBM. In fact, at the present time, even while the corporation is cutting back its middle-level management ranks, it still continues to stress new product development and sales efforts. The culture that Watson mainly created is still alive and well at IBM.

- *McDonald's.* Ray Kroc worked for many years as a salesperson for a food supplier (Lily Tulip Cup). He learned how retail food operations were conducted. He also had an entrepreneurial streak and began a sideline business with a partner. They sold multimixers, machines that were capable of mixing up to six frozen shakes at a time. One day Kroc received a large order for multimixers from the McDonald brothers. The order intrigued Kroc, and he decided to look in on the operation the next time he was in their area. When he did, Kroc became convinced that the McDonald's fast-food concept would sweep the nation. He bought the rights to franchise McDonald's units and eventually bought out the brothers. At the same time, he built the franchise on four basic concepts: quality, cleanliness, service, and price. In order to ensure that each unit offers the customer the best product at the best price, franchisees are required to attend McDonald University, where they are taught how to manage their business. Here they learn the McDonald cultural values and the proper way to run the franchise. This training ensures that franchisees all over the world are operating their units in the same way. Kroc died a few years ago, but the culture he left behind is still very much alive in McDonald's franchises across the world. In fact, new employees receive videotaped messages from the late Mr. Kroc. Some of the more interesting of his pronouncements that reflect and carry on his values are his thoughts on cleanliness: "If you've got time to lean, you've got time to clean." On the competition he says: "If they are drowning to death, I would put a hose in their mouth." And on expanding he declares: "When you're green, you grow; when you're ripe, you rot."[15] So even though he has not been involved in the business for over a decade, his legacy lives on. Even his office at corporate headquarters is preserved as a museum, his reading glasses untouched in their leather case on the desk.

- *Wal-Mart.* Sam Walton, founder of Wal-Mart Stores, Inc., opened his first Wal-Mart store in 1962. Focusing on the sale of discounted name-brand merchandise in small-town markets, he began to set up more and more stores in the Sun Belt. At the same time, he began developing effective inventory control systems and marketing techniques. Today, Wal-Mart has overtaken Sears as the largest retailer in the country with annual sales of about $35 billion. Walton encourages his people to develop new ideas that will increase their store's efficiency. If a policy does not seem to be working, the company quickly changes it. Executives continually encourage the 350,000 associates (employees) to challenge the current system and look for ways to improve it. Those who do these things are rewarded; those who do not perform up to expectations are encouraged to do better. The operating philosophy and environment at Wal-Mart is so attractive that it is consistently rated by *Fortune* at or near the top of the most admired and best managed corporations in America. Walton's founding values permeate the organization. To make sure the cultural values get out to all associates, they have a communication network worthy of the Pentagon. It includes everything from a six-channel satellite system to a private air force of 11 planes.[16] Everyone is taught this culture and is expected to operate within the core cultural values of hard work, efficiency, and customer service.

Maintaining Cultures through Steps of Socialization

Once an organizational culture is started and begins to develop, there are a number of practices that can help solidify the acceptance of core values and ensure that the culture maintains itself. These practices can be described in terms of several socialization steps. Figure 19.1 illustrates the sequence of these steps.

Selection of Entry-Level Personnel. The first step is the careful selection of entry-level candidates.[17] Using standardized procedures and seeking specific traits that tie to effective performance, trained recruiters interview candidates and attempt to screen out those whose personal styles and values do not make a "fit" with the organization's culture. There is accumulating evidence that those who have a realistic preview (called realistic job preview or RJP) of the culture will turn out better.[18]

Placement on the Job. The second step occurs on the job itself, after the person with a fit is hired. New personnel are subjected to a carefully orchestrated series of different experiences whose purpose is to cause them to question the organization's norms and values and to decide whether or not they can accept them. For example, many organizations with strong cultures make it a point to give newly hired personnel more work than they can handle. Sometimes these assignments are beneath the individual's abilities. At Procter & Gamble, for example, new personnel may be required to color in a sales territory map. The experience is designed to convey the

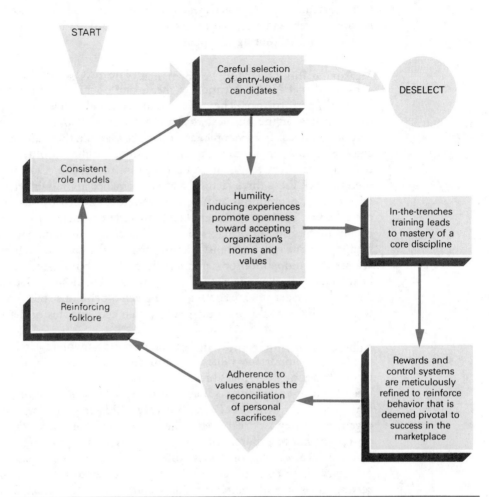

FIGURE 19.1
Steps of organization culture socialization.
(*Source:* Richard Pascale, "The Paradox of Corporate Culture: Reconciling Ourselves to Socialization," Copyright © by the Regents of the University of California. Reprinted from the *California Management Review*, vol. 27, no. 2, Winter 1985, p. 38. By permission of the Regents.)

message, "While you're smart in some ways, you're in kindergarten as far as what you know about this organization." The objective is also to teach the new entrant into the culture the importance of humility. These experiences are designed to make newly hired personnel vulnerable and to cause them to move closer emotionally to their colleagues, thus intensifying group cohesiveness. Campus fraternities and the military have practiced this approach for years.

Job Mastery. Once the initial "cultural shock" is over, the next step is mastery of one's job. This is typically done via extensive and carefully reinforced field experience. For example, IBM puts its new employees through a program that often takes as long as six years to produce an experienced marketing representative and twelve years to turn out a full-fledged controller. As personnel move along their career path, their performance is evaluated and additional responsibilities are assigned on the basis of progress. Quite often companies establish a step-by-step approach to this career plan, which helps reduce efforts by the personnal to use political power or to take shortcuts in order to get ahead at a faster pace. As Pascale notes, "Relationships, staying power, and a constant proven track record are the inescapable requirements of advancement" during this phase.[19]

Measuring and Rewarding Performance. The next step of the socialization process consists of meticulous attention to measuring operational results and to rewarding individual performance. These systems are comprehensive, consistent, and focus on those aspects of the business that are most crucial to competitive success and to corporate values. For example, at Procter & Gamble there are three factors that are considered most important: building volume, building profit, and making changes that increase effectiveness or add satisfaction to the job. Operational measures are used to track these three factors, and performance appraisals are tied to milestones. Importantly, promotions and merit pay are determined by success in each of these critical areas. IBM personnel are taught to adhere to the core cultural values through careful monitoring of managerial performance and through continual training programs. Anyone who commits a crime against the culture such as overzealousness against the competition or harsh handling of a subordinate is sent to the "penalty box." This typically involves a lateral move to a less desirous location. For example, a branch manager in Chicago might be given a nebulous staff position at headquarters. This individual is now off-track, which can slow his or her career progress.

Adherence to Important Values. The next step involves careful adherence to the firm's most important values. Identification with these values helps employees reconcile personal sacrifices brought about by their membership in the organization. They learn to accept these values and to trust the organization not to do anything that would hurt them. As Pascale observes, "Placing one's self 'at the mercy' of an organization imposes real costs. There are long hours of work, missed weekends, bosses one has to endure, criticism that seems unfair, job assignments and rotations that are inconvenient or undesirable."[20] However, the organization attempts to overcome these costs by connecting the sacrifices to higher human values such as serving society with better products and/or services. Companies such as Delta Airlines do this very effectively.

> Prior to joining Delta airlines, candidates hear endlessly about the "Delta family feeling." Numerous anecdotes illustrate that Delta's values require sacrifices: Management takes pay cuts during lean times; senior flight attendants and pilots voluntarily work fewer hours per week in order to avoid laying off more junior employees. Candidates who accept employment with Delta tend to accept this quid pro quo, believing that the restrictions on individual action comprise a reasonable trade-off. In effect, Delta's family philosophy is deemed worthy enough to make their sacrifices worthwhile.[21]

Reinforcing the Stories and Folklore. The next step involves reinforcing organizational folklore. This entails keeping alive stories that validate the organization's culture and way of doing things. The folklore helps explain why the organization does things a particular way. One of the most common forms of folklore is stories with morals the enterprise wants to reinforce. For example, at Procter & Gamble there is a story about the outstanding brand manager who was fired for overstating the features of a product. The moral of the story is that ethical claims are more important than making money. At AT&T there are numerous stories about field employees who made sacrifices to keep the phones working and operators who stayed on the line when a person called in and asked for emergency help because he had suffered a physical calamity. The moral of such stories is that these types of sacrifices are all in the line of duty for telephone employees, who must view their primary responsibility as that of helping the customer.

Recognition and Promotion. The final step is the recognition and promotion of individuals who have done their jobs well and who can serve as role models to new people in the organization. By pointing out these people as winners, the organization encourages others to follow their example. Role models in strong-culture firms are regarded as the most powerful ongoing training program of all. Morgan Stanley, the financial services firm, chooses role models based on energy, aggressiveness, and team play. Procter & Gamble looks for people who exhibit extraordinary consistency in such areas as toughmindedness, motivational skills, energy, and the ability to get things done through others.[22]

Changing Organizational Culture

Sometimes an organization determines that its culture has to be changed. For example, the external environment may undergo drastic change and the organization must either adapt to these new conditions or it may not survive. However, changing old cultures can be quite difficult: a case can even be made that it really can't be done successfully.[23] Predictable obstacles include entrenched skills, staffs, relationships, roles, and structures that work together to reinforce traditional cultural patterns, and powerful stakeholders such as unions, management, or even customers may support the existing culture.[24]

Despite the significant barriers and resistance to change, cultures can be managed and changed over time. This attempt to change culture can take many different forms. Simple guidelines such as developing a sense of history, creating a sense of oneness, promoting a sense of membership, and increasing exchange among members are helpful.[25] Also, organizations attempting to change their culture must be careful not to abandon their roots and blindly copy the so-called "successful" or "excellent" companies.[26] To pragmatically change an organization culture, there will be a need for new criteria for hiring, changes in the reward structure, new criteria for promotion, or a reassignment of organizational priorities. Procter & Gamble is a good example of a firm that has successfully undergone cultural change. After this example is given, the role that Theory Z and Japanese management have played in changing organizational culture will be examined.

Changing the Culture at Procter & Gamble. For years the culture at P&G had supported steady growth and profits. Recently, however, the company found itself under a great deal of pressure from the external competitive environment. For example, Kimberly-Clark had cut deeply into P&G's disposable-diaper market, one of the company's most lucrative market niches. At the same time, Lever Brothers was making inroads into P&G's share of the soap and detergent market. On the new product development front, things were no better. The company was having disappointing results with its Pringles potato chips and was suffering financial losses on its Coldsnap Homemade Ice Cream Mix, Wondra hand cream, and Rely Tampons. These setbacks were reflected on the company's bottom line as pretax earnings fell for the first time in over thirty years. At the same time the firm was having union problems. Its Kansas City plant voted to unionize, and the company went through a long fight with worker representatives in its effort to change work practices and improve efficiency.

These developments led P&G to make changes in its organizational culture. Some of these were:

1. The work team concept, in which production and maintenance workers—called "technicians"—are required to master and use a second skill, was extended throughout P&G's operations.
2. The lifetime-job tradition that once made P&G workers the envy of their blue-collar counterparts elsewhere gave way to layoffs.
3. The corporate paternalism of the past yielded to some hard practicalities as executives and workers alike were put on notice that plants that didn't measure up on productivity, cost, and quality would be shut down.
4. A determined management vigorously resisted attempts by organized labor to dictate how P&G's operations should be run.[27]

In addition to the above, P&G trimmed its work force by 5 percent on the plant floor and 4 percent company-wide. This was accomplished through reduced hiring, early retirement, and, in some cases, layoffs. Changing conditions had led P&G to change its culture.[28]

Changing Culture through Theory Z. Another way in which many organizations are trying to change their culture is by becoming more "Theory Z"–oriented.[29] Drawn from the work of Ouchi,[30] and given coverage as an organization development technique in Chapter 21, Theory Z is an approach to managing that calls for more:

- Consensus decision making
- Participation by the workers in all phases of the operation
- Concern for the overall well-being of employees

The theory draws heavily on the Japanese approach to management. Most accurately, Theory Z is really a combination of the current American and Japanese approaches to management. The accompanying International Application Example, Theory Z in Action, contrasts the typical American and Japanese approaches and the compromising Z approach. The following description of the American subsidiary of Fujitsu Limited (the largest computer and telecommunications company in Japan) shows Theory Z in action:

> Mid-level managers work in interactive teams composed of senior managers, workers and peers. The decision-making approach is consensual, and commitment to employees is long term. Managers are individually responsible for achieving goals, but they

are also expected to encourage employee participation and communication. Recreational condominiums in locations such as California's Lake Tahoe, for example, show a holistic concern for employees' family and recreational needs.[31]

International Application Example

Theory Z in Action

In the early 1980s William Ouchi's book *Theory Z: How American Business Can Meet the Japanese Challenge* pointed out the importance of organizational culture. Many American managers have studied Ouchi's book in order to gain insights regarding how the successful Japanese systems are different from their own and how their firm might successfully modify its culture by drawing on these concepts. In particular, there are seven characteristics that differentiate the approach used by the Americans (Theory A) and that of the Japanese (Theory J). Ouchi's Theory Z is a combination of these theories designed, in most cases, to modify American corporate culture and help firms compete more effectively with the Japanese. Here is how Theory Z modifies Theory A by drawing upon Theory J concepts.

Characteristics	Theory A (American)	Theory J (Japanese)	Theory Z (Modified)
Employment with a firm	Usually short-term; layoffs are quite common.	Especially in some of the large firms, it is for life. Layoffs are rare.	Fairly long term; this will help develop a loyal semipermanent work force.
Evaluation and promotion of the personnel	Very fast; individuals who are not promoted rapidly often seek employment elsewhere.	Very slow; big promotions are generally not given out for years.	Slower; more emphasis is given to training and evaluation than to promotion.
Career paths	Very specialized; people tend to stay in one area (accounting, finance, sales, etc.) for their entire career.	Very general; personnel are rotated from one area to another and become familiar with all areas of operations.	More general; emphasis is on job rotation and more broadly based training in order to give the person a better feel for the entire organization.
Decision making	Carried out by the individual manager.	Carried out via group decision making.	Carried out with more emphasis on group participation and consensus.
Control	Very explicit; people know exactly what to control and how to do it.	Very implicit and informal; people rely heavily on trust and goodwill.	More attention to informal control procedures coupled with explicit performance measures.
Responsibility	Assigned on an individual basis.	Shared collectively by the group.	Assigned on an individual basis.
Concern for the personnel	Organization is concerned primarily with the worker's work life only.	Organization is concerned with the whole life of the worker, business, and social.	Organization's concern is expanded to include more aspects of the worker's whole life.

Problems with Japanese Management. In recent years an increasing number of American firms have attempted to move their culture toward a Japanese-oriented approach in the belief that the Japanese do a much better job of integrating the individual into the workplace. On the other hand, it is important to remember that not all firms believe that Japanese management techniques are the way to go. They prefer American cultural values that emphasize individualism, rapid feedback, and rewards. Additionally, some critics note that in recent years the Japanese economy has suffered setbacks that have brought changes in their organizational cultures.

It has become increasingly popular to note the "myths" of Japanese management. For instance, one myth is that the Japanese people are naturally hard-working. The facts are that foreign production data on Honda, Sony, Matsushita, and other Japanese pioneers of multinationalization show little difference in productivity among local workers in their plants in Japan, Europe, North America, or Asia.[32] Another example is that today some prominent Japanese firms do not give lifetime employment to their new people. (Most of the smaller ones never did.) Lifetime employment is reserved only for those who have been with a big firm for many years. A second change is that some Japanese firms are now putting pressure on their people to retire early so as to reduce the firms' payroll costs and remain competitive. The holistic concern for the well-being of the individual worker may be largely gone. Still another significant change is that many young people in Japan are beginning to question whether the Japanese system can function properly as societal and economic changes become more commonplace. These concerns include the following:

- Decision making by consensus, employed by many large companies, often discourages initiative and the pursuit of imaginative ideas. The basic premise of consensus decision making is homogeneity among members, not heterogeneity.
- Personnel policies such as seniority-based wage and promotion systems cannot better compensate highly specialized employees who are fully aware of the value of their services to the company.
- Probably most important, many Japanese have started to question the notion of single-company loyalty and compensation based on seniority rather than performance. Most Japanese workers still acquire company-specific skills through in-house training and are reluctant to move. This practice is reinforced by strong social norms that make it difficult for employees to find work with other employers.[33]

Theory Z and Japanese Management Approaches in Perspective. Today, most American managers who are drawing on Theory Z and Japanese management approaches to change their organizational culture are doing so on a selective basis. They are choosing those ideas which, when appropriately modified, will result in higher productivity and efficiency. For example, a Japanese-style quality team of Federal Express clerks identified and solved a billing problem that saved the company 2.1 million dollars.[34] In addition, many successful American firms have really been using the so-called "Japanese" concepts for decades. Lincoln Electric, Merck, Delta Airlines, and Johnson & Johnson, to name but a few, have long been outstanding companies because they have encouraged employee participation, rewarded teamwork, and ensured employment to their people. For example, when United States–owned Lincoln Electric experienced a demand slump a few years ago, it trained fifty-four factory and office workers to sell a new welding machine. They went into the field and over a four-year period sold $10 million of this equipment.[35] The "best" American firms have always been concerned with developing the right culture for their social and economic environments.

Summary

Organizational culture is a pattern of basic assumptions that are taught to new personnel as the correct way to perceive, think, and act on a day-to-day basis. Some of the important characteristics of organizational culture are observed behavioral regularities, norms, dominant values, philosophy, rules, and organizational climate.

While everyone in an organization will share the organization's culture, they may not do so to the same degree. There can be a dominant culture, but a number of subcultures. A dominant culture is a set of core values that is shared by a majority of the organization's members. A subculture is a set of values shared by a small percentage of the organization's members.

Some organizations have strong cultures; others have weak cultures. The strength of the culture will depend on sharedness and intensity. Sharedness is the degree to which the organizational members have the same core values. Intensity is the degree of commitment of the organizational members to the core values.

A culture typically is created by a founder or top-level manager who forms a core group that shares a common vision. This group acts in concert to create the cultural values, norms, and climate necessary to carry on this vision. In maintaining this culture, enterprises typically carry out several steps such as the following: careful selection of entry-level candidates; on-the-job experiences to familiarize the personnel with the organization's culture; mastery of one's job; meticulous attention to measuring operational results and to rewarding individual performance; careful adherence to the organization's most important values; a reinforcing of organizational stories and folklore; and, finally, recognition and promotion of individuals who have done their jobs well and who can serve as role models to new personnel in the organization.

In some cases organizations find that they must change their culture in order to remain competitive and even survive in their environment. One of the most common changes occurring in recent years is a trend toward Theory Z and Japanese management approaches. However, in some cases, including Japanese firms themselves, there is actually a trend in the other direction, with lifetime employment and decision making by consensus being eliminated or reduced.

Questions for Discussion and Review

1. What is meant by the term *organizational culture*? Define it and give some examples of its characteristics.

2. There are several important characteristics of organizational culture identified in the chapter. What are these? Describe each.

3. How does a dominant culture differ from a subculture? In your answer be sure to define both terms.

4. How do strong cultures differ from weak cultures? What two factors determine the strength of the culture?

5. In what way do risk taking and feedback help create basic types of organizational culture profiles? Explain, being sure to include a discussion of these profiles in your answer.

6. How do organizational cultures develop? What four steps commonly occur?

7. How do organizations go about maintaining their cultures? What steps are involved? Describe them.

8. Why are some firms turning to a Theory Z approach to help them in modifying their organizational culture? What benefit does this approach offer? Is it best for all American firms?

References

1. Nancy C. Morey and Fred Luthans, "Anthropology: The Forgotten Behavioral Science in Management History," *Best Paper Proceedings of the Academy of Management*, 1987, pp. 128–132.

2. Geert Hofstede, "Editorial: The Usefulness of the 'Organizational Culture' Concept," *Journal of Management Studies*, May 1986, p. 22.

3. Edgar H. Schein, "Organizational Culture," *American Psychologist*, February 1990, p. 110.

4. Edgar H. Schein, *Organizational Culture and Leadership*, Jossey-Bass, San Francisco, 1985, p. 9.

5. Mats Alvesson, "Organizations, Culture, and Ideology," *International Studies of Management and Organization*, vol. 17, 1987, pp. 4–18.

6. Nancy C. Morey and Fred Luthans, "Refining the Displacement of Culture and the Use of Scenes and Themes in Organizational Studies," *Academy of Management Review*, April 1985, p. 221.

7. John J. Keller, "Bob Allen is Turning AT&T into a Live Wire," *Business Week*, November 6, 1989, p. 140.

8. Ibid.

9. "Popular Perks," *The Wall Street Journal*, April 18, 1990, p. R25.

10. Mark R. Edwards, "Integrating Fiefdoms and Subcultures into Organization Networks," in Richard Bellingham, Barry Cohen, Mark Edwards, and Judd Allen (eds.), *The Corporate Culture Sourcebook*, Human Resource Development Press, Amherst, Mass., 1990, p. 175.

11. Terence E. Deal and Allan A. Kennedy, *Corporate Cultures: The Rites and Rituals of Corporate Life*, Addison-Wesley, Reading, Mass., 1982.

12. For more on this topic see Edgar H. Schein, "Coming to a New Awareness of Organizational Culture," *Sloan Management Review*, Winter 1984, pp. 3–16.

13. For a description of some of the work done at Next, Inc., see "The Ultimate Computer Factory," *Fortune*, Feb. 26, 1990, pp. 75–79.

14. Schein, *Organizational Culture and Leadership*, op. cit., p. 210.

15. Robert Johnson, "McDonald's Combines a Dead Man's Advice with Lively Strategy," *The Wall Street Journal*, Dec. 18, 1987, p. 1.

16. Sarah Smith, "Quality of Management," *Fortune*, Jan. 29, 1990, p. 46.

17. This process is described in Richard Pascale, "The Paradox of 'Corporate Culture': Reconciling Ourselves to Socialization," *California Management Review*, Winter 1985, pp. 29–38.

18. See Gregory B. Northcraft and Margaret A. Neale, *Organizational Behavior*, Dryden, Chicago, 1990, pp. 460–461, for a review of this literature, and Robert Vandenberg and Vida Scarpello, "The Matching Model: An Examination of the Processes Underlying Realistic Job Previews,"

Journal of Applied Psychology, February 1990, pp. 60–67, for some recent research.

19. Pascale, op. cit., p. 31.
20. Ibid., p. 32.
21. Ibid., p. 32.
22. For more on this process see Richard Pascale, "Fitting New Employees into the Company Culture," *Fortune,* May 18, 1984, pp. 28–43.
23. See Stephen P. Robbins, *Organization Theory,* 3d ed., Prentice-Hall, Englewood Cliffs, N.J., 1990, pp. 456–457.
24. Michael Beer and Elise Walton, "Developing the Competitive Organization," *American Psychologist,* February 1990, p. 157.
25. Warren Gross and Shula Shichman, "How to Grow an Organization Culture," *Personnel,* September 1987, p. 52.
26. Alan L. Wilkins and Nigel J. Bristow, "For Successful Organization Culture, Honor Your Past," *Academy of Management Executive,* August 1987, pp. 221–228.
27. Thomas M. Rohan, "P&G Fights Back," *Industry Week,* Oct. 15, 1984, pp. 65–66.
28. Jolie B. Solomon and John Bussey, "Pressed by

Its Rivals, Procter & Gamble Co. Is Altering Its Ways," *The Wall Street Journal,* May 20, 1985, p. 22.
29. Charles W. Joiner, Jr., "SMR Forum: Making the 'Z' Concept Work," *Sloan Management Review,* Spring 1985, pp. 57–63.
30. William G. Ouchi, *Theory Z,* Avon, New York, 1981.
31. Richard L. Daft, *Management,* Dryden Press, Chicago, 1988, p. 505. Also see Art Gemmell, "Fujitsu's Cross-Cultural Style," *Management Review,* June 1986, pp. 7–8.
32. Kenichi Ohmae, "Japan's Role in the World Economy," *California Management Review,* Spring 1987, p. 54.
33. S. Prakash Sethi, Nobuaki Namiki, and Carl L. Swanson, "The Decline of the Japanese System of Management," *California Management Review,* Summer 1984, p. 43.
34. Brian Dumaine, "Who Needs a Boss?", *Fortune,* May 7, 1990, p. 52.
35. John Hoerr, "A Japanese Import That's Not Selling," *Business Week,* Feb. 26, 1990, p. 87.

REAL CASE: LOOK OUT WORLD, HERE WE COME

One of the major developments that cause a change in organizational culture is the expansion or contraction of company operations. In the case of American Airlines, recent expansion into fast-growing international markets is causing the company to revise its approach to doing business.

During most of the 1980s, less than 10 percent of American's revenues were generated by global operations. However, in the latter part of the decade, the firm started increasing its overseas business and, in 1990, it bought Eastern Airline's Latin American route system. Now operating out of a strong Miami hub, American is catering strongly to this southern market. These efforts pushed international revenues to over 20 percent of its total, and the firm projects that by the year 2000 it will be generating 30 percent of all revenues from overseas business.

One of the primary ways in which American is changing is through its efforts to cater to these foreign markets. For example, international fliers care a lot more about in-flight service than American realized. For example, when flight attendants warmed the mixed nuts accompanying their cocktails to the precisely correct temperature (98° F), passengers noticed and commented favorably. The airline also learned that many business passengers like to eat soon after the plane is airborne, so that they can then sleep or work undisturbed for the rest of the flight; and they prefer simple, not sumptuous, meals.

American Airlines also adjusts its service features to national preferences. For example, German passengers are particular about the use of titles such as "Herr

Doktor." Japanese passengers dislike being touched. Latin passengers like a main course that consists of beef and French wine.

The company also relies heavily on computer technology to keep ahead of the competition. For example, American's Sabre reservation system is the best in the industry. There currently are more than 85,000 Sabre terminals in use throughout the world, and the system helps ensure that travel agents will book their people on American in more cases than not. As a result of these changes in their organization culture, American Airlines is likely to remain one of the premier carriers in the world.

1. How did American Airlines' international expansion cause changes in its organizational culture?
2. Using Figure 19.1 as a point of reference, which step in the culture model would be most important to top managers at American Airlines? Why?
3. Using Figure 19.1 as a point of reference, which step would be most important in helping ensure that the company continues to adjust its service features to national cultures?

Case:
Out with the Old, In with the New

The Anderson Corporation was started in 1962 as a small consumer products company. During the first twenty years the company's research and development (R&D) staff developed a series of new products that proved to be very popular in the marketplace. Things went so well that the company had to add a second production shift just to keep up with the demand. During this time period the firm expanded its plant on three different occasions. During an interview with a national magazine, the firm's founder, Paul Anderson, said, "We don't sell our products. We allocate them." This comment was in reference to the fact that the firm had only twenty-four salespeople and was able to garner annual revenues in excess of $62 million.

Three years ago Anderson suffered its first financial setback. The company had a net operating loss of $1.2 million. Two years ago the loss was $2.8 million, and last year it was $4.7 million. The accountant estimates that this year the firm will lose approximately $10 million.

Alarmed by this information, Citizen's Bank, the company's largest creditor, insisted that the firm make some changes and start turning things around. In response to this request, Paul Anderson agreed to step aside. The board of directors replaced him with Bill Hartmann, head of the marketing division of one of the country's largest consumer products firms.

After making an analysis of the situation, Bill has come to the conclusion that there are a number of changes that must be made if the firm is to be turned around. The three most important are:

1. More attention must be given to the marketing side of the business. The most vital factor for success in the sale of the consumer goods produced by Anderson is an effective sales force.
2. There must be an improvement in product quality. Two percent of Anderson's output is defective as against ½ of 1 percent for the average firm in the industry. In the past the demand for Anderson's output was so great that quality control was not an important factor. Now it is proving to be a very costly area.
3. There must be reduction in the number of people in the operation. Anderson can get by with two-thirds of its current production personnel and only half of its administrative staff.

Bill has not shared these ideas with the board of directors, but he intends to do so. For the moment he is considering the steps that will have to be taken in making these changes and the effect that all of this might have on the employees and the overall operation.

1. What is wrong with the old organizational culture? What needs to be done to change it?
2. Why might it be difficult for Bill to change the existing culture?
3. What specific steps does Bill need to take in changing the culture? Identify and describe at least two.

Case: Keeping Things the Same

Metropolitan Hospital was built two years ago and currently has a work force of people. The hospital is small, but because it is new, it is extremely efficient. The board has voted to increase its capacity from 60 beds to 190 beds. By this time next year, the hospital will be over three times as large as it is now in terms of both beds and personnel.

The administrator, Clara Hawkins, feels that the major problem with this proposed increase is that the hospital will lose its efficiency. "I want to hire people who are just like our current team of personnel—hard-working, dedicated, talented, and able to interact well with patients. If we triple the number of employees, I don't see how it will be possible to maintain our quality patient care. We are going to lose our family atmosphere. We will be inundated with mediocrity and we'll end up being like every other institution in the local area—large and uncaring!"

The chairman of the board is also concerned about the effect of hiring such a large number of employees. However, he believes that Clara is overreacting. "It can't be that hard to find people who are like our current staff. There must be a lot of people out there who are just as good. What you need to do is develop a plan of action that will allow you to carefully screen those who will fit into your current organizational culture and those who will not. It's not going to be as difficult as you believe. Trust me. Everything will work out just fine."

As a result of the chairman's comments, Clara has decided that the most effective way of dealing with the situation is to develop a plan of action. She intends to meet with her administrative group and determine the best way of screening incoming candidates and then helping those who are hired to become socialized in terms of the hospital's culture. Clara has called a meeting for the day after tomorrow. At that time she intends to discuss her ideas, get suggestions from her people, and then formulate a plan of action. "We've come too far to lose it all now," she told her administrative staff assistant. "If we keep our wits about us, I think we can continue to keep Metropolitan as the showcase hospital in this region."

1. What can Clara and her staff do to select the type of entry-level candidates they want? Explain.
2. How can Clara ensure that those who are hired come to accept the core cultural values of the hospital? What steps would you recommend?
3. Could Clara use this same approach if another 200 people were hired a few years from now?

International Organizational Behavior

■ On a Buying Binge

Many businesses are discovering the importance of international organizational behavior in a direct way—they are investing in or setting up overseas operations. One of the best examples is the Japanese company Mitsubishi which has both invested in and set up operations throughout the world. In the United States, the huge multinational corporation (MNC) is best known for its automobiles and big-screen televisions, but these are only two of its many American businesses. Mitsubishi also owns the Bank of California, Value Rent-a-Car, Aristech Chemical, and 56.7 percent of Rockefeller Center. In addition, the company recently bought Verbatim from Eastman Kodak for $200 million, acquired a $400 million power plant in Virginia, launched a $150 million futures-trading joint venture in Chicago, bought a San Francisco–based oil company for $75 million, and helped finance the purchase of the Pebble Beach golf course in California. At the same time, the MNC is expanding into other geographic areas including Europe and the Far East.

This international expansion is forcing Mitsubishi to closely study and understand the cultural values of the countries in which it does business. The expansion is also fostering a better understanding by Americans of Japanese business strategies. Mitsubishi has twenty-eight core businesses from banks to oil to breweries to manufacturing. Although these core businesses operate independently of each other, they can call on each other for help should they need it. Aware of this fact, the U.S. government has begun to investigate the value of allowing American firms to form cartels or combinations that can work together to fend off foreign competition. The government is also looking into the possibility of restricting expansion in the United States by giant foreign-based MNCs that are able to muscle their way in and push aside local businesses.

So international expansion is proving to be a two-edged sword in encouraging a better understanding of international organizational behavior. Each side is more closely examining the behaviors of the other and learning how to adapt appropriately. In the case of the United States, as one observer recently noted, "American companies want to be individualistic, but the requirement of the new age is that they have to take a few pages out of

Japanese experience to enhance their efficiency." In so doing, the Americans are likely to learn a great deal about how to compete effectively with the Japanese.

Learning Objectives

- **Examine** the role and impact that different cultures have on organizational behavior.
- **Present** the research on organizational behavior across cultures.
- **Discuss** the international implications of interpersonal communication.
- **Analyze** the international implications of employee motivation.
- **Explain** the international implications of managerial leadership.

Just as American businesses have ignored the international context except in recent years, so has the field of organizational behavior. For example, up to recent years organizational behavior textbooks did not even include an international chapter such as this one. However, just as it is becoming increasingly clear that the world is shrinking and America is part of the global economy, requiring new strategies,[1] it is becoming increasingly recognized that the international dimensions of organizational behavior are important. American employees definitely think and behave in a particular way. Many people around the world think and act similarly, but there are also some important differences. Differences even exist in the way knowledge is accumulated. For example, it has been pointed out that the European behavioral scientists tend to be more cognitive and/or psychoanalytically based while their American counterparts are more behavioristic and/or humanistically oriented.[2] In understanding and applying organizational behavior concepts in other countries around the world, it is important to be aware of these differences.

For example, in some countries managers prefer to use—and may be more effective with—an autocratic leadership style than in the typical U.S. organization. Germany is a visible example. Typical American managers who are transferred to Germany may find their leadership style to be too participative. German subordinates may expect the American to make more decisions and to consult with them less. Research on obedience to authority (discussed in Chapter 4) found a higher percentage of Germans were obedient than their American counterparts.[3] Similarly, an American manager in Japan who decides to set up a performance-based incentive system that gives a weekly bonus to the best worker in each work group may be making a mistake. Japanese workers do not like to be singled out for individual attention and go against the group's norms and values. Perhaps this impact of differences across cultures was best stated by the cofounder of Honda Motor, T. Fujisawa, when he stated: "Japanese and American management is 95 percent the same, and differs in all important respects."[4]

This chapter examines organizational behavior from an international perspective and within an international context. It starts by using the last chapter on organizational culture as a point of departure for examining the impact that different cultures can have on organizational behavior. This gives attention both to how cultures vary and how the behaviors within these cultures can differ. The remainder of the chapter analyzes the familiar organizational behavior topics of communication, motivation, and leadership, only in an international context.

THE IMPACT OF CULTURE ON INTERNATIONAL ORGANIZATIONAL BEHAVIOR

Although the last chapter dealt specifically with *organizational* culture, which is somewhat narrower, culture per se was defined in Chapter 2 as the acquired knowledge that people use to interpret experience and generate social behavior. It is important to recognize that culture is learned and helps people in their efforts to interact and communicate with others in the society. When placed in a culture where values and beliefs are different, some people have a great deal of difficulty adjusting. This is particularly true when American businesspeople are assigned to a foreign country. These expatriates quickly learn that the values of American culture are often quite different from those of their host country. As noted by Robbins, "there is a growing body of evidence to indicate that national cultures differ widely and the result is marked differences in behavior patterns worldwide."[5]

How Do Cultures Vary?

There are several basic dimensions that differentiate cultures. The following sections examine the most important of these.

How People See Themselves.   In some countries of the world, people are viewed as basically honest and trustworthy. In others, people are regarded with suspicion and distrust. For example, a reason why some Third World people regard the United States with suspicion and distrust may result from the way these people view themselves. They assume others are like them, that is, prepared to cut corners if they can get away with it. On the other hand, many other people of Third World countries are just the opposite. They do not lock their doors; they are very trusting and assume that no one will break in. It is forbidden to take the property of another person, and the people adhere strictly to that cultural value. In the United States, people also have a mixed view of other people. Most Americans still view others as basically honest but also believe that it is important to be alert for any sign of trouble.

When people travel outside their home country, they carry their values with them just like their baggage. This sometimes results in their being surprised over the way they are treated. The following is an example:

> A young Canadian in Sweden found summer employment working in a restaurant owned by Yugoslavians. As the Canadian explained, "I arrived at the restaurant and was greeted by an effusive Yugoslavian man who set me to work at once washing dishes and preparing the restaurant for the June opening.
>
> "At the end of the first day, I was brought to the back room. The owner took an old cash box out of a large desk. The Yugoslavian owner counted out my wages for the day and was about to return the box to the desk when the phone rang in the front room. The owner hesitated: should he leave me sitting in the room with the money or take it with him? Quite simply, could he trust me?

"After a moment, the man got up to answer the phone, leaving me with the open money box. I sat there in amazement; how could he trust me, someone he had known for less than a day, a person whose last name and address he didn't even know."[6]

People's Relationship to Their World. In some societies people attempt to dominate their environment. In other societies they try to live in harmony with it or are subjugated by it. The Americans and Canadians, for example, attempt to dominate their environment. In agriculture they use fertilizers and insecticides to increase crop yields. Other societies, especially those in the Far East, work in harmony with the environment by planting crops in the right places and at the right time. In still other societies, most notably Third World countries, no action is taken regarding the subjugation of nature, so, for example, when the floods come, there are no dams or irrigation systems for dealing with the impending disaster there. Also, when the Berlin Wall crumbled and Eastern Europe opened up, it was found that there was an ecological disaster there. For example, it was found that almost all of the rivers were heavily polluted, in some areas 90 percent of the children suffered from respiratory and other pollution-related diseases, and sewage treatment was in a terrible state almost everywhere.[7]

Individualism versus Collectivism. Some countries of the world encourage individualism. The United States, Great Britain, and Canada are examples. In other countries collectivism, or group orientation, is important. Japan, China, and the Israeli kibbutzim emphasize group harmony, unity, commitment, and loyalty. The differences reflect themselves in many ways such as in hiring practices. In countries where individualism is important, job applicants are evaluated on the basis of personal, educational, and professional achievements. In group-oriented societies applicants are evaluated on the basis of trustworthiness, loyalty, and compatibility with coworkers.

The Time Dimension. In some societies people are oriented toward the past. In others they tend to be more focused on the present. Still others are futuristic in their orientation. Americans and Canadians are most interested in the present and the near future. Businesspeople in these countries are particularly interested in where their companies are today and where they will be in five to ten years. People who are hired and do not work out are often let go in short order. They seldom last more than one or two years. Most Europeans place more importance on the past than do North Americans. They believe in preserving history and continuing traditions. They are concerned with the past, present, and future. Many Far Eastern countries are futuristic in their approach. The Japanese, for example, have very long-term future-oriented time horizons. When large Japanese firms hire employees, they often retain them for a long time, even for life. The firms will spend a great deal of money to train them, and there is a strong, mutual commitment on both sides. Researchers have even developed ways to measure the time dimensions of organizational members.[8] Scales include those measuring punctuality, allocation, awareness, schedules and deadlines, work pace, and future orientation.

TABLE 20.1 Major Concepts in the Comparative Analysis of U.S. and Japanese Management

Expressions Commonly Used in Management	Principal Meanings, Interpretations, and Images	
	In United States	**In Japan**
Company	Team in sport	Family in village
Business goal	To win	To survive
Employees	Players in a team	Children in a family
Human relations	Functional	Emotional
Competition	Cut-throat	Cooperation or sin
Profit motivation	By all means	Means to an end
Sense of identification	Job pride	Group prestige
Work motivation	Individual income	Group atmosphere
Production	Productivity	Training and diligence
Personnel	Efficiency	Maintenance
Promotion	According to abilities	According to year of service
Pay	Service and results	Considered an award for patience and sacrifice

Source: Adapted from Motofusa Murayama, "A Comparative Analysis of U.S. and Japanese Management Systems," in Sang M. Lee and Gary Schwendiman (eds.), *Management by Japanese Systems,* Praeger, a division of Greenwood Press, Inc., New York, 1982, p. 237. Copyright © 1982 by Praeger Publishers. Used with permission.

Public and Private Space. Some cultures promote the use of public space; others favor private space. For example, in Japan bosses often sit together with their employees in the same large room. The heads of some of the biggest Japanese firms may leave their chaffeur-driven limousines at home and ride the crowded public subways to work in the morning so they can be with their workers. In the Middle East there are often many people present during important meetings. These cultures have a public orientation. In contrast, North Americans prefer private space. The more restricted or confined a manager is, the more important the individual is assumed to be. Anyone coming to see the person must first go past a secretary (and sometimes more than one) before being admitted to the manager's presence.

When comparing societies in terms of the dimensions discussed above, it becomes obvious that there are major differences between the ways in which business is done in one corner of the world and another. Table 20.1, for example, provides a summary comparative analysis of U.S. and Japanese management in terms of some major business-related areas.

Behavior across Cultures

Just as there are many ways that culture per se varies, there are also many ways in which behavior varies across cultures. Tables 20.2 and 20.3 provide insights into the degree to which managers agree (or disagree) regarding the value of a hierarchical structure and the necessity of bypassing that structure in getting things done. Table 20.4 shows how important management feels it is to have a precise answer to subordinate questions about work-related activities. Quite obviously, the way managers function and behave appears to be influenced by their culture.

TABLE 20.2 The Main Reason for a Hierarchical Structure Is so That Everybody Knows Who Has Authority over Whom

	Agreement Rate across Countries to the Above Statement (Least to Greatest)
United States	18%
Germany	24
Great Britain	38
Netherlands	38
France	45
Italy	50
Japan	52
Indonesia	86

Source: Adapted from Andre Laurent, "The Cultural Diversity of Western Conceptions of Management," *International Studies of Management and Organization,* Spring–Summer 1983, p. 82. Used with permission.

TABLE 20.3 In Order to Have Efficient Work Relationships, It Is Often Necessary to Bypass the Hierarchical Line

	Disagreement Rate across Countries to the Above Statement (Least to Greatest)
Sweden	22%
Great Britain	31
United States	32
Netherlands	39
France	42
Germany	46
Italy	75

Source: Adapted from Andre Laurent, "The Cultural Diversity of Western Conceptions of Management," *International Studies of Management and Organization,* Spring–Summer 1983, p. 86. Used with permission.

TABLE 20.4 It Is Important for a Manager to Have at Hand Precise Answers to Most of the Questions That His Subordinates May Raise about Their Work

	Agreement Rate across Countries to the Above Statement (Least to Greatest)
Sweden	10%
Netherlands	17
United States	18
Great Britain	27
Germany	46
France	53
Italy	66
Indonesia	73
Japan	78

Source: Based on Andre Laurent, "The Cultural Diversity of Western Conceptions of Management," *International Studies of Management and Organization,* Spring–Summer 1983, p. 86. Used with permission.

Dimensions of Cultural Difference

One way of examining organizational behavior across cultures and explaining the differences that exist is to look at important dimensions such as those identified by Geert Hofstede, a well-known Dutch researcher. In a huge study involving 116,000 respondents, he found highly significant differences in the behavior and attitudes of employees and managers from 70 different countries who worked for subsidiaries of IBM.[9] Two of these differences were in individualism/collectivism and in power distance. The following sections take a close look at these and other cultural differences important to organizational behavior. A word of caution is in order when reading the results of Hofstede's classic study. It must be remembered that "the position of a culture along a dimension is based on the averages for all the respondents in that particular country. Characterizing a national work culture does not mean that every person in the nation has all the characteristics ascribed to that culture—there are bound to be many individual variations."[10]

Individualism/Collectivism and Power Distance. Individualism is the tendency to take care of oneself and one's immediate family. Collectivism is characterized by a tight social framework in which people distinguish between their own group and other groups. Power distance is the extent to which less powerful members of organizations accept the unequal distribution of power, i.e., the degree to which employees accept that their boss has more power than they do.

When Hofstede examined managers from fifty countries in terms of individualism and power distance, he found four basic clusters. Figure 20.1 shows that the United States has high individualism and small power distance (employees do not grant their boss much power). This is in contrast, for example, to Mexico, which has high collectivism (tight group) and large power distance (a lot of power granted to the boss). Countries that are in the same circled-in area tend to be similar in terms of individualism/collectivism and power distance. Figure 20.1 illustrates that American multinational firms doing business in Mexico would encounter much greater cultural differences than they would in France and still less if they operated in Great Britain.

Uncertainty Avoidance. Another dimension of cultural difference is uncertainty avoidance. Uncertainty avoidance is the extent to which people feel threatened by ambiguous situations and the degree to which they try to avoid these situations by doing such things as:

- Providing greater career stability
- Establishing more formal rules
- Rejecting deviant ideas and behavior
- Accepting the possibility of absolute truths and the attainment of expertise[11]

In Japan, for example, where lifetime employment exists in at least the large companies, there is high uncertainty avoidance. In America, by contrast, where there is relatively high job mobility, there is low uncertainty avoidance.

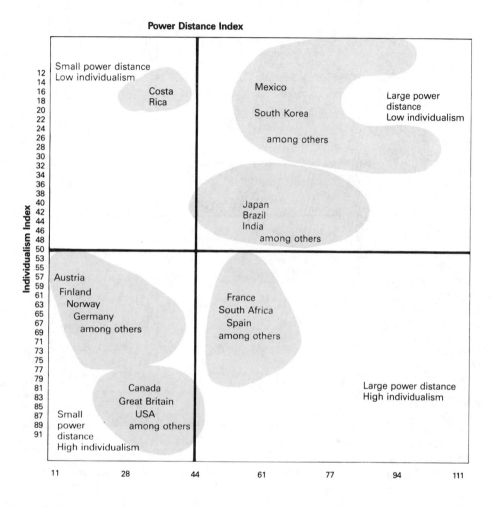

FIGURE 20.1
The position of selected countries on power distance and individualism. (*Source:* Adapted from Geert Hofstede, "The Cultural Relativity of Organizational Practices and Theories," *Journal of International Business Studies,* Fall 1983, p. 82. Used with permission.)

Figure 20.2 shows the position of selected countries on power distance and uncertainty avoidance. Countries like Great Britain, which has weak uncertainty avoidance and low power distance, tend to have less hierarchy and more interaction between people. Additionally, risk taking is both expected and encouraged. Employees in high power distance and low uncertainty avoidance cultures such as India tend to think of their organizations as traditional families. Employees in countries such as Mexico and Brazil tend to think of their organizations as pyramids of people rather than as families. Employees in countries such as Austria and Finland tend to work in organizations that are highly predictable without needing a strong hierarchy. Roles and procedures are clearly defined in these cultures.

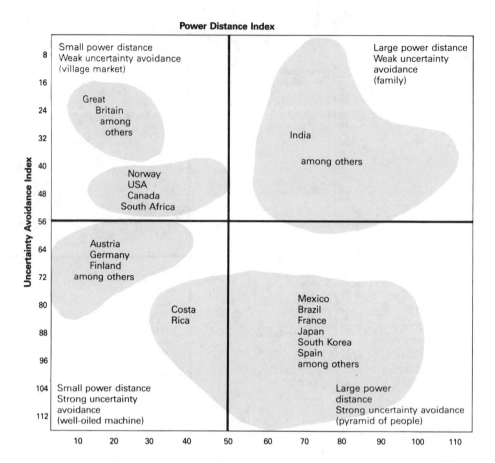

FIGURE 20.2
The position of selected countries on power distance and uncertainty avoidance.
(*Source:* Adapted from Geert Hofstede, "The Cultural Relativity of Organizational Practices and Theories," *Journal of International Business Studies,* Fall 1983, p. 84. Used with permission.)

Masculinity/Femininity. Hofstede also measured the impact of masculinity/femininity. Masculinity is the extent to which the dominant values of a society emphasize assertiveness and the acquisition of money and other material things. Femininity is the extent to which the dominant values in a society emphasize relationships among people, concern for others, and interest in quality of work life. As shown in Figure 20.3, in masculine societies such as Japan the work focus in auto factories is on efficiency. In feminine societies such as Scandinavian countries like Norway the work focus in factories is on quality of work life. This is shown in Figure 20.3.

Overall Categories for Employee Attitudes Worldwide. Figures 20.1, 20.2, and 20.3 show how countries tend to cluster on the basis of particular cultural differences. On an overall employee attitude basis, one comprehensive analysis using eight empirical studies concluded that there are eight basic clusters in which most countries

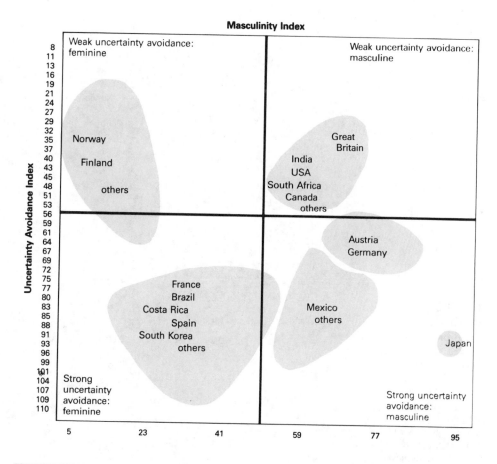

FIGURE 20.3
The position of selected countries on uncertainty avoidance and masculinity/femininity. (*Source:* Adapted from Geert Hofstede, "The Cultural Relativity of Organizational Practices and Theories," *Journal of International Business Studies,* Fall 1983, p. 86. Used with permission.)

of the world can be placed. This is shown in Figure 20.4. Those which do not fit into one of these clusters include Brazil, Japan, India, and Israel. These countries appear in different clusters in different studies so, at least for the time being, more research will have to be conducted before they can be assigned to any specific cluster.[12]

As one would guess, the general attitudes of U.S. employees (work goals, values, needs, and job attitudes) are most culturally similar to those of employees in other "Anglo" countries—Canada, Australia, New Zealand, United Kingdom, Ireland, and South Africa. When American managers are dealing with employees from other clusters—Germanic, Nordic, Near Eastern, Arab, Far Eastern, Latin American, or Independent—they must recognize there will be differences. The theories and application techniques of organizational behavior discussed in the American literature will probably be relevant in the Anglo countries. It remains to be seen if the American version of organizational behavior thought is directly applicable to the other clusters.

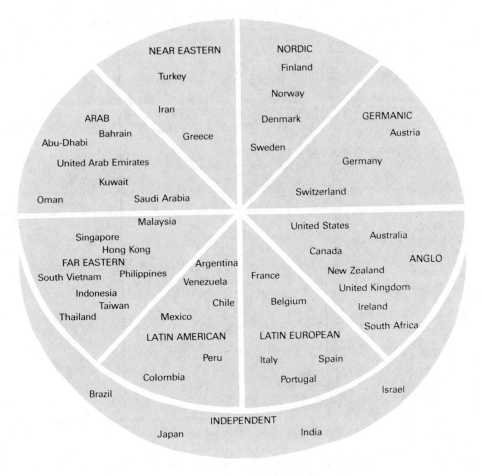

FIGURE 20.4
Country clusters based on employee attitude. (*Source:* Simcha Ronen and Oded Shenkar, "Clustering Countries on Attitudinal Dimensions: A Review and Synthesis," *Academy of Management Review,* July 1985, p. 449. Used with permission.)

Over time, other countries, especially Japan and Korea, may move closer to the Anglo cluster. There is already considerable evidence that this is happening with Japanese consumers, who are increasingly upset that their standard of living doesn't reflect Japan's national wealth.[13] This frustration is being carried over to the workplace as well. The following story told by a Japanese management expert when he went to a nearly empty barber shop in downtown Tokyo on a Saturday afternoon is very revealing about the changing attitudes of Japanese workers:

"Not many customers today, are there?" I said, relieved that I did not have to wait.
"That's right. Lately, business has been off Saturdays."
"When are you busiest?"

"Well, these days, around eleven, then around two or three in the afternoon on weekdays."

"But everyone around here must be working then. You mean during working hours?" I asked in disbelief.

"That's right. People these days don't want to spend their *own time* on things like haircuts."

"And in the past?"

"Well, a decade ago, we'd be busiest during the luncheon break and after five o'clock. Customers would rush to finish in less than 40 minutes."[14]

The recent widespread violent strikes and political protests in Korea, where workers and students are demanding their share of the economic gains, also are indicative of shifting attitudes and values in that fast-developing country.[15]

The rest of the chapter will examine if the cross-cultural similarities and differences do or will have an impact on the generally recognized organizational behavior areas of communication, motivation, and leadership.

COMMUNICATION IN AN INTERNATIONAL ENVIRONMENT

Although Chapter 16 discussed all dimensions of communication, it can be used here to demonstrate the impact of the international context. For example, the people at the home office of a multinational corporation (MNC) and the nationals in the foreign branch or subsidiary may not have the same meanings for the same words. An example is that Japanese managers will rarely come out with a direct "no" to another's request. A way they avoid saying "no" is to say "yes" and then follow the affirmative answer with a detailed explanation which in effect means "no."[16] The following sections examine some of the breakdowns and ways to improve communication across cultures.

Communication Breakdown across Cultures

There are a number of contributing factors leading to communication breakdown across cultures. Perhaps the best way to get at the root causes of this breakdown is through the concepts of perception, stereotyping, and ethnocentrism.

Perceptual Problems. Chapter 3 was specifically devoted to perception. It was simply portrayed as a person's interpretation of reality and was said to be learned. People are taught to "see" things in a given way. For example, when an American manager sees the wife of his Latin American host enter the door of the kitchen, he assumes that the women is putting the finishing touches on the meal. Unknown to him perhaps is the fact that the woman is actually supervising the cooking of the food and is checking to see that everything is in order. If the American were to tell his host's wife, "You're a terrific cook," his comments probably would be greeted with a smile because the hosts would realize he did not mean to be rude. However, a fellow Latin guest would never say this to the wife for it would imply that his hosts were too poor to afford a cook.

Stereotyping Problems. Another barrier to communication is stereotyping, also covered in Chapter 3, which is the tendency to perceive another person as belonging to a single class or category. Stereotyping is a very simple, widely used way of constructing an assumed overall profile of other people. For example, ask Americans which people try to "keep a stiff upper lip during trying times" and the most common answer is the British. Ask Americans what country of the world is famous for its auto engineering and the most common answer is Germany. Whether or not these are accurate stereotypes is immaterial. Most Americans believe them. Similarly, foreigners have their own stereotyped views of Americans. Table 20.5 provides some examples. Note from the table that Americans are regarded as energetic and indus-

TABLE 20.5 How Americans Are Seen by People of Other Countries

Characteristics Most Often Associated with Americans by the People of:		
France	**Japan**	**Germany**
Industrious	Nationalistic	Energetic
Energetic	Friendly	Inventive
Inventive	Decisive	Friendly
Decisive	Rude	Sophisticated
Friendly	Self-indulgent	Intelligent

Characteristics Least Often Associated with Americans by the People of:		
France	**Japan**	**Germany**
Lazy	Industrious	Lazy
Rude	Lazy	Sexy
Honest	Honest	Greedy
Sophisticated	Sexy	Rude

Characteristics Most Often Associated with Americans by the People of:		
Great Britain	**Brazil**	**Mexico**
Friendly	Intelligent	Industrious
Self-indulgent	Inventive	Intelligent
Energetic	Energetic	Inventive
Industrious	Industrious	Decisive
Nationalistic	Greedy	Greedy

Characteristics Least Often Associated with Americans by the People of:		
Great Britain	**Brazil**	**Mexico**
Lazy	Lazy	Lazy
Sophisticated	Self-indulgent	Honest
Sexy	Sexy	Rude
Decisive	Sophisticated	Sexy

Source: Adapted from *Newsweek,* July 11, 1983, p. 50.

trious by most nations and none of these countries stereotype Americans as being lazy.

Ethnocentric Problems. Ethnocentrism refers to the sense of superiority that members of a particular culture have. The Soviet Union, for example, claims that Americans believe they are the best in everything regardless of what area is under discussion. To the extent that this is true, it is an example of ethnocentrism in action. All societies promote ethnocentrism through their value structures and nationalistic spirit. People are taught the "right" way to do things, and, at least for them, it is regarded as the "best" way as well. When interacting with people on an international basis, ethnocentrism can cause communication problems. Here is an example:

> U.S. executives who consider English to be the "best" or the "most logical" language will not apply themselves to learn a foreign language which they consider "inferior" or "illogical." And if they consider their nonverbal system to be the most "civilized" system, they will tend to reject other systems as "primitive." In this sense, ethnocentrism can constitute a formidable block to effective empathy and can lead not only to a complete communication breakdown but also to antagonism, or even hostility.[17]

Improving Communication Effectiveness across Cultures

How can people doing business in other countries sensitize themselves to the culture of these nations and avoid making mistakes? One of the most effective ways is by learning about the culture of that country before going there. Some firms have developed "cultural assimilator" training programs. These programmed learning approaches ask the participants to read about a particular situation and then choose one of four courses of action or type of language that they would use. After the participants have made the choice, they then immediately learn if it was right or wrong, along with an explanation. By being put through a couple of hundred situations that they are likely to encounter in the foreign country, they become somewhat sensitized to the culture of that country and are able to communicate more effectively. There is even evidence that speaking the language correctly is not enough. Pronunciation and accent are even important. More and more foreign-born managers' careers are being stalled because they have thick accents, even though their grammar and vocabulary skills are good.[18]

A second, and often complementary, approach is to provide the trainee with educational background material on the country, including social structure, religion, values, language, and history. In particular, these training programs are designed to help managers going to a foreign assignment to create the right climate between themselves and those with whom they will be communicating. Table 20.6 provides an example of some of the behaviors American managers typically are taught to help build a climate of trust with their subordinates in a host country and those behaviors which should be avoided. Recent research indicates that both types of training methods have additive benefits in preparing managers for intercultural work assignments[19] and that cross-cultural training in general is quite effective.[20]

TABLE 20.6 Managing Cultural Climate

Behaviors That Help *Build* a Trust Climate	Behaviors That Help *Preclude* a Trust Climate
1. Express your doubts, concerns and feelings in an open, natural way. Encourage your subordinates to do so also.	1. Look on expressions of feelings and doubts as signs of weakness.
2. When subordinates express their doubts, concerns and feelings, accept them supportively and discuss them thoroughly.	2. Be sarcastic, but cleverly so.
3. Set honesty as one standard that will not be compromised. Demand it from yourself and from your staff.	3. Let your subordinates know that you expect them to "stretch the truth" a little if it will make the organization look good.
4. Be clear about your expectations when assigning work or eliciting opinions. Explain your reasons, wherever possible, behind requests and directions.	4. Be secretive. Never let them really be sure what's on your mind. This keeps them on their toes.
5. Encourage subordinates to look to you as a possible resource in accomplishing results, but develop and reinforce independence.	5. Discourage subordinates from coming to you for help. After all, they should be "stem-winders" and "self-starters."
6. When something goes wrong, determine what happened, not "who did it."	6. When something goes wrong, blow up, hit the ceiling, and look for the guilty party.
7. Encourage active support and participation in corrective measures from those involved.	7. Gossip about and disparage others on the staff when they are not present. Overrespond to casual comments by others about your people.
8. Share credit for successes; assume the bulk of responsibility for criticism of your unit.	8. Take credit for successes. Plan vendettas and other ploys to make other organizations look bad. Draw on subordinates for carrying these out. Always insist on plenty of documentation to protect yourself.

Source: Adapted from Philip R. Harris and Robert T. Moran, *Managing Cultural Differences*, 2d ed., Gulf Publishing, Houston, 1987, p. 50.

MOTIVATION OF PERSONNEL ACROSS CULTURES

Besides communication, another problem in dealing with people from other countries is the tendency to assume that what motivates Americans also motivates foreign nationals. Although recent research indicates that motivational processes such as equity may be found in the United States, Japan, or Korea, subtle, but important differences still remain,[21] as do, in general, considerable cross-cultural differences in motivating employees. Chapters 6 and 7 were specifically devoted to motivation, but in the international context, the different meanings of work and possible differences in motivation need to be explored.

The Meaning of Work

Traditionally in the United States, work has been generally equated with economic rewards. Although Chapter 6 pointed out that people have diverse needs and individual differences, Americans can still be generally characterized as working because they want to earn money with which to buy things. Thus, for many Americans, time on the job is money. This often is reflected in the way they try to get as much done in as little time as possible. Americans also like to have things spelled out so that they know what is expected of them and by when their tasks are to be accomplished. As Chapter 7 pointed out, they respond to goals that help improve their performance.

The culturally determined needs help dicate the way Americans behave both at home and abroad. Unfortunately, sometimes these behaviors are not regarded in a positive light. Consider some of the following comments made by people from other countries about how Americans behave.

India. Americans seem to be in a perpetual hurry. Just watch the way they walk down the street. They never allow themselves the leisure to enjoy life; there are too many things to do.

Colombia. The tendency in the United States to think that life is only work hits you in the face. Work seems to be the one type of motivation.

Ethiopia. The American is very explicit; he wants a "yes" or "no." If someone tries to speak figuratively, the American is confused.

Turkey. Once we were out in a rural area in the middle of nowhere and saw an American come to a stop sign. Though he could see in both directions for miles and no traffic was coming, he still stopped![22]

Many Americans still believe in the work ethic. Work is a most dominant and important part of life.[23] Do people in other countries feel the same way? Table 20.7 provides a partial answer to this question. Notice that in all of the countries surveyed, work ranked first in terms of its importance in providing income. In Japan and Germany, income was relatively more important than it was to Americans. However, in countries such as Israel and the Netherlands, income was of slightly less relative importance but work that was basically interesting and satisfying was of relatively more importance. In these countries, it would be a mistake to try to

TABLE 20.7 Average Number of Points Assigned to Working Functions by Country Samples

Country	Working Provides You with an Income That Is Needed	Working is Basically Interesting and Satisfying to You	Working Permits You to Have Interesting Contacts with Other People	Working Gives You Status and Prestige
Japan	45.4	13.4	14.7	5.6
Germany	40.5	16.7	13.1	10.1
Belgium	35.5	21.3	17.3	6.9
United Kingdom	34.4	17.9	15.3	10.9
Yugoslavia	34.1	19.8	9.8	9.3
United States	33.1	16.8	15.3	11.9
Israel	31.1	26.2	11.1	8.5
Netherlands	26.2	23.5	17.9	4.9
All countries combined	35.0*	19.5	14.3	8.5

* The combined totals weigh each country equally, regardless of sample size.
Source: Adapted from MOW International Research Team, *The Meaning of Working: An International Perspective,* Academic Press, London and New York, 1985, and reported in Simcha Ronen, *Comparative and Multinational Management,* Wiley, New York, 1986, p. 144.

motivate employees with financial incentives alone. In other words, while there are some similarities, there are also some motivational differences between employees across cultures.

Motivational Differences across Cultures

What contributes to the motivational differences across cultures? The roles of religion, the economy, uncertainty avoidance, and power distance provide some insights to this question.

The Role of Religion. One answer to motivational differences across cultures may be found in religions and the accompanying values. For instance, some religious values put emphasis on allowing events to develop in their own way. Just let things happen. An example would be the Hindus in India. Most Americans, on the other hand, follow religions that teach them to try to control events. Some religions teach that people are reincarnated and will return; most Americans believe they pass this way only once and they want to get as much done here and now as they can. Some religions teach the importance of caring for others as much as oneself (collectivism); most Americans believe that the best way to help others is to ensure one's own success (individualism). These differing religious values may have an indirect and, in some cases, a direct impact on the motivation of the followers.

One international expert recently noted that the old Protestant ethic, which may no longer be dominant in North American and Western European countries, is alive and well in places such as Seoul, Soweto, and Santiago de Chile. He notes that it is operating in these formerly strong Buddhist and Catholic areas of the world much as it did in North America and Western Europe by inculcating religious values and attitudes that are conducive to success in a high-growth, market economy.[24]

The Role of Uncertainty Avoidance. Another contributing factor to motivational differences may revolve around the cultural value of avoiding ambiguity and uncertainty. How willing are people to face uncertainty? How much do they prefer to know what is happening and not take too many risks? If the cultural values of employees make them willing to live with uncertainty, they may be motivated quite differently from those who prefer to know what is going on. For example, those who thrive on uncertainty may not have strong job security needs. Or those with a low tolerance for ambiguity and uncertainty may really respond to objective performance feedback. Table 20.8 illustrates a number of specific guidelines that can be followed in dealing with those who can and those who cannot deal with ambiguity and uncertainty.

Importantly, in light of the present international discussion, this dimension or value of people seems to vary from country to country. Figures 20.2 and 20.3 showed earlier that people in Latin countries (both in Europe and South America) generally do not like uncertainty. Neither do those from Mediterranean nations. On the other hand, those from countries such as Denmark, Sweden, Great Britain,

TABLE 20.8 Ways to Manage People on the Basis of Their Ability to Deal with Uncertainty or Ambiguity

Are Able to Deal with Uncertainty or Ambiguity	Do Not Like to Deal with Uncertainty or Ambiguity
Less structuring of activities	More structuring of activities
Fewer written rules	More written rules
Organizations can take many different forms	Organizations should be as uniform as possible (standardization)
Managers more involved in strategy	Managers more involved in details
Managers more interpersonally oriented and flexible in their style	Managers more task-oriented and consistent in their style
Managers more willing to make individual and risky decisions	Managers less willing to make individual and risky decisions
High labor turnover	Lower labor turnover
More ambitious employees	Less ambitious employees
Lower satisfaction scores	Higher satisfaction scores

Source: Adapted from Geert Hofstede, *Culture's Consequences: International Differences in Work Related Values.* Sage, Beverly Hills, Calif., 1980, p. 187. Copyright © 1980 by Sage Publications, Inc. Used with permission of Sage Publications, Inc.

Ireland, Canada, and the United States function well under conditions of uncertainty or ambiguity. Far Eastern countries such as Japan and Korea tend to fall between these two extremes.[25]

The Role of Power Distance. Still another contributing factor to motivational differences across cultures may revolve around power distance. Can the people in a particular country accept the fact that others have more power than they, or do they find this difficult to live with? As was noted earlier (see Figure 20.3), people in the United States, Britain, Canada, and the Scandinavian countries have trouble accepting that others have more power than they do. On the other hand, people in India, Mexico, Japan, and South Korea do not. Table 20.9 shows some of the ways of managing and organizing both groups.

TABLE 20.9 Ways to Manage People on the Basis of Their Acceptance or Nonacceptance of Power

Are Not Willing to Accept the Fact That Others Have More Power Than They Do	Are Willing to Accept the Fact That Others Have More Power Than They Do
Less centralization	Greater centralization
Flatter organization pyramids	Tall organization pyramids
Smaller proportion of supervisory personnel	Large proportion of supervisory personnel
Manual work same status as clerical work	White-collar jobs valued more than blue-collar jobs

Source: Adapted from Geert Hofstede, *Culture's Consequences: International Differences in Work Related Values,* Sage, Beverly Hills, Calif., 1980, p. 135. Copyright © 1980 by Sage Publications, Inc. Used with permission of Sage Publications, Inc.

MANAGERIAL LEADERSHIP ACROSS CULTURES

Like communication and motivation, the important organizational behavior topic of leadership was given earlier detailed attention in Chapters 10 and 11. Leadership was portrayed as the process of influencing others to direct their efforts toward the pursuit of specific goals.

Because of globalization, leadership will take on added significance. As leadership expert Warren Bennis recently noted, "Given the nature and constancy of change and the transnational challenges facing American business leadership, the key to making the right choices will come from understanding and embodying the leadership qualities necessary to succeed in the volatile and mercurial global economy."[26] In the context of organizational behavior, leadership is mainly concerned with managerial style. The way in which this process is successfully applied, however, will vary across cultures. What is appropriate and effective managerial leadership in one country may not be in another. There are a number of possible contributing factors to the differences in effective managerial leadership across cultures. Some of the more important, and those which have been researched, include personal values, risk preference, the manager's background, interpersonal skills, and decision making.

Personal Values

Managers' personal values help shape their perception of a situation, influence their analysis of alternative solutions to a problem, and have an effect on the ultimate decision. The followers' personal values will also influence their manager. How they accept authority—their power distance—and their loyalty and commitment are examples. Such personal values on the part of both managers and subordinates will differ across cultures. For example, research by George England and his colleagues found that American and Japanese managers tend to be very pragmatic. Their personal values emphasize productivity, profitability, and achievement. Managers from India, on the other hand, tend to be less pragmatic and more moralistic. Their values emphasize equity, fairness, and the overall good of the work force.[27]

Managers' Background

Managers' background may also influence the way their subordinates are led. Research shows that American managers come from all economic strata: lower, middle, and upper.[28] An increasingly large percentage are college-educated, but because performance is important to promotion, there is no guarantee that attending a certain school will lead to success. Although graduates of Ivy League schools and other prestigious institutions may have an advantage, many American managers from all types and sizes of colleges have made it into the upper ranks. The same pattern may not be as true in other countries. For example, in France managers often are chosen from the graduates of the *grandes écoles*. In Japan, those who gain entrance into the prestigious schools have a much better chance of becoming top managers of the large corporations. In Korea, surprisingly perhaps, many of the newly emerging managerial leaders have been educated in the United States. Traditionally, in the Soviet

Union career advancement in management is dependent on engineering or technical education and experience.

Besides educational background, class and family background also make a difference. In the United States, managers come from all classes. However, in Turkey, many of the top managers come from the upper class. In Poland, most of the business leaders come from the lower middle class. In Argentina and Peru, business leaders come from the middle class. In Chile, the landed aristocracy are the managerial leaders.

At the same time, family upbringing is important. For example, in India, it is common to accept the authority of elders. Thus, in superior-subordinate relations there is generally little delegation of authority. Instead, the head of the enterprise exercises a directive leadership style and everyone follows these orders. In the United States, on the other hand, where managers come from all classes, are relatively well educated, and have a liberal upbringing, there is more of an emphasis on participatory decision making and delegation of authority. This background will influence the way the manager exercises leadership.

Interpersonal Skills

There is research evidence that managers differ across cultures in their interpersonal skills. For example, Bass and Burger conducted a comprehensive study of managers in the United States, Belgium, Britain, France, Germany-Austria, Iberia, India, Japan, Latin America, and Scandinavia. Some of their relevant findings in relation to interpersonal styles and skills include the following:

- Spanish and Portuguese managers were most willing to be aware of others' feelings; to be concerned with their subordinates' welfare; and to accept feedback from others. The Germans, Austrians, and French were less willing to do these things. The other countries fell between these two extremely different groups.
- Managers from India were the most concerned about bureaucratic rules; the Japanese were the least concerned.
- Managers from India saw themselves as most dependent on higher authority. German and Austrian managers viewed themselves as very independent.
- Dutch managers were the most willing to cooperate with others; the French were the least willing.
- Japanese managers had a greater desire to be objective rather than intuitive than did managers from any other country.
- Japanese and Dutch managers were most locked in by group commitments and were less likely to deviate from their initial positions. Managers from the United States and Latin America showed the least commitment to their group positions, were able to reach compromises faster than the other groups, and were deadlocked much less often.
- U.S. and Latin American managers demonstrated much greater interpersonal competence than other managers.[29]

What the above once again demonstrates is that interpersonal approaches differ by culture. An American supervisor on an oil rig in Indonesia learned this the hard way. In a moment of anger, he shouted at his timekeeper to take the next boat to shore. Immediately, a mob of outraged Indonesian coworkers grabbed fire axes and went after the supervisor. He saved himself by barricading himself in his quarters. The cultural lesson this American learned: Never berate an Indonesian in public.[30]

International joint ventures (IJVs) also lead to many interpersonal conflicts between members of the same company from vastly different cultures. For example, local managers of IJVs may become frustrated by the lack of promotion opportunities to key jobs if senior positions are reserved for "outsiders" or those whose loyalty lies not with the current IJV but with the parent company. In such instances, conflicts may arise that prevent full cooperation among the staff.[31]

Decision Making

Besides interpersonal skills, managerial leadership is also often expressed through decision-making skills. Chapter 17 gave specific attention to this function of management. Decision making was simply portrayed as the process of choosing between alternatives. However, how managers make these decisions differs across cultures. For example, research by Heller and Yukl has found that in Argentina, Chile, and Uruguay authority is equated with rapid decision making and speed is more important than generating information or carefully analyzing the data.[32]

Boards of directors in these Latin countries often hold meetings without precirculating the minutes of the last meeting or the agenda of the current one. Other researchers have found that Latin American managers also often fail to plan and rely heavily on intuition or improvisation based on emotional arguments and justifica-

International Application Example

The Mighty Deutsche

Decision making in Germany is often carried out in a meticulous, deliberate fashion. A good example is provided by the Deutsche Bank, the largest bank in the country and one of the most profitable in Europe. During the last decade Deutsche Bank (DB) more than doubled its assets and earnings and tripled its capital and reserves. How did it accomplish this feat? By carefully examining its investment opportunities and choosing those that offered the highest returns. In the process, the bank has managed to acquire substantial holdings in some of Germany's biggest and most profitable firms. For example, DB owns 28 percent of Daimler-Benz, Germany's largest industrial corporation; 30 percent of Philipp Holzmann, the country's largest construction company; and 21 percent of Sudzucker, Europe's largest sugar producer.

When asked about the bank's decision-making approach, DB's president hastens to point out that Deutsche has no interest in growth at any price. The bank's retailing operations, for example, are limited to Germany and to select markets in Europe. On the other hand, in the areas of investment banking, securities, assets management, corporate finance, and mergers and acquisitions, DB has a presence in London, Tokyo, Singapore, New York, and the west coast of the United States. In the words of the bank president, "We are not trying to cover the world, nor Europe, with a sprinkling can. We are pursuing a very differentiated policy, country by country, market by market."

tions in making their decisions.[33] Some of them also put off decisions, preferring a "wait and see" attitude that results in eventually having to use stopgap measures to prevent the situation from getting worse.

Other research has found that managers in the United States and Sweden tend to emphasize rationality in their decision making. The same is true of the Germans, as seen in the International Application Example: The Mighty Deutsche. The Japanese, on the other hand, try to balance a concern for rationality and objectivity with the desire for group acceptance and consensus. In the Japanese system, decision making tends to flow from the bottom up. All members of the firm share the responsibility for decisions. After reaching a consensus, the originating group sends its decision to other groups for approval. The more important the decision, the higher it goes for approval within the hierarchy. This is in contrast to the American system in which decisions tend to flow from the top down and individuals, although they may be in a group or committee framework, play a more significant role.

Summary

The international context in which organizational behavior operates is becoming increasingly important as organizations expand beyond their national boundaries. Few would question that there is now a global economy and that cultural differences must be recognized in the study and understanding of organizational behavior.

The chapter started off by defining culture, which is the acquired knowledge that people use to interpret experience and generate social behavior. Whereas the last chapter focused on organizational culture per se, this chapter more directly aimed at the culture of overall societies and countries. Although it must be remembered that it is difficult to make generalizations because of so many subcultures operating in societies and countries, there are several dimensions of culture that do pretty well describe societal orientations. These dimensions were identified in the chapter as follows: how people see themselves; people's relationship to their world; individualism versus collectivism; the time dimension; and public and private space. These lead to organizational behavior differences across cultures. There are many reasons for these differences. The chapter drew heavily from the research of Hofstede, who found that people tend to differ based on individualism/collectivism, power distance, uncertainty avoidance, and masculinity/femininity.

The remainder of the chapter analyzed the major organizational behavior topics of communication, motivation, and managerial leadership across cultures. Communication in an international environment often is influenced by a number of factors such as perception, stereotyping, and ethnocentrism. In helping their managers deal with these communication problems, some companies have developed cultural assimilator training programs.

Another problem in the understanding and application of organizational behavior across cultures is exemplified by the important topic of motivation. What accounts for motivational differences across cultures? A number of factors can be cited, including religion, uncertainty avoidance, and the ways in which the society deals with power acceptance.

Managerial leadership involves influencing others to direct their efforts toward the pursuit of specific goals. There are a number of factors across cultures that influence the way in which managers lead their subordinates. Some of these factors are personal values, the manager's background, interpersonal skills, and decision making. Each of these was discussed in the chapter. When available, research evidence was used to support the conclusions. However, a future challenge for the field of organizational behavior is to do more international research.

Questions for Discussion and Review

1. In your own words, what is meant by the term "culture"? How does it differ from "organizational culture?

2. What are some basic dimensions that describe the cultural orientation of a society? Briefly describe each.

3. In what way do individualism/collectivism, power distance, uncertainty avoidance, and masculinity/femininity help explain cultural differences? Define and give examples of these dimensions.

4. In what way is perception a problem in dealing with employees across cultures?

5. In what way is stereotyping a problem in dealing with employees across cultures?

6. In what way is ethnocentrism a problem in dealing with employees across cultures?

7. How can multinational corporations sensitize their managers to the cultures of host countries before sending them on international assignments?

8. How does work differ in the meaning it takes on in the United States and in other countries?

9. What accounts for some of the motivational differences between employees across cultures?

10. What are some of the major factors that influence the managerial leadership process across cultures?

References

1. For example, see John Naisbitt and Patricia Aburdene, *Megatrends 2000*, Morrow, New York, 1990, chap. 1.

2. Charles J. Cox and Cary L. Cooper, "The Irrelevance of American Organizational Sciences to the UK and Europe," *Journal of General Management*, Winter 1985, pp. 29–30.

3. David G. Myers, *Social Psychology*, 3d ed., McGraw-Hill, New York, 1990, pp. 226–227.

4. Quoted in Nancy J. Adler, Robert Doktor, and S. Gordon Redding, "From the Atlantic to the Pacific Century: Cross-Cultural Management Reviewed," *Journal of Management*, vol. 12, no. 2, 1986, p. 295.

5. Stephen P. Robbins, *Organizational Behavior*, 4th ed., Prentice-Hall, Englewood Cliffs, N.J., 1989, p. 483.

6. Nancy J. Adler, *International Dimensions of Organizational Behavior*, 2d ed., Kent, Boston, 1991, p. 23.

7. Mark Maremont, "Eastern Europe's Big Clean-up," *Business Week,* March 19, 1990, pp. 114–115.

8. Jacquelyn B. Schriber and Barbara A. Gutek, "Some Time Dimensions of Work: Measurement of an Underlying Aspect of Organization Culture," *Journal of Applied Psychology,* vol. 72, 1987, pp. 642–650.

9. Geert Hofstede, *Culture's Consequences: International Differences in Work Related Values,* Sage, Beverly Hills, Calif., 1980. For a recent review and extension of Hofstede's work see Robert G. Westwood and James E. Everett, "Culture's Consequences: A Methodology for Comparative Management Studies in Southeast Asia?" *Asia Pacific Journal of Management,* May 1987, pp. 187–202.

10. Derek S. Pugh and David J. Hickson, *Writers on Organizations,* 4th ed., Sage, Newbury Park, Calif., 1989, p. 94.

11. Adler, op. cit., p. 52.

12. Simcha Ronen, *Comparative and Multinational Management,* Wiley, New York, 1986, pp. 266–267.

13. Barbara Buell, "Japan's Silent Majority Starts to Mumble," *Business Week,* Apr. 23, 1990, p. 52.

14. Kenichi Ohmae, "Japan's Role in the World Economy," *California Management Review,* Spring 1987, p. 54.

15. Laxmi Nakarmi, "The Korean Tiger Has All But Lost Its Claws," *Business Week,* Apr. 30, 1990, pp. 40–41.

16. Don Hellriegel, John W. Slocum, and Richard W. Woodman, *Organizational Behavior,* 4th ed., West, St. Paul, Minn., 1986, p. 219.

17. Adnan Almaney, "Intercultural Communication and the MNC Executive," *Columbia Journal of World Business,* Winter 1974, p. 27.

18. "Lose That Thick Accent to Gain Career Ground," *The Wall Street Journal,* January 4, 1990, p. B1.

19. P. Christopher Earley, "Intercultural Training for Managers: A Comparison of Documentary and Interpersonal Methods," *Academy of Management Journal,* December 1987, pp. 685–698.

20. J. Stewart Black and Mark Mendenhall, "Cross Cultural Training Effectiveness: A Review and a Theoretical Framework for Future Research," *Academy of Management Review,* January 1990, pp. 113–136.

21. Ken I. Kim, Hun-Joon Park, Nori Suzuki, "Reward Allocations in the United States, Japan, and Korea: A Comparison of Individualistic and Collectionistic Cultures," *Academy of Management Journal,* March 1990, pp. 188–198.

22. Adler, op. cit., pp. 77, 79.

23. Robert A. Baron, *Behavior in Organizations,* 2d ed., Allyn & Bacon, Boston, 1986, p. 150.

24. Prof. Peter Berger, quoted in "What Is Culture's Role in Economic Policy?" *The Wall Street Journal,* Dec. 22, 1986, p. 1.

25. Ronen, op. cit., p. 170.

26. Warren G. Bennis, "Managing the Dream: Leadership in the 21st Century," *Journal of Organizational Change Management,* vol. 2, no. 1, 1989, p. 7.

27. George W. England, O. P. Dhingra, and Naresh C. Agarwal, *The Manager and the Man: A Cross-Cultural Study of Personal Values,* Kent State University Press, Kent, Ohio, 1974, p. 20.

28. David C. McClelland, *The Achieving Society,* Van Nostrand, Princeton, N.J., 1961.

29. B. M. Bass and P. C. Burger, *Assessment of Managers: An International Comparison,* Free Press, New York, 1979.

30. Richard L. Daft, *Management,* 2d ed., Dryden, Chicago, 1991, p. 625.

31. Oded Shenkar and Yoram Zeira, "International Joint Ventures: A Tough Test of HR," *Personnel,* January 1990, pp. 27–28.

32. Frank A. Heller and Gary Yukl, "Participation, Managerial Decision-Making, and Situational Variables," *Organizational Behavior and Human Performance,* vol. 4, 1969, pp. 227–241.

33. E. C. McCann, "An Aspect of Management Philosophy in the United States and Latin America," *Academy of Management Journal,* June 1964, pp. 149–152.

**REAL CASE:
EVERY-
BODY'S
EVERYWHERE**

How important is it for managers to understand organizational behavior in the international context? One way to answer this question is by finding out how much business companies are doing internationally. The latest data show that industrial corporations, for example, are becoming more and more international and these firms are now making billions of dollars every year through overseas sales. Going into the 1990s, here is a listing of the top 20 international industrials:

Company	Country	Sales (in millions)
General Motors	United States	$126,974
Ford Motor	United States	96,933
Exxon	United States	86,656
Royal Dutch/Shell	Britain/Netherlands	85,527
IBM	United States	63,438
Toyota Motor	Japan	60,444
General Electric	United States	55,264
Mobil	United States	50,976
Hitachi	Japan	59,894
British Petroleum	Britain	49,484
IRI	Italy	49,077
Matsushita Electric	Japan	43,086
Daimler-Benz	Germany	40,616
Philip Morris	United States	39,069
Fiat	Italy	36,741
Chrysler	United States	36,156
Nissan Motor	Japan	36,078
Unilever	Britain/Netherlands	35,284
DuPont	United States	35,209
Samsung	Korea	35,189

While this is only the top 20 of the largest 500 firms, the two largest national groups are the United States with 167 companies on the list and Japan with 111. Other major countries include Britain with 43, Germany with 32, and France with 29. Moreover, the American firms were the most profitable—with 37 percent of their sales and 40 percent of their profits coming from international operations. The Japanese firms fared poorest with 20 percent of their sales coming from international operations but less than 7 percent of their profits generated this way. Commenting on the overall nature of firms that have an international presence, *Fortune* magazine noted, "Now that the global village is truly upon us, it looks more like a global industrial park. We live in an expansive new world of economic interconnections where business roars through borders and time zones."

1. How important will an understanding of international organizational behavior be to a multinational manager of the 1990s?
2. How can organizations prepare their managers to better understand international organizational behavior?
3. What is the likelihood that by the year 2000 American firms with sales of $100 million or above will be earning at least a portion of this income through international sales? What significance does your answer have for the study of international organizational behavior?

**Case:
I Want Out**

When the Budder Mining Equipment Company decided to set up a branch office in Peru, top management felt that there were two basic avenues it could travel. One was to export its machinery and have an agent in that country be responsible for the selling. The other was to set up on an on-site operation and be directly responsible for the sales effort. After giving the matter a great deal of thought, management decided to assign one of its own people to this overseas market. The person who was chosen, Frank Knight, had expressed an interest in the assignment but had no experience in South America. He was selected because of his selling skills and was given a week to clear out his desk and be on location.

When Frank arrived, he was met at the airport by Pablo Gutierrez, the local who was hired to run the office and break Frank in. Pablo had rented an apartment and car for Frank and taken care of all the chores associated with getting him settled. Frank was very impressed. Thanks to Pablo, he could devote all of his efforts to the business challenge that lay ahead.

After about six months, the vice president for marketing received a call from Frank. In a tired voice Frank indicated that even though sales were okay, he couldn't take it anymore. He wanted to come home. If nothing could be worked out within the next three months, Frank made it clear that he would resign. When his boss pressed him regarding the problems he was having, here is what Frank reported:

> Doing business over here is a nightmare. Everyone comes to work late and leaves early. They also take a two-hour rest period during the afternoon. All the offices close down during this afternoon break. So even if I wanted to conduct some business during this period, there would be no customers around anyway. Also, no one works very hard and they seem to assume no responsibility whatsoever. There seems to be no support for the work ethic among the people. Even Pablo, who looked like he was going to turn out great, has proven to be as lazy as the rest of them. Sales are 5 percent over forecast but a good 30 percent lower than they could be if everyone here would just work a little harder. If I stay here any longer, I'm afraid I'll start becoming like these people. I want out, while I still can.

1. In Frank's view, how important is the work ethic? How is this view causing him problems?
2. Why do the people not work as hard as Frank does? What is the problem?
3. What mistake is Frank making that is undoubtedly causing him problems in managing the branch office?

**Case:
Getting
the Facts**

When California-based Dalton & Dalton (D&D) was contacted by a large conglomerate in Taiwan, the president of D&D was quite surprised. For two years D&D had been looking for an overseas conglomerate that would be interested in building and selling its high-tech medical equipment under a licensing agreement. The company had been unsuccessful because the firms with whom it had spoken were not interested in investing any of their own money. They wanted D&D to provide the financial investment while they handled the actual manufacturing and selling.

The Taiwanese conglomerate has proposed to D&D that the two companies enter into a joint venture type of licensing agreement. The way in which the business deal will work is the following:

- The Taiwanese will set up manufacturing facilities and create a marketing group to sell D&D's high-tech medical equipment.
- D&D will train twenty-five manufacturing and twenty-five salespeople from the conglomerate so that the latter understands how to make and sell this equipment. This training will take place in the States.
- D&D will have the right to send people to the manufacturing facility to ensure that the equipment is being built according to specifications and will also have the right to travel with the salespeople to ensure that the equipment is being sold properly. (Specifically, D&D would be able to monitor the technical side of the sales presentation to ensure that the equipment is being properly represented and that the capabilities of the machinery are not being exaggerated.)

The arrangement sounds fine to the president of D&D. However, before she agrees to anything, she wants to get more information on how to do business with the Taiwanese. "If we're going to enter into a business venture with a foreign company, I think we owe it to ourselves to know something about their culture and customs. I'd like to know how to interact effectively with these people and to get an idea of the types of problems we might have in communicating with them. The better we understand them, the better the chances that there will be no misunderstandings between us."

1. If you were advising the president, what types of information would you suggest be gathered?
2. What types of culturally related problems are there that could result in misunderstanding between the two parties?
3. Overall, is the president right in suggesting that they learn more about the Taiwanese before doing business with them?

Organization Change, Development, and the Future

■ Learning to Keep Customers

One of the major changes in this decade will be recognition of the importance of customers. Companies must realize that every lost customer costs it dearly and every retained customer is highly profitable. For example, in the credit card business it costs approximately $50 to generate a new customer. If the individual remains with the credit card firm for one year, the company can expect to make about $30 in profit from this individual. If the customer stays three years, this total rises to around $115, and after five years it stands at about $220. Since many new customers do not stay one year, the credit card company needs to continually replace them with other new customers. However, if the firm cannot stop defections, it has a losing strategy because the cost of gaining new customers is greater than the profit being generated by loyal ones. Another good example is provided by the auto servicing industry. Gaining a new customer generally costs nothing and provides $25 in profit the first year, and by years four and five the annual profit is up to around $90. Again, loyal customers are the company's bread and butter.

What can organizations do to entice and keep customers? Staples, the Boston-based office products discounter, keeps detailed information on all of its customers regarding their buying habits, frequency of visits, average dollar value spent, and items purchased. If the store notices that a customer is buying less or not shopping there at all, the individual is contacted and Staples attempts to find out if there is a problem. At MBNA America, a Delaware-based credit card company, there is a customer defection "swat" team that talks to customers who have canceled their credit cards and tries to convince them to stay. Over the last eight years the company has been so successful in its effort to keep customers that its loss rate is half that of the industry and its profits have increased sixteenfold. At Great-West Life Assurance Company of Englewood, California, the firm pays a 50 percent premium to group-health-insurance brokers that reach specified customer-retention targets. The system gives brokers a strong incentive to look for customers who are likely to stay with the firm for a long time.

Of course, the amount of profit that is earned as a result of reducing defections will vary from industry to industry. In credit insurance, reducing defections by 5 percent will boost profits by 25 percent. In the insurance brokerage business, the profit boost is 50 percent; for credit cards, it is 75 percent. No wonder so many firms are training their people to give existing accounts the same amount of attention that used to be reserved only for new customers.

Learning Objectives

- **Analyze** the changing environment affecting today's and tomorrow's organizations.
- **Discuss** the background and process of organization development (OD).
- **Explain** the major techniques used in organization development (OD).
- **Identify** the trends that will affect the study and application of organizational behavior in the future.

Whereas the other chapters in this final part were concerned with the organizational and international cultural context of organizations, this chapter is aimed at the change and development of organizations. The term *organization development,* or simply OD, is used to represent an applied, macro-level approach to planned change and development of complex organizations. Many of the concepts and techniques (for example, job enrichment, goal setting, and O.B. Mod.) discussed in previous chapters could be considered part of OD. However, this chapter is directly concerned with the general issue of the management of change and with widely recognized human and structural OD techniques.

After a general discussion of the impact of change, the overall chracteristics of OD will be explored. Then the traditional and more modern OD techniques will be presented and analyzed. The overall track record of OD will be examined. The chapter will conclude with a brief look into the future of organizations and organizational behavior.

THE CHANGING ENVIRONMENT

Most managers today recognize the inevitability of change, that the only constant is change itself. The first chapter identified the new, changing environment facing today's and tomorrow's organizations in terms of the global economy, the second generation of the information age and the quality service revolution. Tom Peters has recently noted that in order for organizations to compete in the years ahead, they are going to need to pursue "six sigma quality" (99.9997 percent perfect, a highly touted Motorola goal); shrink innovation and order cycles by orders of magnitude; use team-based organizations everywhere; and subcontract anything to anyone from anywhere.[1]

Figure 21.1 shows some of the results and overall and organizational/personal impacts of globalization and the information age. As far as quality goes, it has moved

FIGURE 21.1 The Results and Impact of Globalization and Information Technology.
(*Source:* Tom Peters, "Prometheus Barely Unbound," *Academy of Management Executive*, November 1990, p. 71. Used with permission.)

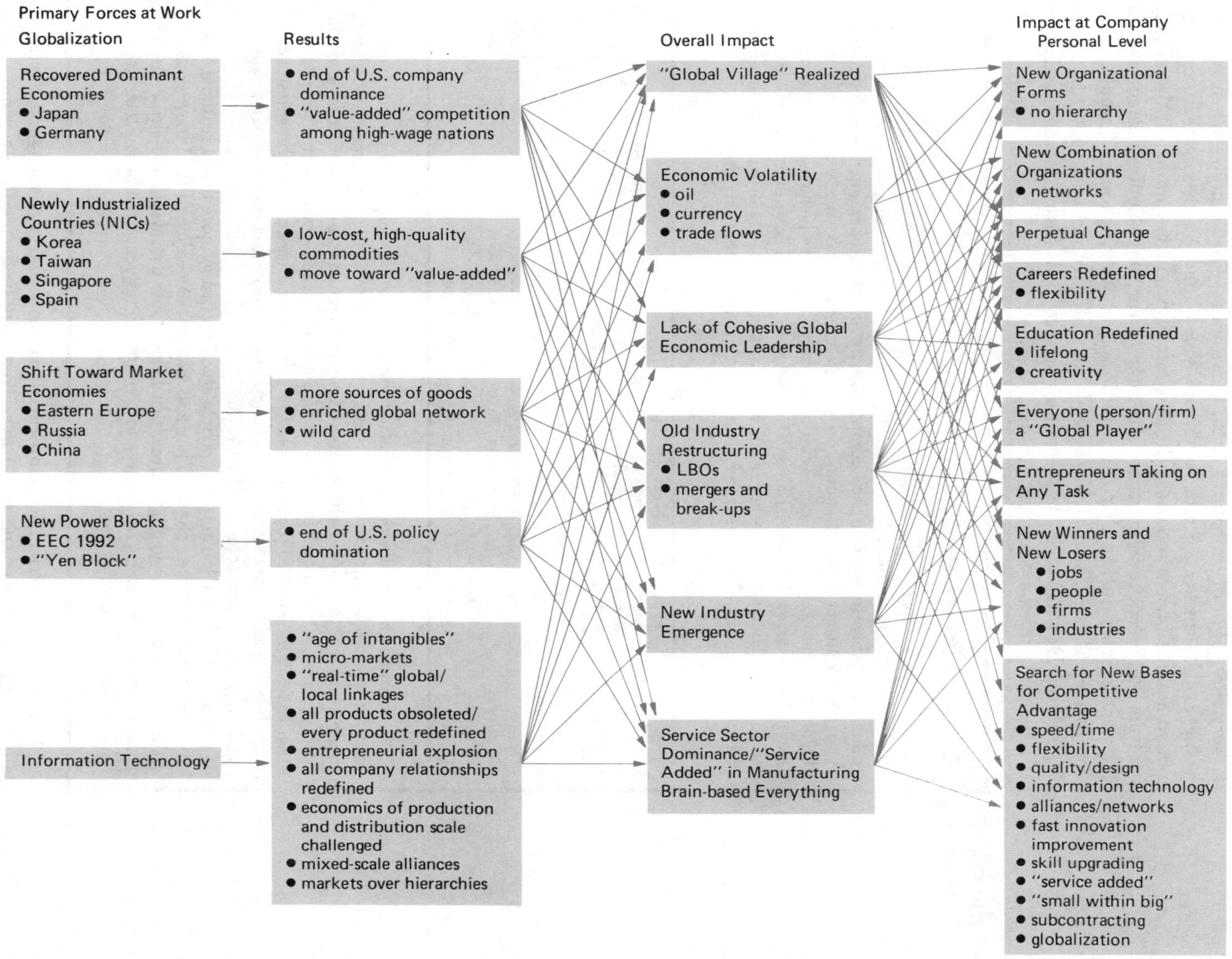

Primary Forces at Work

Globalization

Recovered Dominant Economies
- Japan
- Germany

Newly Industrialized Countries (NICs)
- Korea
- Taiwan
- Singapore
- Spain

Shift Toward Market Economies
- Eastern Europe
- Russia
- China

New Power Blocks
- EEC 1992
- "Yen Block"

Information Technology

Results

- end of U.S. company dominance
- "value-added" competition among high-wage nations

- low-cost, high-quality commodities
- move toward "value-added"

- more sources of goods
- enriched global network
- wild card

- end of U.S. policy domination

- "age of intangibles"
- micro-markets
- "real-time" global/local linkages
- all products obsoleted/every product redefined
- entrepreneurial explosion
- all company relationships redefined
- economics of production and distribution scale challenged
- mixed-scale alliances
- markets over hierarchies

Overall Impact

"Global Village" Realized

Economic Volatility
- oil
- currency
- trade flows

Lack of Cohesive Global Economic Leadership

Old Industry Restructuring
- LBOs
- mergers and break-ups

New Industry Emergence

Service Sector Dominance/"Service Added" in Manufacturing Brain-based Everything

Impact at Company Personal Level

New Organizational Forms
- no hierarchy

New Combination of Organizations
- networks

Perpetual Change

Careers Redefined
- flexibility

Education Redefined
- lifelong
- creativity

Everyone (person/firm) a "Global Player"

Entrepreneurs Taking on Any Task

New Winners and New Losers
- jobs
- people
- firms
- industries

Search for New Bases for Competitive Advantage
- speed/time
- flexibility
- quality/design
- information technology
- alliances/networks
- fast innovation
- improvement
- skill upgrading
- "service added"
- "small within big"
- subcontracting
- globalization

beyond a buzz word and is now recognized as a prerequisite not only for success, but the very survival of organizations in the years ahead. For example, Whistler, one of the biggest U.S. makers of radar detectors, saved hundreds of jobs that might have gone to South Korea by boosting the pass rate of products coming off the assembly line from 75 percent to 99 percent. The same is true for the improvement in white-collar and service quality that companies such as Westinghouse, Campbell Soup, Motorola, and Dow Chemical have greatly benefited from.[2] The Application Example, Calories Down, Profit Up shows how service firms such as commercial airlines are attempting to improve their quality of service.

Application Example ⫸

Calories Down, Profits Up

Until recently most airline food met three requirements: indescribability, indestructibility, and tastelessness. However, this situation is changing as airlines seek to differentiate themselves from their competition by offering nutritious, low-calorie meals designed to attract repeat business. In particular, many passengers now want to eat lightly and healthfully. This means cutting down on cholesterol, spices, and desserts and having more salads and vegetarian and nonmeat offerings. The airlines are also catering to special orders such as kosher meals that, in many cases, are ordered for diet—not religious—reasons. Here are some of the latest offerings from the airlines:

Airline	Types of Special Meals Offered	Most Popular Speciality Meal	Number of Meals Served Daily	% of Specialty Meals Served	Notice Required
American	7	Low cholesterol	170,000	3	6 hours
Continental	12	Kosher	82,000	4	12 hours
Delta	13	Vegetarian	145,000	3	6 hours
Northwest	24	Vegetarian	105,000	4	12 hours
Pan Am	21	Kosher	30,000	3	8 hours
United	12	Vegetarian	183,000	3	6 hours

In addition, the airlines have made some substantial changes in the preparation and selection of their standard coach menus. Beef used to be the most common offering, but no longer. Now most airlines offer it only if there is another choice; it is never the only offering. Other popular dishes include baked chicken—without the fat-retaining skin and sauces—and cold pasta served in olive oil and garlic. Even breakfast menus have been expanded so that the all-too-common cheese omelet now competes with no-yolk Egg Beaters and cold cereal with fruit.

The airlines are learning that people are interested in more than a reasonable fare to the destination of their choice. They also want the same type of food they would eat at home, which means in-flight meals that help people trim down and shape up. The eating habits of passengers are likely to continue to influence the business strategy of airlines for some time to come.

Added to the international, informational, and quality challenges is the dramatically changing nature of the workforce. There will be decidedly fewer new workers entering the job market. In the 1970s, about 3 million new workers entered each year. However, in 1990 there were 1.3 million and by 1995 there will be about 1.3 million *fewer* workers than in the past in the 18–24 age group. There will also be considerably more diversity in terms of skill level, sex, race, and age.[3] For example, by the year 2000: one out of three Americans will be nonwhite; 85 percent of new entrants into the workforce will be members of minority groups, women, or immigrants; and more than one-third of Americans will be age 65 or older.[4] Besides the obvious challenge of providing a climate and practice of equal opportunity in employment for this diverse workforce, there will be a number of other challenges. For instance, with the continued influx of women into the workforce, particularly women with children, there will be a growing challenge of balancing the demands of work and family settings.[5] Also, with the upcoming shortage, the challenge for organizations will be how to recruit new employees and retain the good ones they have.[6]

Does this environment of change spell gloom and doom for today's organizations, or is there really nothing to worry about? One position, although not very popular, is that there is nothing wrong; there should just be business as usual in the years ahead. After all, this argument goes, the American economy has experienced growth for several years and U.S. workers are still the most productive in the world. Quality may not be as high as the Japanese, but it is improving. For example, even beleaguered General Motors went from 740 defects per 100 cars in 1980 to 168 per 100 as the 1990s began, and its Buick and Cadillac models have won prestigious quality awards.[7]

More realistic than this "cheery" view of the situation would be the view that there are definitely challenges ahead. Table 21.1 shows the results of recent Gallup interviews of what American executives feel are the extremely critical issues facing U.S. companies. Obviously, quality and productivity are major challenges that managers foresee, and for good reason. The fact is that from 1980 to 1990 American manufacturers have lost ground to imports in almost every industrial category.[8] A recent *Fortune* report points out this gloomy possible scenario for the future:

Japan, which last year outspent the U.S. for the first time on plant and equipment, could become the world's top industrial power by the year 2000 or soon after. Its manufacturing output, already more than two-thirds as big as America's, is growing

TABLE 21.1 Extremely Critical Issues Facing U.S. Organizations

	Percentage of Executives Rating Each Issue as "Extremely Critical" (Based on 615 interviews of top level executives from large and small U.S. firms)
Service quality	48%
Product quality	39%
Productivity	26%
Government regulation	19%
Product liability	14%
Costs of material and labor	14%
Labor relations	14%

Source: Adapted from Y. K. Shetty and Paul F. Buller, "Regaining Competitiveness Requires HR Solutions," *Personnel*, July 1990, p. 10.

faster. Meanwhile, the U.S. is selling off assets to help pay for an excess of imports over exports, a red ink figure recently running at the equivalent of one Rockefeller Center a week. . . . Will the U.S. increasingly become a branch-office colony of European and Asian owners, stripped of top laboratories, decision-making jobs, and control over its national destiny?[9]

Although the above is perhaps too extreme a view, one thing is clear. Those organizations able to manage the dramatic change they face now and in the years ahead will be more successful than those not able to manage change. Although all chapters of this text deal with how this can be done, the remainder of this concluding chapter is specifically devoted to the management of change per se.

ORGANIZATION DEVELOPMENT: THE MODERN APPROACH TO THE MANAGEMENT OF CHANGE

The modern approach to the management of change and the development of human resources is called *organization development*. Although there is still not a universally agreed-upon definition, one recent applications view stated that "organization development programs" lead to improved organization performance through an improved decision-making climate. OD practitioners (internal or external consultants) may counsel decision makers on an individual basis; work to improve working relationships among the members of a work group or team (often including the top-management team); work to improve relationships among interacting and interdependent organizational groups; and gather attitudinal data throughout the organization and feed this data back to selected individuals and groups, who use this information as a basis for planning and making needed improvements.[10]

More traditionally, French and Bell offered this comprehensive definition:

> Organization development is a long-range effort to improve an organization's problem-solving and renewal processes, particularly through a more effective and collaborative management of organization culture—with special emphasis on the culture of formal work teams—with the assistance of a change agent, or catalyst, and the use of the theory and technology of applied behavior science, including action research.[11]

Burke has a simple definition:

> Organization development is a planned process of change in an organization's culture through the utilization of behavioral science technology, research, and theory.[12]

Using definitions like these as a point of departure and summarizing what the leaders in the OD movement emphasize, Black and Margulies suggest the following elements make up the modern OD approach to the management of change:

1. The OD approach to change is planned.
2. It is system-wide or at least takes a systems perspective.
3. It is designed to improve the organization in both the short and long terms.
4. The OD approach to change is primarily aimed at organizational processes rather than substantive content.

5. It is designed to solve problems.
6. It is primarily focused on human and social relationships.[13]

The desired organizational outcomes of OD efforts include increased effectiveness, problem solving, and adaptability for the future. OD attempts to provide opportunities to be "human" and to increase awareness, participation, and influence. An overriding goal is to integrate individual and organizational objectives.

The Historical Development of OD

As with other behavioral approaches, it is difficult to pinpoint the precise beginning of OD. French and Bell, who have done the most work on the historical development of OD, feel that "organization development has emerged from applied behavioral science and social psychology and from subsequent efforts to apply laboratory training and survey-feedback insights into total systems."[14] Thus, the two major historical stems for OD are laboratory training and survey feedback. The work of the pioneering social psychologist Kurt Lewin was instrumental in both approaches. Today, almost every organization of any size is pursuing some form of organization development.

OD Techniques

Although the beginnings of OD can be traced to laboratory or training group techniques—sometimes called sensitivity training or "T" (for training) groups—the most popular techniques over the years have been grid training, survey feedback, and team building.

Grid Training. Grid training as used in OD is an outgrowth of the managerial grid approach to leadership discussed in Chapter 11. A 9,9 position on Blake and Mouton's leadership grid, shown in Chapter 11, indicating a maximum concern for both people and production, is an implied goal of grid training. A more comprehensive step-by-step approach is taken when grid training is used in OD.

Summarized, the six phases of grid training for OD are the following:

1. *Laboratory-seminar training.* The purpose of this first phase is to introduce the participants to the overall concepts and materials used in grid training. The seminars that are held are not like therapeutic sensitivity training. There is more structure and more concentration on leadership styles than on developing self-insights and group insights.
2. *Team development.* This is an extension of the first phase. Members of the same department are brought together to chart how they are going to attain a 9,9 position on the grid. In this stage, what was learned in the orientation stage is applied to the actual organizational situation.
3. *Intergroup development.* Whereas the first two phases are aimed at managerial development, this phase marks the beginning of overall organization development. There is a shift from the micro level of individual and group development to a macro level of group-to-group organization development. Conflict situations between groups are identified and analyzed.

4. *Organizational goal setting.* In the manner of management by objectives, in this phase the participants contribute to, and agree upon, the important goals for the organization. A sense of commitment and self-control is instilled in the participants.

5. *Goal attainment.* In this phase the participants attempt to accomplish the goals which they set in the fourth phase. As in the first phase, the participants get together, but this time they discuss major organizational issues, and the stakes are real.

6. *Stabilization.* In this final phase, support is marshaled for changes suggested earlier, and an evaluation of the overall program is conducted.[15]

These six phases of grid training may take from three to five years to implement, but in some cases they may be compressed into a shorter period of time.

Most of the support for grid training has come from its founders, Robert R. Blake and Jane S. Mouton. They and their colleagues have maintained over the years that "managerial and team effectiveness *can* be taught by managers with outside assistance. Furthermore, it appears that this type of educational strategy can help to make significant contributions to organizational effectiveness."[16]

In a later work, *The New Managerial Grid*, Blake and Mouton continue to suggest that research indicates that grid training is very effective.[17] A review of the research on OD gives some support to their claims. Although it was found to have the least rigorous research (along with the survey feedback), the four studies reviewed found grid training to have a 43 percent substantial positive impact on process variables, and three studies found a 68 percent positive impact on outcome variables.[18] The impact of grid training on outcome variables was higher than that of any of the other OD techniques, but, again, this finding was based on only three studies. Conclusions are still tentative at this point because more and better research is needed in the future before any firm conclusions can be drawn; nevertheless, the use of grid training does seem to be justified. One thing is certain: It has been very widely used.

Survey Feedback. Besides grid training, another popular OD technique has been survey research and feedback of the data. Once again Kurt Lewin had the original influence, but over the years the survey-feedback approach has been most closely associated with the University of Michigan's Institute for Social Research (ISR).

As the terminology indicates, this approach to OD surveys the unit of analysis (for example, a work group, a department, or a whole organization) by means of questionnaires and feeds back the data to those who generated them. The data are used in the action research sense of diagnosing problems and developing specific action plans to solve the problems. Either the questionnaire can be tailor-made for each situation, or, as has been more common in recent years, a standardized version is researched and developed by the ISR. A number of revisions have been made through the years, but the typical ISR questionnaire provides data in the areas of leadership, organizational climate, and employee satisfaction.

Normally an external consultant will accumulate, present, and interpret the data for the group. The consultant will then, usually in a process-consultation or team-building approach (covered in the next section), help the group diagnose and solve its problems.

In terms of its effectiveness, one review of three rigorous studies on survey feedback indicated it has a 53 percent substantial positive change on outcome variables,[19] and a later review found that three studies yielded an overall 50 percent positive change in productivity. However, the latter analysis found no impact on work-force measures such as turnover, absenteeism, and grievances, and compared with structured laboratory training and team building, survey feedback had the least impact.[20] Used in combination with team building, it had a more positive impact.

Team Building. Both grid training and survey feedback are fairly specialized and associated with a leading advocate (Blake and Mouton in the case of the grid and the Michigan group in the case of survey feedback). Of wider appeal and application is team building. As earlier chapters have brought out, the team approach in general (quality circles, semi-autonomous groups, or self-managed groups) has become quite popular as a human resource management technique.[21] Although similar, team building has actually been around longer as a specific OD intervention. Whereas oldtime sensitivity training "scared off" many managers because of the controversy surrounding it and the potentially harmful psychological implications inherent in it, team building is seen as accomplishing some of the same goals as sensitivity training but tends to be more task-oriented. Table 21.2 shows that team-building activities can be applied to either "family" groups or special groups (for example, task forces, committees, or interdepartmental groups) within the organization.

In general it can be said that team building is an organization development effort aimed at improving overall performance. Perhaps with the exception of widely marketed, commercially based grid training, there is little question that team building has become the most popular OD technique in recent years. French and Bell go as far as to say that "probably the most important single group of interventions in

TABLE 21.2 Various Approaches to Team Building

Family Groups (Members from the Same Organizational Unit)	Special Groups (Start-Up Teams, Task Forces, Committees, and Interdepartmental Groups)
1. Task accomplishment (for example, problem solving, decision making, role clarification, and goal setting)	1. Task accomplishment (special problems, role and goal clarification, resource utilization, etc.)
2. Building and maintaining effective interpersonal relationships (for example, boss-subordinate relationships and peer relationships)	2. Relationships (for example, interpersonal or interunit conflict and underutilization of each other as resources)
3. Understanding and managing group processes and culture	3. Processes (for example, communications, decision making, and task allocations)
4. Role analysis technique for role clarification and definition	4. Role analysis technique for role clarification and definition
5. Role negotiation techniques	5. Role negotiation

Source: Adapted from Wendell L. French and Cecil H. Bell, *Organization Development*, 2d ed., Prentice-Hall, Englewood Cliffs, N.J., 1978, p. 119.

OD are the team-building activities the goals of which are the improvement and increased effectiveness of various teams within the organization."[22]

As an OD process, team building generally follows the classic change procedure originally formulated by Kurt Lewin:

1. *Unfreezing.* The first task is to make the team aware of the need for change. A climate of openness and trust is developed so that the group is ready for change.
2. *Moving.* Basically using a survey-feedback technique, the team makes a diagnosis of where it is and develops action plans to get to where it wants to go.
3. *Refreezing.* Once the plans have been carried out and an evaluation has been made, the team starts to stablilize into more effective performance.

The above, of course, represents only a very general idea of what team building is all about and can also apply to the other OD techniques.

A more specific team-building program actually used in a large industrial plant is described as follows:

1. *Team skills workshop.* The production team in this plant first went through a two-day workshop that consisted mainly of a series of experience-based exercises. The purpose of this first phase was essentially to unfreeze the various teams and get them ready to accept change.
2. *Data collection.* In a questionnaire survey, data were collected on organizational climate, supervisory behavior, and job content from all first-line supervisors in the program.
3. *Data confrontation.* The consultants presented the teams with the data gathered in step 2. The teams, with the consultant present, openly discussed problem areas, established priorities, and made some preliminary recommendations for change.
4. *Action planning.* On the basis of what went on in step 3, the teams developed specific plans for the changes to be actually carried out on the job.
5. *Team building.* The first four phases were preliminary to the actual team building. In this phase, each team met as a whole to identify barriers to effectiveness, developed ways of eliminating the barriers, and agreed upon plans to accomplish the desired changes.
6. *Intergroup building.* In this final phase there were two-day meetings held between various teams that were interdependent in accomplishing goals. The purpose of this phase was to establish collaboration on shared goals and problems and generalize the OD effort to the total organization.[23]

This program took over a year to complete. As an Apple Computer executive experienced in team building recently noted, "Team building is not a fun day away from the office, a strategy for saving a failing manager, a place to go and 'dump' the team's anger, or a group psychotherapy session. Team building is a process for helping a team become more effective."[24]

The advantages of team building are all those which are attributed to old-fashioned teamwork. The process can create a team effort in an open, participatory climate. There can be improved communication and problem solving, and individual team members can experience psychological growth and improve their interpersonal skills. For example, one research study found that four trained teams reported significantly higher levels of group effectiveness, mutual influence, and personal involvement and participation than the eight control groups.[25] Evaluation of the six-step program described above also found that the program produced a positive impact on organizational performance (quality of output and profit but not quantity of output) and favorably affected the attitudes and perceptions of the members of the teams studied.[26]

As the above studies indicate, there is relatively more and better research on team building than on any of the other OD techniques. Porras and Berg found far more acceptable research designs on team building (40 percent of the thirty-five studies met their minimum criteria). Of team-building studies that examined process variables, 45 percent have a substantial positive change, and of the three studies that analyzed the impact on outcome variables, 53 percent were deemed to have a substantial positive change.[27] The later Nicholas review looked at four team-building studies and found that there was a 50 percent overall positive impact on work-force, monetary, and productivity hard measures of performance.[28] It came out better than survey feedback, but was behind structured laboratory training. However, a later study conducted with hard-rock miners produced inconclusive results.[29] So, although there is considerable evidence that team building can be beneficial, it is still open to question *how* and, in some cases, *if* team building works.

Besides having demonstrated that it can have a positive impact on its own as an OD intervention strategy, team building has the strength of being able to be effectively used in combination with other OD techniques. For example, as mentioned earlier, Nicholas found that if it was used in combination with survey feedback, there was a much more positive effect on hard performance measures than if survey feedback was used by itself.[30] Also, there have recently been calls for combining team building with O.B. Mod. approaches. One suggestion along this line was to use a task hierarchy to reinforce the team as it progresses up a behavior skills hierarchy (for example, listening, communicating, monitoring, and feedback skills).[31] There also seem to be successful applications for a team-building approach internationally, but the intervention must be carried out in a culturally sensitive manner.[32] Team building seems to have a bright future.

The Impact of a Possible Paradigm Shift on OD Techniques

In the near future, for reasons including competitive pressures and the accelerated rate of change, there may be an upcoming paradigm shift affecting the management of change. The word "paradigm" comes from the Greek word meaning "pattern," and the new paradigm involves a pattern of behavior that comes from a new way of looking at the world. Whereas the traditional paradigm tried to solve problems with numbers and control from the top, the new paradigm revolves around people—both employees and customers. Here are some events that may signal a paradigm shift:

- Hierarchical organizations are replaced by flexible networks.
- Employees are empowered to make decisions on their own.
- Organizations develop a capacity for group learning instead of waiting for wisdom from above.

- National horizons give way to global thinking.
- Creativity and intuition join numerical analysis as aids to decision making.
- Love and caring become recognized as motivators in the workplace.
- The primacy of the profit motive is questioned by those who argue that the real goal should be the mental and spiritual enrichment of those who participate in the organization.[33]

To help organizations and managers cope with such paradigmatic change, there is a recent call for new OD techniques.[34] There is the argument that the relatively simplistic traditional OD techniques cannot handle the dramatic change of a paradigm shift. Schein offers some recent suggestions of what needs to be done, usually in combination, to produce a new organizational culture that can cope with such change:

1. Leaders may unfreeze the present system by highlighting the threats of the organization if no change occurs, and, at the same time, encourage the organization to believe that change is possible and desirable.
2. Leaders may articulate a new direction and a new set of assumptions, thus providing a clear and new role model.
3. Key positions in the organization may be filled with new incumbents who hold the new assumptions because they are either hybrids, mutants, or brought in from the outside.
4. Leaders may systematically reward the adoption of new directions and punish adherence to the old direction.
5. Organization members may be seduced or coerced into adopting new behaviors that are more consistent with new assumptions.
6. Visible scandals may be created to discredit sacred cows, to explode myths that preserve dysfunctional traditions, and symbolically destroy the artifacts associated with them.
7. Leaders may create new emotionally charged rituals and develop new symbols and artifacts around the new assumptions to be embraced, using the embedding mechanisms described earlier.[35]

Also, there has been a recent call by some OD experts to develop alternatives to the traditional top-down, single-organization OD interventions which have supported top management's outdated definitions of reality. For example, Bradshaw-Camball suggests a radically new approach to OD involving interventions with the organization's board of directors, taking a bottom-up rather than top-down approach, and focusing the OD effort at an interorganizational level.[36] She points out that this new approach to OD demands different values, skills, techniques, and abilities of change agents and that the actual process of change is fundamentally different.[37]

OD in Perspective

OD has matured but, as the above section points out, with a possible paradigm shift underway, many challenges remain. The Application Example, A Rainbow of Talent, notes the challenges organizations face in managing the diverse work force now.

Application
Example
||||➡

A Rainbow of Talent

At the Digital Equipment plant in Boston there are 350 employees. Collectively, these individuals come from forty-four countries and speak nineteen languages including Chinese, English, French, Portuguese, Spanish, and Vietnamese. Is this plant's ethnic breakdown unique? Hardly. All around the country, more and more of the work force is becoming one composed of first- and second-generation immigrants and minorities who have their own language and value systems. As a result, one of the primary areas of managerial focus these days is on "managing diversity."

This trend toward diversity is not limited to immigrants but also includes women and minorities. Organizations in the years ahead are facing a major challenge. What steps can be taken to deal with this diversity? One step is learning to recognize and appreciate individual differences. Rather than having everyone adapt to a "male Anglo culture," organizations are learning how to tap the separate contributions of their diverse work forces. Many of the new entrants into the work force are strong supporters of the work ethic. By using the proper motivation tools, the organization can increase its productivity and maintain its competitive posture. One simple way in which this is being done is by bending the rules and making the work more attractive. For example, in some companies the dress code has been abandoned and people can wear whatever clothing they want. This is important to young people who do not want to wear uniforms or business suits.

Another development is the promotion of minorities and women into the management ranks, thus showing that there is upward mobility for qualified personnel. This development, in turn, is also helping organizations improve the management of their diverse work force and increase their ability to recruit new people from the labor pool. As one observer put it, "In the rest of this decade and beyond, the companies that come out on top will be those that have learned to attract—and keep—the best workers in the rainbow of talent."

and in the future. It is now clear that OD is not going to be a panacea for all management's problems. On the other hand, it is also clear that OD can definitely help management meet the challenges that change and complexity present to modern organizations and their effectiveness. The review articles by Porras and Berg and by Nicholas, which were cited in the discussion of the various OD techniques, shed some important new light on the impact of OD. Although overall they found relatively little systematic research evidence on OD, their conclusions do counter some of the traditional assumptions that OD makes people happier or more satisfied, and, also contrary to common belief, they found that OD had at least as great an impact on outcome variables (for example, openness, self-awareness, goal emphasis, decision making, motivation, and influence).

For those interested in the "bottom-line" impacts of intervention strategies, OD may possess a heretofore overlooked advantage. However, before becoming too optimistc about the value of OD and overturning all the negative assumptions about it, it is well to remember, as Porras and Berg point out, that "the data support the belief that OD does not have an important impact on overall organizational processes but instead impacts primarily on the individual."[38] Nicholas concludes that "the single most apparent finding of this research is that no one change technique or class of techniques works well in all situations."[39]

Another caution is the rigor of the research that has been employed in OD studies. For example, a recent review article by Woodman concludes, "Stated kindly, the quality of research in OD is not always spectacular; indeed, some of it is shoddy."[40] Although there is a clear trend toward more rigorous methods and designs,[41] there are still problems. In fact, one analysis of OD research found an inverse relationship between the degree of methodological rigor and the reported outcome success of OD.[42] But a later study did not verify this.[43] Another recent observation is the role that self-fulfilling expectations may have on OD interventions. Although pointing out that it should not be thought of as detrimental, Dov Eden hypothesizes that an OD intervention's effectiveness is in direct proportion to the expectations for improved performance it arouses.[44]

Thus, the value of OD as a group-wide approach to the management of change is not yet totally supported by the research to date. This conclusion is also consistent with the conclusions of others who have observed OD and argued that it rarely diffuses throughout the entire organization and that it is too limited.[45] Guest makes the point that all the human resource management and behaviorally oriented techniques, not just OD, have come up short. He notes that "much of the innovation is piecemeal and lacking in the crucial ingredient of strategic integration, and that as a result it is unlikely to have a positive impact on organizational performance.[46]

Besides the need for new approaches as suggested in the previous section and strategic intregation as suggested by Guest, there is still a need for common sense guidelines in order to have successful change efforts. Here is a simple list of things that experience says to avoid in major system changes:

1. Do not promise that all employees undergoing a change effort will be winners.
2. Do not blame those who lose out for their negative attitudes.
3. Do not focus only on the new and forget the old.
4. Avoid symbolic or pseudoparticipation in the change effort.
5. Avoid destroying the old culture without building a new one.
6. Do not launch human resource management programs in the context of a major change without the necessary time and resources to support them.[47]

These practical guidelines are not meant to dampen the excitement and enthusiasm for change efforts but to put realistic expectations into the process.

THE FUTURE OF ORGANIZATIONAL BEHAVIOR

The changes discussed in the introductory comments of this chapter dealing with globalization, the information explosion, quality service, and the diverse work force signal the challenges that lie ahead not only for the management of change and organization development, but also for the entire field of organizational behavior. Fortunately, some identifiable trends have emerged in organizational behavior. First, it can be said that organizational behavior has truly arrived as an identifiable field of academic study, with definite implications for the effective management of human resources in modern, complex organizations. This recognition of organizational behavior as a legitimate academic and applied field should become even greater in the future.

Second, there is now a clear distinction between organizational behavior and other areas such as general management and personnel administration. For example, organizational behavior is concerned with human behavior in organizations, while personnel management is recognized as a function of the organization and is concerned mainly with topics such as wage and salary administration and labor relations. The field of organizational behavior is recognized to be very broad, and as one theorist emphasized, "It is the people behaving in them that make organizations what they are."[48] In addition, the micro-macro split in the topics and conceptual framework for organizational behavior, which was at first thought to be getting wider (even in the past editions of this text), now seems to be lessening. Recognition is given to the important role of macro structural variables and the environment in the social learning theoretical framework. Macro variables play a major role, although still not as proportionately great a role as micro variables, in this edition and in the field in general.

Third, the topical coverage of the field of organizational behavior will continue to move away from the traditional specialized topics in behavioral science and toward topics more identified with organizational behavior per se (organizational culture, job stress, job design, goal setting, job satisfaction, organizational behavior modification, behavioral self-management, job conflict, organizational power and politics, informal organization, managerial roles, interpersonal communication, managerial leadership, organization development, and managerial and behavioral decision making). The exceptions here are the mainstays of experimental psychology—attitudes, motivation, and learning. These topics continue to be very important areas in organizational behavior.

Finally—and this, of course, most students and practitioners will be happy to hear—the trend toward making the organizational behavior approach more understandable and applications-oriented should continue. Although there is a definite trend away from simple answers to complex organizational behavior problems at all levels of analysis—individual, group, and organizational—in order to be considered useful it must be both understandable and applicable to the real world.[49] The successive editions of this text have given evidence of this trend. The organizational behavior approach is clearly aimed at the more effective management of human resources. With emphasis on areas such as coping with organizational culture, international management, job stress, job design, goal setting, organizational behavior modification, behavioral self-management, political strategies, leadership styles, organization development, and decision-making techniques, this aim at applications should become clearer and be more likely to hit the target of more effective human resources management in the years to come.

The future of the field of organizational behavior looks very bright and exciting. Although there will be some shifting emphasis in conceptual framework and topical covereage, the "bottom line" is that the study and application of the areas covered in this book will help make better, more effective managers of the most important and underutilized resource in any organization: *people*. The effective management of people (both others and oneself) is really what organizational behavior is all about.

Summary

Organizations today are faced with tremendous forces for change, mainly stemming from globalization, the information explosion, quality service, and work-force diversity. A systematic, planned way of managing this change is through the process of organizational development. The major techniques of OD are grid training, survey feedback, team building, and some new techniques to cope with a possible paradigm shift. However, like the other techniques and approaches, more rigorous research and contingency applications need to be forthcoming. Yet there is little question that OD has a fairly bright future in helping solve some of the tremendous challenges facing today's organizations. The last section of the book looked into the crystal ball of the future and identified some recent trends in the field of organizational behavior and the management of human resources.

Questions for Discussion and Review

1. What are some of the major forces for change that are confronting today's organizations?
2. What are some of the major characteristics of organization development?
3. In your own words, briefly describe three approaches to OD. Discuss some of their major advantages and limitations.
4. What are some of the characteristics of the possible paradigm shift? What new approaches to OD will be required?
5. Do you agree with the view that the future of organizational behavior is bright and exciting? Do you have anything to add to this view?

References

1. Tom Peters, "Prometheus Barely Unbound," *Academy of Management Executive*, November 1990, p. 70.
2. Herbert M. Baum, "White-Collar Quality Comes of Age," *The Journal of Business Strategy*, March–April 1990, p. 34.
3. Lynn R. Offerman and Marilyn K. Gowing, "Organizations of the Future," *American Psychologist*, February 1990, pp. 96–97.
4. William H. Wagel and Hermine Zagat Levine, "HR '90: Challenges and Opportunities," *Personnel*, June 1990, p. 18.
5. Douglas T. Hall, "Promoting Work/Family Balance: An Organization-Change Approach," *Organizational Dynamics*, Winter 1990, pp. 5–18.
6. Jac Fitz-enz, "Getting and Keeping Good Employees," *Personnel*, August 1990, pp. 25–28.
7. See Alex Taylor III, "The New Drive to Revive GM," *Fortune*, Apr. 9, 1990, pp. 52–61.
8. Edmund Faltermayer, "Is 'Made in U.S.A ' Fading Away?" *Fortune*, Sept. 24, 1990, pp. 62–74. Also see Karen Pennar, "Yes, We're Down. No, We're Not Out," *Business Week*, Dec. 17, 1990, pp. 62–63.
9. Faltermayer, op. cit., p. 62.
10. Gerald D. Klein, "Employee-Centered Productivity and QWL Programs: Findings from an Area Study," *National Productivity Review*, Autumn 1986, p. 350.
11. Wendell L. French and Cecil H. Bell, Jr., *Organization Development*, 2d ed., Prentice-Hall, Englewood Cliffs, N.J., 1978, p. 14.
12. W. Warner Burke, *Organization Development*, Little, Brown, Boston, 1982, p. 10.

13. Stewart Black and Newton Margulies, "An Ideological Perspective on Participation: A Case for Integration," *Journal of Organizational Change Management*, vol. 2, no. 1, 1989, p. 16.

14. French and Bell, op. cit., p. 27.

15. Robert R. Blake, Jane S. Mouton, Louis B. Barnes, and Larry E. Greiner, "Breakthrough in Organization Development," *Harvard Business Review*, November–December 1964, pp. 137–138.

16. Ibid., p. 155.

17. Robert R. Blake and Jane S. Mouton, *The New Management Grid*, Gulf, Houston, 1978.

18. Jerry I. Porras and P. O. Berg, "The Impact of Organization Development," *Academy of Management Review*, April 1978, pp. 259–260.

19. Porras and Berg, op. cit.

20. John M. Nicholas, "The Comparative Impact of Organization Development Intervention on Hard Criteria Measures," *Academy of Management Review*, October 1982, p. 536.

21. See Brian Dumaine, "Who Needs a Boss?" *Fortune*, May 7, 1990, pp. 52–60.

22. French and Bell, op. cit., p. 119.

23. Warren R. Nielsen and John R. Kimberly, "The Impact of Organizational Development on the Quality of Organizational Output," *Academy of Management Proceedings*, 1973, pp. 528–529.

24. John Boring, quoted in Wagel and Levine, op. cit., p. 26.

25. Frank Friedlander, "The Impact of Organizational Training Laboratories upon Effectiveness and Intervention of Ongoing Work Groups," *Personnel Psychology*, Autumn 1967, pp. 289–308.

26. John R. Kimberly and Warren R. Nielsen, "Organizational Development and Change in Organizational Performance," *Administrative Science Quarterly*, June 1975, pp. 191–206.

27. Porras and Berg, op. cit.

28. Nicholas, op. cit.

29. Paul F. Buller and Cecil H. Bell, Jr., "Effects of Team Building and Goal Setting on Productivity: A Field Experiment," *Academy of Management Journal*, June 1986, pp. 305–328.

30. Nicholas, op. cit.

31. Ray V. Rasmussen, "Team Training: A Behavior Modification Approach," *Group and Organizational Studies*, March 1982, pp. 51–66.

32. Richard B. Polley, "Intervention and Cultural Context: Mediation in the U.S. and Norway," in Frank Hoy (ed.), *Academy of Management Best Papers Proceedings*, 1987, pp. 236–240; and Alfred M. Jaeger, "Organization Development and National Culture: Where's the Fit?" *Academy of Management Review*, January 1986, pp. 178–190.

33. Frank Rose, "A New Age for Business?" *Fortune*, Oct. 8, 1990, p. 157.

34. Michael Beer and Elise Walton, "Developing the Competitive Organization: Interventions and Strategies," *American Psychologist*, February 1990, p. 160.

35. Edgar H. Schein, "Organizational Culture," *American Psychologist*, February 1990, p. 117.

36. Patricia Bradshaw-Camball, "Organizational Development and the Radical Humanist Paradigm: Exploring the Implications," *Academy of Management Best Papers Proceedings*, 1990, p. 256.

37. Ibid.

38. Porras and Berg, op. cit., p. 264.

39. Nicholas, op. cit., p. 540.

40. Richard W. Woodman, "Organizational Change and Development: New Arenas for Inquiry and Action," *Journal of Management*, vol. 15, no. 2, 1989, p. 223.

41. John M. Nicholas and Marsha Katz, "Research Methods and Reporting Practices in Organization Development: A Review and Some Guidelines," *Academy of Management Review*, October 1985, pp. 737–749.

42. David Terpstra, "Relationship between Methodological Rigor and Reported Outcomes in Organizational Development Evaluation Research," *Journal of Applied Psychology*, October 1981, pp. 541–542.

43. Richard W. Woodman and Sandy J. Wayne, "An Investigation of Positive-Findings Bias in Evaluation of Organization and Development Interventions," *Academy of Management Journal*, December 1985, pp. 889–913.

44. Dov Eden, "OD and Self-Fulfilling Prophecy: Boosting Productivity by Raising Expectations," *Journal of Applied Behavioral Science*, vol. 22, no. 1, 1986, pp. 1–13.

45. Richard Walton, "The Diffusion of New Work Structures: Explaining Why Success Didn't Take," *Organizational Dynamics*, Winter 1975, pp. 3–22; and George Strauss, "Organizational Development: Credits and Debits," *Organizational Dynamics*, Winter 1973, pp. 2–19.

46. David E. Guest, "Human Resource Management

and the American Dream," *Journal of Management Studies,* July 1990, p. 388.

47. Jeffrey K. Liker, David B. Roitman, and Ethel Roskies, "Changing Everything All at Once: Work Life and Technological Change," *Sloan Management Review,* Summer 1987, pp. 43–44.

48. Benjamin Schneider, "The People Make the Place," *Personnel Psychology,* vol. 40, 1987, p. 438.

49. James L. Gibson, John M. Ivancevich, and James H. Donnelly, Jr., *Organizations,* 6th ed., Business Publications, Inc., Plano, Tex., 1988, pp. 755–756.

REAL CASE: MEETING THE CHALLENGES OF THE NEXT CENTURY

There are many areas where organizational change will affect the management of human resources at all levels in the years ahead. One area is the career ladder, where successful managers are often finding that the road to the top is a lot slower than it used to be. "Hurry up and wait" appears to have replaced "hurry up and succeed." In contrasting the organization manager of the 1970s and 1980s with today's manager, some of the primary differences appear to be these: (1) every career move used to be directed toward promotion up the hierarchy but now lateral moves are becoming more routine and, in some cases, even desirable; (2) promotions often used to come every two years but now they come more slowly and while the job title may not change, it is likely that the responsibilities will; (3) success used to mean job security all the way to retirement but today it often means inner fulfillment and money; and (4) the workweek used to be forty hours but now it lasts until the job is done—however long that may take.

In addition, there are other changes that warrant mention. One is the trend toward fewer management levels and the reduction in the overall number of managers in industry, which means slower and fewer promotions. A second is the plateauing of female participation in the labor force. This change is partially accounted for by a desire to stay at home, raise a family, and work either part-time or on a personally acceptable schedule, which means a change in the way organizations recruit and staff some of their positions.

One of the most upsetting of these changes is the slow promotion rate. More firms are moving from a bureaucracy with rewards tied to time on the job to a meritocracy where people are rewarded for effective performance. In measuring the latter, organizations are leaving people in their jobs for a longer period of time so that they can see how well the person has really done. A pet food marketing manager at Quaker Oats put it this way, "I got to see the effects of changes I made and to work through their implications. It helped me learn to approach every job as a long-term opportunity, to stand back and ask what changes we need to make in this whole picture, even if it has been done one way for the last fifteen years." Others point out that it will become more important to be a generalist than a specialist. An executive search recruiter recently noted, "In the future everybody will have strategic alliances with everybody else, and the executives who thrive will be well-rounded. You can't be a specialist at senior levels anymore."

Does this mean that today's managers are pleased with the new trends and that they are more committed to the organization than ever? Hardly. A recent poll comparing managerial responses in 1959 and thirty years later found that, on average, today's managers rank their companies lower in virtually every category, including advancement opportunity, job security, a place to work, and job satisfaction. The only category that was fairly close was job satisfaction. Of the four categories, it is the only one that is most under the personal control of the manager. Simply put, career opportunities are not as good as they were previously, but managers are learning to live with the situation.

1. In what way will new flatter organization structures affect the career potential of managers?
2. Is the trend toward slower promotions good or bad? Why?
3. How can OD be used to help individuals handle career planning problems? Give some examples.

**Case:
The High-
Priced OD
Consultant**

The middle managers of a large firm were told by the corporate personnel office that a group of consultants would be calling on them later in the week. The purpose of the consultants' visit would be to analyze intergroup relations throughout the firm. The consultants had been very effective in using an OD intervention called *team building*. Their particular approach used six steps. When their approach was explained to the managers, a great deal of tension was relieved. They had initially thought that team building was a lot of hocus-pocus, like sensitivity training, where people attack each other and let out their aggressions by heaping abuse on those they dislike. By the same token, these managers generally felt that perhaps the consultants were not needed. One of them put it this way: "Now that we understand what is involved in team building, we can go ahead and conduct the sessions ourselves. All we have to do is to choose a manager who is liked by everyone and put him in the role of the change agent/consultant. After all, you really don't need a high-priced consultant to do this team-building stuff. You just have to have a good feel for human nature." The other managers generally agreed. However, the corporate personnel director turned their suggestion down. He hired the OD consultants to do the team building.

1. What is a team-building approach to organization development? Do you think the managers had an accurate view of the technique?
2. Do you think the managers had an accurate view of the role of the external consultant? Do you agree or disagree with the corporate personnel director's decision to turn down their suggestions? Why?

INTEGRATIVE CONTEMPORARY CASE FOR PART 6

Stepping Up to
the Challenge
of Change*

So it has come to this: You've automated the factory, decimated the inventory, eliminated the unnecessary from the organization chart, and the company still isn't hitting on all cylinders—and you've got an awful feeling you know why. It's the culture. It's the values, heroes, myths, symbols that have been in the organization forever, the attitudes that say, Don't disagree with the boss, or Don't make waves, or Just do enough to get by, or For God's sake, don't take chances. And how on earth are you going to change all *that*?

If your company is like a great many others, it will have to step up to this challenge. The changes businesses are being forced to make merely to stay competitive—improving quality, increasing speed, adopting a customer orientation—are so fundamental that they must take root in a company's very essence, which means in its culture. This news depresses those who remember corporate culture as the trendy concern of the mid-Eighties, when consultants ranging from the super-sober to the wacky tried to change companies' cultures and almost always found they couldn't. But take heart. An increasing number of enterprises are at last figuring out how to alter their cultures, and more than ever are doing it.

The basic lesson sounds like a Confucian principle: Cultural change must come from the bottom, and the CEO must guide it. Despite the apparent contradiction, Du Pont, Tandem Computers, and many others are making that idea work. Says Du Pont CEO Edgar Woolard: "Employees have been underestimated. You have to start with the premise that people at all levels want to contribute and make the business a success."

The CEO must show the direction of the change to make sure it happens coherently. But a cultural transformation is a change in the hearts and minds of the workers, and it won't happen if the CEO just talks. David Nadler, the president of Delta Consulting Group, warns of the plexiglass CEO syndrome: "CEOs encase their mission statement in plexiglass, hand it out, and people laugh. You have to change the way the person who assembles the machine or designs the product acts." This means the CEO must live the new culture, become the walking embodiment of it. He must also spot and celebrate managers and employees who exemplify the values he wants to inculcate.

No cultural change happens easily or quickly. Figure five to ten years for a significant improvment—but since the alternative may be extinction, it's worth a try. Here's how the most successful companies are changing their cultures today:

Beyond Vision. Yes, a CEO must promulgate a vision, but the most brilliant vision statement this side of Paraguay won't budge a culture unless it's backed up by action. At a major manufacturer, a manager who preached quality found

Source: Brian Dumaine, "Creating a New Company Culture," *Fortune*, Jan. 15, 1990, pp. 127–128, 130–131.

that a part in the tractors coming off his assembly line was defective and would burn out after 300 hours of use rather than the specified 1,000 hours—a problem the customer wouldn't notice for quite a while. The manager could ship the tractors and make his quarterly numbers, or he could fix the flaw. He decided to fix the flaw. His people now know he's serious about quality.

Du Pont CEO Woolard, who preaches that "nothing is worthwhile unless it touches the customer," understands that communicating isn't enough. At a number of his plants he has a program called Adopt a Customer, which encourages blue-collar workers to visit a customer once a month, learn his needs, and be his representative on the factory floor. As quality or delivery problems arise, the worker is more likely to see them from the customer's point of view and help make a decision that will keep his "adopted child" happy.

Management at Florida Power & Light is changing its culture from that of a bureaucratic backwater to one that worships quality and service. The company shows it is serious by giving even the lowliest employees extraordinary freedom to practice that religion. Example: The utility discovered that its meter readers suffered more on-the-job injuries than any other type of employee, and they were nasty ones—dog bites. The meter readers in Boca Raton wanted to form a team to study the problem. Under the old culture, management would have scoffed at such a notion as a waste of time. Says executive vice president Wayne Brunetti: "It would have been so easy for us to reject this kind of idea." But the new ethos allowed the meter readers to take the initiative. They formed a team of ten who surveyed households, found out which ones had fierce Fidos, and then programmed hand-held computers to beep just before a visit to a dangerous address. Dog bites (and absenteeism) are down, and morale (and service) is up.

Alter History. A company with the wrong history and myths can get itself in big trouble. For years after Walt Disney's death his ghost stalked the halls of the company's studios in Burbank, California, causing executives to freeze in their tracks and wonder, "What would Walt have done?"

These hero worshipers were driving the studio into the ground with an outdated line of family flicks. Realizing that sometimes history can't be changed without changing the players, CEO Michael Eisner came aboard and cleared the deck, bringing in new managers, most of whom had never met Disney. The new crew, freed of the spectral overseer, began to create a culture that was more sophisticated than stodgy, more adventurous than cautious, more ambitious than content. They have turned the company around by (among other moves) daring to make grown-up films like *The Color of Money* and *Ruthless People*, which would have irked old Walt.

Can something as amorphous as history be changed without spilling blood? Consider what a FORTUNE 500 manufacturer did with a factory that had a history of poor quality, hostile labor relations, and terrible productivity. The company hired a consultant who started out by talking with the employees. They eagerly told him about Sam, the plant manager who was a 300-pound gorilla with a disposition that made King Kong look like Bonzo the chimp.

One time Sam examined a transmission, didn't like the work he saw, picked up a sledgehammer, and smashed it to pieces. A worker summoned to Sam's office threw up on the way. Another time Sam drove his car into the plant, got up on the roof, and started screaming at his workers. One worker, fed up, poured a line of gasoline to the car and lit it.

The stunned consultant made an appointment to see the plant manager. When he walked into the office he saw a slim, pleasant-looking man behind the desk; his name was Paul. "Where's Sam?" asked the consultant. Paul, looking puzzled, replied, "Sam has been dead for nine years."

From then on Paul and the consultant realized they had a serious problem. For years Paul had been trying to instill a sense of fairness and participation, but the plant's nightmarish history was so strong his efforts had failed. To cope, Paul and his supervisors sat down with groups of eight or ten assembly workers to discuss the plant's *history*—300-pound Sam and all. Just discussing it helped clear the air.

Paul also tried hard not to do anything Sam would have done. Once, while on the noisy shop floor, he abruptly pointed at a worker, commanding him to throw away a coffee cup left near a machine. Paul merely thought he was taking care of a safety hazard. The workers on the floor, mindful of the hateful Sam, thought something like, "Ah, he's just another militaristic S.O.B. who loves spit and polish." Better for Paul to have tossed the cup away himself—a small gesture, yet that and a thousand other subtle messages will eventually help transform a culture. After four years of effort, Paul's plant this fall won his company's top award for quality.

Symbols, Symbols, Symbols. As Paul learned, executives often underestimate the power symbolic gestures have on workers. Taking the corporate jet to a Hawaiian retreat to discuss cost cutting isn't exactly going to send the right message to the troops.

At Tandem, the computer company in Cupertino, California, a general manager once told CEO Jimmy Treybig that he wanted to fire an employee. Treybig said OK, but first find out why the person wasn't performing. The general manager discovered the employee had serious family problems and decided to give him another chance, sending a signal to everyone else in the company that we treat people around here with consideration. Says Treybig: "You have to keep remembering what your company is. All your work is done by your people."

Something as simple as an award can help make a culture more innovative. In Japan, Sharp rewards top performers by putting them on a "gold badge" project team that reports directly to the company president. The privilege instills pride and gets other employees scrambling for new ideas and products in the hope that they too may make the team.

Awards can also encourage risk taking. About a year ago, the people in Du Pont's relocation department—who help move executives to new cities—thought they could boost productivity by installing a new computer system.

The experiment failed, but rather than chastise those who suggested it, the company in November presented them with a plaque that told them: We're proud of your effort and hope you try again as hard in years to come.

Create Universities. Michael Beer, a Harvard business school professor, urges CEOs to identify models within the corporation. Scour the company to find some maverick manager who has figured out how to do it right—achieving high quality, good morale, innovative products. Then hold up this department or factory as a kind of university where employees can learn how others have succeeded. It's important not to force managers to adopt everything the university offers. Let them choose what works best for them.

In a study of six FORTUNE 500 companies that wanted to change their cultures, Beer found the only one that truly succeeded used the model approach. "With this one," says Beer, "the change began way before the CEO became fully aware of it. It was started in a small plant by some innovative managers. The top learned about it from the lowest level and spread the best practices around the company."

A caveat: The model concept works only when top management believes that *all* its employees have the ability to learn and grow. Too often a company stereotypes its blue-collar workers as dumb, inarticulate, and mindlessly loyal to archaic values like macho exhibitionism and anti-intellectualism. Shake it. Says Du Pont group vice president Mark Suwyn: "These people manage their lives well outside the factory. They sit on school boards or coach Little League. We have to create a culture where we can bring that creative energy into the work force."

Du Pont considers its plant in Towanda, Pennsylvania, which makes materials for printed circuitboard and other products, a model of the kind Beer is talking about. The plant, organized in self-directed work teams, lets employees find their own solutions to problems, set their own schedules, and even have a say in hiring. Managers call themselves facilitators, not bosses. Their main job is to coach workers and help them understand the tough, external market forces that demand a dedication to quality, teamwork, and speed. Over the past four years productivity at Towanda is up 35 percent.

Last spring Du Pont surveyed 6,600 of its people, including some at Towanda, and found that flexible work hours were a top priority. Working mothers and single parents said it was hard to cope with kids while keeping to a rigid plant schedule. A team at Towanda got together and devised a novel solution: Take vacation time by the hour. During slack times when three of the four team members could easily handle the job, one could take off a few hours in the afternoon to go to a school play or bring a sick kid to the doctor. Today other Du Pont workers and managers visit Towanda to learn about flextime. A few have already borrowed it for their own plants.

Getting the most out of the university idea, CEO Woolard has found it helps to assign different goals of excellence to various Du Pont factories. He may tell the manager of one plant to be the best in team building, another the best in employee benefits, and a third the safety leader. As they improve, he holds up their accomplishments as examples to others. Says he: "It's win-win. You don't have to say one plant is a dog."

Trust Starts from Within. After a decade of restructuring, layoffs, and astronomical CEO salaries, worker trust has taken it on the chin. One of the biggest cultural challenges is to persuade workers to get religion again. It won't be easy. Making an angry, distrustful worker a believer requires fiddling with deep-rooted values. As almost any psychiatrist will tell you, it's a Herculean task to change a single individual. So imagine what it takes to change the beliefs of thousands.

Stephen Covey, a consultant to IBM, Hewlett-Packard, and other major companies, and author of *The 7 Habits of Highly Effective People*, believes every individual from the CEO down must realize that trust starts from within himself. Says he: "It's ludicrous to think that you can build trust unless people view you as trustworthy." In his seminars Covey gets managers to examine their deepest motives and to realize the importance of integrity and openness. And it's not all touchy-feely. Says Covey: "The best way our clients save money is to increase the span of control. When people trust you, you don't have to ride them, and that means fewer managers can oversee more people."

A manager can destroy a lot of trust by acting as if he's better than the people who work for him. Tandem CEO Treybig remembers suggesting that a couple of visiting managers spend a half day on the assembly line. They balked, thinking it a waste of time to mingle with blue-collar workers. "It was like you offered them syphilis," Treybig says.

He thought the idea made sense because much of Tandem's long-term success, he believes, comes from treating people as equals. For the past 15 years Tandem every Friday afternoon has put on its legendary get-togethers, once known as beer busts but now called popcorn parties (the Tandemites don't drink like they used to). Here Treybig and his top managers mix with the troops and exchange ideas about what's bad, what's good, and what can be done better in the company. As a bonus, employees from different parts of the business share ideas about the latest technologies. Four times a year Treybig spends five days in different resorts around the country with a couple of hundred people from all levels of the corporation. They talk business, play, drink beer until 2 A.M., and generally learn to trust each other. Says Treybig: "They'll go back and tell fellow employees that you care about people."

Du Pont CEO Woolard argues that the best way to create a more trusting environment is to reward the right people. "The first thing people watch," says he, "is the kind of people you promote. Are you promoting team builders who spend time on relationships, or those who are autocratic?"

Covey agrees, adding that managers should tailor reward systems to recognize team effort rather than individual accomplishment. As the wrong way to do it, he cites a CEO who would call his managers into his office each week to talk about team spirit. At the end of the meeting he'd point to a large painting of racehorses with photos of the managers' faces pasted over the thoroughbreds' heads. Then he'd announce, "So and so is ahead in the race to win the trip to Bermuda." Says Covey: "It nullified everything he said earlier."

Trying to change an institution's culture is certain to be frustrating. Most people resist change, and when the change goes to the basic character of the place where they earn a living, many people will get upset. Says the University of Pittsburgh's Kilmann: "If you talk about real change and people aren't getting uptight and anxious, they don't believe you." Some will fight. After months of working on cultural change with employees of a company, Kilmann asked the group to write down what they were doing differently. One manager wrote, "I wore a different color tie."

Managers seeking a way to think about the process might reflect that a company trying to improve its culture is like a person trying to improve his or her character. The process is long, difficult, often agonizing. The only reason people put themselves through it is that it's correspondingly satisfying and valuable.

1. In the introductory comments of the case, there is a Confucian-sounding principle that cultural change must come from the bottom, and the CEO must guide it. How is this seeming contradiction resolved, and what are some examples of how such cultural change has actually occurred?
2. Identify the guidelines for how successful companies are changing their cultures. Argue for the one you feel is relatively more important than the others.
3. Can the approaches and examples of organizational culture and the management of change as described in this case also apply to international management? Why and/or why not?

EXPERIENTIAL EXERCISE FOR PART 6

EXERCISE: ORGANIZATION DEVELOPMENT AT J. P. HUNT

Goals: To experience an OD technique—in this case the use of survey feedback—to diagnose strengths and weaknesses and develop an action plan.

Implementation: Set up groups of four to eight members for the one-hour exercise. The groups should be separated from each other and asked to converse only with members of their own group. Each person should read the following:

    J. P. Hunt department stores is a large retail merchandising outlet located in Boston. The company sells an entire range of retail goods (appliances, fashions, furniture, and so on) and has a large downtown store plus six branch stores in various suburban areas.

Survey Results for J. P. Hunt Department Store: Credit and Accounts Receivable Department

Variable	Survey Results*			Industry Norms*		
	Managers	Supervisors	Non-supervisors	Managers	Supervisors	Non-supervisors
Satisfaction and rewards						
Pay	3.30	1.73	2.48	3.31	2.97	2.89
Supervision	3.70	2.42	3.05	3.64	3.58	3.21
Promotion	3.40	2.28	2.76	3.38	3.25	3.23
Coworkers	3.92	3.90	3.72	3.95	3.76	3.43
Work	3.98	2.81	3.15	3.93	3.68	3.52
Performance-to-intrinsic rewards	4.07	3.15	3.20	4.15	3.85	3.81
Performance-to-extrinsic rewards	3.67	2.71	2.70	3.87	3.81	3.76
Supervisory behavior						
Initiating structure	3.42	3.97	3.90	3.40	3.51	3.48
Consideration	3.63	3.09	3.18	3.77	3.72	3.68
Positive rewards	3.99	2.93	3.02	4.24	3.95	3.91
Punitive rewards	3.01	3.61	3.50	2.81	2.91	3.08
Job characterictics						
Autonomy	4.13	4.22	3.80	4.20	4.00	3.87
Feedback	3.88	3.81	3.68	3.87	3.70	3.70
Variety	3.67	3.35	3.22	3.62	3.21	2.62
Challenge	4.13	4.03	3.03	4.10	3.64	3.58
Organizational practices						
Role ambiguity	2.70	2.91	3.34	2.60	2.40	2.20
Role conflict	2.87	3.69	2.94	2.83	3.12	3.02
Job pressure	3.14	4.04	3.23	2.66	2.68	2.72
Performance evaluation process	3.77	3.35	3.19	3.92	3.70	3.62
Worker cooperation	3.67	3.94	3.87	3.65	3.62	3.35
Work-flow planning	3.88	2.62	2.95	4.20	3.80	3.76

* The values are scored from 1, very low, to 5, very high.

As with to most retail stores in the area, employee turnover is high (i.e., 40 to 45 percent annually). In the credit and accounts receivable department, located in the downtown store, turnover is particularly high at both the supervisor and subordinate levels, approaching 75 percent annually. The department employs approximately 150 people, 70 percent of whom are female.

Due to rising hiring and training costs brought on by the high turnover, top department management began a turnover analysis and reduction program. As a first step, a local management consulting firm was contracted to conduct a survey of department employees. Using primarily questionnaires, the consulting firm collected survey data from over 95 percent of the department's employees. The results are shown in the exhibit, by organizational level, along with industry norms developed by the consulting firm in comparative retail organizations.

Instructions for the exercise:

1. Individually, each group member should analyze the data in the exhibit and attempt to identify and diagnose departmental strengths and problem areas.
2. As a group, the members should repeat step 1 above. In addition, suggestions for resolving the problems and an action plan for feedback to the department should be developed.

REFERENCES

CHAPTER 1

A Real World Organizational Behavior Laboratory Adapted from Joseph Szcesney, "The Right Stuff," *Time,* Oct. 29, 1990, pp. 74–84.
International Application Example: Toyota's Rapid Inch-Up Adapted from Alex Taylor III, "Why Toyota Keeps Getting Better and Better and Better," *Fortune,* Nov. 19, 1990, pp. 66–68.
Real Case: It's a Worldwide Problem Adapted from Louis S. Richman, "The Coming World Labor Shortage," *Fortune,* Apr. 9, 1990, pp. 70–77.

CHAPTER 2

The Illumination Studies at the Hawthorne Works of Western Electric: A Serendipitous Discovery The most recent and complete account of the Hawthorne studies can be found in Ronald G. Greenwood and Charles D. Wrege, "The Hawthorne Studies," in Daniel A. Wren (ed.), *Papers Dedicated to the Development of Modern Management,* Academy of Management, 1986, pp. 24–35. Also see Jeffrey A. Sonnenfeld, "Shedding Light on the Hawthorne Studies," *Journal of Occupational Behavior,* vol. 6, 1985, pp. 111–130.
Application Example: A First-Rate Company Adapted from Donald C. Bacon, "A Pursuit of Excellence," *Nation's Business,* Jan. 1990, pp. 27–28.
International Application Example: Do's and Don'ts in the Middle East Adapted from Roger E. Axtell, *Do's and Taboos Around the World,* 2d ed., Wiley, New York, 1990.
Real Case: Things Will Never Be the Same Adapted from Rose Brady and Peter Galuszka, "500 Days," *Business Week,* Oct. 1, 1990, pp. 138–148.

CHAPTER 3

Perceptions in the Author Wars Adapted from "Detroit May Be Missing the Mark that Matters Most," *Business Week,* Oct. 22, 1990, p. 91.
Application Example: Subliminal Perception in the Workplace Adapted from "Whispering Computers Aim to Cut Thefts," *Omaha World-Herald,* May 18, 1985, p. 30.
Real Case: Is Patriotism for Sale? Adapted from Walter Shapiro, "Is Washington in Japan's Pocket?" *Business Week,* Oct. 1, 1990, pp. 106–107.

CHAPTER 4

Winning Personalities for Industrial Leaders Adapted from Roy Rowan, "America's Most Wanted Managers," *Fortune,* Feb. 3, 1986, pp. 18–19.
International Application Example: Gift-Giving in Western Europe Adapted from Roger Axtell, *Do's and Taboos Around the World,* 2d ed., Wiley, New York, 1990.
Application Example: Long Hours and Hard Work Adapted from Thomas A. Stewart, "Do You Push Your People Too Hard?" *Fortune,* Oct. 22, 1990, pp. 121–128.
Real Case: Looking for an Equal Chance Adapted from Jaclyn Fierman, "Why Women Still Don't Hit the Top," *Fortune,* July 30, 1990, pp. 40–62.

CHAPTER 5

?They Just Don't Get Any Respect Adapted from "Unappreciated Workers," *Journal of Accountancy,* June 1989, p. 154; and James S. Hirsch, "Older Workers Chafe Under Young Managers," *Wall Street Journal,* Feb. 26, 1990, pp. B1, B6.
Application Example: Rediscovering the Benefits of Employee Surveys Adapted from Claudia H. Deutsch, "Asking Workers What They Think," *New York Times,* Apr. 22, 1990, sec. 3, part 2, p. 29.
Real Case: Surprisingly, Positive Attitudes Adapted from James P. Womack, Daniel T. Jones, and Daniel Roos, "How Lean Production Can Change the World," *New York Times Magazine,* part 2, Sept. 23, 1990, pp. 20–23, 34–48; and James R. Lincoln, "Employee Work Attitudes and Management Practice in the United States and Japan: Evidence from a Large Comparative Survey," *California Management Review,* Fall 1989, pp. 89–106.

CHAPTER 6

Keeping Money in Perspective Adapted from Claudia H. Deutsch, "Using Money to Change Executive Behavior," *New York Times,* May 29, 1990, sec. 3, part 2, p. 29F; and Michael J. Mandel, "Those Fat Bonuses Don't Seem to Boost Performance," *Business Week,* Jan. 8, 1990, p. 26.
Application Example: High Achievers in Action Adapted from "Expert Advice: How to Reduce Your

Risk as an Entrepreneur," *Working Woman*, January 1987, p. 62.

Application Example: Linking Manager's Rewards with Unit Performance Adapted from Larry Reibstein, "Firms Trim Annual Pay Increases and Focus on Long Term," *The Wall Street Journal*, Apr. 10, 1987, p. 21.

Real Case: Keeping Them Motivated Adapted from Amanda Bennett, "Enticing Stellar Executives to Stay Put," *The Wall Street Journal*, Apr. 9, 1990, pp. B1, B8; and Christopher Knowlton, "11 Men's Million-Dollar Motivator," *Fortune*, Apr. 9, 1990, pp. 66–68.

CHAPTER 7

Good and Getting Better Adapted from Wendy Zellner, "Buick City: The Factory That's Getting Things Right," *Business Week*, Oct. 22, 1990, p. 87.

Application Example: Power to the People Adapted from Ronald Henkoff, "Cost Cutting: How to Do It Just Right," *Fortune*, Apr. 9, 1990, p. 48.

Application Example: Making Personal Goal Setting Pay Off Adapted from "How to Boost Your Career Visibility—For Top Dollar," *Working Woman*, January 1987, p. 55.

Real Case: Made by Hand Adapted from David Woodruff, et al., "A New Era for Auto Quality," *Business Week*, Oct. 22, 1990, pp. 84–96; and Richard A. Melcher, "Rolls-Royce Sees the Future—And It's Still Handmade," *Business Week*, Oct. 22, 1990, p. 96.

CHAPTER 8

Positive Discipline: Punishing Workers with a Day Off Adapted from Laurie Baum, "Punishing Workers with a Day Off," *Business Week*, June 16, 1986, p. 80.

Application Example: Unlearning Adapted from Jack Falvey, "How to Know When to Cut Your Losses," *Working Woman*, Dec. 1986, pp. 27–28.

Application Example: It's Big League Bucks Adapted from "Who Makes What in the Major Leagues," *New York Times*, Nov. 21, 1990, p. B12.

Real Case: Thanks for the Favor Adapted from Carol J. Loomis, "How Drexel Rigged a Stock," *Fortune*, Nov. 19, 1990, pp. 83–91; and Kurt Eichenwald, "Milken Gets 10 Years for Wall Street Crimes," *New York Times*, Nov. 22, 1990, pp. A1, C5.

CHAPTER 9

Things Are Just Going to Have to Change Adapted from David Kirkpatrick, "Why Washington

Dismays CEOs," *Fortune*, Nov. 5, 1990, pp. 83–89.

International Application Example: Giving Them the Power Adapted from Alex Taylor III, "Why Toyota Keeps Getting Better and Better and Better," *Fortune*, Nov. 19, 1990, pp. 74–75.

Real Case: Forget the Raise, How about a Nice Bonus? Adapted from Aaron Bernstein, "How'd You Like a Big Fat Bonus—and No Raise?" *Business Week*, Nov. 3, 1986, pp. 30–31.

CHAPTER 10

The Flight Is Over Adapted from Mark Ivey and Michael Oneal, "Frank Lorenzo: The Final Days," *Business Week*, Aug. 27, 1990, pp. 32–33.

International Application Example: Yeltsin Speaks Adapted from Paul Hofheinz, "The New Russian Revolution," *Fortune*, Nov. 19, 1990, pp. 127–134.

International Application Example: Charismatic Capitalist Adapted from Shawn Tully, "GE in Hungary: Let There Be Light," *Fortune*, Oct. 22, 1990, pp. 137–142.

Real Case: Presidential Leadership Adapted from Ann Reilly Dowd, "What Managers Can Learn from Manager Reagan," *Fortune*, Sept. 15, 1986, pp. 33–41.

CHAPTER 11

An International MBA Adapted from Patricia A. Langan, "Trying to Clone U.S.-Style MBAs," *Fortune*, Oct. 8, 1990, pp. 143–151.

International Application Example: Japanese Versus Korean Leadership Styles Adapted from Laurie Baum, "Korea's Newest Export: Management Style," *Business Week*, Jan. 19, 1987, p. 66.

International Application Example: Balancing People and Profits Adapted from James. B. Hayes, "Wanna Make a Deal in Moscow?" *Fortune*, Oct. 22, 1990, pp. 113–118.

Real Case: Leading Them into the 21st Century Adapted from Peter Nulty, "Batman Shakes BP to Bedrock," *Fortune*, Nov. 19, 1990, pp. 155–162.

CHAPTER 12

It's Just in Time Adapted from Alex Taylor III, "Why Toyota Keeps Getting Better and Better and Better," *Fortune*, Nov. 19, 1990, p. 72.

Application Example: Agreeing to Greater Productivity Adapted from Doron P. Levin, "Chrysler Wants to Go Nonstop," *New York Times*, Nov. 20, 1990, pp. C1, C8.

Application Example: Committees May Not Be the

Answer Adapted from Norman B. Sigband, "The Uses of Meetings," *Nation's Business*, February 1987, p. 28.

Real Case: The Mario Brothers Strike Again Adapted from Susan Moffat, "Can Nintendo Keep Winning," *Fortune*, Nov. 5, 1990, pp. 131–136.

CHAPTER 13

Let's Do It Jointly Adapted from David E. Sanger, "New Rift in U.S.–Japan Jet Project," *New York Times*, Nov. 20, 1990, pp. C1, C17.

International Application Example: Cultural Conflict Adapted from Bill Powell, "Where the Jobs Are," *Newsweek*, Feb. 2, 1987, pp. 42–46.

Application Example: Dealing with Crises Adapted from Mortimer R. Feinberg and Bruce Serlen, "Crash Course in Crisis Management," *Working Woman*, January 1987, pp. 24, 26, 28.

Real Case: Do Just the Opposite Adapted from Brian Dumaine, "How to Manage in a Recession," *Fortune*, Nov. 5, 1990, pp. 58–72.

CHAPTER 14

CEOs Work to Manage Their Stress Adapted from Debra L. Nelson, James Campbell Quick, and Jonathan D. Quick, "Corporate Warfare: Preventing Combat Stress and Battle Fatigue," *Organizational Dynamics*, Summer 1989, pp. 65–79; and Liz Lufkin, "Slow Down, You Move Too Fast: The Time-Sickness Cure," *Working Woman*, April 1990, pp. 111–112.

Application Example: Is Being a Type A Dangerous? Adapted from Joshua Fischman, "Type A on Trial," *Psychology Today*, February 1987, pp. 42–50.

Application Example: Taking Time to Manage Time Some of this example is adapted from "Ten Tricks to Keep Time Eaters Away!" *Working Woman*, August 1986, p. 71.

Real Case: Getting Along without the Boss Adapted from Everett T. Suters, "Overdoing It," *Inc.*, November 1986, pp. 115–116.

CHAPTER 15

The Keating Five Adapted from Nathaniel C. Nash, "Frustration and Relief Mark Start of Keating 5 Hearing," *New York Times*, Nov. 16, 1990, p. A15; and Richard L. Berke, "DeConcini Lashes Out at Counsel in Ethics Case," *New York Times*, Nov. 20, 1990, pp. A1, A12.

International Application Example: Keeping the Inside Track Adapted from Allen R. Myerson,

"Suddenly, the Specter of Capitalism Is Haunting Intourist," *New York Times*, Nov. 18, 1990, p. 4F.

Real Case: Fighting Back Adapted from Donald M. Spero, "Patent Protection or Piracy—A CEO Views Japan," *Harvard Business Review*, September–October 1990, pp. 58–67.

CHAPTER 16

A Tragic Breakdown in Communication Adapted from Michael Brody, "NASA's Challenge: Ending Isolation at the Top," *Fortune*, May 21, 1986, pp. 26–32; and Diane Vaughan, "Autonomy, Interdependence, and Social Control: NASA and the Space Shuttle Challenger," *Administrative Science Quarterly*, vol. 35, 1990, pp. 225–257.

International Application Example: Different Cultures, Different Meanings Adapted from Jane Whitney Gibson, Richard M. Hodgetts, and Charles W. Blackwell, "Cultural Variations in Nonverbal Communication." Paper presented at the 55th Annual Business Communication meetings, San Antonio, Texas, Nov. 9, 1990.

Real Case: 800 to the Rescue Adapted from Faye Rice, "How to Deal with Tougher Customers," *Fortune*, Dec. 3, 1990, pp. 38–48.

CHAPTER 17

Zero Defections Adapted from Christopher W. L. Hart, James L. Heskett, and W. Earl Sasser, Jr., "The Profitable Art of Service Recovery," *Harvard Business Review*, July–August 1990, pp. 148–156.

Application Example: Avon's Calling But No One Answered Adapted from Gretchen Morgenson, "Anyhow, It Was Nice While It Lasted," *Forbes*, Jan. 12, 1987, pp. 50–52.

Real Case: Getting Additional Information Adapted from Anne R. Field and Catherine L. Harris, "The Information Business," *Business Week*, Aug. 25, 1986, pp. 82–90.

CHAPTER 18

Keeping It Simple Adapted from Joshua Levine, "Three-Star Brands," *Forbes*, Nov. 26, 1990, pp. 251–254.

Application Example: Product Diversification Forces Restructuring at Kodak Adapted from Leslie Helm and James Hurlock, "Kicking the Single-Product Habit at Kodak," *Business Week*, Dec. 1, 1986, pp. 36–37.

International Application Example: Executive Epi-

grams by Country: Adapted from Simcha Ronen, *Comparative and Multinational Management*, Wiley, New York, 1986, pp. 318–319. The epigrams in turn were derived from a variety of sources, including Robert M. Worcester of the UK-based Market and Opinion Research International (MORI), Ole Jacob Road of Norway's PM Systems, and anonymous managers.

Real Case: People Are the Real Key Adapted from Christopher A. Bartlett and Sumantra Ghoshal, "Matrix Management: Not a Structure, a Frame of Mind," *Harvard Business Review*, July–August 1990, pp. 138–145.

CHAPTER 19

Apple Seeks a New Culture Adapted from Brenton R. Schlender, "Yet Another Strategy for Apple," *Fortune*, Oct. 22, 1990, pp. 81–87; and Barbara Buell, Jonathan B. Levine, and Neil Gross, "Apple: New Team, New Strategy," *Business Week*, Oct. 15, 1990, pp. 86–96.

Application Example: Strong Managers, Strong Cultures Adapted from Brian Dumaine, "The New Turnaround Champs," *Fortune*, July 16, 1990, pp. 36–44.

Real Case: Look Out World, Here We Come Adapted from Kenneth Labich, "American Takes on the World," *Fortune*, Sept. 24, 1990, pp. 40–48.

CHAPTER 20

On a Buying Binge Adapted from Robert Neff and William J. Holstein, "Mighty Mitsubishi Is on the Move," *Business Week*, Sept. 24, 1990, pp. 98–101; and William J. Holstein, et al., "Hands Across America: The Rise of Mitsubishi," *Business Week*, Sept. 24, 1990, pp. 102–107.

International Application Example: The Mighty Deutsche Adapted from John Dornberg, "The Spreading Might of Deutsche Bank," *New York Times Magazine*, Sept. 23, 1990, pp. 28–30; 60–61.

Real Case: Everybody's Everywhere Adapted from *Fortune*, July 30, 1990, p. 269.

CHAPTER 21

Learning to Keep Customers Frederick F. Reichheld and W. Earl Sasser, Jr., "Zero Defections: Quality Comes to Services," *Harvard Business Review*, September–October 1990, pp. 105–111.

Application Example: Calories Down, Profits Up Adapted from Jean Seligman et. al., "A Lighter Than Airline Load," *Newsweek*, Nov. 26, 1990, pp. 70–72.

Application Example: A Rainbow of Talent Adapted from Joel Dreyfuss, "Get Ready for the New Work Force," *Fortune*, Apr. 23, 1990, pp. 165–181. 165–181.

Real Case: Meeting the Challenges of the Next Century Adapted from Louis Uchitelle, "Women's Push Into Work Place Seems to Have Reached Plateau," *New York Times*, Nov. 24, 1990, pp. 1, 18; and David Kirkpatrick, "Is Your Career on Track?" *Fortune*, July 2, 1990, pp. 38–48.

ACKNOWLEDGMENTS FOR EXPERIENTIAL EXERCISES

EXERCISES FOR PART 1

"Synthesis of Student and Instructor Needs" was suggested by Professor Philip Van Auken and is used with his permission; "Work-Related Organizational Behavior: Implications for the Course" is adapted from "Getting Acquainted Triads," in J. William Pfeiffer and John E. Jones (eds.), *A Handbook of Structured Experiences*, vol. 1, University Associates, San Diego, Calif., 1969, and "Defining Organizational Behavior," in James B. Lau, *Behavior in Organizations*, Irwin, Homewood, Ill., 1975.

EXERCISES FOR PART 2

The exercise "Self-Perception and Development of the Self-Concept" was suggested by Philip Van Auken and is used with his permission. The "He Works She Works" exercise is from Donald D. White and David A. Bednar, *Organizational Behavior*, Allyn and Bacon, Inc., Boston, 1987, pp. 199–200, as adapted from Natasha Josefowitz, *Pathways to Power*, Addison-Wesley, Menlo Park, California, 1980.

EXERCISES FOR PART 3

The "Motivation Questionnaire" is reprinted from "Motivation: A Feedback Exercise," in John E. Jones and J. William Pfeiffer (eds.), *The Annual Handbook for Group Facilitators*, University Associates, San Diego, Calif., 1973, pp. 43–45, and is used with permission; "Job Design Survey" is adapted from J. R. Hackman and G. R. Oldham, "Development of the Job Diagnostic Survey," *Journal of Applied Psychology*, vol. 60, 1975, pp. 159–170; "Role Playing and O.B. Mod." is adapted from Fred Luthans and Mark J. Martinko, *The Power of Positive Reinforcement*, McGraw-Hill, New York, 1978, pp. 35–38; and the "Leadership Questionnaire" is reprinted with permission from J. William Pfeiffer and John E. Jones (eds.), *A Handbook of Structured Experiences for Human Relations Training*, vol. 1, University Associates, San Diego, Calif., 1974. The questionnaire was adapted from Sergiovanni, Metzeus, and Burden's revision of the Leadership Behavior Description Questionnaire, *American Educational Research Journal*, vol. 6, 1969, pp. 62–79.

EXERCISES FOR PART 4

"Groups and Conflict Resolution" is from Alan Filley, *Interpersonal Conflict Resolution*, Scott, Foresman, Glenview, Ill., 1975, pp. 139–142, as adapted from William H. Haney, *Communication and Organizational Behavior*, Irwin, Homewood, Ill., 1967, pp. 319–320; and "Power and Politics" is reprinted with permission from Andrew J. DuBrin, *Human Relations*, Reston Va., 1978, pp. 122–123.

EXERCISES FOR PART 5

"Organizations" is reprinted with permission from Fremont E. Kast and James E. Rosenzweig, "Our Organizational Society," in *Experiential Exercises and Cases in Management*, McGraw-Hill, New York, 1976, pp. 13–15; "Paper Plane Corporation" was contributed by Professor Louis Pothreu and is used with his permission.

EXERCISE FOR PART 6

"Organization Development at J. P. Hunt" is reprinted with permission from Andrew D. Szilagyi and Marc Wallace, "Survey Feedback," *Organizational Behavior and Performance*, Goodyear, Santa Monica, Calif., 1980, pp. 605–606.

NAME INDEX

Abdel-Halim, Ahmed A., 420
Abegglen, James C., 96, 103
Abrahamson, L. Y., 420
Aburdene, Patricia, 15, 604
Adams, Gary L., 39
Adams, J. Stacy, 155, 167–168
Adler, Alfred, 149–150
Adler, Nancy J., 604–605
Adolphus, Gustavus, 529
Agarwal, Naresh C., 605
Albers, Henry H., 543
Alderfer, Clayton, 146, 155–156, 159,
    161–162, 164, 172–173, 178–179
Aldrich, Nelson W., Jr., 488
Allen, Darryl, 549
Allen, David S., 421
Allen, Judd, 578
Allen, Phyllis K., 329
Allie, Stephen M., 419
Almaney, Adnan, 605
Alutto, Joseph A., 291
Alvares, D., 291
Alvarez, Ramon, 552
Alvaris, Kenneth M., 291
Alvesson, Mats, 578
Anderson, Carl R., 175
Andrasik, Frank, 264
Andreas, Dwayne, 303
Andrisani, Paul, 128
Argyris, Chris, 84, 86, 88–90, 102–104,
    393
Ariss, Sonny S., 445
Armenakis, Achilles A., 429
Arnold, Hugh J., 104, 394
Arvey, Richard D., 202
Asch, Solomon E., 79, 498, 512
Ashmos, Donde P., 543
Austin, James T., 203

Baack, Donald, 128
Baetz, J. L., 292
Bailey, Rosetta, 312
Baker, Douglas, 255, 264
Balkin, David B., 231
Bammer, K., 421
Bandura, Albert, 12, 15, 103, 195, 202,
    213, 230, 287, 410, 420
Bannister, Brendan D., 291
Barad, Jill, 312
Barchas, J. D., 420

Barkley, Nella, 138
Barlow, David H., 38
Barnard, Chester I., 427, 445, 468–469,
    487, 493, 512, 530, 542–543
Barneby, Mary Rudie, 104
Barnes, Louis B., 366, 625
Baron, Robert A., 79, 104, 174, 231, 292,
    420, 605
Barrett, Craig R., 330–331
Barrow, J. C., 291
Bartlett, Kay, 103
Bartol, Kathryn M., 445
Bass, Bernard M., 283–285, 290, 292–293,
    311, 322, 601, 605
Bateman, Thomas S., 201, 230
Bateson, Allan G., 79
Baum, Herbert M., 624
Baumeister, R. F., 79
Bazerman, Max H., 15, 500–502, 512–513
Beal, Ilene, 312
Bedeian, Arthur C., 420
Beehr, Terry A., 264, 400, 419–421
Beer, Michael, 579, 625, 631
Bell, Alexander Graham, 564
Bell, Cecil H., Jr., 614–615, 617, 624–625
Bellingham, Richard, 578
Bem, D. J., 155, 169
Bennis, Warren G., 269, 290, 301, 321,
    330, 520–521, 543, 600, 605
Benson, Herbert, 421
Berberich, J. P., 421
Berelson, Bernard, 103
Berg, P. O., 619, 621, 625
Berger, Peter, 605
Berkes, L., 293
Berkley, Stephen, 565
Berkowitz, Leonard, 365
Bernardin, H. John, 79
Bernieri, Frank, 103
Bernstein, Daniel J., 231
Beutell, Nicholas J., 419
Bhagat, Rabi S., 419
Bilhousen, Howard, 68
Bishop, Jerry E., 420
Black, Cathleen, 312
Black, J. Stewart, 513, 605, 614, 625
Blake, Robert R., 302–303, 309, 320–321,
    324, 615–617, 625
Blanchard, Kenneth H., 304–305, 309,
    320–321, 324, 543

Blank, Warren, 321
Blau, Gary J., 201
Blau, Peter M., 519, 542
Bobko, Philip, 203
Boesky, Ivan, 231
Boring, Edwin G., 63
Boring, John, 625
Bortner, R. W., 406
Bowditch, James L., 174, 176, 512
Bradshaw-Camball, Patricia, 620, 625
Bransby, Mike, 488
Braun, Kathryn, 104, 312
Brett, George, 430
Brett, Jeanne M., 395
Bridges, William, 136
Brief, Arthur P., 127, 203, 407, 420
Bristow, Nigel J., 579
Brown, Edward M., 202
Brown, Warner, 68
Bruner, Jerome S., 79
Brunetti, Wayne, 629
Budhraja, Vikram, 522
Buell, Barbara, 605
Buller, Paul F., 613, 625
Buono, Anthony F., 174, 176, 512
Burger, P. C., 601, 605
Burke, M. J., 127
Burke, W. Warner, 614, 624
Burnaska, Robert F., 230
Burns, J. M., 285, 293
Bussey, John, 579
Butler, Sam, 136

Calder, Bobby J., 175
Callahan, Robert E., 174
Cameron, Kim, 135–137
Campbell, A., 419
Campbell, Donald J., 201, 203
Campbell, Donald T., 38, 322
Campion, M. A., 202
Canseco, Jose, 221
Caplan, R. D., 421
Carnegie, Andrew, 19
Carrell, Michael R., 174
Carrick, Jean, 312
Carroll, Glen R., 543
Carroll, Hal O., 543
Carroll, Stephen J., 39
Carson, Kenneth P., 543
Carson, R. C., 15, 230

Cartwright, D., 445
Cascio, Wayne, 39
Cass, Leonard J., 42
Cavanagh, Gerald F., 446
Chemers, Martin M., 291
Chrysler, Walter P., 20, 38
Ciabattari, Jane, 128
Clark, Will, 221
Clegg, C. W., 128
Cleland, David I., 544
Clemens, Roger, 221
Cobb, Anthony T., 445
Cohen, Barry, 578
Cohen, Stephen S., 46
Conger, J. A., 284, 292–293
Connellan, Thomas K., 264
Converse, P. E., 419
Cook, Cathy, 133
Cook, Richard, 466
Cook, Thomas D., 38
Cooper, Cary L., 420–421, 604
Cooper, Joel, 15
Cosier, Richard A., 175, 366
Costello, Timothy W., 79, 111, 373
Cotton, John L., 513
Covey, Stephen, 632–633
Cox, Charles J., 604
Creech, General W. L. (Bill), 523
Cronbach, Lee J., 39
Crosby, Faye, 403
Crowne, Douglas P., 175
Crozier, M., 431, 445
Cummings, Thomas G., 420
Cunningham, David A., 420

Dabbs, James M., Jr., 38
Daft, Richard, 389, 394, 445, 512, 579, 605
Dale, Ernest, 21, 38
Dalkey, N. C., 509
Dalton, Dan R., 175
Dalton, Melville, 363–364, 366, 391–392, 395
Dangerfield, Rodney, 550
Dansereau, Fred, Jr., 291
Darcy, Randy, 452
Darien, Steven M., 329
Davis, Keith, 291, 366
Davis, Tim R. V., 15, 38–39, 116, 260, 262–263, 265, 293
Dawley, Patricia, 312
Dawson, Andre, 221
Deal, Terence E., 567–568, 578
De Bortoli, Silvio, 492
de Charmes, R., 155, 169
Decker, Phillip J., 230
Delbecq, Andre L., 513
DeMeuse, Kenneth P., 365, 513
Deming, W. Edwards, 22
deMontes, Ana I., 231
deMontes, Francisco, 231

DeNisi, Angelo S., 175, 282, 292
Denton, D. Keith, 15
Derr, Den, 303
DeVader, Christy L., 79
Devanna, Mary Anne, 285, 293
DeVris, Manfred F. R. Kets, 175
Dewhirst, H. Dudley, 202
Dhingra, O. P., 605
Di Angelo, Joseph A., Jr., 488
Dickinson, Anthony, 174
Dienesch, Richard M., 291
Dimmick, Thomas F., 299
Distenfano, M. K., 175
Dittrich, John E., 174
Dobbins, Gregory, 175
Doktor, Robert, 604
Dollard, J., 213
Dominguez, Benjamin, 231
Donnellon, Anne, 456
Donnelly, James H., Jr., 394, 543, 626
Dorfman, Peter W., 293
Dossett, Dennis L., 175, 231
Dow, Gregory K., 542
Driver, Michael J., 331
Drucker, Peter F., 21, 38, 197, 488, 520, 527, 543
Dubno, Peter, 128
DuBrin, Andrew J., 441, 445–446
Duchon, Dennis, 175
Duck, Jeanie, 550
Dumaine, Brian, 201, 365, 449, 513, 579, 625, 628
Dumas, MacDonald, 291
Duncan, Robert, 542
Dunnette, Marvin D., 38, 127, 366, 421
du Pont, Pierre S., 20–21
Durand, Douglas E., 175
Durand, V. Mark, 263
Durant, William C., 19–20, 37

Eagly, Alice H., 322
Earley, P. Christopher, 202, 605
Eden, Dov, 622, 625
Edwards, Mark R., 578
Eggert, James, 79
Eichmann, Adolf, 102
Eisenberg, Eric M., 487
Eisner, Michael, 629
Eliot, Robert, 399
Ellertson, Norris, 365
Ellis, A., 421
Enderwick, Peter, 543
Engelhardt, Earl, 454
England, George W., 116, 600, 605
Erez, Miriam, 202
Erikson, Erik, 87, 90
Esrey, Bill, 303
Ettling, Jennifer T., 322
Evans, Martin G., 174, 280, 292
Everett, James E., 605

Fairbank, J. A., 230
Falbe, Cecilia M., 440–441, 445
Faltermayer, Edmund, 624
Fandt, Patricia M., 445
Faulkner, Robert R., 38
Fayol, Henri, 19, 21, 37, 314, 316, 322, 467–469, 484, 487, 493
Fedor, Donald B., 128–129
Feldman, Daniel C., 103–104, 394
Feldman, Robert S., 38, 231, 365, 420, 488, 507, 513
Ferris, Gerald R., 201, 445
Ferry, Jeffrey, 488
Festinger, Leon, 127, 155, 169, 394
Fiedler, Fred E., 273, 276–280, 289–292, 294, 300, 304
Field, R. H. George, 322
Fierman, Jaclyn, 312, 322
Filley, Alan C., 292, 394
Finegan, Jay, 543
Fiore, Michael V., 544
Fisher, Aubrey, 488
Fisher, Cynthia D., 230
Fisher, Dalmor, 488
Fisk, Carlton, 221
Fitz-enz, Jac, 624
Fleenor, C. Patrick, 174
Fleming, Sir Alexander, 18
Fletcher, James C., 465
Fodor, Eugene M., 292, 445
Ford, Henry, 3, 19
Frankenhaeuser, M., 128
Frederiksen, Lee W., 264
Fredrik-juson, M., 128
Freedman, Sara M., 421
Freeman, John J., 543
French, John R. P., 421, 426, 428–431, 436–437, 444–445
French, Wendell L., 614–615, 617, 624–625
Freud, Sigmund, 87, 90, 149, 57, 378–379, 497–498
Fried, Y., 201
Friedlander, Frank, 625
Friedman, Meyer, 406–408, 420
Froggatt, Kirk L., 513
Frost, Peter J., 175
Fry, Fred, 265
Fujisawa, T., 583
Fulk, J., 489
Fussfeld, Nahum, 264
Futrell, David, 365, 513
Fyodorov, Boris, 274

Gabarro, John, 104
Galbraith, James K., 43
Galbraith, Jay, 533, 543–544
Galbraith, John Kenneth, 138
Ganster, Daniel C., 421
Gantt, Henry L., 155

Garber, J., 420
Garcia, Jospeh E., 291–292
Gardell, B., 128
Gardner, William L., 420
Garland, Howard, 203
Garmezy, Norman, 65
Gellerman, Saul W., 103, 543
Gemmell, Art, 579
George, Jennifer M., 109, 127
George, Katie, 419
Georgopoulos, Basil S., 280, 292
Giacalone, Robert A., 79
Gibbons, Barry, 565
Gibson, James L., 394, 543, 626
Gilbreth, Frank, 155, 181
Gillen, Dennis A., 39
Gioia, Dennis A., 230
Glaser, Robert, 229
Glass, Michael, 103
Glick, William H., 201
Glogow, Eli, 175
Glube, Richard, 322
Glucksman, Lewis, 426
Goethals, George, 15
Goldberg, Rube, 450
Goldberg, Stephen B., 395
Golden, Claudia, 104
Goldhaber, Gerald M., 489
Gomez-Mejia, Luis R., 231
Gooden, D., 221
Gorbachev, Mikhail, 274, 303, 522
Gowing, Marilyn K., 624
Graeff, Claude L., 321
Graen, George B., 279, 291, 421
Graham, Katharine, 312
Gray, Barbara, 455
Green, Stephen G., 321
Green, Thad B., 513
Greenberg, Carl I., 175
Greene, Charles N., 290–292
Greenhalgh, Leonard, 138, 455–456
Greenhaus, Jeffrey H., 419
Greer, Jane, 312
Gregory, Doris, 365
Greiner, Larry E., 625
Griffin, Ricky W., 189, 201
Griffith, R. W., 421
Grimes, A. J., 427, 445
Groder, Martin, G., 488
Gross, Bertram M., 360
Gross, Warren, 579
Grove, Andrew S., 329–331, 445, 551, 553
Grove, Byron A., 79
Grunes, Willa Freeman, 79
Guest, David E., 622, 625
Guion, Robert M., 39
Gulick, Luther, 356, 543
Gupta, Nina, 201
Gustafson, David H., 513
Gustafson, S. B., 513

Gutek, Barbara A., 605
Guzzo, Richard A., 366
Gyllenhammar, Pehr, 190

Hackman, J. Richard, 185–188, 200–201, 204, 322, 335, 351, 421
Hadfield, Peter, 552–553
Hadrich, Sherri, 193
Haga, W. J., 291
Haire, Mason, 79
Hales, Colin P., 39
Hall, Douglas T., 84, 86–88, 102, 624
Hall, Trish, 513
Hambrick, Donald C., 328
Hammer, M., 265
Hampton, David R., 513
Hand, H. H., 421
Hanges, P. J., 202
Hannon, Michael T., 543
Harris, Monica, J., 103
Harris, Philip R., 596
Harrison, E. Frank., 512
Hassell, Barbara, 264
Hatter, Norman, Jr., 331
Havemann, Ernest, 68
Hawkins, Brian, 489
Hays, Laurie, 421
Head, Thomas C., 201
Heider, Fritz, 155, 169
Heiman, D. C., 322
Heller, Frank A., 602, 605
Hellriegel, Don, 103, 175, 182, 201, 265, 366, 488, 544, 605
Henderson, A. M., 444, 542
Henderson, R. W., 420
Henkoff, Ronald, 128, 547
Hennessey, Harry W., 39, 421, 489
Hermann, Jaime A., 231
Herold, David M., 230
Herrmann, Ned, 92, 103
Herrnstein, R. J., 15
Hersey, Paul, 304–305, 309, 320–321, 324
Hershock, Robert, 451–452
Herson, Michel, 38
Herzberg, Frederick, 116, 128, 146, 155–156, 159–162, 164–165, 172–174, 178, 181, 183–184, 186, 194, 199, 220, 279, 421
Heskett, James L., 488
Hickson, David J., 543, 605
Hill, Thomas E., 322
Hill, W. E., 63
Himes, John W., 326
Hines, Terence, 103
Hitler, Adolph, 358
Hodgetts, Richard M., 39, 230, 316–317, 322, 366, 446, 467, 487, 489
Hoerr, John, 579
Hofstede, Geert, 578, 588–591, 599, 605
Hogarth, Robin M., 15

Hohenfeld, Jeffrey A., 175
Hollander, Edwin P., 445
Hollenback, John R., 202
Holmes, T. H., 403, 419
Holt, David H., 488
Homans, George C., 155, 365
Hopkins, B. L., 231
Horton, Robert, 323
Horton, Thomas R., 366
Hosenball, S. Neil, 465
Hosking, D., 39, 315
Houghton, Jamie, 449
House, Robert J., 280, 283–284, 292, 322, 394
Howard, Ann, 291
Howard, John H., 420
Howell, Jon P., 293
Hoy, Frank, 625
Huber, George P., 543
Huck, Lud, 451
Hulin, C. L., 114–115, 128, 322
Hultman, Kenneth E., 230
Hunt, James G., 39, 287, 290–293, 315
Hyland, M. E., 202
Hymowitz, Carol, 201–202

Iacocca, Lee, 80, 136, 283
Iffaldano, M. T., 128
Ilgen, Daniel R., 32, 38, 230, 420
Indvik, Julie, 292
Ingham, Harry, 384
Ivancevich, John M., 203, 230, 394, 400, 411, 419–421, 471, 488, 543, 626
Ives, Blake, 488

Jackson, S. E., 420
Jacobs, Rick, 79
Jaeger, Alfred M., 625
Jago, Arthur G., 175, 292, 322
Janis, Irving L., 358–359, 366
Janson, Robert, 188, 201
Jaques, Elliott, 92
Jay, Anthony, 446
Jefferson, Edward G., 268
Jemmott, John B., 420
Jenkins, G. Douglas, 201
Jennings, Kenneth R., 513
Jensen, Arthur, 91
Jermier, John M., 287–288, 293
Jick, Todd D., 419
Jobs, Steve, 133, 568
Johnson, Blair T., 322
Johnson, C. Merle, 264
Johnson, Clifford, 45
Johnson, Harold E., 326
Johnson, J. H., 421
Johnson, Magic, 430
Johnson, Robert, 578
Johnson, Spencer, 543

Johnston, Don, 426
Joiner, Charles W., Jr., 579
Jones, Gareth R., 104
Jones, Nyle W., 292
Jonishi, Asa, 377
Jönsson, Berth, 201
Joyce, William F., 544
Juarez, Robin, 137
Junkins, Jerry, 449

Kagan, Jerome, 68
Kahn, Robert L., 387, 419, 479–490, 488–490
Kahn, S., 420
Kahneman, D., 500, 512–513
Kakabadse, Andrew, 445
Kanter, Rosabeth Moss, 332
Kanungo, R. M., 284, 292–293
Karmel, Barbara, 202, 263, 265, 292
Karren, R. J., 202
Katerberg, Barbara, 201
Katz, Daniel, 109, 127, 479–480, 488–490
Katz, Lawrence F., 44
Katz, Marsha, 625
Katz, Robert, 275, 290
Katzell, Raymond A., 176, 201, 203, 231
Kay, Ira T., 326
Kazanjian, Robert K., 544
Kazdin, Alan E., 39
Keating, Charles H., Jr., 425
Keidel, Robert W., 543
Keller, John J., 578
Keller, Robert T., 419
Kelley, Harold H., 155, 169, 175, 365
Kelly, Robert, 134
Kelly, Joe, 395
Kelman, Herbert C., 435–436
Kemmerer, Barbara, 201
Kempen, R. W., 264
Kendall, Don, 303
Kendall, L. M., 114–115, 128, 322
Kennedy, Allan A., 567–568, 578
Kennedy, M. M., 39
Kerr, Steven, 272, 283, 287–288, 290–293, 394
Kerr, Willard A., 79
Kiechel, Walter, III, 15, 103, 231, 489, 543–544
Kilmann, Ralph, 633
Kim, Ken I., 605
Kim, Sookom, 128
Kimberly, John R., 625
Kimble, Gregory A., 64
King, William R., 544
Klein, Gerald D., 624
Klein, Stephen B., 174
Klein, Tom, 133
Kluckhohn, Clyde, 38, 86, 103
Knudson, Harry R., 174
Kobasa, S. C., 410, 420

Koester, Robert, 512
Kogan, N., 513
Kolb, David, 104
Kolodny, Harvey F., 540, 544
Komaki, Judith L., 38, 229
Konar, Ellen, 128
Kopelman, Richard E., 103, 230
Korman, Abraham K., 103, 292
Korn, Lester, 134
Koslowsky, Meni, 543
Kossek, Ellen Ernst, 264
Kotter, John, 316, 322, 366, 395, 421
Kozlowski, Steve W. J., 79
Krackhardt, David, 444
Kraut, Allen I., 230, 366
Kreitner, Robert, 15, 219, 230, 231, 264, 419
Kriger, Mark P., 366
Kroc, Ray, 569–570
Kroeber, Alfred L., 38
Kuczmarski, Thomas, 455

Landgraf, Kurt M., 328, 330
Lank, Alden G., 201
Larsen, Janet K., 470, 488–489
Larson, James R., Jr., 127
Larson, Lars L., 287, 290–293
Latham, Gary P., 103, 126, 128–129, 174, 195, 197, 202–203, 230–231, 264
Laurent, Andre, 587
Lavin, Bernice, 312
Lawler, Edward E., III, 146, 155, 165–167, 173–174, 185, 194, 201, 329, 351, 450
Lawless, David J., 79
Lawrence, Robert Z., 46
Lawrence, William, 547
Leana, Carrie R., 366
Leary, Mark R., 79
Leatherwood, Marya L., 230
Lederer, Albert L., 488
Lederer, Jerome F., 465
Lee, C., 202
Lee, Sang M., 586
Lee, Thomas W., 128, 202
Leeper, Robert, 63–64
Lena, Carrie R., 513
Lengnick-Hall, Mark L., 513
Leonard, Sugar Ray, 430
Levine, David I., 231, 505, 512
Levine, Hermine Zagat, 624, 625
Levinson, Daniel, 84, 86–87, 102–103
Lewin, Kurt, 155, 162, 169, 270, 346–347, 615–616, 618
Lewis, Kevin J., 513
Lewis, Walker, 547, 550
Liden, Robert C., 291
Lieberman, S., 127
Liker, Jeffrey K., 626

Likert, Rensis, 272, 298, 305–309, 320–322, 324
Linder, Robert C., 230
Lindzey, Gardner, 79
Lippitt, Ronald, 270–271, 280
Lippmann, Walter, 74
Liverant, Shephard, 175
Locke, Christopher, 488
Locke, Edwin A., 38, 79, 103, 114, 119, 126–129, 174, 193–195, 197, 200, 202–203, 230, 265, 513
Lockwood, Diane Lee, 39, 264, 315
Lofquist, L. H., 116
Long, Robert G., 175–176
Longenecker, Clinton O., 128–129
Lord, Robert G., 79, 202, 292, 488
Lorenzo, Frank, 267–268
Lowalski, Robin M., 79
Luft, Joseph, 384
Lundberg, U., 128
Luthans, Fred, 15, 38–39, 89, 103, 128, 201, 203, 219, 230–231, 238, 241, 248, 250–251, 254–255, 260, 262–265, 287, 293, 313, 315–317, 322, 365–366, 383, 421, 446, 467, 470, 478, 487–489, 512, 578
Lynn, Robert, 92

McBride, Dorothy, 365
McCann, E. C., 605
McCartney, Kathleen, 103
McClelland, David C., 151, 420, 436–437, 444–445, 605
McElroy, James C., 79, 175
McFillen, James M., 174
McGee, Gail W., 421
McGrath, J. E., 421
McGregor, Douglas, 13, 157, 299
Machiavelli, Niccolo, 441–442
Maciag, Walter S., 251, 264
McIntyre, James, 104
McKenna, D. Douglas, 366
McKernan, Leo, 565
McKinnow, Arnold B., 134
McLean, A. A., 421
McLemore, Nina, 312
McMahon, J. Timothy, 230
MacNeice, Jill, 488
McNutt, Robert P., 231
Macy, Barry A., 513
Maddi, S. R., 420
Maher, Karen J., 488
Mahar, Linda, 291
Mahoney, Gerald M., 292
Main, Jeremy, 543
Major, Brenda, 128
Mandel, Michael J., 15
Manz, Charles C., 230, 264–265
March, James, 495
Maremont, Mark, 605

Marens, R., 419
Margerison, Charles, 322
Margulies, Newton, 513, 614, 625
Maris, Terry L., 264
Markham, Steven E., 291
Marriott, Bill, Jr., 477
Marshall, Judi, 421
Martella, J. A., 291
Martin, David C., 445
Martinko, Mark J., 241, 264, 383, 420, 478, 488
Marx, Karl, 519
Maslow, Abraham H., 146, 155–162, 164, 172–174, 176, 178, 194, 220, 333, 335
Mason, Richard O., 488
Matsushita, Konosuke, 92
Matteson, Michael T., 400, 411, 419–421, 471, 488
Mattingly, Don, 221
Mausner, Bernard, 128, 421
Mawhinney, Thomas C., 230–231
Mayer, Richard, 565
Mayes, Bronston T., 421
Medford, I. N., 420
Meglino, B. M., 421
Meichenbaum, D. H., 421
Mendenhall, Mark, 605
Mento, A. J., 202
Merlin, B., 128
Merwin, Gerald A., 264
Meyer, Marshall W., 445
Miede, Debbie, 312
Miles, Raymond E., 535, 544
Miles, Robert H., 293, 419, 440, 445
Milgram, Stanley, 100–102, 104
Milken, Michael, 231–232, 425
Milkovich, George T., 231
Miller, Danny, 175
Miller, E. G., 263
Miller, Katharine I., 128, 202
Miller, Lawrence M., 213, 218
Miller, Richard, 565
Mineka, S., 420
Miner, John B., 30, 38, 85, 103, 184, 201, 283, 292
Mintzberg, Henry, 92, 103, 316, 322, 361–362, 365–366, 494, 512
Mirman, Robert, 264
Mishkoff, Henry C., 489
Mitchell, Kevin, 221
Mitchell, Terence R., 38, 127, 174–175, 201, 230, 292, 489, 513
Mitz, Linda F., 419
Moberg, Dennis J., 446
Mobley, W. H., 421
Molloy, John T., 475, 488
Monet, Maria, 104, 312
Money, William H., 291
Monge, Peter R., 128, 202
Montana, Joe, 430

Montanari, John R., 543
Moore, Gordon E., 330
Moore, Thomas, 543
Moorhead, Gregory, 189, 201
Moran, Robert T., 596
Morey, Nancy C., 365, 446, 578
Mornell, Pierre, 133
Morrissette, Arthur, 481
Mott, Paul E., 322
Mouton, Jane S., 302–303, 309, 320–321, 324, 615–617, 625
Mowday, Richard T., 125, 128, 322
Mowrer, Robert R., 174
Muchinsky, P. M., 128
Muczyk, Jan P., 203, 322
Mullen, B., 176
Mumford, M. D., 513
Munchus, George, 513
Murayama, Motofusa, 586
Murray, H. A., 86, 103
Myers, David G., 104, 175–176, 366, 394, 445, 488, 604
Myrsten, A., 128

Nadler, David A., 185, 201, 230, 300, 321, 351, 534, 543, 628
Naisbitt, John, 15, 604
Nakamura, Koichi, 367
Nakarmi, Laxmi, 605
Namiki, Nobuaki, 579
Napolean, 273, 551
Nath, Raghu, 488
Neale, Margaret A., 104, 128, 230, 445, 502, 512–513, 578
Nelson, Debra L., 398, 419
Nestel, Gilbert, 128
Newberry, B. H., 421
Newcomb, Theodore M., 365
Newman, J. E., 400, 419–421
Newstrom, John W., 291, 366
Newton, Lucy A., 129
Nicholas, John M., 619, 621, 625
Nielsen, Warren R., 625
Nixon, Richard M., 358
Nord, Walter R., 175, 439, 445
Northcraft, Gregory B., 104, 128, 230, 445, 502, 512–513, 578
Norton, Larry W., 513
Nottenburg, Gail, 79
Novak, M., 291
Nussbaum, Bruce, 128
Nykodym, Nick, 419
Nystrom, P. C., 293

O'Donnell, Joseph, 426
Offermann, Lynn R., 445, 624
O'Hara, Kirk, 264
Ohmae, Kenichi, 176, 579, 605
Okey, Jack, 455

Oldham, Greg R., 185–186, 188, 200–201, 204, 322, 335, 421
O'Leary, Hazel, 312
O'Neil, Paul, 300
O'Reilly, Brian, 132, 394, 420
O'Reilly, Charles A., 488–489
Organ, Dennis W., 128, 230
Ornstein, Suzyn, 175
Orris, James B., 291
Orsborn, Carol, 136–137
Orsborn, Dan, 137
Ottemann, Robert, 248, 264
Ouchi, William, 574–575, 579

Page, Robert A., Jr., 445
Pankove, E., 513
Park, Hun-Joon, 605
Park, Pat, 377
Parker, Neil, 455
Parkinson, C. Northcote, 520–521, 543
Parnes, Herbert, 128
Parsons, Talcott, 444, 542
Pascale, Richard, 566, 571–572, 578–579
Pate, Larry E., 322
Paul, Robert, 201, 255, 264
Paulson, Robert, 132, 137
Pavlov, Ivan, 11, 208–209
Pearce, John A., 175
Pearce, Jone L., 231, 365, 445
Pedigo, Patricia R., 366
Penley, Larry E., 489
Pennar, Karen, 624
Perroni, Amedeo G., 38
Perry, James L., 231
Peter, Laurence J., 520–521, 543
Peters, Thomas J., 489, 497, 512, 521, 529, 543, 610–611, 624
Peterson, Mark F., 513
Peterson, Peter, 426
Petty, M. M., 293
Pfeffer, Jeffrey, 109, 127, 189, 201, 437, 441, 445
Phillips, James S., 292, 421
Pinkley, Robin L., 395
Podsakoff, Philip M., 128, 174
Polley, Richard B., 625
Porac, Joseph F., 79
Porras, Jerry I., 619, 621, 625
Porter, Lyman W., 13, 118, 125, 128, 146, 155, 165–167, 173–174, 194, 292, 322, 365, 421
Porter, Michael, 548, 553
Postman, Leo, 79
Powell, Gary N., 312–313, 322
Prahalad, C. K., 549–550
Premack, David, 223, 231
Preston, Cynthia, 420
Preston, Paul, 474, 488
Prue, D. M., 230

Pryer, Margaret W., 175
Puder-York, Marilyn, 136, 138
Pugh, Derek S., 543, 605
Purdy, Kenneth A., 188, 201
Pursell, E. D., 231
Pynchon, Thomas, 453

Quick, James C., 398, 419
Quick, Jonathan D., 398, 419
Quinn, Robert P., 419, 544

Rafaeli, Anat, 127
Ragan, James, W., 292
Rahe, R. H., 419
Raisin-ghani, Duru, 494, 512
Randall, Donna M., 128–129
Rasmussen, Ray V., 625
Rathus, Spencer A., 15, 79, 104, 174, 231, 265, 394, 410, 420, 488, 508, 513
Raven, Bertram, 426, 428–431, 436–437, 444-445
Reagan, Ronald, 293–294, 358
Rechnitzer, Peter A., 420
Redding, Gordon, 604
Reibstein, Larry, 291, 489
Reilly, Bernard J., 488
Reimann, Bernard C., 322
Reitz, H. Joseph, 290, 445
Rhodes, Susan R., 421
Rice, Berkeley, 79
Rice, Robert W., 291
Rice, Ronald E., 488
Riggio, Ronald E., 15, 174, 230, 292, 420, 445, 544
Riordan, C. A., 176
Robbins, Stephen P., 394, 427, 445, 544, 579, 584, 604
Roberts, Donald F., 489
Roberts, Karlene H., 489
Robinson, B., 127
Rockefeller, John D., 19
Roderick, Roger, 128
Rodgers, Charles, 137
Rodgers, W. L., 419
Rogers, Donald B., 328
Rogers, Rolf E., 543
Rohan, Thomas M., 579
Rohrbaugh, John, 513
Roitman, David B., 625
Ronen, Simcha, 592, 597, 605
Rose, Frank, 625
Rosenkrantz, Stuart A., 39, 230, 251, 264, 316–317, 322, 366, 421, 446, 467, 487, 489
Rosenman, Ray H., 406–408, 420
Rosenthal, R. A., 419
Roskies, Ethel, 626
Ross, Jerry, 127
Rothman, Andrea, 290

Rotter, Julian B., 155, 170, 175
Rubin, Irwin, 104
Ruch, L. O., 403
Ryan, T. A., 193, 202

Saari, Lise M., 197, 202–203, 230
Saffron, Arlene, 231
St. Mark, Carole, 312
Salancik, Gerald R., 109, 127, 175, 189, 201, 445
Sammons, Mary, 312
Sandler, Marion, 312
Sanford, Eleanor E., 264
Sarson, I. G., 421
Saunders, Carol Stoak, 445
Scanlon, Joseph, 504
Scarpello, Vida, 578
Schachter, Stanley, 350–352, 365
Schein, Edgar H., 97, 104, 562, 578, 620, 625
Scherwitz, Larry, 408
Schlenker, B. R., 79
Schmidt, Warren H., 300–301
Schmitt, Neal, 322
Schnake, Mel E., 231
Schneider, Benjamin, 626
Schneier, Craig Eric, 175
Schopler, Janice H., 394
Schramm, Wilbur, 489
Schriber, Jacquelyn B., 605
Schriesheim, Chester A., 39, 272, 279, 282–283, 290–292, 315
Schuler, Randall S., 404, 420
Schultz, Terri, 421
Schwartz, Richard D., 322
Schweiger, David M., 513
Schweizer, Jason, 250, 264
Schwendiman, Gary, 586
Schwenk, Charles R., 366
Scott, K. Dow, 128
Scott, William G., 489
Sculley, John, 561
Sechrest, Lee, 322
Seers, Anson, 421
Sekaran, Uma, 291
Seligman, M. E. P., 409, 420
Selye, Hans, 400, 418–419, 421
Serey, Timothy T., 421
Sethi, S. Prakash, 579
Seymore, J. D., 231
Shapiro, Irving S., 268
Shapiro, Robert, 135
Sharbaugh, Michael E., 420
Shaw, Karylle A., 202
Shea, Gregory P., 366
Shea, John, 128
Sheldon, Sidney, 94
Shenkar, Oded, 592, 605
Shetty, Y. K., 613
Shichman, Shula, 579

Shook, Douglas E., 488
Shore, Lynn McMarlane, 129
Shrader, Charles B., 79, 175
Siegel, J. S., 421
Sigband, Norman, 357
Silver, William S., 513
Sime, Wesley E., 421
Simison, Robert L., 231
Simon, Herbert A., 493–496, 498, 500, 511–512, 518, 542
Sims, Henry P., Jr., 230, 265, 419
Sirota, Davis R., 184
Skinner, B. F., 11, 207–209, 217, 226, 236, 257, 265
Sloan, Alfred P., 10–21, 37
Slocum, John W., Jr., 103, 175, 182, 201, 265, 293, 366, 488, 544, 605
Sluzer-Azaroff, Beth, 264
Smith, Jonathan E., 176
Smith, Patricia C., 114–115, 117, 128, 202, 265, 322
Smith, Sarah, 578
Smith, Terry, 445
Smyser, Charles M., 175
Snoeck, J. D., 419
Snow, Charles C., 535, 544
Snyder, Charles A., 254, 264
Snyderman, Barbara Bloch, 128, 421
Solo, Sally, 231, 419
Solomon, Jolie B., 579
Sommerkamp, P., 291
Spalding, Carl, 524
Spangler, William D., 292
Sparkes, Boyden, 38
Spector, Paul E., 175
Spradley, J. P., 38
Srull, Thomas K., 15, 201
Stalnecker, Susan M., 329–330
Stanley, Morgan, 573
Starbuck, W. H., 293
Starr, V. Hale, 488
Staskin, Irene Adams, 312
Staw, Barry M., 127, 175, 292, 366, 445
Stayer, Ralph, 450, 452–453, 456
Stedt, Bonnie, 134
Steele, R. P., 202
Steers, Richard M., 125, 128, 292, 322, 420–421
Steiner, Gary A., 103
Stevenson, William B., 231, 365
Stewart, Dave, 221
Stewart, R., 39, 315
Stewart, Thomas A., 15
Stoner, J. A. F., 366
Storrs, Constance, 468, 487
Strauss, George, 625
Strawberry, Darryl, 221
Strohmer, Art F., Jr., 330
Strube, Michael J., 291
Summer, Charles E., 513
Sundstrom, Eric, 365, 513

Super, D. E., 87
Suters, Everett, 422–423
Suttle, J. Lloyd, 201
Sutton, R. I., 127
Suwyn, Mark, 631
Suzuki, Nori, 605
Swain, Bob, 135
Swanda, John, 79
Swanson, Carl L., 579
Swasy, Alecia, 201–202
Swersky, Phyllis, 104
Szilagyi, Andrew D., Jr., 353, 419, 488

Tagiuri, Renato, 79
Tannenbaum, Robert, 300–301
Taylor, Alex, III, 624
Taylor, C. B., 420
Taylor, Frederick W., 19, 22, 37–38, 155,
    181, 193, 202, 352, 493
Taylor, G. Stephen, 128
Taylor, Lew, 128, 201, 264
Taylor, M. Susan, 230
Taylor, Ronald L., 39
Taylor, William, 513
Tehrani, Minoo, 543
Terpening, Will, 203
Terpstra, David, 625
Tharp, Gerald D., 421
Theoret, Andre, 494, 512
Thibaut, John W., 15, 230, 365
Thomas, Joe G., 201
Thomas, Linda T., 89, 103
Thompson, Donna E., 176, 201, 203, 231
Thompson, John A., 264
Thompson, Kenneth R., 203
Thorndike, Edward L., 13, 214, 230
Thornton, George C., 129
Thurow, Lester, 3
Tichy, Noel M., 285, 293
Tiger, Lionel, 38
Tobias, Randall L., 488
Toffler, Alvin, 438, 445
Tolman, Edward, 10, 155, 162, 193,
    210–212, 215
Toman, Walter, 104
Toulouse, Jean-Marie, 175
Tregoe, Benjamin, 548
Treybig, Jimmy, 630, 632
Trotter, Robert J., 93
Tubbs, Mark E., 202

Tuomisto, M., 128
Turner, C. E., 38
Tushman, Michael L., 300, 321, 533, 543
Tversky, A., 500, 512–513

Urwick, Lyndall, 356, 493, 543
Ury, William, L., 395
Uttal, B., 15

Vandenberg, Robert, 578
Vanderbilt, Cornelius, 19
Van deVen, Andrew H., 513
Van Maanen, John, 38, 98, 104
Van Sell, Mary, 404, 420
Varga, George, 283, 294
Vecchio, Robert P., 291, 293, 446
Velasquez, Manuel, 446
Vergé, Roger, 516–517
Villanova, Peter, 79
Vollrath, David A., 513
Vroom, Victor H., 13, 146, 155, 162–165,
    173–174, 194, 298, 309–311, 320, 322

Waddell, Frederick, 548
Wagel, William H., 231, 624–625
Waldron, Hicks, 495
Wallace, Marc J., Jr., 353, 488
Wallace, Robert K., 421
Walter, John, 547, 550
Walton, Elise, 579, 625
Walton, Eugene, 488
Walton, Richard E., 201, 625
Walton, Sam, 570
Ward, W. C., 513
Waterman, Robert H., Jr., 497, 512, 529,
    543–544
Watson, James, 453–455
Watson, John B., 11, 207–208
Watson, Thomas, Sr., 183, 568–569
Watson, William, 456
Wayne, Sandy J., 201, 625
Webb, Eugene J., 322
Webber, Ross A., 38, 184, 326, 366, 513
Weber, Max, 426, 517–519, 530, 541–542
Webster, J., 127
Wedley, William C., 322
Weed, Stan E., 175
Weinbach, Lawrence A., 43

Weiner, Bernard, 175
Weiss, D. J., 116
Weiss, Howard M., 420
Weiss, Richard W., 543
Weitzel, John R., 321
Welch, Jack, 331, 548, 550
Welsh, Dianne H. B., 231
Wendler, E. R., 489
Westwood, Robert G., 605
Wexley, Kenneth N., 231, 264
White, J. Dennis, 264
White, J. Kenneth, 513
White, Ralph K., 270–271, 280
Whitsett, David, 38, 201
Whyte, W. F., 265
Widenmann, Faye, 312
Wilkins, Alan L., 579
Williams, Larry J., 128, 174
Williams, S. L., 420
Wilson, James A., 291
Winfield, Dave, 221
Witten, Marsha G., 487
Wolf, Mark D., 45
Wolfe, D. M., 419
Wood, Robert E., 175
Woodman, Richard W., 103, 182, 201,
    265, 366, 488, 544, 605, 622, 625
Woolard, Edgar, 325, 327, 628–629,
    631–632
Worchel, Stephen, 15
Woycke, James, 292
Wrege, Charles D., 38
Wright, Robert, 439
Wyer, Robert S., Jr., 15, 201

Yavlinsky, Grigori, 274
Yeltsin, Boris, 274
Yetton, Philip W., 298, 309–311, 320, 322
York, Christopher, 135
Yorks, Lyle, 38, 201
Yukl, Gary A., 150, 202, 231, 275, 279,
    290–291, 293, 321, 394, 440–441, 445,
    489, 602, 605

Zaleznik, Abraham, 290
Zalkind, Sheldon S., 79, 111, 373
Zeira, Yoram, 605
Zohar, Dov, 264

SUBJECT INDEX

A type personality, 406–409
Absenteeism and satisfaction, 123–124
Achievement motivation, 150–153
Action tendencies, 118–119
Activity motive, 148
Adams' equity theory, 167–169
Administering reinforcement, 224–227
Adult life stages, 87–90
Affection motive, 148–149
Affiliation motive, 152
Alderfer's theory of motivation (ERG theory), 161–162
Alphanumeric departmentation, 526
Anchoring heuristic, 502
Anthropology, 25–27
Appraisal by results, 197–199
Approach-approach conflict, 374
Approach-avoidance conflict, 374–376
Asch's conformity study, 498
Attitudes:
    antecedents of, 109
    changes in, 111–113
    components of, 108–109
    functions of, 109–111
    international, 590–592
    and job satisfaction, 113–124
    and organizational commitment, 124–126
Attribution theory:
    errors in, 171–172
    locus of control in, 170
    in motivation theory, 169–172
    in perception, 74, 169–172
    self-efficacy in, 172
Authority, 427, 530, 575
Availability heuristic, 501–502
Avoidance-avoidance conflict, 376
Avoidance learning, 217–218

B type personality, 406–409
Balance theory of groups, 347–348
Bank wiring room studies at Hawthorne, 23–24
Barnard's contribution to communication, 468–469
Behavior modification (see Organizational behavior modification)
Behavioral audit, 237–238
Behavioral decision making, 495–503

Behavioral problems from stress, 412–413
Behavioral sciences:
    anthropology, 25–27
    methodology, 29–37
    psychology, 28–29
    sociology, 27–28
Behavioral self-management, 256–261, 415
Behaviorism, 11
    (See also Behavioristic theories of learning)
Behavioristic framework, 11
Behavioristic theories of learning, 208–210, 214–229
"Binging" at Hawthorne, 24
Biofeedback, 92–93, 415
Biological contributions to personality, 90–94
Birth-order data, 96–97
Blake and Mouton's managerial grid, 302–303, 615–616
Bounded rationality model of decision making, 498–500
Brain, role of, in personality, 92
Bureaucracy:
    characteristics of, 518–519
    dysfunctions of, 519–520
    modern view of, 520–522
    modifications of, 522–530

Caller ID in telecommunication, 473
Career planning, 418
Case design, 32–33
Centralization, 522–524
Challenger tragedy, 465–466
Change management, 614–622
Charismatic leadership, 283–284, 300
Citizenship, prosocial behaviors, 124
Classical conditioning, 11, 208–209
Coalitions, 349–350
Coercive power, 428–429
Cognition, 10
    (See also Cognitive approach)
Cognitive approach:
    complexity, 507–508
    definition of, 10
    in general, 10–11
    learning theories, 210–212, 215
    to therapy, 415–416
Cohesiveness in groups, 351–353

Collectivism in international organizational behavior, 588
Commitment, 124–126
Committees, 353–359
Communication:
    definition of, 470–471
    historical background of, 467–470
    interactive, 484–487
    international, 476, 480, 593–596
    interpersonal, 475–479
    management information systems in, 471–472
    nonverbal, 474–476
    organizational, 475–477
    subordinate-initiated, 482–484
    superior-subordinate, 479–482
    telecommunication, 472–474
Conflict:
    cultural, 377
    from frustration, 370–374
    goal, 374–376
    intergroup, 387–390
    interpersonal, 378–387
    intraindividual, 370–378
    organizational, 391–393
    role, 376–378
Connectionist theories of learning, 208–210
    (See also Behaviorism; Behavioristic theories of learning)
Consequence management, 258–259
Construct validity, 36–37
Content theories of work motivation, 156–162
Content validity, 35
Contingency approaches:
    to leadership, 276–280
    to organization theory, 534–535
    to power, 432–437
Contingent time off (CTO) in O.B. Mod., 252–253
Control theory of behavior, 194–195, 409
Coopting strategy of attitude change, 113
Coping strategies for stress, 413–418
Creativity process and techniques, 506–511
Critical incident measurement, 116–117
Cross-cultural analysis, 584–603
    (See also Culture; International organizational behavior)

651

CTO (contingent time off) in O.B. Mod., 252–253
Cultural assimilator training programs, 595
Culture:
in anthropology, 25–27
characteristics of, 26–27
contributions of, to personality, 94–95
definition of, 25
differences in, 584–586
international impact of, 584–593
significance of, 27
(*See also* Organizational culture)
Curiosity motive, 148
Customer departmentation, 526

Decentralization, 522–524
Decision making:
behavioral, 495–503
centralization and decentralization, 523–524
creativity and, 506–511
international, 602–603
models of, 496–503
nature of, 493–494
phases in, 493–494
techniques of, 503–506, 509–511
Decision tree approach to leadership styles, 309–311
Delegation, 522–524
Delphi technique, 509–510
Departmentation, 525–528
Dispositions in stress, 405–410
Divergent thinking, 507
Diverse workforce, 612–613, 621
Dominant culture, 563–564
Downward communication, 479–482
Drives in motivation, 147
Dynamic network design of organizations, 535
Dysfunctions of bureaucracy, 519–520

E-mail (electronic mail), 5, 473
EC (European Community), 5
Ecological organization theory, 534–535
Econologic model of decision making, 497
Economic model of decision making, 497
Effective real managers, 318–319
Ego states in TA, 378–383
Electronic bulletin boards, 473–474
Electronic mail (E-mail), 5, 473
Empowerment of employees, 437
Epigrams, 531
Equipment departmentation, 526
Equity theory of motivation, 167–169
ERG (existence, relatedness, growth) theory of motivation, 161–162
Errors in attribution, 171–172
Escape-avoidance learning, 217–218
Esteem needs, 157

Ethnocentrism, 595
European Community (EC), 5
Evaluation in O.B. Mod., 244–245
Exchange theories:
of groups, 347–348
of leadership, 275–276
Existence needs, 161–162
Expectancy theory:
of learning, 210–212
of motivation, 162–167
roots of, 10
Experimental designs, 31
Expert power, 430–432
External validity, 31–32
Extraorganizational stressors, 401–403

Face validity, 35
Family impact on personality, 95–97
Fayol's gangplank concept of communication, 467–468
Feedback:
in achievement motivation, 151–152
in communication, 477–479
in goal setting, 196
in job design, 185–188
as a reinforcer, 219–220
Femininity in international organizational behavior, 590
Fiber optics, 472–473
Fiedler's contingency approach to leadership, 276–280
Figure-ground perception, 68–69
Fixed interval schedule of reinforcement, 224–225
Fixed ratio schedule of reinforcement, 224
Flat structures, 524–525
Followership in leadership, 275–276
French and Raven's power sources, 428–432
Frustration, 370–374
Functional analysis in O.B. Mod., 240–243
Functional centralization and decentralization, 523
Functional departmentation, 526–527
Fundamental attribution error, 171
Future of organizational behavior, 622–623

Games in TA, 381–383
Gangplank concept of communication, 467–468
General adaptation syndrome (GAS), 400–401
General motives, 148–149
Genetic engineering, 91–92
Geographical centralization and decentralization, 522–523

Goal conflict, 374–376
Goal setting:
and MBO, 197–199
research on, 195–197
and system performance, 197–199
theory of, 193–195
Golden Triangle, 5
"Great man" theory of leadership, 273
"Great Organizers," 21
Grid training in organization development, 615–616
(*See also* Managerial grid)
Grievance procedure, 483
Group decision techniques, 508–511
Group formation theories, 347–348
Group stressors, 405
Group theories of leadership, 275–276
Groups:
as committees, 353–359
formation of, 347–348
as informal organization, 359–364
intergroup behavior and conflict, 387–390
nature of, 346–353
research of, 350–353
types of, 349–350
Groupthink, 358–359
Growth needs, 161–162

Hackman-Oldham model of job design, 184–189
Halo effect, 75–76
Hardiness in stress, 410
"Hawthorne effect," 25
Hawthorne studies, 18, 23–25, 348–350, 352, 405
Health care industry application of O.B. Mod., 253–254
Heredity in personality, 90–91
Hersey and Blanchard's leadership model, 304–305
Herzberg's theory of motivation, 159–161, 183–184
Heuristics in decision making, 500–503
Hierarchy of needs, 156–159, 333–335
Hospital application of O.B. Mod., 253–254
Hygiene factors in motivation, 159–161

Identifying performance behaviors in O.B. Mod., 237–239
Illumination experiments at Hawthorne, 18
Illusions, 63–65
Immaturity characteristics, 88–90
Impression management, 76–78
Incentives in motivation, 147
Individual coping strategies, 414–416
Individual stressors, 405–410

Individualism in international organizational behavior, 588
Informal groups, 359–364
Informal organization, 362
Informal roles of managers and employees, 360–363
Information Age, 5
Information processing approach to organizations, 533–534
Instrumentality in motivation, 163–164
Interaction theory of groups, 347–348
Interactive communication, 484–487
Intergroup conflict, 387–390
Intermittent schedule of reinforcement, 225–226
Internal validity, 31–32
International organizational behavior:
  communication, 476, 480, 593–595
  cultural dimensions, 584–593
  decision making, 602–603
  leadership, 600–602
  motivation, 596–599
Interpersonal communication, 475–479
Interpersonal conflict, 378–387
Interpersonal skills across cultures, 601–602
Intervention strategies for O.B. Mod., 243–244
Intraindividual conflict, 370–378
Iowa University leadership studies, 270–271

JDI (Job Descriptive Index), 115, 117
JDS (Job Diagnostic Survey), 186–187, 335–337
"Jim twins," 90–91
Job characteristics model of job design, 184–189
Job Descriptive Index (JDI), 115, 117
Job design:
  background of, 181–183
  characteristics of, 184–189
  guidelines for, 187–189
  and job enrichment, 183–184
  and quality of work life, 190–193
  and self-managed teams, 191–193
  social information processing approach to, 189
  sociotechnical approach to, 190–193
Job Diagnostic Survey (JDS), 186–187, 335–337
Job engineering, 182–183
Job enrichment, 183–184, 417
Job satisfaction:
  of American employees, 118–121
  and groups, 353
  influences on, 121–122
  meaning of, 113–114
  measuring of, 114–118

Job satisfaction (Cont.):
  outcomes, 122–124
  in Porter-Lawler model, 165–167
Job stress (see Stress)
Johari window, 384–385
Judgmental heuristics and biases model of decision making, 500–503

Kelman's contingency model of power, 435–436

Latent learning experiments, 212
Law of effect, 13, 214–215
Leader Behavior Description Questionnaire (LBDQ), 271
Leader match, 279–280
Leader-member exchange (LMX) model of leadership, 276
Leadership:
  classic studies on, 270–272
  definition of, 268–270
  international, 600–602
  and managerial activities, 313–319
  situational theory of (see Situational theory of leadership)
  styles of, 298–311
  theories of, 273–289
  women in, 311–313
Leadership questionnaire, 339–341
Leadership skills, 275, 319–320
Learned helplessness, 409
Learning:
  classical, 208–209
  cognitive, 210–212
  operant, 209–210
  and perception, 62–65
  punishment in, 227–229
  reinforcement in, 214–227
  social, 213–214
  theories of, 207–214
  types of, 207–214
Legitimate power, 429–430
Levinson's adult life stages, 87–88
Lewin's change procedure, 618
Life-cycle model of leadership, 304–305
Life stages, 87–90
Likert's lag, 307–308
Likert's systems of management leadership, 305–309
Line-staff conflict, 391–392
Lippitt and White leadership studies, 270–271
LMX (leader-member exchange) model of leadership, 276
Locke's theory of goal setting, 193–195
Locus of control, 170
Lose-lose conflict, 386
Love motive, 157

McClelland's two faces of power, 436–437
Management by objectives (MBO), 197–199
Management information systems (MIS), 471–472
Managerial activities, 313–319
Managerial grid, 302–303, 615–616
Managerial roles, 360–362
Managerial thinking, 92
Manipulation motives, 148
Manufacturing applications of O.B. Mod., 247–253
Masculinity in international organizational behavior, 590–591
Maslow's hierarchy of needs, 156–159, 333–335
Matrix organization, 538–541
Maturity characteristics, 88–90, 93–94
MBO (management by objectives), 197–199
Measurement of behaviors in O.B. Mod., 239–240
Media used in communication, 481
  (See also Telecommunication)
Meditation, 415
Methodology in research, 29–37
Michigan University leadership studies, 272
Milgram's obedience to authority study, 100–102
Minnesota Satisfaction Questionnaire (MSQ), 114, 116
Mintzberg's managerial roles, 360–362
Mintzberg's stages of decision making, 494
MIS (management information systems), 471–472
Modeling learning process, 213–214
Monetary reinforcers, 220–223
Motivating potential score (MPS), 186–187
Motivation:
  achievement, 150–153
  affection, 148–149
  affiliation, 152
  Alderfer's theory of, 161–162
  attribution theory of, 169–172
  content theories of, 156–162
  equity theory of, 167–169
  general motives in, 148–149
  Herzberg's theory of, 159–161, 183–184
  international, 596–599
  Locke's theory of, 193–195
  Maslow's theory of, 156–159
  meaning of, 146–147
  and perception, 67
  Porter-Lawler theory of, 165–167
  power as, 149–150, 436–437
  primary needs in, 147–148
  process theories of, 162–172
  secondary, 149–154
  security, 153–154
  status, 154

Motivation (*Cont.*):
techniques, 325–332
Vroom's theory of, 162–165
MPS (motivating potential score), 186–187
MSQ (Minnesota Satisfaction Questionnaire), 114, 116

NA (negative affectivity), 109
Natural reinforcers, 223
Need Satisfaction Questionnaire (NSQ), 115, 118
Needs, 147
(*See also* Motivation)
Negative affectivity (NA), 109
Negative reinforcers, 216–218
Networking, 314–319, 416
Newly industrialized countries (NICs), 5
Nominal group technique (NGT), 510–511
Nomological network, 36–37
Nonverbal communication, 474–476
Normative leadership model, 309–311
Norms of groups, 359–360
NSQ (Need Satisfaction Questionnaire), 115, 118

O.B. Mod. (*see* Organizational behavior modification)
Obedience to authority study, 100–102
OD (*see* Organization development)
Ohio State University leadership studies, 271–272
OJE (orthodox job enrichment), 184
Ombudsperson, 483
Open-door policy, 483
Open system of organization, 532–533
Operant conditioning, 11, 209–210
(*See also* Learning; Organizational behavior modification)
Organization change management, 614–622
Organization designs:
dynamic network, 535
matrix, 538–541
project, 535–538
Organization development (OD):
characteristics of, 614–615
definition of, 8–9, 614–615
historical development of, 615
relation of, to organizational behavior, 8–9
techniques of, 615–619
Organization theory:
bureaucracy in, 517–522
contingency, 534–535
definition of, 8–9
ecological, 534–535
information processing, 533–534

Organization theory (*Cont.*):
as open system, 532–533
and power, 437–438
relation of, to organizational behavior, 8–9
roots of, 530–532
Organizational behavior modification (O.B. Mod.):
ethics in, 261–262
evaluation in, 244–245
experience with, 245–256
functional analysis in, 240–243
identification of behaviors in, 237–239
intervention strategies for, 243–244
measurement of behaviors in, 239–240
model of, 238
research on, 245–256
self-management approach to, 256–261
steps in, 237–245
Organizational change, 610–622
Organizational commitment, 124–126
Organizational communication, 475–477
Organizational conflict, 391–393
Organizational culture:
changing, 573–577
characteristics of, 563
creation of, 567–570
definition of, 562–563
examples of, 569–570, 628–633
international dimensions of, 584–593
maintenance of, 570–573
nature of, 562–568
types of, 568
(*See also* Culture)
Organizational politics, 438–443
Organizational reward systems, 218–223
Organizational specialists, 21
Organizational stressors, 403–405
Organizational symbolism, 170
Orthodox job enrichment (OJE), 184

PA (positive affectivity), 109
Paradigm shift, 619–620
Paralanguage, 474–475
Parkinson's laws, 520–521
Participative decision techniques, 483, 503–506
Path-goal theory of leadership, 280–283
Pavlov's classical conditioning, 208–209
Pay impact on satisfaction, 114
(*See also* Monetary reinforcers)
Perception:
attribution in, 74, 169–172
definition of, 56
equity theory of, 167–169
and impression management, 76–78
international, 593–594
and learning, 62–65
and motivation, 67
nature of, 55

Perception (*Cont.*):
organization of, 68–72
and personality, 67
selectivity in, 58–67
and sensation, 55–56
social, 73–76
subprocesses in, 56–58
Personal control in stress, 409
Personal power, 436–437
Personality:
definition of, 84–86
determinants of, 90–102
development of, 86–90
and perception, 67
situational aspects of, 98–102
Peter principle, 520–521
Peters' and Waterman's model of decision making, 497
Physical problems from stress, 411
Physiological motives, 156–157
PIMS (Profit Impact of Market Strategy) study, 6
Place-learning experiments, 212
Planned change, 614–615
(*See also* Organization development)
Political strategies of power, 440–443
Politics in organizations, 438–443
Population-ecology organization theory, 534–535
Porter-Lawler theory of motivation, 165–167
Porter Need Satisfaction Questionnaire (NSQ), 115, 118
Positive affectivity (PA), 109
Positive control of behavior (*see* Positive reinforcers)
Positive discipline, 206–207
Positive reinforcers, 216, 218–223, 243–244
Power:
classification of, 428–432
contingency approaches to, 431–437
macro view of, 437–438
meaning of, 426–438
as motive, 149–150, 436–437
and politics, 438–443
sources and types of, 428–432
strategies for acquisition of, 440–443
Power distance in international organizational behavior, 588, 599
Power motive, 149–150
Predictive validity, 35–36
Premack principle, 223
Primary groups, 349
Primary motives, 147–148
Process theories of work motivation, 162–172
Product departmentation, 527–528
Productivity:
and O.B. Mod., 245–247
and satisfaction, 123

Profit Impact of Market Strategy (PIMS) study, 6
Project designs of organizations, 535–538
Propinquity in group formation, 347
Prosocial citizenship type behaviors, 124
Psychological hardiness, 410
Psychological problems from stress, 412
Psychology, 28–29
Punishment, 227–229, 244
Punishment strategy for O.B. Mod., 244
    (See also Punishment)

Quality assurance, 180
Quality control (QC) circles, 505
Quality of work life (QWL), 181, 190–193
Quality Service Revolution, 5–6

Rating scales, 114–116
Rationality in decision making, 496–503
Reagan's leadership style, 293–294
Real managers study, 313–319, 466–467, 469–470
Referent power, 430
Reinforcement:
    administering, 224–227
    definition of, 215–216
    law of effect in, 214–215
    negative, 216–218
    in organizational behavior modification (O.B Mod.), 243–244
    organizational reward systems, 218–223
    positive, 216, 218–223, 243–244
Relatedness needs, 161–162
Relay room experiments at Hawthorne, 23
Reliability in measurement, 34–35
Religion across cultures, 598
Representative heuristic, 502
Research methodology, 29–37
Reward power, 428
Rewards (see Reinforcement)
Risk taking, 151
Risky shift phenomenon, 358–359
Role conflict and ambiguity, 376–378, 392–393, 405–406
Role overload or underload, 406
Roles in groups, 359–361

S-O-B-C: functional analysis, 258–261, 286
Safety needs in motivation, 156–157
Safety results under O.B. Mod., 246
Sales performance under O.B. Mod., 246–247, 253–256

Satisfaction:
    and performance, 122–124, 165–167
    (See also Job satisfaction)
Scanlon plan, 503–504
Schachter study of group dynamics, 350–353
Schedules of reinforcement, 224–227
Scientific management, 21–23, 155, 181–182, 352
Scientific methodology, 29–37
Secondary motives, 149–154
Security motive, 153–154
Self-actualization needs, 157–158
Self-concept of personality, 85
Self-efficacy, 85, 172, 215, 409–410
Self-esteem, 85
Self-goal setting, 259
Self-managed groups, 191–193, 350, 449–457
    (See also Team building in organization development)
Self-management in O.B. Mod., 256–261, 415
Self-presentation, 76–78
Self-recording, 259
Self-reinforcement, 258–259
Self-serving bias in attribution, 171–172
Sensation, 55–56
Sensitivity training (see Organization development; Team building in organization development)
Serendipity, 18–19
Service departmentation, 526
Service industries application of O.B. Mod., 253–256
Sex differences in leadership, 311–313
Simon's model of decision making, 498–500
Simon's phases of decision making, 493–494
SIPA (social information processing approach) to job design, 189
Situational impact on personality, 98–102
Situational theory of leadership, 276–280, 304–305
Six sigma quality, 610
Skills, leadership, 275, 319–320
Social decision schemes, 508–509
Social information processing approach (SIPA) to job design, 189
Social learning theory, 11–13, 213–214, 286–287
    of leadership, 286–287
Social model of decision making, 497–498
Social perception, 73–76
Social power, 436–437
Social psychology, 28–29
Socialization, 97–98, 570–573
Sociology, 27–28
Sociotechnical job design, 190–193
Split-brain thinking, 92

Staff organization, 529–520
Stages of personality development, 86–90
Status motive, 154
Stereotyping, 74–75, 594–595
Stimulus management, 258
Stress:
    background of, 400–401
    causes of, 401–410
    coping strategies for, 413–418
    effects of, 410–413
    meaning of, 399–400
Stressors:
    extraorganizational, 401–403
    group, 405
    individual, 405–410
    organizational, 403–405
Strokes in TA, 381–382
Strong culture, 564–565
Structural conflict, 391–392
Styles of leadership, 298–311
Subculture, 564
Subliminal perception, 59
Subordinate-initiated communication, 482–484
Substitutes for leadership, 287–289
Successful real managers, 317
Superior-subordinate communication, 479–482
Survey feedback in organization development, 616–617
Survey research design, 33–34
Symbolism, 170
Systems concept of organization, 532–533
Systems of management leadership, 305–309

TA (transactional analysis), 378–383
Tall structures, 524–525
Tannenbaum and Schmidt leadership continuum, 300–302
Task design (see Job design)
TAT (Thematic Apperception Test), 151
Team building in organization development, 617–619
    (See also Self-managed groups)
Telecommunication, 5, 472–474
Territorial centralization or decentralization, 522–523
Thematic Apperception Test (TAT), 151
Theory A (American), 575
Theory building, 30–31
Theory J (Japanese), 575–576
Theory X, 299
Theory, Y, 299
Theory Z, 574–577
Thinking:
    managerial, 92
    split-brain, 92
Thorndike's law of effect, 13, 214–215
Threats in validity, 31–32

Time departmentation, 526
Time management, 414
Tolman's learning experiments, 210–212
Trait theories of leadership, 273–275
Transactional analysis (TA), 378–383
Transactional leadership, 285
Transformational leadership, 285–286
Turnover and satisfaction, 123
Twin studies, 90–91
Two faces of power, 436–437
Two-factor theory of motivation, 159–161
Type A personality, 406–409
Type B personality, 406–409
Type Z organization, 574–577

Uncertainty avoidance, 588–590, 598–599
Upward communication, 482–484

Valence, 162–164
Validity:
    construct, 36–37
    content, 35
    external, 31–32
    internal, 31–32
    meaning of, 35–37
    predictive, 35–36
Values (*see* Attitudes)
Variable schedule of reinforcement,
    225–226
Vertical dyad linkage (VDL) model of
    leadership, 276
VIE (valence, instrumentality, expectancy)
    theory of motivation, 162–165
Voice messaging, 473
Volvo sociotechnical project, 190–191
Vroom–Yetton model of leadership styles,
    309–311

Vroom's theory of motivation, 162–165

Weak cultures, 564–565
Wellness, 401–402
Win-lose conflict strategy, 386
Win-win conflict strategy, 387
Women and leadership, 311–313
Work motivation, 154–172

Z type organization, 574–577
Zeitgeist theory of leadership, 273